Instructor's Resource Manual

to accompany

Economics

Fifteenth Edition

Campbell R. McConnell
University of Nebraska (emeritus)

Stanley L. Brue
Pacific Lutheran University

Prepared by
Joyce Gleason
Nebraska Wesleyan University

Janet West
University of Nebraska at Omaha

McGraw-Hill
Irwin

Boston   Burr Ridge, IL   Dubuque, IA   Madison, WI   New York   San Francisco   St. Louis
Bangkok   Bogotá   Caracas   Kuala Lumpur   Lisbon   London   Madrid   Mexico City
Milan   Montreal   New Delhi   Santiago   Seoul   Singapore   Sydney   Taipei   Toronto

McGraw-Hill Higher Education

A Division of The McGraw-Hill Companies

Instructor's Resource Manual to accompany
ECONOMICS
Campbell R. McConnell and Stanley L. Brue

1 2 3 4 5 6 7 8 9 0 CUS/CUS 0 9 8 7 6 5 4 3 2 1

ISBN 0-07-246140-3

www.mhhe.com

Table of Contents

Note to Instructors Using *Macroeconomics* and *Microeconomics*

The Chapters in this manual relate to your paperback texts as follows:

Economics	Macro	Micro
1	1	1
2	2	2
3	3	3
4	4	4
5	5	5
6	6	6
7	7	
8	8	
9	9	
10	10	
11	11	
12	12	
13	13	
14	14	
15	15	
16	16	
17	17	
18	18	
19	19	
20		7
21		8
22		9
23		10
24		11
25		12
26		13
27		14
28		15
29		16
30		17
31		18
32		19
33		20
34		21
36		22
36		23
37	20	24
38	21	25
39	22	

GETTING STARTED

Every economy must answer Four Fundamental Questions; similarly, new instructors have four fundamental questions to consider in planning the principles class they are about to teach.

First, *what* topics are to be covered? Second, *how* is the class to be taught and what methods are going to be used? Third, *who* are the students, and what is the likely composition of the class? Last, is there enough *flexibility* in the plans so changes can be made to accommodate student needs and problems?

What and How Much to Teach:

The first step in making a course successful is to prepare the syllabus. A well-written syllabus serves as a contract between student and faculty member and can save many misunderstandings when final evaluations are made. For the student, the syllabus is an important road map for the journey through this course. Students appreciate knowing what to expect. They don't like to be surprised near the end of the term with extra material or unexpected assignments or projects. The syllabus should clearly spell out the requirements for the course and the consequent grade that will be assigned for various levels of achievement.

Decide on the core content by selecting the most important topics. Arrange the content in the order that is most comfortable for you. Prepare a skeleton outline and select the most likely dates or at least the target weeks in the semester for examinations and due dates for written assignments and projects. Try not to schedule tests and due dates for major projects the same week. Setting the time frame in advance allows you to make adjustments throughout the term rather than only at the end. After the outline is in place, select examples that will best illustrate the core principles. Good teaching requires organization knowledge, dependability, and respect for the student's time and effort.

Enthusiasm for your subject is contagious and may be the single most important ingredient for a successful class. Students respond as much to the attitudes of the instructor as they do to the information. Economics can be entertaining and students are usually thrilled to have fun in a class with such a dull reputation. Select current news examples and give active learning lessons that fit your style of teaching and hit the core principles. Some of these examples can be silly and outrageous but are likely to be remembered by the students and incidentally may increase class attendance.

Experience and practice make any task easier, and teaching is no exception. As a new teacher, it is a good idea to prepare your examples in advance and work out all the details. Delivering a reasoned, logical argument while trying not to trip over an electrical cord and doing arithmetic at the same time is akin to trying to kick a football while riding a skateboard.

Efficiency is a key concept in the course and it is a good principle to apply in the classroom as well. As the teacher, it is your set of priorities and value judgments that determine the allocation of time in the classroom. It is, however, helpful to devise some method of communication to get feedback from the students as soon as possible. Make a habit of doing some "classroom research," and acting on the results you receive. Ask the students to write out and turn in one concept that needs to be discussed again in class. Students will often take the opportunity to ask questions anonymously that they are afraid to voice in class. Teaching the class with the least cost combination of your valuable resources, especially time, is difficult. If you are new to the teaching task, ask some of your colleagues about their methods of taking role and other mundane clerical duties. If you assign homework regularly, find a way to minimize the paperwork.

Planning and organization in advance can save hours later. Remember the adage, "many hands make light work," and enlist the students to help in the paper chase.

How? (What methods will be used?)

The best teaching techniques for a class depend to some extent on the physical environment. How large will the class be? (10-16, 25-50, 100, 250, 1500) What capital equipment is available in the classroom? (Chalkboard, white board: overhead projectors, video projector, video-disk player, computers, Internet access?) If you are new to the campus, it is a good idea to find the classroom you will be using and check out the seating arrangement and the supplies. Make sure the equipment is in order before 50 people are staring at your every move. Even if you have years of experience, scouting the campus for new resources and new ideas can be fun. You are likely to meet some wonderful people who are eager to help. Take stock of the services on your campus and urge the students to use them. For example, the tutoring center may be able to assist the less-prepared economics student manage the graphs and applied problems. Forming study groups can also be helpful. If the campus has a computer lab, software for the text can be made available to the students. Even better, a course website can add to the out-of-class learning experience. The possibilities with the new courseware offerings are limited only by your imagination. Such course software also usually enables you to communicate with the class by email, via chat rooms, or using the listserve framework. Shy students often are willing to join discussions online when they wouldn't do so in class. McGraw-Hill has a complimentary CD "The Guide to Web For Economics" by Scott Bellamy and Ron Kardas.

It is a good idea to vary classroom activities, especially if the time frame is longer than an hour. Lecture can be accompanied by techniques that draw the student into the process. Even in large classes small group assignments can be made. This takes some advance planning, but it can increase student involvement significantly. If you are interested in using group work extensively, there are a number of good sources on collaborative learning available. Some examples of small group (usually 3-5 is best) assignments would include having the group: 1) consider one or more discussion questions and write a single response. 2) Read a current news article of interest and ask them to explain how it illustrates an economic principle, or respond to questions that you have prepared in advance. 3) Take a short quiz or write a short essay collectively. One of the advantages of this method is that in large classes, it allows everyone an opportunity to speak and learn from the perspective of others. It also results in fewer papers for the instructor to read, making it easier to give timely feedback to the students.

There are many controversial topics that could be used for discussion, formal debate, essays or term projects. Consider having assignments done orally. Many students prefer to write their essay assignments, but some would be delighted to make a classroom presentation instead, either individually or as a group effort. Assignments that send students into the community for information and observation can be rewarding. Here are some examples:

1. Have the student interview a business owner or manager, banker, stockbroker, an investment counselor, news reporter, city planner or other government official. Tailor your instructions for the interview to reflect the topics you are covering in class.

2. Ask the students to attend a local government meeting (city council, school board, county board of supervisors) and write a report about the economic issues and principles involved. Remind them that opportunity cost is present whenever any decision is made.

3. Have the students investigate local land use. Are there any local "hot topic" areas? Where in the community is growth occurring? Are there areas that are in decline?

4. Have students consider the type of business or industry that is dominant in the area. Why is it dominant? What factors of production contribute? How are local businesses interrelated?

Teaching principles of economics could be called "Current Events 101." Often the best supplemental text available is a good daily newspaper, especially the *Wall Street Journal or New York Times* or a weekly newsmagazine, such as *Time, Fortune,* or *Newsweek*. Consider having students subscribe and use it for class discussion and assignments. All of the above-mentioned periodicals, as well as several others, have special educational-use subscription offers and supplementary materials for classroom use. Term projects based on current information could be focused on domestic issues such as: (1) health care, education, welfare reform, child care, transportation, labor productivity, or (2) specific industries in the news, such as tobacco, computers, utilities and communications or (3) be focused on international issues: trade, financial markets, problems of less developed countries, poverty, world health, and environmental quality.

For Whom:

Before choosing the content of your course take time to consider the students that are in your classroom. Most likely they are not planning to major in economics; it might not even be a required course. Your class may be the first and last exposure they receive to formal economic reasoning. You have a valuable opportunity to make a lasting impression and provide your students with a set of power tools they can use for a lifetime. But remember the principles course is providing economic education, not necessarily training new economists.

Should you alter the course content to fit your audience? Many instructors wishing to maintain high standards bristle at the thought of watering down a transferable academic, principles course. A method for accomplishing both high standards and some flexibility to meet student needs is to break your course outline into two components. First decide on what you consider to be the core topics and principles of the course. Then choose examples, issues and assignments that will appeal to your audience. Also, judge your audience. A brief quiz over basic everyday statistics can be very revealing – What is the population of U.S.? What is the size of the labor force? What is the current GDP? What is the rate of inflation, of unemployment? You will be astonished at the variety of answers you get to such questions in most classes and it indicates that there is a woeful lack of knowledge about basic information, let alone the theories and concepts involved.

Finding the right issues and using appropriate examples and material is easier if your students have a common interest or if they are relatively homogeneous in ability or prior experience. For example, if the class is filled with engineering majors, you can forget about drudging over the basics of reading a graph! If you are facing a group of mature business executives, your examples could be more sophisticated than what you would use for a class filled with 18- to 25-year-old freshmen and sophomores. However, many of us don't have the luxury of having a homogeneous group of students, so use their differences to your advantage. Draw on the experience of those with certain expertise to help others.

Some colleges and high schools have honors programs where a section of the principles of economics could be offered. An honors course is smaller and has well-prepared students. This offers an opportunity for an enriching educational experience for both faculty and students. Teachers who are assigned to honors sections should keep in mind that the purpose of an honors course is to offer a qualitatively different experience. The students are motivated and can work independently. A more sophisticated level of discussion, argument, and debate can take place. It should not degenerate to simply increasing the number of assignments and piling on work. Honors students need a mentor and guide, not a taskmaster clicking off points on a calculator.

The under-prepared student will be the most likely participant in your class. The nature of the discipline means that nearly all students will be unprepared in some area. First, economics is an ESL class, "Economics as a Second Language," which is difficult and tricky. It is especially difficult if English is not your student's native language. Attempting to learn Standard English and economics simultaneously is a difficult assignment and yet foreign students are likely to take, and to major in economics. Second, economics requires the use of graphs and this implies a level of mathematical reasoning that has not been achieved by large numbers of entering college freshman. Third, economic reasoning includes the use of abstract models and the ability to generalize. These three fundamental skills are combined in the arguments that are routinely presented in class. The under-prepared student needs more structure and direct supervision than the well-prepared or mature student. Many of the teaching suggestions in the Instructors Manual are designed to help the struggling student.

Be Flexible:

Even with a great deal of planning, the chosen material may require more time than is available. Monitor your progress throughout the entire course, make adjustments as early as possible, and keep the students informed of any changes. These changes may be necessary because you over estimated the abilities of the students to grasp the material. Also, there may be a major current event that should be discussed in detail in class. As important as a course syllabus is, students appreciate when instructors are willing to be flexible when the result is a course that better suits their needs and interests.

Debt

This revision of the Instructor's Manual is based on the work of those who helped prepare previous editions. The most recent (14/e) was prepared by Arienne Turner of Fullerton College, California. This edition has been prepared cooperatively by Janet West, Assistant Professor of Economics at University of Nebraska at Omaha and by Joyce Gleason, Associate Professor of Economics at Nebraska Wesleyan University in Lincoln. Questions and suggestions related to the Manual's material over Chapters 1-6, 20-36 may be addressed to Professor West at jwest@unomaha.edu and questions or suggestions over Chapters 7-19, 37-39 and web chapter may be addressed to Professor Gleason at jgg@nebrwesleyan.edu

Supplements For McConnell/Brue, Economics, 15e

This package speaks to most any teaching style. It includes the pencil-and-paper basics and offers plenty of resources for the Internet savvy professor. There is also a book-enhancing Website and a CD-ROM version of DiscoverEcon—the best-selling tutorial on the market.

For the Instructor

Three Test Banks
Two Test Banks contain objective, predominately multiple-choice questions. A third Test Bank of short-answer essay questions and problems supplements this edition of **Economics**.

> *Test Bank I* (ISBN 0072461381) now comprises more than 5,200 questions, all written by either the text authors or new Test Bank I co-author, William Harris of the University of Delaware.

> *Test Bank II* (ISBN 0072461365), by Professor Walstad, contains more than 5,000 questions.

> *Test Bank III* (ISBN 007246139X), also prepared by Professor Walstad, contains "constructive response" testing to evaluate student understanding in a manner different from

conventional multiple-choice and true-false questions. Suggested answers to the essay and problem questions are included.

For all test items in Test Banks I and II, the nature of each question is identified as are the numbers of the text pages that are the basis for each question. Also, each chapter in Test Banks I and II includes an outline or table of contents that groups questions by topics. In all, more than 10,000 questions of equal quality offer instructors maximum testing flexibility while assuring the fullest possible correlation with the content of the text.

Computerized Testing
Test Bank I   ISBN 0072461330
Test Bank II   ISBN 0072461349
Test Bank III ISBN 007246142X
These systems include test generation, with the capability of producing high-quality graphs from the Test Banks. They also feature the ability to generate multiple tests, with versions "scrambled" to be distinctive, and other useful features.

PowerPoint Presentations
Macro   ISBN 0072463813
Micro   ISBN 0072474831

Created by Norman Hollingsworth of Georgia Perimeter College, these colorful, dynamic slides help instructors guide students through the key concepts and graphs covered in each chapter. For the first time presentations include built-in hyperlinks that allow instructors to jump to the website for related topics. This is one of the most customizable, robust collections of book slides available on the market today.

Color Transparencies (Graphs and Tables)
Macro   ISBN 0072463805
Micro   ISBN 007247484X

Over 200 new full-color transparencies for overhead projectors have been prepared especially for the **Fifteenth Edition**. They encompass all the graphs and tables appearing in **Economics** and are available on request to adopters.

For the Student

DiscoverEcon

CD-ROM:
Economics   ISBN 0072498951
Macro   ISBN 007249896X
Micro   ISBN 0072498978

Web Versions:
Economics   ISBN 0072498501
Macro   ISBN 0072498528
Micro   ISBN 007249851X

DiscoverEcon by Gerald Nelson at the University of Illinois, Urbana-Champaign, is the most exciting and widely used Economics educational software on the market. Available both on the web and CD, this version is even more closely integrated with the McConnell/Brue text than previous versions. Students who need to explore concepts interactively will find this software especially appealing. And instructors looking for pedagogically sound, easy-to-manage, self-grading exercises for homework need look no further.

Study Guide

Professor William Walstad—one of the world's foremost authorities on economic education—has prepared the 15th edition of the Study Guide, which many students find indispensable. It contains for each chapter an introductory statement, a checklist of behavioral objectives, an outline, a list of important terms, fill-in questions, problems and projects, objective questions, and discussion questions. The glossary found at the end of **Economics** also appears in the Study Guide.

For both Instructor and Student

Website

This Website dovetails with the text better than ever. Web-button icons alert students to points in the book where they can springboard to the Website to learn more. There, they may learn some history behind the concept, build an interactive graph, or read an anecdote.

A wealth of additional exercises, assignments, Last Words, and Web questions give you added flexibility in assigning course work. A password-protected instructor section offers you even more flexibility by having key supplements online—all in one place. There's even a bonus chapter on the Web titled "Transitional Economies: China and Russia."

PageOut

Creating a course Website is easy, especially when you use this "paint by numbers" method of creating one for your course. Simply fill in a series of templates, choose a design, and within minutes your syllabus will be posted on your own Website. Students can then follow your syllabus and be referred to daily assignments and postings.

PowerWeb

This Website is a reservoir of current events. Best of all, searching for those currents is easy because every resource listed at PowerWeb was chosen by professors like you. So a search for "Microsoft appeal," for example, will take you to articles relevant to an economics course. Additionally, students will find weekly news updates, an interactive glossary, and self-grading tests—all specific to economics.

Delivery Platforms

McGraw-Hill content can be delivered online using a number of delivery platforms. These include WebCT, Blackboard, and eCollege, to name just a few. These platforms offer sophisticated features like online quizzing, student tracking, content customization, and professor forums. Best of all, you have complete control over how the McGraw-Hill content is presented to your students.

DiscoverEcon Software

A.   Ordering Information
B.   Software Basics
C.   Using Exercises as Homework
D   Exercise Types
E.   List of Chapter-Specific Exercises
F.   Technical Details: Web and CD versions; course management platforms
G.   Reporting Results: Paper and Electronic Options
H.   Getting Updates for the CD Version

Gerald Nelson of the University of Illinois, Urbana-Champaign designed the DiscoverEcon software to supplement *Economics, 15e*. The software is available both on the web and on CD; both have the same features. Each has a version that accompanies the specific book you adopt (Economics, Macroeconomics, and Microeconomics). See below for directions on how to access the web version and how to order the correct version of book plus software to meet your needs.

Ordering Information

Use the following information to order the right combination of DiscoverEcon and textbook.

DiscoverEcon web access version

Economics and DiscoverEcon web access – Order ISBN 0-07-249850-1
Microeconomics and DiscoverEcon web access– Order ISBN 0-07-249851-X
Macroeconomics and DiscoverEcon web access– Order ISBN 0-07-249852-8

DiscoverEcon CD version

Economics and DiscoverEcon CD – Order ISBN 0-07-249895-1
Microeconomics and DiscoverEcon CD – Order ISBN 0-07-249897-8
Macroeconomics and DiscoverEcon CD – Order ISBN 0-07-249896-X

Software Basics

The software is designed to facilitate active learning. Important graphical concepts are presented step by step with text explaining the construction of each step. In many places the student can change important parameters to see what happens to the shape of the graph. Other concepts are illustrated with fill-in tables and question and answer format. The emphasis is on having the student think rather than just be told. The software is developed using the metaphor of an interactive textbook that parallels the paper textbook. The software has a table of contents for the book and for each chapter. You can click on a chapter name in the book table of contents to go directly to the chapter table of contents. Alternatively, you can click on the chapter number at the side of the page to do the same thing. Each software chapter has pages; each software page has a reference to the relevant pages in the text.

Table 1: Graph and table pages

In this page, (page 7 in chapter 25), the student clicks the arrows below the graph to increase or reduce the number of firms in the industry. As more firms enter, the market demand curve shifts down and eventually excess profits fall to zero for this firm. The top area is for navigating within a chapter; the vertical bar on the left is where you move from chapter to chapter.	
Some exercises, like this one from Chapter 11, involve answering a series of questions.	

In the second exercise in Chapter 22, the student completes a table set up by the software. Each time the page is visited the numbers in the gray columns change.

Note that this exercise topic is covered in pages 422 - 423 of the Economics textbook, see upper right.

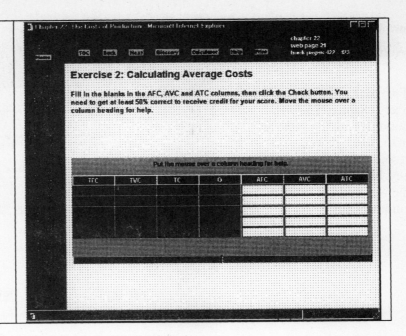

Exercises appear throughout the chapter, coming after an important concept has been covered. The exercises use random numbers so every student sees a different version. A list of these exercises is below. In addition, each chapter contains two essay questions, the web questions from the chapter, a match the terms exercise based on the key terms for the chapter, and a multiple-choice exercise using a test bank of at least 75 questions.

The glossary from the paper textbook is available by clicking the glossary button in the table of contents. In addition, the first time a glossary word appears on a page it is a "hotword" and is blue. If you click on the hotword the glossary entry pops up.

Using Exercises as Homework

All exercise results for a chapter are stored internally. At any time the student can view performance on the exercises by clicking the "Print" button **Print** at the top of the window. The user name, and optionally ID and instructor info, are entered when the software is started, and this information is displayed at the top of the print window. In the print window, the results can be printed, or if the electronic submission feature is available, can be sent to the electronic results management system.

Exercise Types

There are six types of exercises in the DiscoverEcon software. The software grades everything except questions involving essay answers. All grades are between 0 and 100.

- **Short problems** are easy to do. They might involve entering a single number or choosing among a couple of alternatives. Not all chapters have short problems.
- **Interactive Exercises** are more complicated. They also involve repetition with variation. Because exercises are designed with random numbers, they can be repeated as many times as the student wants. Not all chapters have interactive exercises. The Exercises menu lists all exercises in the software.
- The remaining exercise types – essay questions, match the terms, and multiple choice are illustrated in the following table.

Table 2: Exercises available in all chapters

Web and essay questions Two each are available for every chapter. The web questions are the same as in the text. A web resource button opens a new browser window with the web address entered automatically.	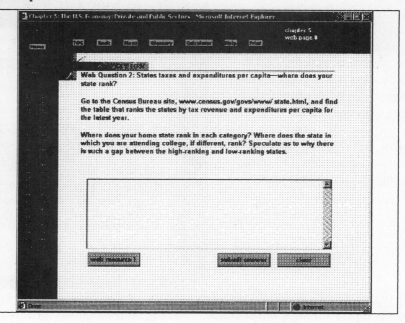
Match the terms This exercise is available for every chapter. You are given six terms taken from the list of key terms at the end of the chapter and 4 glossary entries. Drag the term to the tray next to the correct entry.	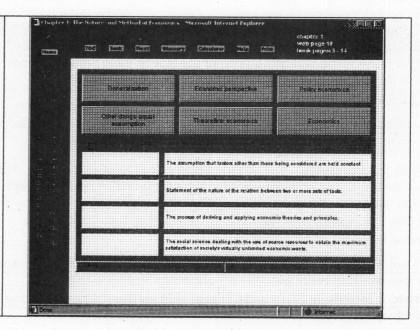

This exercise is available for every chapter. You choose the number of questions in the exercise (minimum of 5, maximum of 15) and software chooses these questions randomly from a test bank with at least 75 questions for each chapter. Only the first answer is graded but the student can check other answers to find the correct one. A page reference to the text is also included.

Chapter 1: The Nature and Method of Economics - Microsoft Internet Explorer

chapter 1
web page 11

The scientific method is:

C A. not applicable to economics, because economics deals with human beings.

C B. also known as the economic perspective.

C C. analysis that moves from broad generalizations called laws to theories and then to hypotheses.

C D. used by economists and other social scientists, as well as by physical scientists and life scientists.

2 out of 10   Attempted 1   Correct 1

List of Chapter-specific Exercises

A list of all the tutorial exercises is below. It is also available from the Exercises popup window (click the exercise button, lower left). For example, if you want to work on the "Identify Shifts and Changes in Demand and Supply Curves" exercise in Chapter 3, choose that item under the Exercises menu or go to the table of contents of Chapter 3 (click on the number 3 above) and click on Exercise 1 in the exercise list there. Note that this list does not include the exercises common to all chapters, nor does it include short problems.

More information on each exercise, including a picture of the exercise, can be found in the chapter-specific material.

Table 3: Chapter-specific exercises

Chapter and Exercise Title	Economics	Macro-economics	Micro-economics
The Nature and Method of Economics	1	1	1
Graphs and their Meaning	1a	1a	1a
Exercise 1: A Graphing Game Exercise 2: Calculate the Slope of a Line Exercise 3: Calculate the Slope of a Curve			
The Economizing Problem	2	2	2
Exercise 1: Identifying Shifts and Changes in Production			
Individual Markets: Supply and Demand	3	3	3
Exercise 1: Identifying Shifts and Changes in Demand and Supply Curves Exercise 2: Identifying Changes in Equilibrium Price and Quantity			
The Market System	4	4	4
The U.S. Economy: Private and Public Sectors	5	5	5
The United States in the Global Economy	6	6	6
Measuring Domestic Output, National Income, and the Price Level	7	7	
Exercise 1: Value Added Chain			

Antitrust Policy, Regulation, and Industrial Policy	32		19
Agriculture: Economics and Policy	33		20
Income Inequality and Poverty	34		21
Labor-Market Issues: Unionism; Discrimination; and Immigration	35		22
The Economics of Health Care	36		23
International Trade	37		24
Exercise 1: Find Comparative Advantage Exercise 2: Identify Equilibrium Values Exercise 3: Effects of an Import Tariff Exercise 4: Effects of an Import Quota Exercise 5: Effects of an Export Tax			
Exchange Rates, the Balance of Payments, and Trade Deficits	38		25
The Developing Economies	39		26
Bonus Web Transitional Economies — China and Russia	See Website	See Website	See Website

Reporting Results: Paper and Electronic Options

All results can be reported on paper. Click on the printer icon in the navigation section (along the top of the DiscoverEcon window). Then click the browser's print button.

For options on electronic submission of DiscoverEcon exercise results, visit the DiscoverEcon website.

Technical Details

Web version

The web version of the software requires Internet Explorer version5.0 or higher. General information about the software is available at:

http://www.mhhe.com/economics/discoverecon/mcbrue15/

There are several ways to use the web version. These depend on how you have set up your course home page.

Using course-delivery software (Pageout, WebCt, or Blackboard)

McGraw-Hill has McConnell/Brue-specific web material for three course development environments – PageOut, WebCt, and Blackboard. PageOut courses are developed on a McGraw-Hill web server. More information regarding PageOut is available at http://www.pageout.net. WebCt and Blackboard courses are developed on your institution's web server, using add-on material provided by McGraw-Hill. More information on how you develop a web site with these products is available from http://www.mhhe.com/catalogs/solutions. In each you have an option of adding a link to the DiscoverEcon web software.

Using a custom-developed web site

If you have developed a course-specific web site that doesn't use one of these products, you can still easily use the DiscoverEcon web software. Add one of the following links to your web site.

Economics

     http://www.mhhe.com/economics/discoverecon/mcbrue15/plain/main

Microeconomics

     http://www.mhhe.com/economics/discoverecon/mcbrue15/plain/micro

Macroeconomics

        http://www.mhhe.com/economics/discoverecon/mcbrue15/plain/macro

CD version

The CD runs on PCs using Windows 95, 98, 2000, and NT. The basic hardware requirements are the same as for the operating system. If your computer can run Windows 95 and has a Pentium or equivalent processor, it can also run the DiscoverEcon software. A PC with the following specifications will run the software comfortably:

        CPU: Intel 586 or equivalent
        Memory: 64 mb
        Free hard disk space: 10 to 60 megabytes depending on installation type

With the CD version your students will be able to print out exercise results but not submit them electronically.

Getting Updates for the CD version

We've worked hard to get the bugs out of this software, but inevitably some remain. Changes are incorporated automatically into the web version. If any updates are available for the CD version, they will be made available at the McConnell/Brue website http://www.mhhe.com/economics/mcconnell15.
We would also like suggestions for modifications and enhancements of this software. Please send them to: DiscEcon@aol.com.

CHAPTER ONE
THE NATURE AND METHOD OF ECONOMICS

CHAPTER OVERVIEW

This chapter begins with a discussion of the meaning and importance of economics. In this first chapter, however, we will not plunge into problems and issues; instead we consider some important preliminaries. We first look at the economic perspective—how economists think about problems. Next, we state some of the benefits of studying economics. Then, we examine the specific methods economists use to examine economic behavior and the economy, distinguishing between macroeconomics and microeconomics. Finally, the problems, limitations, and pitfalls that hinder sound economic reasoning are examined.

The Appendix to Chapter 1 provides an important introduction to graphical analysis. While this will be review material for most students, for some this may be new. Instructors are strongly urged to confirm that their students understand this section before proceeding. The software supplement can provide effective remedial help for those students who are not familiar with graphical analysis.

WHAT'S NEW

There has been substantial rewriting of the material in this chapter. Many of the paragraphs have been shortened and tightened up and the examples have been changed and updated. Note that the term "material wants" has been changed to "economic wants." A major revision has been made in the discussion of "Economic Methodology." The section starts with an explanation of the scientific method and how it is used by economists to study human and institutional behavior. It continues with a discussion of the relationship between facts and theories and the importance of establishing theories, laws, principles, and models within the social scientists' use of the scientific method. The presentation of the material eliminates the references to deductive versus inductive logic. Figure 1.1 has been changed to reflect the changes in the text.

Note that the prices used in Table 2 of the appendix have been doubled to make them more realistic. All of the explanatory numbers in text have been changed to reflect the change in the ticket prices.

There are some changes in the WEB-BASED QUESTIONS at the end of the chapter.

INSTRUCTIONAL OBJECTIVES

After completing this chapter, students should be able to:

1. Define economics.

2. Describe the "economic way of thinking," including definitions of rational behavior, marginal costs, marginal benefits and how these concepts may be used in decision making.

3. State some important reasons for studying economics.

4. Explain how economists use the scientific method to formulate economic principles.

5. Explain the importance of *ceteris paribus* in formulating economic principles.

6. Explain the steps used by policy makers.

7. List eight economic goals and give examples of conflicting and complementary goals.

8. Differentiate between micro- and macroeconomics.

9. Differentiate between positive and normative economics.

10. Explain and give examples of the fallacy of composition and post hoc fallacy.

11. Explain and illustrate a direct relationship between two variables, and define and identify a positive sloping curve.

12. Explain and illustrate an inverse relationship between two variables, and define and identify a negative slope.

13. Identify independent and dependent variables.

14. Define and identify terms and concepts listed at end of chapter and appendix.

COMMENTS AND TEACHING SUGGESTIONS

1. This chapter and related classroom activities will set the tone for the rest of the course. The methods used in the initial class meetings set the expectations and attitudes of the students. Making dramatic changes later can be confusing and the outcome less successful than desired. Please refer to the "Getting Started" section in the introduction for detailed suggestions. If you plan to make current events an integral part of the class, consider offering educational subscriptions to *The Wall Street Journal* or one of the weekly news or business publications.

2. On the level of personal decision making, students might be asked to list all of the economic choices they had to make that day or that week. This impresses upon them that, as Marshall said in the 1890s, "economics is the study of man in the ordinary business of life." To illustrate the rational basis of their decisions, students could analyze one or two of these choices in terms of the alternatives they gave up. What other choices did they have? What criteria were used to judge the alternatives? A discussion of how rational our decisions are might also follow!

3. As the text suggests, it may be useful to discuss several noneconomic examples to illustrate the importance of models or simplification – for example, explaining that a road map is a model or simplification of the real world. The amount of detail on any road map would be determined by the needs of the traveler, i.e., "I need to travel between Chicago and Denver as quickly as possible," versus, "I would like to visit some historical museums as I am traveling through Nebraska." Neither road map would have the details of the real world. Devoting some time and effort to this point can help students see the importance of using economic models to represent the real world.

4. The section on Economic Methodology can be used to explain what economists do when employed in both the private and public sectors. An economist may be asked by his/her railroad employer to determine how the company should best allocate its box cars, or a legislative aide may be asked to research the effects of a state's current welfare-to-work program.

5. A discussion on the Economics Goals allows the instructor to introduce many concepts (Gross Domestic Product, Unemployment Rate, Consumer Price Index, Balance of Trade, etc.) and current statistics (growth rates, unemployment rates, inflation rates, etc.), each of which will be expanded upon in later chapters. The students can be asked to choose the most important goals for them personally and for the nation. In class, students can be asked to explain why they chose a particular goal. The discussion of the goals can illustrate how relevant the goals are to their lives, and the economic and political difficulty of achieving these goals.

6. The first 30-minute segment of the "Economics USA" video series is entitled "What is Economics?" This is one way to introduce the course. The series has 28 half-hour programs on economic concepts designed for a telecourse or supplementary use. Call 1-800-LEARNER for more

information, or ask your McGraw-Hill representative about the possibility of obtaining some or all of this series free of charge.

STUDENT STUMBLING BLOCKS

1. After thirty years of teaching economics, it has become clear to me that instructors cannot take for granted students' background knowledge of economics. Students generally have no idea about the magnitude of common economic measurements and, therefore, their reading of the news may be colored by this lack of knowledge. One teaching tip that has worked for others is to give students a pretest during the first week of class, in which simple questions are asked about the U.S. economy. For example, questions can be asked about the size of population and labor force, unemployment and inflation rates, GDP, federal budget, deficits and debt. You will find wildly different answers to these questions with most far away from "ball park" figures. This exercise accomplishes two things. First, it lets students know that they have a lot to learn about "everyday" news items. Second, the correct answers can give them some early perspective on news events as they relate to the course. As the course progresses, don't forget to reinforce these facts by reminding students of them.

2. The instructor could treat the appendix on graphical analysis as a supplement for those students who have weak backgrounds in reading or constructing simple graphs. There is often a wide disparity among student abilities here. Instructors may wish to have a remedial session and special assignments for students deficient in graphing skills. Comparing graphs to maps seems to help students who have "graph anxiety."

LECTURE NOTES

I.   **Definition of Economics**

    A. The social science concerned with the efficient use of limited or scarce resources to achieve maximum satisfaction of human materials wants.

    B. Human wants are unlimited, but the means to satisfy the wants are limited.

II.   **The Economic Perspective**

    A. Scarcity and choice

        1. Resources can only be used for one purpose at a time.

        2. Scarcity requires that choices be made.

        3. The cost of any good, service, or activity is the value of what must be given up to obtain it. (opportunity cost).

    B. Rational Behavior

        1. Rational self-interest entails making decisions to achieve maximum fulfillment of goals.

        2. Different preferences and circumstances lead to different choices.

        3. Rational self-interest is not the same as selfishness.

    C. Marginalism: benefits and costs

        1. Most decisions concern a change in current conditions; therefore the economic perspective is largely focused on marginal analysis.

        2. Each option considered weighs the marginal benefit against the marginal cost.

3. Whether the decision is personal or one made by business or government, the principle is the same.

4. The marginal cost of an action should not exceed its marginal benefits.

5. There is "no free lunch" and there can be "too much of a good thing."

III. **Why Study Economics?**

A. Economics for citizenship.

1. Most political problems have an economic aspect, whether it is balancing the budget, fighting over the tax structure, welfare reform, international trade, or concern for the environment.

2. Both the voters and the elected officials can fulfill their role more effectively if they have an understanding of economic principles.

B. Professional and personal applications

1. The study of economics helps to develop an individual's analytical skills and allows students to better predict the logical consequences of their actions.

2. Economic principles enable business managers to make more intelligent decisions.

3. Economics can help individuals make better buying decisions, better employment choices, and better financial investments.

4. Economics is however, mainly an academic, not a vocational subject. Its primary objective is to examine problems and decisions from a social rather than personal point of view. It is not a series of "how to make money" examples.

IV. **Economic Methodology**

A. Economists use the scientific method to establish theories, laws, and principles.

1. The scientific method consists of:

a. The observation of facts (real data).

b. The formulations of explanations of cause and effect relationships (hypotheses) based upon the facts.

c. The testing of the hypotheses.

d. The acceptance, reject, or modification of the hypotheses.

The determination of a theory, law, principle, or model.

2. Theoretical economics: The systematic arranging of facts, interpretation of the facts, making generalizations.

3. Principles are used to explain and/or predict the behavior of individuals and institutions.

4. Terminology—Principles, laws, theories, and models are all terms that refer to generalizations about economic behavior. They are used synonymously in the text, with custom or convenience governing the choice in each particular case.

5. Generalization—Economic principles are expressed as the tendencies of the typical or average consumer, worker, or business firm.

6. "Other things equal" or *ceteris paribus* assumption—In order to judge the effect one variable has upon another it is necessary to hold other contributing factors constant.

Natural scientists can test with much greater precision than can economists. They have the advantage of controlled laboratory experiment. Economists must test their theories using the real world as their laboratory.

7. Abstractions—Economic principles, theories or models are abstractions, simplifications, which attempt to find the important connections and relationships of economic behavior. These models are useful precisely because they strip away the clutter and complexity of reality.

8. Graphical Expression—Many economic relationships are quantitative, and are demonstrated efficiently with graphs. The "key graphs" are the most important.

B. Policy economics applies economic facts and principles to help resolve specific problems and to achieve certain economic goals.

1. Steps in formulating economic policy:

   a. State goals.

   b. Recognize various options that can be used to achieve goals.

   c. Evaluate the options on the basis of specific criteria important to decision-makers.

2. Economic goals widely accepted in our economy.

   a. Economic growth

   b. Full employment

   c. Economic efficiency

   d. Price level stability

   e. Economic freedom

   f. Equitable distribution of income

   g. Economic security

   h. Balance of trade

3. Goals may be complementary (full employment and economic security).

4. Some goals may conflict (efficiency and equity). (Key Question 6)

5. All goals cannot be achieved, so priorities must be set.

V.   **Macroeconomics and Microeconomics**

A. Macroeconomics examines the economy as a whole.

1. It includes measures of total output, total employment, total income, aggregate expenditures, and the general price level.

2. It is a general overview examining the forest, not the trees.

B. Microeconomics looks at specific economic units.

1. It is concerned with the individual industry, firm or household and the price of specific products and resources.

2. It is an examination of trees, and not the forest.

C. Positive and Normative Economics.

1. Positive economics describes the economy as it actually is, avoiding value judgments and attempting to establish scientific statements about economic behavior.

2. Normative economics involves value judgments about what the economy should be like and the desirability of the policy options available.

3. Most disagreements among economists involve normative, value-based questions.

VI. **Pitfalls to Objective Thinking**

A. Biases—Preconceptions that are not based on facts.

B. Loaded terminology.

1. Terms that contain the prejudice and value judgments of others.

2. It is very difficult for a person to describe economic behavior without letting their options about that behavior creep into their discussion. The distinction between positive and normative statements is not always clearly apparent.

3. Often, however, there is a deliberate attempt to sway opinion by using loaded terminology. (greedy owners, obscene profits, exploited workers, mindless bureaucrats, costly regulations, creeping socialism)

C. Definitions

1. Economics is a second language.

2. It is often difficult for students to recognize terms as new vocabulary that needs to be studied as diligently as though they had never before encountered the words.

3. Students in a physics class encountering terms like erg, ohm, or foot-pound recognize the need to investigate. Students that are reading a text filled with words like rent, capital, or investment assume that they already have an adequate working definition.

D. Causation Fallacies

1. Post hoc fallacy: When two events occur in time sequence, the first event is not necessarily the cause of the second event.

2. Correlation versus causation: Events may be related without a causal relationship.

a. The positive relationship between education and income does not tell us which causes the increase in the other. (Which is the independent variable and which is the dependent variable?)

b. It may be that the increase income that occurs with increased education is due to some other third factor that is not under direct consideration.

VII. **A Look Ahead**

A. Chapter 2 builds the production possibilities model that visually demonstrates the basic economic principles of scarcity, choice, opportunity cost, and the law of increasing costs.

B. Chapter 3 builds the supply and demand model for individual markets.

C. Chapter 4 combines all the markets in the economy and observes the coordination of economic activity through market prices.

D. Chapters 5 and 6 examine the important sectors of the economy (households, businesses, government, and the international sector) discussing their role and interaction.

VIII. **LAST WORD: Fast Food Lines—An Economic Perspective**

A. People choose the shortest line to reduce time cost.

B. Lines tend to have equal lengths as people shift from longer to shorter lines in effort to save time.

C. Lines are chosen based on length without much other information—cost of obtaining more information is not worth the benefit.

   1. Imperfect information may lead to an unexpected wait.

   2. Imperfect information may cause some people to leave when they see a long line.

D. When a customer reaches the counter, other economic decisions are made about what to order. From an economic perspective, these choices will be made after the consumer compares the costs and benefits of possible choices.

APPENDIX TO CHAPTER 1

This appendix is to prepare students for reading, analyzing, and constructing simple graphs in later chapters. To determine which students need help in this area, the instructor may want to give a brief pretest. In other words, you may want to excuse those students who already have graphing skills from this review. For students who do need help in this area, software graphics tutorials are also very useful, especially the ones designed to accompany the text.

I. **Graphs and Their Meaning**

A. Graphs help students to visualize and understand economic relationships. Most of our economic models explain relationships between just two sets of economic facts.

B. Constructing a two-dimensional graph involves drawing a horizontal and a vertical axis.

   1. Mark the axis using convenient increments and fitting the data given.

   2. Each point on the graph yields *two* pieces of information, the quantity of the variable on the horizontal axis and the corresponding quantity of the variable on the vertical axis.

C. Direct and inverse relationships

   1. If two variables change in the same direction (an increase in one is associated with an increase in the other) it is a direct or positive relationship.

   2. If the two sets of data move in opposite directions, they are inversely or negatively related.

D. Dependent and independent variables:

   1. Economists are often interested in determining which variable is the "cause" and which is the "effect" when two variables appear to be related.

   2. Mathematicians are always consistent in applying the rule that the independent variable or "cause" is placed on the horizontal axis and the dependent variable or outcome (effect) is placed on the vertical axis.

   3. Economists are less tidy, and traditionally have put price and cost data on the vertical axis.

   4. Note that inverse relationships are downward sloping to the right and direct relationships are upward sloping to the right regardless of which variable is placed on the horizontal or vertical axis.

E. Other things equal

1. When economists plot the relationship between two variables, all other influences are assumed to remain exactly the same (ceteris paribus).

2. If any of the other factors do change, a new plot of the original relationship must be made.

3. This point is extremely important for student understanding of the market model developed in chapter 3. It provides the distinction between a "slide" along an existing curve, and the "shift" of a curve that is required if a variable not labeled on the axis is changed.

F. The slope of a straight line is the ratio of the vertical change to horizontal change between any two points on the line.

   1. The slope of a line will be positive if both variables change in the same direction (a positive or direct relationship).

   2. The slope of a line will be negative if the variables change in the opposite direction (an inverse or negative relationship).

   3. The numerical value of the slope will depend on the way the relevant variables are measured.

   4. Economic analysis is often concerned with marginal changes, the relative change in one variable with respect to another; it is this *rate of change* that is measured by the slope.

   5. Lines that are parallel with either the horizontal or vertical axis indicate that the two variables are unrelated, that is, a change in one variable has no effect on the value of the other.

      a. A vertical line has an infinite slope.

      b. A horizontal line has a zero slope.

G. The vertical intercept of a line is the point where the line intersects the vertical axis.

H. Equation of a linear relationship

   1. If the vertical intercept and the slope are known, the general form $y = a + bx$ describes the line.

   2. y represents the variable on the vertical axis (the dependent variable in standard mathematical form) **a** is the vertical intercept, **b** is the slope of the line, and **x** represents the variable on the horizontal axis (the independent variable in standard mathematical form).

   3. The income—consumption example places the dependent and the independent in proper mathematical form.

   4. The price-quantity example reverses their position and places price (the independent variable) on the vertical axis and quantity (the dependent variable) on the horizontal axis.

I. Slope of a nonlinear curve

   1. The slope of a nonlinear relationship changes from one point to another.

   2. The slope of a curve at point **a** is equal to the slope of a line tangent to the curve at point **a**.

ANSWERS TO END-OF-CHAPTER AND APPENDIX QUESTIONS

1-1   (*Key Question*) Use the economic perspective to explain why someone who is normally a light eater at a standard restaurant may become somewhat of a glutton at a buffet-style restaurant which charges a single price for all you can eat.

This behavior can be explained in terms of marginal costs and marginal benefits. At a standard restaurant, items are priced individually—they have a positive marginal cost. If you order more, it will cost you more. You order until the marginal benefit from the extra food no longer exceeds the marginal cost. At a buffet you pay a flat fee no matter how much you eat. Once the fee is paid, additional food items have a zero marginal cost. You therefore continue to eat until your marginal benefit becomes zero.

1-2   What is the scientific method and how does it relate to theoretical economics? What is the difference between a hypothesis and an economic law or principle?

The scientific method is the technique used by economists to determine economic laws or principles. These laws or principles are formulated to explain and/or predict behavior of individuals or institutions.

A hypothesis is a "guessimate" as to the possible cause-and effect relationships between and among the facts. An economic law or principle is formulated after the hypothesis has been tested for validity.

1-3   Why is it significant that economics is not a laboratory science? What problems may be involved in deriving and applying economic principles?

Because the world of reality is cluttered with innumerable interrelated facts, researchers must be highly selective in gathering information. They must determine which facts are relevant to the problem under consideration. But even when this sorting process is complete, the relevant information may at first seem random and unrelated.

The economist seeks principles—generalizations about the way individuals and institutions behave. Deriving principles is called theoretical economics or economic analysis. The role of economic theorizing or economic analysis is to systematically arrange facts, interpret them, and generalize from them.

1-4   Explain the following statements:

a.   "Good economic policy requires good economic theory."

b.   "Generalization and abstraction are nearly synonymous."

c.   "Facts serve to sort out good and bad hypotheses."

d.   "The *other things equal assumption* helps isolate key economic relationships."

(a) Economic theories are the foundation of economic policy. Economic policy is a course of action intended to resolve a specific problem or further a nation's economic goals. Therefore, the action taken (the policy) is effective only if the underlying theory is correct.

(b) The full scope of economic reality is too complex and bewildering to be understood as a whole. Economists abstract—that is, build models—to give meaning to an otherwise overwhelming and confusing maze of facts. Economic principles are generalizations; they are expressed as the tendencies of typical, or average, consumers, workers, or business firms. Generalizations or abstractions are of practical use because the simplification and removal of clutter make analysis of problems easier.

(c) To test a hypothesis, economists must subject it to systematic and repeated comparison with relevant facts. If real-world data confirm the hypothesis repeatedly, we have a good theory, otherwise it must be discarded and a new hypothesis developed.

(d) Natural scientists such as chemists or physicists can much more easily control experiments and test with great precision an assumed relationship between two variables. Economists have a much more difficult time trying to isolate key economic relationships. Nonetheless, the "other things equal assumption" is extremely important. Economists must test their theories using real world data, generated by the actual operation of the economy. Under these conditions "other things" do change and despite sophisticated statistical techniques, controls are less than perfect. As a result economics principles are less precise than those of laboratory sciences.

1-5   (*Key Question*) Explain in detail the interrelationships between economic facts, theory, and policy. Critically evaluate this statement: "The trouble with economic theory is that it is not practical. It is detached from the real world."

Economic theory consists of factually supported generalizations about economic behavior that can be used to formulate economic policies. Economic theory enables policymakers to formulate economic policies that are relevant to real-world goals and problems that are based upon carefully observed facts.

1-6   To what extent do you accept the eight economic goals stated and described in this chapter? What priorities would you assign to them?

The first two parts of this question will be answered differently depending on the basic philosophy or values of the student.

Those who favor especially a high and growing standard of living should favor goals 1 (economic growth) and 2 (full employment).

Those more committed to equity, to "fair shares," and the lessening of poverty, will probably prefer to stress goals 6 (an equitable distribution of income) and 7 (economic security). Such students should also make at least some reference to goals 1 and 2 or at least explain how they expect greater fairness in the economy to come about in the absence of a growing economy that in itself requires at least the absence of heavy unemployment.

Those most committed to free enterprise will probably mention goal 5 (economic freedom) first. But these students should not completely ignore the other goals, for freedom to change jobs or to seek one is of little use in times of high unemployment and no or negative growth. Moreover, such times can well lead to social unrest to such an extent that even the economic freedom of the wealthy is threatened.

Those concerned by the growing international indebtedness of the United States will mention goal 8 (balance of trade) but, at this stage of their studies, should not be expected to go very deeply—if at all—into the need for increasing productivity (implied in goal 3: economic efficiency) and maintaining price stability in relation to America's trading partners in order to improve the balance of international trade in goods and services. Nor should students at this stage be expected to relate the Federal budget deficit and the related Federal borrowing abroad to the trade deficit.

With regard to the third part of this question, most students will probably agree that progress, stability, justice, and freedom are compatible with the list of goals given in the chapter. It is hard to imagine progress without economic growth and at least the absence of substantial unemployment. High inflation and the consequent arbitrary redistribution of incomes preclude stability, as does, in fact, high unemployment. Justice, in the view of most, is bound up with the goal of an equitable distribution of income, as it is defined in the chapter. And freedom, in the broadest sense, is linked with all eight of the goals—even of the eighth, if Americans wish to be free of the undue influence creditors can exert on a debtor.

1-7   (*Key Question*) Indicate whether each of the following statements applies to microeconomics or macroeconomics:

(a), (d), and (f) are macro; (b), (c), and (e) are micro.

1-8   (*Key Question*) Identify each of the following as either a positive or a normative statement:

    a. The high temperature today was 89 degrees.

    b. It was too hot today.

    c. Other things being equal, higher interest rates reduce the total amount of borrowing.

    d. Interest rates are too high.

    (a) and (c) are positive; (b) and (d) are normative..

1-9   (*Key Question*) Explain and give an illustration of (a) the fallacy of composition; and (b) the "after this, therefore because of this" fallacy. Why are cause-and-effect relationships difficult to isolate in the social sciences?

    (a) The fallacy of composition is the mistake of believing that something true for an individual part is necessarily true for the whole. Example: A single auto producer can increase its profits by lowering its price and taking business away from its competitors. But matched price cuts by all auto manufacturers will not necessarily yield higher industry profits.

    (b) The "after this, therefore because of this" fallacy is incorrectly reasoning that when one event precedes another, the first even necessarily caused the second. Example: Interest rates rise, followed by an increase in the rate of inflation, leading to the erroneous conclusion that the rise in interest rates caused the inflation. Actually higher interest rates slow inflation.

    Cause-and-effect relationships are difficult to isolate because "other things" are continually changing.

1-10   Suppose studies show that students who study more hours receive higher grades. Does this relationship guarantee that any particular student who studies longer will get higher grades?

    No, not necessarily, because cause and effect are not clear. The observed relationship could largely reflect the fact that smarter students study more hours than do less able students. A less able student thus might not get better grades by studying longer, at least to the extent suggested by the graph.

1-11   Studies indicate that married men on average earn more income than unmarried men of the same age. Why must we be cautious in concluding that marriage is the cause and higher income is the *effect*?

    Correlation does not necessarily mean that there is causation. The relationship could be purely coincidental or dependent on some other factor not included in the analysis. It is also possible that higher income is the variable that "causes" marriage.

1-12   (*Last Word*) Use the economic perspective to explain the behavior of the *workers* (rather than the customers) observed at a fast-food restaurant. Why are these workers there, rather than, say cruising around in their cars? Why do they work so diligently? Why do so many of them quit these jobs once they have graduated high school?

    Workers at the fast-food restaurant are also engaging in rational behavior attempting to achieve maximum fulfillment of their goals. Each worker is weighing the opportunity cost of being in the restaurant rather than participating in the activity that is perceived as the next best alternative (say, cruising around in their cars).

    The diligence observed is a function of their desire to maintain employment and the marginal benefit they receive from another day's pay. Many of them quit their jobs after high school graduation because they receive more highly valued offers for the use of their time.

Chapter 1 - Appendix

1-1   Briefly explain the use of graphs as a way to present economic relationships. What is an inverse relationship? How does it graph? What is a direct relationship? How does it graph? Graph and explain the relationships you would expect to find between (a) the number of inches of rainfall per month and the sale of umbrellas, (b) the amount of tuition and the level of enrollment at a university, and (c) the popularity of a music artist and the price of her concert tickets.

In each case cite and explain how variables other than those specifically mentioned might upset the expected relationship. Is your graph in part b consistent with the fact that, historically, enrollments and tuition have both increased? If not, explain any difference.

Graphs can be used to illustrate the relationship between two sets of data. An inverse relationship is when the two variables change in opposite directions. The line is downward sloping. A direct relationship is when the two variables change in the same direction. The line is upward sloping. Statements (a) and (c) illustrate direct relationships. Statement (b) illustrates an inverse relationship. The inverse relationship is assuming that everything else remains equal.

1-2   (*Key Question*) Indicate how each of the following might affect the data shown in Table 2 and Figure 2 of this appendix:

a. GSU's athletic director schedules higher-quality opponents.

b. An NBA team locates in the city where GSU plays.

c. GSU contracts to have all its home games televised.

(a) More tickets are bought at each price; the line shifts to the right.

(b) Fewer tickets are bought at each price, the line shifts to the left.

(c) Fewer tickets are bought at each price, the line shifts to the left.

1-3   (*Key Question*) The following table contains data on the relationship between saving and income. Rearrange these data into a meaningful order and graph them on the accompanying grid. What is the slope of the line? The vertical intercept? Interpret the meaning of both the slope and the intercept. Write the equation which represents this line. What would you predict saving to be at the $12,500 level of income?

Income (per year)	Saving (per year)
$15,000	$1,000
0	-500
10,000	500
5,000	0
20,000	1,500

Income column: $0; $5,000; $10,000, $15,000; $20,000. Saving column: $-500; 0; $500; $1,000; $1,500. Slope = 0.1 (= $1,000 - $500)/($15,000 - $10,000). Vertical intercept = $-500. The slope shows the amount saving will increase for every $1 increase in income; the intercept shows the amount of saving (dissaving) occurring when income is zero. Equation: S = $-500 + $0.1Y$ (where S is saving and Y is income). Saving will be $750 at the $12,500 income level.

1-4   Construct a table from the following data shown on the accompanying graph. Which is the dependent variable and which the independent variable? Summarize the data in equation form.

Study time (hours)	Exam scores
0	10
2	30
4	50
6	70
8	90
9	100

The dependent variable (the effect) is the exam score and the independent variable (the cause) is the study time.

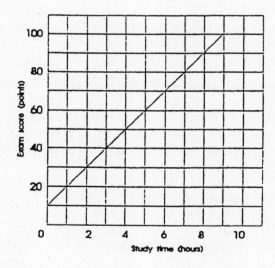

The equation is:

Exam score $= 10 + (50 - 30)/(4 - 2) \times$ Study time

$\quad\quad\quad\quad = 10 + 20/2 \times$ Study time

$\quad\quad\quad\quad = 10 + 10 \times$ Study time

Proof:

Exam score when study time is 6 hours:

$$= 10 + (10 \times 6)$$
$$= 10 + 60$$
$$= 70 \text{ as shown in the table above}$$

1-5 Suppose that when the interest rate is 16 percent, businesses find it unprofitable to invest in machinery and equipment. However, when the interest rate is 14 percent, $5 billion worth of investment is profitable. At 12 percent interest, a total of $10 billion of investment is profitable. Similarly, total investment increases by $5 billion for each successive 2-percentage point decline in the interest rate. Describe the relevant relationship between the interest rate and investment in words, in a table, graphically, and as an equation. Put the interest rate on the vertical axis and investment on the horizontal axis, and in your equation use the form $i = a + bI$, where i is the interest rate, a is the vertical intercept, b is the slope of the line (which is negative), and I is the level of investment. Comment on the advantages and disadvantages of the verbal, tabular, graphic, and equation forms of description.

Interest rate (in percent)	Amount of investment (billions of dollars)
16	$ 0
14	5
12	10
10	15
8	20
6	25
4	30
2	35
0	40

When the interest rate is 16%, investment spending will be zero. When the interest rate is 14%, investment spending will be $5 billion. For each successive drop of 2 percentage points in the interest rate, investment spending will increase by $5 billion.

Using equation $I = a - bI$

$$I = 16 - [(16 - 14)/(5 - 0)] \times I$$
$$= 16 - 2/5I$$

Proof: substituting data from the table when *I* is $25 billion, $i = 16 - 2/5(25) = 16 - 10 = 6$

The verbal presentation can be made, but is hard to visualize. The tabular presentation is precise; all the facts are there, neatly arrayed, and it is easier to visualize than the verbal one. The graphic presentation shows at a glance the relationship between the variables and, moreover, is best for showing large changes, that is, movements of a whole curve. However, the graph requires careful drafting to ensure that it is as accurate as the table. The equation is as precise as the table and, moreover, describes all the intermediate points not set out in the table. For most people, though, the equation form is probably the hardest to visualize.

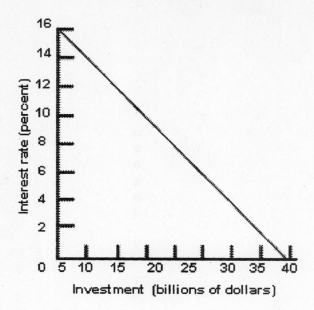

1-6 (*Key Question*) The accompanying graph shows curve *XX* and tangents at points *A*, *B*, and *C*. Calculate the slope of the curve at these three points.

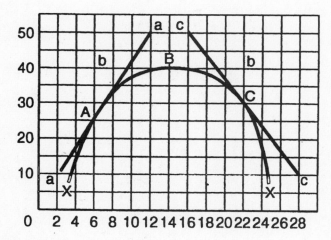

Slopes: at *A* = +4; at *B* = 0; at *C* = -4.

1-7 In the accompanying graph, is the slope of curve *AA'* positive or negative? Does the slope increase or decrease as we move along the curve from *A* to *A'*? Answer the same two questions for curve *BB'*.

Slope of *AA'* is positive (rising from left to right). The slope increases as we move from *A* to *A'*.

Slope of *BB'* is negative (dropping from left to right). The slope increases as we move from **B** to B'.

The slopes of both curves are tending to infinity as they continue to move to the right.

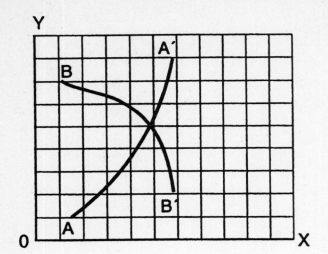

CHAPTER TWO
THE ECONOMIZING PROBLEM

CHAPTER OVERVIEW

This crucial chapter introduces students to a number of important concepts. The first part of the chapter stresses the economizing problem, which results because we have unlimited wants but limited resources. A discussion of full employment and efficiency follows. Both productive and allocative efficiency are defined and emphasized as desirable goals. The production possibilities curve model is introduced to illustrate these important concepts. Using this model, the concepts of opportunity costs and increasing opportunity costs, unemployment, growth, and present vs. future possibilities are all demonstrated. Additional emphasis is placed on allocative efficiency, which is a concept new to most students. Some real-world applications of the production possibilities idea are presented.

The chapter concludes by discussing how market and command economic systems differ, concentrating on who owns the factors of production and the method used to coordinate economic activity. The circular flow model is introduced to provide an overview of the way a market system operates.

WHAT'S NEW

The section on "unlimited wants" has been shortened relative to individual wants. The term "economic wants" is used rather than "material wants" throughout this chapter and the text. The applications/examples at the end of the discussion of the Production Possibilities Model have been reorganized and shortened; the examples are briefer and organized around key elements of the production possibilities model: unemployment, tradeoffs and opportunity costs, and shifts in the production possibilities curve. The section on Economic Systems has been made more concise with the major emphasis on the market and command systems. The discussion of the traditional economy has been dropped. A comparison of the market and command economies is the focus of chapter 4. The section describing the circular flow diagram has been revised; rather than referring to the supplying and demanding of products and resource services, the terms selling and buying are used.

The LAST WORD has been updated. The two WEB-BASED QUESTIONS have been changed.

INSTRUCTIONAL OBJECTIVES

After completing this chapter, students should be able to:

1. Define the economizing problem, incorporating the relationship between limited resources and unlimited wants.

2. Identify types of economic resources and types of income associated with various factors.

3. Differentiate between full employment and full production.

4. Explain the concepts of allocative and productive efficiency and how they differ.

5. Construct a production possibilities curve when given appropriate data.

6. Illustrate economic growth, unemployment and underemployment of resources, allocative and productive efficiency, and increasing costs using a production possibilities curve.

7. Give examples of underallocation and overallocation of resources.

8. Give some real-world applications of the production possibilities concept.

9. Summarize the general relationship between investment and economic growth.

10. Highlight the main features of a market economy and a command economy.

11. Identify the decision makers and the markets in a market system using the circular flow diagram.

12. Identify the two roles each that households and businesses play using the circular flow diagram.

13. Differentiate between product and resource markets.

14. Define and identify the terms and concepts listed at the end of the chapter.

COMMENTS AND TEACHING SUGGESTIONS

1. This Chapter is an important introduction to economic reasoning and provides a foundation and framework for learning the principles of economics. Three topics that should be stressed include: (1) the problem of scarcity and the necessity of choice, (2) the production possibilities model, and (3) the circular flow model.

2. Most students are all too familiar with the problem of scarcity. Although income and time are not resources in the way in which we define resources in economics, these are what are most scarce to students. Explain how making a budget is dealing with the problem of their limited financial resources and their virtually unlimited wants. Other examples can be how businesses choose between two products when allocating their limited resources and choose between two resources when allocating their limited revenues. Further discussion can bring in examples of allocating federal and/or state tax revenues, especially when state revenues compete with funding the state university.

3. To personalize the problem of opportunity cost, ask what else they could be doing during a specific economics class; what are their foregone alternatives? Why might it be more expensive for older students to attend the class than younger ones? Encourage students to find examples of opportunity cost in newspaper articles and magazines. Choice is a necessary part of life; every action has its costs and benefits. Identifying and quantifying these tradeoffs is at the heart of economic analysis.

4. Current news articles can serve many purposes in a principles class. Most instructors assign a high priority to helping students apply the general principles of economics to the specific problems and decisions they make. Short essays, oral reports, class discussion and longer term projects are all examples of how current news could be incorporated into the course. A term project focused on current issues such as health care, welfare reform, environmental problems, defense spending, or education can help students develop an appreciation of the problem of scarcity and the trade-offs that need to be considered when formulating public policy.

   The problems of underdeveloped countries could also be used to illustrate the seriousness of choosing between capital goods and consumer goods. Focusing a project on the problems of a single developing country can be interesting. It would allow students to make many comparisons including the impact of differing economic systems, degree of government regulation, environmental quality standards, differences in resource availability, climate, educational levels, and of course: the choice between consumer and capital goods.

5. Reference is made to the production possibility curve in later chapters. It is essential that students become thoroughly familiar with its use, including the significance of its concave shape.

6. Some instructors may want to insert old Chapter 40 (now an Internet chapter found at www.mhhe.com/economics/mcconnell15) on the Russian transition to capitalism following Chapter 2. Students tend to be fascinated with the contrasts between the former Soviet and American

systems; the contrasts seem to make students more aware of aspects of capitalism that may have been taken for granted. In any case the instructor may want to supplement the chapter by assigning students to find current news items on the economies of the transitional economic systems of the former Eastern bloc countries. This helps to point out that the economizing problem is common to all societies, not just to capitalist systems.

7. The circular flow diagram provides a very useful overview of the market system because it clarifies the interaction between product and resource markets. Follow each of the streams starting with the households, owners of the factors of production, providing the resource services to businesses. The role of business is to combine the inputs and to produce output that then moves through the product markets to the households. The student can then be asked: "Why do they work?" The answer is: to receive a portion of what they have helped to produce. The movement through the money stream starts with the households receiving money income that gives them the ability to purchase goods and services from the product markets. It can be shown that those same dollars are given different names as they move through the economy, i.e., money income becomes consumption expenditures and then business revenue followed by the costs of production, and finally money income again. Also, there can be a discussion about what happens in an economy if one part of the two streams does not function, such as in Russia. The circular flow diagram provides a visual perspective that helps many students.

STUDENT STUMBLING BLOCKS

1. Most students have difficulty with the concept of allocative efficiency as opposed to productive efficiency. Even after mastering the concept, they may downplay its significance until they are given examples of situations where allocative efficiency has not existed. A comparison between capitalist outcomes and those of a centrally planned economic system is helpful, because students can relate to the idea that having planners decide for society what should or should not be produced may result in outcomes that the individual households do not like.

2. The production possibilities curve simplifies many concepts for students who don't have "graph anxiety." However, for those who are uncomfortable with graphs, this model may confuse rather than simplify. Computerized tutorials will be especially helpful for these students.

LECTURE NOTES

I. **The foundation of economics is the economizing problem: society's material wants are unlimited while resources are limited or scarce.**

   A. Unlimited wants (the first fundamental fact):

      1. Economic wants are desires of people to use goods and services that provide utility, which means satisfaction.

      2. Products are sometimes classified as luxuries or necessities, but division is subjective.

      3. Services satisfy wants as well as goods.

      4. Businesses and governments also have wants.

      5. Over time, wants change and multiply.

   B. Scarce resources (the second fundamental fact):

      1. Economic resources are limited relative to wants.

      2. Economic resources are sometimes called factors of production and include four categories:

       a.   Land or natural resources,

       b.   Capital or investment goods which are all manufactured aids to production like tools, equipment, factories, transportation, etc.,

       c.   Labor or human resources, which include physical and mental abilities used in production,

       d.   Entrepreneurial ability, a special kind of human resource that provides four important functions:

           i.   Combines resources needed for production,

           ii.   Makes basic business policy decisions,

           iii. Is an innovator for new products, production techniques, organizational forms,

           iv. Bears the risk of time, effort, and funds.

   3.   Resource payments correspond to resource categories:

       a.   Rent and interest to suppliers of property resources,

       b.   Wages and salaries to labor resources,

       c.   Profits to entrepreneurs.

   4.   Quantities of resources are limited relative to the total amount of goods and services desired.

II.   Economics: Employment and Efficiency

A. Basic definition: Economics is the social science concerned with the problem of using scarce resources to attain the greatest fulfillment of society's unlimited wants.

B. Economics is a science of efficiency in the use of scarce resources. Efficiency requires full employment of available resources and full production.

   1.   Full employment means all available resources should be employed.

   2.   Full production means that employed resources are providing maximum satisfaction of our economic wants. Underemployment occurs if this is not so.

C. Full production implies two kinds of efficiency:

   1.   Allocative efficiency means that resources are used for producing the combination of goods and services most wanted by society—for example, producing compact discs instead of long-playing records with productive resources or computers with word processors rather than manual typewriters.

   2.   Productive efficiency means that least costly production techniques are used to produce wanted goods and services.

D. Full production means producing the "right" goods (allocative efficiency) in the "right" way (productive efficiency). (Key Question 5)

III.   Production possibilities tables and curves are a device to illustrate and clarify the economizing problem.

A. Assumptions:

   1.   Economy is operating efficiently (full employment and full production).

2. Available supply of resources is fixed in quantity and quality at this point in time.

3. Technology is constant during analysis.

4. Economy produces only two types of products.

B. Choices will be necessary because resources and technology are fixed. A production possibilities table illustrates some of the possible choices (see Table 2-1).

C. A production possibilities curve is a graphical representation of choices.

1. Points on the curve represent maximum possible combinations of robots and pizza given resources and technology.

2. Points inside the curve represent underemployment or unemployment.

3. Points outside the curve are unattainable at present.

D. Optimal or best product-mix:

1. It will be some point on the curve.

2. The exact point depends on society; this is a normative decision.

E. Law of increasing opportunity costs:

1. The amount of other products that must be foregone to obtain more of any given product is called the opportunity cost.

2. Opportunity costs are measured in real terms rather than money (market prices are not part of the production possibilities model.)

3. The more of a product produced the greater is its (marginal) opportunity cost.

4. The slope of the production possibilities curve becomes steeper, demonstrating increasing opportunity cost. This makes the curve appear bowed out, concave from the origin.

5. Economic Rationale:

   a. Economic resources are not completely adaptable to alternative uses.

   b. To get increasing amounts of pizza, resources that are not particularly well suited for that purpose must be used. Workers that are accustomed to producing robots on an assembly line may not do well as kitchen help.

F. Allocative efficiency revisited:

1. How does society decide its optimal point on the production possibilities curve?

2. Recall that society receives marginal benefits from each additional product consumed, and as long as this marginal benefit is more than the additional cost of the product, it is advantageous to have the additional product.

3. Conversely, if the additional (marginal) cost of obtaining an additional product is more than the additional benefit received, then it is not "worth" it to society to produce the extra unit.

4. Figure 2-2 reminds us that marginal costs rise as more of a product is produced.

5. Marginal benefits decline as society consumes more and more pizzas. In Figure 2-2 we can see that the optimal amount of pizza is 200,000 units, where marginal benefit just covers marginal cost.

      a.   Beyond that, the added benefits would be less than the added cost.

      b.   At less than 200,000, the added benefits will exceed the added costs, so it makes sense to produce more.

  6. Generalization: The optimal production of any item is where its marginal benefit is equal to its marginal cost. In our example, for robots this must occur at 7,000 robots.

IV.   **Unemployment, Growth, and the Future**

    A. Unemployment and productive inefficiency occur when the economy is producing less than full production or inside the curve (point U in Figure 2-3).

    B. In a growing economy, the production possibilities curve shifts outward.

      1. When resource supplies expand in quantity or quality.

      2. When technological advances are occurring.

    C. Present choices and future possibilities: Using resources to produce consumer goods and services represents a choice for present over future consumption. Using resources to invest in technological advance, education, and capital goods represents a choice for future over present goods. The decision as to how to allocate resources in the present will create more or less economic growth in the future. (Key Questions 10 and 11)

    (See for example Global Perspective 2-1 where various countries are compared with respect to their economic growth rates relative to the share of GDP devoted to investment.)

    D. A Qualification: International Trade

      1. A nation can avoid the output limits of its domestic Production Possibilities through international specialization and trade.

      2. Specialization and trade have the same effect as having more and better resources of improved technology.

    E. Examples and Applications

      1. Unemployment and Productive Inefficiency:

         a.   Depression

         b.   Discrimination in the labor market.

      2. Tradeoffs and Opportunity Costs

         a.   Logging and mining versus wilderness.

         b.   Allocation of tax resources.

      3. Shifts of Production Possibilities Curve

         a.   Technological advances in the U.S.

         b.   The effects of war.

    H. See the Last Word on how a large increase in the number of women in the labor force has shifted the production possibilities curve outward.

V.   **Economic systems differ in two important ways: Who owns the factors of production and the method used to coordinate economic activity.**

    A. The market system:

    1.   There is private ownership of resources.

    2.   Markets and prices coordinate and direct economic activity.

    3.   Each participant acts in his or her own self-interest.

    4.   In pure capitalism the government plays a very limited role.

    5.   In the U.S. version of capitalism, the government plays a substantial role.

  B. Command economy, socialism or communism:

    1.   There is public (state) ownership of resources.

    2.   Economic activity is coordinated by central planning.

VI.   The Circular Flow Model for a Market-Oriented System (Key Graph 2-6)

  A. There are two groups of decision makers in private economy (no government yet): households and businesses.

    1.   The market system coordinates these decisions.

    2.   What happens in the resource markets?

       a.   Households sell resources directly or indirectly (through ownership of corporations).

       b.   Businesses buy resources in order to produce goods and services.

       c.   Interaction of these sellers and buyers determines the price of each resource, which in turn provides income for the owner of that resource.

       d.   Flow of payments from businesses for the resources constitutes business costs and resource owners' incomes.

    3.   What happens in the product markets?

       a.   Households are on the buying side of these markets, purchasing goods and services.

       b.   Businesses are on the selling side of these markets, offering products for sale.

       c.   Interaction of these buyers and sellers determines the price of each product.

       d.   Flow of consumer expenditures constitutes sales receipts for businesses.

    4.   Circular flow model illustrates this complex web of decision-making and economic activity that give rise to the real and money flows.

  B. Limitations of the model:

    1.   Does not depict transactions between households and between businesses.

    2.   Ignores government and the "rest of the world" in the decision-making process.

    3.   Does not explain how prices of products and resources are actually determined, but this is explained in Chapter 3.

VII.   LAST WORD: Women and Expanded Production Possibilities

  A. There has been an increase in the number of women who are working. This has had the effect of shifting the production possibilities curve outward.

  B. Whereas 40% of the women worked in 1965, 60% of the women are now working part time or full time.

    C. There are a number of reasons for this change:

       1. An increase in women's wage rates.

       2. Greater access to jobs.

       3. Changes in preferences and attitudes.

       4. Declining birthrates.

       5. Increasing divorce rates.

       6. Slower growth in male wages.

ANSWERS TO END-OF-CHAPTER QUESTIONS

2-1   Explain this statement: "If resources were unlimited and freely available, there would be no subject called economics."

       If resources were unlimited and freely available, making choices would not be necessary. Every person could have as much as they wanted of any good or service. Economics, the science of choice, would be unnecessary.

2-2   Comment on the following statement from a newspaper article: "Our junior high school serves a splendid hot meal for $1 without costing the taxpayers anything, thanks in part to a government subsidy."

       Obviously the writer is confused. Government subsidies come from government revenues and taxpayers are the source of tax revenues. It may be true that local property taxes that fund the junior high school are not being used for the lunches, but the federal government's funds do come from taxpayers across the country, including those in the town with the junior high. This example helps support the saying, "There ain't no such thing as a free lunch!"

2-3   Critically analyze: "Wants aren't insatiable. I can prove it. I get all the coffee I want to drink every morning at breakfast." Explain: "Goods and services are scarce because resources are scarce." Analyze: "It is the nature of all economic problems that absolute solutions are denied us."

       It may be that you get all the coffee you want on a particular morning, but will that satisfy your wants forever? Not if you want coffee in the future. Therefore, even your desire for coffee is insatiable over time.

       Goods and services are the product of resources. If resources were abundant without limit, then we would not have a scarcity of the products they produce.

       Economic problems are problems of relative scarcity—wants exceed resources in the relative sense. We cannot absolutely solve all of our economic problems; that is, satisfy all of everyone's wants and needs. If all our wants were completely fulfilled, nothing would have a price—why pay for anything if you've got everything already? And if there were no unfulfilled wants there would be no economic resources—why pay for an input when you've got all the outputs you could ever need? The fact that totally free goods and services do not exist provides support for the notion that total fulfillment of our wants is impossible.

2-4   What are economic resources? What are the major functions of the entrepreneur?

       Economic resources are of four main types: labor, land (natural resources), real capital (machines, factories, buildings, etc.,) and entrepreneurs. Economic resources are also called factors of production or inputs in the productive process. As these names imply, economic resources are required to produce the outputs desired by society. Since certain outputs are desired, they command a price and so, therefore, do economic resources. This can lead to some things being economic resources in some circumstances but not in others. Water in the middle of a lake, for example, is not an economic resource: Anyone can have it free. But the same water piped to a factory site is no longer free: Its movement must be paid for by taxes or by a specific charge. It is now an economic resource because the factory owner would not pay for its delivery unless the water was to be used in the factory's production. These four types of resources are highlighted in the circular flow diagram where the type of income accruing to each type of resource is shown.

Entrepreneurs are risk-takers: They coordinate the activities of the other three inputs for profit—or loss, which is why they are called risk-takers. Entrepreneurs sometimes manage companies that they own, but a manager who is not an owner is not necessarily an entrepreneur but may be performing some of the entrepreneurial functions for the company. Entrepreneurs are also innovators, or perhaps inventors, and profits help to motivate such activities.

2-5   (*Key Question*) Why is the problem of unemployment a part of the subject matter of economics? Distinguish between allocative efficiency and productive efficiency. Give an illustration of achieving productive, but not allocative, efficiency.

Economics deals with the "limited resources—unlimited wants" problem. Unemployment represents valuable resources that could have been used to produce more goods and services—to meet more wants and ease the economizing problem.

Allocative efficiency means that resources are being used to produce the goods and services most wanted by society. The economy is then located at the optimal point on its production possibilities curve where marginal benefit equals marginal cost for each good. Productive efficiency means the least costly production techniques are being used to produce wanted goods and services. Example: manual typewriters produced using the least-cost techniques but for which there is no demand.

2-6   (*Key Question*)   Here is a production possibilities table for war goods and civilian goods:

Type of Production	Production Alternatives				
	A	B	C	D	E
Automobiles	0	2	4	6	8
Rockets	30	27	21	12	0

a. Show these data graphically. Upon what specific assumptions is this production possibilities curve based?

b. If the economy is at point C, what is the cost of one more automobile? One more rocket? Explain how this curve reflects increasing opportunity costs.

c. What must the economy do to operate at some point on the production possibilities curve?

(a) See curve EDCBA. The assumptions are full employment and productive efficiency, fixed supplies of resources, and fixed technology.

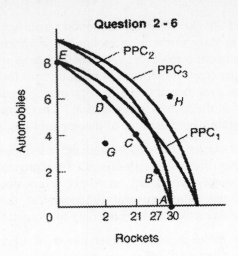

Question 2 - 6

(b) 4.5 rockets; .33 automobiles, as determined from the table. Increasing opportunity costs are

reflected in the concave-from-the-origin shape of the curve. This means the economy must give up larger and larger amounts of rockets to get constant added amounts of automobiles—and vice versa.

(c) It must obtain full employment and productive efficiency.

2-7 What is the opportunity cost of attending college? In 2000, nearly 80% of college-educated Americans held jobs, whereas only about 40% of those who did not finish high school held jobs. How might this difference relate to opportunity costs?

The opportunity cost of attending college (and of doing anything else) consists of the income forgone while attending college (and of doing anything else such as enjoying leisure) and the value of the goods that the student or the student's parents sacrifice in order to pay tuition and buy books, and other items necessary for college but not necessary otherwise.

Those who are college-educated have the potential of earning more income than those who did not finish high school. The opportunity cost (sacrifice of goods and services) of not working is much greater for those with the higher earning potential.

2-8 Suppose you arrive at a store expecting to pay $100 for an item, but learn that a store two miles away is charging $50 for it. Would you drive there and buy it? How does your decision benefit you? What is the opportunity cost of your decision? Now suppose you arrive at a store expecting to pay $6000 for an item, but learn that it costs $5950 at the other store. Do you make the same decision as before? Perhaps surprisingly, you should! Explain why.

Driving to the other store to save $50 does involve some cost in terms of time and inconvenience. However, for most of us the time it takes to drive two miles would be worth $50. For example, if it takes about ten minutes extra time and a negligible amount of gasoline (unless your time is worth $300 an hour, or $50 per each ten-minute period), it would benefit you to drive to the other store. While in the second case, $50 may seem like less compared to the $6000 total price, for you the $50 is still a $50 savings, exactly the same as in the first case. Therefore, you should apply the same reasoning. Is the $50 benefit from driving the extra two miles worth the cost? The conclusion should be the same in both cases.

2-9 (*Key Question*) Specify and explain the shapes of the marginal-benefit and marginal-cost curves and use these curves to determine the optimal allocation of resources to a particular product. If current output is such that marginal cost exceeds marginal benefit, should more or less resources be allocated to this product? Explain.

The marginal benefit curve is downward sloping, MB falls as more of a product is consumed because additional units of a good yield less satisfaction than previous units. The marginal cost curve is upward sloping, MC increases as more of a product is produced since additional units require the use of increasingly unsuitable resource. The optimal amount of a particular product occurs where MB equals MC. If MC exceeds MB, fewer resources should be allocated to this use. The resources are more valuable in some alternative use (as reflected in the higher MC) than in this use (as reflected in the lower MB).

2-10   (*Key Question*) Label point G inside the production possibilities curve you have drawn for question 6. What does it indicate? Label point H outside the curve. What does this point indicate? What must occur before the economy can attain the level of production indicated by point H?

G indicated unemployment, productive inefficiency, or both. H is at present unattainable. Economic growth—through more inputs, better inputs, improved technology—must be achieved to attain H.

2-11   (*Key Question*) Referring again to question 6, suppose improvement occurs in the technology of producing rockets but not in the production of automobiles. Draw the new production possibilities curve. Now assume that a technological advance occurs in producing automobiles but not in producing rockets. Draw the new production possibilities curve. Now draw a production possibilities curve that reflects technological improvement in the production of both products.

See the graph for question 2-6. PPC$_1$ shows improved rocket technology. PPC$_2$ shows improved auto technology. PPC$_3$ shows improved technology in producing both products.

2-12   Explain how, if at all, each of the following affects the location of the production possibilities curve.

a. Standardized examination scores of high school and college students decline.

b. The unemployment rate falls from 9 to 6 percent of the labor force.

c. Defense spending is reduced to allow government to spend more on health care.

d. A new technique improves the efficiency of extracting copper from ore.

 (a) Assuming scores indicate lower skills, then productivity should fall and this would move the curve inward.

(b) Should not affect location of curve. Production moves from inside the curve toward frontier.

(c) Should not affect location of curve. Resources are allocated away from one type of government spending toward another (health care).

(d) The curve should shift outward as more production is possible with existing resources.

2-13   Explain: "Affluence tomorrow requires sacrifice today."

This quote refers to the fact that economic growth and a rising standard of living in the future require investment today. Society can choose to consume all of its income today, or it can set aside some of it for investment purposes. Productive resources that go for investment goods today, e.g., new factories, machines, equipment, are obviously not being used for producing consumer goods. Therefore, consumption is being sacrificed today so that investment goods can be produced with some of today's resources.

2-14   Suppose that, based on a nation's production possibilities curve, an economy must sacrifice 10,000 pizzas domestically to get the one additional industrial robot it desires, but can get that robot from another country in exchange for 9,000 pizzas. Relate this information to the following statement: "Through international specialization and trade, a nation can reduce its opportunity cost of obtaining goods and thus 'get outside its production possibilities curve.'"

The message of the production possibilities curve is that an individual nation is limited to the combinations of output indicated by its production possibilities curve. International specialization means directing domestic resources to output which a nation is highly efficient at producing. International trade involves the exchange of these goods for goods produced abroad. Specialization and trade have the same effect as having more and better resources or discovering improved production techniques. The output gains from greater international specialization and trade are the equivalent of economic growth.

2-15   Contrast how a market system and a command economy try to cope with economic scarcity.

A market system allows for the private ownership of resources and coordinates economic activity through market prices. Participants act in their own self-interest and seek to maximize satisfaction or profit through their own decisions regarding consumption or production. Goods and services are produced and resources are supplied by whoever is willing to do so. The result is competition and widely dispersed economic power.

The command economy is characterized by public ownership of nearly all property resources and economic decisions are made through central planning. The planning board, appointed by the government determines production goals for each enterprise. The division of output between capital and consumer goods is centrally decided based on the board's long-term priorities.

2-16   Distinguish between the resource market and product market in the circular flow model. In what way are businesses and households both *sellers* and *buyers* in this model? What are the flows in the circular flow model?

The resource markets are where the owners of the resources (the households) sell their resources to the buyers of the resources (businesses). In the product markets, businesses sell the goods and services they have produced to the buyers of the goods and services, the households.

Households (individuals) either own all economic resources directly or own them indirectly through their ownership of business corporations. These households are willing to sell their resources to businesses because attractive prices draw them into specific resource markets. Businesses buy resources because they are necessary for producing goods and services. The interaction of the buyers and sellers establishes the price of each resource.

In the product market, businesses are the sellers and householders are the buyers; their role in the market has been reversed. Each group of economic units both buys and sells.

One flow is the flow of real goods and services (including resource services) and the other flow is the flow of money (money income, consumption expenditures, revenue, production costs).

2-17   (*Last Word*) Which *two* of the six reasons listed in the Last Word do you think are the *most important* in explaining the rise in participation of women in the workplace? Explain your reasoning.

A poll taken in a class of 60 college freshman gave the first three reasons (women's rising wage rates, expanded job accessibility, and changing preferences and attitudes) nearly all the votes. Each of these explanations received about one third of the votes. Surprisingly, not a single student voted for "declining birth rates" as a reason for the rise in the number of women in the workforce. The consensus of the class was that the last three explanations (declining birth rates, rising divorce rates, and stagnating male earnings) were the effects, rather than the cause of more women joining the workforce. Because wage rates are higher the opportunity cost of raising children has risen. Women have chosen to bear fewer children, because they are now relatively more expensive. Similarly, women who have a higher earning capacity find the opportunity cost of getting a divorce reduced. Finally, male earnings may have stagnated partially because of the entrance of large numbers of well-educated women into the workforce, increasing the competition for the available jobs.

CHAPTER THREE
INDIVIDUAL MARKETS:
DEMAND AND SUPPLY

CHAPTER OVERVIEW

This chapter provides a basic, but rather detailed introduction to how markets operate as well as an introduction to demand and supply concepts. Both demand and supply are defined and illustrated; determinants of demand and supply are listed and explained. The concept of equilibrium and the effects of changes in demand and supply on equilibrium price and quantity are explained and illustrated. The chapter also includes brief discussions of supply and demand factors in resource markets and the importance of the ceteris paribus assumption.

WHAT'S NEW?

This chapter contains most of what was in the previous edition, but has several new examples. The examples in Tables 3-3 and 3-7 have been changed

INSTRUCTIONAL OBJECTIVES

After completing this chapter, students should be able to:

1. Identify why price and quantity demanded are inversely related and why price and quantity supplied are directly related.

2. Differentiate between demand and quantity demanded; and supply and quantity supplied.

3. Graph demand and supply curves when given demand and supply schedules.

4. State the Law of Demand and the Law of Supply.

5. List the major determinants of demand.

6. List the major determinants of supply.

7. Explain the concept of equilibrium price and quantity.

8. Illustrate graphically equilibrium price and quantity.

9. Explain the effects of changes in demand and supply on equilibrium price and quantity.

10. Explain the effects of a price change for one good on the demand for its substitutes or complements.

11. Give an example of the rationing function of prices.

12. Explain briefly how concepts of supply and demand apply to resource markets.

13. Define and identify terms and concepts listed at the end of the chapter.

COMMENTS AND TEACHING SUGGESTIONS

1. Emphasis in this chapter should be placed on: (a) The fact that demand and supply are schedules; (b) the intuitive understanding of the downward slope of demand and upward slope of supply curves; (c) the determinants of demand and supply; and (d) the distinction between a shift or change in demand (supply) and a change in quantity demanded (supplied).

2. Walk through the definition of supply and demand. Emphasize the distinction between a reaction to price and the influence of other variables. Point out that finding the equilibrium price and quantity is not the end of the process: It is only the beginning. The market model is powerful because it can be used to forecast what the likely outcome will be if one of the determinants of demand or the determinants of supply is changed. Do examples that use actual numbers on the axis of the graphs. Most students who have not used graphs extensively will get lost without specific examples. Approach the process systematically, and offer an example of each type of shift. Spend extra time on examples of substitute and complementary goods.

3. The concepts introduced in Chapter 3 are extremely important for an understanding of a market system. In later chapters more sophisticated explanations are introduced. Most instructors will want to wait until that point to discuss marginal utility, elasticity, and other related ideas. However, it may be useful to briefly discuss government price controls in looking at market equilibrium concepts. If they see what happens when price controls are attempted, it helps students understand how powerful market forces are. For example, attempts to control the price of gasoline below its equilibrium level in the 1970's led to shortages and long lines at the gas pumps. On the other hand, attempts to support the price of farm products above equilibrium prices has led to large surpluses in the markets for many agricultural products in the U.S. and Europe. Usually attempts to control prices are a response to the view that market prices are not always "fair." Therefore, government regulation of prices is based on equity issues. Students may discuss the dilemma: markets may not be always "fair," but attempts to interfere with its operation may lead to other problems. More discussion of these policies occurs in Chapters 20 (on elasticities) and Chapter 33 (on agriculture).

4. Emphasize that the students are already very experienced demanders, and what the instructor is doing is analyzing their behavior and using the vocabulary of economics when describing this behavior. Whereas the demand discussion can use real-world examples that are familiar to the students, the supply discussion is more theoretical.

5. Emphasize that the separate demand and supply discussions are lacking in reality because only one side of the market is being examined, i.e., demand or supply. Particularly with the changes in the determinants of supply (the imposition of a tax), students are going to conclude that the market price will change (increase). Explain that their intuitive conclusion will be correct once demand and supply are discussed together. Introduce each determinant systematically, offering an example of each type. Discuss the difference between determinants "change in price of a related good" when it is a demand determinant as opposed to a supply determinant. There are some products (cars and pickup trucks) that can be both demand and supply-related products.

6. When graphically showing a "change in demand" and simultaneously a "change in supply," show these changes separately on two graphs and ask the students to compare the changes in price and quantity exchanges.

7. It is useful to point out that in the real world it may be hard to pinpoint the equilibrium price and quantity exactly, but it is easy to establish when the price is too high because surpluses will develop, or too low because shortages will result.

8. Depending upon how the material in the micro course is organized, Chapter 3 could be combined with Chapter 20 (elasticity, administered pricing) and Chapter 21 (consumer behavior, utility).

9. The Last Word on ticket scalping illustrates the fact that equilibrium price may not be what many would consider a "fair" price. This is a good opportunity for a discussion of the fairness of market prices.

10. Good market simulation games exist. Some of these will be found in the inexpensive teaching materials designed for secondary teachers (but useful at the introductory college level also) from Economics America, National Council on Economic Education, 1140 Avenue of the Americas, New

York, NY 10036. Call 1-800-338-1192. The Stock Market Game sponsored by the NYSE can now be accessed over the internet.

STUDENT STUMBLING BLOCK

Vocabulary in this chapter is extremely important. The word "market" sounds familiar to students and they have already assigned another "everyday" meaning to the word. The competitive process described in this chapter does not fit the common experience of most students as they shop at the mall or at the grocery store. They are accustomed to prices that are "set" by a few producers. Careful definition of terms is not enough. Repetition and reinforcement with classroom exercises, homework, assignments from the study guide or computer software are essential in this chapter.

Change in quantity demanded (supplied) versus change in demand (supply) are concepts that students will need to master to be successful in the class and future economic classes. It is also very easy for the instructor to misstate these changes. We often say "change in demand" when what we mean is "change in the quantity demanded." Be careful not to further confuse students by making this mistake! End-of-chapter questions 2, 5, and 8 help clarify the difference, and why the semantics are so important to understanding this difference. For both instructor and student this distinction may seem like "nit-picking," but if the distinction is not made, more than the usual confusion may result. Whereas the discussion of demand fits the common experiences of most students, the discussion of supply is more theoretical and does not.

LECTURE NOTES

I. **Markets Defined**

   A. A market is an institution or mechanism that brings together buyers (demanders) and sellers (suppliers) of particular goods and services.

      1. A market may be local, national, or international in scope.

      2. Some markets are highly personal, face-to-face exchanges; others are impersonal and remote.

      3. This chapter concerns purely competitive markets with a large number of independent buyers and sellers.

      4. Product market involves goods and services.

      5. Resource market involves factors of production.

   B. The goal of the chapter is to explain the way in which markets adjust to changes and the role of prices in bringing the markets toward equilibrium.

II. **Demand**

   A. Demand is a schedule that shows the various amounts of a product consumers are willing and able to buy at each specific price in a series of possible prices during a specified time period.

      1. Example of demand schedule for corn is Table 3-1.

      2. The schedule shows how much buyers are willing and able to purchase at five possible prices.

      3. The market price depends on demand and supply.

      4. To be meaningful, the demand schedule must have a period of time associated with it.

B. Law of demand is a fundamental characteristic of demand behavior.

   1. Other things being equal, as price increases, the corresponding quantity demanded falls.

   2. Restated, there is an inverse relationship between price and quantity demanded.

   3. Note the "other things being constant" assumption refers to consumer income and tastes, prices of related goods, and other things besides the price of the product being discussed.

   4. Explanation of the law of demand:

      a. Diminishing marginal utility: The decrease in added satisfaction that results as one consumes additional units of a good or service, i.e., the second "Big Mac" yields less extra satisfaction (or utility) than the first.

      b. Income effect: A lower price increases the purchasing power of money income enabling the consumer to buy more at lower price (or less at a higher price).

      c. Substitution effect: A lower price gives an incentive to substitute the lower-priced good for now relatively higher-priced goods.

C. The demand curve:

   1. Illustrates the inverse relationship between price and quantity (see corn example, Figure 3-1).

   2. The downward slope indicates lower quantity (horizontal axis) at higher price (vertical axis), higher quantity at lower price.

D. Individual vs. market demand:

   1. Transition from an individual to a market demand schedule is accomplished by summing individual quantities at various price levels.

   2. Market curve is horizontal sum of individual curves (see corn example, Tables 3-2, 3-3 and Figure 3-2).

E. Class example: This is a good place to involve the class if your classroom setting allows. Select an item that students typically buy, such as a can of soft drink or donuts. It works especially well if one student already has the item, and you can use that student for your individual demand schedule. Select five to ten representative prices for the item and create a demand schedule based on this student's responses. It is usually interesting to include the zero price to see how many the student would want if the item were free. You can then construct an individual demand schedule on board or overhead transparency. Don't worry if it isn't a straight line, it will undoubtedly still represent the law of demand. If your class isn't too large, you could then construct a class market schedule using a show of fingers to indicate amounts students would purchase at each price level.

F. There are several determinants of demand or the "other things," besides price, which affect demand. Changes in determinants cause changes in demand.

   1. Table 3-4 provides additional illustrations. (Key Question 2)

      a. Tastes—-favorable change leads to increase in demand; unfavorable change to decrease.

      b. Number of buyers—the more buyers lead to an increase in demand; fewer buyers lead to decrease.

   c. Income—more leads to increase in demand; less leads to decrease in demand for normal goods. (The rare case of goods whose demand varies inversely with income is called inferior goods).

   d. Prices of related goods also affect demand.

    i. Substitute goods (those that can be used in place of each other): The price of the substitute good and demand for the other good are directly related. If price of Budweiser rises, demand for Miller should increase.

    ii. Complementary goods (those that are used together like tennis balls and rackets): When goods are complements, there is an inverse relationship between the price of one and the demand for the other.

   e. Expectations—consumer views about future prices, product availability, and income can shift demand.

2. A summary of what can cause an increase in demand:

   a. Favorable change in consumer tastes.

   b. Increase in the number of buyers.

   c. Rising income if product is a normal good.

   d. Falling incomes if product is an inferior good.

   e. Increase in the price of a substitute good.

   f. Decrease in the price of a complementary good.

   g. Consumers expect higher prices in the future.

3. A summary of what can cause a decrease in demand:

   a. Unfavorable change in consumer tastes,

   b. Decrease in number of buyers,

   c. Falling income if product is a normal good,

   d. Rising income if product is an inferior good,

   e. Decrease in price of a substitute good,

   f. Increase in price of a complementary good,

   g. Consumers' expectations of lower prices, or incomes in the future.

G. Review the distinction between a change in quantity demanded caused by price change and a change in demand caused by change in determinants.

III. Supply

A. Supply is a schedule that shows amounts of a product a producer is willing and able to produce and sell at each specific price in a series of possible prices during a specified time period.

1. A supply schedule portrays this such as the corn example in Table 3-5.

2. Schedule shows what quantities will be offered at various prices or what price will be required to induce various quantities to be offered.

B. Law of supply:

1. Producers will produce and sell more of their product at a high price than at a low price.

2. Restated: There is a direct relationship between price and quantity supplied.

3. Explanation: Given product costs, a higher price means greater profits and thus an incentive to increase the quantity supplied.

4. Beyond some production quantity producers usually encounter increasing costs per added unit of output.

   Note: A detailed explanation of diminishing returns is probably not necessary at this point and can be delayed until a later consideration of the costs of production.

C. The supply curve:

1. The graph of supply schedule appears in Figure 3-4, which graphs data from Table 3-6.

2. It shows direct relationship in upward sloping curve.

D. Determinants of supply:

1. A change in any of the supply determinants causes a change in supply and a shift in the supply curve. An increase in supply involves a rightward shift, and a decrease in supply involves a leftward shift.

2. Six basic determinants of supply, other than price. (See examples of curve shifts in Figure 3-4 and summary Table 3-7 and Key Question 5.)

   a. Resource prices—a rise in resource prices will cause a decrease in supply or leftward shift in supply curve; a decrease in resource prices will cause an increase in supply or rightward shift in the supply curve.

   b. Technology—a technological improvement means more efficient production and lower costs, so an increase in supply or rightward shift in the curve results.

   c. Taxes and subsidies—a business tax is treated as a cost, so decreases supply; a subsidy lowers cost of production, so increases supply.

   d. Prices of related goods—if price of substitute production good rises, producers might shift production toward the higher priced good, causing a decrease in supply of the original good.

   e. Expectations—expectations about the future price of a product can cause producers to increase or decrease current supply.

   f. Number of sellers—generally, the larger the number of sellers the greater the supply.

E. Review the distinction between a change in quantity supplied due to price changes and a change or shift in supply due to change in determinants of supply.

IV. **Supply and Demand: Market Equilibrium**

A. Review the text example, Table 3-8, which combines data from supply and demand schedules for corn.

B. Have students find the point where *quantity supplied equals the quantity demanded,* and note this equilibrium price and quantity. Emphasize the correct terminology!

1. At prices above this equilibrium, note that there is an excess quantity or surplus.

2. At prices below this equilibrium, note that there is an excess quantity demanded or shortage.

C. Market clearing or market price is another name for equilibrium price.

D. Graphically, note that the equilibrium price and quantity are where the supply and demand curves intersect (See Figure 3-5). This is an IMPORTANT point for students to recognize and remember. Note that it is NOT correct to say supply equals demand!

E. Rationing function of prices is the ability of competitive forces of supply and demand to establish a price where buying and selling decisions are coordinated. (Key Question 7)

V. **Changes in Supply and Demand, and Equilibrium**

A. Changing demand with supply held constant:

1. Increase in demand will have effect of increasing equilibrium price and quantity (Figure 3-6a).

2. Decrease in demand will have effect of decreasing equilibrium price and quantity (Figure 3-6b).

B. Changing supply with demand held constant:

1. Increase in supply will have effect of decreasing equilibrium price and increasing quantity (Fig 3-6c).

2. Decrease in supply will have effect of increasing equilibrium price and decreasing quantity (Fig 3-6d).

C. Complex cases—when both supply and demand shift (see Table 3-9):

1. If supply increases and demand decreases, price declines, but new equilibrium quantity depends on relative sizes of shifts in demand and supply.

2. If supply decreases and demand increases, price rises, but new equilibrium quantity depends again on relative sizes of shifts in demand and supply.

3. If supply and demand change in the same direction (both increase or both decrease), the change in equilibrium quantity will be in the direction of the shift but the change in equilibrium price now depends on the relative shifts in demand or supply.

D. A Reminder: Other things equal:

1 Demand is an inverse relationship between price and quantity demanded, other things equal (unchanged).

2. Supply is a direct relationship showing the relationship between price and quantity supplied, other things equal (unchanged).

3. It can appear that these rules have been violated over time, when tracking the price and the quantity sold of a product such as salsa or coffee.

4. Many factors *other* than price determine the outcome.

5. If neither the buyers nor the sellers have changed, the equilibrium price will remain the same.

6. The most important distinction to make is to determine if a change has occurred because of something that has affected the buyers or something that is influencing the sellers.

7. A change in any of the determinants of demand will shift the demand curve and cause a change in quantity supplied. (See Figure 3-6 a & b)

8. A change in any of the determinants of supply will shift the supply curve and cause a change in the quantity demanded. (See Figure 3-6 c & d)

VI. "Other Things Equal" Revisited

A. Remember that the "laws" of supply and demand depend on the assumption that the "other things" or "determinants" of demand and supply are constant.

B. Confusion results if "other things" (determinants) change and one does not take this into account. For example, sometimes more is demanded at higher prices because incomes rise, but if that fact is ignored, the law of demand seems to be violated. If income changes, however, there is a shift or increase in demand that could cause more to be purchased at a higher price. In this example, "other things" did not remain constant.

VII. Application: Pink Salmon

A. This is an example of simultaneous changes in both supply and demand.

B. An increase in supply occurs because of more efficient fishing boats, the development of fish farms and new entrants to the industry.

C. There is a decrease in demand because of changes in consumer preference, and an increase in income shows pink salmon to be an inferior good.

VIII. LAST WORD: "Ticket Scalping: A Bum Rap?"

A. "Scalping" refers to the practice of reselling tickets at a higher-than-original price, which happens often with athletic and artistic events. Is this "ripping off" justified?

B. Ticket re-sales are voluntary—both buyer and seller must feel that they gain or they would not agree to the transaction.

C. "Scalping" market simply redistributes assets (tickets) from those who value them less than money to those who value them more than the money they're willing to pay.

D. Sponsors may be injured, but if that is the case, they should have priced the tickets higher.

E. Spectators are not damaged, according to economic theory, because those who want to go the most are getting the tickets.

F. Conclusion: Both seller and buyer benefit and event sponsors are the only ones who may lose, but that is due to their own error in pricing and they would have lost from this error whether or not the scalping took place.

ANSWERS TO END-OF-CHAPTER QUESTIONS

3-1   Explain the law of demand. Why does a demand curve slope downward? What are the determinants of demand? What happens to the demand curve when each of these determinants changes? Distinguish between a change in demand and a change in the quantity demanded, noting the cause(s) of each.

As prices change because of a change in supply for a commodity, buyers will change the quantity they demand of that item. If the price drops, a larger quantity will be demanded. If the price rises, a lesser quantity will be demanded.

The demand curve slopes downward because of the substitution and income effects. When the price of a commodity decreases relative to that of substitutes, a buyer will substitute the now cheaper commodity for those whose prices have not changed. At the same time, the decreased price of the commodity under discussion will make the buyer wealthier in real terms. More can be bought of this commodity (as well as of others whose prices have not changed). Thus, the substitution and income effects reinforce each other: More will be bought of a normal (or superior) commodity as its price decreases. On a graph with price on the vertical axis and quantity on the horizontal, this is shown as a demand curve sloping downward from left to right.

The fundamental determinant of demand is the price of the commodity under consideration: a change in price causes movement along the commodity's demand curve. This movement is called a change in quantity demanded. Decreased price leads to movement down the demand curve: There is an increase in quantity demanded. Increased price leads to movement up the demand curve: There is a decrease in quantity demanded.

In addition, there are determinants of demand, which are factors that may shift the demand curve, i.e., cause a "change in demand." These are the number of buyers, the tastes (or desire) of the buyers for the commodity, the income of the buyers, the changes in price of related commodities (substitutes and complements), and expectations of the buyers regarding the future price of the commodity under discussion.

The following will lead to increased demand: more buyers, greater desire for the commodity, higher incomes (assuming a normal good), lower incomes (assuming an inferior good), an increased price of substitutes, a decreased price of complements, and an expectation of higher future prices. This increased demand will show as a shift of the entire demand curve to the right.

The reverse of all the above will lead to decreased demand and will show as a shift of the entire demand curve to the left.

3-2　(*Key Question*) What effect will each of the following have on the demand for product B?

a. Product B becomes more fashionable.

b. The price of substitute product C falls.

c. Income declines and product B is an inferior good.

d. Consumers anticipate the price of B will be lower in the near future.

e. The price of complementary product D falls.

f. Foreign tariff barriers on B are eliminated.

Demand increases in (a), (c), (e), and (f); decreases in (b) and (d).

3-3　Explain the following news dispatch from Hull, England: "The fish market here slumped today to what local commentators called a 'disastrous level'—all because of a shortage of potatoes. The potatoes are one of the main ingredients in a dish that figures on almost every café menu—fish and chips [French fries]."

The shortage of potatoes either meant they were not available in the required quantities at any price (i.e., that the quantity demanded greatly exceeded the quantity supplied at the market price, for that is how a "shortage" is defined) or that there was an exceptional scarcity of potatoes so that their price was far above normal. In any event, the restaurants could not get enough potatoes at what they considered profitable prices.

Fish and chips are complements. The sharp increase in the price of potatoes (because of decreased supply) has led to a decreased demand for fish and to a subsequent drop in its price to "a disastrous level."

3-4   Explain the law of supply. Why does the supply curve slope upward? What are the determinants of supply? What happens to the supply curve when each of these determinants changes? Distinguish between a change in supply and a change in the quantity supplied, noting the cause(s) of each.

As prices rise because of increased demand for a commodity, producers find it more and more profitable to increase the quantity they offer for sale; that is, the supply curve will slope upward from left to right. Clearly, firms would rather sell at a higher price than at a lower price. Moreover, it is necessary for firms to demand a higher price as they increase production. This comes about because as they produce more and more, they start to run up against capacity constraints and costs rise. At any given time, a plant has a given size. As production increases, the firm will need to add an extra shift and then a third shift, both perhaps at higher wages. It may run out of warehouse space and have to rent at higher cost from another firm. It may have to pay extra to get increasingly urgent raw material, and so on.

The fundamental determinant of supply is the price of the commodity. As price increases, the quantity supplied increases. An increase in price causes a movement up a given supply curve. A decrease in price causes a movement down a given supply curve.

The non-price determinants of supply are: resource (input) prices, technology, taxes and subsidies, prices of other related goods, expectations, and the number of sellers. If one or more of these change, there will be a change in supply and the whole supply curve will shift to the right or the left.

The following will cause an increase in supply: a decrease in resource (input) prices; improved (lower cost) technology; a decrease in business taxes, an increase in subsidies to business; a decrease in the price of another commodity that this firm was making, provided that commodity is a substitute in production (the firm can switch from the now lower priced one to our commodity); an expectation of lower prices in the future; and an increase in the number of sellers. The increase in supply caused by the noted change in one or more of the above will cause the entire supply curve to shift to the right. More will now be supplied at any given price. Alternatively expressed, any given amount will now be supplied at a lower price.

The reverse of any or all the above changes in the determinants of demand will cause a decrease in demand and will be shown as a shift of the supply curve to the left. Less will now be supplied at any given price. Alternatively expressed, any given amount will now be supplied at a higher price.

3-5   (*Key Question*) What effect will each of the following have on the supply of product B?

a.   A technological advance in the methods of producing B.

b.   A decline in the number of firms in industry B.

c.   An increase in the price of resources required in the production of B.

d.   The expectation that the equilibrium price of B will be lower in the future than it is currently.

e.   A decline in the price of product A, a good whose production requires substantially the same techniques as does the production of B.

f.   The levying of a specific sales tax upon B.

g.   The granting of a 50-cent per unit subsidy for each unit of B produced.

Supply increases in (a), (d), (e), and (g); decreases in (b), (c), and (f).

3-6   "In the corn market, demand often exceeds supply and supply sometimes exceeds demand." "The price of corn rises and falls in response to changes in supply and demand." In which of these two statements are the terms "supply" and "demand" used correctly? Explain.

In the first statement "supply" and "demand" are used incorrectly. Supply and demand are both schedules or curves that intersect where quantity supplied and quantity demanded are equal. One cannot talk of curves that intersect as exceeding or not exceeding each other.

Supply and/or demand can change (the entire curves can shift). Each time this happens, it will create a new intersection of the two curves that will lead to changes in the equilibrium quantity and price of corn. Thus, the terms "supply" and "demand" are used correctly in the second statement.

3-7   (*Key Question*) Suppose the total demand for wheat and the total supply of wheat per month in the Kansas City grain market are as follows:

Thousands of bushels demanded	Price per bushel	Thousand of bushels supplied	Surplus (+) or shortage (-)
85	$3.40	72	_____
80	3.70	73	_____
75	4.00	75	_____
70	4.30	77	_____
65	4.60	79	_____
60	4.90	81	_____

a. What will be the market or equilibrium price? What is the equilibrium quantity? Using the surplus-shortage column, explain why your answers are correct.

b. Graph the demand for wheat and the supply of wheat. Be sure to label the axes of your graph correctly. Label equilibrium price "P" and the equilibrium quantity "Q."

c. Why will $3.40 not be the equilibrium price in this market? Why not $4.90? "Surpluses drive prices up; shortages drive them down." Do you agree?

d. Now suppose that the government establishes a ceiling price of, say, $3.70 for wheat. Explain carefully the effects of this ceiling price. Demonstrate your answer graphically. What might prompt the government to establish a ceiling price?

Data from top to bottom: -13; -7; 0; +7; +14; and +21.

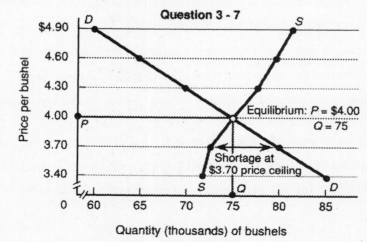

40

(a) P_e = \$4.00; Q_e = 75,000. Equilibrium occurs where there is neither a shortage nor surplus of wheat. At the immediately lower price of \$3.70, there is a shortage of 7,000 bushels. At the immediately higher price of \$4.30, there is a surplus of 7,000 bushels. (See Graph top of next page.

(b) Quantity (thousands) of bushels.

(c) Because at \$3.40 there will be a 13,000 bushel shortage which will drive price up. Because at \$4.90 there will be a 21,000 bushel surplus which will drive the price down. Quotation is incorrect; just the opposite is true.

(d) A \$3.70 ceiling causes a persistent shortage. This product may be a necessity and the government is concerned that some consumers might not being able to afford it.

3-8   (*Key Question*)   How will each of the following changes in demand and/or supply affect equilibrium price and equilibrium quantity in a competitive market; that is do price and quantity rise, fall, remain unchanged, or are the answers indeterminate, depending on the magnitudes of the shifts in supply and demand? You should rely on a supply and demand diagram to verify answers.

a.   Supply decreases and demand remains constant.

b.   Demand decreases and supply remains constant.

c.   Supply increases and demand is constant.

d.   Demand increases and supply increases.

e.   Demand increases and supply is constant.

f.   Supply increases and demand decreases.

g.   Demand increases and supply decreases.

h.   Demand decreases and supply decreases.

(a) Price up; quantity down;

(b) Price down; quantity down;

(c) Price down; quantity up;

(d) Price indeterminate; quantity up;

(e) Price up; quantity up;

(f) Price down; quantity indeterminate;

(g) Price up, quantity indeterminate;

(h) Price indeterminate and quantity down.

3-9   "Prices are the automatic regulator that tends to keep production and consumption in line with each other." Explain.

When demand increases, prices rise. This induces producers to increase the quantity supplied as they move up their supply curves toward the new (higher) equilibrium point. The same happens in reverse when demand decreases.

When supply increases, prices drop. This induces buyers to increase the quantity demanded as they move down their demand curves toward the new (lower) equilibrium point. The same happens in reverse when supply decreases.

In each case, it is the change in price caused by the change in demand or supply that brings about the change in quantity supplied (in the case of a change in demand) and a change in quantity demanded (in the case of a change in supply). Thus, price is the automatic regulator that keeps production and consumption in line with each other.

3-10   Explain: "Even though parking meters may yield little or no net revenue, they should nevertheless be retained because of the rationing function they perform."

Even parking meters that charge, say, 25 cents an hour do perform a useful parking-spot-rationing function: When the hour is up, the car owner must either move the car or rush out to feed the meter to avoid getting a ticket. In this case it is not money or ration coupons that ration the parking space but the timing device on the meter.

3-11   Use two market diagrams to explain how an increase in state subsidies to public colleges might affect tuition and enrollments in both public and private colleges.

The state subsidies to public colleges shift the supply curve of the public colleges to the right, thus reducing tuition and increasing enrollments in these institutions. The decreased cost of public college education leads to some substitution away from the private colleges, where the enrollment demand curve shifts to the left. The final result is a lower cost of tuition in both public and private colleges. (See Figure 3-6c.)

3-12   Critically evaluate: "In comparing the two equilibrium positions in Figure 3-6a, I note that a larger amount is actually purchased at a higher price. This refutes the law of demand."

The key point here is that the second equilibrium occurs after demand has increased, that is demand has shifted because of a change in determinants, which has caused buyers to want more at every price compared to the original D1 demand curve and schedule. Each equilibrium price refers to a different demand situation. Therefore, the fact that more is purchased at a higher price when demand increases does not refute the law of demand. Note that on the second demand curve and schedule, more would still be purchased at a lower price.

3-13   Suppose you go to a recycling center and are paid 25 cents per pound for your aluminum cans. However, the recycler charges you $.20 per bundle to accept your old newspapers. Use demand and supply diagrams to portray both markets. Can you explain how different government policies with respect to the recycling of aluminum and paper might account for these different market outcomes?

The equilibrium price of aluminum cans is not only higher than that for newspapers, but the price of newspapers is actually negative, meaning that the demand is very low relative to the supply. The demand is so low that the equilibrium quantity is at a negative price and consumers pay to have the papers "purchased." Diagrams (a) and (b) illustrate the two situations. (One might even suggest that there is a current abundance of old newspapers, and the demand is for environmental quality rather than for old newspapers. However, this complicating idea will probably confuse students and is probably not worth mentioning unless a student raises the issue.)

Various government policies could cause these different market outcomes. For example, requiring the use of recycled aluminum in can production could raise its demand; requiring refundable deposits on cans at the time of purchase could give them a value not given to newspapers; giving tax breaks for the use of recycled aluminum and not for recycled newspapers would also encourage demand for aluminum and not for newspapers.

3-14   Advanced analysis: Assume that the demand for a commodity is represented by the equation $P = 10 - .2Q_d$ and supply by the equation $P = 2 + .2Q_s$, where Q_d and Q_s are quantity demanded and quantity supplied, respectively, and P is price. Using the equilibrium condition $Q_s = Q_d$, solve the equations to determine equilibrium price. Now determine equilibrium quantity. Graph the two equations to substantiate your answers.

Demand is $P = 10 - 2Q$

Therefore $5P = 50 - Q_d = 50 - 5P$

Supply is $P = 2 + 2Q_s$

Therefore $5P = 10 + Q_s$ and $Q_s = -10 + 5P$

Substitute Q_d and Q_s into $Q_s = Q_d$ equilibrium condition

$50 - 5P = -10 + 5P$

$60 = 10P$ and $6 = P$

Now substitue $P = 6$ in either Q_d or Q_s to determine equilibrium quantity :

$Q_d = 50 - 5P = 50 - 5(6) = 20$

or

$Q_s = -10 + 5P = -10 + 5(6) = 20$

3-15   (*Last Word*) Discuss the economic aspects of ticket scalping, specifying the gainers and losers.

Ticket scalping occurs in situations in which the original ticket price is set below the equilibrium price. This means that holders of tickets can find buyers who are willing to pay a higher price than that printed on the ticket. Basically, there is a shortage or the quantity demanded exceeds the quantity supplied at the original price. Some ticket holders are willing to part with their tickets by selling them at a higher price than the price they paid, and some buyers are willing to pay this higher price. In other words, both the buyers and sellers voluntarily enter into the "scalping" transaction because both expect to benefit. The buyers value the tickets more than the money, and the sellers value the money more than the tickets. The only losers in this case would be the sponsors of the event, who could have charged higher prices for the tickets originally. However, they don't lose because of the scalping, but because they originally priced the tickets below equilibrium.

CHAPTER FOUR
THE MARKET SYSTEM

CHAPTER OVERVIEW

This chapter begins with a discussion of the institutional framework of the American market system. Brief explanations are given for these characteristics of the market system: private property, freedom of enterprise and choice, the role of self-interest, competition, markets and prices, the reliance on technology and capital goods, specialization, use of money, and the active, but limited role of government. In the final section of the chapter, the authors address the Four Fundamental Questions faced by every economy and explain how a market economy answers each one.

WHAT'S NEW

This chapter has a new focus and organization. The overriding change throughout the chapter is a focus on the American market system rather than on pure capitalism. Many of the sections have been rewritten and made more concise. Added to the role of private property is the notion of maintaining and improving property. The discussion on Freedom of Enterprise and Choice has been made more concise. The Five Fundamental Questions have been consolidated to Four Fundamental Questions. The concept of normal profit and the difference between normal profit and economic profit has been clarified. The discussion of "Profits and Expanding Industries" and "Losses and Declining Industries" has been simplified and the products chosen as examples for the two industries have been changes. In the section on technological advance, the concept of creative destruction has been added. The students should find this chapter more readable and more relevant to the economy within which they function.

The Last Word and the two Web-Based Questions have been changed.

INSTRUCTIONAL OBJECTIVES

After completing this chapter, students should be able to:

1. List and explain nine important characteristics of the American market system.

2. State the Four Fundamental Questions faced by any economic system.

3. Describe how the market system answers each of these four fundamental questions.

4. Define normal profits and economic profits and explain the difference between them.

5. Identify the relationship between profits and expanding industries; losses and declining industries.

6. Explain how the consumer influences the "What goods and services will be produced?" question.

7. Explain how a market system achieves economic efficiency.

8. Explain the role of income distribution on the "Who will get the goods and services?" question.

9. Describe the guiding function of prices.

10. Describe how the market system promotes technological improvements and capital accumulation.

11. Explain the role of competition and "invisible hand" in promoting economic efficiency.

12. Define and identify terms and concepts at the end of the chapter.

COMMENTS AND TEACHING SUGGESTIONS

1. A surprising number of students do not really understand the characteristics of the American market system. Many students have no idea how prices are set and even after the chapter on supply and demand may still believe that most prices are determined by an external government agency or by producers arbitrarily.

2. If you haven't already talked about Adam Smith and his role in economics, this may be a good time to introduce the "father of economics." His emphasis on the role of self-interest in motivating economic activity is especially relevant here. You might place copies of the "Wealth of Nations" on reserve at the library to encourage students to sample the original work. You could use short excerpts as the basis for discussion or essays. "Adam Smith and the Wealth of Nations," a 28-minute video/film, is an excellent supplement. Check with your Federal Reserve District Bank's public information office or your nearest Center for Economic Education for availability.

3. Markets coordinate economic activity and changes in prices (products and resources) signal that changes have occurred within particular markets. A simple example of product X and product Y can be used. Assume an increase in the demand for X. This change will lead to an increase in the price of X, an increase in the profitability of X, an increase in the quantity supplied of X, an increase in the demand for the resources used to produce X, and an increase in the prices of the those resources. Because of a limit in consumer income, the demand for Y is assumed to decrease followed by all of the changes that will occur in response to the decrease in the demand of Y. After all of these changes have occurred, explain how the transferable resources will move from Y to X. This illustrates the concepts of the "invisible hand" and allocative efficiency.

4. This is a good time to reintroduce the concept of goods for the future from chapter 2. In discussing the importance of producing goods for the future for the market system, remind the students of the impact upon the production of consumption goods in the present.

5. Use this chapter as a way of introducing the students to the terminology and concepts in chapters 22 (Costs of Production), 23 (Pure Competition), and 26 (Technology, R&D, and Efficiency) in the Principles of Microeconomics course. Be sure that the terminology and concepts are presented in a way that is consistent with the way in which they will be used in these micro chapters.

6. The four fundamental questions must be answered by all types of economic systems. Although the emphasis of this chapter is on the American market system, current economic changes in Russia and China and areas of the developing world can be discussed to illustrate how different types of economics answer these questions differently.

7. When discussing the first two of the fundamental questions, ask who in the market economy are most responsible for answering each of the questions. Explain that the "Who will get the goods and services?" question is an income distribution question and is determined by the distribution and productivity of the resources and the demand for the resources. Discuss how differing demand and supply conditions in the market for fast food workers and computer system workers determine the differences in the workers' wages and incomes.

STUDENT STUMBLING BLOCK

This chapter introduces students to many important concepts and terms that will be expanded upon in later chapters, particularly in the Principles of Microeconomics course. These concepts and terms are vital to the understanding of economics. Current event examples can be helpful.

LECTURE NOTES

I.   **Characteristics of the Market System**

    A. Private individuals and firms own most of the private property (land and capital).

        1. Private property, coupled with the freedom to negotiate binding legal contracts, enables individuals and businesses to obtain, control, use, and dispose of this property.

        2. Private property rights encourage investment, innovation, exchange of assets, maintenance of property, and economic growth.

        3. Property rights extend to intellectual property through patents, copyrights, and trademarks.

    B. Freedom of enterprise and choice exist.

        1. Freedom of enterprise means that entrepreneurs and businesses have the freedom to obtain and use resources, to produce products of their choice, and to sell these products in the markets of their choice.

        2. Freedom of choice means:

            a. Owners of property and money resources can use resources as they choose.

            b. Workers can choose the training, occupations, and job of their choice.

            c. Consumers are free to spend their income in such a way as to best satisfy their wants (consumer sovereignty).

    C. Self-interest

            a. Self interest is one of the driving forces in a market system. Entrepreneurs try to maximize profits or minimize losses; resource suppliers try to maximize income; consumers maximize satisfaction.

            b. As each tries to maximize profits, income, satisfaction, the economy will benefit if competition is present.

    D. Competition among buyers and sellers is a controlling mechanism.

        1. Large numbers of sellers mean that no single producer or seller can control the price or market supply.

        2. Large number of buyers means that no single consumer or employer can control the price or market demand.

        3. Depending upon market conditions, producers can enter or leave industry easily.

    E. Markets and prices

        1. A market system conveys the decisions of the many buyers and sellers of the product and resource markets. Recall the demand and supply model in Chapter 3.

        2. A change in the market price signals that a change in the market has occurred.

        3. Those who respond to the market signals will be rewarded with profits and income.

    F. Reliance on technology and capital goods

        1. Competition, freedom of choice, self-interest, and the potential of profits provide the incentive for capital accumulation (investment).

        2. Advanced technology and capital goods uses the more efficient roundabout method of technology.

G. Specialization
   1. Division of labor allows workers to specialize.
      a. People can take advantage of differences in abilities and skills.
      b. People with identical skills may still benefit from specialization and improving certain skills.
      c. Specialization saves time involved in shifting from one task to another.
   2. Geographic specialization: Regional and international specialization take advantage of localized resources.

H. Use of money as a medium of exchange
   1. Money substitutes for barter, which requires a coincidence of wants. (I may want what you produce but you may not want to exchange for what I have.)
   2. Willingness to accept money in place of goods permits 3-way trades (or multilateral trades). See Figure 4-1 and examples in text.
      a. Floridians give money to Nebraskans for wheat who give money to Idahoans for potatoes who give money to Florida for oranges.
      b. Foreign exchange markets permit Americans, Japanese, Germans, Britons, and Mexicans to complete international exchanges of goods and services.
      c. Detroit autoworker produces crankshafts for Buicks. If the worker were paid in crankshafts, he would have to find grocers, clothing retailers, etc., who would be willing to exchange their products for a crankshaft. It is much more efficient to use money wages than to accept one's wages in crankshafts!

I. Active, but limited government
   1. Although the market system promotes efficiency, it has certain shortcomings (over production of goods with social costs, under production of goods with social benefits, tendency for business to increase monopoly power, macro instability).
   2. Chapter 5 deals with how the government can increase the overall effectiveness of the market system.

III. **The Market System at Work**

A. The market system is made up of millions of individual decision makers who make trillions of decisions all of which are attempting to maximize their individual or business self-interest.

B. The market is a mechanism by which the consumers and producers can come together to respond to each other's desires and wants in an efficient way.

C. Although the focus of this chapter is on the market system, the four fundamental questions must be answered by all economic systems.
   1. What goods and services will to be produced?
   2. How will these goods and services be produced?
   3. Who will get the goods and services?
   4. How will the system accommodate change?

D. What will be produced?
   1. In order to be profitable, businesses must respond to consumers' (individuals, other businesses, and the government) wants and desires.

2. When businesses allocate resources in a way that is responsive, businesses will be profitable and allocative efficiency will be achieved.
3. Accounting profits are total revenue minus total accounting costs.
4. In economics, the return to the entrepreneur is treated just like the return to the worker, i.e., it is an economic cost and must be received if the entrepreneur is going to continue to produce in that industry.
5. Normal profits are the return to the entrepreneur that is necessary for him/her to continue to produce that product. Any revenue received beyond normal profits is pure or economic profit.
6. If producers in an industry are receiving pure or economic profits, additional producers will move into the industry, the industry supply will increase, and the price will decrease thus squeezing out the economic profits. Refer to Figure 3-6(c).
7. If producers in an industry are experiencing economic losses, some of these producers will exit the industry, the industry supply will decrease, and the price will increase thus eliminating the economic losses. Refer to 3-6(d).
8. Consumer sovereignty is the key to determining the types and quantities of the various products that will be produced. "Dollar votes" for a product when purchases are made and "dollar votes" against a product when products are ignored will determine which industries continue to exist and which individual products survive or fail.
9. Businesses are not really "free" to produce what they wish. They must match their production choices with consumer choices or face losses and eventual bankruptcy. Profit-seeking firms must consider the allocation of the "dollar votes" when they make their production decisions.
10. Resource demand is a "derived" demand, i.e., it depends on the demand for the products produced by the resource.

E. How will the goods and services be produced?
 1. The market system encourages and rewards those producers who are achieving productive efficiency, i.e., least-cost production.
 2. Least-cost production techniques include: locating firms in the optimum location considering resource prices, resource productivity, and transportation costs, available technology, and resource prices in general.
 3. The most efficient technique will be the one that produces a given amount of output with the smallest input of scarce resources when both inputs and outputs are measured in dollars and cents. (Key Question 7)

F. Who will get the goods and services?
 1. The answer to this question is directly related to how the income is distributed among the individuals and the households and the tastes and preferences of consumers.
 2. Products go to those who are willing and able to pay for them.
 3. The productivity of the resources, the relative supply of particular resources, and the ownership of the resources will determine the income of individuals and households.
 4. The resource markets, which determine income, are linked to this decision.

G. How will the system accommodate change?
 1. Accommodating changes in consumer tastes and the guiding function of prices:
   a. An increase in demand for some products will lead to higher prices in those markets.
   b. A decrease in demand for other products will lead to lower prices in those markets.

    c. Increased demand leads to higher prices that induce greater quantities of output. The opposite is true for a decrease in demand.

    d. Higher prices lead to more profits and new firms entering the market.

    e. Lower prices lead to losses and firms leaving the industry.

2. The market system promotes technological improvements and capital accumulation.
    a. An entrepreneur or firm that introduces a popular new product will be rewarded with increased revenue and profits.
    b. New technologies that reduce production costs, and thus product price, will spread throughout the industry as a result of competition.
    c. Creative destruction occurs when new products and production methods destroy the market positions of firms that are not able or willing to adjust.

III.   **Competition and the "Invisible Hand":**

    A. Competition is the mechanism of control for the market system. It not only guarantees that industry responds to consumer wants, but it also forces firms to adopt the most efficient production techniques.

    B. Adam Smith talked of the "invisible hand" which promotes public interest through a market system where the primary motivation is self-interest. By attempting to maximize profits, firms will also be producing the goods and services most wanted by society.

IV.   **LAST WORD: Shuffling the Deck**

    A. If one thoroughly shuffles a deck of cards, there is a virtual 100% chance that the resulting arrangement of cards will be unlike any previous arrangement.

    B. Yet, even though there are tens of billions of resources in the world, these resources are arranged in such a way as to produce the products and services that serve human needs.

    C. Private property eliminates the possibility that resource arrangements will be random because each resource owner will choose a particular course of action if it promises rewards to the owner that exceed the rewards promised by all other available actions.

    D. The result is a complex and productive arrangement of countless resources.

ANSWERS TO END-OF-CHAPTER QUESTIONS

4-1   Explain each of these statements:

    a. The market system not only *accepts* self-interest as a fact of human existence; it *relies* on self-interest to achieve society's material goals.

    b. The market system provides such a variety of desired goods and services precisely because no single individual or small groups is deciding what the economy will produce.

    c. Entrepreneurs and business are at the helm of the economy, but their commanders are consumers.

    (a) The motive of self-interest gives direction and consistency to the economy. The primary driving force of the market system is self-interest. Entrepreneurs try to maximize their profits; property owners want the highest price for their resources; workers choose the job with the best wages, fringe benefits and working conditions. Consumers apportion their expenditures to maximize their utility, while seeking the lowest possible prices. As individuals express their free choice, the economy is directed to produce the most wanted goods at the lowest possible cost.

(b) Each individual consumer will choose a variety of goods and services that in combination will maximize his/her satisfaction (utility). To maximize profits, producers must respond to the desires of the individual consumer.

(c) Although producers are free to choose what products they will produce, if the producers are to maximize profits, these good and services must be what consumers desire.

4-2   Why is private property, and the protection of property rights, so critical to the success of the market system?

The ownership of private property and the protection of property rights encourages investment, innovation, and, therefore, economic growth. Property rights encourage the maintaining of the property and they facilitate the exchange of the property.

4-3   What are the advantages of "roundabout" production? What is meant by the term "division of labor"? What are the advantages of specialization in the use of human and material resources? Explain: "Exchange is the necessary consequence of specialization."

"Roundabout production" means using capital goods in the production process. This enables producers to operate more efficiently and to produce more output.

"Division of labor" means that workers perform those tasks that are best suited to their individual abilities and skills.

The advantages of specialization for workers are that they can choose work according to their natural aptitudes, have the opportunity to perfect those skills, and save time in not having to shift continually from one task to another. Material resources will be developed and adapted for a specific use. On a regional basis, each region will produce those products for which it is best suited. By specializing in its comparative advantage, each region or set of human and material resources is being used to maximize efficiency.

When resources are specialized, they are no longer self-sufficient. To obtain the goods and services one needs, exchange is necessary. Also, specialization will result in a surplus of a specific good being produced. The surplus of one good will be exchanged for the surplus production of other goods.

4-4   What problem does barter entail? Indicate the economic significance of money as a medium of exchange. What is meant by the statement: "We want money only to part with it"?

Barter requires the "double coincidence of wants." If someone wants something, he/she will have to find someone who wishes to part with that good and at the same time wishes to exchange the good for something that the first party wishes to part with.

With money, as a medium of exchange, one knows the purchase price of the item to be purchased and it relative price to other items. Money is a very convenient common denominator, a common measure of value that is also used as a medium of exchange. Money also encourages specialization. Without money, workers and other resources could not be paid except in the output produced. All those who participated in the production of the good would have to collectively exchange it for all the goods and service desired by the resource owners.

Money itself has value only in relation to the resources, goods, and services that can be obtained with it. When people say that they want money, they really mean that they want the things that money can buy. In this sense, money imparts value only when someone parts with it.

4-5   Evaluate and explain the following statements:

a.   The market system is a profit-and-loss economy.

b. Competition is the indispensable disciplinarian of the market economy.

c. Production methods that are inferior in the engineering sense may be the most efficient methods in the economic sense, once resource prices are considered.

(a) The quotation is accurate. In a market system, producer decisions are motivated by the attempt to earn profits. Those products that enable a firm to earn at least a normal profit will be produced. If the product cannot be produced for a profit—in other words, if losses are involved in production—the capitalist firm will respond by seeking lower cost production methods and may halt the production of goods completely. Because profits and/or losses are the motivation behind the fundamental decisions made in a market system, it could be called a "profit and loss economy."

(b) Competition provides discipline in two ways. First, it forces firms to seek the least-cost production methods or face being driven out of business by their rivals. Second, it prevents successful producers from charging whatever the market will bear. Competition keeps prices at a level where total revenue will just cover the total cost of production including a normal profit, but no more in the long run. If sellers try to charge a price that will earn them economic profits, new firms will enter the industry, increasing supply, and lowering prices until the economic profits are eliminated. Competition is indispensable in this role, because otherwise some other method would have to be found to direct firms to use the least-cost production technique and to charge a price that provides only a normal return. Where competition does not exist, such as in natural monopolies like public utility companies, regulators or publicly owned companies must assume the role of disciplinarian. Experience has shown that this is a difficult process and does not achieve the same results as easily as a competitive market situation.

(c) There are some very effective engineering techniques that may be too costly in terms of the scarce resources that they would employ. For example, using computerized word processors may be a superior way to write essays and papers. However, investing in enough computers for every school child would not be efficient in the economic sense. Education can be provided more efficiently by using more labor-intensive methods, i.e., with the teacher at the chalkboard and the student using pencil and paper. In another example, using a shovel to scoop snow may be inferior to a snow blower in the engineering sense, but it may be a more efficient use of resources for the middle- or low-income family who has to decide between buying groceries and using better technology to clean its driveway and sidewalk.

4-6   Explain fully the meaning and implications of the following quotation.

"The beautiful consequence of the market is that it is its own guardian. If output prices or certain kinds of remuneration stray away from their socially ordained levels, forces are set into motion to bring them back to the fold. A curious paradox thus ensues: The market, which is the acme of individual economic freedom, is the strictest taskmaster of all. One may appeal the ruling of a planning board or win the dispensation of a [government] minister; but there is no appeal, no dispensation from the anonymous pressures of the market mechanism. Economic freedom is thus more illusory than at first appears. One can do as one pleases in the market. But if one pleases to do what the market disapproves, the price of individual freedom is economic ruination."

The statement that the market is its own guardian implies that there really is an invisible hand or taskmaster that watches over the decision makers in the marketplace. In a pure capitalist system where free markets exist, freedom of enterprise and freedom of choice exist. However, if one chooses to produce that which the consumer does not want, or at least doesn't want enough to cover the cost of the scarce resources employed, the producer-entrepreneur will find this freedom of enterprise limited by the decisions of consumers in the marketplace. On the demand side, consumer choice is limited by the prices of products that the consumer wants and the consumer's income, which is limited by the value that the consumer's own resources can earn in resource markets.

In other words, the freedom is to some extent illusory, because if producers ignored consumer wishes, they would likely suffer losses and eventually find themselves with no income or means to support themselves. If consumers make choices that ignore their own income potential, they, too, will soon find themselves unable to buy even the basic necessities. Personal freedom exists only in the fact that no single individual or command agency is telling economic decision makers what to do with regard to their production and consumption decisions. One is free to make one's own decisions subject to the limitations of the anonymous marketplace.

4-7   (*Key Question*) Assume that a business firm finds that its profits will be at maximum when it produces $40 worth of product A. Suppose also that each of the three techniques shown in the following table will produce the desired output.

		Resource Units Required		
Resource	Price per unit of resource	Technique No. 1	Technique No. 2	Technique No. 3
Labor	$3	5	2	3
Land	4	2	4	2
Capital	2	2	4	5
Entrepreneurial ability	2	4	2	4

a. With the resource prices shown, which technique will the firm choose? Why? Will production entail profits or losses? Will the industry expand or contract? When is a new equilibrium output achieved?

b. Assume now that a new technique, technique No. 4, is developed. It entails the use of 2 units of labor, 2 of land, 6 of capital, and 3 of entrepreneurial ability. Given the resource prices in the table, will the firm adopt the new technique? Explain your answers.

c. Suppose now that an increase in labor supply causes the price of labor to fall to $1.50 per unit, all other resource prices being unchanged. Which technique will the producer now choose? Explain.

d. "The market system causes the economy to conserve most in the use of those resources which are particularly scarce in supply. Resources that are scarcest relative to the demand for them have the highest prices. As a result, producers use these resources as sparingly as is possible." Evaluate this statement. Does your answer to part c, above, bear out this contention? Explain.

(a) Technique 2. Because it produces the output with least cost ($34 compared to $35 each for the other two). Economic profit will be $6 (= 40 - $34), which will cause the industry to expand. Expansion will continue until prices decline to where total revenue is $34 (equal to total cost).

(b) Adopt technique 4 because its cost is now lowest at $32.

(c) Technique 1 because its cost is now lowest at $27.50.

(d) The statement is logical. Increasing scarcity causes prices to rise. Firms ignoring higher resource prices will become high-cost producers and be competed out of business by firms switching to the less expensive inputs. The market system forces producers to conserve on the use of highly scarce resources. Question 8c confirms this: Technique 1 was adopted because labor had become less expensive.

4-8   Suppose the demand for bagels rises dramatically while the demand for breakfast cereal falls. Briefly explain how the competitive market economy will make the needed adjustments to reestablish an efficient allocation of society's scarce resources?

Consumers can redirect resources through their "dollar votes." The increased demand for bagels will raise their market price, while the decrease in demand for cereal will cause its market price to fall. A higher price for bagels provides an incentive for producers to increase output.

They will also be able to pay higher wages and bid workers away from alternative employment. Bagel manufacturing firms will also be willing to pay higher prices for flour and other ingredients. They will be likely to buy additional capital equipment and expand their facilities. Cereal manufacturers will cut production, lay off workers and reduce purchases of materials. They may have to close facilities and offer their used capital equipment and unneeded land for sale at reduced prices.

4-9   (*Key Question*) Some large hardware stores such as Home Depot boast of carrying as many as 20,000 different products in each store. What motivated the producers of those products—everything from screwdrivers to ladders to water heaters—to make them and offer them for sale? How did producers decide on the best combinations of resources to use? Who made these resources available, and why? Who decides whether these particular hardware products should continue to get produced and offered for sale?

The quest for profit led firms to produce these goods. Producers looked for and found the least-cost combination of resources in producing their output. Resource suppliers, seeking income, made these resources available. Consumers, through their dollar votes, ultimately decide on what will continue to be produced.

4-10   In a single sentence, describe the meaning of the term "invisible hand."

Market prices act as an "invisible hand" coordinating an economy by rationing what is scare and providing incentives to produce the most desired goods and services.

4-11   (*Last Word*) What explains why millions of economic resources tend to get arranged logically and productively rather than haphazard and unproductively?

Through the ownership of private property, resource owners will choose to use their resources in a manner that will maximize benefits to themselves (the invisible hand). This will result in the resources being utilized in the way that will best serve human goals (allocative efficiency).

CHAPTER FIVE
THE U.S. ECONOMY: PRIVATE AND PUBLIC SECTORS

CHAPTER OVERVIEW

This chapter provides descriptive details about both the private sector (households and businesses) and the public sector (government) in our market economy. The goal is to understand households, businesses, and governmental units as the primary decision makers in our economy. The circular flow diagram has been expanded to show how the public sector interacts with two parts of the private sector.

WHAT'S NEW

The new chapter title is in keeping with the focus of previous chapter. The term "mixed market system" is no longer used. The introductions to many of the sections and subsection have been made more concise. The material on components of personal consumption is presented as a pie chart rather than a table. The section on the business population has been reorganized and the terminology "horizontal, vertical, conglomerate combinations" has been changed to "horizontally and vertically organized firms" and "conglomerates." The three types of business organizations are defined prior to the discussion of the advantages and disadvantages of each. The advantages and disadvantages are presented in narrative form rather than in numeric lists. The discussion on business "Hybrid Structures" and "The Principle-Agent Problem" are presented as separate subsections. The circular flow diagram, Figure 5-6, that adds the governmental sector, has been revised for clarification. There is a new Figure 5-7 that compares government purchases of goods and services and transfer payments in 1960 as a percentage of the 1960 GDP and government purchases and transfer payments in 2000 as a percentage of 2000 GDP.

The second Web-Based Question has been changed.

INSTRUCTIONAL OBJECTIVES

After completing this chapter, students should be able to:

1. Define, explain, and give relative importance of the five shares in the functional distribution of income and explain what is included in the fifth share – proprietors' income.

2. Define and explain the personal distribution of income, and state the relative shares going to the top 20 percent compared to the bottom 20 percent (or one-fifth).

3. State the three major categories of household spending or income disposition and relative shares of each.

4. Explain the terms durable goods, nondurable goods, and services.

5. Explain the difference between a plant, a firm, and an industry.

6. State the advantages and disadvantages of the three legal forms of business in comparative terms, including the hybrid structures.

7. Describe the principal-agent problem.

8. Explain how the government promotes competition.

9. Explain how government alters the income distribution.

10. Define and explain the effects of spillover benefits and spillover costs.

11. Describe how the government can correct the effects of spillover costs and benefits.

12. Explain what is meant by a "public good" and why government must provide these goods and services.

13. Explain the methods government can use to reduce unemployment and inflation.

14. Understand the circular flow model with the addition of the government sector.

15. Differentiate between government purchases and transfer payments and the relative and absolute importance of each over time.

16. Identify the major categories of federal spending and the major sources of federal revenue.

17. Differentiate between marginal and average tax rates.

18. Identify the major categories of spending for state and local governments and the major sources of revenue for each.

19. Define and identify terms and concepts listed at the end of the chapter.

COMMENTS AND TEACHING SUGGESTIONS

1. Because the numbers change from year to year, students should not be expected to learn exact figures. However, it is reasonable to expect students to recall "ballpark" figures, especially for relative shares of income distribution, household spending, the corporate share of total output in the private sector, and relative importance of public sector output in GDP. In making the distinction between functional income distribution and personal income distribution, you can make the distinction between national income and personal income. National income is earned market income from the four factors of production. Personal income includes transfer payments such as social security, unemployment benefits and cash welfare grants. Personal taxes have not been deducted. Specify clearly the students' responsibility for the statistical knowledge that you expect from this chapter, or they may become overwhelmed by the data and not remember the meaningful relationships. Emphasize that the figures being presented in the discussion of personal income are examples of positive economics, and that the students' individual views on income distribution and equity are examples of normative economics. If Chapter 34, "Income Inequality and Poverty," is not going to be included in the semester, the section on "Trends in Income Inequality" and "Causes of Growth Inequality" could be covered when discussing the personal distribution of income in this chapter.

2. In comparing the legal forms of business, a matrix or grid diagram helps students to compare advantages and disadvantages of each form at a glance. Have students interview a local business owner to find out what kinds of government regulation applies to their business. How much does it cost them? How much time is spent in compliance activity?

3. While most students will have a basic knowledge of the corporate form, it is a very new concept to those who do not. The nature of the corporation as a legal entity and the concept of limited liability should be stressed. Limited liability companies are becoming more prevalent and this category should not be left to a footnote. It is also useful in today's global economy to point out that the symbols Ltd. and S.A. are the abbreviations for words that mean incorporated in the United Kingdom and Latin America, respectively.

4. Information in many of the tables in this chapter can be updated with current editions of *Economic Indicators* or *Economic Report of the President* or *Survey of Current Business*.

5. The degree of government involvement in the economy is a controversial topic in most of the areas discussed in this chapter. Good debates can center on questions related to government's role in

protecting the environment, the social security program, welfare programs, health care, and tax policy, among others.

6. A game can be played with the budget of any level of government, ranging from the local school district's budget to the federal budget. Provide students with the figures (or have students research them) for current spending in each of the major budget categories. Then have students play the role of decision makers who are to cut 10 percent out of this budget. Where would they cut? Have them justify their answers on the basis of a decision-making grid, where they list the possible alternatives vs. the criteria for making the decision.

   Another version of this game gives the decision-makers an extra amount of dollars to spend, and they have to decide which category gets top priority for spending that amount. Before the discussion, group students according to their choices. For example, all wanting to spend more on defense would be in one group. Then, representative members of each group can discuss the reasons for their choice for the rest of the class.

7. Make up four or five different scenarios that include households with different number of members, different incomes, and different deductions. Have the students calculate the average tax rate based upon the household's adjusted gross income using the Federal 1040 tax form. By working through the tax form, the students will understand the difference between a tax deduction and a tax credit and will be able to better evaluate proposed changes in the Federal tax system.

STUDENT STUMBLING BLOCKS

1. Terminology can cause confusion among students in separating public and private sectors. For example, corporations are often referred to as public corporations to reflect the fact that stock is offered to the public. Some "public" utilities are publicly owned while others are privately held. It may be even more confusing to address these points at the introductory level, but keep in mind that these contradictions in terms do mislead some students.

2. One stumbling block originates from misinformation students learn before they arrive in class. Students have difficulty differentiating between marginal and average tax rates. They tend to believe that people in the 28 percent tax brackets are paying 28 percent of their incomes in taxes. Although the chapter does a good job of highlighting the difference between the marginal and average rates, it bears emphasis. Students may already believe that people are taxed too much, without the added misconception of what the top tax bracket rates mean.

3. The Last Word on corporate finance covers some important definitions. It also explains the inverse relationship between bond prices and interest rates which will be used later in discussing monetary policy. One way to help students understand this is to use an actual bond, or replica of a bond, with its par value and stated interest rate on it. Then you can ask what price would be offered for that bond if interest rates rose above or fell below the rate paid by that bond.

LECTURE NOTES

I. **Goals of Chapter**

    A. To acquire basic factual information about the household and business components of the private sector economy.

    B. To acquire basic factual information about the public (or government) sector in the U.S. economy.

    C. To understand the role of the public sector in the U.S. economy.

II. **Households as Income Receivers**

A. Functional distribution of income is shown in Figure 5-1. (This figure is based on NI—National Income.)

  1. Wages and salaries are 70 percent of total.

  2. Proprietors' income (income to self-employed business owners, doctors, lawyers, etc.) is under 10 percent of total. (This is a combination of wage and profit income.)

  3. Capitalist income—corporation profits, rent, interest—is less than one-fifth of total. (Note: rent may be negative because of the depreciation charged against rental income.)

B. Personal distribution of income is shown in Figure 5-2. (This figure is based on PI—Personal Income.)

  1. It is often described by dividing the population into quintiles or five numerically equal parts.

  2. Proportions of total income going to each quintile are then compared.

  3. Comparison shows unequal distribution of income. For example, see how many times greater the share of income going to the top quintile is relative to the bottom fifth. (Key Question 2)

III. **Households As Spenders (Figure 5-3) (Figure is based on PI—Personal Income)**

A. Use Figure 5.3 or most recent data from *Survey of Current Business,* January issue of current year, to describe the following.

B. How do households dispose of their income?

  1. Personal taxes, of which Federal personal income tax is the major component, has increased over the years.

  2. Saving (dissaving if spending exceeds income) is the smallest fraction of personal income disposition.

  3. Most of household income goes to consumer spending (Figure 5.3). There are several categories of spending categories (Figure 5.4):

    a. Durable goods are those with life of three or more years.

    b. Nondurable goods include things such as food and clothing.

    c. Services are today more than one-half of all consumer spending, which demonstrates that ours is a service-oriented economy.

IV. **The Business Population**

A. Related definitions:

  1. Plant: physical establishment where production or distribution takes place (factory, farm, store).

  2. Firm: business organization that owns and operates the plants. (The legal entity.)

  3. Industry: a group of related firms, producing the same or similar products.

    a. Examples include the automobile industry or the tobacco industry.

    b. Confusion often occurs because many businesses are multiproduct firms.

  4. Types of multiplant firms:

      a. Horizontal integrated: a multiplant firm with plants in the same stage, like a retail chain store such as J. C. Penney or Safeway.

      b. Vertical integrated: a multiplant firm in which the company owns plants at different production stages. Example: A steel company may own ore and coal mines as well as different plants in different stages of the manufacturing process.

      c. Conglomerate: a firm that owns plants in different industries or markets.

B. Legal forms of businesses (Figure 5.5):

   1. Definition:

      a. Sole proprietorship: a business owned by a single individual.

      b. Partnership: two or more individuals own and operate the business in a partnership agreement.

      c. Corporation: a legal entity distinct from its individual owners. The organization acts as "legal person."

   2. Discussion of Figure 5-5 relative to most important – percentage of firms versus percentage of sales.

   3. Sole proprietorship

      a. Advantages: easy to set up; proprietor is his/her own boss; because profit is proprietor's income, there is an incentive to operate the business efficiently.

      b. Disadvantages: financial resources are limited and insufficient; the proprietor is responsible for all of management functions; the proprietor is subject to unlimited liability.

   4. Partnership

      a. Advantages: easy to organize; greater specialization; better access to financial resources than proprietorships.

      b. Disadvantages: some of the same shortcomings of the proprietorship; possible difficulties in sharing management responsibilities; still limited financial resources; problems if one of the partners leaves; still unlimited liabilities.

   5. Corporations

      a. Advantages: improved ability to raise financial capital (money); defining and comparing stocks and bonds; limited liabilities; corporations have a permanence that is conducive to long-run planning and growth.

      b. Disadvantages: red tape and expense in obtaining a corporate charter; unscrupulous business owners sometimes avoid responsibility for questionable business activities.

   6. Hybrid structures

   7. Principle-agent problem

V.   The Public Sector: Government's Role

A. Providing the legal structure:

   1. Government ensures property rights, provides enforcement of contracts, acts as a referee and imposes penalties for foul play.

2. Government intervention improves the allocation of resources by supplying a medium of exchange, ensuring product quality, defining ownership rights, and enforcing contracts.

3. These interventions widen the market and foster greater specialization in the use of property and human resources.

4. The appropriate amount of regulation is at the level where the marginal benefit and marginal cost are equal.

B. Maintain competition:

1. Competition is the market mechanism that encourages producers and resource suppliers to respond to consumer sovereignty.

2. If producers (and/or resource suppliers) have monopoly power, the monopolist can charge higher-than-competitive prices and supplant consumer sovereignty with producer sovereignty (or economic rent).

3. If "natural monopoly" exists, government regulates price and service. (Natural monopoly exists when technology or economic realities make a monopoly more efficient than competition.)

3. Where competitive markets are more efficient, anti-monopoly laws (Sherman Act of 1890; Clayton Act of 1913) are designed to regulate business behavior and promote competition.

C. Redistribution of income:

1. Transfer payments provide relief to the poor, dependent, handicapped, and unemployment compensation to those unemployed who qualify for benefits. Social Security and Medicare programs support the sick and aged.

2. Government intervenes in markets by modifying prices. Price support programs for farmers; minimum wage laws are examples.

3. Taxation takes a larger proportion of incomes of the rich than the poor.

D. Reallocation of resources:

1. Market failure occurs when the competitive market system produces the "wrong" amounts of certain goods or services or fails to provide any at all.

2. Spillovers and externalities

   a. Spillovers or externalities occur when some of the benefits or costs of production are not fully reflected in market demand or supply schedules. Some of the benefits or costs of a good may "spill over" to third parties.

   b. An example of a spillover cost is pollution, which allows polluters to enjoy lower production costs because the firm is passing along the cost of pollution damage or cleanup to society. Because the firm does not bear the entire cost, it will overallocate resources.

   c. Correcting for spillover costs requires that government get producers to internalize these costs.

      1. Legislation can limit or prohibit pollution, which means the producer must bear costs of antipollution effort.

      2. Specific taxes on the amounts of pollution can be assessed, which causes the firm to cut back on pollution as well as provide funds for government cleanup.

    d.   Spillover benefits occur when direct consumption by some individuals impacts third parties. Public health vaccinations and education are two examples. Because some of the benefits accrue to others, individuals will demand too little for themselves and resources will be underallocated by the market.

    e.   Correcting for spillover benefits requires that the government somehow increase demand to increase benefits to socially desirable amounts.

        1.   Government can increase demand by providing subsidies like food stamps and education grants to subsidize consumers.

        2.   Government can finance production of good or service such as public education or public health.

        3.   Government can increase supply by subsidizing production, such as higher education, immunization programs, or public hospitals.

  2.   Government provides public goods and quasi-public goods and services.

    a.   Private goods are produced through the market because they are divisible and come in units small enough to be afforded by individual buyers. Private goods are subject to the exclusion principle, the idea that those unable and unwilling to pay are excluded from the benefits of the product.

    b.   Public or social goods would not be produced through the market, because they are indivisible and are not subject to the exclusion principle.

        1.   A lighthouse is a good example of a public good. The light is there for all to see whether or not they paid for it. Those who receive benefits without paying are part of the so-called free-rider problem.

        2.   Other examples include national defense, flood-control, public health.

    c.   Producers would not be able to find enough paying buyers for "public goods" because of the free-rider problem mentioned above. Therefore, "public goods" are not produced voluntarily through the market but must be provided by the public sector and financed by compulsory taxes.

    d.   Quasi-public goods are those that have large spillover benefits, so government will sponsor their provision. Otherwise, they would be underproduced. Medical care, education, and public housing are examples.

    e.   Resources are reallocated from private to public use by levying taxes on households and businesses, thus reducing their purchasing power and using the proceeds to purchase public and quasi-public goods. This can bring about a significant change in the composition of the economy's total output.

E. Promoting stability:

  1.   An economy's level of output is dependent on its level of total spending relative to its productive capacity.

  2.   The government may promote macroeconomic stability through changes in government spending and taxation.

    a.   When total spending is too low, the government may increase its spending and/or lower taxes to reduce unemployment.

    b.   When total spending is excessive, the government may cut its spending and/or raise taxes to foster price stability.

VI. Circular Flow Revisited

A. Figure 5.6 shows the circular flow model with the addition of the government sector.

B. There are several modifications to the Chapter 2 model.

1. Flows (5) through (8) illustrate that government makes purchases and expenditures in both the product and resource markets.

2. Flows (9) and (10) illustrate that the government provides public good and services to households and businesses.

3. Flows (11) and (12) illustrate that government receives taxes from and distributes subsidies to households and businesses.

C. These flows suggest ways that the government might alter the distribution of income, reallocate resources, and change the level of economic activity.

VII. Government Finance

A. Government expenditures on goods and services and transfer payments.

1. Government purchases directly use or employ resources to produce goods or services measured in domestic output.

2. Government transfer payments are not directly part of domestic output, but include payments like social security, unemployment compensation, welfare payments.

B. Changes in government purchases of goods and services, expenditures on transfer payments, and total spending as percentages of U.S. output, 1960 and 2000 (Figure 5.7).

C. Major growth in government spending since the 1960s has been in transfer payment area.

VIII. Federal Finance (see Figure 5.8)

A. Expenditures emphasize four important areas.

1. Income security,

2. National defense,

3. Health, and

4. Interest on national debt.

B. Receipts come from several sources.

1. Personal income tax is a major source.

    a. The Federal personal income tax is progressive. People with higher incomes pay a higher *percentage* of that income as tax than do people with lower incomes.

    b. A marginal tax rate is the rate at which the tax is paid on each additional unit of taxable income (Table 5.1).

    c. The average tax rate is the total tax paid divided by total taxable income.

    d. A tax whose average tax rises as income increases is progressive.

2. Payroll taxes, such as social security contributions, are a close second as source of revenue.

3. Corporate income taxes on corporation profits are the third largest source of revenue.

   4. Excise taxes are similar to sales taxes on specific commodities, like alcoholic beverages, tobacco, and gasoline. They are levied at the wholesale level, so are hidden from the consumer.

C. Global Perspective 5-2 shows that Australia, the United States, and Japan enjoy relatively low tax burdens.

IX. **State and Local Finance**

A. State expenditures and receipts for all states in 1998 are illustrated in Figure 5.9.

   1. State revenues primarily come from sales taxes and secondly from personal income taxes.

   2. State spending goes for public welfare, education, highways, and health care.

B. Local expenditures and receipts for all local governmental units in 1996 are shown in Figure 5.10.

   1. Revenue is primarily from property taxes.

   2. Spending is primarily on education.

   3. Gap between local tax revenues and spending is largely filled by grants from state and Federal government. (This system of intergovernmental transfers is called fiscal federalism.)

X. **LAST WORD: The Financing of Corporate Activity**

A. A major advantage of corporate form of organization is the ability to finance operations through sale of stock and bonds. This Last Word examines corporate finance in more detail.

B. There are three ways to finance corporate activity:

   1. Internally out of undistributed profits,

   2. Borrowing from financial institutions, and

   3. Issuing stocks and/or bonds.

      a. Common stock is a share of ownership in the corporation and gives the holder a voting right and share of dividends.

      b. A bond is an IOU whereby the corporation promises to pay the holder a fixed amount in the future plus annual interest.

C. Differences between stocks and bonds:

   1. Bondholder is not an owner, only a lender.

   2. Bonds are less risky usually because of certain factors.

      a. Bondholders can claim interest payments before stockholder dividends are calculated.

      b. Interest is guaranteed as long as company is healthy, whereas dividends depend on profits.

   3. Risks involved with bonds include:

      a. Capital risk, which means that the market price of a bond can change if market interest rates change and a holder needs to sell a bond before its maturity date. Note that the market price of a bond varies inversely with market interest rates.

b. Risk of unexpected inflation means that the purchasing power of the bond will fall because its interest rate is less than the inflation rate.

ANSWERS TO END-OF-CHAPTER QUESTIONS

5-1 Distinguish between the functional and personal distribution of income.

The functional distribution of income shows the sources of income, i.e., as payments to the four factors of production: labor, entrepreneurs, physical capital, and land (natural resources). The breakdown is: wages and salaries, proprietors' income, corporate profits, interest, and rents. There are five categories whereas there are only four factors of production, because proprietors' income includes profits as well as wages, interest, and rents.

The personal distribution of income shows how income, regardless of its source, is divided by quintiles among all the families in the country. Whereas the worst-off 20 percent of families, the lowest quintile, gets most of its income from wages and transfer payments, the best-off 20 percent gets considerable income from profits, interest, and rent.

5-2 (*Key Question*) Assume that the five residents of Econoville receive incomes of $50, $75, $125, $250, and $500. Present the resulting personal distribution of income as a graph similar to Figure 5-2. Compare the incomes of the lowest and highest fifth of the income receivers.

The distribution of income is quite unequal. The highest 20 percent of the residents receive 10 times more income than the lowest 20 percent.

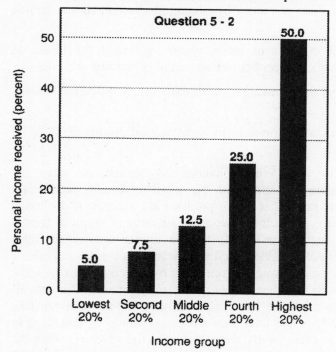

5-3 Distinguish clearly between a plant, a firm, and an industry. Contrast a vertically integrated firm, a horizontally integrated firm, and a conglomerate.

A plant is an operating unit where production takes place. This production can be manufacturing, farming, mining, retailing, wholesaling, warehousing—anything, in short, necessary for the production and distribution of goods and services.

A firm is the business organization that owns one or more plants. A firm can be very large, such as General Motors, which owns many plants in many countries, or very small, such as an independent corner grocery.

An industry is a somewhat arbitrary grouping of firms producing similar products—such as the steel industry. There may be a problem defining which firms belong to an industry; the firms in the automobile industry produce many non-automotive products.

A vertically integrated firm contains plants that are involved in various stages of the production process. A horizontally integrated firm contains plants that are involved in the same function of business. A conglomerate firm has plants that are producing products in several industries.

5-4   (*Key Question*) What are the major legal forms of business organization? Briefly state the advantages and disadvantages of each. How do you account for the dominant role of corporations in the U.S. economy?

The legal forms of business organizations are: sole proprietorship, partnership, and corporation.

Proprietorship advantages: easy to start and provides maximum freedom for the proprietor to do what she/he thinks best. Proprietorship disadvantages: limited financial resources; the owner must be a Jack-or-Jill-of-all-trades; unlimited liability.

Partnership advantages: easy to organize; greater specialization of management; and greater financial resources. Disadvantages: financial resources are still limited; unlimited liability; possibility of disagreement among the partners; and precarious continuity.

Corporation advantages: can raise large amounts of money by issuing stocks and bonds; limited liability; continuity.

Corporation disadvantages: red tape and expense in incorporating; potential for abuse of stockholder and bondholder funds; double taxation of profits; separation of ownership and control.

The dominant role of corporations stems from the advantages cited, particularly unlimited liability and the ability to raise money.

5-5   "The legal form an enterprise assumes is dictated primarily by the financial requirements of its particular line of production." Do you agree?

It is possible to agree with this statement in part. Where financial requirements are large, the corporate form is advantageous because financial capital can be raised by issuing stocks and bonds.   The new bondholder or stockholders know that the corporation has an unlimited life and that their shares or bonds are transferable. It is difficult to raise large amounts of financial capital for sole proprietorships because financial institutions usually have a limited amount of funds available to loan to any single borrower; it is not possible to sell shares or issue bonds; individuals fear loaning large amounts of money to any single owner. Even if the owner could borrow large amounts of financial capital, it still might not be done because of the unlimited liability that puts all of the owner's assets at risk. Partnerships might be better able to raise capital than are sole proprietorships, but they have similar difficulties and their only advantage would be that there is more than one owner with ability to invest. In other words, there is truth in the statement when the financial requirements are large as opposed to small.

Other factors may play a role in the decision about the legal form of business organization, but it does seem that the financial requirements will be a primary determinant.

5-6   Enumerate and briefly discuss the main economic functions of government. Which of these functions do you think is the most controversial? Why?

One role is to provide the legal and social framework. This goes beyond the elementary policing of keeping people from assaulting and stealing from each other. Government attempts to regulate business in terms of setting standards and rules. Some examples include establishing rules regarding contract negotiations and enforcement; setting standards on safety of food, drugs and other products; educating the public about respect for private property; devising zoning laws, etc.

A second function is to promote and maintain competition. Government does this through antitrust laws to make anti-competitive behavior illegal, and by regulating monopoly power in the case of "natural monopolies," where competition is not efficient, as is the case with many public utilities.

Third, the government redistributes income to help alleviate poverty. This is done by progressive taxation of income, which taxes low incomes proportionately less than high incomes, and by transfer payment programs such as unemployment compensation, social security benefits and Medicare, food stamps, aid to low-income families with dependent children, and other programs that provide support for the poor.

A fourth role is the reallocation of resources. This includes the provision of public or social goods, such as education, lighthouses, streetlights, and national defense. It also includes government programs that correct misallocation of resources, which may occur when there are spillover costs or benefits. When spillover costs occur, resource allocation would be more than is socially desirable, because some of the production costs have been passed on to third parties. The government designs programs to force producers to internalize these costs by regulation or specific taxes, so that the spillover costs are reduced or eliminated. In the case of spillover benefits, too few resources are allocated, because there are social gains to be gotten from production of some products, like education, but without government intervention, only those who reap direct benefits may pay. These purchasers would see no reason to support more of the product on an individual basis, so the government intervenes through subsidies or public production.

Stabilization is the fifth government role. The Federal government, through fiscal policy (taxation and government spending) attempts to prevent inflation and unemployment. The government's role is to attempt to dampen or stabilize the effect of business cycles.

5-7   What divergences arise between equilibrium and an efficient output when (a) spillover costs and (b) spillover benefits are present? How might government correct for these divergences? "The presence of spillover costs suggests under-allocation of resources to that product and the need for government subsides." Do you agree? Explain how zoning and seat belt laws might be used to deal with a problem of spillover costs.

(a) When spillover costs are present, the equilibrium output will be greater than the efficient output. This is because the producer, who is not bearing the full cost of production, will be able to produce more at a lower price than the efficient level, which would exist if true costs were reflected in the production decision.

(b) When spillover benefits are present, the equilibrium output will be smaller than the efficient output because the consumer is willing to pay a price equal to the consumer's individual marginal benefit, but no more. Since social benefits exist in addition to the private benefit, the government must either aid the producer to encourage more output or engage in its own production of the item with the spillover benefits.

Government might correct spillover costs through regulation, which requires firms to internalize these spillover costs, or it might tax the spillover until it becomes too expensive for the firm to incur these costs. This effectively shifts the supply curve to the left as costs of production rise, and the new equilibrium output will be less and closer to the efficient level. Spillover benefits can be encouraged by government subsidies to the producers of these products or by government production. In either case, the supply curve shifts to the right which lowers the equilibrium price and leads to a greater equilibrium output level.

The quote is incorrect. Spillover "costs" should be changed to spillover "benefits" to make this a true statement. Zoning could force businesses producing spillover costs to locate in regions where these costs would not spill over onto third parties, or where such costs would at least be reduced. Seat belt laws reduce injury and death from accidents, which, in turn, reduce the cost of public rescue units, hospital care, etc. Such laws should also reduce premiums for accident insurance, which benefits all of the insured.

5-8   Researchers have concluded that injuries caused by firearms cost about $500 million a year in hospital expenses alone. Because the majority of those shot are poor and without insurance, almost 85 percent of hospital costs must be borne by taxpayers. Use your understanding of externalities to recommend appropriate policies.

Taxpayers in general are bearing most of the $500 million cost of injuries caused by firearms. This is an example of spillover cost. The injured person is bearing part of the cost in terms of lost work time and, of course, the injury itself, but much of the cost of treating the injury is paid by taxpayers. Several solutions come to mind in terms of correcting this misallocation of resources.

One solution would be to impose a tax or license fee on firearms to pay for the cost of injuries caused by guns. Then only firearms manufacturers and purchasers would bear the cost of injuries caused by these weapons. Of course, this would place a burden on responsible gun owners who do not cause injury as well as those who do, but the cost would not be borne by non-owners, who seem to be totally innocent parties here.

Other solutions to reduce the external cost would include forcing the poor to carry injury insurance and/or forcing the perpetrators to pay the cost of injuries they cause. If any evidence exists on ways to prevent such injuries, it would be better to subsidize the cost of these methods of prevention and provide the external benefits of a safer, healthier society. This could include subsidizing safety education programs, recreation programs to keep would-be criminals off the street, and other ideas that might cut down on injuries. The present method does not prevent injury or violent crime. Whether or not these solutions are politically feasible may be more of a problem than their economic feasibility.

5-9   (*Key Question*) What are the basic characteristics of public goods? Explain the significance of the exclusion principle. By what means does government provide public goods?

Public goods are indivisible (they are produced in such large units they cannot be sold to individuals) and the exclusion principle does not apply to them (once the goods are produced nobody—including free riders—can be excluded from the goods' benefits). The free-rider problem explains the significance of the exclusion principle. The exclusion principle separates goods and services that private firms will supply because those who do not pay for them can be excluded from their benefits and goods and services which government must supply (because people can obtain the benefits without paying). Government must levy taxes to get revenues to pay for public goods.

5-10   (*Key Question*) Draw a production possibilities curve with public goods on the vertical axis and private goods on the horizontal axis. Assuming the economy is initially operating on the curve, indicate the means by which the production of public goods might be increased. How might output of public goods be increased if the economy is initially functioning at a point inside the curve?

On the curve, the only way to obtain more public goods is to reduce the production of private goods (from *C* to *B*).

An economy operating inside the curve can expand the production of public goods without sacrificing private goods (say, from *A* to *B*) by making use of unemployed resources.

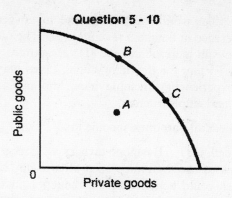

5-11 Use your understanding of the characteristics of private and public goods to determine whether the following should be produced through the market system or provided by government: (a) bread; (b) street lighting; (c) bridges; (d) parks; (e) swimming pools; (f) medical care; (g) mail delivery; (h) housing; (i) air traffic control; (j) libraries.

(a) bread—market system

(b) street lighting—government

(c) bridges—government (although one could answer quasi-government, as toll bridges exist)

(d) parks—government (although user fees could make them quasi-public goods)

(e) swimming pools—combination of market system pools (with fees for members or users) government provided or subsidized pools (for neighborhoods where funding is not be feasible)

(f) medical care—combined market and government; the mix of private and public production is a controversial topic addressed in the chapter on the economics of health care

(g) mail delivery—government, as long as the law gives postal service a monopoly

(h) housing—market system

(i) air traffic control—government

(j) libraries—government

5-12 Explain how government might manipulate its expenditures and tax revenues to reduce (a) unemployment and (b) the rate of inflation.

(a) To reduce unemployment, government must increase total or aggregate spending in the economy to encourage more production and employment. It can do so by increasing its own spending on goods and services and, by reducing taxes, inducing the population to spend more. Reduced taxes on businesses might also have a supply-side effect, allowing businesses to produce more as a result of the lower tax cost burden. Monetary authorities should be encouraged to increase the supply of money and credit available.

(b) To reduce the rate of inflation, government should reduce aggregate spending for goods and services in the economy. It can do so by decreasing its own spending and/or by increasing taxes, which would induce consumers to spend less. It could also encourage the monetary authorities to reduce the supply of money and credit.

5-13 "Most governmental actions simultaneously affect the distribution of income, the allocation of resources, and the levels of unemployment and prices." Use the circular flow model to confirm this assertion for each of the following:

a. The construction of a new high school in Blackhawk county.

In building the school, the effect would be an increase in government expenditures to the product market (5) and an increase in business revenues (3). The owners of the resources used to building the school will have an increase income (1). Resources will be diverted away from the private sector (5 and 6). To pay for the high school, taxes may have to be increased (11 and 12). If the economy is experiencing unemployment, the increase in government spending (5) may increase total output and employment.

b. A 2 percent reduction in the Federal corporate income tax.

Business taxes will be reduced (11). Business owners will receive a larger percent of the money income (1). If businesses use the increased profits to buy capital goods, labor and the owners of the other resources could benefit. If the reduction in the corporate income taxes results in a decrease in government spending (5) and an increase in corporate spending (1), there would be a reallocation of resources. If the economy is experiencing unemployment and government spending does not decrease, there could be an increase in spending if businesses increase their spending on capital goods (1).

c. An expansion of preschool programs for disadvantaged children.

This is shown as an increase in goods and services from government to households (9) or as a decrease in net taxes, which is equivalent to an increase in transfer payments (12). In either case, this is a redistribution of income or services in favor of the less well off. As additional teachers are hired and paid, there will be an increase in resources paid by the government (7).

There will be some reallocation of resources from private enterprise to government and some decrease in unemployment, unless the economy is already at full employment. In this case, there will some upward pressure on prices since, to the extent the program is a transfer payment, there will be no increase in production.

d. $50 million increase in spending for space research.

If this increased government spending were channeled entirely to outside contractors, the effects would be an increase in government expenditures to the product market (5) and an increase in business revenues (3). To the extent that some (or most) of the spending is "in-house," the government expenditures will be directed to the resource markets (7 and 8). In both cases, income going to households will increase (1), which will then increase their consumption (3), and an increase in the goods and services flowing from businesses (4).

If government increases net taxes (11) and (12) to pay for increased spending, there will be a reallocation of some resources from private business and household products to government products.

The increased government spending will redistribute income mostly toward better-paid labor: scientists, technicians, computer programmers. It will reduce whatever unemployment exists among the better-paid labor. It will tend to be inflationary since the $50 million paid out for goods and services will go to households without producing output that households could purchase. (This is always true of defense spending: the military does not produce for sale or have things produced for sale. But defense spending does create incomes, which are spent.)

e. The levying of a tax on air polluters.

This will be an increase in net taxes paid by business (11). Since business will regard this as an increase in costs, it will decrease its demand for resources (2), leading to a decreased flow of income to the resource markets (1). With less money income, households will decrease their consumption demand for goods and services from businesses (4) and business receipts (3) will be less. Also, the decrease in household income will lead to a decrease in net household taxes paid to government (12).

The distribution of income will be slightly away from profits and therefore toward the other three categories. To the extent that total tax revenues increase (11) - (12), there will be a slight increase in allocation of resources to government away from private enterprise. There will also likely be a reallocation of resources towards pollution control equipment. The increased costs to business, having caused decrease in supply, will tend to increase unemployment and prices.

f. A $1 per hour increase in the minimum wage.

This will increase costs of some businesses immediately and most businesses eventually, as better paid labor demands and gets what it considers its rightful historic percentage premium over the minimum wage. This will shift businesses' supply curve to the left, leading to a decreased demand for resources (2) though total business costs paid to labor (1) will likely have increased. With increased income, labor households will most likely increase consumption by more than the decrease of capitalist households (those getting at least part of their income as rents, interest, and profits). Thus flow (4) of goods and services to households increases as does flow (3), receipts of businesses from households.

The distribution of income will be toward labor. There will be increased wages—especially for the lowest paid workers. There will also be a small reallocation of resources towards labor. Unemployment may rise for the lowest paid workers and so will prices.

5-14 What is the most important source of revenue and the major type of expenditure at the Federal level? At the state level? At the local level?

At the Federal level, the most important source of revenue is the personal income tax. The main expenditure is for income security.

At the state level the most important sources of revenue are sales, excise, and gross receipts taxes, followed by personal income taxes. The main expenditures are for public welfare, with education running a very close second.

At the local level the most important source of revenue is, by far, property taxes. Education is by far the most important expenditure.

5-15 (*Key Question*) Suppose Fiscalville has no tax on the first $10,000 of income, but earnings between $10,000-20,000 are taxed at 20 percent and income between $20,000 and $30,000 at 30 percent. Any income above $30,000 is taxed at 40 percent. If your income is $50,000, how much in taxes will you pay? Determine your marginal and average tax rates. Is it a progressive tax?

Total tax = $13,000; marginal tax rate = 40% average tax rate = 26%. This is a progressive tax; the average tax rate rises as income goes up.

5-16 (Last Word) Describe three ways to finance corporate activity. Make a case that stocks are more risky for the financial investor than are bonds.

There are three ways to finance corporate activity: it can be done internally out of undistributed profits, or Corporations can borrow from financial institutions or issue their own stocks or bonds.

Common stock is an ownership share in a corporation that gives a holder voting rights and a share of dividends. Bonds are promissory notes where the corporation promises to pay the holder a fixed amount in the future plus annual interest on the loan. A bondholder is not an owner, only a lender. Stocks are usually riskier than bonds. Bondholders have a "legally prior claim" against corporate earnings. Stock dividends cannot be paid until all interest payments due to bondholders are paid. Interest is guaranteed as long as the company is healthy, whereas dividend depends on profits.

CHAPTER SIX
THE UNITED STATES IN THE GLOBAL ECONOMY

CHAPTER OVERVIEW

This chapter introduces the basic principles underlying the global economy; a more advanced discussion of international economics follows in Part Eight. The growth of world trade, and the United States' role in it, is examined first. The concept of comparative advantage is introduced as the basis for world trade followed by a discussion of foreign currencies and international exchange rates. Restrictive trade practices are examined, and this leads to a discussion of multilateral trade agreements and free-trade regions of the globe. The chapter concludes with an update of how well U.S. firms are competing in an increasingly competitive global economy.

WHAT'S NEW

This chapter has been condensed and updated both in terms of the statistics as well as the institutional changes that have occurred in the global economy. The chapter begins with a section that describes international linkages – trade flows, resource flows, information and technology flows, and financial flows. The old Figure 6-1 that illustrated where the component parts for a Boeing 777 were produced has been replaced with a diagram that indicates the flows between the U.S. economy and other national economies. Note that the Last Word, "Buy American: The Global Refrigerator" has been retained. Also omitted is the circular flow model with the foreign sector and the discussion that accompanied the diagram. A summary table has been added to the discussion of comparative advantage. This table will help students understand the relative costs of avocados and soybeans in Mexico and the U.S. The section on Multilateral Trade Agreements and Free-Trade Zones has been reorganized. The discussion on the WTO has been expanded and updated and a subsection on the euro has been added.

INSTRUCTIONAL OBJECTIVES

After completing this chapter, students should be able to:

1. Identify and give an example of the four types of flows that link the U.S. economy with the economies of other nations.

2. Describe the relative importance of U.S. exports of goods when compared to other industrialized countries and the position of the U.S. exports as a percentage of total world trade.

3. Describe the pattern of U.S exports and imports of goods and services since 1975 both in terms of percentage of GDP and absolute dollars.

4. Compare the dollar value of U.S. exports and imports of goods and the dollar value of U.S. exports and imports of services.

5. Name three of our principle imports and exports.

6. Identify our most important trading partner.

7. Explain the principles of comparative advantage, terms of trade, and gains from trade.

8. Explain how foreign exchange rates are determined and how a change in the international price of a currency can affect the price of exports and imports and the volume of exports and imports.

9. Describe four ways in which governments interfere with free trade among nations.

10. Describe the political reasons that influence governments to impose trade barriers.

11. Describe the purposes of the GATT and the WTO and explain the criticisms of the WTO.

12. Explain what is meant by a trade bloc or a free-trade zone and name two regional trade blocs.

13. Define and identity terms and concepts at the end of the chapter.

COMMENTS AND TEACHING SUGGESTIONS

1. Some of the best examples of Comparative Advantage can be found in the simple specialization and exchange that take place at home or in local businesses. Why does a parent ask their seven year old to set the table? Why does a parent have their twelve year old trim the hedge? Parents have absolute advantage in performing all household tasks. They can do jobs faster and with less errors. But while Tommy is trimming the hedge parents can complete tasks of higher value. Besides teaching a child responsibility, chores for children are economically efficient. They illustrate comparative advantage and demonstrate clearly that specialization increases total output even when one of the trading partners has an absolute advantage in producing all output. This example also demonstrates the undesirability of having resources sit idle. "Tommy, do get out of bed and finish the lawn."

   Local business examples of Comparative Advantage would include a lawyer that can type 80wpm hiring a secretary that can only type 50wpm; a dentist using the services of a laboratory to make crowns when he is more proficient at the job.

2. A 13-part video series, *Inside the Global Economy*, presents an in-depth examination of basic principles of international economics. Each 60-minute program features two documentary case studies, which illustrate the connection between economic theory and global trade, business, and finance in concrete, visual terms. The series is offered as a telecourse by some universities, but it is available for classroom use as well from the Annenberg/CPB Collection. Call 1-800-LEARNER for information. Several programs are appropriate to supplement this chapter and Chapters 37 and 38.

3. The Federal Reserve system's public information materials catalog also lists materials relevant for this chapter: "Wild About Trade" is part of the "World of Economics" audiovisual series published by the San Francisco Fed; "Their Money" is an instructional unit on monetary units in various countries and explains exchange rates and the international payments process. Contact the individual district or your district Fed Public Information Department for assistance in ordering these materials. A particularly good teaching aid is a comic book, "The Story of Foreign Trade and Exchange," which covers the principle of comparative advantage, exchange rates and forward rates in an entertaining and easy-to-understand format. These comic books are available free from the Fed in classroom quantities, and although they are written for high-school level students, college students love them! (You may need to mention that you think they're "corny," but nevertheless present some very sophisticated concepts.)

4. Economics America, The National Council on Education, has instructional materials on international topics available at reasonable prices. Call 1-800-338-1192 for their catalog. Particularly interesting would be issues of the "Senior Economist" on "The Pacific Age," "The Global Environment," and "Immigrants and the Economy." There is also an instructional volume on "International Trade, Teaching Strategies," with 23 complete lessons. Contact your regional university Center for Economic Education about borrowing or purchasing materials directly from them as well.

5. The most current trade information can be found in several periodical publications including: Federal Reserve Bulletin, International Economic Conditions (St. Louis Fed quarterly), Survey of Current Business, and the International Monetary Fund's International Financial Statistics.

STUDENT STUMBLING BLOCK

The principle of absolute advantage is easy to understand, but the principle of comparative advantage always gives students problems. It seems counterintuitive for trade to be advantageous to a country that can produce many things more efficiently than its trading partners. Yet this principle is the foundation for much of our gains from trade. Most students require practice with several applications before they understand this concept. Likewise, students have difficulty thinking in two currencies. An exercise in which students are asked to calculate the price of a McDonald's meal in various other currencies can help.

LECTURE NOTES

I. **Introduction**

    A. Even on a wilderness backpacking trip, Americans are not leaving the world behind. Much of backpacking equipment may be imported, not to mention the vehicle they used to arrive at the trail, the coffee they sip, etc.

    B. Many "American" products are made with components from abroad or are manufactured there. For example, the Chevrolet Lumina is made in Canada; the Gerber baby food company is owned by a Swiss company; Burger King is owned by a British corporation. The component parts of many "American" products are manufactured abroad.

II. **Linkages**

    A. Several economic flows link the U.S. economy with the economies of other nations.

    B. These linkages are:

        1. Goods and services flows;

        2. Capital and labor (resource) flows;

        3. Information and technology flows;

        4. Financial flows.

III. **U.S. and World Trade**

    A. Volume and Pattern:

        1. Table 6.1 gives an index of the importance of world trade to several countries.

        2. Figure 6.2 reveals the growth in U.S. imports and exports over past decades. Currently, exports and imports are 12 percent and 17 percent of GDP, which is more than double their importance of twenty-five years ago.

        3. The U.S. is world's leading trading nation, although its share has diminished from post-World War II level of one-third of total trade to one-eighth today.

    B. Dependence:

        1. U.S. depends on imports for many food items (bananas, coffee, tea, spices); raw silk, diamonds, natural rubber, much petroleum.

        2. On the export side, agriculture relies on foreign markets for one-fourth to one-half of sales; chemical, aircraft, auto, machine tool, coal, and computer industries also sell major portions of output in international markets (see Table 6-2).

    C. Trade pattern:

1. The U.S. has a trade deficit in goods. In 1999 U.S. imports exceeded exports of goods by $346 billion.

2. While we have a deficit in goods trade, U.S. export of services exceeds the import of services by $81 billion.

3. The U.S. imports some of the same categories it exports. Specifically, automobiles, computers, chemicals, and semiconductors. (See Table 6-2)

4. Most U.S. trade is with industrially advanced countries. (See Table 6-3)

5. Canada is the United States' most important trade partner quantitatively. Twenty-four percent of U.S. exports sold went to Canadians, who in turn provided 20 percent of U.S. imports. (See Table 6-3)

6. The U.S. has sizable trade deficits with Japan and China. In 1999, the U.S. trade deficit with Japan was $75 billion. There was also a sizable trade deficit with China. (See Table 6-3)

7. In 1999 the U.S. imported $24 billion of goods (mainly oil) from OPEC nations, while exporting $12 billion to those countries.

D. Financial Linkages: (International trade implies complex financial linkages among nations.) Trade deficits must be financed by borrowing or earning foreign exchange, which is accomplished by selling U.S. assets through foreign investment in the U.S. The U.S. borrows from citizens of other nations; the U.S. is the world's largest debtor nation.

E. Facilitating factors that explain the growth of trade:

1. Transportation technology has improved over the years.

2. Communications technology allows traders to make deals in trade and global finance very easily.

3. Trade barriers declined dramatically since 1940, and the trend toward free trade continues.

F. Participants in international trade:

1. Global Perspective 6-1 shows the major participants in world trade.

2. New participants have become important, especially the Asian countries of Hong Kong, Singapore, South Korea, and Taiwan. China is also emerging as important in global trade. Collapse of communism has led to the emergence of former Soviet republics and Eastern bloc countries as world trade participants.

IV. **Specialization and Comparative Advantage**

A. The U.S. is referred to as an "open economy" when it is placed in the global economy.

B. Adam Smith observed in 1776 that specialization and trade increase the productivity of a nation's resources. His observation related to the principle of absolute advantage whereby a country should buy a good from other countries if they can supply it cheaper than we can.

C. Basic principle of comparative advantage was first observed and explained in early 1800s by David Ricardo. This principle says that it pays for a person or a country to specialize and exchange even if that person or nation is more productive than potential trading partners in all economic activities. Specialization should take place if there are relative cost differences in production of different items.

D. Example: A CPA can paint her house faster and better than a painter. She earns $50 per hour as accountant and can hire a painter for $15 per hour. The CPA can do the painting job in 30 hours; it takes the painter 40 hours. Should she hire the painter? On economic grounds, the opportunity cost is greater for the accountant to paint her house. She is better off to specialize in accounting rather than sacrifice 30 x $50, or $1500, to paint her house, when she can hire the painter for 40 x $15, or $600. The accountant will gain, and the painter will also gain because he is very inefficient in accounting. It may take him 10 hours to prepare his tax return which would mean 10 x $15, hours or $150, in opportunity cost, whereas the accountant could probably complete the forms in 2 hours for a cost of $100. This example shows that even if a person (the accountant) has an absolute advantage in production of two products (painting and accounting), it is still advantageous to specialize and trade. The same is true for nations.

E. Comparative advantage and terms of trade: Tables 6-4 and 6-5 illustrate the principle of comparative advantage for two countries, U.S. and Mexico, with a simplified example. In Mexico, the opportunity cost of 1 ton of soybeans is giving up 4 tons of avocados. In the U.S., the opportunity cost of 1 ton of soybeans is 3 tons of avocados. In other words, the comparative cost of soybeans is less in U.S. than in Mexico when the alternative is producing avocados. Thus the U.S. should specialize in soybeans, and Mexico should specialize in avocados.

1. If the two nations specialize according to comparative advantage, then to get the other product they must trade. A nation has a comparative advantage in some product when it can produce that product at a lower domestic opportunity cost than can a potential trading partner.

2. Table 6-6 summarizes which nation has a comparative advantage in each product.

3. The rate of exchange of these two products will be determined through negotiation; the outcome is called the terms of trade.

4. The terms of trade will be limited by the relative costs of production within each country. The U.S. will not forgo more than 1 ton of soybeans to get 3 tons of avocados and Mexico will not give up more than 4 tons of avocados for 1 ton of soybeans.

5. Somewhere between these limits, trade is possible. In the text example, the terms of trade are assumed to be 3.5 tons of avocados for each ton of soybeans. Americans would specialize in soybeans only if they could obtain more than 3 tons of avocados for 1 ton of soybeans by trading with Mexico.

F. Gains from specialization and trade:

1. Table 6-7, column 1, shows the optimal outputs for Mexico and U.S. in soybeans and avocados before specialization and trade.

2. Column 2 of Table 6-7 shows the amount each country produces when it specializes.

3. Column 3 of Table 6-7 shows quantities in each country after trade takes place at the rate of 1S = 3.5Av.

4. Mexico will give up 35 tons of avocados for 10 tons of U.S. soybeans.

5. Now each country will have more than they had originally: Mexico now has 25 tons of avocados left plus 10 tons of soybeans. U.S. now has 35 tons of avocados and keeps 20 tons of soybeans. Mexico has gained 1 ton of each; U.S. has gained 2 tons of avocados and 1 ton of soybeans, and these gains have occurred using the same resources as before specialization.

6. This example illustrates that specialization and trade can improve overall output even when one country (U.S.) can produce more of both items compared to the other without trade. Specialization and trade have the same effect as an increase in resources or technological progress. (Key Question 4)

V.   Foreign Exchange Markets

A. In a foreign exchange market, various national currencies are exchanged for one another so that international trade can take place. Germans want euros, Mexicans want pesos, and the Japanese want yen when they sell their products.

B. Two points require emphasis with respect to these markets.

   1. Real-world foreign exchange markets are competitive, with large numbers of buyers and sellers dealing with a standardized product, the currency of some country.

   2. Exchange rates link domestic (one country's) prices with all foreign prices. They enable you to translate the price of foreign products into dollars. For example, if the dollar/yen exchange rate is 1 cent/per yen, a Sony T.V. set priced at ¥20,000 will cost an American $200 = (20,000 x .01).

C. The dollar-yen exchange market is depicted in Figure 6.3. The demand for yen and the supply of yen curve will establish the equilibrium dollar price of yen.

D. Changing rates: Appreciation and Depreciation.

   1. If the demand for yen rises, the dollar price of yen rises. That means the dollar depreciates relative to the yen. This could happen for many reasons including an increase in U.S. incomes that enables Americans to buy more Japanese goods, or an increase in preference for Japanese products. The result is that Japanese goods would become more expensive to Americans and U.S. products would become less expensive to us. (See Figure 6-4.)

   2. If the opposite occurred and Japanese incomes increased more than U.S. incomes and/or Japanese preferences for U.S. products increased, then the dollar would appreciate relative to the yen as the yen supply increased. Americans will purchase a greater quantity of Japanese products because they have become less expensive in dollar terms. (Key Questions 6 and 7)

   3. Chapter 38 has more detailed explanations of the foreign exchange markets.

VI.   Government and Trade

A. Several trade impediments are sometimes enacted by governments.

   1. Protective tariffs are excise taxes or duties on imported goods. Governments enact these tariffs to protect domestic producers by making foreign goods more expensive.

   2. Import quotas are maximum limits on the number or total value of specific imports. Once quotas are filled, no more imports are allowed into the country.

   3. Nontariff barriers include licensing requirements, unreasonable standards, and unnecessary bureaucratic "red tape."

   4. Governments have used export subsidies to promote the sale of products aboard.

B. Why do governments enact trade barriers?

   1. They don't understand the benefits from international trade and see only the damage in certain industries that can't compete successfully with imports.

2. Political considerations are important because consumers don't see the effects of a tariff or quota directly, but they do see the impact of import competition on some workers. Also, the benefits of free trade tend to be spread among all consumers, but the benefits of a protective policy are realized almost immediately in the short run by the affected industry may have a large and vocal stake in the outcome.

C. Trade barriers hurt American consumers who must pay higher than world prices. Interference with international trade through protective tariffs and quotas is shown to cost society more than the benefits that are received by the protected firms and workers.

VII. **Multilateral Agreements and Free-Trade Zones**

A. Trade barriers can cause a "trade war," in which all nations retaliate with trade barriers of their own. The Smoot-Hawley Tariff Act of 1930 was a classic example of this. It prompted other nations to increase tariffs and global trade fell as well as U.S. output. (See Figure 6-5.)

B. Reciprocal Trade Agreements Act had the goal of reducing tariffs.

1. It gave the President the power to negotiate reductions up to 50 percent if the trading partner also reduced its tariffs.

2. It included "most-favored-nation" clauses in agreements so other nations also benefit when negotiations succeeded with one particular country. For example, if the U.S. negotiated a reduction in tariffs with France, to lower American tariffs on French imports, the imports of other nations having most-favored-nation status, say, Sweden would also be reduced.

C. The General Agreement of Tariffs and Trade (GATT):

1. In 1947 after WWII, the U.S. signed an agreement to negotiate reductions on a multilateral basis. Twenty-three nations originally signed, but now 128 nations belong to GATT.

2. The latest round of GATT negotiations was the eighth set of negotiations. It began in Uruguay in 1986 and concluded at the end of 1993. The agreement was passed by Congress in the fall of 1994, went into effect in 1995, and will be phased in through 2005. Its major provisions include the following.

a. Tariff reductions will average 33 percent.

b. Services are included in the treaty's trade rules.

c. Quotas on textiles and apparel imports will be replaced by tariffs and these, too, will be eliminated gradually.

d. Agriculture will also be affected with members agreeing to cut subsidies to agriculture and quotas on agricultural imports.

e. Intellectual property will be protected by international patent, trademark, and copyright agreements.

f. When fully implemented, experts estimate the GATT agreement will boost world GDP by $6 trillion or 8 percent, and U.S. consumers will save about $30 billion each year.

D. World Trade Organization (WTO)

1. The Uruguay Round of the GATT established the WTO as the GATT's successor.

2. The WTO oversees trade agreements and rules on trade disputes.

3. Critics of the WTO are concerned that the rules crafted to expand trade and investment enables firms to circumvent national laws that protect workers and the environment.

4   Proponents argue promotion of free trade will raise output and incomes and that the higher standards of living will likely result in more protections for workers and the environment.

E. European Union (EU):

1. In many regions of the world, countries have formed free-trade zones to reduce tariffs.

2. The EU, formed in 1958 as the Common Market, now is comprised of 15 western European countries.

F. The Euro:

1. The euro is a currency established by the EU that is now being used by eleven of the fifteen EU nations.

2. Starting in 1999, the euro has been used as electronic payments for credit card purchases and transfer of funds among banks.

3. By July 2002, only the euro will be accepted for payments in the EU countries that have adopted the currency.

G. North American Free Trade Agreement (NAFTA):

1. This free-trade zone was established in 1993 among Canada, U.S. and Mexico with about the same combined output as EU, but a larger geographical area.

2. Free trade with Mexico was controversial because critics fear a loss of American jobs as firms can move to Mexico more easily. Also, they fear Japanese and South Korean firms will build plants there and import goods duty-free to U.S.

3. The increased trade has increased domestic employment, reduced unemployment, and increased the standard of living in all three countries.

VIII.   Increased global competition

A. Although imports of many products have decreased the share of American firms in the U.S. market, hundreds of U.S. firms have prospered in the global market.

B. Although some domestic producers will get hurt and their workers will have to find employment elsewhere, freer trade benefits the consumer and society.

IX.   LAST WORD: Buy American: The Global Refrigerator

A. This essay is by humorist Art Buchwald, and illustrates how hard it is to define what is "American made" in today's global economy.

B. The conversation takes place at the Baleful Refrigerator Co. (an American company) where an executive is insisting that Americans should not buy foreign refrigerators because this hurts his company. While he is talking, several things occur:

1. He orders steel from Japan because it is less expensive.

2. He orders handles from Taiwan for his refrigerators.

3. Icemakers come from Hong Kong or South Korea.

4. Motors come from a German company in Brazil.

5. The defroster comes from Finland.

6. Shipping crates are arriving from Singapore, and he cancels an order from Boise Cascade.

C. After demonstrating that the "American" refrigerator is made from foreign parts and assembled here, the executive shows Art the beautiful American refrigerator made by American workers for the American consumer. Art dutifully says, "It puts foreign imports to shame!"

ANSWERS TO END-OF-CHAPTER QUESTIONS

6-1   Describe the four major economic flows that link the U.S. with other nations. Provide an example to illustrate each flow. Explain the relationship between the top and bottom flows in Figure 6-1.

The four major economic flows are: the flows of goods and services; the flows of capital equipment and labor; the flows of information and technology; and the flows of money.

The financial flows provide the money necessary to pay for exports and imports.

6-2   How important is international trade to the U.S. economy? In terms of volume, does the United States trade more with industrially advanced economies or with developing economies? What country is the United States' most important trading partner, quantitatively?

Exports and imports constituted 12 percent and 17 percent of GDP respectively in 2000. These proportions have more than doubled since 1975. The United States trades more with industrially advanced economies although the U.S. trade with Mexico is substantial. The U.S.'s most important trading partner quantitatively is Canada, buying 24 percent of our exports and providing 20 percent of our imports in 1999.

6-3   What factors account for the rapid growth of world trade since the Second World War? Who are the major players in international trade today? Besides Japan, what other Asian nations play significant roles in international trade?

The rapid growth in world trade has been facilitated by a reduction in trade barriers, by increasing prosperity of nations around the world, and by improved communication and transportation that have made trade easier among the world's major industrial powers.

The major players in international trade are the United States, Japan and Germany along with Canada and the members of the European Union. China is an emerging power along with the newly industrializing economies of Hong Kong, Singapore, South Korea and Taiwan who have increased their share of global trade from about 3 percent of the total to 10 percent since 1972.

6-4   (*Key Question*) The following are production possibilities tables for South Korea and the United States. Assume that before specialization and trade the optimal product-mix for South Korea is alternative B and for the United States alternative U.

Product	South Korea's production possibilities					
	A	**B**	**C**	**D**	**E**	**F**
Radios (in 1000s)	30	24	18	12	6	0
chemicals (tons)	0	6	12	18	24	30

Product	U.S. production possibilities					
	R	**S**	**T**	**U**	**V**	**W**
Radios (in 1000s)	10	8	6	4	2	0
chemicals (tons)	0	4	8	12	16	20

a. Are comparative cost conditions such that the two areas should specialize? If so, what product should each produce?

b. What is the total gain in radio and chemical output that results from this specialization?

c. What are the limits of the terms of trade? Suppose actual terms of trade are 1 unit of radios for 1-1/2 units of chemicals and that 4 units of radios are exchanged for 6 units of chemicals. What are the gains from specialization and trade for each area?

d. Can you conclude from this illustration that specialization according to comparative advantage results in more efficient use of world resources? Explain.

(a) Yes, because the opportunity cost of radios is less (1R = 1C) in South Korea than in the United States (1R = 2C). South Korea should produce radios and the United States should produce chemicals.

(b) If they specialize, the United States can produce 20 tons of chemicals and South Korea can produce 30,000 radios. Before specialization South Korea produced alternative B and the United States alternative U for a total of 28,000 radios (24,000 + 4,000) and 18 tons of chemicals (6 tons + 12 tons). The gain is 2,000 radios and 2 tons of chemicals.

(c) The limits of the terms of trade are determined by the comparative cost conditions in each country before trade: 1R = 1C in South Korea and 1R = 2C in the United States. The terms of trade must be somewhere between these two ratios for trade to occur.

If the terms of trade are 1R = 1-1/2C, South Korea would end up with 26,000 radios (= 30,000 - 4,000) and 6 tons of chemicals. The United States would have 4,000 radios and 14 tons of chemicals (= 20 - 6). South Korea has gained 2,000 radios. The United States has gained 2 tons of chemicals.

(d) Yes, the world is obtaining more output from its fixed resources.

6-5   Suppose that the comparative-cost ratios of two products—baby formula and tuna fish—are as follows in the hypothetical nations of Canswicki and Tunata.

Canswicki: 1 can baby formula = 2 cans tuna fish

Tunata: 1 can baby formula = 4 cans tuna fish

In what product should each nation specialize? Explain why terms of trade of 1 can baby formula = 2-1/2 cans tuna fish would be acceptable to both nations.

Canswicki should specialize in baby formula and Tunata in tuna fish because the opportunity cost of producing baby formula in Canswicki is less than in Tunata. (In other words, the opportunity cost of producing tuna in Canswicki is greater at 1/2 can formula per can of tuna than in Tunata, where each can of tuna means giving up only 1/4 can of formula.)

Since neither country can do as well as this trade if they produce both products for themselves, they should benefit from these terms of trade. The best that Canswicki can do on its own without trade is 2 cans of tuna fish for each can of baby formula given up, so 2-1/2 cans of tuna would be an improvement. The best that Tunata can do without trade is to give up 4 cans of tuna produced for each can of baby formula, so 2-1/2 cans would be less of a sacrifice in exchange for a can of baby formula.

6-6   (Key Question) True or false? "U.S. exports create a demand for foreign currencies; foreign imports of U.S. goods generate supplies of foreign currencies." Explain. Would a decline in U.S. consumer income or a weakening of U.S. preferences for foreign products cause the dollar to depreciate or appreciate? Other things equal, what would be the effects of that depreciation or appreciation on U.S. exports and imports?

The first part of this statement is incorrect. U.S. exports create a domestic *supply* of foreign currencies, not a domestic demand for them. The second part of the statement is accurate. The foreign demand for dollars (from US. exports) generates a supply of foreign currencies to the United States.

A decline in U.S. incomes or a weakening of U.S. preferences for foreign goods would reduce U.S. imports, reducing U.S. demand for foreign currencies. These currencies would depreciate (the dollar would appreciate). Dollar appreciation means U.S. exports would decline and U.S. imports would increase.

6-7   If the European euro declines in value (depreciates) in the foreign exchange market, would it be easier or harder for the French to sell their wine in the United States? Suppose you were planning a trip to Paris. How would the depreciation of the euro change the dollar price of this trip?

If the European euro declines in value, it means that Americans can receive more francs for each dollar. Therefore, they do not need as many dollars to pay the franc price of a bottle of French wine, so the quantity demanded would rise and it should be easier to sell French wine in the U.S. Likewise, the franc depreciation would make it less costly for Americans to travel in France, since the dollar would now buy more francs (assuming that prices inside France have not risen to entirely offset the depreciation of the franc).

6-8   True or False? "An increase in the American dollar price of the South Korean won implies that the South Korean won has depreciated in value." Explain.

This is a false statement. It implies just the opposite. If the price of the South Korean won has risen, this means it has appreciated in value by definition. It now takes more dollars to buy a won, which means the dollar has lost purchasing power vis à vis the won. It is the dollar that has depreciated against the won.

6-9   What measures do governments use to promote exports and restrict imports? Who benefits and who loses from protectionist policies? What is the net outcome for society?

Governments promote exports by providing subsidies to export producers, which effectively lowers their costs and enables them to sell their products at lower prices on world markets. Subsidies enable export firms or industries to compete against other nations, but the fact the subsidy was necessary for this competition means that the most efficient use of resources is not taking place.

Restriction of imports can be accomplished by protective tariffs, by import quotas, and by non-tariff barriers such as licensing requirements, unreasonable quality standards, and unnecessary import procedures.

The benefits of protectionist policies are to the industry that is having to compete on world markets either with its exports or against imports. Even this may be a short-run benefit, because industries that are protected may become so inefficient and outmoded that they are unable to stay afloat even with the protection in the long run. There may also be some political benefits as those protected groups have a strong self interest in this protection and are vocal opponents of free trade for their industries, whereas the benefits of free trade are more diffuse and the benefits to any single group of voters is less noticeable.

The costs of protectionist policies are more widespread. The costs of protectionist policies arise because resources are not being used as efficiently as they might be under free trade. This raises the cost of production and raises prices, and means the total quantity of world output produced and consumed is not as great as it could be without such barriers. Consumers lose since they must pay higher prices, but worldwide producers also lose because productivity is not as high as it could be.

The net outcome to society is negative. Costs outweigh the benefits for the reasons stated above.

6-10   (*Key Question*) Identify and state the significance of each of the following: (a) WTO; (b) EU; (c) euro; and (d) NAFTA. What commonality do they share?

(a) The WTO oversees trade agreements reached by member nations and arbitrates trade disputes among them. (b) The EU is a trading bloc of 15 European countries who have agreed to abolish tariffs and import quotas on most products and have liberalized the movement of labor and capital within the EU. (c) The euro is the common currency that will be used by 11 of the 15 EU countries. (d) NAFTA is a trade bloc made up of the United Sates, Canada, and Mexico whose purpose is to reduced tariffs and other trade barriers among the three countries.

All of the above have the goals of increasing international trade and leading to a better allocation of the world's resources.

6-11   Explain: "Free-trade zones such as the EU and NAFTA lead a double life. They can promote free trade among members, but pose serious trade obstacles for nonmembers." Do you think the net effects of these trade blocs are good or bad for world trade? Why? How do the efforts of the WTO relate to these trade blocs?

Free-trade zones increase the efficient use of resources within the zones by eliminating trade barriers and allowing for the freer movement of resources across international borders among the member nations. On the other hand, if trade barriers are retained against imports from nations outside the zone, this results in less efficient allocation of resources in the larger global economy.

The evidence seems to point to the net effect of trade blocs as being good for world trade. They seem to be a first step in breaking down trade barriers as can be seen from the expansion of the original European Economic Community to today's 15-member European Union, and the expansion of the U.S.-Canada free trade agreement to NAFTA several years later. Also, the attraction of the large consumer markets within each trade zone makes other trade blocs more likely to conclude agreements between blocs that would further lower trade barriers.

Some might argue that such blocs are bad for world trade because the unity and self-sufficiency gained inside the trade zone may inhibit further overtures for trade expansion outside the bloc, but so far this does not seem to have been the case.

The WTO provides a forum for the trade blocs to meet and negotiate further reductions in trade barriers among the trade blocs.

6-12   Speculate as to why some U.S. firms strongly support trade liberalization while other U.S. firms favor protectionism. Speculate as to why some U.S. labor unions strongly support trade liberalization while other U.S. labor unions strongly oppose it.

When trade barriers are eliminated, some U.S. firms will be hurt by the increased competition from foreign companies. On the other hand, if trade barriers against U.S. products are eliminated, the U.S. companies producing those products will be able to sell more of their products outside the U.S. Likewise, the union workers working for the firm that face increased international competition may lose their jobs, whereas union workers working for companies that are expanding due to international trade will experience an increase in job opportunities.

6-13   (*Last Word*) What point is Art Buchwald making in his humorous essay on the Baleful Refrigerator Company? Why might Mr. Baleful *oppose* tariffs on imported goods, even though he wants consumers to buy "American" refrigerators?

Art Buchwald is pointing out that even when the manufacturer himself believes in "buying American," his belief is hypocritical. The "American" refrigerator is made from components manufactured in many different countries because it is less costly to buy these imported parts, which means they can be made more efficiently elsewhere. Based on the long list of the important components in the Baleful refrigerator that are made in other nations, it seems that the major American aspect to this appliance is the fact that it was assembled in the U.S. by American workers (we assume). Buchwald is pointing out how hard it is to tell what is "Made in America" in today's global economy. One recent advertisement illustrates the point, with Honda claiming to be the only car that is completely made in the U.S. with parts made in the U.S. Their claim is that the Hondas that are manufactured here are more "American" than cars made by General Motors, Ford, or Chrysler, which either make their cars in another country or buy many of their parts from other countries.

Mr. Baleful would oppose tariffs on imports because he would not want to pay higher prices on the supplies he uses to make his company's refrigerators, and most of the important components are imported.

CHAPTER SEVEN
MEASURING DOMESTIC OUTPUT, NATIONAL INCOME, AND THE PRICE LEVEL

CHAPTER OVERVIEW

News headlines frequently report the status of the nation's economic conditions, but to many citizens the information is confusing or incomprehensible. This chapter acquaints students with the basic language of macroeconomics and national income accounting. GDP is defined and explained. Then, the differences between the expenditure and income approaches to determining GDP are discussed and analyzed in terms of their component parts. The income and expenditure approaches are developed gradually from the basic expenditure-income identity, through tables and figures.

The importance of investment is given considerable emphasis, including the nature of investment, the distinction between gross and net investment, the role of inventory changes, and the impact of net investment on economic growth. On the income side, nonincome charges—depreciation and indirect business taxes—are covered in detail because these usually give students the most trouble.

Other measures of economic activity are defined and discussed, with special emphasis on price indexes. The purpose and procedure of deflating and inflating nominal GDP are carefully explained and illustrated. Finally, the shortcomings of current GDP measurement techniques are examined. Global comparisons are made with respect to size of national GDP and size of the underground economy.

The Last Word looks at the sources of data for the GDP accounts.

WHAT'S NEW

The chapter is updated and slightly revised from the 14th edition. The last sections on GDP as a measure of well-being and the underground economy have been shortened and consolidated. Finally, a new Last Word on GDP data sources replaces the previous editions discussion of the consumer price index.

INSTRUCTIONAL OBJECTIVES

After completing this chapter, students should be able to:

1. State the purposes of national income accounting.

2. List the components of GDP in the output (expenditures) approach and in the income approach.

3. Compute GDP using either the expenditure or income approach when given national income data.

4. Differentiate between gross and net investment.

5. Explain why changes in inventories are investments.

6. Discuss the relationship between net investment and economic growth.

7. Compute NDP, NI, PI, and DI when given relevant data.

8. Describe the system represented by the circular flow in this chapter when given a copy of the diagram.

9. Calculate a GDP price index using simple hypothetical data.

10. Find real GDP by adjusting nominal GDP with use of a price index.

11. List eight shortcomings of GDP as an index of social welfare.

12. Explain what is meant by the underground economy and state its approximate size in the U.S. and how that compares to other nations.

13. Give an estimate of actual 1999 (or later) U.S. GDP in trillions of dollars and be able to rank U.S. relative to a few other countries.

14. Define and identify terms and concepts listed at the end of the chapter.

COMMENTS AND TEACHING SUGGESTIONS

1. National income accounts are detailed and can be very time-consuming for students. Some instructors choose to treat them selectively. For example, focus only on expenditures approach to GDP. Decide what priorities are most important and plan accordingly.

2. Encourage students to look for news items on Chapter 7 concepts. Students could be asked to keep a weekly journal summarizing reports or follow a particular measure like unemployment.

   Political cartoons are often about macroeconomic issues. Keeping a collection of them and asking students to contribute enlivens the classroom and builds understanding.

3. Use of circular flow diagrams in this section may be helpful. The national income accounts are built on the identity of income and output. Once a good is produced it generates a like amount of income; this is clearly demonstrated in the sum of the transactions in the product and resource markets.

4. Discuss the difference between "stock" concepts and "flows." The national accounts are measured over a period of time, so GDP and the related aggregates are all flow concepts. A "stock" is a measure of a variable at a point in time. Consider these pairs of terms: income and wealth; saving and savings; deficit and debt. Contrast the income statement of a firm with the firm's balance sheet.

5. For discussion: Why is a hurricane or an earthquake good for the economy? How does a divorce add to GDP? How can the depletion of a natural resource add to GDP?

6. Ask students how they think a researcher might get information about the size of the underground economy. Obviously a drug dealer is not going to include sales information on his 1040 tax return. Discuss how the presence of the underground economy might influence tax structure and policies.

7. Have the students construct a market basket of goods that reflects their own typical purchases. Price the items early in the semester and again near the end of the class. What was the value of their CPI? Was it difficult to define the items, so as to insure a constant market basket of goods? How did the composition of their market basket compare to others in the class or to the current contents of the official market basket of goods?

STUDENT STUMBLING BLOCK

There is a lot of memorization required to learn the various measures used in the national accounts. In the interest of time, you might choose to have your students focus on the expenditures approach to calculating GDP. It will prove to be the most useful in understanding the analysis in subsequent chapters which use C + I + G + X_n formulation frequently.

Special Problems: Investment is a word that all of the students in the class think they understand. The meaning of the term in ordinary conversation interferes with their ability to acquire a new definition and use that new definition consistently.

Changes in business inventory is an entry that represents the difference between what has been produced and what is sold. Although this entry is very small compared to total GDP, it is one of the most important indicators of future business activity. It has an important role in the income determination models presented later in the text.

Many of the exclusions from the GDP accounts involve financial transactions that transfer the ownership of existing assets. The sale of stock in a corporation is a transfer of part ownership of existing assets. New stock issues only dilute the share of ownership and are excluded as well. The sale of corporate bonds also represents a purely financial transaction. Corporations that are seeking to expand use the proceeds of these sales to purchase capital equipment or engage in new construction, and this is included in GDP. To also include the purchase of the securities would be an example of double counting.

Remind the students that entries beginning with the word *net* could be negative and have been in the case of net exports for many years in U.S.

LECTURE NOTES

I. **Assessing the Economy's Performance**

    A. National income accounting measures the economy's performance by measuring the flows of income and expenditures over a period of time.

    B. National income accounts serve a similar purpose for the economy, as do income statements for business firms.

    C. Consistent definition of terms and measurement techniques allows us to use the national accounts in comparing conditions over time and across countries.

    D. The national income accounts provide a basis for of appropriate public policies to improve economic performance.

II. **Gross Domestic Product**

    A. GDP is the monetary measure of the total *market value* of all *final* goods and services *produced within a country* in one year.

       1. Money valuation allows the summing of apples and oranges; money acts as the common denominator.

       2. GDP includes only final products and services; it avoids double or multiple counting, by eliminating any intermediate goods used in production of these final goods or services.

       3. GDP is the value of what has been produced in the economy over the year, not what was actually sold.

    B. GDP Excludes Nonproduction Transactions

       1. GDP is designed to measure what is produced or created over the current time period. Existing assets or property that sold or transferred, including used items, are not counted.

       2. Purely financial transactions are excluded.

         a. Public transfer payments, like social security or cash welfare benefits.

         b. Private transfer payments, like student allowances or alimony payments.

         c. The sale of stocks and bonds represent a transfer of existing assets. (However, the brokers' fees are included for services rendered.)

3. Secondhand sales are excluded, they do not represent current output.

C. Two Ways to Look at GDP: Spending and Income.

1. What is spent on a product is income to those who helped to produce and sell it.

2. This is an important identity and the foundation of the national accounting process.

D. Expenditures Approach (See Figure 7.1 and Table 7.3)

1. GDP is divided into the categories of buyers in the market; household consumers, businesses, government, and foreign buyers.

2. Personal Consumption Expenditures—(C)—includes durable goods, nondurable goods and services.

3. Gross Private Domestic Investment—(I_g)

   a. All final purchases of machinery, equipment, and tools by businesses.

   b. All construction (including residential).

   c. *Changes* in business inventory.

      i. If total output exceeds current sales, inventories build up.

      ii. If businesses are able to sell more than they currently produce, this entry will be a negative number.

   d. Net Private Domestic Investment—(I_n).

      i. Each year as current output is being produced, existing capital equipment is wearing out and buildings are deteriorating; this is called depreciation or capital consumption allowance.

      ii. Gross Investment minus depreciation (*capital consumption allowance)* is called net investment.

      iii. If more new structures and capital equipment are produced in a given year than are used up, the productive capacity of the economy will expand.

      iv. When gross investment and depreciation are equal, a nation's productive capacity is static.

      v. When gross investment is less than depreciation, an economy's production capacity declines.

4. Government Purchases (of consumption goods and capital goods) – (G)

   a. Includes spending by all levels of government (federal, state and local).

   b. Includes all direct purchases of resources (labor in particular).

   c. This entry excludes transfer payments since these outlays do not reflect current production.

5. Net Exports—(X_n)

   a. All spending on goods produced in the U.S. must be included in GDP, whether the purchase is made here or abroad.

   b. Often goods purchased and measured in the U.S. are produced elsewhere (Imports).

    c. Therefore, net exports, (X_n) is the difference: (exports minus imports) and can be either a positive or negative number depending on which is the larger amount.

  6. Summary: $GDP = C + I_g + G + X_n$

E. Income Approach to GDP (See Table 7.3): Demonstrates how the expenditures on final products are allocated to resource suppliers.

  1. Compensation of employees includes wages, salaries, fringe benefits, salary and supplements, and payments made on behalf of workers like social security and other health and pension plans.

  2. Rents: payments for supplying property resources (adjusted for depreciation it is *net rent*).

  3. Interest: payments from private business to suppliers of money capital.

  4. Proprietors' income: income of incorporated businesses, sole proprietorships, partnerships, and cooperatives.

  5. Corporate profits: After corporate income taxes are paid to government, dividends are distributed to the shareholders, and the remainder is left as *undistributed corporate profits*.

  6. The sum of the above entries equals *national income*: all income earned by American supplied resources, whether here or abroad.

  7. Adjustments required to balance both sides of the account.

    a. Indirect business taxes: general sales taxes, excise taxes, business property taxes, license fees and customs duties (the seller treats these taxes as a cost of production).

    b. Depreciation Consumption of Fixed Capital: The firm also regards the decline of its capital stock as a cost of production. The capital consumption allowance is set aside to replace the machinery and equipment used up. In addition to the depreciation of private capital, public capital (government buildings, port facilities, etc.), must be included in this entry.

    c. Net foreign factor income: National income measures the income of Americans both here and abroad. GDP measures the output of the geographical U.S. regardless of the nationality of the contributors. To make this final adjustment, the income of foreign nationals must be added and American income earned abroad must be subtracted. Sometimes this entry is a negative number.

III. **Other National Accounts (see Table 7.4)**

A. Net domestic product (NDP) is equal to GDP minus depreciation allowance (consumption of fixed capital).

B. National income (NI) is income earned by American-owned resources here or abroad. Adjust NDP by subtracting indirect business taxes and adding net American income earned abroad. (Note: This may be a negative number if foreigners earned more in U.S. than American resources earned abroad.)

C. Personal income (PI) is income received by households. To calculate, take NI minus payroll taxes (social security contributions), minus corporate profits taxes, minus undistributed corporate profits, and add transfer payments.

D. Disposable income (DI) is personal income less personal taxes.

IV.   **Circular Flow Revisited (see Figure 7.3)**

A. Compare to the simpler model presented in earlier chapters. Now both government and foreign trade sectors are added.

B. Note that the inside covers of the text contain a useful historical summary of national income accounts and related statistics.

V.   **Nominal Versus Real GDP**

A. Nominal GDP is the market value of all final goods and services produced in a year.

1. GDP is a (P ∞ Q) figure including every item produced in the economy. Money is the common denominator that allows us to sum the total output.

2. To measure changes in the quantity of output, we need a yardstick that stays the same size. To make comparisons of length, a yard must remain 36 inches. To make comparisons of real output, a dollar must keep the same purchasing power.

3. Nominal GDP is calculated using the current prices prevailing when the output was produced but real GDP is a figure that has been adjusted for price level changes.

B. The adjustment process in a one-good economy (Table 7.5). Valid comparisons can not be made with nominal GDP alone, since both prices and quantities are subject to change. Some method to separate the two effects must be devised.

1. One method is to first determine a price index, (see equation 1) and then adjust the nominal GDP figures by dividing by the price index (in hundredths) (see equation 1).

2. An alternative method is to gather separate data on the quantity of physical output and determine what it would sell for in the base year. The result is Real GDP. The price index is implied in the ratio: Nominal GDP/Real GDP. Multiply by 100 to put it in standard index form (see equation 3).

C. Real World Considerations and Data

1. The actual GDP price index in the U.S. is called the *chain-type annual weights price index*, and is more complex than can be illustrated here.

2. Once nominal GDP and the GDP price index are established, the relationship between them and real GDP is clear (see Table 7.7).

3. The base year price index is always 100, since Nominal GDP and Real GDP use the same prices. Because the long-term trend has been for prices to rise, adjusting Nominal GDP to Real GDP involves inflating the lower prices before the base year and deflating the higher prices after the base year.

4. Real GDP values allow more direct comparison of physical output from one year to the next, because a "constant dollar" measuring device has been used. (The purchase power of the dollar has been standardized at the base year level.)

VI.   **The Consumer Price Index (CPI)**

A. Characteristics of the CPI

1. The CPI is designed to measure the changes in the cost of a constant standard of living for a typical urban consumer. This *fixed weight* approach means that the items in the market basket remain the same.

2. The market basket of goods is changed about every 10 years. The present composition was determined from a survey of urban consumers in the 1993-1995 period and contains about 300 goods and services purchased by the *typical* urban consumer.

B. The CPI differs from the GDP price index, which is broader and changes its market basket each year to reflect the current composition of output.

VII. Shortcomings of GDP

A. GDP doesn't measure some very useful output because it is unpaid (homemakers' services, parental child care, volunteer efforts, home improvement projects).

B. GDP does not measure improvements in product quality or make allowances for increased leisure time.

C. GDP doesn't measure improved living conditions as a result of more leisure.

D. GDP makes no value adjustments for changes in the composition of output or the distribution of income.

1. Nominal GDP simply adds the dollar value of what is produced; it makes no difference if the product is a semi-automatic rifle or a jar of baby food.

2. Per capital GDP may give some hint as to the relative standard of living in the economy; but GDP figures do not provide information about how the income is distributed.

E. The Underground Economy

1. Illegal activities are not counted in GDP.

2. Legal economic activity may also be part of the "underground," usually in an effort to avoid taxation.

F. GDP and the environment.

1. The harmful effects of pollution are not deducted from GDP (oil spills, increased incidence of cancer, destruction of habitat for wildlife, the loss of a clear unobstructed view).

2. GDP does include payments made for cleaning up the oil spills, and the cost of health care for the cancer victim.

G. Per Capita GDP (GDP per person) is a better measure of standard of living than total GDP.

H. Noneconomic Sources of Well-Being like courtesy, crime reduction, etc., are not covered in GDP.

VIII. LAST WORD: Feeding the GDP Accounts

A. GDP is compiled by the Bureau of Economic Analysis (BEA) in U.S. Commerce Department. Where does it get its data? Explanation follows.

B. Consumption data comes from:

1. Census Bureau's "Retain Trade Survey" from sample of 22,000 firms.

2. Census Bureau's "Survey of Manufacturers," which gets information on consumer goods shipments from 50,000 firms.

3. Census Bureau's "Service Survey" of 30,000 service businesses.

4. Industry trade sources like auto and aircraft sales.

C. Investment data comes from:

1. All the consumption sources listed above.

2. Census construction surveys.

D. Government purchase data is obtained from:

1. U.S. Office of Personnel Management, which collects data on wages and benefits.

2. Census construction surveys of public projects.

3. Census Bureau's "Survey of Government Finance."

E. Net export information comes from:

1. U.S. Customs Service data on exports and imports.

2. BEA surveys on service exports and imports.

ANSWERS TO END-OF-CHAPTER QUESTIONS

7-1   In what ways are national income statistics useful?

National income accounting does for the economy as a whole what private accounting does for businesses. Firms measure income and expenditures to assess their economic health.

The national income accounting system measures the level of production in the economy at some particular time and helps explain that level. By comparing national accounts over a number of years, we can track the long-run course of the economy. Information supplied by national accounts provide a basis for designing and applying public policies to improve the performance of the economy. Without national accounts, economic policy would be guesswork. National income accounting allows us to assess the health of an economy and formulate policies to maintain and improve that health.

7-2   Explain why an economy's output is also its income?

Everything that is produced is sold, even if the "selling," in the case of inventory, is to the producing firm itself. Since the same amount of money paid out by the buyers of the economy's output is received by the sellers as income (looking only at a private-sector economy at this point), "an economy's output is also its income."

7-3   (*Key Question*) Why do national income accountants include only final goods in measuring GDP for a particular year? Why don't they include the value of stocks and bonds sold? Why don't they include the value of used furniture bought and sold?

The dollar value of final goods includes the dollar value of intermediate goods. If intermediate goods were counted, then multiple counting would occur. The value of steel (intermediate good) used in autos is included in the price of the auto (the final product).

This value is not included in GDP because such sales and purchases simply transfer the ownership of existing assets; such sales and purchases are not themselves (economic) investment and thus should not be counted as production of final goods and services.

Used furniture was produced in some previous year; it was counted as GDP then. Its resale does not measure new production.

7-4   What is the difference between gross private domestic investment and net private domestic investment? If you were to determine net domestic product (NDP) through the expenditures approach, which of these two measures of investment spending would be appropriate? Explain.

Gross private domestic investment less depreciation is net private domestic investment. Depreciation is the value of all the physical capital—machines, equipment, buildings—used up in producing the year's output.

Since net domestic product is gross domestic product less depreciation, in determining net domestic product through the expenditures approach it would be appropriate to use the net investment measure that excludes depreciation, that is, net private domestic investment.

7-5   Why are changes in inventories included as part of investment spending? Suppose inventories declined by $1 billion during 2001. How would this affect the size of gross private domestic investment and gross domestic product in 2001? Explain.

Anything produced by business that has not been sold during the accounting period is something in which business has invested—even if the "investment" is involuntary, as often is the case with inventories. But all inventories in the hands of business are expected eventually to be used by business—for instance, a pile of bricks for extending a factory building—or to be sold—for instance, a can of beans on the supermarket shelf. In the hands of business both the bricks and the beans are equally assets to the business, something in which business has invested.

If inventories declined by $1 billion in 2001, $1 billion would be subtracted from both gross private domestic investment and gross domestic product. A decline in inventories indicates that goods produced in a previous year have been used up in this year's production. If $1 billion is not subtracted as stated, then $1 billion of goods produced in a previous year would be counted as having been produced in 2001, leading to an overstatement of 2001's production.

7-6   Use the concepts of gross and net investment to distinguish between an economy that has a rising stock of capital and one that has a falling stock of capital. "In 1933 net private domestic investment was minus $6 billion. This means in that particular year the economy produced no capital goods at all." Do you agree? Explain: "Though net investment can be positive, negative, or zero, it is quite impossible for gross investment to be less than zero."

When gross investment exceeds depreciation, net investment is positive and production capacity expands; the economy ends the year with more physical capital than it started with. When gross investment equals depreciation, net investment is zero and production capacity is said to be static; the economy ends the year with the same amount of physical capital. When depreciation exceeds gross investment, net investment is negative and production capacity declines; the economy ends the year with less physical capital.

The first statement in wrong. Just because *net* investment was a minus $6 billion in 1993 does not mean the economy produced no new capital goods in that year. It simply means depreciation exceeded gross investment by $6 billion. So the economy ended the year with $6 billion less capital.

The second statement is correct. If only one $20 spade is bought by a construction firm in the entire economy in a year and no other physical capital is bought, then gross investment is $20—a positive amount. This is true even if *net* investment is highly negative because depreciation is well above $20. If not even this $20 spade has been bought, then gross investment would have been zero. But gross investment can never be less than zero.

7-7   Define net exports. Explain how the United States' exports and imports each affect domestic production. Suppose foreigners spend $7 billion on American exports in a given year and Americans spend $5 billion on imports from abroad in the same year. What is the amount of America's net exports? Explain how net exports might be a negative amount.

Net exports are a country's exports of goods and services less its imports of goods and services. The United States' exports are as much a part of the nation's production as are the expenditures of its own consumers on goods and services made in the United States. Therefore, the United States' exports must be counted as part of GDP. On the other hand, imports, being produced in foreign countries, are part of those countries' GDPs. When Americans buy imports, these expenditures must be subtracted from the United States' GDP, for these expenditures are not made on the United States' production.

If American exports are $7 billion and imports are $5 billion, then American net exports are +$2 billion. If the figures are reversed, so that Americans export $5 billion and import $7 billion, then net exports are -$2 billion—a negative amount. For this to come about, Americans must either decrease their holdings of foreign currencies by $2 billion, or borrow $2 billion from foreigners— or do a bit of both. (Another option is to sell back to foreigners some of the previous American investments abroad.)

7-8   (*Key Question*) Below is a list of domestic output and national income figures for a given year. All figures are in billions. The questions that follow ask you to determine the major national income measures by both the expenditure and income methods. The results you obtain with the different methods should be the same.

Personal consumption expenditures	$245
Net foreign factor income earned	4
Transfer payments	12
Rents	14
Consumption of fixed capital (depreciation)	27
Social security contributions	20
Interest	13
Proprietors' income	33
Net exports	11
Dividends	16
Compensation of employees	223
Indirect business taxes	18
Undistributed corporate profits	21
Personal taxes	26
Corporate income taxes	19
Corporate profits	56
Government purchases	72
Net private domestic investment	33
Personal saving	20

a. Using the above data, determine GDP and NDP by both the expenditure and income methods.

b. Now determine NI: first, by making the required additions and subtractions from GDP; and second, by adding up the types of income which comprise NI.

c. Adjust NI from (b) as required to obtain PI.

d. Adjust PI from part c as required to obtain DI.

(a) GDP = $388, NDP = $362;

(b) NI = $399;

(c) PI = $291;

(d) DI = $265.

7-9   Using the following national income accounting data, compute (a) GDP, (b) NDP, (c) NI. All figures are in billions.

Compensation of employees	**$194.2**
U.S. exports of goods and services	**17.8**
Consumption of fixed capital	**11.8**
Government purchases of goods and services	**59.4**
Indirect business taxes	**14.4**
Net private domestic investment	**52.1**
Transfer payments	**13.9**
U.S. imports of goods and services	**16.5**
Personal taxes	**40.5**
Net foreign factor income earned in U.S.	**2.2**
Personal consumption expenditures	**219.1**

(a) Personal consumption expenditures (C)	**$219.1**
Government purchases (G)	59.4
Gross private domestic investment (I_g)	63.9
(52.1 + 11.8)	
Net exports (X_n) (17.8 - 16.5)	1.3
Gross domestic product (GDP)	$343.7
(b) Consumption of fixed capital	**-11.8**
Net domestic product (NDP)	$331.9
(c) Net foreign factor income earned in U.S.	**-2.2**
Indirect business taxes	-14.4
National income (NI)	$315.3

7-10   Why do national income accountants compare the market value of the total outputs in various years rather than actual physical volumes of production? What problem is posed by any comparison over time of the market values of various total outputs? How is this problem resolved?

If it is impossible to summarize oranges and apples as one statistic, as the saying goes, it is surely even more impossible to add oranges and, say, computers. If the production of oranges increases by 100 percent and that of computers by 10 percent, it does not make any sense to add the 100 percent to the 10 percent, then divide by 2 to get the average and say total production has increased by 55 percent.

Since oranges and computers have different values, the quantities of each commodity are multiplied by their values or prices. Adding together all the results of the price times quantity figures leads to the aggregate figure showing the total value of all the final goods and services produced in the economy. Thus, to return to oranges and computers, if the value of orange production increases by 100 percent from $100 million to $200 million, while that of computers increases 10 percent from $2 billion to $2.2 billion, we can see that total production has increased from $2.1 billion (= $100 million + $2 billion) to $2.4 billion (= $200 million + $2.2 billion). This is an increase of 14.29 percent [= ($2.4 billion - $2.1 billion)/$2.1 billion]—and not the 55 percent incorrectly derived earlier.

Comparing market values over time has the disadvantage that prices change. If the market value in year 2 is 10 percent greater than in year 1, we cannot say the economy's production has increased

10 percent. It depends on what has been happening to prices; on whether the economy has been experiencing inflation or deflation.

To resolve this problem, statisticians deflate (in the case of inflation) or inflate (in the case of deflation) the value figures for the total output so that only "real" changes in production are recorded. To do this, each item is assigned a "weight" corresponding to its relative importance in the economy. Housing, for example, is given a high weight because of its importance in the average budget. A book of matches would be given a very low weight. Thus, the price of housing increasing by 5 percent has a much greater effect on the price index used to compare prices from one year to the next, than would the price of a book of matches increasing by 100 percent.

7-11   (*Key Question*) Suppose that in 1984 the total output in a single-good economy was 7,000 buckets of chicken. Also suppose that in 1984 each bucket of chicken was priced at $10. Finally, assume that in 1992 the price per bucket of chicken was $16 and that 22,000 buckets were purchased. Determine the GDP price index for 1984, using 1992 as the base year. By what percentage did the price level, as measured by this index, rise between 1984 and 1992? Use the two methods listed in Table 7-6 to determine real GDP for 1984 and 1992.

X/100 = $10/$16 = .625 or 62.5 when put in percentage or index form (.625 x 100)

$\frac{100 - 62.5}{62.5} = .60$ or 60%   (Easily calculated $\frac{16-10}{10} = \frac{6}{10} = .6 = 60\%$)

Method 1:   1992 = (22,000 x $16) ÷ 1.0 = $352,000

1984 = ($7,000 x $10) ÷ .625 = $112,000

Method 2:   1992 = 22,000 x $16 = $352,000

1984 = 7,000 x $16 = $112,000

7-12   (*Key Question*) The following table shows nominal GDP and an appropriate price index for a group of selected years. Compute real GDP. Indicate in each calculation whether you are inflating or deflating the nominal GDP data.

Year	Normal GDP, Billions	Price index (1996 – 100)	Real GDP billions
1960	$527.4	22.19	$ _____
1968	911.5	26.29	$ _____
1978	2295.9	48.22	$ _____
1988	4742.5	80.22	$ _____
1998	8790.2	103.22	$ _____

Values for real GDP, top to bottom of the column: $2,376.7 (inflating); $3,467.1 (inflating); $4,761.3 (inflating); $5,911.9 (inflating); $8,516 (deflating).

7-13 Which of the following are actually included in this year's GDP? Explain your answer in each case.

   a. Interest on an AT&T bond

   b. Social security payments received by a retired factory worker

   c. The services of a painter in painting the family home

   d. The income of a dentist

   e. The money received by Smith when she sells her economics textbook to a book buyer

   f. The monthly allowance a college student receives from home

   g. Rent received on a two-bedroom apartment

   h. The money received by Mac when he resells his current-year model Plymouth Prowler to Stan

   i. Interest received on corporate bonds

   j. A 2-hour decline in the length of the workweek

   k. The purchase of an AT&T bond

   l. A $2 billion increase in business inventories

   m. The purchase of 100 shares of GM common stock

   n. The purchase of an insurance policy

(a) Included. Income received by the bondholder for the services derived by the corporation for the loan of money.

(b) Excluded. A transfer payment from taxpayers for which no service is rendered (in this year).

(c) Excluded. Not a market transaction. If any payment is made, it will be within the family.

(d) Included. Payment for a final service. You cannot pass on a tooth extraction!

(e) Excluded. Secondhand sales are not counted; the textbook is counted only when sold for the first time.

(f) Excluded. A private transfer payment; simply a transfer of income from one private individual to another for which no transaction in the market occurs.

(g) Included. Payment for the final service of housing.

(h) Excluded. The production of the car had already been counted at the time of the initial sale.

(i) Included. The income received by the bondholders is paid by the corporations for the current use of the "money capital" (the loan).

(j) Excluded. The effect of the decline will be counted, but the change in the work week itself is not the production of a final good or service or a payment for work done.

(k) Excluded. A non-investment transaction; it is merely the transfer of ownership of financial assets. (If AT&T uses the money from the sale of a new bond to carry out an investment in real physical assets, that will be counted.)

(l) Included. The increase in inventories could only occur as a result of increased production.

(m) Excluded. Merely the transfer of ownership of existing financial assets.

(n) Included. Insurance is a final service. If bought by a household, it will be shown as consumption; if bought by a business, as investment—as a cost added to its real investment in physical capital.

7-13   (*Last Word*) What government agency compiles the U.S. GDP accounts? In what U.S. Department is it located? Of the several sources of information, name one source for each of the four components of GDP: consumption, investment, government purchases and net exports.

The Bureau of Economic Analysis (BEA) in the Department of Commerce compiles GDP statistics.

The Census Bureau provides survey data for consumption, investment, and government purchases Consumption figures also come from industry trade sources as does some investment data. The U.S. Office of Personnel Management also provides data on government spending on services.

Net export figures come from the U.S. Customs Service and BEA surveys on service exports and imports.

CHAPTER EIGHT
INTRODUCTION TO ECONOMIC GROWTH AND INSTABILITY

CHAPTER OVERVIEW

This chapter previews economic growth, the business cycle, unemployment, and inflation. It sets the stage for the analytical presentation in later chapters.

Economic growth is defined and the arithmetic and sources of economic growth are examined. The record of growth in the U.S. is viewed from several perspectives including an international comparison in Global Perspective. The business cycle is introduced in historical perspective and is presented in stylized form (Figure 8-1). While hinting at various business cycle theories, the authors stress the general belief that changes in aggregate spending, especially durable goods and investment spending, are the immediate cause of economic instability. Non-cyclical fluctuations are also treated briefly before the analysis of unemployment and inflation.

In the section on unemployment, the various types of unemployment—frictional, structural, and cyclical—are described. Then the problems involved in measuring unemployment and in defining the full-employment unemployment rate are considered. The economic and non-economic costs of unemployment are presented, and finally, Global Perspective 8-2 gives an international comparison of unemployment rates.

Inflation is accorded a rather detailed treatment from both a cause and an effect perspective. International comparisons of inflation rates in the post-1983 period are given in Global Perspective 8-3. Demand-pull and cost-push inflation are described. Considerable emphasis is placed on the fact that the redistributive effects of inflation will differ, depending on whether inflation is anticipated or unanticipated. The chapter ends with historical cases of extreme inflation to remind students that inflationary fears have some basis in fact.

WHAT'S NEW

This chapter has a new title, which includes an introduction to economic growth as well as macroeconomic instability. Chapter 17 now examines the analytical aspects of growth.

Many sections have been revised and abridged, with Figures 8-1 and 8-3 from the 14th edition now deleted. All of the discussion on unemployment is now in the unemployment section, which has also been updated. A new Figure 8-4 shows inflation rates over the years rather than tracing out CPI. Sections on the effects of inflation have been reorganized and revised.

The Last Word on the stock market and macroeconomic instability has been updated.

INSTRUCTIONAL OBJECTIVES

After completing this chapter, students should be able to:

1. Define two measures of economic growth.
2. Explain why growth is a desirable goal.
3. Identify two main sources of growth.
4. Explain the "rule of 70."

5. Give average long-term growth rates for U.S. and qualifications of raw data.

6. Summarize Global Perspective 8-1.

7. Explain what is meant by a business cycle.

8. Describe the four phases of an idealized business cycle.

9. Identify two types of non-cyclical fluctuations in business activity.

10. Describe how innovation and/or random events might cause business cycles.

11. Explain why business cycles affect capital and consumer durable goods industries more than non-durable goods industries.

12. State causes of frictional, cyclical, and structural unemployment.

13. Identify the full employment or natural rate of unemployment.

14. Describe how unemployment is measured by the Bureau of Labor Statistics (BLS).

15. Evaluate strengths and limitations of BLS unemployment statistics.

16. Identify the economic costs of unemployment and the groups that bear unusually heavy unemployment burdens.

17. Define inflation and list two types of inflation.

18. Describe the predicted outcome of increased total demand on employment and inflation in ranges 1, 2, and 3 when presented with the diagram.

19. List three groups who are hurt and two groups who may benefit from unanticipated inflation.

20. Present three possible effects of inflation on output and employment.

21. Compare U.S. inflation and unemployment rates to one or more industrialized nations.

22. Define and identify terms and concepts at the end of the chapter.

COMMENTS AND TEACHING SUGGESTIONS

1. Most students have a vague idea of what is meant by unemployment or inflation. Nor have they considered how these problems impact the economy or themselves.

2. It makes this chapter more relevant to have students find the latest data on these measures. See Web-based questions at end of chapter or an Internet source such as www.dismal.com.

3. Table 8-3 can be used to discuss the definition of unemployment and its limitations. Current data to update the table can be found in the *Monthly Labor Review, Employment and Earnings, Economic Indicators, or see Web-based question 16.* Make it clear that a portion of each unemployment statistic is due to frictional and structural unemployment, which are found even in a "full employment" economy. Frictional unemployment indicates a healthy economy with labor mobility. Structural unemployment is viewed as serious, but not responsive to economic policies alone.

4. Have students consider the losses from unemployment. Perhaps they could write a feature article on losses due to GDP gap, higher inflation, or the social and personal losses incurred by those unemployed.

5. Try Web Exercise 17 for latest inflation data. While we have been concerned with inflation since World War II, it is interesting to note that past economists have been as concerned about deflation. A good topic is to ask students how deflation can be a problem. Presently it is in Japan.

6. *The Wall Street Journal* is a good source of information on the most current economic situation. They have a "Newspaper-in-Education" program which provides various teaching aids, in addition to favorable subscription rates for students. Call 1-800-JOURNAL contact their website for more information. Among their aids is a stylized *Wall Street Journal Education* edition, which gives information on dates on which important economic statistics are announced each month or each quarter. Your local newspaper and other business periodicals may have similar education programs.

7. Unemployment and inflation have a human face. A dramatic reading of quotes from a book such as Studs Terkel's *Hard Times* can be used to bring statistics to life. You or your students may be acquainted with individuals who lived through the depression years or who have suffered from periods of unemployment. Inviting them to discuss the impact of these experiences also helps to make this material more interesting for students.

STUDENT STUMBLING BLOCKS

1. This chapter includes lots of descriptive detail. Help your students sort out the forest from the trees—be clear about what you expect them to know from this chapter.

2. Struggling students often have difficulty because they lack very basic math skills. Sometimes, they simply have not used fractions, percentages or decimals lately. Do not take it for granted that college students will be prepared for the simple calculations in this chapter. One skill that is frequently missing is the ability to make reasonable estimates of a correct answer (a ball park guess) without actually crunching the numbers. Give students practice with simple questions first – for example, GDP loss when the unemployment rate is 1% above the natural rate (applying Okun's Law). Then demonstrate the gap for every 1% beyond that.

3. In anticipation of future chapters, the sections on demand-pull and cost-push inflation will be helpful. Emphasize the analysis of Figure 8-6. It also helps to reinforce Chapter 7's distinction between nominal and real GDP.

LECTURE NOTES

I.   **Introduction: This chapter provides an introductory look at trends of real GDP growth and the macroeconomic problems of the business cycle, unemployment and inflation.**

II. **Economic Growth-how to increase the economy's productive capacity over time.**

   A. Two definitions of economics growth are given.

      1. The increase in real GDP, which occurs over a period of time.

      2. The increase in real GDP per capita, which occurs over time. This definition is superior if comparison of living standards is desired. For example, China's GDP is $744 billion compared to Denmark's $155 billion, but per capita GDP's are $620 and $29,890 respectively.

   B. Growth is an important economic goal because it means more material abundance and ability to meet the economizing problem. Growth lessens the burden of scarcity.

   C. The arithmetic of growth is impressive. Using the "rule of 70," a growth rate of 2 percent annually would take 35 years for GDP to double, but a growth rate of 4 percent annually would only take about 18 years for GDP to double. (The "rule of 70" uses the absolute value of a rate of change, divides it into 70, and the result is the number of years it takes the underlying quantity to double.)

   D. Main sources of growth are increasing inputs or increasing productivity of existing inputs.

    1. About one-third of U.S. growth comes from more inputs.

    2. About two-thirds comes from increased productivity.

  E. Growth Record of the United States (Table 8-1) is impressive.

    1. Real GDP has increased more than sixfold since 1940, and real per capita GDP has risen almost fourfold. (See columns 2 and 4, Table 8-1)

    2. Rate of growth record shows that real GDP has grown 3.1 percent per year since 1950 and real GDP per capita has grown about 2 percent per year. But the arithmetic needs to be qualified.

      a. Growth doesn't measure quality improvements.

      b. Growth doesn't measure increased leisure time.

      c. Growth doesn't take into account adverse effects on environment or human security.

      d. International comparisons are useful in evaluating U.S. performance. For example, Japan grew more than twice as fast as U.S. until the 1990s when the U.S. far surpassed Japan. (see Global Perspective 8-1).

III. Overview of the Business Cycle

  A. Historical record:

    1. The United States' impressive long-run economic growth has been interrupted by periods of instability.

    2. Uneven growth has been the pattern, with inflation often accompanying rapid growth, and declines in employment and output during periods of recession and depression (see Figure 8-1 and Table 8-2).

  B. Four phases of the business cycle are identified over a several-year period. (See Figure 8-1)

    1. A peak is when business activity reaches a temporary maximum with full employment and near-capacity output.

    2. A recession is a decline in total output, income, employment, and trade lasting six months or more.

    3. The trough is the bottom of the recession period.

    4. Recovery is when output and employment are expanding toward full-employment level.

  C. There are several theories about causation.

    1. Major innovations may trigger new investment and/or consumption spending.

    2. Changes in productivity may be a related cause.

    3. Most agree that the level of aggregate spending is important, especially changes on capital goods and consumer durables.

  D. Cyclical fluctuations: Durable goods output is more unstable than non-durables and services because spending on latter usually can not be postponed.

IV. Unemployment (One Result of Economic Downturns)

  A. Types of unemployment:

1. Frictional unemployment consists of those searching for jobs or waiting to take jobs soon; it is regarded as somewhat desirable, because it indicates that there is mobility as people change or seek jobs.

2. Structural unemployment: due to changes in the structure of demand for labor; e.g., when certain skills become obsolete or geographic distribution of jobs changes.

   a. Glass blowers were replaced by bottle-making machines.

   b. Oil-field workers were displaced when oil demand fell in 1980s.

   c. Airline mergers displaced many airline workers in 1980s.

   d. Foreign competition has led to downsizing in U.S. industry and loss of jobs.

   e. Military cutbacks have led to displacement of workers in military-related industries.

3. Cyclical unemployment is caused by the recession phase of the business cycle, which is sometimes called deficient demand unemployment.

B. Definition of "Full Employment"

   1. Full employment does not mean zero unemployment.

   2. The full-employment unemployment rate is equal to the total frictional and structural unemployment.

   3. The full-employment rate of unemployment is also referred to as the natural rate of unemployment.

   4. The natural rate is achieved when labor markets are in balance; the number of job seekers equals the number of job vacancies. At this point the economy's potential output is being achieved. The natural rate of unemployment is not fixed, but depends on the demographic makeup of the labor force and the laws and customs of the nations. The recent drop in the natural rate from 6% to 5.5% has occurred mainly because of the aging of the work force and increased competition in product and labor markets.

   5. The natural rate of unemployment is not fixed but depends on the demographic makeup of the labor force and the laws and customs of the nations.

   6. The recent drop in the natural rate of 6% to 5.5% has occurred mainly because of the aging of the work force and increased competition in product and labor markets.

C. Measuring unemployment (see Figure 8-4 for 1994):

   1. The population is divided into three groups: those under age 16 or institutionalized, those "not in labor force," and the labor force that includes those age 16 and over who are willing and able to work.

   2. The unemployment rate is defined as the percentage of the labor force that is not employed

   3. The unemployment rate is calculated by random survey of 60,000 households nationwide.

      a. Part-time workers are counted as "employed."

      b. "Discouraged workers" who want a job, but are not actively seeking one, are not counted as being in the labor force, so they are not part of unemployment statistic.

D. Economic cost of unemployment:

   1. GDP gap and Okun's Law: GDP gap is the difference between potential and actual GDP. (See Figure 8-5) Economist Okun quantified relationship between unemployment and

GDP as follows: For every 1 percent of unemployment above the natural rate, a 2 percent GDP gap occurs. This has become known as "Okun's law."

2. Unequal burdens of unemployment exist. (See Table 8-2)

   a. Rates are lower for white-collar workers.

   b. Teenagers have the highest rates.

   c. Blacks have higher rates than whites.

   d. Rates for males and females are comparable, though females had a lower rate in 1992.

   e. Less educated workers, on average, have higher unemployment rates than workers with more education.

   f. "Long-term" (15 weeks or more) unemployment rate is much lower than the overall rate.

E. Noneconomic costs include loss of self-respect and social and political unrest.

F. International comparisons. (See Global Perspective 8-1)

V. **Inflation: Defined and Measured**

A. Definition: Inflation is a rising general level of prices (not all prices rise at the same rate, and some may fall).

B. To measure inflation, subtract last year's price index from this year's price index and divide by last year's index; then multiply by 100 to express as a percentage.

C. "Rule of 70" permits quick calculation of the time it takes the price level to double: Divide 70 by the percentage rate of inflation and the result is the approximate number of years for the price level to double. If the inflation rate is 10 percent, then it will take about ten years for prices to double. (Note: You can also use this rule to calculate how long it takes savings to double at a given compounded interest rate.)

D. Facts of inflation:

1. In the past, deflation has been as much a problem as inflation. For example, the 1930s depression was a period of declining prices and wages.

2. All industrial nations have experienced the problem (see Global Perspective 8-2).

3. Some nations experience astronomical rates of inflation (Angola's was 4,145 percent in 1996).

4. The inside covers of the text contain historical rates for the U.S.

E. Causes and theories of inflation:

1. Demand-pull inflation: Spending increases faster than production. (See Figure 8-7) Inflation will occur in range 2 and range 3 of this illustration. Bottlenecks occur in some industries in range 2, and output cannot expand to meet demand in these industries so producers raise prices; in Range 3 full employment has been reached and resource prices will rise with increasing demand, causing producers to raise prices. Note: Chapter 7's distinction between nominal and real GDP is helpful here.

2. Cost-push or supply-side inflation: Prices rise because of rise in per-unit production costs (Unit cost = total input cost/units of output).

   a. Wage-push can occur as result of union strength.

    b. Supply shocks may occur with unexpected increases in the price of raw materials.

   3. Complexities: It is difficult to distinguish between demand-pull and cost-push causes of inflation, although cost-push will die out in a recession if spending does not also rise.

VI. Redistributive effects of inflation:

A. Fixed-income groups will be hurt because their real income suffers. Their nominal income does not rise with prices.

B. Savers will be hurt by unanticipated inflation, because interest rate returns may not cover the cost of inflation. Their savings will lose purchasing power.

C. Debtors (borrowers) can be helped and lenders hurt by unanticipated inflation. Interest payments may be less than the inflation rate, so borrowers receive "dear" money and are paying back "cheap" dollars that have less purchasing power for the lender.

D. If inflation is anticipated, the effects of inflation may be less severe, since wage and pension contracts may have inflation clauses built in, and interest rates will be high enough to cover the cost of inflation to savers and lenders.

   1. "Inflation premium" is amount that interest rate is raised to cover effects of anticipated inflation.

   2. "Real interest rate" is defined as nominal rate minus inflation premium. (See Figure 8-6)

E. Final points

   1. Unexpected deflation, a decline in price level, will have the opposite effect of unexpected inflation.

   2. Many families are simultaneously helped and hurt by inflation because they are both borrowers *and* earners and savers.

   3. Effects of inflation are arbitrary, regardless of society's goals.

   4. See Quick Review 8-4.

VII. Output Effects of Inflation

A. Cost-push inflation, where resource prices rise unexpectedly, could cause both output and employment to decline. Real income falls.

B. Mild inflation (<3%) has uncertain effects. It may be a healthy by-product of a prosperous economy, or it may have an undesirable impact on real income.

C. Danger of creeping inflation turning into hyperinflation, which can cause speculation, reckless spending, and more inflation (see examples in text of Hungary and Japan following World War II, and Germany following World War I).

VIII. LAST WORD: The Stock Market and The Economy: How, if at all, do changes in stock prices relate to macroeconomic stability?

A. Do changes in stock prices and stock market wealth cause instability? The answer is yes, but usually the effect is weak.

   1. There is a wealth effect: Consumer spending rises as asset values rise and vice versa if stock prices decline substantially.

   2. Also, there is an investment effect: Rising share prices lead to more capital goods investment and the reverse in true for falling share prices.

B. Stock market "bubbles" can hurt the economy by encouraging reckless speculation with borrowed funds or savings needed for other purposes. A "crash" can cause unwarranted pessimism about the underlying economy.

C. A related question concerns forecasting value of stock market averages. Stock price averages are included as one of ten "Leading Indicators" used to forecast the future direction of the economy. (See Last Word, Chapter 12). However, by themselves, stock values are not a reliable predictor of economic conditions.

ANSWERS TO END-OF-CHAPTER QUESTIONS

8-1   Why is economic growth important? Why could the difference between a 2.5 percent and a 3.0 percent annual growth rate make a great difference over several decades?

Economic growth means a higher standard of living, provided population does not grow even faster. And if it does, then economic growth is even more important to maintain the current standard of living. Economic growth allows the lessening of poverty even without an outright redistribution of wealth.

If population is growing at 2.5 percent a year—and it is in some of the poorest nations—then a 2.5 percent growth rate of real GDP means no change in living standards. A 3.0 percent growth rate means a gradual rise in living standards. For a wealthy nation, such as the United States, with a GDP in the neighborhood of $10 trillion, the 0.5 percentage point difference between 2.5 and 3.0 percent amounts to $50 billion a year, or more than $150 per person per year.

8-2   (*Key Question*) Suppose an economy's real GDP is $30,000 in year 1 and $31,200 in year 2. What is the growth rate of its real GDP? Assume that population was 100 in year 1 and 102 in year 2. What is the growth rate of GDP per capita?

Growth rate of real GDP = 4 percent (= $31,200 - $30,000)/$30,000). GDP per capita in year 1 = $300 (= $30,000/100). GDP per capita in year 2 = $305.88 (= $31,200/102). Growth rate of GDP per capita is 1.96 percent = ($305.88 - $300)/300).

8-3   Briefly describe the growth record of the United States. Compare the rates of growth in real GDP and real GDP per capita, explaining any differences. How do the average growth rates compare between Japan and the U.S. between 1950 and 2000? Between 1990 and 2000? To what extent might growth rates understate or overstate economic well-being?

The growth record of the United States is seen in Table 8-1, which shows that per capita GDP (in 1992 constant dollars) has grown from $6,484 in 1929 to $25,635 in 1995. The rate of growth of real GDP per capita in the 1950-2000 period was just under 2 percent; the growth rate of real GDP during the same period was 3.1 percent. It is evident that real GDP grows more rapidly than real GDP per capita because the population is growing at the same time that GDP is growing. Since GDP per capita is GDP/population, this will show a smaller rate of growth than GDP if the denominator, population, is expanding.

Looking at Global Perspective 8-1, we can see that the average annual growth rates of real GDP have been more rapid in Japan, averaging more than 6 percent in the 1950-2000 period. But, in 1990s the U.S. surged ahead of Japan from 1992 until the present.

The real GDP and per capita real GDP figures may understate economic well-being to the extent they do not fully take into account improvements in product quality; and they take no account at all of the very considerable increase in leisure since 1929. On the other hand, the measures of growth also leave out increases in pollution and the possible increase in stress caused by growth, and also do not measure the extent of inequality in distribution. If inequality is great, many may have less GDP per capita than shown..

8-4   (*Key Question*) What are the four phases of the business cycle? How long do business cycles last? How do seasonal variations and secular trends complicate measurement of the business cycle? Why does the business cycle affect output and employment in capital goods and consumer durable goods industries more severely than in industries producing non-durables?

The four phases of a typical business cycle, starting at the bottom, are trough, recovery, peak, and recession. As seen in Figure 8-1, the length of a complete cycle varies from about 2 to 3 years to as long as 15 years.

There is a pre-Christmas spurt in production and sales and a January slackening. This normal seasonal variation does not signal boom or recession. From decade to decade, the long-term trend (the secular trend) of the U.S. economy has been upward. A period of no GDP growth thus does not mean all is normal, but that the economy is operating below its trend growth of output.

Because capital goods and durable goods last, purchases can be postponed. This may happen when a recession is forecast. Capital and durable goods industries therefore suffer large output declines during recessions. In contrast, consumers cannot long postpone the buying of nondurables such as food; therefore recessions only slightly reduce non-durable output. Also, capital and durable goods expenditures tend to be "lumpy." Usually, a large expenditure is needed to purchase them, and this shrinks to zero after purchase is made.

8-5   What factors make it difficult to determine the unemployment rate? Why is it difficult to distinguish between frictional, structural, and cyclical unemployment? Why is unemployment an economic problem? What are the consequences of a GDP gap? What are the noneconomic effects of unemployment?

Measuring the unemployment rate means first determining who is eligible and available to work. The total U.S. population is divided into three groups. One group is made up of people under 16 years of age and people who are institutionalized. The second group, labeled "not in the labor force" are adults who are potential workers but for some reason—age, in school, or homemakers are not seeking work. The third group is the labor force, those who are employed and those who are unemployed but actively seeking work.

It is not easy to distinguish between these three types and since the unavoidable minimum of frictional and structural unemployment is itself changing, it is difficult to determine the full-employment unemployment rate. For example, a person who quits a job in search of a better one would normally be considered frictionally unemployed. But suppose the former job then disappears completely because the firm is in a declining industry and can no longer make money. Our still jobless worker could now be considered structurally unemployed. And then suppose the economy slips into a severe recession so that our worker cannot find any job and has become cyclically unemployed. To complicate things further, the unavoidable minimums of frictional and structural unemployment have increased in the past thirty years as the labor force structure has changed. In other words, there is no automatic label on the type of unemployment when someone is counted as unemployed.

Unemployment is an economic problem because of the concept of opportunity cost. Quite apart from any idea of consideration for others, unemployment is a total economic waste: A unit of labor resource that could be engaged in production is sitting idle.

The "GDP gap" is the difference between what the economy could produce its potential GDP and what it is producing its actual GDP. The consequence is that what is not produced – the amount represented by the gap—is lost forever. Moreover, to the extent that this lost production represents capital goods, the potential production for the future is impaired. Future economic growth will be less.

The noneconomic effects of unemployment include the sense of failure created in parents and in their children, the feeling of being useless to society, of no longer belonging.

8-6   (*Key Question*) Use the following data to calculate (a) the size of the labor force and (b) the official unemployment rate: total population, 500; population under 16 years of age or institutionalized, 120; not in labor force, 150; unemployed, 23; part-time workers looking for full-time jobs, 10.

Labor force = #230 [= 500 - (120 + 150)]; official unemployment rate = 10% [(23/230)×100].

8-7   Since the U.S. has an unemployment compensation program which provides income for those out of work, why should we worry about unemployment?

The unemployment compensation program merely gives the unemployed enough funds for basic needs. Furthermore, many of the unemployed do not qualify for unemployment benefits. The programs apply only to those workers who were covered by the insurance, and this may be as few as one-third of those without jobs. Most of the unemployed get no sense of self-worth or accomplishment out of drawing this compensation. Moreover, from the economic point of view, unemployment is a total waste of resources; when the unemployed go back to work, nothing is forgone except undesired leisure. Finally, unemployment could be inflationary and costly to taxpayers: The unemployed are producing nothing—their supply is zero – but the compensation helps keep demand in the economy high.

8-8   (*Key Question*) Assume that in a particular year the natural rate of unemployment is 5 percent and the actual rate of unemployment is 9 percent. Use Okun's law to determine the size of the GDP gap in percentage-point terms. If the nominal GDP is $500 billion in that year, how much output is being foregone because of cyclical unemployment?

GDP gap = 8 percent [= (9 - 5)] × 2; forgone output estimated at $40 billion (= 8% of $500 billion)

8-9   Explain how an *increase* in your nominal income and a *decrease* in your real income might occur simultaneously. Who loses from inflation? From unemployment? If you had to choose between (a) full employment with a 6 percent annual rate of inflation or (b) price stability with an 8 percent unemployment rate, which would you select? Why?

If a person's nominal income increases by 10 percent while the cost of living increases by 15 percent, then her real income has decreased from 100 to 95.65 (= 110/1.15). Alternatively expressed, her real income has decreased by 4.35 percent (= 100 - 95.65). Generally, whenever the cost of living increases faster than my nominal income, real income decreases.

The losers from inflation are those on incomes fixed in nominal terms or, at least, those with incomes that do not increase as fast as the rate of inflation. In the worst recession since the Great Depression, those who lost the most from unemployment were, in descending order, blacks (who also suffer the most in good times), teenagers, and blue-collar workers generally. In addition to the specific groups who lose the most, the economy as a whole loses in terms of the living standards of its members because of the lost production.

Choosing between (a) and (b) is truly a Hobson's choice! But if one must choose, it would probably be (b) because with inflation at zero, the central bank will have no cause to raise interest rates and cut off the economic expansion needed to get unemployment down from the unforgivable 8 percent. If one chose (a), we would not stay at full employment because the central bank would be raising interest rates to choke off demand to get inflation down from 6 percent. And we might soon have stagflation—increasing unemployment in the presence of high inflation.

8-10　(*Key Question*) If the price index was 110 last year and is 121 this year, what is this year's rate of inflation? What is the "rule of 70"? How long would it take for the price level to double if inflation persisted at (a) 2, (b) 5, and (c) 10 percent per year?

This year's rate of inflation is 10% or $[(121-110)/110]\times100$.

Dividing 70 by the annual percentage rate of increase of any variable (for instance, the rate of inflation or population growth) will give the approximate number of years for doubling of the variable.

(a) 35 years (= 70/2); (b) 14 years (= 70/5); (c) 7 years (= 70/10).

8-11　Describe the relationship between total spending and the level of output and employment. Explain what happens to the price level as increases in total spending move the economy from substantial unemployment to moderate unemployment, to full employment, and, finally, to full-capacity output.

As total spending rises and falls, so does output and employment. Cyclical unemployment is caused by a deficiency in total spending in the economy. If this deficiency begins to disappear—as total spending increases—output increases and unemployment decreases.

With substantial unemployment, an increase in total spending can occur without any increase in the price level. After a while (range 2 in Figure 8-7), if total spending continues to increase and unemployment to decrease, the price level will start to rise, because some sectors will begin to experience full employment and a demand for resources rising faster than their supply in that sector. This price-level increase will become more and more pronounced as full employment is approached. The economy may reach the formal definition of full employment and still be able to produce more by working overtime, for example. Finally, at absolute capacity, when, by definition, no more can be produced, any further increase in total spending will be entirely inflationary (range 3 in Figure 8-7).

8-12　Explain how "hyperinflation" might lead to a depression.

With inflation running into the double, triple, quadruple, or even greater number of digits per year, it makes little sense to save. The only sensible thing to do with money is to spend it before its value is cut in half within a month, a week, or a day. This very fact of everyone trying to spend as fast as possible will speed the inflationary spiral and cause people to spend more and more time trying to figure out what goods are most likely to go up fastest in price. More and more people will turn away from productive activity, because wages and salaries are not keeping up with inflation. Instead, they will spend their time speculating, transferring goods already in existence and producing nothing.

Eventually, money may become worthless. No one will work for money. Barter and living by one's wits become the only means of survival. Production falls for this reason and also because investment in productive capital practically ceases. Unemployment soars. A massive depression is at hand.

8-13　Evaluate as accurately as you can how each of the following individuals would be affected by unanticipated inflation of 10 percent per year:

a.　A pensioned railroad worker

b.　A department-store clerk

c. A unionized automobile assembly-line worker

d. A heavily indebted farmer

e. A retired business executive whose current income comes entirely from interest on government bonds

f. The owner of an independent small-town department store

(a) Assuming the pensioned railway worker has no other income and that the pension is not indexed against inflation, the retired worker's real income would decrease by approximately 10 percent of its former value.

(b) Assuming the clerk was unionized and the contract had over a year to run, the clerk's real income would decrease in the same manner as the pensioner. However, the clerk could expect to recoup at least part of the loss at contract renewal time. In the more likely event of the clerk not being unionized, the clerk's real income would decrease, possibly by as much as the pensioned railroad worker.

(c) Since the UAW worker is unionized, the loss in the first year would be the same as in (b) but we can be sure—barring a deep recession—that the loss will be made up at contract renewal time plus the usual real increase that may or may not be related to increased productivity. If the contract had a cost-of-living allowance clause in it, the wage would automatically be raised at the end of the year to cover the loss in purchasing power. Next year's wage would rise by 10 percent.

(d) If the inflation is also in the price the farmer gets for his products, he could gain. But more likely the price increases are mostly in what he buys, since farm machinery, fertilizer, etc., tend to be sold by less competitive sellers with more power to raise their prices. The farmer faces a lot of competition and has to rely on the market price to go up—the farmer has little control over prices on an individual basis. Moreover, if interest rates on the farmer's new debts have gone up with the prices, the farmer could be even worse off. The other side of the coin is that if no new borrowing is necessary, the inflation will reduce the real burden of the farmer's debt, because the purchasing power declines on the fixed payments he contracted to make before inflation.

(e) The retired executive is in the same boat as the pensioned railroad worker, except that the executive's income from the bonds or other interest bearing assets is probably greater than that of the worker from the pension. The increase in inflation has most probably been accompanied by rising interest rates, with a proportional drop in the price of bonds. Therefore, the retired executive would suffer a capital loss if he or she decided to cash in some of the bonds at this time and the fixed interest received on these existing bonds is worth less in terms of purchasing power. In other words, the executive, although wealthier than the retired worker, may be affected just as much or more from inflation.

(f) Assuming the store owner's prices and revenues have been keeping pace with inflation, his or her real income will not change unless the costs have risen more than the product prices.

8-14 A noted television comedian once defined inflation as follows: "Inflation? That means your money today won't buy as much as it would have during the depression when you didn't have any." Was his definition accurate?

Humorous, but largely correct!

8-15 (*Last Word*) Suppose that stock prices fall by 10 percent in the stock market. All else being equal, are these lower stock prices likely to *cause* a decrease in real GDP? How might they predict a decline in real GDP?

GDP could be reduced if stock owners feel significantly poorer and reduce their spending on goods and services, including investment in real capital goods. However, research indicates that downturns in the stock market have not had major impacts on GDP.

A fall in stock prices might signal a change in expectations. Evidence does suggest that there is a link between falling stock prices and future recessions. However, this is only one factor related to predicting recessions and, by itself, a fall in stock prices is not a reliable predictor of recession.

CHAPTER OVERVIEW

The central purpose of this chapter is to introduce the basic analytical tools that will help us organize our thinking about macroeconomic theories and controversies. First, the historical backdrop of the aggregate expenditures model is established. Next, the focus is on the consumption-income and saving-income relationships that are part of the model. Third, investment is examined, and finally, the consumption, saving, and investment concepts are combined to explain the equilibrium levels of output, income, and employment in a private (no government), domestic (no foreign sector) economy.

WHAT'S NEW

This chapter has been condensed with a focus on "aggregate expenditures-aggregate output" approach. The previous "leakage-injection" approach has been eliminated here and in Chapter 10. The "historical backdrop" section has been converted to the Last Word section. Also, simplified terminology is used when discussing the role of inventory changes, by referring to "unplanned changes in inventories" for both increases and decreases in inventories. There is a greater stress on the wealth effect to reflect its current role as an important nonincome determinant of consumption. Finally, as stated, the new Last Word incorporates the content from previous editions on the historical backdrop to these theories.

INSTRUCTIONAL OBJECTIVES

After completing this chapter, students should be able to:

1. Recognize, construct, and explain the consumption, saving, and investment schedules.

2. Identify the determinants of the location of the consumption and saving schedules.

3. Differentiate between the average and marginal propensities to consume (and save).

4. Identify the immediate determinants of investment and construct an investment demand curve.

5. Identify the factors that may cause a shift in the investment-demand curve or schedule.

6. Describe the reasons for the instability in investment spending.

7. Explain verbally and graphically the equilibrium level of GDP.

8. Explain why above-equilibrium or below-equilibrium GDP levels will not persist.

9. Explain the basics of the classical view that the economy would generally provide full employment levels of output.

10. Trace the changes in GDP that will occur when there is a discrepancy between saving and planned investment.

11. Define and identify terms and concepts at the end of the chapter.

COMMENTS AND TEACHING SUGGESTIONS

1. For those who feel that it is important for students to grasp the multiplier concept, it is possible to explain the multiplier concept without going into the theoretical discussions of Chapters 9 and 10. One suggestion would be to use the humorous Last Word for Chapter 10 and some simple role-playing exercises mentioned in this manual for Chapter 10.

2. The Last Word for this chapter provides historical backdrop for Keynesian theory. Impress upon students that Keynes developed the theory that emphasizes the importance of aggregate demand for economic performance. You may want to point out that his theory changed the way economists viewed the modern capitalist system and that he has been credited with the development of macroeconomics as a separate field. Stress that debate still lingers over whether the system is self-correcting during periods of unemployment or inflation.

3. Data to update Figure 9-1 may be found in the most recent issue of *Survey of Current Business* or *Economic Indicators*. Web-based questions at the end of the chapter also point to sources.

4. Investment expenditures are the most volatile segment of aggregate expenditures. Ask students to research a particular industry to find out what factors are most likely to influence investment decisions for that industry, or have students interview a local business manager or owner about their decision to add capital equipment. Make a list of the factors that they consider when making their decisions. Are they similar to the reasons given in the text? How were they different?

STUDENT STUMBLING BLOCKS

1. The concept of equilibrium GDP seems to be easy for students to grasp intuitively, but difficult for them to apply. Give them a lot of practice in finding equilibrium GDP using questions similar to the quantitative Key Questions at the end of the chapter.

2. Non-business majors may not be familiar with the term "inventory," or with the idea that business inventories represent an investment expenditure to businesses. This is key to understanding the difference between actual and planned investment. Make sure the distinction is emphasized.

3. If your class is filled with struggling students consider using only one "macro model." It is very difficult for beginning students to switch from one set of assumptions to another. The concept of equilibrium can be presented using Aggregate Expenditures or the AD-AS model presented in Chapter 11. The model in this chapter uses income as the main determinant. AD-AS emphasizes the price level. An emphasis on only one model may help students understand the macro economy better.

LECTURE NOTES

I. **Introduction—What Determines GDP?**

   A. This chapter and the next focus on the aggregate expenditures model. We use the definitions and facts from previous chapters to shift our study to the analysis of economic performance. The aggregate expenditures model is one tool in this analysis. Recall that "aggregate" means total.

   B. As explained in this chapter's Last Word, the model originated with John Maynard Keynes (Pronounced Canes).

   C. The focus is on the relationship between income and consumption and savings.

   D. Investment spending, an important part of aggregate expenditures, is also examined.

   E. Finally, these spending categories are combined to explain the equilibrium levels output and employment in a private (no government), domestic (no foreign sector) economy. Therefore, GDP=NI=PI=DI in this very simple model.

II. **Simplifying Assumptions for this Chapter**

   A. We assume a "closed economy" with no international trade.

   B. Government is ignored; focus is on private sector markets until next chapter.

C. Although both households and businesses save, we assume here that all saving is personal.

D. Depreciation and net foreign income are assumed to be zero for simplicity.

E. There are two reminders concerning these assumptions.

    1. They leave out two key components of aggregate demand (government spending and foreign trade), because they are largely affected by influences outside the domestic market system.

    2. With no government or foreign trade, GDP, national income (NI), personal income (PI), and disposable income (DI) are all the same.

III. **Tools of Aggregate Expenditures Theory: Consumption and Saving**

A. The theory assumes that the level of output and employment depend directly on the level of aggregate expenditures. Changes in output reflect changes in aggregate spending.

B. Consumption and saving: Since consumption is the largest component of aggregate spending, we analyze its determinants.

    1. Disposable income is the most important determinant of consumer spending (see Figure 9-1 in text which presents historical evidence).

        a. What is not spent is called saving.

        b. Therefore, $DI - C = S$ or $C + I = DI$

    2. In Figure 9-1 we see a 45-degree line which represents all points where consumer spending is equal to disposable income; other points represent actual C, DI relationships for each year from 1980-2000.

    3. If the actual graph of the relationship between consumption and income is below the 45-degree line, then the difference must represent the amount of income that is saved.

    4. Look at 1996 where consumption was $5238 billion and disposable income was $5678 billion. Hence, saving was $440 billion.

    5. The graph illustrates that as disposable income increases both consumption and saving increase.

    6. Some conclusions can be drawn:

        a. Households consume a large portion of their disposable income.

        b. Both consumption and saving are directly related to the level of income.

C. The consumption schedule:

    1. The dots in Figure 9-1 represent actual historical data.

    2. A hypothetical consumption schedule (Table 9-1 and Key Graph 9-2a) shows that households spend a larger proportion of a small income than of a large income.

    3. A hypothetical saving schedule (Table 1, column 3) is illustrated in Key Graph 9-2b.

    4. Note that "dissaving" occurs at low levels of disposable income, where consumption exceeds income and households must borrow or use up some of their wealth.

D. Average and marginal propensities to consume and save:

    1. Define average propensity to consume (APC) as the fraction or % of income consumed (APC = consumption/income). See Column 4 in Table 9-1.

2. Define average propensity to save (APS) as a the fraction or % of income saved (APS = saving/income). See Column 5 in Table 9-1.

3. Global Perspective 9-1 shows the APCs for several nations in 1999. Note the high APC for both U.S. and Canada.

4. Marginal propensity to consume (MPC) is the fraction or proportion of any change in income that is consumed. (MPC = change in consumption/change in income.) See Column 6 in Table 9-1.

5. Marginal propensity to save (MPS) is the fraction or proportion of any change in income that is saved. (MPS = change in saving/change in income.) See Column 7 in Table 9-1.

6. Note that APC + APS = 1 and MPC + MPS = 1.

7. Note that Figure 9-3 illustrates that MPC is the slope of the consumption schedule, and MPS is the slope of the saving schedule.

8. Test Yourself: Try the Self-Quiz below Key Graph 9-2.

E. Nonincome determinants of consumption and saving can cause people to spend or save more or less at various income levels, although the level of income is the basic determinant.

1. Wealth: An increase in wealth shifts the consumption schedule up and saving schedule down. In recent years major fluctuations in stock market values have increased the importance of this wealth effect.

2. Expectations: Changes in expected inflation or future wealth can affect consumption spending today.

3. Household debt: Lower debt levels shift consumption schedule up and saving schedule down.

4. Taxation: Lower taxes will shift both schedules up since taxation affects both spending and saving, and vice versa for higher taxes.

F. Shifts and stability: See Figure 9-4.

1. Terminology: Movement from one point to another on a given schedule is called a change in amount consumed; a shift in the schedule is called a change in consumption schedule.

2. Schedule shifts: Consumption and saving schedules will always shift in opposite directions unless a shift is caused by a tax change.

4. Stability: Economists believe that consumption and saving schedules are generally stable unless deliberately shifted by government action.

G. Review these aggregate expenditures concepts with Quick Review 9-1.

IV. Investment

A. Investment, the second component of private spending, consists of spending on new plants, capital equipment, machinery, inventories, construction, etc.

1. The investment decision weighs marginal benefits and marginal costs.

2. The expected rate of return is the marginal benefit and the interest rate represents the marginal cost.

B. Expected rate of return is found by comparing the expected economic profit (total revenue minus total cost) to cost of investment to get expected rate of return. The text's example gives $100 expected profit, $1000 investment for a 10% expected rate of return. Thus, the business would not want to pay more than 10% interest rate on investment.

C. The real interest rate, i (nominal rate corrected for expected inflation), is the cost of investment.

    1. Interest rate is either the cost of borrowed funds or the cost of investing your own funds, which is income forgone.

    2. If real interest rate exceeds the expected rate of return, the investment should not be made.

D. Investment demand schedule, or curve, shows an inverse relationship between the interest rate and amount of investment.

    1. As long as expected return exceeds interest rate, the investment is expected to be profitable (see Table 9-2 example).

    2. Key Graph 9-5 shows the relationship when the investment rule is followed. Fewer projects are expected to provide high return, so less will be invested if interest rates are high.

    3. Test yourself with Quick Quiz 9-5.

E. Shifts in investment demand occur when any determinant apart from the interest rate changes.

    1. Greater expected returns create more investment demand; shift curve to right. The reverse causes a leftward shift.

        a. Acquisition, maintenance, and operating costs of capital goods may change.

        b. Business taxes may change.

        c. Technology may change.

        d. Stock of capital goods on hand will affect new investment.

        e. Expectations can change the view of expected profits.

F. In addition to the investment demand schedule, economists also define an investment schedule that shows the amounts business firms collectively intend to invest at each possible level of GDP or DI.

    1. In developing the investment schedule, it is assumed that investment is independent of the current income. The line I_g (gross investment) in Figure 9-7b shows this graphically related to the level determined by Figure 9-7a.

    2. The assumption that investment is independent of income is a simplification, but will be used here.

    3. Table 9-3 shows the investment schedule from GDP levels given in Table 9-1.

G. Investment is a very unstable type of spending; I is more volatile than GDP (See Figure 9-8).

    1. Capital goods are durable, so spending can be postponed or not. This is unpredictable.

    2. Innovation occurs irregularly.

    3. Profits vary considerably.

    4. Expectations can be easily changed.

V.   **Equilibrium GDP: Expenditures-Output Approach**

A. Look at Table 9-4, which combines data of Tables 9-1 and 9-3.

B. Real domestic output in column 2 shows ten possible levels that producers are willing to offer, assuming their sales would meet the output planned. In other words, they will produce $370 billion of output if they expect to receive $370 billion in revenue.

C. Ten levels of aggregate expenditures are shown in column 6. The column shows the amount of consumption and planned gross investment spending ($C + I_g$) forthcoming at each output level.

   1. Recall that consumption level is directly related to the level of income and that here income is equal to output level.

   2. Investment is independent of income here and is planned or intended regardless of the current income situation.

D. Equilibrium GDP is the level of output whose production will create total spending just sufficient to purchase that output. Otherwise there will be a disequilibrium situation.

   1. In Table 9-4, this occurs only at $470 billion.

   2. At $410 billion GDP level, total expenditures ($C + I_g$) would be $425 = $405(C) + $20 ($I_g$) and businesses will adjust to this excess demand by stepping up production. They will expand production at any level of GDP less than the $470 billion equilibrium.

   3. At levels of GDP above $470 billion, such as $510 billion, aggregate expenditures will be less than GDP. At $510 billion level, $C + I_g$ = $500 billion. Businesses will have unsold, unplanned inventory investment and will cut back on the rate of production. As GDP declines, the number of jobs and total income will also decline, but eventually the GDP and aggregate spending will be in equilibrium at $470 billion.

E. Graphical analysis is shown in Figure 9-9 (Key Graph). At $470 billion it shows the $C + I_g$ schedule intersecting the 45-degree line which is where output = aggregate expenditures, or the equilibrium position.

   1. Observe that the aggregate expenditures line rises with output and income, but not as much as income, due to the marginal propensity to consume (the slope) being less than 1.

   2. A part of every increase in disposable income will not be spent but will be saved.

   3. Test yourself with Quick Quiz 9-9.

VI. **Two Other Features of Equilibrium GDP**

A. Savings and planned investment are equal.

   1. It is important to note that in our analysis above we spoke of "planned" investment. At GDP = $470 billion in Table 9-4, both saving and planned investment are $20 billion.

   2. Saving represents a "leakage" from spending stream and causes C to be less than GDP.

   3. Some of output is planned for business investment and not consumption, so this investment spending can replace the leakage due to saving.

      a. If aggregate spending is less than equilibrium GDP as it is in Table 9-4, line 8 when GDP is $510 billion, then businesses will find themselves with unplanned inventory investment on top of what was already planned. This unplanned portion is reflected as a business expenditure, even though the business may not have desired it, because the total output has a value that belongs to someone—either as a planned purchase or as an unplanned inventory.

    b. If aggregate expenditures exceed GDP, then there will be less inventory investment than businesses planned as businesses sell more than they expected. This is reflected as a negative amount of unplanned investment in inventory. For example, at $450 billion GDP, there will be $435 billion of consumer spending, $20 billion of planned investment, so businesses must have experienced a $5 billion unplanned decline in inventory because sales exceed that expected.

B. In equilibrium there are no unplanned changes in inventory.

    1. Consider row 7 of Table 9-4 where GDP is $490 billion, here C + Ig is only $485 billion and will be less than output by $5 billion. Firms retain the extra $5 billion as unplanned inventory investment. Actual investment is $25 billion or more than $20 billion planned. So $490 billion is an above-equilibrium output level.

    2. Consider row 5, Table 9-4. Here $450 billion is a below-equilibrium output level because actual investment will be $5 billion less than planned. Inventories decline below what was planned. GDP will rise to $470 billion.

C. Quick Review: Equilibrium GDP is where aggregate expenditures equal real domestic output. (C + planned Ig = GDP)

    1. A difference between saving and planned investment causes a difference between the production and spending plans of the economy as a whole.

    2. This difference between production and spending plans leads to unintended inventory investment or unintended decline in inventories.

    3. As long as unplanned changes in inventories occur, businesses will revise their production plans upward or downward until the investment in inventory is equal to what they planned. This will occur at the point that household saving is equal to planned investment.

    4. Only where planned investment and saving are equal will there be no unintended investment or disinvestment in inventories to drive the GDP down or up.

VII. Last Word: Say's Law, The Great Depression, and Keynes

A. Until the Great Depression of the 1930, most economists going back to Adam Smith had believed that a market system would ensure full employment of the economy's resources except for temporary, short-term upheavals.

B. If there were deviations, they would be self-correcting. A slump in output and employment would reduce prices, which would increase consumer spending; would lower wages, which would increase employment again; and would lower interest rates, which would expand investment spending.

C. Say's law, attributed to the French economist J. B. Say in the early 1800s, summarized the view in a few words: "Supply creates its own demand."

D. Say's law is easiest to understand in terms of barter. The woodworker produces furniture in order to trade for other needed products and services. All the products would be traded for something, or else there would be no need to make them. Thus, supply creates its own demand.

E.   Reformulated versions of these classical views are still prevalent among some modern economists today.

F.   The Great Depression of the 1930s was worldwide. GDP fell by 40 percent in U.S. and the unemployment rate rose to nearly 25 percent (when most families had only one breadwinner). The Depression seemed to refute the classical idea that markets were self-correcting and would provide full employment.

G.   John Maynard Keynes in 1936 in his *General Theory of Employment, Interest, and Money,* provided an alternative to classical theory, which helped explain periods of recession.

  1.   Not all income is always spent, contrary to Say's law.

  2.   Producers may respond to unsold inventories by reducing output rather than cutting prices.

  3.   A recession or depression could follow this decline in employment and incomes.

H.   The modern aggregate expenditures model is based on Keynesian economics or the ideas that have arisen from Keynes and his followers since. It is based on the idea that saving and investment decisions may not be coordinated, and prices and wages are not very flexible downward. Internal market forces can therefore cause depressions and government should play an active role in stabilizing the economy.

ANSWERS TO END-OF-CHAPTER QUESTIONS

9-1   Explain what relationships are shown by (a) the consumption schedule, (b) the saving schedule, (c) the investment-demand curve, and (d) the investment schedule.

  (a)   The consumption schedule or curve shows how much households plan to consume at various levels of disposable income at a specific point in time, assuming there is no change in the nonincome determinants of consumption, namely, wealth, the price level, expectations, indebtedness, and taxes. A change in disposable income causes movement along a given consumption curve. A change in a nonincome determinant causes the entire schedule or curve to shift.

  (b)   The saving schedule or curve shows how much households plan to save at various levels of disposable income at a specific point in time, assuming there is no change in the nonincome determinants of saving, namely, wealth, the price level, expectations, indebtedness, and taxes. A change in disposable income causes movement along a given saving curve. A change in a nonincome determinant causes the entire schedule or curve to shift.

  (c)   The investment-demand curve shows how much will be invested at all possible interest rates, given the expected rate of net profit from the proposed investments, assuming there is no change in the noninterest-rate determinants of investment, namely, acquisition, maintenance, operating costs, business taxes, technological change, the stock of capital goods on hand, and expectations. A change in any of these will affect the expected rate of net profit and shift the curve. A change in the interest rate will cause movement along a given curve.

  (d)   The investment schedule shows how much businesses plan to invest at each of the possible levels of output or income.

9-2   Precisely how are the APC and the MPC different? Why must the sum of the MPC and the MPS equal 1? What are the basic determinants of the consumption and saving schedules? Of your own level of consumption?

APC is an average whereby total spending on consumption (C) is compared to total income (Y): APC = C/Y. MPC refers to changes in spending and income at the margin. Here we compare a change in consumer spending to a change in income: MPC = change in C / change in Y.

When your income changes there are only two possible options regarding what to do with it: You either spend it or you save it. MPC is the fraction of the change in income spent; therefore, the fraction not spent must be saved and this is the MPS. The change in the dollars spent or saved will appear in the numerator and together they must add to the total change in income. Since the denominator is the total change in income, the sum of the MPC and MPS is one.

The basic determinants of the consumption and saving schedules are the levels of income and output. Once the schedules are set, the determinants of where the schedules are located would be the amount of household wealth (the more wealth, the more is spent at each income level); expectations of future income, prices and product availability; the relative size of consumer debt; and the amount of taxation.

Chances are that most of us would answer that our income is the basic determinant of our levels of spending and saving, but a few may have low incomes, but with large family wealth that determines the level of spending. Likewise, other factors may enter into the pattern, as listed in the preceding paragraph. Answers will vary depending on the student's situation.

9-3   Explain how each of the following will affect the consumption and saving schedules or the investment schedule:

a. A large increase in the value of real estate, including private houses.

b. The threat of limited, non-nuclear war, leading the public to expect future shortages of consumer durables.

c. A decline in the real interest rate.

d. A sharp, sustained decline in stock prices.

e. An increase in the rate of population growth.

f. The development of a cheaper method of manufacturing computer chips.

g. A sizable increase in the retirement age for collecting social security benefits.

h. The expectation that mild inflation will persist in the next decade.

i. An increase in the Federal personal income tax.

(a) If this simply means households have become more wealthy, then consumption will increase at each income level. The consumption schedule should shift upward and the saving schedule shift leftward. The investment schedule may shift rightward if owners of existing homes sell them and invest in construction of new homes more than previously.

(b) This threat will lead people to stock up; the consumption schedule will shift up and the saving schedule down. If this puts pressure on the consumer goods industry, the investment schedule will shift up. The investment schedule may shift up again later because of increased military procurement orders.

(c) The decline in the real interest rate will increase interest-sensitive consumer spending; the consumption schedule will shift up and the saving schedule down. Investors will increase investment as they move down the investment-demand curve; the investment schedule will shift upward.

(d) Though this did not happen after October 19, 1987, a sharp decline in stock prices can normally be expected to decrease consumer spending because of the decrease in wealth; the consumption schedule shifts down and the saving schedule upwards. Because of the depressed share prices and the number of speculators forced out of the market, it will be harder to float new issues on the stock market. Therefore, the investment schedule will shift downward.

(e) The increase in the rate of population growth will, over time, increase the rate of income growth. In itself this will not shift any of the schedules but will lead to movement upward to the right along the upward sloping investment schedule.

(f) This innovation will in itself shift the investment schedule upward. Also, as the innovation starts to lower the costs of producing everything using these chips, prices will decrease leading to increased quantities demanded. This, again, could shift the investment schedule upward.

(g) The postponement of benefits may cause households to save more if they planned to retire before they qualify for benefits; the saving schedule will shift upward, the consumption schedule downward. This impact is uncertain, however, if people continue to work and earn productive incomes.

(h) If this is a new expectation, the consumption schedule will shift upwards and the saving schedule downwards until people have stocked up enough. After about a year, if the mild inflation is not increasing, the household schedules will revert to where they were before.

(i) Because this reduces disposable income, consumption will decline in proportion to the marginal propensity to consume. Consumption will be less at each level of real output, and so the curve shifts down. The saving schedule will also fall because the disposable income has decreased at each level of output, so less would be saved.

9-4   Explain why an upward shift in the consumption schedule typically involves an equal downshift in the saving schedule. What is the exception?

If, by definition, all that you can do with your income is use it for consumption or saving, then if you consume more out of any given income, you will necessarily save less. And if you consume less, you will save more. This being so, when your consumption schedule shifts upward (meaning you are consuming more out of any given income), your saving schedule shifts downward (meaning you are consuming less out of the same given income).

The exception is a change in personal taxes. When these change, your disposable income changes, and, therefore, your consumption and saving both change in the same direction and opposite to the change in taxes. If your MPC, say, is 0.9, then your MPS is 0.1. Now, if your taxes increase by $100, your consumption will decrease by $90 and your saving will decrease by $10.

9-5   (*Key Question*) Complete the accompanying table (top of next page).

a.   Show the consumption and saving schedules graphically.

b.   Locate the break-even level of income. How is it possible for households to dissave at very low income levels?

c.   If the proportion of total income consumed (APC) decreases and the proportion saved (APS) increases as income rises, explain both verbally and graphically how the MPC and MPS can be constant at various levels of income.

Level of Output and income (GDP = DI)	Consumption	Saving	APC	APS	MPC	MPS
$240	$ _____	$-4	_____	_____	_____	_____
260	$ _____	0	_____	_____	_____	_____
280	$ _____	4	_____	_____	_____	_____
300	$ _____	8	_____	_____	_____	_____
320	$ _____	12	_____	_____	_____	_____
340	$ _____	16	_____	_____	_____	_____
360	$ _____	20	_____	_____	_____	_____
380	$ _____	24	_____	_____	_____	_____
400	$ _____	28	_____	_____	_____	_____

Data for completing the table (top to bottom). Consumption: $244; $260; $276; $292; $308; $324; $340; $356; $372. APC: 1.02; 1.00; .99; .97; .96; .95; .94; .94; .93. APS: -.02; .00; .01; .03; .04; .05; .06; .06; .07. MPC: 80 throughout. MPS: 20 throughout.

(a) See the graphs.

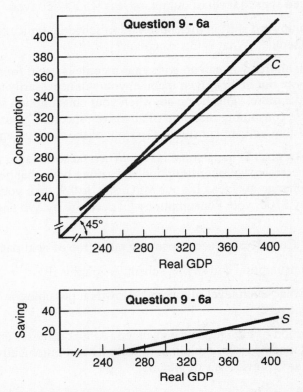

(b) Break-even income = $260. Households dissave borrowing or using past savings.

(c) Technically, the APC diminishes and the APS increases because the consumption and saving schedules have positive and negative vertical intercepts respectively. (Appendix to Chapter

1). MPC and MPS measure *changes* in consumption and saving as income changes; they are the *slopes* of the consumption and saving schedules. For straight-line consumption and saving schedules, these slopes do not change as the level of income changes; the slopes and thus the MPC and MPS remain constant.

9-6 What are the basic determinants of investment? Explain the relationship between the real interest rate and the level of investment. Why is the investment schedule less stable than the consumption and saving schedules?

The basic determinants of investment are the expected rate of net profit that businesses hope to realize from investment spending and the real rate of interest.

When the real interest rate rises, investment decreases; and when the real interest rate drops, investment increases—other things equal in both cases. The reason for this relationship is that it makes sense to borrow money at, say, 10 percent, if the expected rate of net profit is higher than 10 percent, for then one makes a profit on the borrowed money. But if the expected rate of net profit is less than 10 percent, borrowing the money would be expected to result in a negative rate of return on the borrowed money. Even if the firm has money of its own to invest, the principle still holds: The firm would not be maximizing profit if it used its own money to carry out an investment returning, say, 9 percent when it could lend the money at an interest rate of 10 percent.

For the great majority of people, their only saving is to buy a house and to make the mortgage payments on it. Apart from that, practically their entire income is consumed. Since for the majority of people their incomes are quite stable and since almost all their income is consumed, the consumption and saving schedules are also quite stable. After all, most consumption is for the essentials of food, shelter, and clothing. These cannot vary much.

Investment, on the other hand, is variable because, unlike consumption, it can be put off. In good times, with demand strong and rising, businesses will bring in more machines and replace old ones. In times of economic downturn, no new machines will be ordered. A firm can continue for years with, say, a tenth of the investment it was carrying out in the boom. Very few families could cut their consumption so drastically.

New business ideas and the innovations that spring from them do not come at a constant rate. This is another reason for the irregularity of investment. Profits and the expectations of profits also vary. Since profits, in the absence of easy access to borrowed money, are essential for investment and since, moreover, the object of investment is to make a profit, investment, too, must vary.

9-7 (*Key Question*) Assume there are no investment projects in the economy which yield an expected rate of return of 25 percent or more. But suppose there are $10 billion of investment projects yielding expected rate of return of between 20 and 25 percent; another $10 billion yielding between 15 and 20 percent; another $10 billion between 10 and 15 percent; and so forth. Cumulate these data and present them graphically, putting the expected rate of net return on the vertical axis and the amount of investment on the horizontal axis. What will be the equilibrium level of aggregate investment if the real interest rate is (a) 15 percent, (b) 10 percent, and (c) 5 percent? Explain why this curve is the investment-demand curve.

See the graph on following page. Aggregate investment: (a) $20 billion; (b) $30 billion; (c) $40 billion. This is the investment-demand curve because we have applied the rule of undertaking all investment up to the point where the expected rate of return, r, equals the interest rate, *i*.

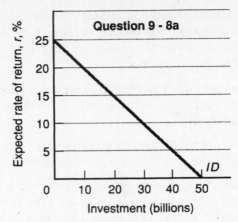

9-8.   Explain graphically the determination of the equilibrium GDP for a private closed economy. Explain why the intersection of aggregate expenditures schedule and the 45-degree line determines the equilibrium GDP.

These two approaches must always yield the same equilibrium GDP because they are simply two sides of the same coin, so to speak. Equilibrium GDP is where aggregate expenditures equal real output. Aggregate expenditures consist of consumer expenditures (C) + planned investment spending (I_g). If there is no government or foreign sector, then the level of income is the same as the level of output. In equilibrium, I_g makes up the difference between C and the value of the output.

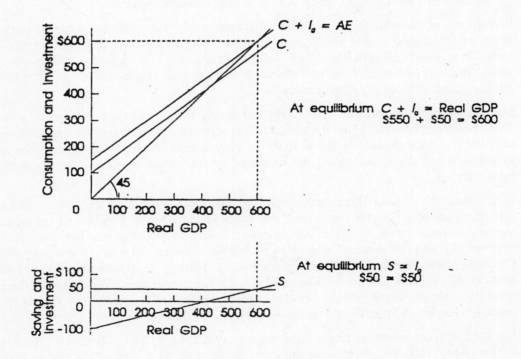

If we let Y be the value of the output, which is also the value of the real income, then whatever households have not spent is Y - C = S. But at equilibrium, Y - C also equals I_g so at equilibrium the value of S must be equal to I_g. This is another way of saying that saving (S) is a leakage from the income stream, and investment is an injection. If the amount of investment is equal to S, then the leakage from saving is replenished and all of the output will be purchased which is the definition of equilibrium. At this GDP, $C + S = C + I_g$, so $S = I_g$.

Alternatively, one could explain why there would not be an equilibrium if (a) S were greater than I_g or (b) S were less than I_g. In case (a), we would find that aggregate spending is less than output and output would contract; in (b) we would find that $C + I_g$ would be greater than output and output would expand. Therefore, when S and I_g are not equal, output level is not at equilibrium.

The 45-degree line represents all the points at which real output is equal to aggregate expenditures. Since this is our definition of equilibrium GDP, then wherever aggregate expenditure schedule coincides (intersects) with the 45-degree line, there is an equilibrium output level.

9-9   (*Key Question*) Assuming the level of investment is $16 billion and independent of the level of total output, complete the following table and determine the equilibrium levels of output and employment which this private closed economy would provide. What are the sizes of the MPC and MPS?

Possible levels of employment (millions)	Real domestic output (GDP=DI) (billions)	Consumption (billions)	Saving (billions)
40	$240	$244	$ ___
45	260	260	$ ___
50	280	276	$ ___
55	300	292	$ ___
60	320	308	$ ___
65	340	324	$ ___
70	360	340	$ ___
75	380	356	$ ___
80	400	372	$ ___

Saving data for completing the table (top to bottom): $-4; $0; $4; $8; $12; $16; $20; $24; $28.

Equilibrium GDP = $340 billion, determined where (1) aggregate expenditures equal GDP (C of $324 billion + *I* of $16 billion = GDP of $340 billion); or (2) where planned *I* = *S* (*I* of $16 billion = *S* of $16 billion). Equilibrium level of employment = 65 million; MCP = .8; MPS = .2.

9-10   (*Key Question*) Using the consumption and saving data given in question 9 and assuming the level of investment is $16 billion, what are the levels of saving and planned investment at the $380 billion level of domestic output? What are the levels of saving and actual investment at that level? What are saving and planned investment at the $300 billion level of domestic output? What are the levels of saving and actual investment? Use the concept of unplanned investment to explain adjustments toward equilibrium from both the $380 and $300 billion levels of domestic output.

At the $380 billion level of GDP, saving = $24 billion; planned investment = $16 billion (from the question). This deficiency of $8 billion of planned investment causes an unplanned $8 billion *increase* in inventories. Actual investment is $24 billion (= $16 billion of planned investment *plus* $8 billion of unplanned inventory investment), matching the $24 billion of actual saving.

At the $300 billion level of GDP, saving = $8 billion; planned investment = $16 billion (from the question). This excess of $8 billion of planned investment causes an unplanned $8 billion *decline* in inventories. Actual investment is $8 billion (= $16 billion of planned investment *minus* $8 billion of unplanned inventory disinvestment) matching the actual of $8 billion.

When unplanned investments in inventories occur, as at the $380 billion level of GDP, businesses revise their production plans downward and GDP falls. When unplanned disinvestments in inventories occur, as at the $300 billion level of GDP; businesses revise their production plans upward and GDP rises. Equilibrium GDP—in this case, $340 billion—occurs where planned investment equals saving.

9-11 Why is saving called a *leakage?* Why is planned investment called an *injection?* Are unplanned changes in inventories rising, falling, or constant at equilibrium GDP? Explain.

Saving is like a leakage from the flow of aggregate consumption expenditures because saving represents income not spent. Planned investment is an injection because it is spending on capital goods that businesses plan to make regardless of their current level of income. At equilibrium GDP there will be no changes in unplanned inventories because expenditures will exactly equal planned output levels which include consumer goods and services and planned investment. Thus there is no unplanned investment including no unplanned inventory changes.

9-12 "Planned investment is equal to saving at all levels of GDP; actual investment equals saving only at the equilibrium GDP." Do you agree? Explain. Critically evaluate: "The fact that households may save more than businesses want to invest is of no consequence, because events will in time force households and businesses to save and invest at the same rates."

You should not agree. The statement is backward—reverse the placement of the planned investment and actual investment. Actual investment is always present—it is the amount that actually takes place at any output level because it includes unintended changes in inventories (a type of investment) as well as the level of planned investment. If saving is greater than planned investment, the total level of aggregate spending will not be enough to support the existing level of output, causing businesses to reduce their output. If saving is less than planned investment, the total level of aggregate expenditures will be greater than the existing output level and inventories will drop below the planned level of inventory investment, causing businesses to increase their output to replenish their inventories. The only stable output level will be the equilibrium level, at which saving and planned investment are equal.

The events described in the second quote are predictable, but most would argue that this is of great consequence. When households save more than businesses want to invest, it means they are consuming less. This, in turn, means that aggregate spending (consumption plus investment) will be less than the level of output and current real income. Businesses will experience unplanned inventory buildup and will cut their output levels, which means a decline in employment. The resulting unemployment is not inconsequential—especially to those who lose their jobs, but also in terms of lost potential output for the entire economy.

9-13 Advanced analysis: Linear equations (see appendix to Chapter 1) for the consumption and saving schedules take the general form $C = a + bY$ and $S = -a + (1-b)Y$, where C, S, and Y are consumption, saving, and national income respectively. The constant a represents the vertical intercept, and b is the slope of the consumption schedule.

a. Use the following data to substitute specific numerical values into the consumption and saving equations.

National Income (Y)	Consumption (C)
$ 0	$ 80
100	140
200	200
300	260
400	320

b. What is the economic meaning of b? Of (1 - b)?

c. Suppose the amount of saving that occurs at each level of national income falls by $20, but that the values for b and (1 - b) remain unchanged. Restate the saving and consumption equations for the new numerical values and cite a factor which might have caused the change.

(a) $C = \$80 + 0.6Y \quad S = -\$80 + 0.4Y$

(b) Since b is the slope of the consumption function, it is the value of the MPC. (In this case the slope is 6/10, which means for every $10 increase in income (movement to the right on the horizontal axis of the graph), consumption will increase by $6 (movement upwards on the vertical axis of the graph). (1 - b) would be 1 - .6 = .4, which is the MPS.

Since (1 - b) is the slope of the saving function, it is the value of the MPS. (With the slope of the MPC being 6/10, the MPS will be 4/10. This means for every $10 increase in income (movement to the right on the horizontal axis of the graph), saving will increase by $4 (movement upward on the vertical axis of the graph).

(c) $C = 100 + 0.6Y \qquad S = -\$100 + 0.4Y$

A factor that might have caused the decrease in saving—the increased consumption—is the belief that inflation will accelerate. Consumers wish to stock up before prices increase. Other factors might include a sudden decline in wealth or increase in indebtedness, or an increase in personal taxes.

9-14 Advanced analysis: Suppose that the linear equation for consumption in a hypothetical economy is $C = \$40 + .8Y$. Also suppose that income (Y) is $400. Determine (a) the marginal propensity to consume, (b) the marginal propensity to save, (c) the level of consumption, (d) the average propensity to consume, (e) the level of saving, and (f) the average propensity to save.

(a) MPC is .8

(b) MPS is $(1-8) = .2$

(c) $C = \$40 + .8(\$400) = \$40 + \$320 = \$360$

(d) $APC = \$360 / \$400 = .9$

(e) $S = Y - C = \$400 - \$360 = \$40$

(f) $APS = \$40 / \$400 = .1$ or $1 - APC$

9-15 Advanced analysis: Assume that the linear equation for consumption in a hypothetical private closed economy is $C = 10 + .9Y$, where Y is total real income (output). Also suppose that the equation for investment is $I_g = I_{g0} = 40$, meaning that I_g is 40 at all levels of real income (output). Using the equation $Y = C + I_g$, determine the equilibrium level of Y. What are the total amounts of consumption, saving, and investment at equilibrium Y?

$$Y = 500, C = 460, I_g = 40, S = 40$$

To obtain these results, recognize that at equilibrium aggregate demand $(C + I_g)$ must equal Y which represents output. Therefore the solution for equilibrium Y is where:

$$Y = C + 40 = (10 + 9Y) + 40 \text{ or } Y = 9Y + 50 \text{ or } Y - 9Y = 50, \text{ which means that } Y = 500$$

From this we can find $C = 10 + 9(500)$, which is 460

Since saving equals Investment at equilibrium, S = 40

9-16   (Last Word) What is Say's law? How does it relate to the view held by classical economists that the economy generally will operate at a position on its production possibilities curve (Chapter 2). Use production possibilities to demonstrate Keynes's view on this matter.

Say's law states that "supply creates its own demand." People work in order to earn income to and plan to spend the income on output – why else would they work? Basically, the classical economists would say that the economy will operate at full employment or on the production possibilities curve because income earned will be recycled or spent on output. Thus the spending flow is continuously recycled in production and earning income. If consumers don't spend all their income, it would be redirected via saving to investment spending on capital goods.

The Keynesian perspective, on the other hand, suggests that society's savings will not necessarily all be channeled into investment spending. If this occurs, we have a situation in which aggregate demand is less than potential production. Because producers cannot sell all of the output produced at a full employment level, they will reduce output and employment to meet the aggregate demand (consumption plus investment) and the equilibrium output will be at a point inside the production possibilities curve at less than full employment.

CHAPTER TEN
AGGREGATE EXPENDITURES: THE MULTIPLIER, NET EXPORTS AND GOVERNMENT

CHAPTER OVERVIEW

We have seen in Chapter 9 why a particular level of real GDP exists in a private, closed economy. Now we examine how and why that level might change. By adding the foreign sector and government to the model we gain complexity and realism.

First, the chapter analyzes changes in investment spending and how they could affect real GDP, income, and employment, finding that changes in investment are multiplied in their impact on output and incomes. The simplified "closed" economy is "opened" to show how it would be affected by exports and imports. Government spending and taxes are brought into the model to reflect the "mixed" nature of our system. Finally, the model is applied to two historical periods in order to consider some of the model's deficiencies. The price level is assumed constant in this chapter unless stated otherwise, so the focus is on real GDP.

WHAT'S NEW

This chapter continues the focus on aggregate expenditures (AE) analysis rather than the dual emphasis on AE and leakages-injections approach. The student is simply reminded that at equilibrium, leakages equal injections, and there are no unplanned changes in inventories.

A new application, "Recession in Japan in the 1990's," supports references in Chapter 15 to ineffective monetary policy in Japan.

The closing section is an abridged version of the earlier edition and is now called "Limitations of the Model." Finally, a new Internet question replaces on of those in the 14th edition.

INSTRUCTIONAL OBJECTIVES

After completing this chapter, students should be able to:

1. Describe and define the multiplier effect.
2. State the relationships between the multiplier and the MPS and the MPC.
3. Define the net export schedule.
4. Explain the impact of positive (or negative) net exports on aggregate expenditures and the equilibrium level of real GDP.
5. Explain the effect of increases (or decreases) in exports on real GDP.
6. Explain the effect of increases (or decreases) in imports on real GDP.
7. Describe how government purchases affect equilibrium GDP.
8. Describe how personal taxes affect equilibrium GDP.
9. Explain what is meant by the balanced-budget multiplier and why it equals 1.
10. Identify a recessionary gap and explain its effect on real GDP.

11. Identify an inflationary gap and explain its effect.

12. Explain the relationship between the concept of recessionary gap and the Great Depression or Japan's recession.

13. Explain the relationship between the Vietnam era inflation and the inflationary gap concept.

14. List four limitations of the aggregate expenditures model.

15. Define and identify terms and concepts listed at the end of the chapter.

COMMENTS AND TEACHING SUGGESTIONS

1. As stated earlier, some instructors may choose to skip this chapter as well as Chapter 9 which develop the aggregate expenditures model. Time limitations may force the macro theory focus to begin with Chapter 11, on the aggregate demand-aggregate supply model. The text is organized for this possibility. However, as suggested in Chapter 9, students could still benefit from the Last Word sections for both Chapters 9 and 10, and the multiplier concept can still be successfully presented, as suggested in #2 below.

2. The multiplier concept can be demonstrated effectively by a role-playing exercise in which you have students pretend that one row (group) of students are construction workers who benefit from a $1 million increase in investment spending. (Some instructors use an oversized paper $1-million bill.) If their MPC is .9, then they will spend $900,000 of this at stores "owned" by a second row (group) of students, who will in turn spend $810,000 or .9 x $900,000. At the end of the exercise, each row can add up its new income and it will be well in excess of the initial $1 million. In fact, if played out to its conclusion, the final change in GDP should approximate $10 million, given the MPS is .1 in this example.

   If you decide to use an oversized paper $1-million bill, then students will have to clip off one-tenth of it at every stage to represent saving. By the end of the process, each row (group) of students has seen its income increase by nine-tenths of what the previous group received. Adding up all of these increases illustrates the idea that the original $1 million increase in spending has resulted in many times that amount in terms of the students' increased incomes. Obviously, you won't be able to illustrate the final multiplier, but it should give them a good idea of how the final multiplier could be equal to 10 in this example. In other words, if the process were carried to its conclusion, the original $1 million of new investment would result in a $10 million increase in student incomes and $10 million of new saving.

   If you don't want to use the prop, students are good at imagining that this could happen if you'll simply ask them to imagine that a new $1 million injection of investment spending (or government or export sales) occurs, and then go through the chain of events described above.

3. Note that the multiplier effect can work in reverse as well as the forward direction. The closing of a military base or a factory shutting down has a multiplied negative impact on the local community, reducing retail sales and placing a hardship on other businesses. Ask students to offer examples of the multiplier effect that they have witnessed. They enjoy making up their own versions of Buchwald's Last Word for this chapter.

4. Note that net exports are kept as independent of the level of GDP to keep the analysis simple. You may want to note in passing that, in fact, there tends to be a direct relationship between import spending and the level of GDP.

5. The Last Word by Art Buchwald is a humorous look at the multiplier. Not only is it funny, but it provides a good demonstration of the concept.

STUDENT STUMBLING BLOCK

As with equilibrium GDP, the multiplier is not a difficult concept to grasp with intuitive applications, but quantitative applications are often difficult for students. If you expect them to be able to solve problems involving the multiplier, give them practice on assignments such as Key Questions #2, 5, 8, and 10. A recent paper by leading economic educators suggests neglect of the multiplier formula in favor of the intuitive approach.

LECTURE NOTES

I.   **Introduction**

   A. This chapter examines why real GDP might be unstable and subject to cyclical fluctuations.

   B. The revised model adds realism by including the foreign sector and government in the aggregate expenditures model.

   C. Applications of the new model include two U.S. historical periods and the current situation in Japan. The focus remains on real GDP.

II. **Changes in Equilibrium GDP and the Multiplier**

   A. Equilibrium GDP changes in response to changes in the investment schedule or to changes in the consumption schedule. Because investment spending is less stable than the consumption schedule, this chapter's focus will be on investment changes.

   B. Figure 10-1 shows the impact of changes in investment. Suppose investment spending rises (due to a rise in profit expectations or to a decline in interest rates).

   1. Figure 10-1 shows the increase in aggregate expenditures from $(C + I_g)_0$ to $(C + I_g)_1$. In this case, the $5 billion increase in investment leads to a $20 billion increase in equilibrium GDP.

   2. Conversely, a decline in investment spending of $5 billion is shown to create a decrease in equilibrium GDP of $20 billion to $450 billion.

   C. The multiplier effect:

   1. A $5 billion change in investment led to a $20 billion change in GDP. This result is known as the multiplier effect.

   2. Multiplier = change in real GDP / initial change in spending. In our example M = 4.

   3. Three points to remember about the multiplier:

   a. The initial change in spending is usually associated with investment because it is so volatile.

   b. The initial change refers to an upshift or downshift in the aggregate expenditures schedule due to a change in one of its components, like investment.

   c. The multiplier works in both directions (up or down).

   D. The multiplier is based on two facts.

   1. The economy has continuous flows of expenditures and income—a ripple effect—in which income received by Jones comes from money spent by Smith.

   2. Any change in income will cause both consumption and saving to vary in the same direction as the initial change in income, and by a fraction of that change.

a. The fraction of the change in income that is spent is called the marginal propensity to consume (MPC).

b. The fraction of the change in income that is saved is called the marginal propensity to save (MPS).

c. This is illustrated in Table 10-1 and Figure 10-2 which is derived from the Table.

3. The size of the MPC and the multiplier are directly related; the size of the MPS and the multiplier are inversely related. See Figure 10-3 for an illustration of this point. In equation form $M = 1 / MPS$ or $1 / (1-MPC)$.

E. The significance of the multiplier is that a small change in investment plans or consumption-saving plans can trigger a much larger change in the equilibrium level of GDP.

F. The simple multiplier given above can be generalized to include other "leakages" from the spending flow besides savings. For example, the realistic multiplier is derived by including taxes and imports as well as savings in the equation. In other words, the denominator is the fraction of a change in income not spent on domestic output. (Key Question 2.)

III.   **International Trade and Equilibrium Output**

A. Net exports (exports minus imports) affect aggregate expenditures in an open economy. Exports expand and imports contract aggregate spending on domestic output.

1. Exports (X) create domestic production, income, and employment due to foreign spending on U.S. produced goods and services.

2. Imports (M) reduce the sum of consumption and investment expenditures by the amount expended on imported goods, so this figure must be subtracted so as not to overstate aggregate expenditures on U.S. produced goods and services.

B. The net export schedule (Table 10-2):

1. Shows hypothetical amount of net exports (X - M) that will occur at each level of GDP given in Tables 9-1 and 9-4.

2. Assumes that net exports are autonomous or independent of the current GDP level.

3. Figure 10-4b shows Table 10-2 graphically.

a. X_{n1} shows a positive $5 billion in net exports.

b. X_{n2} shows a negative $5 billion in net exports.

C. The impact of net exports on equilibrium GDP is illustrated in Figure 10-4.

1. Positive net exports increase aggregate expenditures beyond what they would be in a closed economy and thus have an expansionary effect. The multiplier effect also is at work. In Figure 10-4a we see that positive net exports of $5 billion lead to a positive change in equilibrium GDP of $20 billion (to $490 from $470 billion). This comes from Table 9-4 and Figure 9-9.

2. Negative net exports decrease aggregate expenditures beyond what they would be in a closed economy and thus have a contractionary effect. The multiplier effect also is at work here. In Figure 10-4a we see that negative net exports of $5 billion lead to a negative change in equilibrium GDP of $20 billion (to $450 from $470 billion).

D. Global Perspective 10-1 shows 1999 net exports for various nations.

E. International economic linkages:

1. Prosperity abroad generally raises our exports and transfers some of their prosperity to us. (Conversely, recession abroad has the reverse effect.)

2. Tariffs on U.S. products may reduce our exports and depress our economy, causing us to retaliate and worsen the situation. Trade barriers in the 1930s contributed to the Great Depression.

3. Depreciation of the dollar (Chapter 6) lowers the cost of American goods to foreigners and encourages exports from the U.S. while discouraging the purchase of imports in the U.S. This could lead to higher real GDP or to inflation, depending on the domestic employment situation. Appreciation of the dollar could have the opposite impact.

IV. **Adding the Public Sector**

A. Simplifying assumptions are helpful for clarity when we include the government sector in our analysis. (Many of these simplifications are dropped in Chapter 12, where there is further analysis on the government sector.)

1. Simplified investment and net export schedules are used. We assume they are independent of the level of current GDP.

2. We assume government purchases do not impact private spending schedules.

3. We assume that net tax revenues are derived entirely from personal taxes so that GDP, NI, and PI remain equal. DI is PI minus net personal taxes.

4. We assume tax collections are independent of GDP level.

5. The price level is assumed to be constant unless otherwise indicated.

B. Table 10-3 gives a tabular example of a $20 billion increase in government spending and Figure 10-5 gives the graphical illustration.

1. Increases in government spending boost aggregate expenditures.

2. Government spending is subject to the multiplier.

C. Table 10-4 and Figure 10-6 show the impact of a tax increase. (Key Question 8)

1. Taxes reduce DI and, therefore, consumption and saving at each level of GDP.

2. An increase in taxes will lower the aggregate expenditures schedule relative to the 45-degree line and reduce the equilibrium GDP.

3. Table 10-4 confirms that, at equilibrium GDP, the sum of leakages equals the sum of injections. Saving + Imports + Taxes = Investment + Exports + Government Purchases.

D. Balanced-budget multiplier is a curious result of this effect. (See Figure 10-7)

1. Equal increases in government spending and taxation increase the equilibrium GDP.

a. If G and T are each increased by a particular amount, the equilibrium level of real output will rise by that same amount.

b. In the text's example, an increase of $20 billion in G and an offsetting increase of $20 billion in T will increase equilibrium GDP by $20 billion (from $470 billion to $490 billion).

2. The example reveals the rationale.

a. An increase in G is direct and adds $20 billion to aggregate expenditures.

      b.   An increase in T has an indirect effect on aggregate expenditures because T reduces disposable incomes first, and then C falls by the amount of the tax times MPC.

      c.   The overall result is a rise in initial spending of $20 billion minus a fall in initial spending of $15 billion (.75 ∞ $20 billion), which is a net upward shift in aggregate expenditures of $5 billion. When this is subject to the multiplier effect, which is 4 in this example, the increase in GDP will be equal to 4 ∞ $5 billion or $20 billion, which is the size of the change in G.

      d.   It can be seen, therefore, that the balanced-budget multiplier is equal to 1.

      e.   This can be verified by using different MPCs .

V.   Equilibrium vs. Full-Employment GDP

A. A recessionary gap exists when equilibrium GDP is below full-employment GDP. (See Figure 10-8a)

    1. Recessionary gap of $5 billion is the amount by which aggregate expenditures fall short of those required to achieve the full-employment level of GDP.

    2. In Table 10-4, assuming the full-employment GDP is $510 billion, the corresponding level of total expenditures there is only $505 billion. The gap would be $5 billion, the amount by which the schedule would have to shift upward to realize the full-employment GDP.

    3. Graphically, the recessionary gap is the vertical distance by which the aggregate expenditures schedule $(C_a + I_g + X_n + G)_1$ lies below the full-employment point on the 45-degree line.

    4. Because the multiplier is 4, we observe a $20-billion differential (the recessionary gap of $5 billion times the multiplier of 4) between the equilibrium GDP and the full-employment GDP. This is the $20 billion GDP gap we encountered in Chapter 8's Figure 8-4.

B. An inflationary gap exists when aggregate expenditures exceed full-employment GDP.

    1. Figure 10-8b shows that a demand-pull inflationary gap of $5 billion exists when aggregate spending exceeds what is necessary to achieve full employment.

    2. The inflationary gap is the amount by which the aggregate expenditures schedule must shift downward to realize the full-employment noninflationary GDP.

    3. The effect of the inflationary gap is to pull up the prices of the economy's output.

    4. In this model, if output can't expand, pure demand-pull inflation will occur (Key Question 10).

C. Table 10-5 gives steps needed to determine the recessionary or inflationary gap.

D. Try Quick Quiz 10-8.

VI.   Historical Applications

A. The Great Depression of the 1930s provides a significant case study. In the U.S. a major factor was the decline in investment spending, which fell by about 90% in the 1930s. Global Perspective 10-2 shows the depression was worldwide.

    1. In the U.S. overcapacity and business indebtedness had resulted from excessive expansion by businesses in the 1920s, during a period of prosperity. Expansion of the

auto industry ended as the market became saturated, and this affected related industries of petroleum, rubber, steels, glass, and textiles.

2. A decline in residential construction followed the boom of the 1920s, which had resulted from population growth and a need for housing following World War I.

3. In October 1929, a dramatic crash in stock market values occurred, causing pessimism and highly unfavorable conditions for acquiring additional investment funds.

4. The nation's money supply fell as a result of Federal Reserve monetary policies and other forces.

B. The Vietnam War era inflation provides an example of an inflationary gap period.

1. The policies of the Kennedy and Johnson administrations had called for fiscal incentives to increase aggregate demand. A tax credit encouraged investment spending.

2. Unemployment levels had fallen from 5.2 percent in 1964 to 4.5 percent in 1965.

3. The Vietnam War resulted in a 40 percent rise in government defense expenditures and a draft that removed young people from potential unemployment. The unemployment rate fell below 4 percent from 1966 to 1969.

4. In terms of Figure 10-8, the boom in investment and government spending boosted the aggregate expenditures schedule upward and created a sizable inflationary gap.

C. The End of the Japanese Growth "Miracle."

1. Japanese economic growth was high, 9.7% annual average from 1966-1974 and 3.9% annually from 1974-1990. Unemployment was very low.

2. In 1990s its economy slowed to a halt.

3. Why did growth stop? Japan has a high saving rate, and when planned investment fell below saving, aggregate expenditures were below output. An unplanned inventory rise led firms to cut back production and a recessionary gap results.

4. It is difficult to reverse this cycle.

VII. **Limitations of the Model**

A. The aggregate expenditures model has four limitations.

1. The model can account for demand-pull inflation, but it does not indicate the extent of inflation when there is an inflationary gap. It doesn't measure inflation.

2. It doesn't explain how inflation can occur before the economy reaches full employment.

3. It doesn't indicate how the economy could produce beyond full-employment output for a time.

4. The model does not address the possibility of cost-push type of inflation.

B. In Chapter 11, these deficiencies are remedied with a related aggregate demand-aggregate supply model.

VIII. **LAST WORD: Squaring the Economic Circle**

A. Humorist Art Buchwald illustrates the concept of the multiplier with this funny essay.

B. Hofberger, a Chevy salesman in Tomcat, Va., called up Littleton of Littleton Menswear & Haberdashery, and told him that a new Nova had been set aside for Littleton and his wife.

C. Littleton said he was sorry, but he couldn't buy a car because he and Mrs. Littleton were getting a divorce.

D. Soon afterward, Bedcheck the painter called Hofberger to ask when to begin painting the Hofbergers' home. Hofberger said he couldn't, because Littleton was getting a divorce, not buying a new car, and, therefore, Hofberger could not afford to paint his house.

E. When Bedcheck went home that evening, he told his wife to return their new television set to Gladstone's TV store. When she returned it the next day, Gladstone immediately called his travel agent and canceled his trip. He said he couldn't go because Bedcheck returned the TV set because Hofberger didn't sell a car to Littleton because Littletons are divorcing.

F. Sandstorm, the travel agent, tore up Gladstone's plane tickets, and immediately called his banker, Gripsholm, to tell him that he couldn't pay back his loan that month.

G. When Rudemaker came to the bank to borrow money for a new kitchen for his restaurant, the banker told him that he had no money to lend because Sandstorm had not repaid his loan yet.

H. Rudemaker called his contractor, Eagleton, who had to lay off eight men.

I. Meanwhile, General Motors announced it would give a rebate on its new models. Hofberger called Littleton to tell him that he could probably afford a car even with the divorce. Littleton said that he and his wife had made up and were not divorcing. However, his business was so lousy that he couldn't afford a car now. His regular customers, Bedcheck, Gladstone, Sandstorm, Gripsholm, Rudemaker, and Eagleton had not been in for over a month!

ANSWERS TO END-OF-CHAPTER QUESTIONS

10-1 What effect will each of the changes designated in question 3 at the end of Chapter 9 have on the equilibrium level of GDP? Explain your answers.

a. A large increase in the value of real estate, including private houses.

b. The threat of limited, nonnuclear war, leading the public to expect future shortages of consumer durables.

c. A decline in the real interest rate.

d. A sharp, sustained decline in stock prices.

e. An increase in the rate of population growth.

f. The development of a cheaper method of manufacturing computer chips.

g. A sizable increase in the retirement age for collecting social security benefits.

h. The expectation that mild inflation will persist in the next decade.

i. An increase in the Federal personal income tax.

(a) If this means people have become more wealthy, then their consumption schedule will shift up and GDP will rise by a multiple of the increase in consumption.

(b) The increased consumption will increase GDP temporarily.

(c) This will increase interest-sensitive consumer purchases and investment, causing GDP to increase.

(d) By reducing consumption (because households will feel—or be—less wealthy, or because they fear a recession) and by decreasing investment, the AE schedule will shift downward, causing the GDP to decline.

(e) This will increase AE, causing GDP to increase.

(f) Investment will increase both because of increased profitability and because of increased innovations, causing GDP to increase.

(g) The announcement will lead to an upward shift of the current saving schedule (downward shift of the consumption schedule), causing GDP to decline.

(h) To the extent that this leads to increased buying for, say, a year, the AE schedule will shift upward for a year, leading to a temporary increase in GDP.

(i) An increase in the personal income tax will decrease the level of disposable income, and decrease consumer spending, which could mean a decline in aggregate expenditures. But if the government increases its purchases to the extent of the tax increase, then aggregate expenditures will actually increase, since consumer expenditures fall only by a fraction of the decline in income and government spending is more than offsetting this decline. If this happens, the equilibrium level of GDP should rise. On the other hand, if government spending does not rise, then the equilibrium level of GDP may fall as private spending falls.

10-2 (*Key Question*) What is the multiplier effect? What relationship does the MPC bear to the size of the multiplier? The MPS? What will the multiplier be when the MPS is 0, .4, .6, and 1? When the MPC is 1, .90, .67, .50, and 0? How much of a change in GDP will result if businesses increase their level of investment by \$8 billion and the MPC in the economy is .80? If the MPC is .67? Explain the difference between the simple and the complex multiplier.

The multiplier effect is the magnified increase in equilibrium GDP that occurs when any component of aggregate expenditures changes. The greater the MPC (the smaller the MPS), the greater the multiplier.

MPS = 0, multiplier = infinity; MPS = .4, multiplier = 2.5; MPS = .6, multiplier = 1.67; MPS = 1, multiplier = 1.

MPC = 1; multiplier = infinity; MPC = .9, multiplier = 10; MPC = .67; multiplier = 3; MPC = .5, multiplier = 2; MPC = 0, multiplier = 1.

MPC = .8: Change in GDP = \$40 billion (= \$8 billion ∞ multiplier of 5); MPC = .67: Change in GDP = \$24 billion (\$8 billion ∞ multiplier of 3). The simple multiplier takes account of only the leakage of saving. The complex multiplier also takes account of leakages of taxes and imports, making the complex multiplier less than the simple multiplier.

10-3 Graphically depict the aggregate expenditures model for a private closed economy. Next, show a decrease in the aggregate expenditures schedule and explain why the decrease in real GDP in your diagram is greater than the initial decline in aggregate expenditures. What would be the ratio of a decline in real GDP to the initial drop in aggregate expenditures if the slope of your aggregate expenditures schedule were .8?

If the slope of the aggregate expenditures schedule were .75, then the MPC = .75 and the MPS = .25. Therefore, the multiplier would be 1/(.25) = 4. The ratio of decline in real GDP to the initial drop of expenditures would be a ratio of 4:1. That is, if expenditures declined by \$5 billion, GDP should decline by \$20 billion. On the graph it can be seen that a one-unit decline in (C + I) leads to a four-unit decline in real GDP.

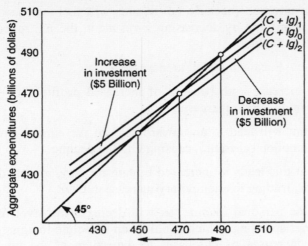

Real domestic product, GDP (billions of dollars)

10-4   Suppose that Zumo has an MPC of .9 and real GDP of $400 billion. If investment spending falls by $4 billion, what will be its new level of real GDP? The multiplier is 10 or $1/(1-.9)$ so $10 \times -\$4$ billion = -$40 billion. The new GDP is $400 billion - $40 billion = $360 billion.

10-5   (*Key Question*) The data in columns 1 and 2 of the table below are for a private closed economy.

(1) Real domestic output (GDP=DI) billions	(2) Aggregate expenditures private closed economy, billions	(3) Exports, billions	(4) Imports, billions	(5) Net exports, private economy	(6) Aggregate expenditures, open billions
$200	$240	$20	$30	$_____	$_____
$250	$280	$20	$30	$_____	$_____
$300	$320	$20	$30	$_____	$_____
$350	$360	$20	$30	$_____	$_____
$400	$400	$20	$30	$_____	$_____
$450	$440	$20	$30	$_____	$_____
$500	$480	$20	$30	$_____	$_____
$550	$520	$20	$30	$_____	$_____

a.   Use columns 1 and 2 to determine the equilibrium GDP for this hypothetical economy.

b.   Now open this economy for international trade by including the export and import figures of columns 3 and 4. Calculate net exports and determine the equilibrium GDP for the open economy. Explain why equilibrium GDP differs from the closed economy.

c.   Given the original $20 billion level of exports, what would be the equilibrium GDP if imports were $10 billion greater at each level of GDP? Or $10 billion less at each level of GDP? What generalization concerning the level of imports and the equilibrium GDP do these examples illustrate?

d.   What is the size of the multiplier in these examples?

(a) Equilibrium GDP for closed economy = $400 billion.

(b) Net export data for column 5 (top to bottom); $-10 billion in each space. Aggregate expenditure data for column 6 (top to bottom): $230; $270; $310; $350; $390; $430; $470; $510. Equilibrium GDP for the open economy is $350 billion, $50 billion below the $400 billion equilibrium GDP for the closed economy. The $-10 billion of net exports is a leakage which reduces equilibrium GDP by $50 billion.

(c) Imports = $40 billion: Aggregate expenditures in the private open economy would fall by $10 billion at each GDP level and the new equilibrium GDP would be $300 billion. Imports = $20 billion: Aggregate expenditures would increase by $10 billion; new equilibrium GDP would be $400 billion. Exports constant, increases in imports reduce GDP; decreases in imports increase GDP.

(d) Since every rise of $50 billion in GDP increases aggregate expenditures by $40 billion, the MPC is .8 and so the multiplier is 5.

10-6   Assume that, without taxes, the consumption schedule of an economy is as shown below:

GDP, billions	Consumption, billions
$100	$120
200	200
300	280
400	360
500	440
600	520
700	600

a. Graph this consumption schedule and note the size of the MPC.

b. Assume now a lump-sum tax system is imposed such that the government collects $10 billion in taxes at all levels of GDP. Graph the resulting consumption schedule and compare the MPC and the multiplier with that of the pretax consumption schedule.

(a) The size of the MPC is 80/100 or .8 because consumption changes by 80 when GDP changes by 100.

(b) The resulting consumption schedule will be exactly $10 billion below the original at all levels of GDP, because people now have to pay $10 billion in tax out of each level of income. The multiplier should be 5 because the MPS is .2 and 1/.2 is 5. We see on the graph that the equilibrium GDP has fallen to $150 billion. That is equilibrium GDP fell by $50 billion when expenditures fell by $10 billion, a multiple of 5 times the decline in expenditures.

10-7   Explain graphically the determination of equilibrium GDP for a private economy through the aggregate expenditures model. Now add government spending (any amount that you choose) to your graph, showing its impact on equilibrium GDP. Finally, add taxation (any amount of lump-sum tax that you choose) to your graph and show its effect on equilibrium GDP. Looking at your graph, determine whether equilibrium GDP has increased, decreased, or stayed the same in view of the sizes of the government spending and taxes that you selected.

Figure 10-5 and 10-6 show how to do this. Graphs and answers will differ depending on magnitude of changes.

10-8   (*Key Question*) Refer to columns 1 and 6 of the tabular data for question 5. Incorporate government into the table by assuming that it plans to tax and spend $20 billion at each possible level of GDP. Also assume that all taxes are personal taxes and that government spending does not induce a shift in the private aggregate expenditures schedule. Compute and explain the changes in equilibrium GDP caused by the addition of government.

Before G is added, open private sector equilibrium will be at 350. The addition of government expenditures of G to our analysis raises the aggregate expenditures ($C + I_g + X_n + G$) schedule and increases the equilibrium level of GDP as would an increase in C, 1_g, or X_n. Note that changes in government spending are subject to the multiplier effect. Government spending supplements private investment and export spending ($I_g + X + G$), increasing the equilibrium GDP to 450.

The addition of $20 billion of government expenditures and $20 billion of personal taxes increases equilibrium GDP from $350 to $370 billion. The $20 billion increase in *G raises* equilibrium GDP by $100 billion (= $20 billion x the multiplier of 5); the $20 billion increase in *T reduces* consumption by $16 billion at every level. (= $20 billion x the MPC of .8). This $16 billion decline in turn reduces equilibrium GDP by $80 billion ($16 billion x multiplier of 5). The net change from including balanced government spending and taxes is $20 billion (= $100 billion - $80 billion).

10-9   What is the balanced-budget multiplier? Demonstrate the balanced-budget multiplier in terms of your answer to question 8. Explain: "Equal increases in government spending and tax revenues of *n* dollars will increase the equilibrium GDP by *n* dollars." Does this hold true regardless of the size of MPS? Why or why not?

The balanced-budget multiplier stems from the fact that increases in government spending go directly into the flow of aggregate expenditures. Whereas the tax increase first reduces incomes by the amount of the tax, but spending will be reduced by a fraction of the income reduction (the fraction will be equal to the MPC), and the multiplier effect will work in opposite directions on the increase and the reduction in spending. But the reduction will be less than the increase due to the initial government spending influx, which was not affected by the MPC. Since this initial "shot" of government spending was not offset by an equal and opposite effect on the downside from the tax increase, it is an addition to the aggregate expenditures flow which just equals the change in government spending. Thus, we say the balanced budget multiplier is equal to 1.

In question 8, the added government spending alone would increase GDP by 5 ∞ $20 billion, and the tax increase would reduce GDP by 5 ∞ $16 billion, for a net change of ($ 100 - $80) billion or $20 billion. This is equal to 1 ∞ the change in G so the balanced budget multiplier is 1 in this example. (Note: The multiplier is 5 because MPS = .2 and 1/.2 = 5. The tax increase reduces consumer spending by $16 billion because the tax reduces incomes by $20, and this will reduce spending by a factor equal to the MPC, or 8 x $20 billion.)

The quote does hold true regardless of the size of the MPS. This is true because the only increase in expenditures that will occur is a result of the initial change in government spending. Beyond that, increases in spending from the "ripple" effect of the initial change in G will be exactly offset by decreases in spending which result from the "ripple" effect caused by the higher taxes. It doesn't matter whether the multiplier is 10 or 2, the offsetting effect will occur on all changes except the initial increase in government spending.

10-10   (*Key Question*) Refer to the accompanying table in answering the questions which follow:

(1) Possible levels of employment, millions	(2) Real domestic output, billions	(2) Real domestic output, billions
90	$500	$520
100	550	560
110	600	600
120	650	640
130	700	680

a. If full employment in this economy is 130 million, will there be an inflationary or recessionary gap? What will be the consequence of this gap? By how much would aggregate expenditures in column 3 have to change at each level of GDP to eliminate the inflationary or recessionary gap? Explain.

b. Will there be an inflationary or recessionary gap if the full-employment level of output is $500 billion? Explain the consequences. By how much would aggregate expenditures in column 3 have to change at each level of GDP to eliminate the inflationary or recessionary gap? Explain.

c. Assuming that investment, net exports, and government expenditures do not change with changes in real GDP, what are the sizes of the MPC, the MPS, and the multiplier?

(a) A recessionary gap. Equilibrium GDP is $600 billion, while full employment GDP is $700 billion. Employment will be 20 million less than at full employment. Aggregate expenditures would have to increase by $20 billion (= $700 billion -$680 billion) at each level of GDP to eliminate the recessionary gap.

(b) An inflationary gap. Aggregate expenditures will be excessive, causing demand-pull inflation. Aggregate expenditures would have to *fall* by $20 billion (= $520 billion -$500 billion) at each level of GDP to eliminate the inflationary gap.

(c) MPC = .8 (= $40 billion/$50 billion); MPS = .2 (= 1 -.8); multiplier = 5 (= 1/.2).

10-11 (*Advanced analysis*) Assume the consumption schedule for a private open economy is such that $C = 50 + 0.8Y$. Assume further that planned investment and net exports are independent of the level of income and constant at $I_g = 30$ and $X_n = 10$. Recall also that in equilibrium the real output produced (Y) is equal to the aggregate expenditures: $Y = C + I_g + X_n$.

a Calculate the equilibrium level of income for this economy. Check your work by expressing the consumption, investment, and net export schedules in tabular form and determining the equilibrium GDP.

b What will happen to equilibrium Y if I_g changes to 10? What does this tell you about the size of the multiplier?

(a) $Y = C + I_g + X_n = \$50 + 0.8Y + \$30 + \$10 = 0.8Y + \$90$

Therefore $Y - 0.8Y = \$90$, and $0.2Y = \$90$, so $Y = \$450$ at equilibrium.

Real domestic output (GDP = YI)	C	I_g	X_n	Aggregate expenditures, open economy
$ 0	$ 50	$30	$10	$90
50	90	30	10	130
100	130	30	10	170
150	170	30	10	210
200	210	30	10	250
250	250	30	10	290
300	290	30	10	330
350	330	30	10	370
400	370	30	10	410
450	410	30	10	450
500	450	30	10	490

(b) If I_g decreases from $30 to $10, the new equilibrium GDP will be at GDP of $350, for with I_g now $10 this is where AE also equals $350. This indicates that the multiplier equals 5, for a decline in AE of $20 has led to a decline in equilibrium GDP of $100. The size of the multiplier could also have been calculated directly from the MPC of 0.8 .

10-12 (*Last Word*) What is the central economic idea humorously illustrated in Art Buchwald's piece, "Squaring the Economic Circle"?

The central idea illustrated is the multiplier effect that exists in a market economic system. One independently determined change in spending has an effect on another's income, which then sets in motion a chain of events whereby spending changes directly with the income changes. A decline in spending begins a chain of declines, or, in other words, the initial decrease in spending is multiplied in terms of the final effect of this single decision. This occurs because of the observation that any change in income causes a change in spending that is directly proportional to it.

CHAPTER ELEVEN
AGGREGATE DEMAND AND AGGREGATE SUPPLY

CHAPTER OVERVIEW

The aggregate expenditures model developed in Chapters 9 and 10 is a fixed-price-level model. Its focus is on changes in real GDP, not on changes in the price level. This chapter introduces a variable-price model in which it is possible to simultaneously analyze changes in real GDP and the price level. This distinction should be made explicit for those students who have covered Chapters 9 and 10. What students learn in this chapter will help organize their thoughts about equilibrium GDP, the price level, and government macroeconomic policies. The tools learned will be applied in later chapters.

The present chapter introduces the concepts of aggregate demand and aggregate supply, explaining the shapes of the aggregate demand and aggregate supply curves and the forces causing them to shift. The equilibrium levels of prices and real GDP are considered. Finally, the chapter analyzes the effects of shifts in the aggregate demand and/or aggregate supply curves on the price level and size of real GDP.

WHAT'S NEW

Major revisions are under the heading "Changes in Equilibrium." The new subtitles are related to demand-pull inflation, the multiplier in presence of price level changes, decreases in aggregate demand and employment, cost-push inflation, and increases in aggregate supply with full-employment and price stability. The derivation of the AD curve from AE has been reworked.

Discussion of the "ratchet effect" has been deleted. The term "wealth effect" is changed to "real balances effect" through out. Other changes improve clarity. The Last Word has been updated. Finally, a new Internet Question was added.

INSTRUCTIONAL OBJECTIVES

After completing this chapter, students should be able to:

1. Define aggregate demand and aggregate supply.

2. Give three reasons why the aggregate demand curve slopes downward.

3. Illustrate, label, and explain the three ranges of the aggregate supply curve.

4. State the determinants of the aggregate demand curve's location.

5. Explain the shape of the aggregate supply curve.

6. Indicate the determinants of the supply curve's location.

7. Explain how a market economy moves to equilibrium price and output level.

8. Predict effects of an increase in aggregate demand when economy is in (a) horizontal range, (b) intermediate range, and (c) vertical range.

9. Explain how the multiplier is weakened in the intermediate or vertical range of aggregate supply.

10. State three basic causes of changes in aggregate supply differentiating between leftward and rightward shifts of the curve.

11. Define and identify terms and concepts at the end of the chapter.

COMMENTS AND TEACHING SUGGESTIONS

1. The aggregate demand-aggregate supply model will be used repeatedly for discussion of unemployment, inflation, and economic growth in other chapters. It is important for students to understand the basics in this chapter.

2. While it is helpful to show the similarities between the aggregate model and single-product supply and demand markets explained in Chapter 3, you need to highlight the differences between the two models.

3. The concepts of demand-pull and cost-push inflation, which were introduced earlier, can be analyzed graphically by using the aggregate demand-aggregate supply model (see Figures 11-11 and 11-12).

4. If you have a number of students in your class who are business majors or pursuing careers in business, you may wish to emphasize the section on productivity. The relationship between productivity growth and lower per unit cost of output is important.

STUDENT STUMBLING BLOCKS

1. The difference between aggregate demand-aggregate supply (AD-AS) model and the demand-supply analysis for a single product market is difficult for students to grasp. The similarities are so great that students often don't focus on the important differences between the two models.

2. Students will to confuse changes in demand and changes in supply. For example, if asked about an increase in export sales of wheat, some students will inevitably view this as a decrease in supply, because wheat leaves the country. Repetition of the determinants of demand and supply can help clarify the distinction.

LECTURE NOTES

I. **Introduction to AD-AS Model**

   A. AD-AS model is a variable price model. The aggregate expenditures model in Chapters 9 and 10 assumed constant price.

   B. AD-AS model provides insights on inflation, unemployment and economic growth.

II. **Aggregate demand is a schedule that shows the various amounts of real domestic output that domestic and foreign buyers will desire to purchase at each possible price level.**

   A. The aggregate demand curve is shown in Figure 11-1.

   1. It shows an inverse relationship between price level and domestic output.

   2. The explanation of the inverse relationship is not the same as for demand for a single product, which centered on substitution and income effects.

      a. Substitution effect doesn't apply in the aggregate case, since there is no substitute for "everything."

      b. Income effect also doesn't apply in the aggregate case, since income now varies with aggregate output.

   3. What is the explanation of inverse relationship between price level and real output in aggregate demand?

a. Real balances effect: When price level falls, the purchasing power of existing financial balances rises, which can increase spending.

b. Interest-rate effect: A decline in price level means lower interest rates which can increase levels of certain types of spending.

c. Foreign purchases effect: When price level falls, other things being equal, U.S. prices will fall relative to foreign prices, which will tend to increase spending on U.S. exports and also decrease import spending in favor of U.S. products that compete with imports.

B. Deriving AD-curve from aggregate expenditures model. (See Figure 11-2)

1. Both models measure real GDP on horizontal axis.

2. Suppose initial price level is P_1 and aggregate expenditures AE_1 as shown in Figure 11-2a. Then equilibrium GDP is GDP_1. This is shown in Figure 11-2b.

3. If price rises to P_2, aggregate expenditures will fall to AE_2 because purchasing power of wealth falls, interest rates may rise, and net exports fall. (See Figure 11-2a) Then new equilibrium is at GDP_2 shown also in Figure 11-2b.

4. If price rises to P_3, real asset balance value falls, interest rates rise again, net exports fall and new equilibrium is at GDP_3. Again see Figures 11-2a and 11-2b.

C. Determinants of aggregate demand: Determinants are the "other things" (besides price level) that can cause a shift or change in demand (see Figure 11-3 in text). Effects of the following determinants are discussed in more detail in the text.

1. Changes in consumer spending, which can be caused by changes in several factors.

a. Consumer wealth,

b. Consumer expectations,

c. Consumer indebtedness, and

d. Taxes.

2. Changes in investment spending, which can be caused by changes in several factors.

a. Interest rates,

b. Profit expectations,

c. Business taxes,

d. Technology, and

e. Amount of excess capacity.

3. A change in government spending is another determinant.

4. Changes in net export spending unrelated to price level, which may be caused by changes in other factors such as:

a. Income abroad, and

b. Exchange rates: Depreciation of the dollar encourages U.S. exports since U.S. products become less expensive when foreign buyers can obtain more dollars for their currency. Conversely, dollar depreciation discourages import buying in the U.S. because our dollars can't be exchanged for as much foreign currency.

C. Aggregate demand shifts and the aggregate expenditures model:

1. When there is a change in one of the determinants of aggregate demand, there will be a change in the aggregate expenditures as well. Look at Figure 11-4.

2. If price level remains constant, then a change in aggregate expenditures is multiplied and the real output rises by more than the initial change in spending (see the lower part of Figure 11-4). The text illustrates the multiplier effect of a change in investment spending.

III. **Aggregate supply is a schedule showing level of real domestic output available at each possible price level.**

A. Aggregate supply curve may be viewed as having three distinct segments. See Figure 11-5.

1. Horizontal range: where the price level remains constant with substantial output variation. In this range substantial unemployment and excess capacity exist. Economy is far below full-employment output level.

2. Intermediate (upsloping) range: where the expansion of real output is accompanied by rising price level, near to where the full-employment level of output exists. Per unit production costs rise in this stage because as resource markets near full employment their prices will be bid up and, therefore, producer costs rise.

3. Vertical range: where absolute full capacity is assumed, and any attempt to increase output will bid up resource and product prices. We assume full-employment occurs at the "natural rate of unemployment."

B. Determinants of aggregate supply: Determinants are the "other things" besides price level that cause changes or shifts in aggregate supply (see Figure 11-6 in text). The following determinants are discussed in more detail in the text.

1. A change in input prices, which can be caused by changes in several factors.

    a. Availability of resources (land, labor, capital, entrepreneurial ability),

    b. Prices of imported resources, and

    c. Market power in certain industries.

2. Change in productivity (productivity = real output / input) can cause changes in per-unit production cost (production cost per unit = total input cost / units of output). If productivity rises, unit production costs will fall. This can shift aggregate supply to the right and lower prices. The reverse is true when productivity falls. Productivity improvement is very important in business efforts to reduce costs.

3. Change in legal-institutional environment, which can be caused by changes in other factors.

    a. Business taxes and/or subsidies,

    b. Government regulation.

IV. **Equilibrium: Real Output and the Price Level**

A. Equilibrium price and quantity are found where the aggregate demand and supply curves intersect. (See Key Graph 11-7a,b for illustration of why quantity will seek equilibrium where curves intersect.) (Key Questions 4 and 7)

B. Try Quick Quiz 11-7.

C. Shifting aggregate demand when a determinant changes will change the equilibrium.

1. Demand-pull inflation: Shifts in the intermediate and vertical ranges will cause demand-pull inflation with an increase in aggregate demand (Figures 11-8b and c).

2. Shifts in the horizontal range will cause quantity changes but not price level (Figure 11-8a).

D. The multiplier effect is weakened with price level changes in intermediate and vertical ranges of aggregate supply. Real GDP does not change as much in Figure 11-8c as it does in Figures 11-8a even though the aggregate demand shifts are of equal magnitude. Figure 11-9 combines the effects of Figures 11-8a and b. Conclusion: The more price level increases, the less effect any increase in aggregate demand will have in increasing real GDP.

E. Decreases in AD: If AD decreases, recession and cyclical unemployment may result. See Figure 11-10. Prices don't fall easily.

1. Wage contracts are not flexible so businesses can't afford to reduce prices.

2. Also, employers are reluctant to cut wages because of impact on employee effort, etc.

3. Minimum wage laws keep wages above that level.

4. So-called menu costs are difficult to change.

5. Fear of price wars keep prices from being reduced also.

F. Shifting aggregate supply occurs when a supply determinant changes. (See Key Questions 5, 7, 8):

1. Leftward shift in curve illustrates cost-push inflation (see Figure 11-11).

2. Rightward shift in curve will cause a decline in price level (see Figure 11-12). See text for discussion of this desirable outcome.

V. **LAST WORD: Why Is Unemployment in Europe So High?**

A. Several European economies have had high rates of unemployment in the past several years, even before their recessions.

1. In 2000: France, 9.7 percent; Italy, 10.7 percent; Germany, 8.3 percent.

2. These rates compare to a 4.0 percent unemployment rate at the same time in U.S.

B. Reasons for high European unemployment rates:

1. High natural rates of unemployment exist due to frictional and structural unemployment. This results from government policies and union contracts, which increase the costs of hiring and reduce the cost of being unemployed.

   a. High minimum wages exist.

   b. Generous welfare benefits exist for unemployed.

   c. Restrictions against firings discourage employment.

   d. Thirty to forty days of paid vacation and holidays boost the cost of hiring.

   e. High worker absenteeism reduces productivity.

   f. High employer cost of fringe benefits discourages hiring.

2. Deficient aggregate demand may also be a cause as shown in Figure 11-7b. European governments have feared inflation and have not undertaken expansionary monetary or fiscal policies. If they did, aggregate demand would expand, and unemployment rates might drop without inflation.

3. Conclusion: Economists in Europe are not sure whether aggregate demand is near full-employment (Figure 11-7a) or is below full employment.

ANSWERS TO END-OF-CHAPTER QUESTIONS

11-1 Why is the aggregate demand curve downsloping? Specify how your explanation differs from the explanation for the downsloping demand curve for a single product.

The aggregate demand (AD) curve shows that as the price level drops, purchases of real domestic output increase. The AD curve slopes downward for three reasons. The first is the interest-rate effect. We assume the supply of money to be fixed. When the price level increases, more money is needed to make purchases and pay for inputs. With the money supply fixed, the increased demand for it will drive up its price, the rate of interest. These higher rates will decrease the buying of goods with borrowed money, thus decreasing the amount of real output demanded.

The second reason is the wealth or real balances effect. As the price level rises, the real value—the purchasing power—of money and other accumulated financial assets (bonds, for instance) will decrease. People will therefore become poorer in real terms and decrease the quantity demanded of real output.

The third reason is the foreign purchases effect. As the United States' price level rises relative to other countries, Americans will buy more abroad in preference to their own output. At the same time foreigners, finding American goods and services relatively more expensive, will decrease their buying of American exports. Thus, with increased imports and decreased exports, American net exports decrease and so, therefore, does the quantity demanded of American real output.

These reasons for the downsloping AD curve have nothing to do with the reasons for the downsloping single-product demand curve. In the case of the dropping price of a single product, the consumer with a constant money income substitutes more of the now relatively cheaper product for those whose prices have not changed. Also, the consumer has become richer in real terms, because of the lower price of the one product, and can buy more of it and all other products. But with the AD curve, moving down the curve means all prices are dropping—the price level is dropping. Therefore, the single-product substitution effect does not apply. Also, whereas when dealing with the demand for a single product the consumer's income is assumed to be fixed, the AD curve specifically excludes this assumption. Movement down the AD curve indicates lower prices but, with regard to the circular flow of economic activity, it also indicates lower incomes. If prices are dropping, so must the receipts or revenues or incomes of the sellers. Thus, a decline in the price level does not necessarily imply an increase in the nominal income of the economy as a whole.

11-2 Explain the shape of the aggregate supply curve, and account for the horizontal, intermediate, and vertical ranges of the curve.

In the horizontal range of the aggregate supply (AS) curve, the economy is in a severe recession, so that there is a large GDP gap—much excess capacity—because of deficient aggregate demand (AD). In these circumstances, AD can increase without pulling the price level upward.

In the intermediate, or upsloping, range of the AS curve, the economy is clearly in the recovery phase of the business cycle and the price level moves up more and more as AD increases. The economy as a whole nears the full employment level of output, as some firms, some industries, are at or close enough to their capacity production that they believe they can—or are forced to—raise their prices to equate the quantity they supply with increasing demand. Moreover, some essential inputs are fully employed—some skilled labor, certain raw materials—and firms must bid against each other in order to increase their production. Thus, costs—and prices—start to rise in the economy, pushing up the price level as full employment is reached.

In the vertical range of the AS curve, absolute full capacity has been reached; the economy, by definition, cannot produce any more (not until, through economic growth, the potential output of the economy has increased). Since the economy has attained its potential, any further increase in AD cannot be met by an increase in output. Therefore, the increase in AD results only in pure demand-pull inflation.

11-3   (*Optional Section Question*) Explain: "A change in the price level shifts the aggregate expenditures curve but not the aggregate demand curve."

A change in the price level does not shift the aggregate demand curve. It simply represents a movement along the curve, because there is an inverse relationship between the price level and aggregate quantity demanded.

However, a change in the price level will shift the aggregate expenditures curve, which responds to the wealth, interest-rate, and foreign purchases effects occurring with a change in price level. When the price level declines, aggregate expenditures will rise, and when the price level rises, aggregate expenditures will fall. The aggregate expenditures model assumes a constant price level, so it is expressed in "real" terms. Figure 11-2 graphically illustrates the relationship between the two models.

11-4   (*Key Question*) Suppose that aggregate demand and supply for a hypothetical economy are as shown:

Amount of real domestic output demanded, billions	Price level (price index)	Amount of real domestic output supplied, billions
$100	300	$400
200	250	400
300	200	300
400	150	200
500	150	100

a. Use these sets of data to graph the aggregate demand and supply curves. What will be the equilibrium price level and level of real domestic output in this hypothetical economy? Is the equilibrium real output also the absolute full-capacity real output? Explain.

b. Why will a price level of 150 not be an equilibrium price level in this economy? Why not 250?

c. Suppose that buyers desire to purchase $200 billion of extra real domestic output at each price level. What factors might cause this change in aggregate demand? What is the new equilibrium price level and level of real output? Over which range of the aggregate supply curve—horizontal, intermediate, or vertical—has equilibrium changed?

(a) See the graph. Equilibrium price level = 200. Equilibrium real output = $300 billion. No, the full-capacity level of GDP is $400 billion, where the AS curve becomes vertical

(b) At a price level of 150, real GDP supplied is a maximum of $200 billion, less than the real GDP demanded of $400 billion. The shortage of real output will drive the price level up. At a price level of 250, real GDP supplied is $400 billion, which is more than the real GDP demanded of $200 billion. The surplus of real output will drive down the price level. Equilibrium occurs at the price level at which AS and AD intersect.

See the graph. Increases in consumer, investment, government, or net export spending might shift the AD curve rightward. New equilibrium price level = 250. New equilibrium GDP = $400 billion. The intermediate range.

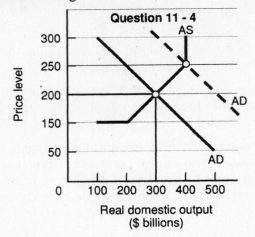

Question 11 - 4

11-5   (*Key Question*)   Suppose that the hypothetical economy in question 4 had the following relationship between its real domestic output and the input quantities necessary for producing that level of output:

a.   What is productivity in this economy?

b.   What is the per unit cost of production if the price of each input is $2?

c.   Assume that the input price increases from $2 to $3 with no accompanying change in productivity. What is the new per unit cost of production? In what direction did the $1 increase in input price push the aggregate supply curve? What effect would this shift in aggregate supply have upon the price level and the level of real output?

d.   Suppose that the increase in input price does not occur but instead that productivity increases by 100 percent. What would be the new per unit cost of production? What effect would this change in per unit production cost have on the aggregate supply curve? What effect would this shift in aggregate supply have on the price level and the level of real output?

Input quantity	Real domestic output
150.0	400
112.5	300
75.0	200

(a)   Productivity = 2.67(= 300/112.5).

(b)   Pre - unit cost of production = $.75(= $2×112.5/300).

(c)   New per unit production cost = $1.13.   The AS curve would shift leftward.   The price level would rise and real output would decrease.

(d)   New per unit cost of production = $0.375(= $2×112.5/600).
AS curve shifts to the right; price level declines and real output increases.

11-6   Distinguish between the "real-balances effect" and the "wealth effect," as the terms are used in this chapter. How does each relate to the aggregate demand curve?

The "real balances effect" refers to the impact of price level on the purchasing power of asset balances. If prices decline, the purchasing power of assets will rise, so spending at each income level should rise because people's assets are more valuable. The reverse outcome would occur at higher price levels. The "real balances effect" is one explanation of the inverse relationship between price level and quantity of expenditures.

The "wealth effect" assumes the price level is constant, but a change in consumer wealth causes a shift in consumer spending; the aggregate expenditures curve will shift right. For example, the value of stock market shares may rise and cause people to feel wealthier and spend more. A stock decline can cause a decline in consumer spending.

11-7   (*Key Question*) What effects would each of the following have on aggregate demand or aggregate supply? In each case use a diagram to show the expected effects on the equilibrium price level and level of real output. Assume that all other things remain constant.

   a.   A widespread fear of depression on the part of consumers.

   b.   A large purchase of U.S. wheat by Russia.

   c.   A $1 increase in the excise tax on cigarettes.

   d.   A reduction in interest rates at each price level.

   e.   A major cut in Federal spending for health care.

   f.   The expectation of a rapid rise in the price level.

   g.   The complete disintegration of OPEC, causing oil prices to fall by one-half.

   h.   A 10 percent reduction in personal income tax rates.

   i.   An increase in labor productivity.

   j.   A 12 percent increase in nominal wages.

   k.   Depreciation in the international value of the dollar.

   l.   A sharp decline in the national incomes of our western European trading partners.

   m.   A sizable increase in U.S. immigration.

   (a)   AD curve left

   (b)   AD curve right

   (c)   AS curve left

   (d)   AD curve right

   (e)   AD curve left

   (f)   AD curve right

   (g)   AS curve right

   (h)   AD curve right

   (i)   AS curve right

   (j)   AS curve left

   (k)   AD curve right; AS curve left

    (l) AD curve left

    (m) AS curve right.

11-8   (*Key Question*) Other things being equal, what effect will each of the following have on the equilibrium price level and level of real output:

    a. An increase in aggregate demand in the vertical range of aggregate supply.

    b. An increase in aggregate supply with no change in aggregate demand (assume prices and wages are flexible).

    c. Equal increases in aggregate demand and aggregate supply.

    d. A reduction in aggregate demand in the horizontal range of aggregate supply.

    e. An increase in aggregate demand and a decrease in aggregate supply.

    f. A decrease in aggregate demand in the intermediate range of aggregate supply

    (a) Price level rises and no change in real output

    (b) Price level drops and real output increases

    (c) Price level does not change, but real output rises

    (d) Price level does not change, but real output declines

    (e) Price level increases, but the change in real output is indeterminate

    (f) Price level may not change, but real output declines (if prices are flexible downward, then output will decline but not as much as if prices stay high)

11-9   (*Optional Section Question*) Suppose that the price level is constant and investment spending increases sharply. How would you show this increase in the aggregate expenditures model? What would be the outcome? How would you show this rise in investment in the aggregate demand-aggregate supply model? What range of the aggregate supply curve is involved?

An increase in investment spending represents an increase in aggregate expenditures and an upward shift in the aggregate expenditures curve. The outcome would be a new, greater equilibrium output level. This rise in output would be equal to a multiple of the initial change in investment spending based on the multiplier effect. The multiplier is 1/MPS in this model.

Because we are assuming the price level is constant with increased aggregate demand, the shift in aggregate demand occurs in the horizontal range of the aggregate supply curve. It would be a rightward shift of aggregate demand, and the new equilibrium output would fall to the right of the original equilibrium by the full extent of the shift in aggregate demand.

11-10   (*Optional Section Question*) Explain how an upsloping aggregate supply curve might weaken the multiplier.

An upward sloping aggregate supply curve weakens the effect of the multiplier because any increase in aggregate demand will have both a price and an output effect. For example, if aggregate demand grows by $110 million, this could represent an increase of $100 million in real output and $10 million in higher prices if the inflation rate averages 10 percent. The multiplier is weakened because some of the increase in aggregate demand is absorbed by the higher prices and real output does not change by the full extent of the change in aggregate demand.

11-11   Why does a reduction in aggregate demand reduce real output, rather than the price level?

A reduction in aggregate demand causes a decline in real output rather than the price level because prices are "sticky" or inflexible downward. If we assume prices are completely inflexible downward, then a reduction in demand is essentially moving leftward in the horizontal range of aggregate supply, which means reduced output at a constant price. To say prices are completely inflexible downward may exaggerate but prices don't fall easily for several reasons: wage contracts, minimum wage laws, employee morale, fear of price wars and the "menu cost" notion.

11-12 "Unemployment can be caused by a decrease in aggregate demand or a decrease in aggregate supply." Do you agree? Explain. In each case specify price-level effects.

Assuming the economy was not operating in the vertical range of the AS curve, the statement is true. In either case, the new point of intersection is to the left of the previous position, denoting a decrease in real domestic output and, therefore, assuming no change in productivity, necessarily an increase in unemployment.

However, assuming complete flexibility of prices and wages, the decrease in AD will result in a lower price level, whereas the decrease in AS will result in a higher price level. From the point of view of price stability, therefore, the decrease in AD is preferable. If the economy were in the horizontal range initially, there would be no price changes in either case.

11-13 Use shifts in the AD and AS curves to explain (a) the U.S. experience of strong economic growth, full employment, and price stability in the late 1990s and early 2000s; (b) how a strong positive wealth effect could cause demand-pull inflation even though productivity growth in surging; and (c) how a strong negative wealth effect from say, a precipitous drop in the stock market, could cause a recession even though productivity is surging.

(a) While AD is increasing and shifting to right, AS is shifting rightward as well, because of productivity increasing and growing labor force. Thus, both output and employment can rise while price level remains constant. The equilibrium shifts rightward, not upward because AS and AD shift by similar magnitudes.

(b) In this situation both AD and AS shift right, but AD increases by more so that the increase in AD ends up in vertical range of AS.

(c) In this situation AD shifts left while AS shifts right. Price level may even decline, but real output could decline if the reduction in AD exceeds the increase is AS. Figure 11-10 shows how this could happen even if AS shifted to the right.

11-14 (*Last Word*) State the alternative views on why unemployment in Europe has recently been so high. Discuss the policy implications of each view.

There are two views on this question. One is that there is a high natural rate of unemployment in each of the European countries in question. This view holds that there are high levels of frictional and structural unemployment which accompany the full-employment level of output. Any increase in aggregate demand would cause demand-pull inflation. The sources of the high frictional and structural unemployment are government policies and union contracts, which increase the costs of hiring and reduce the costs of not having a job. For example, there are high minimum wages; generous welfare benefits; restrictions against firing, which discourage firms from employing workers; thirty to forty days of paid vacation per year; high worker absenteeism, which reduces productivity; and high employer costs of health, pension, disability, and other benefits.

The second explanation disagrees with the first and sees the major problem as being deficient aggregate demand. Those economists who hold this view point to government policies that are aimed at preventing inflation and not at increasing aggregate demand. In this view, the European economies are operating in the horizontal range of their aggregate supply curves and, increases in aggregate demand would not be inflationary but would, instead, increase output and employment.

CHAPTER TWELVE
FISCAL POLICY

CHAPTER OVERVIEW

This chapter looks briefly at the legislative mandates given to government to pursue stabilization of the economy; it then explores the tools of government stabilization policy in terms of the aggregate demand-aggregate (AD-AS) model. Next, some fiscal policy measures that automatically adjust government expenditures and tax revenues when the economy moves through the business cycle phases are examined. Finally, problems, criticism, and complications of government's fiscal policy are addressed.

WHAT'S NEW

The full-employment budget discussion has been revised and clarified in a section entitled "Evaluating Fiscal Policy." Current real-world budget surpluses eliminated the need to emphasize the structural deficit. Also the section on budget's expansionary bias has been deleted. Tables and graphs have been updated and revised for clarity. End-of-chapter questions 7 and 9 and Internet questions are new.

INSTRUCTIONAL OBJECTIVES

After completing this chapter, students should be able to:

1. Identify the Employment Act of 1946 and the roles of the CEA and JEC.

2. Distinguish between discretionary and nondiscretionary fiscal policy.

3. Differentiate between expansionary and contractionary fiscal policy.

4. Recognize the conditions for recommending an expansionary or contractionary fiscal policy.

5. Explain expansionary fiscal policy and its effects on the economy and Federal budget.

6. Explain contractionary fiscal policy and its effects on the economy and Federal budget.

7. Describe the two ways to finance a government budget deficit and how each affects the economy.

8. Describe the two ways to handle a government budget surplus and how each affects the economy.

9. Give two examples of how built-in stabilizers help eliminate recession or inflation.

10. Explain the differential impacts of progressive, proportional, and regressive taxes in terms of stabilization policy.

11. Explain the significance of the "full-employment budget" concept.

12. List three timing problems encountered with fiscal policy.

13. State political problems that limit effective fiscal policy.

14. Explain and recognize graphically how crowding out and inflation can reduce the effectiveness of fiscal policy.

15. Give two examples of complications that may arise when fiscal policy interacts with international trade.

16. Give an example of supply-side fiscal policy and three possible positive effects from it.

17. Define and identify terms and concepts at the end of the chapter.

COMMENTS AND TEACHING SUGGESTIONS

1. Fiscal policy, especially tax policy, is one of the subjects that students usually find very interesting. The chapter provides an excellent opportunity to establish the ties between theory and real-world applications.

2. To give a more human dimension to this chapter, students may identify current members of the Council of Economic Advisers (end-of-chapter question #1). You could assign excerpts from the latest Economic Report of the President, which the Council helps to prepare.

3. Current federal tax or spending issues can illustrate the timing, administrative, and political problems with discretionary fiscal policy. The 2001 tax cut proposal illustrated many of these issues.

4. Current data on the federal budget can be obtained from the *Federal Reserve Bulletin*, *Economic Indicators*, the *Survey of Current Business*, or the *Economic Report of the President* or websiste given in web-based question #18.

5. Remind students of the multiplier impact that results from changes in government spending and/or taxes. Most students can understand these concepts without reference to the numerical examples. Numbers often confuse those with "math anxiety," and if you skipped Chapters 9 and 10, they will benefit from a brief overview of the concept.

6. The Last Word for the chapter is on the "leading indicators." The stock market often reacts immediately to changes in various indicators. One assignment could focus on the impact of latest report.

STUDENT STUMBLING BLOCKS

1. The biggest concern is with the magnitude of information in this chapter. Give students an opportunity to focus on a few concepts at a time rather than assigning the entire chapter at once.

2. Although most students know this, some need to be reminded how Congress and the President establish fiscal policy. This is particularly important when highlighting the different policy-making process for monetary policy.

LECTURE NOTES

I. **Introduction**

    A. One major function of the government is to stabilize the economy (prevent unemployment or inflation).

    B. Stabilization can be achieved in part by manipulating the public budget—government spending and tax collections—to increase output and employment or to reduce inflation.

    C. This chapter will examine a number of topics.

        1. It will look at the legislative mandates given government to pursue stabilization.

        2. It explores the tools of government fiscal stabilization policy using AD-AS model.

        3. Both discretionary and automatic fiscal adjustments are examined.

        4. The problems, criticisms, and complications of fiscal policy are addressed.

II. **Legislative mandates—The Employment Act of 1946**

    A. Congress proclaimed government's role in promoting maximum employment, production, and purchasing power.

B. The Act created the Council of Economic Advisers to advise the President on economic matters.

C. It created the Joint Economic Committee of Congress to investigate economic problems of national interest.

III. **Fiscal Policy and the AD/AS Model**

A. Discretionary fiscal policy refers to the deliberate manipulation of taxes and government spending by Congress to alter real domestic output and employment, control inflation, and stimulate economic growth. "Discretionary" means the changes are at the option of the Federal government.

B. Simplifying assumptions:

1. Assume initial government purchases don't depress or stimulate private spending.

2. Assume fiscal policy affects only demand, not supply, side of the economy.

C. Fiscal policy choices: Expansionary fiscal policy is used to combat a recession (see examples illustrated in Figure 12-1).

1. Expansionary Policy needed: In Figure 12-1, a decline in investment has decreased AD from AD_1 to AD_2 so real GDP has fallen and also employment declined. Possible fiscal policy solutions follow:

   a. An increase in government spending (shifts AD to right by more than change in G due to multiplier),

   b. A decrease in taxes (raises income, and consumption rises by MPC ∞ change in income; AD shifts to right by a multiple of the change in consumption).

   c. A combination of increased spending and reduced taxes.

   d. If the budget was initially balanced, expansionary fiscal policy creates a budget deficit.

2. Contractionary fiscal policy needed: When demand-pull inflation occurs as illustrated by a shift from AD_3 to AD_4 in the vertical range of aggregate supply in Figure 12-2. Then contractionary policy is the remedy:

   a. A decrease government spending shifts AD_4 back to AD_3 once the multiplier process is complete. Here price level returns to its preinflationary level P_3 but GDP remains at full-employment level.

   b. An increase in taxes will reduce income and then consumption at first by MPC ∞ fall in income, and then multiplier process leads AD to shift leftward still further. In Figure 12-2 a tax increase of $6.67 billion decreases consumption by 5 and multiplier causes eventual shift to AD_3.

   c. A combined spending decrease and tax increase could have the same effect with the right combination ($2 billion decline in G and $4 billion rise in T will have this effect).

D. Financing deficits or disposing of surpluses: The method used influences fiscal policy effect.

1. Financing deficits can be done in two ways.

   a. Borrowing: The government competes with private borrowers for funds and could drive up interest rates; the government may "crowd out" private borrowing, and this offsets the government expansion.

  b. Money creation: When the Federal Reserve loans directly to the government by buying bonds, the expansionary effect is greater since private investors are not buying bonds. (Note: Monetarists argue that this is monetary, not fiscal, policy that is having the expansionary effect in such a situation.)

 2. Disposing of surpluses can be handled two ways.

  a. Debt reduction is good but may cause interest rates to fall and stimulate spending. This could be inflationary.

  b. Impounding or letting the surplus funds remain idle would have greater anti-inflationary impact. The government holds surplus tax revenues which keeps these funds from being spent.

E. Policy options: G or T?

 1. Economists tend to favor higher G during recessions and higher taxes during inflationary times if they are concerned about unmet social needs or infrastructure.

 2. Others tend to favor lower T for recessions and lower G during inflationary periods when they think government is too large and inefficient.

IV. Built-In Stability

A. Built-in stability arises because net taxes (taxes minus transfers and subsidies) change with GDP (recall that taxes reduce incomes and therefore, spending). It is desirable for spending to rise when the economy is slumping and vice versa when the economy is becoming inflationary. Figure 12-3 illustrates how the built-in stability system behaves.

 1. Taxes automatically rise with GDP because incomes rise and tax revenues fall when GDP falls.

 2. Transfers and subsidies rise when GDP falls; when these government payments (welfare, unemployment, etc.) rise, net tax revenues fall along with GDP.

B. The size of automatic stability depends on responsiveness of changes in taxes to changes in GDP: The more progressive the tax system, the greater the economy's built-in stability. In Figure 12-3 line T is steepest with a progressive tax system.

 1. A 1993 law increased the highest marginal tax rate on personal income from 31 percent to 39.6 percent and corporate income tax rate to 35% by 1 percentage. This helped prevent demand-pull inflation.

 2. Automatic stability reduces instability, but does not correct economic instability.

V. Evaluating Fiscal Policy

A. A full-employment budget in Year 1 is illustrated in Figure 12-4(a) because budget revenues equal expenditures when full-employment exists at GDP_1.

B. At GDP_2 there is unemployment and assume no discretionary government action, so lines G and T remain as shown.

 1. Because of built-in stability, the actual budget deficit will rise with decline of GDP; therefore, actual budget varies with GDP.

 2. The government is not engaging in expansionary policy since budget is balanced at F.E. output.

 3. The full-employment budget measures what the Federal budget deficit or surplus would be with existing taxes and government spending if the economy is at full employment.

4. Actual budget deficit or surplus may differ greatly from full-employment budget deficit or surplus estimates.

C. In Figure 12-4b, the government reduced tax rates from T_1 to T_2, now there is a F.E. deficit.

   1. Structural deficits occur when there is a deficit in the full-employment budget as well as the actual budget.

   2. This is expansionary policy because true expansionary policy occurs when the full-employment budget has a deficit.

D. If the F.E. deficit of zero was followed by a F.E. budget surplus, fiscal policy is contractionary.

E. Recent U.S. fiscal policy is summarized in Table 12-1.

   1. Observe that F.E. deficits are less than actual deficits.

   2. Column 3 indicates expansionary fiscal policy of early 1990s became contractionary in the later years shown.

   3. Actual deficits have disappeared and the U.S. budget has actual surpluses since 1999. (Key Question 7)

F. Global Perspectives 12-1 gives a fiscal policy snapshot for selected countries.

VI. **Problems, Criticisms and Complications**

A. Problems of timing

   1. Recognition lag is the elapsed time between the beginning of recession or inflation and awareness of this occurrence.

   2. Administrative lag is the difficulty in changing policy once the problem has been recognized.

   3. Operational lag is the time elapsed between change in policy and its impact on the economy.

B. Political considerations: Government has other goals besides economic stability, and these may conflict with stabilization policy.

   1. A political business cycle may destabilize the economy: Election years have been characterized by more expansionary policies regardless of economic conditions.

      a. political business cycle?

   2. State and local finance policies may offset federal stabilization policies. They are often procyclical, because balanced-budget requirements cause states and local governments to raise taxes in a recession or cut spending making the recession possibly worse. In an inflationary period, they may increase spending or cut taxes as their budgets head for surplus.

   3. The crowding-out effect may be caused by fiscal policy.

      a. "Crowding-out" may occur with government deficit spending. It may increase the interest rate and reduce private spending which weakens or cancels the stimulus of fiscal policy. (See Figure 12-5)

      b. Some economists argue that little crowding out will occur during a recession.

       c. Economists agree that government deficits should not occur at F.E., it is also argued that monetary authorities could counteract the crowding-out by increasing the money supply to accommodate the expansionary fiscal policy.

    C. With an upward sloping AS curve, some portion of the potential impact of an expansionary fiscal policy on real output may be dissipated in the form of inflation. (See Figure 12-5c)

VI.   Fiscal Policy in an Open Economy (See Table 12-2)

    A. Shocks or changes from abroad will cause changes in net exports which can shift aggregate demand leftward or rightward.

    B. The net export effect reduces effectiveness of fiscal policy: For example, expansionary fiscal policy may affect interest rates, which can cause the dollar to appreciate and exports to decline (or rise).

VII.   Supply-Side Fiscal Policy

    A. Fiscal policy may affect aggregate supply as well as demand (see Figure 12-6 example).

    B. Assume that AS is upward sloping for simplicity.

    C. Tax changes may shift aggregate supply. An increase in business taxes raises costs and shifts supply to left; decrease shifts supply to the right.

        1. Also, lower taxes could increase saving and investment.

        2. Lower personal taxes may increase effort, productivity and, therefore, shift supply to the right.

        3. Lower personal taxes may also increase risk-taking and, therefore, shift supply to the right.

    D. If lower taxes raise GDP, tax revenues may actually rise.

    E. Many economists are skeptical of supply-side theories.

        1. Effect of lower taxes on a supply is not supported by evidence.

        2. Tax impact on supply takes extended time, but demand impact is more immediate.

VIII.   LAST WORD: The Leading Indicators

    A. This index comprises 10 variables that have indicated forthcoming changes in real GDP in the past.

    B. The variables are the foundation of this index consisting of a weighted average of ten economic measurements. A rise in the index predicts a rise in the GDP; a fall predicts declining GDP.

    C. Ten components comprise the index:

        1. Average workweek: A decrease signals future GDP decline.

        2. Initial claims for unemployment insurance: An increase signals future GDP decline.

        3. New orders for consumer goods: A decrease signals GDP decline.

        4. Vendor performance: Better performance by suppliers in meeting business demand indicates decline in GDP.

        5. New orders for capital goods: A decrease signals GDP decline.

        6. Building permits for houses: A decrease signals GDP decline.

7. Stock market prices: Declines signal GDP decline.

8. Money supply: A decrease is associated with falling GDP.

9. Interest-rate spread: when short-term rates rise, there is a smaller spread between short-term and long-term rates which are usually higher. This indicates restrictive monetary policy.

10. Index of consumer expectations: Declines in consumer confidence foreshadow declining GDP.

D. None of these factors alone is sufficient to predict changes in GDP, but the composite index has correctly predicted business fluctuations many times (although not perfectly). The index is a useful signal, but not totally reliable.

ANSWERS TO END-OF-CHAPTER QUESTIONS

12-1 What is the central thrust of the Employment Act of 1946? What is the role of the Council of Economic Advisers (CEA) in responding to this law? Class assignment: Determine the names and educational backgrounds of the present members of the CEA.

The central thrust of the Employment Act of 1946 is that the government does have a role to play in stabilizing prices (purchasing power), employment, and output. It formally recognized that the government had a role to play in stabilizing economic conditions.

The CEA advises the President on economic matters. Its members and staff gather and analyze relevant economic data, make forecasts, formulate policy, and help to "educate" the public and public officials on matters related to the nation's economic health.

Try www.whitehouse.gov for information on CEA.

12-2 (*Key Question*) Assume that a hypothetical economy with an MPC of .8 is experiencing severe recession. By how much would government spending have to increase to shift the aggregate demand curve rightward by $25 billion? How large a tax cut would be needed to achieve this same increase in aggregate demand? Why the difference? Determine one possible combination of government spending increases and tax decreases that would accomplish this same goal. (See Figure 12-1 for illustration).

In this problem, the multiplier is 1/.2 or 5 so, the increase in government spending = $5 billion.

For tax cut question, initial spending of $5 billion is still required, but only .8 (= MPC) of a tax cut will be spent. So .8 x tax cut = $5 billion or tax cut = $6.25 billion. Part of the tax reduction ($1.25 billion) is saved, not spent.

One combination: a $1 billion increase in government spending and a $5 billion tax cut.

12-3 (*Key Question*) What are government's fiscal policy options for ending severe demand-pull inflation? Use the aggregate demand-aggregate supply model to show the impact of these policies on the price level. Which of these fiscal policy options do you think a "conservative" economist might favor? A "liberal" economist?

Options are to reduce government spending, increase taxes, or some combination of both. See Figure 12-2. If the price level is flexible downward, it will fall. In the real world, the goal is to reduce inflation—to keep prices from rising so rapidly—not to reduce the price level. A "conservative" economist might favor cuts in government spending since this would reduce the size of government. A "liberal" economist might favor a tax hike; it would preserve government spending programs.

12-4   (*For students who were assigned Chapters 9 and 10*) Use the aggregate expenditures model to show how government fiscal policy could eliminate either a recessionary gap or an inflationary gap (Figure 10-8). Use the concept of the balanced budget multiplier to explain how equal increases in *G* and *T* could eliminate a recessionary gap and how equal decreases in *G* and *T* could eliminate an inflationary gap.

A recessionary gap could be eliminated by increasing government spending and/or decreasing personal taxes. Both of these policies have the effect of raising aggregate demand and shifting the aggregate expenditures schedule upward toward full-employment GDP.

An inflationary gap could be eliminated by pursuing the opposite policies: either decreasing government spending or raising taxes or both. This would reduce aggregate expenditures and would shift actual spending downward toward the full-employment level of real GDP.

Because the balanced budget multiplier essentially multiplies any change in government spending by a factor of 1, an increase in government spending and taxes would still have a positive effect on aggregate expenditures, increasing them by the amount of the initial increase in G. If G were large enough, the recessionary gap could be eliminated. Likewise, a balanced decrease in G and T could eliminate an inflationary gap, because the decline in aggregate expenditures would be equal to G. If the decrease in G were large enough to bring aggregate expenditures to the level of full-employment GDP, then the inflationary gap would be eliminated.

12-5   Designate each statement *true* or *false* and justify your answer.

   a. Expansionary fiscal policy during a depression will have a greater positive effect on real GDP if government borrows the money to finance the budget deficit than if it creates new money to finance the deficit.

   b. Contractionary fiscal policy during severe demand-pull inflation will be more effective if government impounds the budget surplus rather than using the surplus to pay off some of its past debt.

   (a) The statement is false. The truth is the opposite because when government creates new money during a depression, there is little danger of inflation and all of the new expenditures will be felt through increased aggregate demand as government's net spending increases. If the government finances its deficit by borrowing, there is danger that this will crowd out some private borrowing and investment spending. The resulting reduction in private spending offsets the expansionary effect of the fiscal deficit.

   (b) The statement is true. When the government impounds the surplus, these funds are removed from the spending flow. If the government used the surplus to pay of some of its past debt, money is returned to the private sector and at least a portion of it will be pumped into the economy in new expenditures. These expenditures will offset the contractionary effect of the budget surplus.

12-6   Explain how built-in (or automatic) stabilizers work. What are the differences between a proportional, progressive, and regressive tax system as they relate to an economy's built-in stability?

In a phrase, "net tax revenues vary directly with GDP." When GDP is rising so are tax collections, both income taxes and sales taxes. At the same time, government payouts—transfer payments such as unemployment compensation, and welfare—are decreasing. Since net taxes are taxes less transfer payments, net taxes definitely rise with GDP, which dampens the rise in GDP. On the other hand, when GDP drops in a recession, tax collections slow down or actually diminish while transfer payments rise quickly. Thus, net taxes decrease along with GDP, which softens the decline in GDP.

A progressive tax system would have the most stabilizing effect of the three tax systems and the regressive tax would have the least built-in stability. This follows from the previous paragraph. A progressive tax increases at an increasing rate as incomes rise, thus having more of a dampening effect on rising incomes and expenditures than would either a proportional or regressive tax. The latter rate would rise more slowly than the rate of increase in GDP with the least effect of the three types. Conversely, in an economic slowdown, a progressive tax falls faster because not only does it decline with income, but it becomes proportionately less as incomes fall. This acts as a cushion on declining incomes—the tax bite is less, which leaves more of the lower income for spending. The reverse would be true of a regressive tax that falls, but more slowly than the progressive tax, as incomes decline.

12-7   (*Key Question*) Define the "full-employment budget," explain its significance, and state why it may differ from the "actual budget." Suppose the full-employment, noninflationary level of real output is GDP$_3$ (not GDP$_2$) in the economy depicted in Figure 12-3. If the economy is operating at GDP$_2$ instead of GDP$_3$, what is the status of its full-employment budget? Of its current fiscal policy? What change in fiscal policy would you recommend? How would you accomplish that in terms of the G and T lines in the figure?

The full-employment budget (also call standardized) measures what the Federal deficit or surplus would be if the economy reached full-employment level of GDP with existing tax and spending policies. If the full-employment budget is balanced, then the government is not engaging in either expansionary not contractionary policy, even if, for example, a deficit automatically results when GDP declines. The "actual" budget is the deficit or surplus that results when revenues and expenditures occur over a year if the economy is not operating at full-employment.

Looking at Figure 12-3, if full-employment GDP level was GDP$_3$, then the full-employment budget is contractionary since a surplus would exist. Even though the "actual" budget has no deficit at GDP$_2$, fiscal policy is contractionary. To move the economy to full-employment, government should cut taxes or increase spending. You would raise G line or lower T line or combination of each until they intersect at GDP$_3$.

12-8   As shown in Table 12-1, between 1990 and 1991 the actual budget as a percent of GDP grew more rapidly than the full-employment budget deficit. What could explain this fact?

The explanation must be that the economy entered a recessionary phase during those years (it did, in fact), and for that reason the deficit was greater than it would have been in a full-employment economic situation. During a recession, tax revenues are lower than they would be at full employment and government expenditures for entitlement programs rise more than they would at full employment. Therefore, the actual deficit is greater than the full-employment budget deficit.

12-10   (*Key Question*) Briefly state and evaluate the problem of time lags in enacting and applying fiscal policy. Explain the notion of a political business cycle. What is the crowding-out effect and why is it relevant to fiscal policy? In what respect is the net export effect similar to the crowding-out effect?

It takes time to ascertain the direction in which the economy is moving (recognition lag), to get a fiscal policy enacted into law (administrative lag); and for the policy to have its full effect on the economy (operational lag). Meanwhile, other factors may change, rendering inappropriate a particular fiscal policy. Nevertheless, discretionary fiscal policy is a valuable tool in preventing severe recession or severe demand-pull inflation.

A political business cycle is the concept that politicians are more interested in reelection than in stabilizing the economy. Before the election, they enact tax cuts and spending increases to please voters even though this may fuel inflation. After the election, they apply the brakes to restrain inflation; the economy will slow and unemployment will rise. In this view the political process creates economic instability.

The crowding-out effect is the reduction in investment spending caused by the increase in interest rates arising from an increase in government spending, financed by borrowing. The increase in G was designed to increase AD but the resulting increase in interest rates may decrease I. Thus the impact of the expansionary fiscal policy may be reduced.

The next export effect also arises from the higher interest rates accompanying expansionary fiscal policy. The higher interest rates make U.S. bonds more attractive to foreign buyers. The inflow of foreign currency to buy dollars to purchase the bonds drives up the international value of the dollar, making imports less expensive for the United States, and U.S. exports more expensive for people abroad. Net exports in the United States decline, and like the crowding-out effect, diminish the expansionary fiscal policy.

12-11   In view of your answers to question 10, explain the following statement: "While fiscal policy clearly is useful in combating the extremes of severe recession and demand-pull inflation, it is impossible to use fiscal policy to 'fine-tune' the economy to the full-employment, noninflationary level of real GDP and keep the economy there indefinitely."

As suggested, the answer to question 9 explains this quote. While fiscal policy is useful in combating the extremes of severe recession with its built-in "safety nets" and stabilization tools, and while the built-in stabilizers can also dampen spending during inflationary periods, it is undoubtedly not possible to keep the economy at its full-employment, noninflationary level of real GDP indefinitely. There is the problem of timing. Each period is different, and the impact of fiscal policy will affect the economy differently depending on the timing of the policy and the severity of the situation. Fiscal policy operates in a political environment in which the unpopularity of higher taxes and specific cuts in spending may dictate that the most appropriate economic policies are ignored for political reasons. Finally, there are offsetting decisions which may be made at any time in the private and/or international sectors. For example, efforts to revive the economy with more government spending could result in reduced private investment or lower net export levels.

Even if it were possible to do any fine tuning to get the economy to its ideal level in the first place, it would be virtually impossible to design a continuing fiscal policy that would keep it there for all of the reasons mentioned above.

12-12   Suppose that government engages in deficit spending to push the economy away from recession and that this spending is directed toward new "public capital" such as roads, bridges, dams, harbors, office parks, and industrial sites. How might this spending increase the expected rate of return on some types of potential *private* investment projects? What are the implications for the crowding-out effect?

Government spending which is directed toward the improvement of the infrastructure (roads, bridges, dams, and harbors) provides additional "public capital" which increases the "production possibilities" of the nation. Private business firms benefit from these improvements through more convenient and reliable transportation systems and other amenities that lower production costs and make their business locations more desirable. Business firms that benefit from these public projects are, in effect, being subsidized by the government spending. These firms are likely to find that the publicly funded improvements increase the expected rate of return on their own investment projects.

Some economists argue that little crowding out will occur if the deficit spending is carried out during a recession. In addition, if the increased government spending improves business profit expectations, as suggested above, private investment need not fall, even though interest rates rise.

12-13 Use Figure 12-4(a) to explain why a deliberate increase in the full-employment budget (resulting from the tax cut) will reduce the size of the actual deficit if the fiscal policy succeeds in pushing the economy to its full-employment output of GDP$_3$. In requesting a tax cut in the early 1960s, President Kennedy said, "It is a paradoxical truth that tax rates are too high today and tax revenues are too low, and the soundest way to raise tax revenues in the long run is to cut tax rates now." Relate this quotation to your previous answer.

To the extent the deficit increase is successful in expanding the economy, equilibrium GDP will be to the right of its original position in Figure 12-4. The higher GDP means greater income and employment, which should raise total tax revenues despite lower rates and automatically reduce government spending on many social programs as fewer recipients qualify for support. The expansionary policy could have a beneficial effect on both the economy and the actual budget deficit.

Especially in the relatively noninflationary early 1960s, President Kennedy was right. The cut in tax rates, finally achieved under President Johnson, did indeed increase real GDP. The cut in taxes boosted production, so that out of the increased real GDP, tax revenues became greater than they had been before the tax cut—as Figure 12-4 would have predicted.

12-14 Discuss: "Mainstream economists tend to focus on the aggregate demand effects of tax-rate reductions; supply-side economists emphasize the aggregate supply effects." Identify three routes through which a tax cut might increase aggregate supply. If tax cuts are so good for the economy, why don't we cut taxes to zero?

Mainstream economists come from the Keynesian tradition, which focused on the demand side of the economy. Keynes emphasized deficient aggregate demand as the major cause of recessions and depressions, and the recessionary gap concept implies that shifting demand is the solution to the unemployment problem. Supply-side economists take their name from their focus on the supply side of the economy. They argue that the tax structure has a major effect on the supply side of the economy through its impact on work incentives and productivity as well as its impact on saving and investment. They argue that a lighter tax burden has an encouraging effect in all of these areas.

Taking these factors one by one, tax cuts may provide more incentive to work harder and longer, as workers and employers keep more of their after-tax earnings; encourage investment, especially if the tax cuts are aimed at promoting saving and business investment via such avenues as tax-free interest on certain types of saving, investment tax credits, and/or lower capital gains income taxes; the latter tax cuts might also encourage risk-taking and more innovation and new business.

Of course, zero taxes are absurd because there is a certain level of government that all agree is necessary, and we must pay for it. Lower taxes might provide additional revenue under circumstances where the existing structure has imposed an excessive burden, but there is a point below which lower tax rates will mean lower revenue. One might think of the incentive factor of lower taxes as producing diminishing returns.

12-15 Advanced analysis: (For students assigned Chapters 9 and 10) Assume that, without taxes, the consumption schedule for an economy is as shown below:

GDP, billions	Consumption, billions
$100	$120
200	200
300	280
400	360
500	440
600	520
700	600

a. Graph this consumption schedule and determine the size of the MPC.

b. Assume a lump-sum (regressive) tax is imposed such that the government collects $10 billion in taxes at all levels of GDP. Calculate the tax rate at each level of GDP. Graph the resulting consumption schedule and compare the MPC and the multiplier with that of the pretax consumption schedule.

c. Now suppose a proportional tax system with a 10 percent tax rate is imposed instead of the regressive system. Calculate the new consumption schedule, graph it, and note the MPC and the multiplier.

d. Impose a progressive tax system such that the tax rate is zero percent when GDP is $100, 5 percent at $200, 10 percent at $300, 15 percent at $400, and so forth. Determine and graph the new consumption schedule, noting the effect of the tax system on the MPC and multiplier.

e. Explain why proportional and progressive tax systems contribute to greater economic stability, while a regressive system does not. Demonstrate using a graph similar to Figure 12-3.

(a) The MPC = $(\$200 - \$120)$ billion/$(\$200 - \$100)$ billion $= 80/100 = 0.8$

(b)

GDP, billions	Tax, billions	DI, billions	Consumption after tax	Tax rate, percent billions
$100	$10	$ 90	$112	10%
200	10	190	192	5.0
300	10	290	272	3.33
400	10	390	352	2.5
500	10	490	432	2.0
600	10	590	512	1.67
700	10	690	592	1.43

The MPC is $0.8[= (\$192 - \$112)$ billion$/(\$200 - \$100)$ billion $= 80/100]$, as before the tax increase.
And the spending multiplier remains $5[1/(1 - 0.8 = 1/0.2)]$.

(c)

GDP, billions	Tax, billions	DIs billions	Consumption after tax, billions
$100	10%	$90	$112
200	10	180	184
300	10	270	256
400	10	360	328
500	10	450	400
600	10	540	472
700	10	630	544

The MPC is $0.72 \left[= (\$184 - \$112) \text{ billion} / (\$200 - \$100) \text{ billion} = 72/100 \right]$.

And the spending multiplier is now $3.57 \left[= 1/(1 - .072) = 1/0.28 \right]$.

(d)

GDP billions	Tax, billions	DI, billions	Consumption after tax	Tax rate, percent billions	MPC
$100	$ 0	$100	$120	0%	undefined
200	10	190	192	5	0.72
300	30	270	256	10	0.64
400	60	340	312	15	0.56
500	100	400	360	20	0.48
600	150	450	400	25	0.40
700	210	490	432	30	0.32

(e) The MPC decreases as shown in the right-hand column above. Proportional and (especially) progressive tax systems reduce the size of the MPC and, therefore, the size of the multiplier. A lump-sum tax does not alter the MPC or the multiplier.

NOTE: For instructors who assign the graphs, the following would be true. For each graph (a) through (d), plot the consumption schedule against the GDP. Graph (a) will have a slope of .8 and will cross the 45 degree line at C = GDP = 200. Graph (b) is parallel to (a) but $10 billion below it and will cross the 45 degree line at C = GDP = 150, indicating the multiplier of 5 ($10 billion loss in income leads to $50 billion drop in equilibrium GDP). Graph (c) will not be as steep as (a) or (b) with a slope of .72 and equilibrium between GDP = 200 and GDP = 300 on the diagram. Graph (d) has a decreasing slope so it will not be a straight line. Equilibrium is just beyond GDP = 200. The multiplier is illustrated by noting the change in equilibrium GDP if any curve were to be shifted by a given amount. The multiplier is the ratio of change in equilibrium GDP to the vertical shift.

12-16 (*Last Word*) What is the index of leading economic indicators and how does it relate to discretionary fiscal policy?

The index of leading indicators is a monthly composite index of a group of variables that in the past has provided advance notice of changes in GDP. Changes in the index provide a clue to the future direction of the economy and may shorten the length of the "recognition lag" associated with the implementation of discretionary fiscal policy.

CHAPTER THIRTEEN
MONEY AND BANKING

CHAPTER OVERVIEW

Chapters 13, 14, and 15 form a conventional unit on money and banking. These chapters provide the foundation for the discussion of modern monetary theory and for the discussion and analysis of the monetarist and competing theories which follow.

Chapter 13 introduces the student to the U.S. financial system. The chapter first covers the nature and functions of money and then discusses the Federal Reserve System's definition of the money supply. Next, the chapter addresses the question of what "backs" money by looking at the value of money, money and prices, and the management of the money supply. The demand for money is then covered, and it is followed by an introduction and discussion of the money market. Finally, there is a rather comprehensive description of the U.S. financial system, which focuses on the features and functions of the Federal Reserve System and recent difficulties in the U.S. financial system.

WHAT'S NEW

The entire chapter has been updated and streamlined with revised discussion of money as a store of value, updated the "Recent Developments" section, and revised Key Questions. This edition deletes sections on "near money," reciprocal relationship between prices and money value, and previews of monetary policy.

The Last Word, "The Global Greenback," has been updated.

INSTRUCTIONAL OBJECTIVES

After completing this chapter, students should be able to:

1. List and explain the three functions of money.

2. Define the money supply, M1 and near-monies, M2, and M3.

3. State three reasons why currency and checkable deposits are money and why they have value.

4. Identify two types of demand for money and the main determinant of each.

5. Describe the relationship between GDP and the interest rate and each type of money demand.

6. Explain what is meant by equilibrium in the money market and the equilibrium rate of interest.

7. Explain the relationship between bond prices and the money market.

8. Describe the structure of the U.S. banking system.

9. Explain why Federal Reserve Banks are central, quasi-public, and bankers' banks.

10. Describe seven functions of the Federal Reserve System and point out which role is the most important.

11. Summarize and evaluate the arguments for and against the Federal Reserve System remaining an independent institution.

12. Describe the conditions that have caused the loss of market share of banks and thrifts to pension funds, insurance companies, mutual funds, and securities-related firms.

13. Identify three major changes continuing to occur in the financial services industry.

14. Define and identify terms and concepts listed at the end of the chapter.

COMMENTS AND TEACHING SUGGESTIONS

1. Definitions of the money supply are arbitrary, and this should be stressed. The definition of M1 changes over time as different instruments become acceptable as money.

2. The Federal Reserve Banks publish a number of excellent low-cost or free educational materials. A comprehensive guide to these, along with ordering information, is found in *Public Information Materials*, available from the Federal Reserve Bank in your district. It could be ordered from any district, or from the New York Federal Reserve Bank, 33 Liberty Street, New York, NY 10045. Address your requests to the Public Information Department of the district bank that you write. The *Federal Reserve Bulletin* contains a wealth of financial and economic statistics. Write The Board of Governors, Federal Reserve System, Washington, D.C. 20551 for subscription information or check their website given in the first web-based question.

3. As an in-class exercise, have the students collectively identify some or all of the Federal Reserve districts by finding the bank of issue on bills they have in their possession. The issuing bank is shown in the circle on the left side of the face of the bill. See if all twelve are represented among the bills present in your classroom.

4. Ask students to give examples of each one of the functions of money and point out that in some contemporary countries, inflation has undermined these functions. In these countries, people often prefer U.S. dollars instead of their own currencies because their currencies don't store value or work for long as a unit of account since prices change rapidly.

5. Discuss the use of barter as an alternative means of exchange in places like Russia and Ukraine. Ask students to relate examples of barter exchanges they have made. Note the conditions required for barter. Give students an opportunity to explain why barter exchanges are inconvenient.

6. The Federal Reserve banks, including their branches, offer guided tours of their facilities, and many of the district banks also have exhibits in their public lobby areas. It is definitely a good "field trip" if you have the opportunity to take your students. If not, the bank's public information department may be willing to schedule a presentation at your institution.

STUDENT STUMBLING BLOCKS

1. It is hard for students to believe that nothing intrinsic backs the money supply. Make sure they realize that the gold in Fort Knox (or elsewhere) has no function in terms of the value of our money. Returning to the gold standard continues to be advocated by some. It is a good topic for debate.

2. Point out to the students that the phrase "central bank" refers to the Federal Reserve System and the Board of Governors. It acts as our Central Bank, whereas other countries have a single institution as their central bank.

3. Another common error that students make is to equate money with income. Focus on the distinction between the amount of money in one's possession and one's income. This helps students to understand that money and income are not synonyms. For example, you could ask them to estimate how much M1 money they have at the moment in currency and checking. If they are typical, this will be much less than their annual income. In other words, the student's average money supply is less than the student's income. The concept of velocity is introduced later, but it could be mentioned at this point as a way of helping students to contrast the money supply with income concepts.

4. If you want students to understand why interest rates on bonds vary as described in Money Market section, you must explain carefully. If bond price : rate relationship is not important for you, focus only on money : rate relationships. See question 9 at end of chapter for practice on relating bond prices to interest rates.

LECTURE NOTES

I. Functions of Money

A. Medium of exchange: Money can be used for buying and selling goods and services.

B. Unit of account: Prices are quoted in dollars and cents.

C. Store of value: Money allows us to transfer purchasing power from present to future. It is the most liquid (spendable) of all assets, a convenient way to store wealth.

II. Supply of Money

A. Narrow definition of money: M1 includes currency and checkable deposits (see Table 13-1).

   1. Currency (coins + paper money) held by public.

      a. Is "token" money, which means its intrinsic value is less than actual value. The metal in a dime is worth less than 10¢.

      b. All paper currency consists of Federal Reserve Notes issued by the Federal Reserve.

   2. Checkable deposits are included in M1, since they can be spent almost as readily as currency and can easily be changed into currency.

      a. Commercial banks are a main source of checkable deposits for households and businesses.

      b. Thrift institutions (savings & loans, credit unions, mutual savings banks) also have checkable deposits.

   3. Qualification: Currency and checkable deposits held by the federal government, Federal Reserve, or other financial institutions are not included in M1.

B. Money Definition: M2 = M1 + some near-monies which include: (See Table 13-1)

   1. Savings deposits and money market deposit accounts.

   2. Certificates of deposit (time accounts) less than $100,000.

   3. Money market mutual fund balances, which can be redeemed by phone calls, checks, or through the Internet.

C. Money Definition: M3 = M2 + large certificates of deposit (time accounts) $100,000 or more (See Table 13-1)

D. Which definitions are used? M1 will be used in this text, but M2 is watched closely by the Federal Reserve in determining monetary policy.

   1. M2 and M3 are important because they can easily be changed into M1 types of money and influence people's spending of income.

   2. The ease of shifting between M1, M2, and M3 complicates the task of controlling spendable money supply.

3. The definition becomes important when authorities attempt to measure control and the money supply.

E. Credit cards are not money, but their use involves short-term loans; their convenience allows you to keep M1 balances low because you need less for daily purchases.

III. **What "backs" the money supply?**

A. The government's ability to keep its value stable provides the backing.

B. Money is debt; paper money is a debt of Federal Reserve Banks and checkable deposits are liabilities of banks and thrifts because depositors own them.

C. Value of money arises not from its intrinsic value, but its value in exchange for goods and services.

1. It is acceptable as a medium of exchange.

2. Currency is legal tender or fiat money. It must be accepted by law. (Note that checks are not legal tender but, in fact, are generally acceptable in exchange for goods, services, and resources.)

3. The relative scarcity of money compared to goods and services will allow money to retain its purchasing power.

D. Money's purchasing power determines its value. Higher prices mean less purchasing power. (Key Question #6) (See Figure 13-1)

E. Excessive inflation may make money worthless and unacceptable. An extreme example of this was German hyperinflation after World War I, which made the mark worth less than 1 billionth of its former value within a four-year period.

1. Worthless money leads to use of other currencies that are more stable.

2. Worthless money may lead to barter exchange system.

F. Maintaining the value of money

1. The government tries to keep supply stable with appropriate fiscal policy.

2. Monetary policy tries to keep money relatively scarce to maintain its purchasing power, while expanding enough to allow the economy to grow.

IV. **The Demand for Money : Two Components**

A. Transactions demand, D_t, is money kept for purchases and will vary directly with GDP (Figure 13-1a).

B. Asset demand, D_a, is money kept as a store of value for later use. Asset demand varies inversely with the interest rate, since that is the price of holding idle money (Figure 13-1b).

C. Total demand will equal quantities of money demanded for assets plus that for transactions (Figure 13-1c).

V. **The Money Market: Interaction of Money Supply and Demand**

A. Key Graph 13-1c illustrates the money market. It combines demand with supply of money.

B. Figure 13-2 illustrates how equilibrium changes with a shift in the supply of money.

C. If the quantity demanded exceeds the quantity supplied, people sell assets like bonds to get money. This causes bond supply to rise, bond prices to fall, and a higher market rate of interest.

D. If the quantity supplied exceeds the quantity demanded, people reduce money holdings by buying other assets like bonds. Bond prices rise, and lower market rates of interest result (see example in text).

E. Monetary authorities can shift supply to affect interest rates, which in turn affect investment and consumption and aggregate demand and, ultimately, output, employment, and prices. (Key Question #7)

F. Try Quick Quiz 13-2.

VI. **The Federal Reserve and the Banking System**

A. The Federal Reserve System (the "Fed") was established by Congress in 1913 and holds power over the money and banking system.

1. Figure 13-3 gives framework of Fed and its relationship to the public.

2. The central controlling authority for the system is the Board of Governors and has seven members appointed by the President for staggered 14-year terms. Its power means the system operates like a central bank.

3. Assistance and Advice:

   a. Federal Open Market Committee includes the seven governors plus five regional Federal Reserve Bank presidents whose terms alternate. They set policy on buying and selling of government bonds, the most important type of monetary policy, and meet several times each year.

   b. Three advisory councils exist: Federal Advisory Council includes twelve prominent commercial bankers, one from each Fed district, who act as advisors to the Board, Thrift Institutions Advisory Council advises on thrift institution matters, the Consumer Advisory Council advises on more general issues. (See Figure 13-4)

4. The system has twelve districts, each with its own district bank and two or three branch banks. They help implement Fed policy and are advisory. (See Figure 13-4)

   a. Each is quasi-public: It is owned by member banks but controlled by the government's Federal Reserve Board, and any profits go to the U.S. Treasury.

   b. They act as bankers' banks by accepting reserve deposits and making loans to banks and other financial institutions.

3. About 8,600 commercial banks existed in 2001. They are privately owned and consist of state banks (three-fourths of total) and large national banks (chartered by the Federal government).

4. Thrift institutions consist of savings and loan associations and mutual savings banks. They are regulated by the Treasury Dept. Office of Thrift Supervision, but they may use services of the Fed and keep reserves on deposit at the Fed. See Figure 13-4.

5. Global Perspective 13-1 gives the world's ten largest banks.

B. Functions of the Fed and money supply:

1. The Fed issues "Federal Reserve Notes," the paper currency used in the U.S. monetary system.

2. The Fed sets reserve requirements and holds the reserves of banks and thrifts not held as vault cash.

3. The Fed may lend money to banks and thrifts, charging them an interest rate called the discount rate.

4. The Fed provides a check collection service for banks (checks are also cleared locally or by private clearing firms).

5. Federal Reserve System acts as the fiscal agent for the Federal government.

6. The Federal Reserve System supervises member banks.

7. Monetary policy and control of the money supply is the "major function" of the Fed.

C. Federal Reserve independence is important but is also controversial from time to time. Advocates of independence fear that more political ties would cause the Fed to follow expansionary policies and create too much inflation, leading to an unstable currency such as that in other countries (see Last Word for this chapter).

VII. **Recent Developments in Money and Banking**

A. Relative decline of banks and thrifts: Several other types of firms offer financial services.

B. Consolidation among banks and thrifts: Because of failures and mergers, there are fewer banks and thrifts today. Since 1990, there has been a decline of 5000 banks.

C. Convergence of services provided has made financial institutions more similar: See text on new laws of 1996 and 1999 that made many changes possible.

D. Globalization of financial markets: Significant integration of world financial markets is occurring and recent advances in computer and communications technology suggest the trend is likely to accelerate.

E. Electronic transactions: Internet buying and selling, electronic cash and "smart cards" are examples.

1. In the future, nearly all payments could be made with a personal computer or "smart card."

2. Unlike currency, E-cash is "issued" by private firms rather than by government. To control the money supply the Fed will need to find ways to control the total amount of E-cash, including that created through Internet loans.

VIII. **LAST WORD: The Global Greenback**

A. Two-thirds of all U.S. currency is circulating abroad.

1. Russians hold about $40 billion because dollar value is stable.

2. Argentina holds $7 billion and fixes its own peso exchange rate to dollar reserves.

B. U.S. profits when dollars stay overseas: It costs us 4¢ to print each dollar and to get the dollar; foreigners must sell Americans $1 worth of products. Americans gain 96¢ over cost of printing the dollar. It's like someone buying a travelers check and never cashing it.

C. Black markets and illegal activity overseas also are usually conducted in dollars because they are such a stable form of currency.

D. Overall, the "global greenback" is a positive economic force. It is a reliable medium of exchange, measure, and store of value that facilitates transactions everywhere and there is little danger that all the dollars will return to U.S.

ANSWERS TO END-OF-CHAPTER QUESTIONS

13-1 What are the three basic functions of money? Describe how rapid inflation can undermine money's ability to perform each of the three functions.

Money is used as a medium of exchange for goods and services, as a unit of account for expressing price, and as a store of value.

People will only accept money in exchange for goods and services and for the work they perform if they can be reasonably certain that the medium of exchange—money—will retain its value until they are ready to spend it. In runaway inflations of the thousands or tens of thousands of percent a year, people revert to barter.

Again, drastic inflation greatly reduces money's use as a measure of value, for it is impossible to adjust instantaneously all prices strictly in line with their relative values. Thus, opportunities are afforded to speculators to profit at the expense of the less sophisticated who, eventually, will learn to distrust money's usefulness as a measure of value.

Finally, and most obviously, money's usefulness as a store of value is destroyed in a drastic inflation. The "rule of 70" is instructive here. By dividing the absolute inflation rate into 70, one can estimate how long it takes one's dollar savings to lose half their purchasing power. At 7 percent inflation, the dollar will be worth half as much in ten years.

13-2 Which two of the following financial institutions offer checkable deposits included within the M1 money supply: mutual fund companies, insurance companies, commercial banks, securities firms, thrift institutions? Which of the following is not included in either M1 or M2: currency held by the public; checkable deposits, money market mutual fund balances; small (less than $10,000) deposits; currency held by banks; savings deposits?

Commercial banks and thrift institutions offer checkable deposits.

Currency held by banks is not counted in either M1 or M2.

13-3 Explain and evaluate the following statements:

a. The invention of money is one of the great achievements of humankind, for without it the enrichment that comes from broadening trade would have been impossible.

b. Money is whatever society says it is.

c. In most economies of the world, the debts of government and commercial banks are used as money.

d. People often say they would like to have more money, but what they usually mean is that they would like to have more goods and services.

e. When the prices of everything go up it is because the currency is worth less.

f. Any central bank can create money; the trick is to create enough of it, but not too much of it.

(a) Without money, trade must occur through barter. And barter requires the "double coincidence of wants," the requirement that a seller find a buyer who not only desires what the seller has to offer but also has to offer what the buyer desires. A wheat grower desiring milk must find a dairy farmer desiring wheat or, at least, a merchant in the middle trading in both wheat and milk. Maybe one can imagine a merchant owning both a grain elevator and refrigerated milk holding tanks. But suppose the wheat farmer desires a new suit or a new combine?

And so far all we have been talking about is local trade. Suppose the dairy farmer desires oriental spices, to use an example from the beginning of trade after the ending of the Dark Ages in Europe. The dairy farmer could hardly ship the milk to the Orient, so a buyer must be found in Europe who desires milk and who has something our dairy farmer can trade for oriental spices. And how are the terms of trade to be determined in the absence of money? Is a quart of milk worth an ounce of pepper? Or how much of what the dairy farmer got locally for milk is worth an ounce of pepper? As one can see, without a measure of value the complications are enormous.

(b) Money must be acceptable in exchange. That is its fundamental requirement. A person will accept payment in whatever is called money only if that person knows that the money can subsequently be used in exchange for something else. If the money is easily, cheaply predicable by a monetary authority, it will only be acceptable if the conviction exists that the authority will keep the rate of increase below the hyperinflationary level. If the money is a commodity such as cigarettes in a prisoner-of-war camp, the commodity will be acceptable as money not only because of its intrinsic value, but also, again, because there is no fear of the supply suddenly increasing to a hyperinflationary level. Note that checks are our primary medium of exchange, although they have not been deemed legal tender by government.

(c) All accounts (saving and checking) in the commercial banks are money owed by these banks to their customers, who own these deposits. Since checks drawn on checking accounts are accepted as money (since they demand payment out of these checking accounts), it follows that the debts of the commercial banks are used as moneys. Paper money is merely the circulating debt of the government.

(d) People often use the term "money" when they are referring to wealth or income. Wealth refers to accumulated assets, measured at a point in time. Money is an asset, and can be used as a store of value. However, holding wealth in the form of money provides no creature comforts, nor does it return much additional income (before interest was paid on checking balances, the return was zero). Money is also a unit of account, a means of measurement, literally a yardstick, that is used for comparison purposes. When people say they want more money, they are saying they want to be richer—to have more things.

(e) The equation is accurate. The great advantage of paper money is that its supply does not rely on the chance discovery of laborious production of whatever commodity is used as money. The cost of printing paper money is trivial compared to the values that can be printed on it. However, the very convenience and ease of producing paper money can be their downfall or the downfall of the economies that use it. Since it can be produced without limit at virtually no cost, sometimes it is. Hyperinflation and economic breakdown may result. However, this is not a fault of paper money in itself: Colonial Pennsylvania issued paper money completely unbacked by gold and silver for forty-four years, from 1723 to 1767, without any inflation at all.

(f) The most important function of the Federal Reserve is to manage the nation's money supply and thus interest rates. This involves making an amount of money available that is consistent with high and rising levels of output and employment and a relatively constant price level.

13-4 (*Key Question*) What are the components of the $M1$ money supply? What is the largest component? Which of the components is legal tender? Why is the face value of a coin greater than its intrinsic value? What near-monies are included in M2 money supply? What distinguishes the M2 and M3 money supplies?

$M1$ = currency (in circulation) + checkable deposits. The largest component of $M1$ is checkable deposits, but only currency is legal tender. If the face value of a coin were not greater than its intrinsic (metallic) value, people would remove coins from circulation and sell them for their metallic content. $M2 = M1$ + noncheckable savings deposits + money market deposit accounts + small time deposits money market mutual fund balances. $M3 = M2$ + large time deposits (those of $100,000 or more). Near-monies are components of $M2$ and $M3$ not included in $M1$. $M3$ is distinguished from $M2$ by large time deposits (certificates of deposits).

13-5   What "backs" the money supply in the United States? What determines the value (domestic purchasing power) of money? How does the value of money relate to the price level? Who is the U.S. is responsible for maintaining money's value? Why is it important to be able to alter the money supply?

There is no concrete backing to the money supply in the United States. Paper money, which has no intrinsic value, has value only because people are willing to accept it in exchange for goods and services, including their labor services as employees. And people are willing to accept paper as money because they know that everyone else is also willing to do so. If the monetary authorities were issuing new banknotes at a rate far in excess of available output, the acceptability of paper money would diminish. People would start to worry about whether the banknotes would be worth much after they received them. Checks are part of the money supply and are not legal tender, but people accept them willingly from people believed trustworthy.

The value or purchasing power of money is inversely related to the price level.

The Board of Governors of the Federal Reserve System (the Fed) is responsible for managing the United States' money supply so that money retains its value.

13-6   (*Key Question*) Suppose the price level and value of the dollar in year 1 are 1.0 and $1.00, respectively. If the price level rises to 1.25 in year 2, what is the new value of the dollar? If instead the price level had fallen to .50, what would have been the value of the dollar? What generalization can you draw from your answer?

In the first case, the value of the dollar (in year 2, relative to year 1) is $.80 (= 1/1.25); in the second case the value is $2 (= 1/.50). Generalization: The price level and the value of the dollar are inversely related.

13-7   (*Key Question*) What is the basic determinant of (a) the transactions demand and (b) the asset demand for money? Explain how these two demands might be combined graphically to determine total money demand. How is the equilibrium interest rate in the money market determined? How might (a) the expanded use of credit cards, (b) a shortening of worker pay periods, and (c) an increase in nominal GDP each independently affect the transactions demand for money and the equilibrium interest rate?

(a) The level of nominal GDP. The higher this level, the greater the amount of money demanded for transactions. (b) The interest rate. The higher the interest rate, the smaller the amount of money demanded as an asset.

On a graph measuring the interest rate vertically and the amount of money demanded horizontally, the two demands for the money curves can be summed horizontally to get the total demand for money. This total demand shows the total amount of money demanded at each interest rate. The equilibrium interest rate is determined at the intersection of the total demand for money curve and the supply of money curve.

(a) Expanded use of credit cards: transaction demand for money declines; total demand for money declines; interest rate falls. (b) Shortening of worker pay periods: transaction demand for money declines; total demand for money declines; interest rate falls. (c) Increase in nominal GDP: transaction demand for money increases; total demand for money increases; interest rate rises.

13-8 Assume that the following data characterize a hypothetical economy: money supply = $200 billion; quantity of money demanded for transactions = $150 billion; quantity of money demanded as an asset = $10 billion at 12 percent interest, increasing by $10 billion for each 2-percentage-point fall in the interest rate.

 a. What is the equilibrium interest rate? Explain.

 b. At the equilibrium interest rate, what are the quantity of money supplied, the total quantity of money demanded, the amount of money demanded for transactions, and the amount of money demanded as an asset?

 (a) The equilibrium interest rate is 4% where the quantity of money supplied is equal to the total quantity demanded.

 (b) At the equilibrium interest rate the quantity of money supplied is 200 and the asset demand for money is 50, the transactions demand for money is 150 and the total quantity of money demanded is 200.

13-9 Suppose a bond having no expiration date has a face value of $10,000 and annually pays a fixed amount on interest of $800. Compute and enter in the space provided either the interest rate which a bond buyer could secure at each of the bond prices listed or the bond price at each of the interest rates shown. What generalization can be drawn from the completed table?

Bond Price	Interest rate %
$ 8,000	10.0
9,000	8.9
10,000	8.0
11,000	7.3
13,000	6.2

Generalization: Bond price and interest rate are inversely related.

13-10 Assume the money market is initially in equilibrium and that the money supply is then increased. Explain the adjustments toward a new equilibrium interest rate. Will bond prices be higher at the new equilibrium rate of interest? What effects would you expect that interest-rate change to have on the levels of output, employment, and prices? Answer the same questions for a decrease in the money supply.

Assuming there is no initial change in GDP, there will be no change in the transactions demand for money. Therefore, the entire increase in the money supply will initially go toward the purchase of financial assets that people prefer to the holding of noninterest-bearing cash. Assuming that these purchases are entirely for bonds (some undoubtedly will be, anyway), the increased demand for bonds will drive their price up and the rate of return on them down; that is, the interest rate in the market will drop.

The lower interest rate will encourage investment and interest-rate-sensitive consumer buying, that is, for big-ticket items, such as cars. Output and employment will rise and so will prices, unless the economy is in a deep recession in the Keynesian range of the AS curve. The increase in output (in GDP) will increase the transactions demand for money and, thus, the total demand for money.

This will tend to force interest rates back up, but not all the way back to where they were before the money supply was increased.

If the money supply is decreased, everything works in reverse. The quantity of money demanded exceeds the quantity supplied at the previous equilibrium interest rate. To get the money they desire, people will sell some of their financial assets, some of which, at least, will be bonds. The increased supply of bonds in the market will drive down their price. This means the rate of return on them will rise; the market rate of interest rises. This will lead to a decrease in investment and interest-sensitive consumer purchases. Output and employment will drop, leading to a decrease in the transactions demand for money and, thus, to a decrease in the total demand for money. This will tend to lower the interest rate, but not all the way back to where it was before the money supply decreased. Prices likely will not decrease, because of the ratchet effect, unless the economy is in a very deep recession; in which case the monetary authorities, having learned something from 1929-33, would not have decreased the money supply.

13-11   How is the chairperson of the Federal Reserve Board selected? Describe the relationship between the Board of Governors of the Federal Reserve System and the 12 Federal Reserve Banks. What is meant when economists say that the Federal Reserve Banks are central banks, quasipublic banks, and bankers' banks? What are the seven basic functions of the Federal Reserve System?

The Board of Governors of the Federal Reserve is selected by the U.S. president with the confirmation of the Senate. The seven board members have long terms—14 years—and staggered so that one member is replaced every 2 years. The president selects the chairperson and vice-chairperson of the board from among the members, and they serve 4-year terms. Several entities assist the Board of Governors in determining banking and monetary policy. The Federal Open Market Committee is the most important, voting on the Fed's monetary policy and directing the purchase or sale of government securities. Five of the presidents of the Federal Reserve Banks have voting rights on the FOMC each year, rotating the membership among the 12 banks, except for the president of the NY Fed who has a permanent voting seat.

The 12 Federal Reserve Banks are "central" banks whose policies are coordinated by the Board of Governors. They are quasipublic banks, meaning that they are a blend of private ownership and public control. They are also banker's banks in that they perform essentially the same functions for banks and thrifts as those institutions perform for the public.

The Federal Reserve performs 7 basic functions:

1. The Fed issues Federal Reserve Notes, the paper currency used in the U.S. monetary system.

2. The Fed sets reserve requirements and holds the mandated reserves that are not held as vault cash.

3. The Fed lends money to banks and thrifts.

4. The Fed provides for check collection.

5. The Fed acts as fiscal agent for the Federal government.

6. The Fed supervises the operation of banks.

7. Finally, and most importantly, the Fed has responsibility for regulating the supply of money, and this in turn enables it to affect interest rates.

13-12   Following are two hypothetical ways in which the Federal Reserve Board might be appointed. Would you favor either of these two methods over the present method? Why or why not?

a. Upon taking office, the U.S. President appoints 7 people to the Federal Reserve Board, including a chair. Each appointee must be confirmed by a majority vote of the Senate, and each serves the same 4-year term as the president.

b. Congress selects 7 members from its ranks (4 from the House of Representatives and 3 from the Senate) to serve as its pleasure as the Board of Governors of the Federal Reserve System.

In the opinion of most economists, the Fed should be protected from political pressures so that it can effectively control the money supply and maintain price stability. Option (a) would create a Board of Governors that sat at the pleasure of the president, placing the monetary policy of the country in the hands of the executive branch. Option (b) would place the BOG under the control of Congress. Neither of the options would maintain the independence needed for effective monetary policy.

13-13   What are the major categories of firms that make up the U.S. financial services industry? Did the bank and thrift share of the financial services market rise, fall, or stay the same between 1980 and 2000? Are there more or fewer bank firms today than a decade ago? Why are the lines between the categories of financial firms becoming more blurred than in the past?

The major categories of firms that make up the U.S. financial services industry include: commercial banks, thrifts, insurance companies, mutual fund companies, pension funds, and securities related firms. Commercial banks and thrifts have declined in market share substantially since 1980. In response they have offered a variety of new services, purchased or merged with other institutions, and pushed Congress for regulatory reform.

13-14   In what way are electronic money and smart cards potentially related? Do you think electronic money and smart cards will dominate transactions sometime within the next 20 years? Why or why not?

Electronic money is simply an entry in an electronic file stored in a computer. The internet and the widespread availability of personal computers have made it possible for individuals to use E-cash instead of checks or currency in making transactions. E-cash is "loaded" into the account through Internet payments, or other asset transfer. It can then be withdrawn or used through the Internet to make a variety of payments. Smart cards are like credit cards with prepaid balances. Each time it is used for a transaction, the value of the card account is decreased by the price of the purchase. Smart card balances can be replenished by adding new prepayments to the account. Both also represent a new form of money outside the narrower definitions of M1, and as such are outside the current control of monetary authorities. Increased usage of electronic cash and smart cards is certain to take place.

13-15   (*Last Word*) Over the years the Federal Reserve Banks have printed many billions of dollars more in currency than American households, businesses, and financial institutions now hold. Where is this "missing" money? Why is it there?

This missing money is outside of the country. It originally left the country to pay for imports of goods and services purchased by Americans from producers abroad. Now it is in circulation outside the country, especially in countries whose currencies are not very stable. For example, it is estimated that Russians hold about $40 billion worth of U.S. dollars. Transactions are conducted in dollars inside Russia, because Russians fear that when they accept the Russian ruble, it may lose its value very quickly. The same is true in other countries with high rates of inflation. The dollar is also used in international transactions, both legal and illegal, where it is acceptable because of its stability.

CHAPTER FOURTEEN
HOW BANKS AND THRIFTS CREATE MONEY

CHAPTER OVERVIEW

The central topic of this chapter is the creation of checkable (demand) deposit money by commercial banks. First, a number of routine but significant introductory transactions are covered, followed by an assessment of the lending ability of a single commercial bank. Second, the lending ability and the money multiplier of the commercial banking system are traced through the balance statements of individual banks and through the summary Table 14-2. The chapter concludes with a discussion of how the earlier analysis must be modified, but not changed in its essentials, to take account of actions that may offset the money-creating power of the banking system.

WHAT'S NEW

Other than inclusion of "thrifts" into the title, this chapter has only minor revisions, updates and clarification. For example, "checkable deposits" replaces "demand deposits" throughout.

INSTRUCTIONAL OBJECTIVES

After completing this chapter, students should be able to:

1. Recount the story of how fractional reserves began with goldsmiths.

2. Explain the effects of a currency deposit in a checking account on the composition and size of the money supply.

3. Compute a bank's required and excess reserves when you are given its balance-sheet figures.

4. Explain why a commercial bank is required to maintain a reserve and why it isn't sufficient to cover deposits.

5. Describe what happens to the money supply when a commercial bank makes a loan or buys securities.

6. Describe what happens to the money supply when a loan is repaid or a bank sells its securities.

7. Explain what happens to a commercial bank's reserves and checkable deposits after it has made a loan.

8. Describe how a check drawn on one commercial bank and deposited in another will affect the reserves and excess reserves in each bank after the check clears.

9. Describe what would happen to a single bank's reserves if it made loans that exceeded its excess reserves.

10. Explain how it is possible for the banking system to create an amount of money that is a multiple of its excess reserves when no single bank ever creates money greater than its excess reserves.

11. Compute the size of the monetary multiplier and the money-creating potential of the banking system when provided with appropriate data.

12. State the two leakages that reduce the money-creating potential of the banking system.

13. Define and identify the terms and concepts at the end of the chapter.

COMMENTS AND TEACHING SUGGESTIONS

1. Emphasize that the money multiplier in this chapter is distinct from the income multiplier that was discussed in earlier chapters.

2. Current data on the money multiplier can be obtained from two publications: *Monetary Trends* (monthly) and *US Financial Data* (weekly), which are published by the Federal Reserve Bank of St. Louis, (P.O. Box 442, St. Louis, MO 63166).

3. Remind the student that the chapter's discussion of bank credit is in terms of the maximum money-creating potential that would probably not ever be reached due to these modifications introduced at the end of this chapter.

4. Have the students act out the process of requesting a loan. Appoint one student as the loan officer and another as the customer. Encourage all students to participate in deciding what questions the loan officer should ask and what criteria should be used to decide credit worthiness. Have the student (customer) sign a promissory note and demonstrate the change in the bank's balance sheet on the overhead projector or blackboard. Point out to the students that the promissory note is viewed as a debt by the customer but is treated as an asset by the bank. It is in fact an income-earning asset that can be held by the bank or sold to someone else if desired.

    The customer, of course, spends the proceeds of the loan. This is brand new spendable money, money created by the loan. The customer's IOU is literally a promise to pay, a promise to pay that was monetized by the bank. The customer's IOU is not generally accepted in the economy as money. However, the bank's IOU—the liabilities of the bank—in the form of checkable deposits are generally accepted as money. This demonstration may help students remember that the nation's money supply is circulating debt and that promissory notes "back up" the money supply. Make it clear to students that banks make loans because much of their profitability depends on it.

STUDENT STUMBLING BLOCKS

1. The fact that banks can create money seems somewhat like magic. Part of the mystery lies in forgetting that checkable deposits are money. Many students fall back on their old understanding of money as currency and forget that the bulk of the money supply is in checkable deposits. Federal Reserve Banks have published simulations to make the money creation process more interesting and concrete. Although designed for high schools, the simulations are perfectly suitable for use with most college students. Check the publications catalog of the Federal Reserve Banks for their educational materials. Even their comic books are enjoyed by college students.

2. Students without an accounting background may not understand T-accounts. Especially confusing is the idea that checkable deposits are liabilities for banks. Emphasize that deposits belong to the depositor and can be withdrawn at any time. Thus, they are not assets for the bank. On the asset side there will be reserves or cash to back up the claim when the depositor first puts his/her money in the bank. When the depositor withdraws funds or writes a check to someone who banks elsewhere, both deposits and reserves decrease in the home bank. Problems at the end of the chapter, or those found in the *Study Guide* or the computer tutorial provide practice.

3. The distinction between the money-creating potential of a single bank and the multiplied potential of the entire system is difficult for students to grasp. When discussing the consolidated balance sheet concept, it may be helpful to have students imagine that all banks are linked through an imaginary island parent bank where there is no cash and no leakages of reserves or deposits from this system. This may help them understand the difference between the situation in which a single bank is one among many and the system as a whole.

LECTURE NOTES

I. **Introduction: Although we are fascinated by large sums of currency, people use checkable deposits for most transactions.**

   A. Most transaction accounts are "created" as a result of loans from banks or thrifts.

   B. This chapter demonstrates the money-creating abilities of a single bank or thrift and then looks at that of the system as a whole.

   C. The term depository institution refers to banks and thrift institutions, but in this chapter the term bank will be often used generically to apply to all depository institutions.

II. **Balance Sheet of a Single Commercial Bank**

   A. A balance sheet states the assets and claims of a bank at some point in time.

   B. All balance sheets must balance, that is, the value of assets must equal value of claims.

   1. The bank owners' claim is called net worth.

   2. Nonowners' claims are called liabilities.

   3. Basic equation: Assets = liabilities + net worth.

III. **History of Fractional Reserve Banking: The Goldsmiths**

   A. In the 16th century goldsmiths had safes for gold and precious metals, which they often kept for consumers and merchants. They issued receipts for these deposits.

   B. Receipts came to be used as money in place of gold because of their convenience, and goldsmiths became aware that much of the stored gold was never redeemed.

   C. Goldsmiths realized they could "loan" gold by issuing receipts to borrowers, who agreed to pay back gold plus interest.

   D. Such loans began "fractional reserve banking," because the actual gold in the vaults became only a fraction of the receipts held by borrowers and owners of gold.

   E. Significance of fractional reserve banking:

   1. Banks can create money by lending more than the original reserves on hand. (Note: Today gold is not used as reserves).

   2. Lending policies must be prudent to prevent bank "panics" or "runs" by depositors worried about their funds. Also, the U.S. deposit insurance system prevents panics.

IV. **Money Creation Potential by a Single Bank in the Banking System**

   A. Formation of a commercial bank: Following is an example of the process.

   1. In Wahoo, Nebraska, the Wahoo bank is formed with $250,000 worth of owners' capital stock (see Balance Sheet 1).

   2. This bank obtains property and equipment with some of its capital funds (see Balance Sheet 2).

   3. The bank begins operations by accepting deposits (see Balance Sheet 3).

   4. Bank must keep reserve deposits in its district Federal Reserve Bank (see Table 14-1 for requirements).

   a. Banks can keep reserves at Fed or in cash in vaults.

b. Banks keep cash on hand to meet depositors' needs.

c. Required reserves are a fraction of deposits, as noted above.

B. Other important points:

1. Terminology: Actual reserves minus required reserves are called excess reserves.

2. Control: Required reserves do not exist to protect against "runs," because banks must keep their required reserves. Required reserves are to give the Federal Reserve control over the amount of lending or deposits that banks can create. In other words, required reserves help the Fed control credit and money creation. Banks cannot loan beyond their fraction required reserves.

3. Asset and liability: Reserves are an asset to banks but a liability to the Federal Reserve Bank system, since now they are deposit claims by banks at the Fed.

C. Continuation of Wahoo Bank's transactions:

1. Transaction 5: A $50,000 check is drawn against Wahoo Bank by Mr. Bradshaw, who buys farm equipment in Surprise, Nebraska. (Yes, both Wahoo and Surprise exist).

2. The Surprise company deposits the check in Surprise Bank, which gains reserves at the Fed, and Wahoo Bank loses $50,000 reserves at Fed; Mr. Bradshaw's account goes down, and Surprise implement company's account increases in Surprise Bank.

3. The effects of this transaction are traced in Figure 14-1 and Balance Sheet 5.

D. Money-creating transactions of a commercial bank are shown in the next 3 transactions.

1. Transaction 6: Wahoo Bank grants a loan of $50,000 to Gristly in Wahoo (see Balance Sheet 6a).

a. Money ($50,000) has been created in the form of new demand deposit worth $50,000.

b. Wahoo Bank has reached its lending limit: It has no more excess reserves as soon as Gristly Meat Packing writes a check for $50,000 to Quickbuck Construction (See Balance Sheet 6b).

c. Legally, a bank can lend only to the extent of its excess reserves.

2. Transaction 7: Loan repayments result in a decline in demand deposits and, therefore, a decrease in money supply at the time the loan is repaid (see Balance Sheet 7). Gristly repays its $50,000 loan.

3. Transaction 8: When banks or the Federal Reserve buy government securities from the public, they create money in much the same way as a loan does (see Balance Sheet 8). Wahoo bank buys $50,000 of bonds from a securities dealer. The dealer's checkable deposits rise by $50,000. This increases the money supply in same way as the bank making the loan to Gristly.

4. Likewise, when banks or the Federal Reserve sell government securities to the public, they decrease supply of money like a loan repayment does.

E. Profits, liquidity, and the federal funds market:

1. Profits: Banks are in business to make a profit like other firms. They earn profits primarily from interest on loans and securities they hold.

2. Liquidity: Banks must seek safety by having liquidity to meet cash needs of depositors and to meet check clearing transactions.

3. Federal funds rate: Banks can borrow from one another to meet cash needs in the federal funds market, where banks borrow from each other's available reserves on an overnight basis. The rate paid is called the federal funds rate.

V. **The Entire Banking System and Multiple-Deposit Expansion (all banks combined)**

A. The entire banking system can create an amount of money which is a multiple of the system's excess reserves, even though each bank in the system can only lend dollar for dollar with its excess reserves.

B. Three simplifying assumptions:

1. Required reserve ratio assumed to be 20 percent. (The actual reserve ratio averages 10 percent of checkable deposits.)

2. Initially banks have no excess reserves; they are "loaned up."

3. When banks have excess reserves, they loan it all to one borrower, who writes check for entire amount to give to someone else, who deposits it at another bank. The check clears against original lender.

C. System's lending potential: Suppose a junkyard owner finds a $100 bill and deposits it in Bank A. The system's lending begins with Bank A having $80 in excess reserves, lending this amount, and having the borrower write an $80 check which is deposited in Bank B. See further lending effects on Banks C and D. The possible further transactions are summarized in Table 14-2.

D. Monetary multiplier is illustrated in Table 14-2.

1. Formula for monetary or checkable deposit multiplier is:

Monetary multiplier = 1/required reserve ratio or m = 1/R or 1/.20 in our example.

2. Maximum deposit expansion possible is equal to: excess reserves ∞ monetary multiplier, or $D = M \times e$.

3. Figure 14-2 illustrates this process in a diagram.

4. Modifications to simple monetary multiplier concept reduce the final result and include complications due to "leakages."

   a. Currency drains (cash kept by customers) dampen M, because that money is not part of bank reserves so can't be loaned out further.

   b. Excess reserves kept on hand by banks also dampen M, because those reserves are not loaned out and therefore not expanded.

E. Need for monetary control:

1. During prosperity, banks will lend as much as possible and reserve requirements provide a limit to expansion of loans.

2. During recession, banks may cut lending, which can worsen recession. Federal Reserve has ways to encourage lending in such cases.

3. The conclusion is that profit-seeking bankers will be motivated to expand or contract loans that could worsen business cycle. The Federal Reserve uses monetary policy to counteract such results in order to prevent worsening recessions or inflation. Chapter 15 explains this.

VI. **LAST WORD: The Bank Panics of 1930-1933**

A. Bank panics in 1930-33 led to a multiple contraction of the money supply, which worsened Depression.

B. Many of failed banks were healthy, but they suffered when worried depositors panicked and withdrew funds all at once. More than 9000 banks failed in three years.

C. As people withdrew funds, this reduced banks' reserves and, in turn, their lending power fell significantly.

D. Contraction of excess reserves leads to multiple contraction in the money supply, or the reverse of situation in Table 14-2. Money supply was reduced by 25 percent in those years.

E. President Roosevelt declared a "bank holiday," closing banks temporarily while Congress started the Federal Deposit Insurance Corporation (FDIC), which ended bank panics on insured accounts.

ANSWERS TO END-OF-CHAPTER QUESTIONS

14-1 Why must a balance sheet always balance? What are the major assets and claims on a commercial bank's balance sheet?

A balance sheet is a statement of assets and claims (or liabilities and net worth). It must balance because every asset is claimed by someone, so that assets (the left-hand side) = liabilities + net worth (the right-hand side).

The major assets of a bank are: cash (including cash reserves held by the Fed), its property, the loans it has made, and the securities it holds over and above general loans. Its liabilities are the deposits of its customers. The difference between the assets and liabilities is the bank's net worth, which is shown on the liabilities side, thus ensuring that the balance sheet balances.

14-2 (*Key Question*) Why are commercial banks required to have reserves? Explain why reserves are an asset to commercial banks but a liability to the Federal Reserve Banks. What are excess reserves? How do you calculate the amount of excess reserves held by a bank? What is their significance?

Reserves provide the Fed a means of controlling the money supply. It is through increasing and decreasing excess reserves that the Fed is able to achieve a money supply of the size it thinks best for the economy.

Reserves are assets of commercial banks because these funds are cash belonging to them; they are a claim the commercial banks have against the Federal Reserve Bank. Reserves deposited at the Fed are a liability to the Fed because they are funds it owes; they are claims that commercial banks have against it.

Excess reserves are the amount by which actual reserves exceed required reserves: Excess reserves: Excess reserves = actual reserves - required reserves. Commercial banks can safely lend excess reserves, thereby increasing the money supply.

14-3 "Whenever currency is deposited into a commercial bank, cash goes out of circulation and, as a result, the supply of money is reduced." Do you agree? Explain.

Students should not agree. The M1 money supply consists of currency outside of the banks (cash in the hands of the public) and checking account deposits of the public in the commercial banks. The deposit of currency into a checking account in a bank has changed the form of the money supply but not the amount.

14-4 (*Key Question*) "When a commercial bank makes loans, it creates money; when loans are repaid, money is destroyed." Explain.

Banks add to checking account balances when they make loans; these checkable deposits are part of the money supply. People pay off loans by writing checks; checkable deposits fall, meaning the money supply drops. Money is "destroyed."

14-5   Explain why a single commercial bank can safely lend only an amount equal to its excess reserves but the commercial banking system can lend by a multiple of its excess reserves. What is the monetary multiplier? How does it relate to the reserve ratio?

When a bank grants a loan, it can expect that the borrower will not leave the proceeds of the loan sitting idle in his or her account. Most people borrow to spend. Therefore the lending bank can expect that checks will be written against the loan and that the bank will shortly lose reserves to other banks, as the checks are presented for payment, to the full extent of the loan. In short, when a bank grants loans to the full extent of its excess reserves, it can shortly expect to lose these excess reserves to other banks. From this it can be seen why a bank cannot safely lend more than its excess reserves. If it did, it would soon find that its cash reserves were below its legal reserve requirement.

From the above it can be seen why the commercial banking system can safely lend a multiple of its excess reserves. Whereas one bank loses reserves to other banks, the system does not. With a legal cash reserve requirement of, say, 20 percent, Bank "B" on receiving as a new deposit the $100 loaned by Bank "A" (the excess reserves of Bank "A"), may safely lend $80 (80 percent of $100). Bank "C", on receiving as a new deposit the $80 loan of Bank "B", loans 80 percent of that, namely $64. Note that the $100 initial excess reserves of the banking system have already resulted in the money supply increasing by $244 (= $100 + $80 + $64). The money supply will continue to increase, at a diminishing rate (Bank "D" will increase the money supply by $51.20 in loaning this amount), until the total increase in the money supply is $500.

The algebra underlying the monetary multiplier is that of an infinite geometric progression. Designating the fixed fraction of the previous number as b (0.8 in our case) and k as the sum of the progression, we have:

$$k = 1 + b + b2 + b3 + \ldots\ldots + bn$$

Solving this for a very large n, we get, $k = 1/(1 - b)$

In our example, the multiplier k is $1/(1 - 0.8) = 1/.2 = 5$. And 5 is the reciprocal of the reserve ratio of 20 percent of 0.2. The multiplier is inversely related to the reserve ratio.

14-6   Assume that Jones deposits $500 in currency into her checkable deposit account in the First National Bank. A half-hour later Smith negotiates a loan for $750 at this bank. By how much and in what direction has the money supply changed? Explain.

The loan of $750 to Smith increases the money supply by $750, and that is the only change. The deposit of $500 by Jones does not change the money supply. Whether Jones' $500 is in her purse or in her demand deposit, the $500 are still part of the money supply.

14-7   Suppose the National Bank of Commerce has excess reserves of $8,000 and outstanding checkable deposits of $150,000. If the reserve ratio is 20 percent, what is the size of the bank's actual reserves?

Required reserves = 20 percent of $150,000 = $30,000

Therefore, required reserves = $30,000; Excess reserves = $ 8,000; Actual reserves = $38,000.

14-8   (Key Question) Suppose the Continental Bank has the following simplified balance sheet. The reserve ratio is 20 percent.

	Assets			Liabilities and net worth		
		(1)	(2)		(1)	(2)
Reserves	$22,000	___	___	Demand deposits $100,000	___	___
Securities	38,000					
Loans	40,000	___	___			
		___	___			

a. What is the maximum amount of new loans which this bank can make? Show in column 1 how the bank's balance sheet will appear after the bank has loaned this additional amount.

b. By how much has the supply of money changed? Explain.

c. How will the bank's balance sheet appear after checks drawn for the entire amount of the new loans have been cleared against this bank? Show this new balance sheet in column 2.

d. Answer questions a, b, and c on the assumption that the reserve ratio is 15 percent.

(a) $2,000. Column 1 of Assets (top to bottom): $22,000; $38,000; $42,000. Column 1 of Liabilities: $102,000.

(b) $2,000. The bank has lent out its excess reserves, creating $2,000 of new demand-deposit money.

(c) Column 2 of Assets (top to bottom): $20,000; $38,000; $42,000. Column 2 of Liabilities; $100,000.

(d) $7,000.

14-9   The Third National Bank has reserves of $20,000 and demand deposits of $100,000. The reserve ratio is 20 percent. Households deposit $5,000 in currency into the bank which is added to reserves. How much excess reserves does the bank now have?

Demand deposits have risen to $105,000. Twenty percent of this is $21,000, which is its required reserves. The bank's actual reserves have risen to $25,000. Therefore, its excess reserves are $4,000 ($25,000 - $21,000).

14-10   Suppose again that the Third National Bank has reserves of $20,000 and demand deposits of $100,000. The reserve ratio is 20 percent. The bank now sells $5,000 in securities to the Federal Reserve Bank in its district, receiving a $5,000 increase in reserves in return. What level of excess reserves does the bank now have? Why does your answer differ (yes, it does!) from the answer to question 9?

The bank now has excess reserves of $5,000 (rather than $4,000) because in this case the demand deposits on the liabilities side of its balance sheet did not change. In the former case, $1,000 of new cash reserves were needed against the $5,000 increase in demand deposits. In the present case, nothing occurred on the liabilities side of the balance sheet. The sale of the securities to the Fed caused changes on the assets side only—one asset (securities) was exchanged for another (reserves).

14-11   Suppose a bank discovers its reserves will temporarily fall slightly short of those legally required. How might it remedy this situation through the Federal funds market? Next, assume the bank finds that its reserves will be substantially and permanently deficient. What remedy is available to this bank? (*Hint*: Recall your answer to question 4.)

Banks can borrow temporarily from other banks that have temporary excess reserves. These funds are transferred from one bank's reserve account to the other and allow the lending bank to earn interest on otherwise idle excess reserve funds for an overnight period, while replenishing the reserves of the deficient bank.

If a bank finds that its reserves are substantially deficient, it should suspend lending and gradually build up its reserves as borrowers repay loans made by the bank earlier.

14-12   Suppose that Bob withdraws $100 of cash from his checking account at Security Bank and uses it to buy a camera from Joe, who deposits the $100 in his checking account in Serenity Bank. Assuming a reserve ratio of 10 percent and no initial excess reserves, determine the extent to which (a) Security Bank must reduce its loans and demand deposits because of the cash withdrawal and (b) Serenity Bank can safely increase its loans as demand deposits because of the cash deposit. Have the cash withdrawal and deposit changed the money supply?

(a) Security Bank will have to reduce its loans and demand deposits by $90, the amount of its new deficiency of reserves.

(b) Serenity Bank can safely increase its loans and demand deposits by $90, the amount of its new excess reserves.

The money supply has not changed. Bob's checking account has decreased by $100 and Joe's checking account has increased by $100. There has been no change in the overall excess reserves in the banking system.

14-13   (*Key Question*) Suppose the simplified consolidated balance sheet shown below is for the commercial banking system. All figures are in billions. The reserve ratio is 25 percent.

Assets			Liabilities and Net Worth		
	(1)				(2)
Reserves	$ 52	___	Demand deposits	$200	___
Securities	48	___			
Loans	100	___			

a.   What amount of excess reserves does the commercial banking system have? What is the maximum amount the banking system might lend? Show in column 1 how the consolidated balance sheet would look after this amount has been lent. What is the monetary multiplier?

b.   Answer question 13a assuming that the reserve ratio is 20 percent. Explain the resulting difference in the lending ability of the commercial banking system.

(a) Required reserves = $50 billion (= 25% of $200 billion); so excess reserves = $2 billion (= $52 billion - $50 billion). Maximum amount banking system can lend = $8 billion (= 1/.25 ∞ $2 billion). Column (1) of Assets data (top to bottom): $52 billion; $48 billion; $108 billion. Column (1) of Liabilities data: $208 billion. Monetary multiplier = 4 (= 1/.25).

(b) Required reserves = $40 billion (= 20% of $200 billion); so excess reserves = $12 billion (= $52 billion - $40 billion). Maximum amount banking system can lend = $60 billion (= 1/.20 ∞ $12 billion). Column (1) data for assets after loans (top to bottom); $52 billion; $48 billion;

$160 billion. Column (1) data for liabilities after loans: $260 billion. Monetary multiplier = 5 (= 1/.20). The decrease in the reserve ratio increases the banking system's excess reserves from $2 billion to $12 billion and increases the size of the monetary multiplier from 4 to 5. Lending capacity becomes 5 ∞ $12 = $609 billion.

14-14 What are banking "leakages"? How might they affect the money-creating potential of the banking system?

Banking leakages are reductions in the money available to banks in each successive round of money-supply creation that occurs as banks lend money deposited with them. The first leakage is government-ordained: The banks are required to keep a certain percentage of their deposits as cash reserves. Thus, when Bank "A" receives a deposit of $100 it may only loan, say, $80. And when the $80 is deposited in Bank "B," it, too, may only loan 80 percent, or $64; and so on. The $20 Bank "A" must retain is a leakage, as is the $16 that Bank "B" must retain. If these and all other leakages did not exist, the monetary multiplier would be infinite, for the initial deposit would be continuously relent without any part being retained in the system.

There are, in fact, two other leakages. The first is called "currency drains." If those who borrow from a bank take part of the loan in cash and they or others retain it as additional cash in hand, then less than the amount of the loan will be redeposited in other banks in the system. For instance, Bank "B" would not be able to lend $80, but only, say, $40 if only $50 of the $100 loan was deposited in it.

The third leakage is "excess reserves" that are not loaned out; that is, that are retained by a bank in excess of the legal reserve required by law. Since reserves earn no interest for the bank, it is not usual for a bank to hold excess reserves, but when it does happen (presumably because the bank is not satisfied that it can lend safely), the monetary multiplier is diminished.

14-15 Explain why there is a need for the Federal Reserve System to control the money supply.

Without the Fed, in a boom the commercial banks would lend as much as they could, subject only to the legal reserve requirement. This could well increase the inflationary pressures that might already be building. Therefore, the Fed has the means to decrease the money supply (or its rate of increase) and thus the inflationary lending ability of the commercial banks.

Again, in a recession, without the Fed, the commercial banks might well be disinclined to lend because they fear loans will not be repaid. The banking system thus would fail to provide the liquidity needed for recovery.

14-16 (*Last Word*) Explain how the bank panics of 1930 to 1933 produced a decline in the nation's money supply. Why are such panics highly unlikely today?

Because we have a fractional reserve banking system, bank reserves support a multiple amount of demand deposit money. When depositors collectively withdraw funds and "cash out" their accounts, bank reserves fall. Although demand deposits fall by the amount of cash withdrawn, the remaining demand deposits are too high relative to the reduced reserves. Banks therefore must call in loans or sell securities to get reserves. Both actions reduce the money supply.

Such panics are unlikely today because deposits are insured by the Federal Deposit Insurance Corporation (FDIC), which covers the Bank Insurance Fund (BIF) for bank deposits up to $100,000 for each depositor, and also the Savings Association Insurance Fund (SAIF), which covers deposits up to $100,000 in savings and loan associations. Because Congress stands behind these insurance funds, depositors are not worried about the loss of their funds and, therefore, will not rush to withdraw them whenever they might be slightly worried about a particular institution's financial health.

CHAPTER FIFTEEN
MONETARY POLICY

CHAPTER OVERVIEW

The objectives and the mechanics of monetary policy are covered in this chapter. It is organized around seven major topics: (1) the balance sheet of the Federal Reserve Banks; (2) the techniques of monetary policy; (3) a graphic restatement of monetary policy; (4) the cause-effect chain of monetary policy; (5) a survey of the advantages and disadvantages of monetary policy; (6) the dilemma of which targets should be the goal of monetary policy, interest rates or money supply; (7) the impact of monetary policy operating in an open world economy. Finally, there is a brief, but important, synopsis of mainstream theory and policies. The purpose of the concluding sections is to summarize all the macro theory developed so far and fit the pieces together as an integrated whole for students.

WHAT'S NEW

The section on the "relative importance" of monetary policy tools is reorganized and has been clarified. Also revised and updated is the section on the strengths and weaknesses of monetary policy. Discussion of the potential asymmetry of monetary policy is stronger with a focus on recent monetary policy weakness in Japan. As in the earlier chapter, former references to demand deposits are changed to checkable deposits.

INSTRUCTIONAL OBJECTIVES

After completing this chapter, students should be able to:

1. Identify the goals of monetary policy.

2. List the principal assets and liabilities of the Federal Reserve Banks.

3. Explain how each of the three quantitative controls may be used by the Fed to expand and to contract the money supply.

4. Describe three monetary policies the Fed could use to reduce unemployment.

5. Describe three monetary policies the Fed could use to reduce inflationary pressures in the economy.

6. Explain the cause-effect chain between monetary policy and changes in equilibrium GDP.

7. Demonstrate graphically the money market and how a change in the money supply will affect the interest rate.

8. Show the effects of interest rate changes on investment spending.

9. Describe the impact of changes in investment on aggregate demand and equilibrium GDP.

10. Contrast the effects of an easy money policy with the effects of a tight money policy.

11. Identify the federal funds rate and its importance for monetary policy.

12. List four shortcomings and three strengths of monetary policy.

13. Explain the net export effect of an expansionary and a contractionary monetary policy.

14. Define and identify terms and concepts at the end of the chapter.

COMMENTS AND TEACHING SUGGESTIONS

1. The Federal Reserve Banks have numerous educational publications and videos available for classroom distribution or use. Ask your district Fed for a catalog of materials available. Most of the high school level materials are suitable for adults as well.

2. Plan a visual demonstration of open market operations. The creation of new reserves in the banking system seems like a magician's trick to most students and the further expansion of the money supply through bank loans, just more smoke and mirrors. This is a good opportunity to get students involved through role playing. Assign individual students or small groups parts in the process: the Fed, commercial banks, bank customers. Walk through several transactions to show how purchases by the Fed monetize U.S. Government securities, putting dollars in the hands of bank customers. When the Fed sells U.S. Government securities, the money supply declines as buyers pay for the bonds.

3. The discussion of the Federal Reserve Bank's consolidated balance sheet demonstrates the changes that take place on the Fed's balance sheet and the commercial bank's balance sheets as open market operations are carried out. Note the focus on open market operations.

STUDENT STUMBLING BLOCKS

1. Open market operations are puzzling to students who may not be familiar with bonds in the first place. Begin by a brief review of the federal government's debt, which will inform them that there are trillions of dollars worth of government bonds in existence. The latest Federal Reserve Bulletin, will have a table giving the amount of this debt currently held by the Fed. In other words, the Fed has significant power to affect the money supply by buying or selling these securities. Also remind students that the Fed deals only in federal government bonds, not corporate stock or bonds.

2. One memory tip suggested by a teacher is to tell students that when the Fed "sells" securities that "soaks" up money, i.e., the money supply decreases. The link between "sell" and "soak" should be an easy one for students to remember. Likewise, the Fed's "purchase" can be associated with "pump or push."

LECTURE NOTES

I.   **Introduction to Monetary Policy**

A. Reemphasize Chapter 13's points: The Fed's Board of Governors formulates policy, and twelve Federal Reserve Banks implement policy.

B. The fundamental objective of monetary policy is to aid the economy in achieving full-employment output with stable prices.

1. To do this, the Fed changes the nation's money supply.

2. To change money supply, the Fed manipulates size of excess reserves held by banks.

C. Monetary policy has a very powerful impact on the economy, and the Chairman of the Fed's Board of Governors, Alan Greenspan currently, is sometimes called the second most powerful person in the U.S.

II. **Consolidated Balance Sheet of the Federal Reserve Banks**

A. The assets on the Fed's balance sheet contains two major items.

1. Securities which are federal government bonds purchased by Fed, and

2. Loans to commercial banks (Note: again commercial banks term is used even though the chapter analysis also applies to other thrift institutions.)

B. The liability side of the balance sheet contains three major items.

1. Reserves of banks held as deposits at Federal Reserve Banks,

2. U.S. Treasury deposits of tax receipts and borrowed funds, and

3. Federal Reserve Notes outstanding, our paper currency.

III. **The Fed has Three Major "Tools" of Monetary Policy**

A. Open-market operations refer to the Fed's buying and selling of government bonds.

1. Buying securities will increase bank reserves and the money supply (see Figure 15-1).

a. If the Fed buys directly from banks, then bank reserves go up by the value of the securities sold to the Fed. See impact on balance sheets using text example.

b. If the Fed buys from the general public, people receive checks from the Fed and then deposit the checks at their bank. Bank customer deposits rise and therefore bank reserves rise by the same amount. Follow text example to see the impact.

i. Banks' lending ability rises with new excess reserves.

ii. Money supply rises directly with increased deposits by the public.

c. When Fed buys bonds from bankers, reserves rise and excess reserves rise by same amount since no checkable deposit was created.

d. When Fed buys from public, some of the new reserves are required reserves for the new checkable deposits.

e. Conclusion: When the Fed buys securities, bank reserves will increase and the money supply potentially can rise by a multiple of these reserves.

f. Note: When the Fed sells securities, points a-e above will be reversed. Bank reserves will go down, and eventually the money supply will go down by a multiple of the banks' decrease in reserves.

g. How the Fed attracts buyers or sellers:

i. When Fed buys, it raises demand and price of bonds which in turn lowers effective interest rate on bonds. The higher price and lower interest rates make selling bonds to Fed attractive.

ii. When Fed sells, the bond supply increases and bond prices fall, which raises the effective interest rate yield on bonds. The lower price and higher interest rates make buying bonds from Fed attractive.

B. The reserve ratio is another "tool" of monetary policy. It is the fraction of reserves required relative to their customer deposits.

1. Raising the reserve ratio increases required reserves and shrinks excess reserves. Any loss of excess reserves shrinks banks' lending ability and, therefore, the potential money supply by a multiple amount of the change in excess reserves.

2. Lowering the reserve ratio decreases the required reserves and expands excess reserves. Gain in excess reserves increases banks' lending ability and, therefore, the potential money supply by a multiple amount of the increase in excess reserves.

191

3. Changing the reserve ratio has two effects.

    a. It affects the size of excess reserves.

    b. It changes the size of the monetary multiplier. For example, if ratio is raised from 10 percent to 20 percent, the multiplier falls from 10 to 5.

4. Changing the reserve ratio is very powerful since it affects banks' lending ability immediately. It could create instability, so Fed rarely changes it.

5. Table 15-2 provides illustrations.

C. The third "tool" is the discount rate which is the interest rate that the Fed charges to commercial banks that borrow from the Fed.

1. An increase in the discount rate signals that borrowing reserves is more difficult and will tend to shrink excess reserves.

2. A decrease in the discount rate signals that borrowing reserves will be easier and will tend to expand excess reserves.

D. "Easy" monetary policy occurs when the Fed tries to increase money supply by expanding excess reserves in order to stimulate the economy. The Fed will enact one or more of the following measures.

1. The Fed will buy securities.

2. The Fed may reduce reserve ratio, although this is rarely changed because of its powerful impact.

3. The Fed could reduce the discount rate, although this has little direct impact on the money supply.

E. "Tight" monetary policy occurs when Fed tries to decrease money supply by decreasing excess reserves in order to slow spending in the economy during an inflationary period. The Fed will enact one or more of the following policies:

1. The Fed will sell securities.

2. The Fed may raise the reserve ratio, although this is rarely changed because of its powerful impact.

3. The Fed could raise the discount rate, although it has little direct impact on money supply.

F. For several reasons, open-market operations give the Fed most control of the three "tools."

1. Open-market operations are most important. This decision is flexible because securities can be bought or sold quickly and in great quantities. Reserves change quickly in response.

2. The reserve ratio is rarely changed since this could destabilize bank's lending and profit positions.

3. Changing the discount rate has little direct effect, since only 2-3 percent of bank reserves are borrowed from Fed. At best it has an "announcement effect" that signals direction of monetary policy.

IV. **Monetary Policy, Real GDP, and the Price Level: How Policy Affects the Economy**

A. Cause-effect chain:

1. Money market impact is shown in Key Graph 15-2.

    a. Demand for money is comprised of two parts (Recall Chapter 13).

        i. Transactions demand is directly related to GDP.

        ii. Asset demand is inversely related to interest rates, so total money demands is inversely related to interest rates.

    b. Supply of money is assumed to be set by the Fed.

    c. Interaction of supply and demand determines the market rate of interest, as seen in Figure 15-2(a).

    d. Interest rate determines amount of investment businesses will be willing to make. Investment demand is inversely related to interest rates, as seen in Figure 15-2(b).

    e. Effect of interest rate changes on level of investment is great because interest cost of large, long-term investment is sizable part of investment cost.

    f. As investment rises or falls, equilibrium GDP rises or falls by a multiple amount, as seen in Figure 15-2(c).

2. Expansionary or easy money policy: The Fed takes steps to increase excess reserves, which lowers the interest rate and increases investment which, in turn, increases GDP by a multiple amount. (See Column 1, Table 15-3)

3. Contractionary or tight money policy is the reverse of an easy policy: Excess reserves fall, which raises interest rate, which decreases investment, which, in turn, decreases GDP by a multiple amount of the change in investment. (See Column 2, Table 15-3)

4. Aggregate supply and monetary policy:

    a. Easy monetary policy may be inflationary if initial equilibrium is at or near full-employment.

    b. If economy is below full-employment, easy monetary policy can shift aggregate demand and GDP toward full-employment equilibrium.

    c. Likewise a tight monetary policy can reduce inflation if economy is near full-employment, but can make unemployment worse in a recession.

5. Try Quick Quiz 15-2.

V. **Effectiveness of Monetary Policy**

A. Strengths of monetary policy:

    1. It is speedier and more flexible than fiscal policy since the Fed can buy and sell securities daily.

    2. It is less political. Fed Board members are isolated from political pressure, since they serve 14-year terms, and policy changes are more subtle and not noticed as much as fiscal policy changes. It is easier to make good, but unpopular decisions.

    3. In the 1980s and 1990s Fed policy is given much credit for achieving a prosperous economy with low inflation and high employment.

B. Shortcomings of monetary policy:

    1. Control is weakening as technology makes it possible to shift from money assets to other types; also global finance gives nations less power.

2. Cyclical asymmetry may exist: a tight monetary policy works effectively to brake inflation, but an easy monetary policy is not always as effective in stimulating the economy from recession.

3. The velocity of money (number of times the average dollar is spent in a year) may be unpredictable, especially in the short run and can offset the desired impact of changes in money supply. Tight money policy may cause people to spend faster; velocity rises.

4. The impact on investment may be less than traditionally thought. Japan provides a case example. Despite interest rates of zero, investment spending remained low during the recession.

C. Currently the Fed communicates changes in monetary policy through changes in its target for the Federal funds rate. (Key Question 5)

1. The Fed does not set either the Federal funds rate or the prime rate; (see Figure 15-3) each is established by the interaction of lenders and borrowers, but rates generally follow the Fed funds rate.

2. The Fed acts through open market operations, selling bonds to raise interest rates and buying bonds to lower interest rates.

D. Links between monetary policy and the international economy:

1. Net export effect occurs when foreign financial investors respond to a change in interest rates.

    a. Tight monetary policy and higher interest rates lead to appreciation of dollar value in foreign exchange markets; lower interest rates from an easy monetary policy will lead to dollar depreciation in foreign exchange markets (see Figure 12-6d).

    b. When dollar appreciates, American goods become more costly to foreigners, and this lowers demand for U.S. exports, which tends to lower GDP. This is the desired effect of a tight money policy. Conversely, an easy money policy leads to depreciation of dollar, greater demand for U.S. exports and higher GDP. This policy has the desired outcome for expanding GDP.

2. Monetary policy works to correct both trade balance and GDP problems together. An easy monetary policy leads to increased domestic spending and increased GDP, but it also leads to depreciated dollar and higher U.S. export demand, which enhances GDP and erases a trade deficit. The reverse is true for a tight monetary policy, which would tend to reduce net exports and worsen a trade deficit.

3. Table 15-4 illustrates these points.

VI.   **The Big Picture (see Key Graph, Figure 15-4) Shows Many Interrelationships**

A. Fiscal and monetary policy are interrelated. The impact of an increase in government spending will depend on whether it is accommodated by monetary policy. For example, if government spending comes from money borrowed from the general public, it may be offset by a decline in private spending, but if the government borrows from the Fed or if the Fed increases the money supply, then the initial increase in government spending may not be counteracted by a decline in private spending.

B. Study Key Graph 15-4 and you will see that the levels of output, employment, income, and prices all result from the interaction of aggregate supply and aggregate demand. In particular, note the items shown in red that constitute, or are strongly influenced by, public policy.

C. Try Quick Quiz 15-4.

VII. **LAST WORD: For the Fed Life is a Metaphor**

A. The media use colorful terms to describe the Federal Reserve Board and its chair, Alan Greenspan. They may loosen or tighten reins while riding herd on a rambunctious economy!

B. The Fed has been depicted as a mechanic, with references to loosening or tightening things, and to the economy running beautifully or acting sluggish, accelerating, or going out of control.

C. The warrior metaphor has been used—fighting inflation, plotting strategy, protecting the dollar from attack.

D. The Fed has been depicted as the fall guy in terms of administration officials "leaning heavily" on it and telling the Fed to ease up or to relax.

E. As a cosmic force, the Fed satisfies three criteria—power, mystery, and a New York office.

ANSWERS TO END-OF-CHAPTER QUESTIONS

15-1 Use commercial bank and Federal Reserve Bank balance sheets to demonstrate the impact of each of the following transactions on commercial bank reserves:

a. Federal Reserve Banks purchase securities from private businesses and consumers.

b. Commercial banks borrow from the Federal Reserve Banks.

c. The Board of Governors reduces the reserve ratio.

In the tables below, columns "a" through "c" show the changes caused by the answers to the questions. It is assumed the initial reserve ratio is 20 percent. Thus, as the first column shows, the commercial banks are initially completely loaned up. The answers are not cumulated: We return to the first column each time to show the resulting change in column a, b, or c. If you would rather not use numbers, it would be acceptable to substitute with + or - signs, using symbols to represent numbers. For example, part (a) could read "the Fed purchases 'x dollars' worth of securities," and instead of the $2 billion changes on the balance sheet, you would indicate + x. Note: Any numbers could demonstrate this if direction is same.

(a) It is assumed the Fed buys $2 billion worth of securities. This should increase checkable deposits and commercial bank reserves by $2 billion. With demand deposits of $202 billion, required reserves are $40.4 billion, (= 20 percent of $202 billion). Therefore, excess reserves are $1.6 billion (= $42 billion - $40.4 billion) and the banking system can increase the money supply (by making loans) by $8 billion more (= $1.6 billion ∞ 5).

(b) It is assumed the commercial banks borrow $1 billion from the Fed. The commercial banks may now increase the money supply (through making loans) by $5 billion (= $1 billion ∞ 5).

(c) Changing the reserve ratio in itself does not change the balance sheets. However, if we assume the reserve ratio has been decreased from 20 percent to 19 percent, required reserves are now $38 billion (= 19 percent of $200 billion) and the commercial banks can now increase the money supply (through making loans) by $10.53 billion [= $2 billion ∞ (1/0.19)]. Proof: 19 percent of $210.53 billion is $40 billion.

CONSOLIDATED BALANCE SHEET: ALL COMMERCIAL BANKS

		a	b	c
Assets:				
Reserves	$ 40	$ 42	$ 41	$ 40
Securities	60	60	60	60
Loans	102	102	102	102
Liabilities and net worth:				
Checkable deposits	200	202	200	200
Loans from the Federal Reserve Banks	2	2	3	2

CONSOLIDATED BALANCE SHEET: TWELVE FEDERAL RESERVE BANKS

		A	b	c
Assets:				
Securities	$283	$285	$283	$283
Loans to commercial banks	2	2	3	2
Liabilities and net worth:				
Reserves of commercial banks	40	42	41	40
Treasury deposits	5	5	5	5
Federal Reserve Notes	225	225	225	225
Other liabilities and net worth	15	15	15	15

15-2 (*Key Question*) In the table below you will find simplified consolidated balance sheets for the commercial banking system and the twelve Federal Reserve Banks. In columns 1 through 3, indicate how the balance sheets would read after each transaction of a to c is completed. Do not cumulate your answers; that is, analyze each transaction separately, starting in each case from the figures provided. All accounts are in billions of dollars.

CONSOLIDATED BALANCE SHEET: ALL COMMERCIAL BANKS

		(1)	(2)	(3)
Assets:				
Reserves	$ 33	____	____	____
Securities	60	____	____	____
Loans	60	____	____	____
Liabilities and net worth:				
Checkable deposits	150	____	____	____
Loans from the Federal Reserve Banks	3	____	____	____

CONSOLIDATED BALANCE SHEET:
TWELVE FEDERAL RESERVE BANKS

	(1)	(2)	(3)
Assets:			
Securities	$60 ___	___	___
Loans to commercial banks	3 ___	___	___
Liabilities and net worth:			
Reserves of commercial banks	$33 ___	___	___
Treasury deposits	3 ___	___	___
Federal Reserve Notes	27 ___	___	___

---

a. Suppose a decline in the discount rate prompts commercial banks to borrow an additional $1 billion from the Federal Reserve Banks. Show the new balance-sheet figures in column 1.

b. The Federal Reserve Banks sell $3 billion in securities to the public, who pay for the bonds with checks. Show the new balance-sheet figures in column 2.

c. The Federal Reserve Banks buy $2 billion of securities from commercial banks. Show the new balance-sheet figures in column 3.

d. Now review each of the above three transactions, asking yourself these three questions: (1) What change, if any, took place in the money supply as a direct and immediate result of each transaction? (2) What increase or decrease in commercial banks' reserves took place in each transaction? (3) Assuming a reserve ratio of 20 percent, what change in the money-creating potential of the commercial banking system occurred as a result of each transaction?

(a) Column (1) data, top to bottom: Bank Assets: $34, 60, 60; Liabilities: $150, 4; Fed Assets: $60, 4; Liabilities: $34, 3, 27.

(b) Column (2) data: Bank Assets: $30, 60, 60; Liabilities: $147, 3; Fed Assets: $57, 3, 30, 3, 27.

(c) Column (3) data (top to bottom): $35; $58; $60; $150; $3; (Fed banks) $62; $3; $35; $3; $27.

(d) (d1) Money supply (checkable deposits) directly changes only in (b), where it decreases by $3 billion; (d2) See balance sheets; (d3) Money-creating potential of the banking system increases by $5 billion in (a); decreases by $12 billion in (b) (not by $15 billion—the writing of $3 billion of checks by the public to buy bonds reduces demand deposits by $3 billion, thus freeing $0.6 billion of reserves. Three billion dollars minus $0.6 billion equals $2.4 billion of reduced reserves, and this multiplied by the monetary multiplier of 5 equals $12 billion); and increases by $10 billion in (c).

15-3 (*Key Question*) Suppose that you are a member of the Board of Governors of the Federal Reserve System. The economy is experiencing a sharp and prolonged inflationary trend. What changes in (a) the reserve ratio, (b) the discount rate, and (c) open-market operations would you recommend? Explain in each case how the change you advocate would affect commercial bank reserves, the money supply, interest rates, and aggregate demand.

(a) Increase the reserve ratio. This would increase the size of required reserves. If the commercial banks were fully loaned up, they would have to call in loans. The money supply would decrease, interest rates would rise, and aggregate demand would decline.

(b) Increase the discount rate. This would decrease commercial bank borrowing from the Fed. Actual reserves of the commercial banks would fall, as would excess reserves and lending. The money supply would drop, interest rates would rise, and aggregate demand would decline.

(c) Sell government securities in the open market. Buyers of the bonds would write checks to the Fed on their demand deposits. When these checks cleared, reserves would flow from the banking system to the Fed. the decline in reserves would reduce the money supply, which would increase interest rates and reduce aggregate demand.

15-4   (*Key Question*) What is the basic objective of monetary policy? State the cause-effect chain through which monetary policy is made effective. What are the major strengths and weaknesses of monetary policy?

The basic objective of monetary policy is to assist the economy in achieving a full-employment, non-inflationary level of total output. Changes in the money supply affect interest rates, which affect investment spending and therefore aggregate demand.

The major strengths of monetary policy are its speed and flexibility compared to fiscal policy, the Board of Governors is somewhat removed from political pressure, and its successful record in preventing inflation and keeping prices stable. The Fed is given some credit for prosperity in the 1990s.

The major weaknesses are that the Fed's control may weaken with bank reforms and electronic banking that diminish the importance of the traditional money supply, changes in velocity may offset changes in money supply and weaken monetary policy results, and monetary policy has asymmetrical impact – it combats inflation better than it helps recovery from recession.

15-5   (*Key Question*) Distinguish between the Federal funds rate and the prime interest rate. In what way is the Federal funds rate a measure of the tightness or looseness of monetary policy? In 1999 and 2000 the Fed used open-market operations to increase the Federal funds rate. What was the logic of those actions? What was the effect on the prime interest rate?

The Federal funds interest rate is the interest rate banks charge one another on overnight loans needed to meet the reserve requirement. The prime interest rate is the interest rate banks change on loans to their most creditworthy customers. The tighter the monetary policy, the less the supply of excess reserves in the banking system and the higher the Federal funds rate. The reverse is true of a loose or easy monetary policy, which expands excess reserves, and the federal funds rate will fall.

The Fed wanted to reduce the excess reserves, slowing the growth of the money supply. This would slow the expansion of aggregate demand and prevent inflation. The prime interest rate went up.

15-6   (*Key Question*) Suppose the Federal Reserve decides to engage in a tight money policy as a way to reduce demand-pull inflation. Use the aggregate demand-aggregate supply model to show what this policy is intended to accomplish in a closed economy. Now introduce the open economy and explain how changes in the international value of the dollar might affect the location of your aggregate demand curve.

The intent of a tight money policy would be shown as a leftward shift of the aggregate demand curve and a decline in the price level (or, in the real world, a reduction in the rate of inflation). In an open economy, the interest rate hike resulting from the tight money policy would entice people abroad to buy U.S. securities. Because they would need U.S. dollars to buy these securities, the international demand for dollars would rise, causing the dollar to appreciate. Net exports would fall, pushing the aggregate demand curve farther leftward than in the closed economy.

15-7   (*Last Word*) How do each of the following metaphors apply to the Federal Reserve's role in the economy: Fed as a mechanic; Fed as a warrior; Fed as a fall guy?

The Fed is a mechanic in the sense that it is responsible for "tightening" or "loosening" the money supply. It uses terms like a "sluggish" economy or an economy "out of control" in discussing the proper policy to follow. In other words, if we view the economy as a machine and the money supply as one of its components, the Fed takes on the task of adjusting that part in order to "fix" the economy machine!

The Fed is a warrior in the sense that it is asked to "fight" inflation. Policies that reduce inflation are generally unpopular and inflation is often very persistent, hence the term "fight" is used in the "battle" against inflation.

Because the Fed is independent, its policies are often blamed for many of the economy's ills or its failure to perform as desired. It is easy for politicians to blame their own failures to enact appropriate fiscal policies on the Fed. The Fed is thus a "fall guy" whenever the economy does not behave as desired.

CHAPTER SIXTEEN
EXTENDING THE ANALYSIS OF AGGREGATE SUPPLY

CHAPTER OVERVIEW

This is the first chapter of renamed and reorganized Part IV, "Long Run Perspectives and Macroeconomic Debates." This chapter explains the difference between long-run and short-run aggregate supply; it examines the unemployment-inflation relationship and assesses the effect of taxes on aggregate supply.

WHAT'S NEW

Changes from the 14th edition include shortened and simplified analysis of the inflation-unemployment tradeoff. Three generalizations are now addressed: normal, short-run tradeoff between inflation and unemployment; the impact of aggregate supply shocks; the long-run Phillips curve compared to the short-run situation.

Discussion of "adaptive expectations" is deleted and rational expectations theory appears now in Chapter 19.

A new Last Word on the "Impact of Oil" appears along with an associated new question. Also, the Web-Based Questions have been improved.

INSTRUCTIONAL OBJECTIVES

After completing this chapter, students should be able to:

1. Explain the difference between the short-run and long-run aggregate supply curves and their significance for economic policy.

2. Distinguish between demand-pull and cost-push inflation using the aggregate demand-aggregate supply model.

3. Explain and construct a traditional short-run Phillips Curve using the aggregate demand-aggregate supply model.

4. Differentiate between the short-run and long-run Phillips Curves.

5. Identify the supply-side shocks to the U.S. economy in the 1970s and 1980s.

6. Use an aggregate demand-aggregate supply graph to show how supply-side shocks led to stagflation in the 1970s and 1980s.

7. Explain why demand-management policies cannot eliminate stagflation.

8. Distinguish between demand-pull and cost-push inflation using the aggregate demand-aggregate supply model.

9. Explain two possible effects of taxation on aggregate supply.

10. Explain the Laffer Curve concept and list three criticisms of this theory.

11. Define and identify terms at the end of the chapter.

COMMENTS AND TEACHING SUGGESTIONS

1. The Phillips Curve controversy can be introduced by using actual data such as that shown in Figure 16-7b. Ask students if they can see any discernible pattern between unemployment and inflation data without viewing the curves.

2. The aggregate supply and demand model can also be helpful in explaining why demand management policies might entail supply-side effects that limit the attainment of policy goals. The shifts in Figures 16-4 and 16-5 illustrate this problem.

3. Demand-pull and cost-push inflation were introduced earlier, so they should be familiar. However, a review of the aggregate demand and supply model would be a useful way to begin the discussion. Explain that it is difficult to distinguish the two types of inflation in the real world, since the causes of inflation are complex. Use Figure 16-3 and 16-4 to illustrate.

4. A speaker who can recall a time or country where wage-price controls were used, and the problems associated with them might be interesting for students, who might otherwise believe these controls are a simple solution.

5. Throughout the discussion of the Phillips Curve, be sure to point out that the vertical axis measures changes in the price level, not the price level itself (as in AD-AS model).

STUDENT STUMBLING BLOCKS

1. Students may not see why employment usually declines when policies to reduce inflation are implemented.

2. Students may have difficulty with the extended AD-AS model. Have them review Figure 16-1 carefully. Current events may give practice in deciding how the event will impact the economy, through the demand side or the supply side. For example, the potential impact of tax cut proposals made in 2001 could be analyzed.

LECTURE NOTES

I. **Introduction**

    A. Recent focus on the long-run adjustments and economic outcomes has renewed debates about stabilization policy and causes of instability.

    B. This chapter makes the distinction between short run and long run aggregate supply.

    C. The extended model is then used to glean new insights on demand-pull and cost-push inflation.

    D. The relationship between inflation and unemployment is examined; we look at how expectations can affect the economy, and assess the effect of taxes on aggregate supply.

II. **Short-Run and Long-Run Aggregate Supply**

    A. Definition: Short-run and long-run.

        1. For macroeconomics the short-run is a period in which nominal wages (and other input prices) remain fixed as the price level changes.

            a. Workers may not be fully aware of the change in their real wages due to inflation (or deflation) and thus have not adjusted their labor supply decisions and wage demands accordingly.

            b. Employees hired under fixed wage contracts must wait to renegotiate regardless of changes in the price level.

2. Long run aggregate supply (See Figure 16-1b). Formed by long-run equilibrium points a_1, b_1, c_1.

    a. In the long run, nominal wages are fully responsive to price level changes.

    b. The long run aggregate supply curve is a vertical line at the full employment level of real GDP. (See Figure 16-1b) (b_1, a_1, c_1).

B. Short-run aggregate supply curve AS_1, is constructed with three assumptions. (see Figure 16-1a)

    1. The initial price level is given at P_1.

    2. Nominal wages have been established on the expectation that this specific price level will persist.

    3. The price level is flexible both upward and downward.

    4. If the price level rises, higher product prices with constant wages will bring higher profits and increased output. (See Figure 16-1a) (The economy moves from a_1 to a_2 on curve AS_1.)

    5. If the price level falls, lower product price with constant wages will bring lower profits and decreased output. (See Figure 16-1a) (The economy moves from a_1 to a_3 on curve AS_1.)

C. The extended AD-AS makes the distinction between the short run and long run aggregate supply curves. (See Figure 16-2) Equilibrium occurs at point a where aggregate demand intersects both the vertical long run supply curve and the short run supply at full employment output.

III.   **Applying the Extended AD-AS Model**

A. Demand-pull inflation: In the short run it drives up the price level and increases real output; in the long run, only price level rises. (See Figure 16-3)

B. Cost push inflation arises from factors that increase the cost of production at each price level; the increase in the price of a key resource, for example. This shifts the short run supply to the left, not as a response to a price level increase, but as its initiating *cause*. Cost-push inflation creates a dilemma for policymakers. (See Figure 16-4)

    1. If government attempts to maintain full employment when there is cost-push inflation an inflationary spiral may occur.

    2. If government takes a hands-off approach to cost push inflation, a recession will occur. The recession may eventually undo the initial rise in per unit production costs, but in the meantime unemployment and loss of real output will occur.

C. Recession and the extended AD-AS model.

    1. When aggregate demand shifts leftward a recession occurs. If prices and wages are downwardly flexible, the price level falls. The decline in the price level reduces nominal wages, which then eventually shifts the aggregate supply curve to the right. The price level declines and output returns to the full employment level. (See Figure 16-5)

    2. This is the most controversial application of the extended AD-AS model. The key point of dispute is how long it would take in the real world for the necessary price and wage adjustments to take place to achieve the indicated outcome.

IV. **The Phillips Curve and the Inflation – Unemployment Tradeoff**

A. Both low inflation and low unemployment are major goals. But are they compatible?

B. The Phillips Curve is named after A.W. Phillips, who developed his theory in Great Britain by observing the British relationship between unemployment and wage inflation.

C. The basic idea is that given the short run aggregate supply curve, an increase in aggregate demand will cause the price level to increase and real output to expand, and the reverse for a decrease in AD. (Figure 16-b)

D. This tradeoff between output and inflation does not occur over long time periods.

E. Empirical work in the 1960s verified the inverse relationship between the unemployment rate and the rate of inflation in the United States for 1961-1969. (See Figure 16-7b)

F. The stable Phillips Curve of the 1960s gave way to great instability of the curve in the 1970s and 1980s. The obvious inverse relationship of 1961-1969 had become obscure and highly questionable. (See Figure 16-8)

1. In the 1970s the economy experienced increasing inflation and rising unemployment: stagflation.

2. At best, the date in Figure 16-8 suggests a less desirable combination of unemployment and inflation. At worse, the data imply no predictable trade off between unemployment and inflation.

G. Adverse aggregate supply shocks—the stagflation of the 1970s and early 1980s may have been caused by a series of adverse aggregate supply shocks. (Rapid and significant increases in resource costs.)

1. The most significant of these supply shocks was a quadrupling of oil prices by the Organization of Petroleum Exporting Countries (OPEC).

2. Other factors included agricultural shortfalls, a greatly depreciated dollar, wage increases and declining productivity.

3. Leftward shifts of the short run aggregate supply curve make a difference. The Phillips Curve trade off is derived from shifting the aggregate demand curve along a stable short-run aggregate supply curve. (See Figure 16-6)

4. The "Great Stagflation" of the 1970s made it clear that the Phillips Curve did not represent a stable inflation/unemployment relationship.

H. Stagflation's Demise.

1. Another look at Figure 16-8 reveals a generally inward movement of the inflation/unemployment points between 1982 and 1989.

2. The recession of 1981-1982, largely caused by a tight money policy, reduced double-digit inflation and raised the unemployment rate to 9.5% in 1982.

3. With so many workers unemployed, wage increases were smaller and in some cases reduced wages were accepted.

4. Firms restrained their price increases to try to retain their relative shares of diminished markets.

5. Foreign competition throughout this period held down wages and price hikes.

6. Deregulation of the airline and trucking industries also resulted in wage and price reductions.

7. A significant decline in OPEC's monopoly power produced a stunning fall in the price of oil.

I. Global Perspective 16-1 portrays the "misery index" in 1999-2000 for several nations. The index adds unemployment and inflation rates.

V.   Long-Run Vertical Phillips Curve

A. This view is that the economy is generally stable at its natural rate of unemployment (or full-employment rate of output).

1. The hypothesis questions the existence of a long-run inverse relationship between the rate of unemployment and the rate of inflation.

2. Figure 16-9 explains how a short-run tradeoff exists, but not a long-run tradeoff.

3. In the short run we assume that people form their expectations of future inflation on the basis of previous and present rates of inflation and only gradually change their expectations and wage demands.

4. Fully anticipated inflation by labor in the nominal wage demands of workers generates a vertical Phillips Curve. (See Figure 16-9) This occurs over time.

B. Interpretations of the Phillips Curve have changed dramatically over the past three decades.

1. The original idea of a stable tradeoff between inflation and unemployment has given way to other views that focus more on long-run effects.

2. Most economists accept the idea of a short-run tradeoff—where the short run may last several years—while recognizing that in the long run such a tradeoff is much less likely.

VI.   Taxation and Aggregate Supply

A. Economic disturbances can be generated on the supply side, as well as on the demand side of the economy. Certain government policies may reduce the growth of aggregate supply. "Supply-side" economists advocate policies that promote output growth. They argue that:

1. The U.S. tax transfer system has negatively affected incentives to work, invest, innovate and assume entrepreneurial risks.

a. To induce more work government should reduce marginal tax rates on earned income.

b. Unemployment compensation and welfare programs have made job loss less of an economic crisis for some people. Many transfer programs are structured to discourage work.

2. The rewards for saving and investing have also been reduced by high marginal tax rates. A critical determinant of investment spending is the expected after-tax return.

3. Lower marginal tax rates may encourage more people to enter the labor force and to work longer. The lower rates should reduce periods of unemployment and raise capital investment, which increases worker productivity. Aggregate supply will expand and keep inflation low.

B. The Laffer Curve is an idea relating tax rates and tax revenues. It is named after economist Arthur Laffer, who originated the theory. (See Figure 16-10)

1. As tax rates increase from zero, tax revenues increase from zero to some maximum level (m) and then decline.

2. Tax rates above or below this maximum rate will cause a decrease in tax revenue.

3. Laffer argued that tax rates were above the optimal level and by lowering tax rates government could increase the tax revenue collected.

4. The lower tax rates would trigger an expansion of real output and income enlarging the tax base. The main impact would be on supply rather than aggregate demand.

C. Supply side economists offer two additional reasons for lowering the tax rate.

1. Tax avoidance (legal) and tax evasion (illegal) both decline when taxes are reduced.

2. Reduced transfers—tax cuts stimulate production and employment, reducing the need for transfer payments such as welfare and unemployment compensation.

D. Criticisms of the Laffer Curve.

1. There is empirical evidence that the impact on incentives to work, save and invest are small.

2. Tax cuts also increase demand, which can fuel inflation. Demand impact exceeds supply impact.

3. The Laffer Curve (Figure 16-10) is based on a logical premise, but where the economy is located is an empirical question and difficult to determine. It may be hard to know in advance the impact of a tax cut on supply.

VII. **LAST WORD: Has the Impact of Oil Prices Diminished?**

ANSWERS TO END-OF-CHAPTER QUESTIONS

16-1 Distinguish between the short run and the long run as they relate to macroeconomics.

For macroeconomists the short run is a period in which normal wages (and other input prices) remain fixed as output price level changes. There are at least two reasons why nominal wages may remain constant for a while even though the price level has changed.

1. Workers may not be aware of price level changes, and thus have not adjusted their demands.

2. Many employees are hired under fixed wage contracts.

Once sufficient time has elapsed for contracts to expire and nominal wage adjustments to occur, the economy enters the long run a period in which nominal wages are fully responsive to changes in the price level.

16-2 Which of the following statements are true? Which are false? Explain why the false statements are untrue.

a. Short-run aggregate supply curves reflect an inverse relationship between the price level and the level of real output.

b. The long-run aggregate supply curve assumes that nominal wages are fixed.

c. In the long run, an increase in the price level will result in an increase in nominal wages.

(a) False, short run aggregate supply curves reflect a direct relationship between the price level and the level of real output. If there is an increase in the price level, the higher product prices bring an increase in revenue from sales to business firms. Since the nominal wage they are paying are fixed, their profits rise. In response firms collectively increase their output. Produce respond to a decrease in the price level by cutting output. When product prices fall with nominal wages constant firms will discover their revenue and profits have diminished.

(b) False, by definition, nominal wages in the long run are fully responsive to changes in the price level.

(c) True, as above.

16-3 (*Key Question*) Suppose the full-employment level of real output (Q) for a hypothetical economy is $250 and the price level (P) initially is 100. Use the short-run aggregate supply schedules below to answer the questions which follow:

AS(P=100)		AS(P=125)		AS(P=75)	
P	Q	P	Q	P	Q
125	280	125	250	125	310
100	250	100	220	100	280
75	220	75	190	75	250

a. What will be the level of real output in the *short run* if the price level unexpectedly rises from 100 to 125 because of an increase in aggregate demand? What if the price level falls unexpectedly from 100 to 75 because of a decrease in aggregate demand? Explain each situation, using numbers from the table.

b. What will the level of real output in the long run when the price level rises from 100 to 125? When it falls from 100 to 75? Explain each situation.

c. Show the circumstances described in parts a and b on graph paper, and derive the long-run aggregate supply curve.

(a) $280; $220. When the price level rises from 100 to 125 [in aggregate supply schedule AS(P_{100})], producers experience higher prices for their products. Because nominal wages are constant, profits rise and producers increase output to Q = $280. When the price level decreases from 100 to 75, profits decline and producers adjust their output to Q = $75. These are short-run responses to changes in the price level.

(b) $250; $250. In the long run a rise in the price-level to 125 leads to nominal wage increases. The AS(P_{100}) schedule changes to AS(P_{125}) and Q returns to $250, now at a price level of 125. In the long run a decrease in price level to 75 leads to lower nominal wages, yielding aggregate supply schedule AS(P_{75}). Equilibrium Q returns to $250, now at a price level of 75.

(c) Graphically, the explanation is identical to Figure 16-1b. Short-run AS: P_1 = 100; P_2 = 125; P_3 = 75; and Q_1 = $250; Q_2 = $280; and Q_3 = $220. Long-run aggregate supply = Q_1 = $250 at each of the three price levels.

16-4 (*Key Question*) Use graphical analysis to show how each of the following would affect the economy first in the short run and then in the long run. Assume that the United States is initially operating at its full-employment level of output, that prices and wages are eventually flexible both upward and downward, and that there is no counteracting fiscal or monetary policy.

a. Because of a war abroad, the oil supply to the United States is disrupted, sending oil prices rocketing upward.

b. Construction spending on new homes rises dramatically, greatly increasing total U.S. investment spending.

c. Economic recession occurs abroad, significantly reducing foreign purchases of U.S. exports.

(a) See Figure 16-4 in the chapter. Short run: The aggregate supply curve shifts to the left, the price level rises, and real output declines. Long run: The aggregate supply curve shifts back rightward (due to declining nominal wages), the price level falls, and real output increases.

(b) See Figure 16-3. Short run: The aggregate demand curve shifts to the right, and both the price level and real output increase. Long run: The aggregate supply curve shifts to the left (due to higher nominal wages), the price level rises, and real output declines.

(c) See Figure 16-5. Short run: The aggregate demand curve shifts to the left, both the price level and real output decline. Long run: The aggregate supply curve shifts to the right, the price level falls further, and real output increases.

16-5   Assume that a particular short-run aggregate supply curve exists for an economy and that the curve is relevant for several years. Use the AD-AS analysis to show graphically why higher rates of inflation over this period would be associated with lower rates of unemployment, and vice versa. What is the inverse relationship called?

As aggregate demand increases given a particular short-run aggregate supply curve, increases in real output are associated with increases in the price level. When real output increases, the unemployment rate decreases. The Phillips Curve shown on the right expresses the same relationship as the AD-AS model, but graphs as an inverse relationship because unemployment is on the horizontal axis rather than real output.

Question 16 - 5

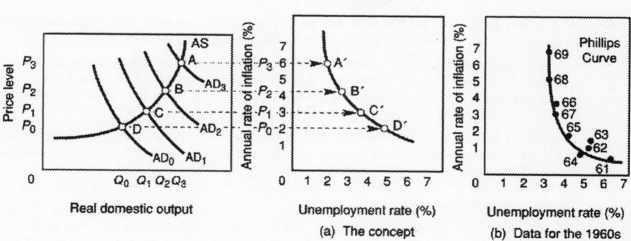

(a) The concept   (b) Data for the 1960s

16-6   (*Key Question*) Suppose the government misjudges the natural rate of unemployment to be much lower than it actually is, and thus undertakes expansionary fiscal and monetary policy to try to achieve the lower rate. Use the concept of the short-run Phillips Curve to explain why these policies might at first succeed. Use the concept of the long-run Phillips Curve to explain the long-run outcome of these policies.

In the short-run there is probably a tradeoff between unemployment and inflation. The government's expansionary policy should reduce unemployment as aggregate demand increases. However, the government has misjudged the natural rate and will continue its expansionary policy beyond the point of the natural level of unemployment. As aggregate demand continues to rise, prices begin to rise. In the long-run, workers demand higher wages to compensate for these higher prices. Aggregate supply will decrease (shift leftward) toward the natural rate of unemployment.

In other words, any reduction of unemployment below the natural rate is only temporary and involves a short-run rise in inflation. This, in turn, causes long-run costs to rise and a decrease in aggregate supply. The end result should be an equilibrium at the natural rate of unemployment and a higher price level than the beginning level. The long-run Phillips curve is thus a vertical line connecting the price levels possible at the natural rate of unemployment found on the horizontal axis. (See Figure 16-9)

16-7   What do the distinction between short-run and long-run aggregate supply have in common with the distinction between the short-run and long-run Phillips Curves? Explain.

In the short-run, economists assume that production costs don't change so the aggregate supply curve is fixed. Therefore, changes in aggregate demand are the sole determinant of unemployment and inflation rates. (Figure 16-1a) In the long-run, wages and input prices adjust to price changes causing rise (or fall) in production costs and aggregate supply decreases (or increases) as shown in Figure 16-1b. This means the long-run relationship between price-level and output is vertical at the full-employment level of output.

The long-run Phillips curve illustrates this latter point with the natural rate of unemployment (sometimes called full-employment rate) being measured on the horizontal axis and price level on the vertical axis. The long-run curve is vertical as shown in Figure 16-9. However, the short-run Phillips curve reflects what happens with unemployment at different price levels using the short-run aggregate supply curve. (See Figures 16-6 and 16-7)

16-8   What is the Laffer Curve and how does it relate to supply side economics? Why is determining the location where the economy is on the curve so important in assessing tax policy?

Economist Arthur Laffer observed that tax revenues would obviously be zero when the tax rate was either at 0% or 100%. In between these two extremes would have to be an optimal rate where aggregate output and income produced the maximum tax revenues. This idea is presented as the Laffer Curve shown in Figure 16-10.

The difficult decision involves the analysis to determine what is the optimum tax rate for producing maximum tax revenue and the related maximum economic output level. Laffer argued that low tax rates would actually increase revenues because low rates improved productivity, saving and investment incentives. The expansion in output and employment and thus, revenue, would more than compensate for the lower rates.

16-9   Why might one person work more, earn more, and pay more income tax when his or her tax rate is cut, while another person will work less, earn less, and pay less income tax under the same circumstance?

Proponents of supply-side economics argue that cuts in the marginal tax rate on earned income will make work more attractive because the opportunity cost of leisure is higher. Thus, individuals choose to substitute work for leisure. Critics of supply-side reasoning contend that workers are just as likely to reduce their efforts because the after-tax pay increases their ability to "buy leisure." They can meet their after-tax income goals by working fewer hours.

16-10   (*Last Word*) Do oil prices play a smaller role or large role in the U.S. economy today compared to the 1970s and 1980s? Explain why or why not.

Changes in oil prices have a smaller impact today than in the 1970s and 1980s for several reasons. First, the beneficial effects on cost reduction of technology improvements offset higher energy costs. Second, the Federal Reserve has become better at maintaining overall price stability through monetary policy. Third, energy costs are not as large a proportion of production costs as they used to be. Experts estimate that the U.S. economy is one-third less sensitive to oil price changes than in early 1980s.

CHAPTER SEVENTEEN
ECONOMIC GROWTH AND THE NEW ECONOMY

CHAPTER OVERVIEW

In Chapter 8 we looked at the impact of economic growth in general and concentrated on the causes of short-run fluctuations in employment and price levels and on policies that might mitigate such instability. The issue of long-run economic growth is equally important. Although punctuated by periods of cyclical instability, economic growth in the United States has been impressive. For example, during the last half century, real output has increased 450 percent and population has increased only 80 percent, to yield approximately a tripling of the goods and services available to the average American.

The discussion of growth in this chapter explores economic growth in more depth than in Chapter 8. We question whether the United States is achieving a "new economy" which might deliver a stronger future rate of growth. Finally, we explore both positive and negative aspects of growth.

WHAT'S NEW

Chapter 17 is a highly revised version of Chapter 18 in the 14th edition. The introduction to economic growth is now found in Chapter 8. Here there is an expanded numerical example demonstrating real GDP growth. Also, productivity growth and the new economy are topics that replace the previous edition's discussion of productivity slowdown.

Figures 17-3 and 17-5 are new and Table 17-1 has been adjusted for clarity. Finally, the 14th edition's Last Word on "Is Growth Desirable and Sustainable?" is in the text of the new chapter and a new Last Word discusses side effects of the "new economy."

INSTRUCTIONAL OBJECTIVES

After completing this chapter, students should be able to:

1. Identify six main ingredients in economic growth.

2. Show economic growth using production possibilities analysis and aggregate demand-aggregate supply analysis.

3. Describe the growth record of the U.S. economy since 1940, including two measures of its long-term growth rates.

4. Identify six major factors that contributed to U.S. economic growth according to empirical studies.

5. List five reasons for increasing returns in the New Economy.

6. Give four positive side effects to New Economy besides improved living standards.

7. Define and identify terms and concepts at the end of the chapter.

COMMENTS AND TEACHING SUGGESTIONS

1. The record of U.S. economic growth is made more meaningful if you can take time to put it in comparative perspective. Global Perspectives 17-1 is a start. World Bank publications such as the *World Development Report or World Bank Atlas* give population and growth statistics for most countries of the world.

2. An interesting source for debate on whether or not growth is desirable would be the classic, E. F. Schumacher's *Small is Beautiful*. Other books that touch on U.S. economic growth issues are Lester Thurow's *Zero-Sum Society* and *Zero-Sum Solution* and Wallace Peterson's *Our Overloaded Economy*. The many articles and books related to environmental issues highlight the gap between rich and poor.

3. The information economy raises many questions about concepts we teach in economics. Two excellent books *are Information Rules* and *Blown to Bits*. The January 1, 2000, issue of *The Wall Street Journal* had an entire section entitled "Good-By Supply and Demand."

LECTURE NOTES

I. **Introduction**

   A. Two definitions of economics growth were given in Chapter 8.

      1. The increase in real GDP, which occurs over a period of time.

      2. The increase in real GDP per capita, which occurs over time. This definition is superior if comparison of living standards is desired.

   B. Growth has been impressive in capitalist countries during the past half century. Real GDP in the U.S. increased by 450 percent.

   C. This chapter explores economic growth in more depth than Chapter 8.

II. **Six Main Ingredients of Growth**

   A. Four supply factors relate to the ability to grow.

      1. The quantity and quality of natural resources,

      2. The quantity and quality of human resources,

      3. The supply or stock of capital goods, and

      4. Technology.

   B. Two demand and efficiency factors are also related to growth.

      1. Aggregate demand must increase for production to expand.

      2. Full employment of resources and both productive and allocative efficiency are necessary to get the maximum amount of production possible.

III. **Production Possibilities Analysis (Figure 17-1)**

   A. Growth can be illustrated with a production possibilities curve (Figure 17-1), where growth is indicated as an outward shift of the curve from AB to CD.

      1. Aggregate demand must increase to sustain full employment at each new level of production possible.

      2. Additional resources that shift the curve outward must be employed efficiently to make the maximum possible contribution to domestic output.

      3. And for economy to achieve the maximum increase in monetary value, the optimal combination of goods must be achieved (allocative efficiency).

   B. Focus on the supply side is illustrated in Figure 17-2, where growth depends on labor inputs multiplied by labor productivity.

1. Increased labor inputs depend on size of population and labor force participation rate (the percent of population actually in the labor force).

2. Productivity is determined by technological progress, the availability of capital goods, quality of labor itself, and efficiency with which inputs are allocated, combined, and managed.

C. Aggregate demand-aggregate supply framework can also be used to illustrate growth, as seen in Figure 17-3. Aggregate supply shifts outward with economic growth, and in recent decades aggregate demand has shifted outward by an even greater amount. Nominal GDP rises faster than real GDP. (Key Question 3)

D. Extended AD-AD model is shown in figure 17-4 where short-term and long-term aggregate supply are differentiated in Figure 17-4.

1. Long-run potential output is shown at Q_1. It depends on resources and productive efficiency.

2. If potential output increases, the long-run supply curve shifts from AS_{LR1} to AS_{LR2}.

3. If aggregate demand rises from AD_1 to AD_2, real output rises to Q_2 and prices to P_2.

4. At P_2 there will be a different short-run AS curve, AS_2.

5. The result is some mild inflation and increases in real GDP.

IV. **Growth Record of the United States (Table 17-5)**

A. Real GDP has increased more than sixfold since 1940, and real per capita GDP has risen by a multiple of three.

B. Rate of growth record shows that real GDP has grown 3.1 percent per year since 1948 and real GDP per capita has grown about 2 percent per year. In last four years of century, U.S. economic growth surged and averaged more than 4 percent per year. But the arithmetic needs to be qualified.

1. Growth doesn't measure quality improvements.

2. Growth doesn't measure increased leisure time.

3. Growth doesn't take into account adverse effects on environment.

4. International comparisons are useful in evaluating U.S. performance. For example, Japan has grown more than twice as fast as U.S. since 1948 (see Global Perspective 17-1) but less in past decade.

V. **Accounting for growth is an attempt to quantify factors contributing to economic growth as shown in Table 17-1. Important research has been done in the area by Edward Denison.**

A. More labor input is one source of growth. Labor force has grown about 2 million workers per year for past 25 years and accounts for about one-third of total economic growth.

B. Technological advance, the most important factor, has been estimated to contribute to about 26 percent of the U.S. growth record since 1929.

C. Increases in quantity of capital are estimated to have contributed 18% to economic growth in U.S. since 1929.

D. Education and training improve the quality of labor. (See Figure 17-6 and Table 17-1)

E. Improved resource allocation and economies of scale also contribute to growth and explain about 12% of total.

   1. Improved resource allocation has occurred as discrimination disappears and labor moves where it is most productive, and as tariffs and other trade barriers are lowered.

   2. Economies of scale occur as the size of markets and firms that serve them have grown.

F. Other factors influence growth and are more difficult to measure.

   1. Social cultural environment and political stability are "growth friendly" in U.S.

      a. Respect for material success provides incentive to increase incomes.

      b. Market system rewards actions that increase output.

      c. Property rights and legal system encourage growth.

   2. Positive attitudes toward work and flow of energetic immigrants also add to growth.

VI. **Productivity Growth and the New Economy (Figure 17-7)**

A. Improvement in standard of living is linked to labor productivity – output per worker per hour.

B. The U.S. is experiencing a resurgence of productivity growth based on innovations in computers and communications, coupled with global capitalism. Since 1995 productivity growth has averaged 2.9% annually – up from 1.4% over 1973-95 period. "Rule of 70" projects real income will double in 23 years rather than 50 years.

C. Much recent improvement in productivity is due to "new economy" factors such as:

   1. Microchips and information technology are the basis for improved productivity. Many new inventions are based on microchip technology.

   2. New firms and increasing returns characterize the new economy.

      a. Some of today's most successful firms didn't exist 25 years ago: Dell, Compaq, Microsoft, Oracle, Cisco Systems, America Online, Yahoo and Amazon.com are just a few of many.

      b. Economies of sale and increasing returns in new firms encourage rapid growth. (See Table 17-1)

   3. Sources of increasing returns include:

      a. More specialized inputs.

      b. Ability to spread development costs over large output quantities since marginal costs are low.

      c. Simultaneous consumption of many customers at same time.

      d. Network effects make widespread use of information goods more valuable as more use the products.

      e. Learning increases with practice.

   4. Global competition encourages innovation and efficiency.

D. Macroeconomic outcomes include increases in aggregate supply (shift to right). See Figure 17-3.

E. Faster growth without inflation is possible with higher productivity.

F.   The natural rate of unemployment seems to be lower (4.5 – 5.0%).

G.   Federal revenues increase with economic growth; a 1995 deficit of $160 billion became a $167 billion surplus in 2000.

H.   Skepticism about long-term continued growth remains.

VII.   **Is Growth Desirable and Sustainable?**

A.   An antigrowth view exists.

1.   Growth causes pollution, global warming, ozone depletion, and other problems.

2.   "More" is not always better if it means dead-end jobs, burnout, and alienation from one's job.

3.   High growth creates high stress.

B.   Others argue in defense of growth.

1.   Growth leads to improved standard of living.

2.   Growth helps to reduce poverty in poor countries.

3.   Growth has improved working conditions.

4.   Growth allows more leisure and less alienation from work.

6.   Environmental concerns are important, but growth actually has allowed more sensitivity to environmental concerns and the ability to deal with them.

C.   Is growth sustainable? Yes, say proponents of growth.

1.   Resource prices are not rising.

2.   Growth today has more to do with expansion and application of knowledge and information, so is limited only by human imagination.

VIII.   **LAST WORD: Some Pleasant Side Effects of the New Economy**

A.   Economists Jason Saving and W. Michael Cox point to other benefits of New Economy besides improved living standards.

B.   Crime rates are down possible due to better job and income prospects.

C.   Welfare rolls have fallen from 5.5% of U.S. population in 1995 to 2.5% in 1999.

D.   Charitable contributions increased an average 9% annually, much higher than previous increases in giving.

E.   Minority well being improved with decreased poverty and unemployment rates.

ANSWERS TO END-OF-CHAPTER QUESTIONS

17-1   *(Key Question)* What are the four supply factors of economic growth? What is the demand factor? What is the efficiency factor? Illustrate these factors in terms of the production possibilities curve.

The four supply factors are the quantity and quality of natural resources; the quantity and quality of human resources; the stock of capital goods; and the level of technology. The demand factor is the level of purchases needed to maintain full employment. The efficiency factor refers to both productive and allocative efficiency. Figure 18-1 illustrates these growth factors by showing movement from curve AB to curve CD.

17-2 Suppose that Alpha and Omega have identically sized working aged populations, but that annual work hours are much greater in Alpha than in Omega. Provide two possible explanations.

One explanation might be that Omega's labor force is underemployed, producing at a point inside the production possibilities curve. Another explanation could be that the two populations have different attitudes and preferences about work and leisure with Omega workers placing a higher value on leisure than those in Alpha.

17-3 Suppose that work-hours in New Zombie are 200 in year 1 and productivity is $8. What is New Zombie's real GDP? If work-hours increase to 210 in year 2 and productivity rises to $10, what is New Zombie's rate of economic growth?

NZ's GDP in year 1 is $1600; GDP in year 2 is $2100

Rate of growth is (2100-1600)/1600 or .3125 =31.25% (assumes constant prices)

17-4 What is the relationship between a nation's production possibilities curve and its long-run aggregate supply curve? How do each relate to the idea of a New Economy?

The same supply factors that shift the production possibilities curve outward and explain economic growth are the same factors that shift its long-run aggregate supply curve rightward. This is shown in Figure 17-3 in the text. The new economy has hastened these shifts by improving technology and the efficiency factor. These, in turn, have caused businesses new invest in new capital and have made worker quality better as new skills are learned

17-5 *(Key Question)* Between 1990 and 1999 the U.S. price level rose by about 20 percent while its real output increased by about 33 percent. Use the aggregate demand-aggregate supply model to illustrate these outcomes graphically.

In the graph shown, both AD and AS expanded over the 1990-1999 period. Because aggregate supply increased as well as aggregate demand, the new equilibrium output rose at a faster pace than did the price level. P2 is 20% above P1 and GDP2 is 33% greater than GDP1. Note that it is also possible that in early 1990s when unemployment was above natural rate that some of the expansion of AD took place in the horizontal portion of AS curve, but that is not the situation depicted here.

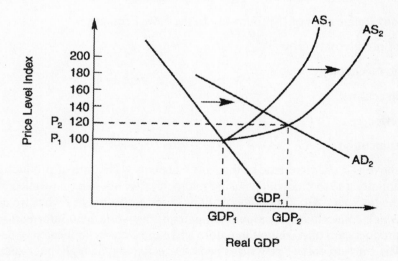

17-6   (*Key Question*) To what extent have increases in U.S. real GDP resulted from more labor inputs? Rearrange the following contributors to the growth of real GDP in order of their quantitative importance: economies of scale, quantity of capital, improved resource allocation, education and training, technological advance.

The U.S. labor force grew by about 2 million workers per year for each of the past 25 years, and this explains much of the growth in real GDP. Other factors have also been important. Refer to Table 17-1. Factor importance in descending order: (1) Technological advance—the discovery of new knowledge which results in the combining of resources in more productive ways. (2) The quantity of capital. (3) Education and training.   (4) Economies of scale and (5) improved resource allocation.

17-7   True or false? If false, explain why.

a.   Technological advance, which to date has played a relatively small role in U.S. economic growth, is destined to play a more important role in the future.

b.   Many public capital goods are complementary to private capital goods.

c.   Immigration has slowed economic growth in the U.S.

(a) Is false at the beginning because technology has played the most important role in U.S. economic growth of any growth factor. However, the second part of the statement is probably true.

(b) Is true

(c) False, immigration has been a source for expanded labor force and labor inputs and also for expansion in aggregate demand.

17-8   Explain why there is such a close relationship between changes in a nation's rate of productivity growth and changes in its average real hourly wage.

Real hourly wage average represents the average purchasing power of the wage each worker receives. Purchasing power refers to the amount of output that can be obtained with that wage. If output per worker is not increasing, then the amount of output available per capita for workers to buy will not be growing either. In other words the "real" wage changes only if there is an increase in productivity. Nominal wages don't represent purchasing power.

17-9   (*Kwy Question*) Relate each of the following to the New Economy:

a.   the rate of productivity growth

b.   information technology

c.   increasing returns

d.   network effects

e.   global competition

Each of the above is a characteristic of the New Economy. The rate of productivity growth has grown substantially due to innovations using microchips, computers, new telecommunications devices and the Internet. All of these innovations describe features of what we call information technology, which connects information in all parts of the world with information seekers. New information products are often digital in nature and can be easily replicated once they have been developed. The start-up cost of new firms and new technology is high, but expanding production has a very low marginal cost which leads to economies of scale – firms' output grows faster than their inputs. Network effects refer to a type of economy of scale whereby certain information products become more valuable to each user as the number of buyers grows. For example, a fax machine is more useful to you when lots of other people and firms have one; the same is true for compatible word-processing programs. Global competition is a feature of the New Economy because both transportation and communication can be accomplished at much lower cost and faster speed than previously which expands market possibilities for both consumers and producers who are not very limited by national boundaries today.

17-10   Provide three examples of products or services that can be simultaneously consumed by many people. Explain why labor productivity greatly rises as the firm sells more units of the product or service, and explain why the higher level of sales greatly reduces the per-unit cost of the product.

Text examples include films, CD entertainment, television programs, software programs, internet information. Labor productivity rises with some of these products when they are used as inputs because sharing compatible software programs, Internet information and the same video training programs, for example, can expand output potential for many workers who benefit from the effects of using or learning from the information simultaneously.

Production of information goods has a high start-up or development cost, but additional units can be produced at little or no cost. Therefore the more units that are produced, the denominator rises, but the total cost won't rise much and the cost per unit, therefore, will fall.

17-11   What is meant when economists say that the U.S. economy has a "higher safe speed limit" than previously? If the New Economy has a higher safe speed limit, what explains the series of interest rate hikes engineered by the Federal Reserve in 1999 and 2000?

If productivity growth (output per worker) is fueling economic growth, then the economy is able to grow more rapidly without experiencing increasing production costs. Cost per unit does not increase if total output is growing as fast as increases in input costs. The increased efficiency of the New Economy has allowed the economy to grow without increasing resource costs substantially. However, the Federal Reserve probably bases its concern about inflation on past history and declining unemployment is usually a signal that inflationary pressures will heat up. Therefore, the Fed acted to dampen these pressures, but it may have raised interest rates too high and slowed the economy when inflation was not so great a threat in the new environment.

17-12   Productivity often rises during economic expansions and falls during economic recessions. Can you think of reasons why? Briefly explain. (*Hint*: Remember that the level of productivity involves both levels of output and levels of labor input.)

Productivity would be likely to rise during economic expansions because the low rate of unemployment would encourage the more intensive use of existing plant and equipment and current workforce. Worker productivity would be likely to fall during recessions because employers would be reluctant to discharge valuable workers until absolutely necessary.

17-13   (*Last Word*) Explain how rapid U.S. economic growth can reduce crime rates, trim welfare rolls, increase charitable giving, and enhance the well-being of racial and ethnic minorities.

Rapid economic growth increases incomes, which enhance everyone's well-being and allow more generous donations to charity – especially if there are tax benefits to be gained as higher taxes apply to higher taxable income levels. Also, economic growth reduces unemployment so that welfare rolls decrease in favor of paying jobs and crime rates probably fall as people are able to find jobs to support themselves. It is also likely that expanded tax revenues have allowed for better police services.

CHAPTER EIGHTEEN
DEFICIT, SURPLUSES AND THE PUBLIC DEBT

CHAPTER OVERVIEW

Three interrelated topics of national concern—Federal budget deficits, surpluses and the public debt—are the focus of this chapter. It begins by considering several contrasting budget philosophies. Table 18-1 provides statistical evidence that is useful in tracing the growth of the debt and assessing its current quantitative significance.

The material on the public debt is designed to explode two popular misconceptions as to the character and problems associated with a large public debt: (1) the debt will force the U.S. into bankruptcy; and (2) the debt imposes a burden on future generations. The debt discussion, however, also entails a look at substantive economic issues. Potential problems of a large public debt include greater income inequality, reduced economic incentives, and crowding out of private investment. Now attention turns to what to do about budget surpluses.

The chapter examines the Federal deficits of the 1990s and recent and projected surpluses. The relationship between budget and trade deficits is highlighted in The Last Word.

WHAT'S NEW

This was Chapter 19 in the 14th edition. The new title reflects recent budget surpluses.

In defining public debt, the text names the types of government securities that finance the debt. Also, the list of causes of public debt is shortened to three, and printing money is no longer listed as one of the reasons the government can't go bankrupt.

Other changes include more discussion of the social security fund and the budget, less discussion of crowding out, new mention of complementarity of public and private capital, and a new examination of current and projected surpluses.

A new Last Word examines the relationship between the "U.S. Trade Deficit and Debt Reduction."

INSTRUCTIONAL OBJECTIVES

After completing this chapter, students should be able to:

1. Differentiate between deficit and debt.

2. Explain each of the three budget philosophies.

3. Identify three principal causes of the public debt.

4. State the absolute size of the debt and the relative size as a percentage of GDP.

5. Describe the annual interest charges on the debt, who holds the debt, and the impact of inflation on the debt.

6. Explain why the debt can also be considered public credit.

7. Identify and discuss two widely held myths about the public debt.

8. Explain the real or potential effect of the debt on income distribution, economic incentives, fiscal policy, and private investment.

9. State how debt plays a positive role in society.

10. Explain the four policy options for the current and future surpluses.

11. Describe how budget deficits are related to trade deficits.

12. Define and identify the terms and concepts at the end of the chapter.

COMMENTS AND TEACHING SUGGESTIONS

1. In the discussion of myths about the debt, remind students that the debt is not completely harmless. Explode the myths, but also discuss the substantive impact of the debt. Also, note the Global Perspectives on debt in other nations.

2. Current data on the public debt and on the Federal budget are reported in the most recent *Economic Report of the President*, the *Survey of Current Business*, or *Federal Reserve Bulletins*. These sources can be used to update chapter data. The Federal deficit can be measured in several ways, and these differences can lead to different conclusions about its impact.

STUDENT STUMBLING BLOCK

1. The national debt has been an issue of great concern to politicians and citizens. Students probably have major misconceptions based on the publicity surrounding the deficit and debt. The concern is most often centered around the "myths" that the government can go bankrupt or that debt necessarily is a burden on future generations. Spend some time discussing why these particular concerns are not the major issues about which we should worry. Paying down the debt using current surplus is a policy option discussed in this chapter. Point to pro's and con's.

2. "Millions, billions, trillions," most people have a difficult time maintaining perspective and proportion when using really large numbers. For most of us, $100 million dollars sounds like an incredible fortune. Ask students to calculate the percentage $100 million dollars represents out of one trillion dollars. Check your figures before you try this in class. (The answer is .01 percent.) This demonstration may help students understand why cutting a government budget can be so difficult. What sounds like a huge sum of money may represent an extremely small percentage of the total amount. Remind students of current GDP, budget and surplus statistics.

LECTURE NOTES

I. **Definitions of deficit, surplus and debt**

    A. A budget deficit is the amount by which government's expenditures exceed its revenues during a particular year. In contrast, a surplus is the amount by which its revenues exceed expenditures.

        1. In 1997 there was a Federal deficit of $22 billion.

        2. In 1999 there was a surplus of $125 billion.

    B. The national or public debt is the total accumulation of the Federal government's total deficits and surpluses that have occurred through time. State and local governments historically have a collective budget surplus.

II. **Three Budget Philosophies**

A. The annually balanced budget was the goal until the 1930s Depression, but this ruled out using fiscal policy as a countercyclical, stabilizing force and even makes recession or depression worse.

1. The balanced budget is not neutral, but is procyclical, that is, it worsens the business cycle.

2. In a recession, the government would have to raise taxes and lower spending to balance the budget as tax revenues fell with recessionary income levels. This policy would worsen recession.

3. In an inflationary boom period, a balanced budget would intensify the inflation. As tax revenues increased, the government would need to cut taxes or raise spending to avoid a budget surplus. This strategy would make the inflation worse.

4. Those who argue for the annually balanced budget want to limit the growth of government.

B. The cyclically balanced budget is a spending philosophy which allows for some government stabilization policy over the length of the business cycle. Deficit spending is allowed during a recession, and surpluses during an inflationary period. Over the business cycle, deficits would be offset by surpluses. But in reality, surpluses and deficits do not equally offset each other.

C. Functional finance is the third budget philosophy. Advocates argue that the budget is secondary, but the primary purpose of Federal finance is to achieve noninflationary full employment. Government should do what is necessary to achieve this goal regardless of the deficit or surplus in the budget. Proponents offer several responses to critics.

III. **The Public Debt: Facts and Figures**

A. The public debt in 2000 was $5.7 trillion. This is a large number. One million seconds ago was 12 days back. One trillion seconds ago was around 30,000 B.C.

B. Causes of the expansion in debt:

1. National defense and military spending have soared, especially during wartime. During World Wars I and II debt grew rapidly. See Table 18-1 for facts that show World War II debt exceeded GDP.

2. Recessions cause a decline in revenues and growth in government spending on programs for income maintenance. Such periods included 1974-75, 1980-82, 1990-91.

3. Tax cuts are another cause. Tax cuts in the 1980s without equivalent spending cuts led to increasing debt. The Clinton administration in 1993 is an example of how hard it is to reduce spending and raise taxes to reduce the deficit. An unpopular deficit reduction act was passed in that year and many Democrats lost elections later.

B. Quantitative aspects of the debt are found in Table 18-1. Note that the absolute level in column 2 is not meaningful without comparison of the relative size of debt and interest payments to the nation's ability to pay, as estimated by GDP and shown in column 5.

1. Comparing the debt to GDP is more meaningful than the absolute level of debt by itself. Use the example of a family or corporate borrowing. For a prosperous family or firm, $100,000 worth of debt may be a small fraction of their income; for others, $100,000 worth of debt may mean they're unable to make payments on the debt. The amount is not as important as the amount relative to the ability to pay. Also, most borrowing is made to purchase physical assets such as buildings, equipment, etc. Another way to judge government debt is to compare it to an estimate of public assets.

2. International comparisons show that other nations have relative public debts as great or greater than that of the U.S. when compared to their GDPs. See Global Perspective 18-1.

3. Interest charges as a percentage of GDP represent the primary burden of the debt today.

4. Who owns the debt is also an important question. About one-fourth of U.S. debt is held by government agencies and the Federal Reserve; the rest is held by individuals, banks, investment and insurance companies, and about 23 percent was held by foreign investors in 2000. See Figure 18-1.

5. Social Security Trust Fund considerations may obscure the true debt picture. Payroll taxes currently exceed social security payments so the fund's surplus is counted as part of the Federal surplus. Some economists say this fund should not be part of the calculation of Federal deficits or surpluses because social security funds are earmarked for future beneficiaries. For example, the Federal surplus in 2000 would be only $87 billion without the fund surplus of $80 billion.

C. False concerns about the federal debt include several popular misconceptions:

1. Can the federal government cannot go bankrupt? There are reasons why it cannot.

   a. The government does not need to raise taxes to pay back the debt, but it can refinance bonds when they mature by more borrowing, that is, selling new bonds. Corporations use similar methods—they almost always have outstanding debt.

   b. The government has the power to tax, which businesses and individuals do not have when they are in debt.

2. Does the debt impose a burden on future generations? In 2000 the per person federal debt in U.S. was $20,667. But the public debt is a public credit—your grandmother may own the bonds on which taxpayers are paying interest. Some day you may inherit those bonds which are assets to those who have them. The true burden is borne by those who pay taxes or loan government money today to finance government spending. If the spending is for productive purposes, it will enhance future earning power and the size of the debt relative to future GDP and population could actually decline. Borrowing allows growth to occur when it is invested in productive capital.

D. Substantive issues do exist.

1. Repayment of the debt affects income distribution. If working taxpayers will be paying interest to the mainly wealthier groups who hold the bonds, this probably increases income inequality.

2. Since interest must be paid out of government revenues, a large debt and high interest can increase tax burden and may decrease incentives to work, save, and invest for taxpayers.

3. A higher proportion of the debt is owed to foreigners (about 23 percent) than in the past, and this can increase the burden since payments leave the country. But Americans also own foreign bonds and this offsets the concern.

4. Some economists believe that public borrowing crowds out private investment, but the extent of this effect is not clear (see Figure 18-2).

5. There are some positive aspects of borrowing even with crowding out.

   a. If borrowing is for public investment that causes the economy to grow more in the future, the burden on future generations will be less than if the government had not borrowed for this purpose.

      b. Public investment makes private investment more attractive. For example, new federal buildings generate private business; good highways help private shipping, etc.

IV.   **Deficits and Surpluses: 1990-2010**

   A. Figure 18-3 shows huge absolute size of deficits in early 1990s.

   B. In 1993 Congress passed <u>Deficit Reduction Act</u> to increase tax revenues by $250 billion over 5 years and to reduce spending by a similar amount.

      1. Top marginal tax rate went from 31 to 39.6%.

      2. Corporate income tax rate went up 1% to 35%.

      3. Gasoline excise tax rose by 4.3 cents per gallon.

      4. Spending was held at 1993 levels (unless increases already mandated by law).

   C. By 1998 there was a budget surplus for the first time since 1969.

   D. There are four main options for the surpluses.

      1. Pay off part of the public debt.

         a. Less government borrowing could mean more private investment.

         b. Critics contend that the debt is shrinking relative to GDP and we need government securities as safe investments, for monetary policy, and for social security trust fund assets.

      2. Reduce taxes and reduce surplus.

         a. Returns money directly to those who earned it.

         b. Helps to limit size of government.

         c. Critics fear this surplus may be temporary and tax reduction may be poorly timed if economy is prosperous anyway.

      3. Increase government spending and reduce the surplus.

         a. Several areas of need exist where federal spending programs could help, especially Medicare drug coverage.

         b. Critics say new spending could be inflationary and interfere with private investment.

      4. Add to the Social Security trust fund. See Figure 18-4.

         a. We could pay off debt and use interest savings for the trust fund.

         b. More funds will be needed in future as population ages and fewer workers remain to support larger proportion of retired population.

      5. Combine any or all of these four proposals.

V.   **Last Word: Debt Reduction and the U.S. Trade Deficit**

   A. Some economists believe the debt and trade deficits are connected.

   B. Here's why. Higher interest rates may result from government borrowing, which has an international impact because:

      1. The dollar will appreciate as foreigners demand more dollars to invest in the U.S. to earn higher interest rates.

2. As the dollar appreciates, American goods become more expensive to foreigners and foreign goods become less costly to Americans. This contributes to the trade deficits more imports and fewer exports.

3. Since net exports are a component of aggregate demand, the net export effect will be negative and slow economic growth.

C. If the U.S. pays down the national debt, it will be borrowing less, which should reduce interest rates. Then, the reverse process will occur: the dollar will depreciate and trade deficit will shrink.

D. There are other related effects.

1. Foreign investment helps to finance U.S. borrowing so less foreign investment may offset some of the decline in interest rates.

2. Lower U.S. interest rates may reduce the burden on foreign borrowers of U.S. funds as their debt is refinanced at lower rates. This can help developing countries.

3. A trade deficit means we are not exporting enough to pay for the imports. The difference must be paid by borrowing from people and institutions abroad, or by selling U.S. assets to foreigners for the dollars they earned from our import buying.

E. However, many factors besides real interest rates affect the trade balance so reducing the debt may not reduce the trade deficit.

ANSWERS TO END-OF-CHAPTER QUESTIONS

18-1 (*Key Question*) Assess the potential for using fiscal policy as a stabilization tool under (a) an annually balanced budget, (b) a cyclically balanced budget, and (c) functional finance.

(a) There is practically no potential for using fiscal policy as a stabilization tool under an annually balanced budget. In an economic downturn, tax revenues fall. To keep the budget in balance, fiscal policy would require the government to reduce its spending or increase its tax rates, adding to the deficiency in spending and accelerating the downturn. If the economy were booming and tax revenues were mounting, to keep the budget balanced fiscal policy would have to increase government spending or reduce taxes, thus adding to the already excessive demand and accelerating the inflationary pressures. An annually balanced budget would intensify cyclical ups and downs.

(b) A cyclically balanced budget would be countercyclical, as it should be, since it would bolster demand by lowering taxes and increasing government spending during a recession and restrain demand by raising taxes and reducing government spending during an inflationary boom. However, because boom and bust are not always of equal intensity and duration, budget surpluses during the upswing need not automatically match budget deficits during the downswing. Requiring the budget to be balanced over the cycle may necessitate inappropriate changes in tax rates or levels of government expenditures.

(c) Functional finance pays no attention to the balance of deficits and surpluses annually or over the cycle. What counts is the maintenance of a noninflationary full-employment level of spending. Balancing the economy is what counts, not the budget.

18-2 What have been three major sources of the public debt historically? Why were annual deficits so large in the 1980s? Why did the deficit rise sharply in 1991 and 1992? What explains the large budget surpluses of the late 1990s and early 2000s?

Historically, wars and recessions have caused the public debt to increase. It would have been possible to finance World War II entirely through taxes, but this would have greatly decreased the work incentives deemed essential to get the job done. It would have been possible to finance the war effort by printing new money but, in the conditions of the already excessive demand then existing, this would have been highly inflationary. So, the government borrowed from the public. This reduced purchasing power without greatly impairing the growing wealth and work incentives of the civilian labor force. Recessions have also been responsible for the growing debt. Government deficits to bolster the economy during recessions have not been equaled by surpluses during booms.

The Economic Recovery Tax Act of 1981 was responsible for much of the large deficits in the 1980s. ERTA reduced personal and corporate income tax rates without also reducing government spending. Indeed, defense spending rose considerably during the Reagan administration. Thus, the Federal budget has had a structural deficit built into it: Even at full employment, the Federal budget was deficit.

In 1991 and 1992 three unique events contributed to the deficit: Operation Desert Storm, more funding for the S&L bailout, and a recession that was followed by a slow recovery.

Recent large surpluses result from several years of economic prosperity coupled with the results of the Deficit Reduction Act of 1993 which increased marginal tax rates on high income earners and corporate income tax rates. Also, Congress made a commitment to limit government spending, and it has been a period of relative peace.

18-3 (*Key Question*) What are the two main ways the size of the public debt is measured. Distinguish between refinancing and retiring the debt. How does an internally held public debt differ from an externally held public debt? Contrast the effects of retiring an internally held debt from an externally held debt.

Two ways of measuring the public debt: (1) measure its absolute dollar size; (2) measure its size as a percentage of GDP.

Refinancing the public debt simply means rolling over outstanding debt—selling "new" bonds to retire maturing bonds. Retiring the debt means purchasing bonds back from those who hold them or paying the bonds off at maturity.

An internally held debt is one in which the bondholders live in the nation having the debt; an externally held debt is one in which the bondholders are citizens of other nations. Paying off an internally held debt would involve buying back government bonds. This could present a problem of income distribution because holders of the government bonds generally have higher incomes than the average taxpayer. But paying off an internally held debt would not burden the economy as a whole—the money used to pay off the debt would stay within the domestic economy. In paying off an externally held debt, people abroad could use the proceeds of the bonds sales to buy products or other assets from the U.S. However, the dollars gained could be simply exchanged for foreign currency and brought back to their home country. This reduces U.S. foreign reserves holdings and may lower dollar exchange rate.

18-4 True or false? If false, explain why.

a. "A internally held debt is like a debt of the left hand to the right hand."

b. The Federal Reserve and Federal government agencies hold more than half of the public debt.

c. The U.S. public debt was smaller in percentage terms in 2000 than it was in 1990.

d. In recent years, social security payments have exceeded social security tax revenues.

(a) The statement is true about a national debt held internally, but this does not mean a large debt is entirely problem free.

(b) False, the general public held 61 percent of the public debt in 2000.

(c) True.

(d) False, much of the Federal budget surplus consists of the surplus from the social security trust fund, which is included in the general Federal budget. However, by 2040 there will only be two workers for each recipient of Social Security funds. Today the ratio is 3 to 1. Therefore, some economists believe the future of the trust fund will be enhanced if more of the Federal debt is paid down and interest savings used to bolster the trust fund for future needs.

18-5 Why might economists be quite concerned if the annual interest payments on the debt sharply increased as a percentage of the GDP?

The weight of the debt is not its absolute size. Indeed, if there were no interest to be paid on the debt and refinancing were automatic, there would be no debt-load at all. But interest does have to be paid. Lenders expect that. And to pay the interest the government must either use tax revenues or go deeper into debt. Interest on the debt, then, is important and its weight can best be assessed by noting the size of the interest payments in relation to GDP, since the size of the GDP is a measure of total national income or how much the government can raise in taxes to pay the interest.

18-6 Do you think that paying off the public debt would increase or decrease inequality? Explain.

Probably those who hold bonds are in the upper-income, higher wealth proportion of taxpayers and since middle-income groups pay a sizable portion of taxes, interest payments on the debt increase income inequality since recipients are primarily wealthy. In the long run, therefore, paying down the debt should reduce inequality since interest payments would be diminished.

18-7 (*Key Question*) Trace the cause-and-effect chain through which financing and refinancing of the public debt might affect real interest rates, private investment, and the stock of capital and economic growth. How might investment in public capital and complementarities between public and private capital alter the outcome of the cause-effect chain?

Cause and effect chain: Government borrowing to finance the debt competes with private borrowing and drives up the interest rate; the higher interest rate causes a decline in private capital and economic growth slows.

However, if public investment complements private investment, private borrowers may be willing to pay higher rates for positive growth opportunities. Productivity and economic growth could rise.

18-8 Relate the Laffer Curve (Figure 16-10) to the Deficit Reduction Act of 1993 and its effect on U.S. budget deficits.

The Deficit Reduction Act increased tax rates and subsequently tax revenues expanded and the deficit disappeared. Therefore, using the Laffer Curve concept, we would say that tax rates before 1993 were below their optimal level.

18-9 What role do the components of the public debt play in the day-to-day conduct of monetary policy?

Buying and selling U.S. government securities is called open market operations, which is the main instrument of the Federal Reserve's monetary policy. For this tool to work, government securities (debt instruments) must be available.

18-10 What are the broad policy options for eliminating the large budget surpluses projected for the 2000s? If you were forced to choose only one of the options, which would it be? Explain your choice.

There are four broad options: pay off part of existing public debt; reduce taxes; increase government spending; or boost the Social Security trust fund.

Support for each of these views depends on your preferences, but the text does give some arguments supporting each view. See section entitled "Options for the Surpluses."

18-11 How might large U.S. budget surpluses reduce the large U.S. trade deficit?

U.S. budget surpluses mean the government won't need to borrow more loanable funds and may pay back existing debt rather than refinance. This should reduce interest rates, which will reduce demand for U.S. dollars by foreign investors. If this causes the exchange rate to fall, U.S. exports are less expensive for foreigners to buy and import prices will rise in U.S. dollars. The deficit will fall by definition.

18-12 (*Last Word*) Explain how a substantial reduction of the public debt could greatly reduce the U.S. trade deficit.

A significant decline in the Federal debt should reduce the sale of government bonds in the financial markets, which means that interest rates would decline. This will eventually reverse the flow of foreign demand for U.S. bonds. Then the international value of the dollar will decline, exports will increase, and imports should decrease. In other words, the trade deficit will fall.

CHAPTER NINETEEN
DISPUTES OVER MACRO THEORY AND POLICY

CHAPTER OVERVIEW

One of the great traditions in scholarship is the challenge to mainstream thinking. Many such challenges to the "conventional wisdom" fail; either the new theories are not logical or they don't conform to facts. At the opposite extreme, some new theories gain full support and replace the existing theories. More often, the new ideas modify mainstream thinking, which thereafter is improved or extended. This is true in economics.

In this chapter we examine some of the major disputes in macro theory and policy. We initially provide historical background by contrasting classical and Keynesian macroeconomic theories. Then we turn to contemporary disagreements on three interrelated questions: 1) What causes instability in the economy? 2) Is the economy self-correcting? 3) Should government adhere to rules or use discretion in setting economic policy?

WHAT'S NEW

This chapter covers topics that were in Chapter 17 of the 14th edition. Otherwise, changes are few and mainly editorial. References to "natural rate hypothesis" and "adoptive expectations" are no longer used.

A new Last Word appears at the end of the chapter on the "Taylor Rule" for monetary policy.

INSTRUCTIONAL OBJECTIVES

After completing this chapter, students should be able to:

1. Contrast the classical and Keynesian views of the aggregate supply curve.

2. Compare the classical and Keynesian views of the stability of the aggregate demand curve.

3. Give two reasons for macroeconomic instability according to mainstream economists.

4. Explain the equation of exchange.

5. Identify the single most important cause of macroeconomic instability according to the monetarists.

6. Explain the main reasons for macro economic instability according to the real-business-cycle theory.

7. Construct an example to demonstrate a coordination failure.

8. Explain the view of self-correction held by mainstream economists.

9. List three reasons why a higher wage could result in greater efficiency.

10. Explain how insider-outsider relationships contribute to downward wage inflexibility.

11. Describe the monetary rule and explain why monetarists prefer it to discretionary monetary policy.

12. Compare the views of mainstream economists with monetarists and RET economists regarding the use of discretionary fiscal policy and the need for an annually balanced budget.

13. Compare and contrast Taylor Rule with Monetary Rule advocated by monetarists.

14. Define and explain the terms and concepts listed at the end of the chapter.

COMMENTS AND TEACHING SUGGESTIONS

1. This chapter illuminates basic disagreements and controversies in macroeconomic theory. Stress that, despite the disagreements, there is considerable agreement about the basic macro concepts, the tools of analysis, and the framework for discussion.

2. This may be a good time to reemphasize the difference between positive and normative economics. Remind students that value judgments about the economy, that is, which economic goals are most important, influence opinions about a particular economic policy, as much as any empirical data.

3. Ask students to evaluate the last presidential election. Can they identify the school of thought most closely associated with each candidate for president? Consider the candidates for local elective office; is there enough information available to make a judgment about the candidates' opinions about economic policies?

4. Mainstream economists believe that nominal wages are inflexible downward because of labor contracts, efficiency wages, and insider-outsider relationships. Have students interview a business manager with first-hand experience in this area; or ask students to consider what kind of empirical data they would need to collect to evaluate the flexibility or inflexibility of wages.

5. Arthur Okun published a work in the 1960s that is still a good basis for discussion, *Equality and Efficiency, the Big Tradeoff.*

STUDENT STUMBLING BLOCK

This is not easy material. Students may become frustrated when they consider more than one point of view. It may be helpful to point out that acceptance or rejection of a theory depends on opinions about which economic goals are most important for the country.

LECTURE NOTES

I.   **Introduction: Disagreements about Macro Theory and Policy**

    A. This chapter contrasts the classical and Keynesian macroeconomic theories.

    B. Contemporary disagreements on three inter-related questions are considered.

        1. What causes instability in the economy?

        2. Is the economy self-orrecting?

        3. Should government adhere to rules or use discretion in setting economic policy?

II. **Some History: Classical Economics**

    A. Classical economics dominated the discipline from Adam Smith (1776) until the 1930s. It maintained that full employment was normal and that a "laissez-faire" (let it be) policy by government is best.

    B. Keynes observed in the 1930s that laissez-faire capitalism is subject to recurring recessions or depressions with widespread unemployment, and contended that active government stabilization policy is required to avoid the waste of idle resources.

    C. Classical View.

        1. The aggregate supply curve is vertical and located at the full-employment level of real output.

2. Stress that classical economists believed that real output does not change in response to changes in the price level because wages and other input prices would be flexible.

3. The economy would operate at its full employment level of output because of:

    a. Say's law (See Chapter 9) which states "supply creates its own demand."

    b. responsive, flexible prices and wages in cases where there might be temporary over-supply.

4. Money underlies aggregate demand. Classical economists theorize that aggregate demand will be stable as long as the supply of money is controlled with limited growth.

5. The downward sloping demand curve is stable and is solely responsible for setting the price level. (See Figure 19-1a)

6. Changes in the money supply would shift AD right for an increase and left for decrease, but responsive, flexible prices and wages will insure that full employment output is maintained.

D. Keynesian View.

1. The core of Keynesianism is that product prices and wages are downwardly inflexible (don't fall easily). This is graphically represented as a horizontal aggregate supply curve. (See Figure 19-1b)

2. A decline in real output will have no impact on the price level. Once full employment is reached at Q_f, the aggregate supply curve is vertical.

3. Keynesian economists view aggregate demand as unstable from one period to the next, even without changes in the money supply.

4. The investment component of aggregate demand is especially likely to fluctuate and the sole impact is on output and employment, while the price level remains unchanged. (See shift AD_1, to AD_2 in Figure 19-1)

5. Active government policies are essential to increase aggregate demand and move the economy back toward full employment.

III. **What Causes Macro Instability such as Great Depression, Recessions, Inflationary Periods?**

A. Mainstream View: This term is used to characterize prevailing perspective of most economists.

1. Mainstream macroeconomics is Keynesian-based, and focuses on aggregate demand and its components. $C(a) + I(g) + X(n) + G = GDP$ (Aggregate expenditures) = (real output)

2. Any change in one of the spending components in the aggregate expenditure equation shifts the aggregate demand curve. This, in turn, changes equilibrium real output, the price level or both.

    a. Investment spending is particularly subject to variation.

    b. Instability can also arise from the supply side. Artificial supply restriction, wars, or increased costs of production can decrease supply, destabilizing the economy by simultaneously causing cost-push inflation and recession.

B. Monetarist View: This label is applied to a modern form of classical economics.

1. Money supply is the focus of monetarist theory.

2. Monetarism argues that the price and wage flexibility provided by competitive markets cause fluctuations in product and resource prices, rather than output and employment.

3. Therefore, a competitive market system would provide substantial macroeconomic stability if there were no government interference in the economy.

   a It is government that has caused downward inflexibility through the minimum wage law, pro-union legislation, and guaranteed prices for some products as in agriculture.

   b. Monetarists say that government also contributes to the economy's business cycles through clumsy, mistaken, monetary policies.

4. The fundamental equation of monetarism is the equation of exchange. $MV = PQ$

   a. The left side, MV, represents the total amount spent [M, the money supply x V, the velocity of money, (the number of times per year the average dollar is spent on final goods and services)]

   b. The right side, PQ, equals the nation's nominal GDP [P is the price level or more specifically, the average price at which each unit of output is sold x Q is the physical volume of all goods and services produced.]

   c. Monetarists say that velocity, V, is stable, meaning that the factors altering velocity change gradually and predictably. People and firms have a stable pattern to holding money.

   d. If velocity is stable, the equation of exchange suggests there is a predictable relationship between the money supply and nominal GDP (PQ).

5. Monetarists say that inappropriate monetary policy is the single most important cause of macroeconomic instability. An increase in money supply will increase aggregate demand.

6. Mainstream economists view instability of investment as the main cause of the economy's instability. They see monetary policy as a stabilizing factor since it can adjust interest rates to keep investment and aggregate demand stable.

C. Real Business Cycle View: A third perspective on macroeconomic stability focuses on a aggregate supply. (See Figure 19-2)

   1. The view that business cycles are caused by real factors affecting aggregate supply such as a decline in productivity, which causes a decline in AS.

   2. In the real-business cycle theory declines in GDP mean less demand for money. Here, the supply of money is decreased after the demand declines. AD falls, but price level is the same because AS also declined.

D. Coordination Failures: A fourth view relates to so-called coordination failures.

   1. Macroeconomic instability can occur "when people do not reach a mutually beneficial equilibrium because they lack some way to jointly coordinate their actions."

   2. There is no mechanism for firms and households to agree on actions that would make them all better off if such a failure occurs. The initial problem may be due to expectations that are not justified, but if everyone believes that a recession may come, they reduce spending, firms reduce output and the recession occurs. The economy can be stuck in a recession because of a failure of households and businesses to coordinate positive expectations.

IV.   **Does the Economy "Self-Correct"?**

A. New Classical View of Self-Correction

1. Monetarist and rational expectation economists believe that the economy has automatic, internal mechanisms for self-correction.

2. Figure 19a-b demonstrates the adjustment process, which retains full employment output according to this view.

3. The disagreement among new classical economists is over the speed of the adjustment process.

   a. Monetarists usually hold the adaptive expectations view of gradual change. The supply curve shifts, show in figure 19-3 may take 2 or 3 years or longer.

   b. Rational expectations theory (RET) holds that people anticipate some future outcomes before they occur, making change very quick, even instantaneous.

      i. Where there is adequate information, people's beliefs about future outcomes accurately reflect the likelihood that those outcomes will occur.

      ii. RET assumes that new information about events with known outcomes will be assimilated quickly.

4. In RET unanticipated price-level changes do cause temporary changes in real output. Firms mistakenly adjust their production levels in response to what they perceive to be a relative price change in their product alone. Any change in GDP is corrected as prices are flexible and firms readjust output to its previous level.

5. In RET fully anticipated price-level changes do not change real output, even for short periods. Firms are able to maintain profit and production levels.

B. Mainstream View of Self-Correction

1. There is ample evidence that many prices and wages are inflexible downward for long periods of time. However, some aspects of RET have been incorporated into the more rigorous model; of the mainstream.

2. Graphical analysis shown in Figure 19-3b demonstrates the adjustment process along a horizontal aggregate supply curve.

3. Downward wage inflexibility may occur because firms are unable to cut wages due to contracts and the legal minimum wage. Firms may not want to reduce wages if they fear problems with morale effort, and efficiency.

4. An efficiency wage is one that minimizes the firm's labor cost per unit of output. Firms may discover that paying higher than market wages lowers wage cost per unit of output.

   a. Workers have an incentive to retain an above-market wage job and may put forth greater work effort.

   b. Lower supervision costs prevail if workers have more incentive to work hard.

   c. An above-market wage reduces job turnover.

5. Some economists believe wages don't fall easily because already employed workers (insiders) keep their jobs even though unemployed outsiders might accept lower pay. Employers prefer a stable work force. (Key Question 7)

V.   **Rules or Discretion?**

A. Monetarists and other new classical economists believe that policy rules would reduce instability in the economy.

1. A monetary rule would direct the Fed to expand the money supply each year at the same annual rate as the typical growth of GDP. (See Figure 19-4)

   a. The rule would tie increases in the money supply to the typical rightward shift of long-run aggregate supply, and ensure that aggregate demand shifts rightward along with it.

   b. A monetary rule, then, would promote steady growth of real output along with price stability.

2. A few economists favor a constitutional amendment to require the federal government to balance its budget annually.

   a. Others simply suggest that government be "passive" in its fiscal policy and not intentionally create budget deficits of surpluses.

   b. Monetarists and new classical economists believe that fiscal policy is ineffective. Expansionary policy is bad because it crowds out private investment.

   c. RET economists reject discretionary fiscal policy for the same reason they reject active monetary policy. They don't believe it works because the effects are fully anticipated by private sector.

B. Mainstream economists defend discretionary stabilization policy.

1. In supporting discretionary monetary policy, mainstream economists argue that the velocity of money is more variable and unpredictable, in short run monetary policy can help offset changes in AD than monetarists contend.

2. Mainstream economists oppose requirements to balance the budget annually because it would require actions that would intensify the business cycle, such as raising taxes and cutting spending during recession and the opposite during booms. They support discretionary fiscal policy to combat recession or inflation even if it causes a deficit or surplus budget.

C. The U.S. economy has been about one-third more stable since 1946 than in earlier periods. Discretionary fiscal and monetary policy were used during this period and not before. This makes a strong case for its success.

D. A summary of alternative views presents the central ideas and policy implications of four main macroeconomic theories: Mainstream macroeconomics, monetarism, rational expectations theory and supply side economics. (See Table 19-1)

VI. **Last Word: The Taylor Rule: Could a Robot Replace Alan Greenspan?**

A. Macroeconomist John Taylor of Stanford University calls for a new monetary rule that would institutionalize appropriate Fed policy responses to changes in real output and inflation.

B. Traditional "monetarist rule" is passive. It required Fed to expand money supply at a fixed annual rate regardless of economic conditions.

C. "Discretion" is associated with the opposite: an active monetary policy where Fed changes the money supply and interest rates in response to changes in the economy or to prevent undesirable results.

D. Taylor's policy proposal would dictate active monetary actions that are precisely defined. It combines monetarism and the more mainstream view.

E. Taylor's rule has three parts:

1. If real GDP rises 1% above potential GDP, the Fed should raise the Federal funds rate by 0.5% relative to the current inflation rate.

2. If inflation is 1% above its target of 2%, the Fed should raise Federal funds rate by 0.5% above the inflation rate.

3. If real GDP equals potential GDP and inflation is 2%, the Federal funds rate should be about 4% implying real interest rate of 2%.

F. Taylor would retain Fed's power to override rule, so a robot really couldn't replace the Board. But a rule increases predictability and credibility.

G. Critics of the proposal see no reason for this rule given the success of monetary policy in the past decade.

ANSWERS TO END-OF-CHAPTER QUESTIONS

19-1   (*Key Question*) Use the aggregate demand-aggregate supply model to compare classical and Keynesian interpretations of (a) the aggregate supply curve, and (b) the stability of the aggregate demand curve. Which of these interpretations seems more consistent with the realities of the Great Depression?

(a) Classical economists envisioned the AS curve as being perfectly vertical. When prices fall, real profits do not decrease because wage rates fall in the same proportion. With constant real profits, firms have no reason to change the quantities of output they supply. Keynesians viewed the AS curve as being horizontal at outputs less than the full-employment output and vertical only at full employment. Declines in aggregate demand do not change the price level because wages and prices are assumed to be inflexible downward.

(b) Classical economists viewed AD as stable so long as the monetary authorities hold the money supply constant. Therefore inflation and deflation are unlikely. Keynesians viewed the AD curve as unstable—even if the money supply is constant—since investment spending is volatile. Decreases in AD can cause a recession; rapid increases in AD can cause demand-pull inflation.

(c) The Keynesian view seems more consistent with the facts of the Great Depression; in that period, real output declined by nearly 40 percent in the United States and remained low for a decade.

19-2   According to mainstream economists what is the usual cause of macroeconomic instability? What role does the spending-income multiplier play in creating instability? How might adverse aggregate supply factors cause instability, according to mainstream economists?

The mainstream view of macroeconomic instability is Keynesian-based and focuses on aggregate spending and its components. Particularly significant are changes in investment spending, which change aggregate demand and, occasionally, adverse supply shocks which change aggregate supply.

Investment spending is subject to wide variations, and a "multiplier effect" magnifies these changes into even greater changes in aggregate demand, which can cause demand pull inflation in the forward direction or a recession if investment spending falls.

In the mainstream view, a second source of instability could arise on the supply side. Wars or artificial supply restrictions boost may raise per unit production costs. The result is a sizable decline in a nation's aggregate supply, which could destabilize the economy by simultaneously causing cost-push inflation and recession.

19-3   State and explain the basic equation of monetarism. What is the major cause of macroeconomic instability, as viewed by monetarists?.

The fundamental equation of monetarism is the equation of exchange. MV = PQ. The left side, MV, represents the total amount spent [M, the money supply X V, the velocity of money, (the number of times per year the average dollar is spent on final goods and services)]. The right side, PQ, equals the nation's nominal GDP [P is the price level or more specifically, the average price at which each unit of output is sold]. Q is the physical volume of all goods and services produced.

Monetarists believe changes in the money supply, in particular, inappropriate monetary policy, is the single most important cause of macroeconomic stability.

19-4   (*Key Question*) Suppose that the money supply and the nominal GDP for a hypothetical economy are $96 billion and $336 billion, respectively.   What is the velocity of money? How will households and businesses react if the central bank reduces the money supply by $20 billion? By how much will nominal GDP have to fall to restore equilibrium, according to the monetarist perspective?

Velocity = 3.5 or 336/96. They will cut back on their spending to try to restore their desired ratio of money to other items of wealth. Nominal GDP will fall to $266 billion (= $76 billion remaining money supply x 3.5) to restore equilibrium.

19-5   Briefly describe the difference between a so-called real business cycle and a more traditional "spending" business cycle.

In the real-business-cycle theory, business fluctuations result from significant changes in technology and resource availability. These changes affect productivity and thus the long-run growth trend of aggregate supply. The changes in aggregate supply then induce changes in the demand for money, which in this controversial scenario then leads to a change in the money supply, which allows adjustment without changes in the price level. The conclusion of the real-business-cycle theory is that macro instability arises on the aggregate supply side of the economy, not on the aggregate demand side as both mainstream economists and monetarists generally say.

19-6   Andrew and Kris were walking directly toward each other in a congested store aisle. Andrew moved to his left to avoid Kris, and at the same time Kris moved to his right to avoid Andrew. They bumped into each other. What concept does this example illustrate? How does this idea relate to macroeconomic instability?

This example illustrates a coordination failure which occurs in macroeconomics, when people do not reach a mutually beneficial equilibrium because they lack some way to jointly coordinate their actions.

Expectations of households and business firms can create an undesirable outcome. If individuals expect others to cut spending and anticipate excess capacity, they will cut their own investment and consumption as well. Aggregate demand will decline and the economy will experience a recession due to self-fulfilling prophecy. Once the economy is depressed, producers and households have no individual incentive to increase spending. If all participants would agree to simultaneously increase spending, then aggregate demand would rise and real output and real income would expand. Each producer and consumer would be better off. But this mutually beneficial outcome will not occur because there is no mechanism by which to coordinate their actions.

19-7   (*Key Question*) Use an AD-AS graph to demonstrate and explain the price-level and real-output outcome of an anticipated decline in aggregate demand, as viewed by RET economists. (Assume that the economy initially is operating at its full-employment level of output.) Then, demonstrate and explain on the same graph the outcome, as viewed by mainstream economists.

See the graph and the decline in aggregate demand from AD_1 to AD_2. RET view: The Economy anticipates the decline in the price level and immediate moves from a to d. Mainstream view: The economy first moves from a to b and then to c. In view of historical evidence, the mainstream view seems more plausible to us than the RET view; only when aggregate demand shifts from AD_2 to AD_1 will full-employment output Q_1 be restored in the mainstream view.

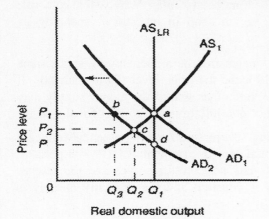

19-8   What is an efficiency wage? How might payment of an above-market wage reduce shirking by employees and reduce worker turnover? How might efficiency wages contribute to downward wage inflexibility, at least for a time, when aggregate demand declines?

An efficiency wage is one that minimizes the firm's labor cost per unit of output. Normally, we could assume that the market wage for the particular type of labor would be efficient, since it is the lowest wage that could be paid to obtain workers in the classification. Firms may discover, however, that paying a wage that is higher than the market wage will lower their wage cost per unit of output. There are a number of reasons for this possible outcome:

> First, the above average wage raises the opportunity cost of losing the job and gives workers an incentive to retain their relatively high-paying job. Worker productivity is likely to be higher and in a sense the higher wage more than pays for itself.

> Second, motivated workers require less supervision. If the firm needs fewer supervisory personnel to monitor work performance, the overall wage cost per unit of output can be lower.

> Third, the above-market pay discourages workers from voluntarily leaving their jobs and the lower turnover rate reduces the firm's cost of hiring and training new workers. It also gives the firm a better selection of potential workers, since the above-market wage would increase applications. With a high retention rate and a good pool of applicants, the firm is likely to maintain a more experienced and productive workforce.

Efficiency wages are likely to contribute to downward wage inflexibility. Wage cuts may encourage shirking, require more supervising personnel and increased turnover. Wage cuts that reduce productivity and raise per-unit labor costs are self-defeating.

19-9   How might relationships between so-called insiders and outsiders contribute to downward wage inflexibility?

Insiders are workers who retain employment even during recession. Outsiders are workers laid off from a particular firm and other unemployed workers who would like to work at that firm. Insider-outsider theory suggests that wages will be inflexible downward even when aggregate demand declines. Employers seem to believe that hiring unemployed workers at a reduced wage is not worth the disruption it could cause the business. Insiders are already trained, know their jobs and may work in teams. Replacing them with outsiders may cost more than the saving in reduced wages.

19-10   Use the equation of exchange to explain the rationale for a monetary rule. Why will such a rule run into trouble if V unexpectedly falls because of, say, a drop in investment spending by businesses?

MV = PQ. If we assume that V (velocity) is constant, increasing the money supply at the same rate as the anticipated increase in real output (Q) would leave the price level (P) unchanged. If velocity is not stable and changes unexpectedly, a steady rate of growth of the money supply may not be sufficient to keep the economy on the desired path of non-inflationary growth of real output.

19-11   Answer questions (a) and (b) on the basis of the following information for a hypothetical economy in year 1: money supply = $400 billion; long-term annual growth of potential GDP = 3 percent; velocity = 4. Assume that the banking system initially has no excess reserves and the reserve requirement is 10 percent. Also assume that velocity is constant and the economy initially is operating at its full-employment real output.

(a) What is the level of nominal GDP in year 1?

(b) Suppose the Fed adheres to a monetary rule through open-market operations. What amount of U.S. securities will it have to sell to, or buy from, banks or the public between years 1 and 2 to meet its monetary rule?

The equation of exchange MV = PQ allows us to calculate nominal GDP by multiplying M(400 billion) times V(4).

(a) nominal GDP is 1,600 billion in year 1

(b) to achieve a 3% growth rate, an increase in nominal GDP of 48 billion, the money supply would have to increase by $12 billion.

MV = 1,648 (412 ∞ 4) = 1,648.

Assuming a 10% reserve requirement and all money in the form of bank deposits, a money multiplier of 10 would suggest that the Federal Reserve would need to purchase $1.2 billion in U.S. Government securities in order to achieve the required monetary growth over the course of the year.

19-12   Explain the difference between "active" discretionary fiscal policy advocated by mainstream economists and "passive" fiscal policy advocated by new classical economists. Explain: "The problem with a balanced-budget amendment is that it would, in a sense, require active fiscal policy—but in the *wrong* direction—as the economy slides into recession."

Active discretionary fiscal policy entails the use of deficit spending during recessions, that is, increasing government spending, and/or cutting taxes to expand aggregate demand and to use contractionary fiscal policy, running a budget surplus, all to ward off inflationary pressures when necessary.

New classical economists, monetarists and rational expectationlists see the economy as automatically self-correcting when disturbed from its full-employment level of real output. They are opposed to using discretionary fiscal policy to create budget deficits or budget surpluses.

Mainstream economists vigorously defend the use of both discretionary fiscal and monetary policies. They believe that both theory and empirical data support the use of countercyclical measures. Requiring an annually balanced budget would require the use of fiscal policy that would intensify the swings in the business cycle, rather than help reduce variations in output.

19-13 (*Key Question*) Place MON, RET, or MAIN besides the statements that most closely reflect monetarist, rational expectations, or mainstream views, respectively.

    a. Anticipated changes in aggregate demand affect only the price level; they have no effect on real output.

    b. Downward wage inflexibility means that declines in aggregate demand can cause long-lasting recession.

    c. Changes in the money supply M increase PQ; at first only Q rises because nominal wages are fixed, but once workers adapt their expectations to new realities, P rises and Q returns to its former level.

    d. Fiscal and monetary policy smooth out the business cycle.

    e. The Fed should increase the money supply at a fixed annual rate.

    (a) RET;

    (b) MAIN;

    (c) MON;

    (d) MAIN;

    (e) MON.

19-14 You have just been elected president of the United States, and the present chairman of the Federal Reserve Board has resigned. You need to appoint a new person to this position, was well as a person to chair your Council of Economic Advisers. Using Table 19-1 and your knowledge of macroeconomics, identify the views on macro theory and policy you would want your appointees to hold. Remember, the economic health of the entire nation—and your chances for reelection—may depend on these selections.

The appointments to chair the Federal Reserve Board and the Council of Economic Advisors would depend on what coalition of interest groups contributed to my campaign and helped put me in office.

A Democratic president is likely to appoint economists with a mainstream approach and who are in favor of active fiscal and monetary policies. Since labor unions may have contributed, supply siders need not apply.

During the Reagan administration (1981-1988) supply side policies were implemented. One of the first actions taken was to fire striking air traffic controllers. Labor unions were shaken by the action, since they are usually most successful representing highly skilled workers and air traffic controllers are among the most specialized and skilled workers in the nation. This risky but successful move set the tone for supply side policies which were designed to reduce the costs of production, increase worker productivity and shift aggregate supply to the right. In addition to reducing the power of labor unions the Reagan administration tried to reduce government regulation of business in many areas and cut marginal tax rates in an effort to increase saving and investment.

Conservative Republican candidates for president are most likely to surround themselves with economic advisers who are monetarists or rational expectationalists since both favor a reduced role for government and would be against the use of discretionary fiscal policy to manage aggregate demand. Both would favor the use of a monetary rule and reliance upon the market system to be self-adjusting.

19-15 (*Last Word*) Compare and contrast the Taylor Rule for monetary policy with the older, simpler monetary rule advocated by Milton Friedman.

The monetary rule advocated by Friedman, the "monetarist rule," is passive. It requires consistent expansion of money supply regardless of economic conditions. The "Taylor rule" is activist and counter cyclical. It allows the Fed to adjust the money supply and interest rates in expansionary or contractionary fashion depending on economic conditions. However, it is similar to the monetarist prescription by stating the Fed's policy changes precisely in response to a variety of economic conditions.

CHAPTER TWENTY
DEMAND AND SUPPLY:
ELASTICITIES AND GOVERNMENT-SET PRICES

CHAPTER OVERVIEW

This chapter is the first of the chapters in Part Five, "Microeconomics of Product Markets." Students will benefit by reviewing Chapter 3's demand and supply analysis prior to reading this chapter. Depending upon the course outline used in the micro principles course, this chapter could be taught after Chapter 3.

Both the elasticity coefficient and the total receipts test for measuring price elasticity of demand are presented in the chapter. The text attempts to sharpen students' ability to estimate price elasticity by discussing its major determinants. The chapter reviews a number of applications and presents empirical estimates for a variety of products. Cross and income elasticities of demand and price elasticity of supply are also addressed.

Finally, price ceilings and price floors are discussed as well as the economic consequences on the market of government-set prices.

WHAT'S NEW

The chapter title has been expanded to include the second topic – government-set prices. Throughout the discussion on price elasticity, examples (popcorn, movie tickets, etc.) are used instead of product X and product Y. An application section has been added to the cross elasticity discussion. The section on government-set prices has been rewritten with more current examples being included in the price ceiling discussion. Finally, the example of rock concert promoters using below-equilibrium prices has been moved to an Internet problem.

The Last Word has been changed. One of the Web-Based Questions has been revised.

INSTRUCTIONAL OBJECTIVES

After completing this chapter, students should be able to:

1. Define demand and supply and state the laws of demand and supply (review from Chapter 3).

2. Determine equilibrium price and quantity from supply and demand graphs and schedules (from Chapter 3).

3. Define price elasticity of demand and compute the coefficient of elasticity given appropriate data on prices and quantities.

4. Explain the meaning of elastic, inelastic, and unitary price elasticity of demand.

5. Recognize graphs of perfectly elastic and perfectly inelastic demand.

6. Use the total-revenue test to determine whether elasticity of demand is elastic, inelastic, or unitary.

7. List four major determinants of price elasticity of demand.

8. Explain how a change in each of the determinants of price elasticity would affect the elasticity coefficient.

9. Define price elasticity of supply and explain how the producer's ability to shift resources to alternative uses and time affect price elasticity of supply.

10. Explain cross elasticity of demand and how it is used to determine substitute or complementary products.

11. Define income elasticity and its relationship to superior and inferior goods.

12. Define ceiling price and floor price in relationship to the equilibrium price.

13. Explain by examples the economic effects of price ceilings and floors.

14. Define and identify the terms and concepts listed at end of the chapter.

COMMENTS AND TEACHING SUGGESTIONS

1. Suggestions given for chapter 3 are also pertinent to this chapter, as an understanding of demand and supply is essential to understanding this chapter.

2. Find, or have the students find, real-world examples of changing prices to explore the forces of the changing demand and supply. Any daily newspaper or business periodical should have such articles. Articles on impacts of a drought, freeze, strike, or a new fad product would provide such examples. Use the examples to differentiate between changes in quantity demanded and change in demand.

3. Draw demand curves that illustrate relatively elastic, relatively inelastic and unitary elastic. When discussing the idea that every downward sloping demand curve has all three properties, use salt as an example. Ask the students if anyone knows what a box of salt costs. Probably no one will. Then ask them if anyone cares what a box of salt costs and if they would hesitate buying a box if the price were to increase from 30 cents to 33 cents. Then ask if they would answer the same way if the price were to increase from $100 per box to $110.

4. Emphasize the total revenue test for elasticity. Many important applications turn on whether a price change is directly or inversely related to the change in total revenue. Most students assume that if you raise the price of a product or service, more money will be collected. Ask students how the theater department could increase revenue from ticket sales. The following discussion illustrates the point that they must know the coefficient of elasticity in order to make the correct choice to raise or lower the price for more revenue. It also will give you an opportunity to explain why economists often give more than one answer to a question.

5. Chapter 33 (Agriculture) and Chapter 35 (Health Care) both illustrate the special problems of industries characterized by a relatively inelastic demand. You might want to use some of the material in these chapters as examples in your discussion about elasticity.

6. The discussion on income elasticity and cross elasticity provides an opportunity to review the difference between "change in demand" and "change in quantity demanded" and substitute good and complementary goods.

STUDENT STUMBLING BLOCKS

1. The general concept of price elasticity of demand is relative easy for the students to understand particularly if they have a good grasp of the demand concepts in chapter 3. Where students run into problems is when they are introduced to the calculation of the coefficient of elasticity of demand. Use an example of an elastic demand schedule and a demand curve. Calculate the percentage changes in both price and quantity and ask them to identify whether the demand is elastic or inelastic by comparing the two percentages. Repeat the process with an inelastic demand schedule and demand curve.

2. A related problem is for the students to remember whether the percentage change in quantity or the percentage price is the numerator or the denominator of the coefficient ratio. A way of overcoming this problem is to explain that the coefficient is greater than "1" when the demand is elastic, and thus the larger of the two percentages (percentage change in quantity demanded) must be divided by the smaller of the two percentages (percentage in change in price). Use the same analysis for the inelastic demand.

LECTURE NOTES

I. **Introduction**

   A. Elasticity of demand measures how much the quantity demanded changes with a given change in price of the item, change in consumers' income, or change in price of related product.

   B. Price elasticity is a concept that also relates to supply.

   C. The chapter explores both elasticity of supply and demand and applications of the concept.

   D. The chapter also looks at the effects of government-set prices on individual markets.

II. **Price Elasticity of Demand**

   A. Law of demand tells us that consumers will respond to a price decrease by buying more of a product (other things remaining constant), but it does not tell us how much more.

   B. The degree of responsiveness or sensitivity of consumers to a change in price is measured by the concept of price elasticity of demand.

      1. If consumers are relatively responsive to price changes, demand is said to be elastic.

      2. If consumers are relatively unresponsive to price changes, demand is said to be inelastic.

      3. Note that with both elastic and inelastic demand, consumers behave according to the law of demand; that is, they are responsive to price changes. The terms elastic or inelastic describe the degree of responsiveness. A precise definition of what we mean by "responsive" or "unresponsive" follows.

   C. Price elasticity formula:

   Quantitative measure of elasticity, E_d = percentage change in quantity/ percentage change in price.

      1. Using two price-quantity combinations of a demand schedule, calculate the percentage change in quantity by dividing the absolute change in quantity by one of the two original quantities. Then calculate the percentage change in price by dividing the absolute change in price by one of the two original prices.

      2. Estimate the elasticity of this region of the demand schedule by comparing the percentage change in quantity and the percentage change in price. Do not use the ratio formula at this time. Emphasize that it is the two percentage changes that are being compared when determining elasticity.

      4. Show that if the other original quantity and price were used as the denominator that the percentage changes would be different. Explain that a way to deal with this problem is to use the average of the two quantities and the average of the two prices.

      5. Emphasis: What is being compared are the percentages changes, not the absolute changes.

a. Absolute changes depend on choice of units. For example, a change in the price of a $10,000 car by $1 and is very different than a change in the price a of $1 can of beer by $1. The auto's price is rising by a fraction of a percent while the beer rice is rising 100 percent.

b. Percentages also make it possible to compare elasticities of demand for different products.

6. Because of the inverse relationship between price and quantity demanded, the actual elasticity of demand will be a negative number. However, we ignore the minus sign and use absolute value of both percentage changes.

7. If the coefficient of elasticity of demand is a number greater than one, we say demand is elastic; if the coefficient is less than one, we say demand is inelastic. In other words, the quantity demanded is "relatively responsive" when Ed is greater than 1 and "relatively unresponsive" when Ed is less than 1. A special case is if the coefficient equals one; this is called unit elasticity.

8. Note: Inelastic demand does not mean that consumers are completely unresponsive. This extreme situation called perfectly inelastic demand would be very rare, and the demand curve would be vertical.

9. Likewise, elastic demand does not mean consumers are completely responsive to a price change. This extreme situation, in which a small price reduction would cause buyers to increase their purchases from zero to all that it is possible to obtain, is perfectly elastic demand, and the demand curve would be horizontal.

D. The best formula for elasticity is:

E_d = [(change in Q)/(sum of Q's/2)] divided by [(change in P)/(sum of P's/2)]

1. Have the students calculate each of the percentage changes separately using to determine whether the demand is elastic or inelastic. After the students have determined the type of elasticity, then have them insert the percentage changes into the formula.

2. Students should practice the exercise in Table 20.1. (Key Question 2)

E. Graphical analysis:

1. Illustrate graphically perfectly elastic, relatively elastic, unitary elastic, relative inelastic, and perfectly inelastic.

2. Using Figure 20.2, explain that elasticity varies over range of prices.

a. Demand is more elastic in upper left portion of curve (because price is higher, quantity smaller).

b. Demand is more inelastic in lower right portion of curve (because price is lower, quantity larger).

3. It is impossible to judge elasticity of a single demand curve by its flatness or steepness, since demand elasticity can measure both elastic and inelastic at different points on the same demand curve.

F. Total-revenue test is the easiest way to judge whether demand is elastic or inelastic. This test can be used in place of elasticity formula, unless there is a need to determine the elasticity coefficient.

1. Elastic demand and the total-revenue test: Demand is elastic if a decrease in price results in a rise in total revenue, or if an increase in price results in a decline in total revenue. (Price and revenue move in opposite directions).

2. Inelastic demand and total revenue test: Demand is inelastic if a decrease in price results in a fall in total revenue, or an increase in price results in a rise in total revenue. (Price and revenue move in same direction).

3. Unit elasticity and the total revenue test: Demand has unit elasticity if total revenue does not change when the price changes.

4. The graphical representation of the relationship between total revenue and price elasticity is shown in Figure 20.2.

5. Table 20.2 provides a summary of the rules and concepts related to elasticity of demand.

G. There are several determinants of the price elasticity of demand.

1. Substitutes for the product: Generally, the more substitutes, the more elastic the demand.

2. The proportion of price relative to income: Generally, the larger the expenditure relative to one's budget, the more elastic the demand, because buyers notice the change in price more.

3. Whether the product is a luxury or a necessity: Generally, the less necessary the item, the more elastic the demand.

4. The amount of time involved: Generally, the longer the time period involved, the more elastic the demand becomes.

H. Table 20.3 presents some real-world price elasticities. Use the determinants discussed to see if the actual elasticities are equivalent to what one would predict. (Questions 9 and 10)

I. There are many practical applications of elasticity.

1. Inelastic demand for agricultural products helps to explain why bumper crops depress the prices and total revenues for farmers.

2. Governments look at elasticity of demand when levying excise taxes. Excise taxes on products with inelastic demand will raise the most revenue and have the least impact on quantity demanded for those products.

3. Demand for cocaine is highly inelastic and presents problems for law enforcement. Stricter enforcement reduces supply, raises prices and revenues for sellers, and provides more incentives for sellers to remain in business. Crime may also increase as buyers have to find more money to buy their drugs.

   a. Opponents of legalization think that occasional users or "dabblers" have a more elastic demand and would increase their use at lower, legal prices.

   b. Removal of the legal prohibitions might make drug use more socially acceptable and shift demand to the right.

4. The impact of minimum-wage laws will be less harmful to employment if the demand for minimum-wage workers is inelastic.

III. Price Elasticity of Supply

A. The concept of price elasticity also applies to supply. The elasticity formula is the same as that for demand, but we must substitute the word "supplied" for the word "demanded" everywhere in the formula.

E_s = percentage change in quantity supplied / percentage change in price

As with price elasticity of demand, the midpoints formula is more accurate.

B. The time period involved is very important in price elasticity of supply because it will determine how much flexibility a producer has to adjust his/her resources to a change in the price. The degree of flexibility, and therefore the time period, will be different in different industries. (Figure 20.3)

    1. The market period is so short that elasticity of supply is inelastic; it could be almost perfectly inelastic or vertical. In this situation, it is virtually impossible for producers to adjust their resources and change the quantity supplied. (Think of adjustments on a farm once the crop has been planted.)

    2. The short-run supply elasticity is more elastic than the market period and will depend on the ability of producers to respond to price change. Industrial producers are able to make some output changes by having workers work overtime or by bringing on an extra shift.

    3. The long-run supply elasticity is the most elastic, because more adjustments can be made over time and quantity can be changed more relative to a small change in price, as in Figure 20.3c. The producer has time to build a new plant.

IV. **Cross and income elasticity of demand:**

A. Cross elasticity of demand refers to the effect of a change in a product's price on the quantity demanded for another product. Numerically, the formula is shown for products X and Y.

E_{xy} = (percentage change in quantity of X) / (percentage change in price of Y)

    1. If cross elasticity is positive, then X and Y are substitutes.

    2. If cross elasticity is negative, then X and Y are complements.

    3. Note: if cross elasticity is zero, then X and Y are unrelated, independent products.

B. Income elasticity of demand refers to the percentage change in quantity demanded that results from some percentage change in consumer incomes.

E_i = (percentage change in quantity demanded) / (percentage change in income)

    1. A positive income elasticity indicates a normal or superior good.

    2. A negative income elasticity indicates an inferior good.

    3. Those industries that are income elastic will expand at a higher rate as the economy grows.

V. **Government-Set Prices**

A. Price ceilings are maximum legal prices a seller may charge for a product or service; they have been established historically to enable consumers to obtain some "essential" good or service that they could not afford at the market equilibrium price.

    1. Figure 20.4 illustrates the problem that arises when the price is set below the equilibrium price. Shortages will result, since the quantity demanded will be greater than the quantity supplied at the lower price. This presents problems to the government.

        a. How should the available supply be apportioned among buyers? Some possibilities include first-come, first-served or ration cards.

b. Black markets arise as some consumers obtain the item at the fixed price and resell it at the higher price that many consumers are willing and able to pay.

2. Rent controls also create special problems because they make it less attractive for landlords to offer housing in that market, and so shortages of housing will develop.

3. Interest ceilings on credit cards have also been proposed but might create problems, according to a Federal Reserve study.

a. Card issuers might tighten credit standards.

b. The annual fee would probably rise or transaction fees would emerge.

c. The interest-free "grace period" available on most cards might disappear.

d. Retail stores might raise prices to offset decline in interest income on their credit cards.

B. Price floors are minimum prices set by government above the equilibrium. Examples include farm price subsidies and minimum wage laws.

1. Price floors result in persistent surpluses, since the quantity supplied will be above the quantity demanded (see Figure 20.5).

2. There are government policies to cope with surpluses.

a. Government may obtain agreement of the sellers to restrict supplies in exchange for the price floor.

b. Government may purchase the surplus if efforts to restrict supply are not successful.

C. Controversial Tradeoffs: Price ceilings or price floors destroy the rationing function of the market-price system. Price ceilings cause shortages; price floors create surpluses.

1. Price ceilings or price floors destroy the rationing and guiding functions of the market-price system.

2. Government must step in and provide a rationing system for product shortages created by price ceilings, and devise methods to eliminate product surpluses from price floors.

3. Government interference with market processes imposes administrative costs and unwanted side effects that must be weighed against the alleged benefits.

VI.   LAST WORD: Luxury on $8 Day

A. Rent controls in New York City have allowed long-term residents of some high-priced hotels to continue to live in the hotel for a fraction of the usual room rent.

B. New York City regulations allow landlords to increase rents on apartments that are vacant, but they cannot increase the rent on an apartment that continues to be occupied by the same tenant.

C. Some hotels have tried to encourage the permanent residents to move by offering to pay them as much as $250,000. Few have taken the offer.

ANSWERS TO END-OF-CHAPTER QUESTIONS

20-1   Explain why the choice between 1, 2, 3, 4, 5, 6, 7, and 8 "units" or 1000, 2000, 3000, 4000, 5000, 6000, 7000, and 8000 movie tickets, makes no difference in determining elasticity in Table 20.1.

Price elasticity of demand is determined by comparing the percentage change in price and the percentage change in quantity demanded. The percentage change in quantity will remain the same regardless of whether the difference is between 1 unit and 2 units or 1000 units and 2000 units.

20-2   (*Key Question*) Graph the accompanying demand data and then use the midpoints formula for Ed to determine price elasticity of demand for each of the four possible $1 price changes. What can you conclude about the relationship between the slope of a curve and its elasticity? Explain in a nontechnical way why demand is elastic in the northwest segment of the demand curve and inelastic in the southeast segment.

Product price	Quantity demanded
$5	1
4	2
3	3
2	4
1	5

See the graph accompanying the answer to 20-4. Elasticities, top to bottom: 3; 1.4; .714; .333. Slope does not measure elasticity. This demand curve has a constant slope of -1 (= -1/1), but elasticity declines as we move down the curve. When the initial price is high and initial quantity is low, a unit change in price is a *low* percentage while a unit change in quantity is a *high* percentage change.   The percentage change in quantity exceeds the percentage change in price, making demand elastic. When the initial price is low and initial quantity is high, a unit change in price is a *high* percentage change while a unit change in quantity is a *low* percentage change.   The percentage change in quantity is less than the percentage change in price, making demand inelastic.

20-3   Draw two linear demand curves parallel to one another. Demonstrate that for any specific price change demand is more elastic on the curve closer to the origin.

Two linear demand curves that are parallel to one another will have the same slope. (Slope is equal to the absolute vertical change divided by the absolute horizontal change.) For any specific change in price, the absolute change in quantity demanded would be the same on both of the parallel demand curves. This absolute change in quantity will represent a larger percentage change on the demand curve closest to the origin. The percentage change in the price will be the same for both demand curves. Since the formula for price elasticity places the percentage change in quantity demanded in the numerator and the percentage change in price in the denominator, elasticity will be greater on the curve closest to the origin.

In the example given Ed, equals 4—between points A and B on D1, the demand curve closest to the origin. Ed equals 2—between points C and D, the corresponding change on D2.

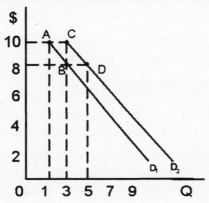

20-4   (*Key Question*) Calculate total-revenue data from the demand schedule in question 2. Graph total revenue below your demand curve. Generalize on the relationship between price elasticity and total revenue.

See the graph. Total revenue data, top to bottom: $5; $8; $9; $8; $5. When demand is elastic, price and total revenue move in the opposite direction. When demand is inelastic, price and total revenue move in the same direction.

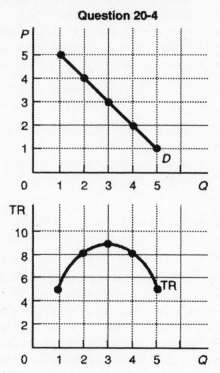

Question 20-4

20-5   (*Key Question*) How would the following changes in price affect total revenue. That is, would total revenue increase, decline, or remain unchanged?

a.   Price falls and demand is inelastic.

b.   Price rises and demand is elastic.

c.   Price rises and supply is elastic.

d.   Price rises and supply is inelastic.

e.   Price rises and demand is inelastic.

f.   Price falls and demand is elastic.

g.   Price falls and demand is of unit elasticity.

Total revenue would increase in (c), (d), (e), and (f); decrease in (a) and (b); and remain the same in (g).

20-6   (*Key Question*) What are the major determinants of price elasticity of demand? Use these determinants and your own reasoning in judging whether demand for each of the following products is elastic or inelastic:

(a) bottled water, (b) tooth paste; (c) Crest toothpaste; (d) ketchup, (e) diamond bracelets; (f) Microsoft Windows operating system.

Substitutability, proportion of income; luxury versus necessity, and time. Elastic: (a), (c), (e). Inelastic: (b), (d), and (f).

20-7 What effect would a rule stating that university students must live in university dormitories have on the price elasticity of demand for dormitory space? What impact might this in turn have on room rates?

The ruling would make the price elasticity of demand more inelastic than if there were no such rule, assuming that there is not another equivalent university nearby to which students could transfer. Although universities are nonprofit organizations, the rule would certainly allow them to raise rates without worrying so much about students moving out to live elsewhere.

20-8 "If the demand for farm products is highly price inelastic, a bumper crop may reduce farm incomes." Evaluate and illustrate graphically.

The statement is true. As shown on the graph, the increased supply, S2, results in a considerably reduced income compared to the pre-bumper crop situation, S1. When demand is highly price inelastic, as it is here, the increase in quantity demanded as a result of a price decline is proportionately far less than the decline in price. Note that the decline in price from $9 to $4 results in a decline in farm revenue or income of $21 (= $45-$24).

20-9 You are chairperson of a state tax commission responsible for establishing a program to raise new revenue through excise taxes. Would elasticity of demand be important to you in determining those products on which excises should be levied? Explain.

Elasticity of demand would be very important to me. I would select goods for which the demand was price inelastic. When demand is price inelastic, the decrease in quantity demanded as a result of the price increase caused by the excise tax is proportionately less than the increase in price. As a result, tax revenues will increase. An ideal good would be one for which the demand was perfectly inelastic. In such a case, there would be no decrease in quantity demanded at all when an excise tax was levied. Also, it would be helpful to find a good whose consumption is harmful. On these two counts, cigarettes and liquor make excellent candidates for excise taxes; to the extent that there is any cutback in consumption at all, the majority view now is that this is a good thing.

20-10 (*Key Question*) In November 1998 Vincent van Gogh's self-portrait sold at auction for $71.5 million. Portray this sale in a demand and supply diagram and comment on the elasticity of supply. Comedian George Carlin once mused, "If a painting can be forged well enough to fool some experts, why is the original so valuable?" Provide an answer.

The supply is perfectly inelastic—vertical—at a quantity of 1 unit. The $71.5 million price is determined where the downward sloping demand curve intersected this supply curve.

If more than one picture where available (all but one having to be a copy), the demand would likely decrease enormously.

20-11 Because of a legal settlement over state health care claims, in 1999 the U.S. tobacco companies had to raise the average price of a pack of cigarettes from $1.95 to $2.45. The projected decline in cigarette sales was 8 percent. What does this imply for the elasticity of cigarettes? Explain.

The price elasticity of demand for cigarettes was inelastic. The percentage change in price was 23 percent whereas the percentage change in quantity demanded was only 8 percent. For those hooked on cigarettes, even a 23 percent increase will not discourage them from smoking.

20-12   (*Key Question*) Suppose the cross elasticity of demand for products A and B is +3.6 and for products C and D it is -5.4. What can you conclude about how products A and B are related? Products C and D?

A and B are substitutes; C and D are complements.

20-13   (*Key Question*) The income elasticities of demand for movies, dental services, and clothing have been estimated to be +3.4, +1.0, and +0.5 respectively. Interpret these coefficients. What does it mean if the income elasticity coefficient is negative?

All are normal goods—income and quantity demanded move in the same direction. These coefficients reveal that a 1 percent increase in income will increase the quantity of movies demanded by 3.4 percent, of dental services by 1.0 percent, and of clothing by 0.5 percent. A negative coefficient indicates an inferior good—income and quantity demanded move in the opposite direction.

20-14   A recent study found that an increase in the price of beer would reduce the amount of marijuana consumed. Is cross elasticity between the two products positive or negative? Are these products substitutes or complements? What might be the logical relationship?

The cross elasticity of the two products is negative. The products appear to be complementary. As one drinks beer, one also smokes marijuana.

20-15   Why is it desirable for ceiling prices to be accompanied by government rationing? And for price floors to be accompanied by programs that purchase surpluses, restrict output, or increase demand? Show graphically why price ceilings entail shortages and price floors result in surpluses. What effect, if any, does elasticity of demand and supply have on the size of these shortages and surpluses? Explain.

A ceiling price that is set below the equilibrium price necessarily results in the quantity demanded being greater than the quantity supplied. This creates a shortage, as shown in Figure 20.4. To ensure that the restricted supply may be shared fairly among all those desiring it, government rationing is necessary.

A floor price that is set above the equilibrium price necessarily results in the quantity supplied being greater than the quantity demanded. This creates a surplus, as shown in Figure 20.5. The government must purchase the surplus (and store it and/or sell it abroad), or restrict supply to the quantity that will be bought at the floor price, or develop new uses for the product.

If the elasticity of demand and/or supply were inelastic, the shortage or surplus created by the government-set price will be less than if the demand and/or supply were elastic.

20-15   (*Last Word*) What unusual side effect have rent controls in New York City produced? Use the economic perspectives to explain why a substantial "buyout" may not in all cases correct the problem.

Rent controls have resulted in extremely low rents for individuals who continue to live in the same apartment for many years. For these long-term tenants, the cost of moving far exceeds the benefit of the "buyout."

CHAPTER TWENTY-ONE
CONSUMER BEHAVIOR
AND UTILITY MAXIMIZATION

CHAPTER OVERVIEW

This chapter may be omitted without damaging the continuity or understanding of the material in ensuing chapters. Those instructors who think it important to explain the law of demand on a more sophisticated level than that of previous chapters should assign this chapter. It may also be used as an enrichment chapter for brighter students. This chapter may be combined with Chapters 3 and 20.

The law of demand is explained in terms of (1) the income and substitution effects and (2) diminishing marginal utility. The latter approach leads into a detailed discussion of the theory of consumer choice. The numerical illustrations of the utility-maximizing rule should be viewed as a pedagogical technique, rather than an attempt to portray the actual choice-making process of consumers. When this illustration is explained by "order of purchase," the brief algebraic summary of consumer equilibrium should pose no great difficulties for most students. The discussion of the diamond-water paradox helps students look beyond what may be their first conclusions about the importance and value of products.

The opportunity cost of time may be considered as a component of product price. This chapter concludes with a simplified integration of time into the theory of consumer behavior.

The appendix to this chapter introduces indifference curve analysis for those intending to pursue further study in economic, or for those who desire a more rigorous explanation of consumer choice. This material is linked to the coverage provided in the rest of the chapter by using indifference curve analysis to develop an individual's demand curve for a product.

WHAT'S NEW

Many of the examples have been changed to make them more relevant to the students, but the numbers used in the tables have not been altered. The section on "transfers and gifts" has been revised and changed to "cash and in-kind gifts." Note that "budget constraint" is used rather than "budget restraint."

The Last Word is new. One of the Web-Based Questions has been revised.

INSTRUCTIONAL OBJECTIVES

After completing this chapter, students should be able to:

1. Define and distinguish between the income and substitution effects of a price change.

2. Explain why a consumer will buy more (less) of a commodity when its price falls (rises) by using the income and substitution effects.

3. Define marginal utility and state the law of diminishing marginal utility.

4. Explain how the law of diminishing marginal utility and price elasticity of demand are related.

5. List four assumptions made in the theory of consumer behavior.

6. State the utility-maximizing rule.

7. Use the utility-maximizing rule to determine a consumer's spending when given income, utility, and price data.

8. Use the theory of consumer behavior to define the market shift to compact discs from records since the early 1980s.

9. Explain the diamond-water paradox.

10. Explain how the value of time fits in the theory of consumer behavior and give two examples of implications that result.

11. Describe how the theory of consumer behavior helps us understand different values placed on time.

12. Explain why a cash gift will give the receiver more utility than a noncash gift costing the same amount.

13. Define and identify terms and concepts listed at the end of the chapter.

After completing the appendix, students should be able to:

1. Define a budget constraint line and explain shifts in a budget constraint line.

2. Explain three characteristics of indifference curves.

3. Identify a consumer's equilibrium position, given a set of indifference curves and a budget constraint line.

4. Use indifference curve analysis to derive an individual's demand curve for a product by showing consumption responses to a change in the price of the product.

5. Define and identify terms and concepts listed at the end of the appendix

COMMENTS AND TEACHING SUGGESTIONS

1. Demonstrate the law of diminishing marginal utility, and perhaps even the idea of a saturation point (MU = 0), by having a student consume jelly beans or something similar while you review the law of demand, income and substitution effects, etc. Normally, the student will stop eating in a few minutes even though the candy is "free."

2. Imagine a case in which marginal utility rises rather than diminishes with increased consumption. (Drug addiction comes to mind.) Reason with students how this would ultimately result in a consumer spending all of his/her income on this one good. Emphasize that this is fortunately not consistent with most consumer behavior. This helps support the law of diminishing marginal utility and the process by which consumers allocate their incomes among many different goods and services.

3. Ask students to identify people who would be likely to value time very highly and others who would place a low value on time. Have them discuss how those two groups of people would react to such situations as: (a) waiting in line to buy a product; (b) shopping for hours to find the best prices on products such as cars, stereo equipment, and soft drinks; or (c) hiring cleaning, laundry, and gardening services.

4. The marginal-total relationship presented in this chapter is the first of many the students will be asked to learn as they go through the Microeconomics chapters. Spend a little extra time on this relationship and explain that they will be using the concept in somewhat altered forms later in the course.

5. What consumers decide to purchase depends on their personal preferences and priorities. No two people will make exactly the same decisions. Test this hypothesis by handing out monopoly money in different amounts and asking students to write down the purchases they would make with the sum given. Then have the students compare their choices. (This would be a good group activity.) Were

there any identical lists? Some students got much more "money" than others. Was this "fair"? This exercise can be used to demonstrate the problem of making interpersonal comparisons and the problem of income inequality. Explain that the concept of consumer equilibrium puts each person in charge of his/her own satisfaction. The objective is to maximize their satisfaction but to stay within their budget.

6. The final objective of the chapter is to illustrate the concept of a constrained maximum. Without the use of calculus this demonstration can be time consuming and confusing. Yet the equimarginal principle is a powerful tool and is central to the concept of efficiency with many applications. Consumer equilibrium, (where total utility is maximum) occurs when marginal utility per dollar is the same for every good consumed. This means that the consumer's dollars are doing equal work at the margin. A dollar's worth of taffy apples is giving the same satisfaction as a dollar's worth of peanut butter cookies. Students may be able to grasp the concept intuitively by using physical examples (refer to the Last Word Chapter 1). Fast food customers try to join the shortest line and, in the process they make the food servers do equal work. The same thing happens in the grocery store as shoppers jockey for position at the check-out stand. A foreman of an assembly line achieves efficiency when he assigns workers tasks requiring equal time.

7. Ask students to think about the silliest, most undesirable, ugliest or useless gift they ever received. Assuming the giver had good intentions, why was there a loss of efficiency?

8. Debate: Resolved welfare recipients should be provided income in kind (food, clothing, shelter, etc.) not cash.

STUDENT STUMBLING BLOCK

The indifference curve analysis found in the appendix is most appropriate for advanced students or those who have had beginning calculus. While other students can grasp these concepts without calculus, the amount of time spent in explaining indifference curves has a great opportunity cost in terms of the topics that must be sacrificed later in most 12-to-15-week semesters. The topic is covered thoroughly in an intermediate microeconomic theory course.

LECTURE NOTES

I.   **Introduction**

A. Americans spend trillions of dollars on goods and services each year—more than 95 percent of their after-tax incomes, yet no two consumers spend their incomes in the same way. How can this be explained?

B. Why does a consumer buy a particular bundle of goods and services rather than others? Examining these issues will help us understand consumer behavior and the law of demand.

II. **Two Explanations of the Law of Demand**

A. Income and substitution effects explain the inverse relationship between price and quantity demanded.

1. The income effect is the impact of a change in price on consumers' real incomes and consequently on the quantity of that product demanded. An increase in price means that less real income is available to buy subsequent amounts of the product.

2. The substitution effect is the impact of a change in a product's price on its expensiveness relative to other substitute products' prices. A higher price for a particular product with no change in the prices of substitutes means that the item has become relatively more

expensive compared to its substitutes. Therefore, consumers will buy less of this product and more of the substitutes, whose prices are relatively lower than before.

B. The law of diminishing marginal utility is a second explanation of the downward sloping demand curve. Although consumer wants in general are insatiable, wants for specific commodities can be fulfilled. The more of a specific product consumers obtain, the less they will desire more units of that product. This can be illustrated with almost any item. The text uses the automobile example, but houses, clothing, and even food items work just as well.

1. Utility is a subjective notion in economics, referring to the amount of satisfaction a person gets from consumption of a certain item.

2. Marginal utility refers to the extra utility a consumer gets from one additional unit of a specific product. In a short period of time, the marginal utility derived from successive units of a given product will decline. This is known as diminishing marginal utility.

3. Figure 21.1 and the accompanying table illustrate the relationship between total and marginal-utility.

   a. Total utility increases as each additional tacos is purchased through the first five, but utility rises at a diminishing rate since each tacos adds less and less to the consumer's satisfaction.

   b. At some point, marginal utility becomes zero and then even negative at the seventh unit and beyond. If more than six tacos were purchased, total utility would begin to fall. This illustrates the law of diminishing marginal utility.

4. The law of diminishing marginal utility is related to demand and elasticity.

   a. Successive units of a product yield smaller and smaller amounts of marginal utility, so the consumer will buy more only if the price falls. Otherwise, it is not worth it to buy more.

   b. If marginal utility falls sharply as successive units are consumed, demand is predicted to be inelastic. That is, price must fall a relatively large amount before consumers will buy more of an item.

III. **Theory of consumer behavior uses the law of diminishing marginal utility to explain how consumers allocate their income.**

A. Consumer choice and the budget constraint:

1. Consumers are assumed to be rational, i.e. they are trying to get the most value for their money.

2. Consumers have clear-cut preferences for various goods and services and can judge the utility they receive from successive units of various purchases.

3. Consumers' incomes are limited because their individual resources are limited. Thus, consumers face a budget constraint.

4. Goods and services have prices and are scarce relative to the demand for them. Consumers must choose among alternative goods with their limited money incomes.

B. Utility maximizing rule explains how consumers decide to allocate their money incomes so that the last dollar spent on each product purchased yields the same amount of extra (marginal) utility.

1. A consumer is in equilibrium when utility is "balanced (per dollar) at the margin." When this is true, there is no incentive to alter the expenditure pattern unless tastes, income, or prices change.

2. Table 21.1 provides a numerical example of this for an individual named Holly with $10 to spend. Follow the reasoning process to see why 4 units of A and 4 of B will maximize Holly's utility, given the $10 spending limit.

3. It is marginal utility per dollar spent that is equalized; that is, consumers compare the extra utility from each product with its cost.

4. As long as one good provides more utility per dollar than another, the consumer will buy more of the first good; as more of the first product is bought, its marginal utility diminishes until the amount of utility per dollar just equals that of the other product.

5. Table 21.2 summarizes the step-by-step decision-making process the rational consumer will pursue to reach the utility-maximizing combination of goods and services attainable.

6. The algebraic statement of this utility-maximizing state is that the consumer will allocate income in such a way that:

   MU of product A/price of A = MU of product B/price of B = etc.

IV. **Utility Maximization and the Demand Curve**

   A. Determinants of an individual's demand curve are tastes, income, and prices of other goods.

   B. Deriving the demand curve can be illustrated using item B in Table 21.1 and considering alternative prices at which B might be sold. At lower prices, using the utility-maximizing rule, we see that more will be purchased as the price falls.

   C. The utility-maximizing rule helps to explain the substitution effect and the income effect.

   1. When the price of an item declines, the consumer will no longer be in equilibrium until more of the item is purchased and the marginal utility of the item declines to match the decline in price. More of this item is purchased rather than another relatively more expensive substitute.

   2. The income effect is shown by the fact that a decline in price expands the consumer's real income and the consumer must purchase more of this and other products until equilibrium is once again attained for the new level of real income.

V. **Applications and Extensions**

   A. The compact disc (CD) takeover:

   1. CDs have revolutionized the music industry since 1983, when fewer than 1 million were sold as compared to 210 million LPs. In 1999, 939 million CDs were sold, while only 2.9 million LPs were sold.

      a. Preferences changed due to improved quality and the amount of music available on one CD.

      b. CD player prices fell from over $1,000 or more to under $200.

   2. CD players and CDs have a higher ratio of marginal utility to price than do LP players and LPs. To maximize their utility, consumers will switch from LPs to CDs.

   B. The diamond-water paradox:

1. Before marginal analysis, economists were puzzled by the fact that some essential goods like water had lower prices than luxuries like diamonds.

2. The paradox is resolved when we look at the abundance of water relative to diamonds.

3. Theory tells us that consumers should purchase any good until the ratio of its marginal utility to price is the same as that ratio for all other goods.

   a. The marginal utility of an extra unit of water may be low as is its price, but the total utility derived from water is very large.

   b. The total utility of all water consumed is much larger than the total utility of all diamonds purchased.

   c. However, society prefers an additional diamond to an additional drop of water, because of the abundant stock of water available.

C. Time also has a value, so this must be considered in decision-making and utility maximization. The total price of an item must include the value of the time spent in consuming the product, i.e., the wage value of an hour of time. When time is considered, consumer behavior appears to be much more rational.

   1. Highly paid doctors may not spend hours hunting for bargains because their time is more valuable than the money to be saved from finding the best buy.

   2. Foreigners observe that Americans waste material goods but conserve time. This could be because our high productivity makes our time more valuable than many of the goods we waste.

D. Buying medical care or eating at a buffet:

   1. Most Americans have health insurance for which they pay a fixed monthly premium, which covers, say, 80 percent of their health care costs. Therefore, the cost of obtaining care is only 20 percent of its stated price for the insured patient.

   2. Following the law of demand, people purchase a larger quantity of medical care than if they had to pay the full price for each visit.

   3. If you buy a meal at an "all-you-can-eat" buffet, you eat more than if you paid separately for each item.

E. Cash and noncash gifts:

   1. Noncash gifts may yield less utility to the receiver than a cash gift of equal monetary value because the noncash gift may not match the receiver's preferences.

   2. Individuals know their own preferences better than the gift giver.

   3. Look back at Table 21.1. If Holly had no income and was given $2 worth, she would rather have the cash transfer to spend on B than to be given 2 units of A. (She gets more utility or satisfaction by spending her $2 on B.)

VI. **LAST WORD: Criminal Behavior**

A. The theory of consumer behavior can provide some useful insights into criminal behavior.

B. A person who steals from a store imposes uncompensated costs on others – the store owner, customers.

C. Whereas a person who is thinking about buying an item weighs the cost (the price) and the benefit (utility) of a particular purchase, a person who steals also weighs the cost and benefit of stealing the item.

D. The cost to the potential criminal is the possible guilt felt, the tools of the trade, the income forgone while engaging in an illegitimate activity, and possible fines and imprisonment. The potential criminal will engage in criminal behavior if the benefits exceed the costs.

E. Society can reduce criminal behavior by increasing the cost of guilt through family, educational, and religious efforts and by increasing the direct costs by using more sophisticated security systems. Society can also increase the penalties on those who are caught.

APPENDIX TO CHAPTER 21: INDIFFERENCE CURVE ANALYSIS

I. **The Budget Constraint Line**

A. Show various combinations of two products which can be purchased with a given money income with knowledge of the prices of the two products. Table 1 and Figure 1.

B. A decrease in money income shifts the budget constraint line inward to the left in Figure 1; an increase in money income shifts the budget constraint line outward to the right in Figure 1.

C. Price changes in either of the two products will rotate the budget constraint line. For example, in Figure 1, if the price of A rises, less of A will be purchased at each of the possible combinations of A and B, so the curve will fan downward along the vertical A-axis. A decrease in A's price would have the curve fanning upward along the A-axis. See Figure 5 (a).

II. **Indifference curves show all combinations of two products that will yield the same level of satisfaction or utility to the consumer. (Figure 2)**

A. Curves are downward sloping because the consumer will be able to maintain the same level of total utility by substituting more of B for less of A.

B. Curves are convex to the origin.

1. The slope of the curve measures the marginal rate of substitution of one good for the other (B for A) for the consumer to have a constant level of satisfaction.

2. Rationale for this shape is related to diminishing marginal utility. If the consumer has a lot of A and very little of B, B is more valuable at the margin, while A has a lower marginal utility. The consumer will then be willing to give up a substantial amount of product A to get more units of B. However, as the consumer obtains more and more of B and gives up more and more A, this relationship changes. The consumer will not be willing to give up much A to get more of B. In other words, the slope of the curve diminishes, and the curve is, by definition, convex to the origin.

3. An indifference map refers to successive indifference curves where each entails a different level of utility. As one moves away from the origin on the map, the level of utility increases. Figure 3.

C. The consumer's utility-maximizing combination of A and B will occur on the highest attainable indifference curve. This is where the budget constraint line is tangent to an indifference curve, which is the highest attainable level of utility. Higher levels will be unattainable or off the budget line. Figure 4. (Key Question 4)

D. The measurement of utility is not necessary when decisions are being made on a relative basis. The marginal rate of substitution is the ratio of the prices of the two goods, A and B. Also, the ratio of the marginal utilities at the maximizing point is equivalent to the ratio of the two prices. Therefore, the marginal rate of substitution is equivalent to the ratio of marginal utilities of two goods, and it is not necessary to find the absolute measure of marginal utility.

E. The demand curve can be derived using the indifference curve approach and determining how the quantity purchased will change when the price of one good changes to various levels. Figure 5 illustrates this procedure.

ANSWERS TO END-OF-CHAPTER QUESTIONS

21-1 Explain the law of demand through the income and substitution effects, using a price increase as a point of departure for your discussion. Explain the law of demand in terms of diminishing marginal utility.

When the price of a good rises, the real income of those who demand it is reduced; they now can buy less of this good (and of all other commodities). The second reason for buying less of the good whose price has risen is that it has become more expensive in relation to substitute goods. People will, therefore, substitute the now relatively cheaper goods for the one whose price has risen. For these two reasons— a decrease in real income and the now relatively higher price of the good in question—people buy less of a good when its price rises.

This reasoning also works in reverse; people's real income rises when the price of a good drops and they tend to substitute it for other goods whose prices have not changed. This is the law of demand: People tend to buy more of a commodity as its price drops.

As people acquire more and more of any commodity, eventually their desire for yet more of it decreases. In other words, the extra or marginal utility they derive from additional units of the commodity decreases. This being so, people can only be induced to buy more and more of a commodity if its price gets progressively less.

21-2 (*Key Question*) Complete the following table and answer the questions below:

Units consumed	Total utility	Marginal utility
0	0	—
1	10	10
2		8
3	25	—
4	30	—
5		3
6	34	—

a. At which rate is total utility increasing: a constant rate, a decreasing rate, or an increasing rate? How do you know?

b. "A rational consumer will purchase only 1 unit of the product represented by these data, since that amount maximizes marginal utility." Do you agree? Explain why or why not.

c. "It is possible that a rational consumer will not purchase any units of the product represented by these data." Do you agree? Explain why or why not.

Missing total utility data top – bottom: 18; 33. Missing marginal utility data, top – bottom: 7; 5; 1.

(a) A decreasing rate; because marginal utility is declining.

(b) Disagree. The marginal utility of a unit beyond the first may be sufficiently great (relative to product price) to make it a worthwhile purchase.

(c) Agree. This product's price could be so high relative to the first unit's marginal utility that the consumer would buy none of it.

21-3 Mrs. Wilson buys loaves of bread and quarts of milk each week at prices of $1 and 80 cents, respectively. At present she is buying these two products in amounts such that the marginal utilities from the last units purchased of the two products are 80 and 70 utils, respectively. Is she buying the utility-maximizing combination of bread and milk? If not, how should she reallocate her expenditures between the two goods?

Mrs. Wilson is not buying the utility-maximizing combination of bread and milk since the marginal utility per cent spent on each good is not equal. The marginal utility per cent of bread is 0.8 (= 80 utils/100 cents); the utility per cent of milk is 0.875 (= 70 utils/80 cents). Mrs. Wilson should buy more milk and less bread.

21-4 (Key Question) Columns 1 through 4 of the accompanying table show the marginal utility, measured in terms of utils, which Ricardo would get by purchasing various amounts of products A, B, C, and D. Column 5 shows the marginal utility Ricardo gets from saving. Assume that the prices of A, B, C, and D are $18, $6, $4, and $24, respectively, and that Ricardo has a money income of $106.

Column 1		Column 2		Column 3		Column 4		Column 5	
Units of A	MU	Units of B	MU	Units of C	MU	Units of D	MU	No. of $ saved	MU
1	72	1	24	1	15	1	36	1	5
2	54	2	15	2	12	2	30	2	4
3	45	3	12	3	8	3	24	3	3
4	36	4	9	4	7	4	18	4	2
5	27	5	7	5	5	5	13	5	1
6	18	6	5	6	4	6	7	6	1/2
7	15	7	2	7	3.5	7	4	7	1/4
8	12	8	1	8	3	8	2	8	1/8

a. What quantities of A, B, C, and D will Ricardo purchase in maximizing his utility?

b. How many dollars will Ricardo choose to save?

c. Check your answers by substituting them into the algebraic statement of the utility-maximizing rule.

(a) 4 units of A; 3 units of B; 3 units of C, and 0 units of D.

(b) Save $4.

(c) 36/$18 = 12/$6 = 8/$4 = 2/$1. The marginal utility per dollar of the last unit of each product purchased is 2.

21-5 (Key Question) You are choosing between two goods, X and Y, and your marginal utility from each is as shown below. If your income is $9 and the prices of X and Y are $2 and $1, respectively, what quantities of each will you purchase in maximizing utility? What total utility will you realize? Assume that, other things remaining unchanged, the price of X falls to $1. What quantities of X and Y will you now purchase? Using the two prices and quantities for X, derive a demand schedule (price-quantity-demanded table) for X.

Units of X	MU$_x$	Units of Y	MU$_y$
1	10	1	8
2	8	2	7
3	6	3	6
4	4	4	5
5	3	5	4
6	2	6	3

Buy 2 units of X and 5 units of Y. Marginal utility of last dollar spent will be equal at 4 (= 8/$2 for X and 4/$1 for Y) and the $9 income will be spent. Total utility = 48 (= 10 + 8 for X plus 8 + 7 + 6 + 5 + 4 for Y). When the price of X falls to $1, the quantity of X demanded increases from 2 to 4. Total utility is now 58 (= 10 + 8 + 6 + 4 for X plus 8 + 7 + 6 + 5 + 4 for Y).

Demand schedule: $P = \$2; Q = 2.$ $P = \$1; Q = 4.$

21-6   How can time be incorporated into the theory of consumer behavior? Explain the following comment: "Want to make a million dollars? Devise a product that saves Americans time."

Time is money. This expression is a time-saving way of making the point that for a person who can make so much per hour, every hour spent not working is so much money not made. A person can be said to "consume" a ball game or an evening at the theater. If the ball game costs $10 and the theater $20, at first sight one could say the ball game is a better deal. But if the person makes $20 an hour and is forgoing this in taking the time off, then we must take into account the time spent at the ball game and at the theater. If the ball game goes into extra innings and takes 4 hours, then its total cost is $90 (= $10 + $80). If the theater takes 3 hours, its total cost is $80 (= $20 + $60). Assuming the marginal utility of the ball game and attending the theater are the same, the theory of consumer behavior (with time taken into account) would therefore have this consumer going to the theater.

A time-saving device would free the individual up to earn more income. As long as the amount of extra income earned is greater than the cost of the device, many Americans will buy the device. For many Americans, what is scarcest in their lives is time.

21-7   Explain:

a.   "Before economic growth, there were too few goods; after growth, there is too little time."

b.   "It is irrational for an individual to take the time to be completely rational in economic decision making."

c.   "Telling Santa what you want for Christmas make sense in terms of utility maximization."

(a) Before economic growth, most people live at the subsistence level. By practically anyone's definition, this implies "too few goods." After economic growth, goods are in relative abundance. To make more takes time, but the relative abundance of goods means that there are already many goods to enjoy. So, now there is a clash between the use of time to make more goods and the use of time to relax and enjoy the goods one already has. There just isn't enough time.

(b) To be completely rational in economic decision making, provided one does not take time into consideration, one has to take account of every factor. This would take a great deal of time.

One could not, for example, make any purchase without first searching the classifieds to see whether a better deal could be had, rather than simply heading for the nearest store. However, this would be most irrational, for time does have value. While making an extensive search before making any deal, one would be forgoing the income to make this or any deal. For every penny saved to make the perfect deal, one would be losing dollars in income because of the time spent in making the perfect deal.

(c) There is little time sacrificed in making a request to Santa for a specific item. If one receives it, the benefit will likely exceed the cost.

21-8   In the last decade or so there has been a dramatic expansion of small retail convenience stores (such as Kwik Shops, 7-Elevens, Gas 'N Shops) although their prices are generally much higher than those in the large supermarkets. What explains the success of the convenience stores?

These stores are selling convenience as well as the goods that are purchased there. Because of their small size and convenient locations, they save busy consumers time. In an era when most consumers are working at least 40 hours per week, their time is valuable, and when only a few items are needed, the time saved must be worth the additional cost one pays for shopping at these convenience stores. (You seldom, if ever, see anyone buying a week's worth of groceries at such shops.)

21-9   Many apartment-complex owners are installing water meters for each individual apartment and billing the occupants according to the amount of water they use. This is in contrast to the former procedure of having a central meter for the entire complex and dividing up the water expense as part of the rent. Where individual meters have been installed, water usage has declined 10 to 40 percent. Explain this drop, referring to price and marginal utility.

The way we pay for a good or service can significantly alter the amount purchased. An individual living in an apartment complex who paid a share of the water expense measured by a central meter would have little incentive to conserve. Individual restraint would not have much impact on the total amount of water used.

Suppose there were 10 apartments in the complex, each apartment would be billed for one tenth of the cost of the water. A single gallon of water would carry a price equal to one tenth the amount charged by the water district. The very low price per gallon would encourage the use of water until the marginal utility of an additional gallon was correspondingly low. If the tenants paid separately for their own water, the full market price of water would be considered when making their consumption choices.

21-10   Advanced analysis: A mathematically "fair bet" is one in which a gambler bets, say $100, for a 10 percent chance to win $1000 dollars ($100 = .10 x 1000). Assuming diminishing marginal utility of dollars, explain why this is not a fair bet in terms of utility. Why is it even less fair a bet when the "house" takes a cut of each dollar bet? So is gambling irrational?

Because of marginal utility of money diminishes the more you have, the utility of the $100 used to make the bet is greater than the $100 that you might gain ($1000 - $900) if you win the bet.

It is even less of a "fair bet' when the "house" takes its cut, because the $100 bet has the possibility of yielding less than $100 in winnings.

Maybe. The activity of gambling may provide enough extra utility to offset the poor utility odds of winning.

21-11   Advanced analysis: Let $MU_a = z = 10 - x$ and $MU_b = z = 21 - 2y$, where z is marginal utility measured in utils, x is the amount spent on product A, and y is the amount spent on B. Assume the consumer has $10 to spend on A and B; that is, $x + y = 10$. How is this $10 best allocated between A and B? How much utility will the marginal dollar yield?

The consumer should spend $3 on A and $7 on B. The marginal dollar will yield 7 utils.

Proof:

Substituting in $z = 10 - x$, $z = 10 - 3 = 7$

Substituting in $z = 21 - 2y$, $z = 21 - 2 \times 7 = 21 - 14 = 7$

21-12 (*Last Word*) In what way is criminal behavior similar to consumer behavior? Why do most people obtain goods via legal behavior as opposed to illegal behavior?

Both criminal behavior and consumer behavior uses cost/benefit analysis. Consumers weigh the cost of purchasing the product against the benefits received from the product. Criminals also use cost/benefit analysis. The cost to the criminal includes "guilt costs," the cost of tools, the forgone income from not engaging in legitimate activities, and the possibility of fines and imprisonment. For most people, the costs of illegal behavior outweigh the benefits. Society must increase the costs by increasing the guilt factor, make it more difficult for a person to engage in criminal activity by improved security systems, enhance the possibilities to legitimate earnings through education and training programs, and impose greater penalties on those who get caught and convicted.

Chapter 21-Appendix Questions

21A-1 What information is embodied in a budget line? What shifts will occur in the budget line as money income (a) increases and (b) decreases? What shifts will occur in the budget line as the product price shown on the horizontal axis (a) increases and (b) decreases?

A budget line shows all the combinations of any two products that a consumer can purchase, given the prices of the products and the consumer's income.

As money income (a) increases, the budget line shifts to the right (outward); (b) decreases, the budget line shifts to the left (inward).

As the price of the product on the horizontal axis (a) increases, the budget line, while remaining anchored at its original position on the vertical axis, will fan to the left (inward); (b) decreases, the budget line, while remaining anchored at its original position on the vertical axis, will fan to the right (outward).

21A-2 What information is contained in an indifference curve? Why are such curves (a) downsloping and (b) convex to the origin? Why does total utility increase as the consumer moves to indifference curves further from the origin? Why can't indifference curves intersect?

Every point on an indifference curve shows some combination of two products that will give equal utility to a consumer; that is, each combination of the two products has the same level of total utility. Indifference curves are:

(a) downsloping because both products yield utility to the consumer. Going down the curve means more of one commodity is being consumed, thus increasing the consumer's total utility. To keep total utility constant, some amount of the other commodity must be given up to precisely offset the gain in total utility. Thus, the quantities of the two commodities are inversely related. Any curve showing an inverse relationship is downsloping.

(b) convex to the origin because the consumer's willingness to give up more of one commodity to get more of another diminishes as more and more of one commodity is substituted for the other. When the consumer has much of one commodity but little of the other, the consumer will resist more and more giving up what little still remains of the first commodity. This resistance is shown by the consumer demanding a great deal of the abundant commodity in exchange for a small amount of the scarce commodity. Technically expressed, the marginal rate of substitution declines as one moves southeast along an indifference curve.

Total utility increases as the consumer moves to indifference curves further from the origin because each successive curve embodies larger amounts of both commodities.

Indifference curves cannot intersect, because each curve shows a different level of total utility over its entire length, but a point of intersection of two curves would necessarily mean that at that point the two curves had the same total utility.

21A-3 (*Key Question*) Using Figure 4, explain why the point of tangency of the budget line with an indifference curve is the consumer's equilibrium position. Explain why any point where the budget line intersects an indifference curve will not be equilibrium. Explain: "The consumer is in equilibrium where MRS = P_B/P_A."

The tangency point places the consumer on the highest attainable indifference curve; it identifies the combination of goods yielding the highest total utility. All intersection points place the consumer on a lower indifference curve. MRS is the slope of the indifference curve; PB/PA is the slope of the budge line. Only at the tangency point are these two slopes equal. If MRS > P_B/P_A or MRS < P_B/P_A, adjustments in the combination of products can be made to increase total utility (get to a higher indifference curve).

21A-4 Assume that the data in the accompanying table indicate an indifference curve for Mr. Chen. Graph this curve, putting A on the vertical and B on the horizontal axis. Assuming the prices of A and B are $1.50 and $1.00, respectively, and that Chen has $24 to spend, add the resulting budget line to your graph. What combination of A and B will Chen purchase? Does your answer meet the MRS = P_B/P_A rule for equilibrium?

Units of A	Units of B
16	6
12	8
8	12
4	24

As shown in the graph, Mr. Chen will purchase 8A and 12B, spending his 24[$= (8 \times \$1.50) + (12 \times \$1.00)$]. The answer does meet the MRS = P_B / P_A rule. Thus, MRS = $8/12$ = P_B / P_A = $\$1.00 / \$1.50 = 2/3$.

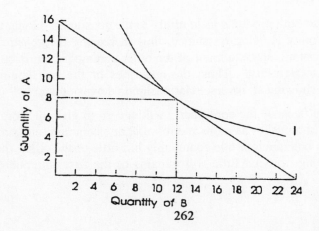

21A-5 Explain graphically how indifference analysis can be used to derive a demand curve.

In the top graph, the initial equilibrium is at X, where the budget line is tangent to indifference curve I_2. Money income is $12; the price of A is $1.50 and the price of B is $1.00. Dropping a perpendicular from X in the top diagram to the bottom diagram, we obtain X', a point on the demand curve of B. We note that at the price of $1.00, Q is 7.

We now assume that the price of B rises to $2.00, causing the budget line to fan to the left (inwards) from its anchor on the vertical (A) axis to Q of 6 on the horizontal (B) axis. This causes the new budget line to be tangent, at Y, to an indifference curve, I_1, closer to the origin—one that gives less utility. Dropping a perpendicular from Y in the top diagram to the bottom diagram, we obtain Y', the second point on the demand curve of B. We note that at the higher price of $2.00, Q is 3.

We can continue this procedure to obtain more points on the demand curve of B.

21A-6 Advanced analysis: Demonstrate mathematically that the equilibrium condition MRS $= P_B/P_A$ is the equivalent of the utility maximizing rule $MU_A/P_A = MU_B/P_B$.

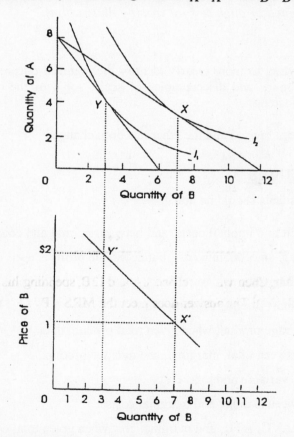

Since MRS $= MU_B/MU_A$, we have $MU_B/MU_A = P_B/PA$. Multiplying both sides of the equation by MU_A/P_B, we have: $MU_B/P_B = MU_A/P_A$.

CHAPTER TWENTY-TWO
THE COST OF PRODUCTION

CHAPTER OVERVIEW

This chapter develops a number of crucial cost concepts that will be employed in the succeeding three chapters to analyze the four basic market models. A firm's implicit and explicit costs are explained for both short- and long-run periods. The explanation of short-run costs includes arithmetic and graphic analyses of both the total-, unit-, and marginal-cost concepts. These concepts prepare students for both total-revenue—total-cost and marginal-revenue — andmarginal-cost approaches to profit maximization, which are presented in the next few chapters.

The law of diminishing returns is explained as an essential concept for understanding average and marginal cost curves. The general shape of each cost curve and the relationship they bear to one another are analyzed with special care.

The final part of the chapter develops the long-run average cost curve and analyzes the character and factors involved in economies and diseconomies of scale. The role of technology as a determinant of the structure of the industry is presented through several specific illustrations.

WHAT'S NEW

The chapter opener has been revised to more clearly identify the material covered in the chapter. In the section on applications of economies and diseconomies of scale, some of the old examples have been replaced and others have been updated.

One Web-Based Question has been revised and the other has been changed.

INSTRUCTIONAL OBJECTIVES

After completing this chapter, students should be able to:

1. Distinguish between explicit and implicit costs, and between normal and economic profits.

2. Explain why normal profit is an economic cost, but economic profit is not.

3. Explain the law of diminishing returns.

4. Differentiate between the short run and the long run.

5. Compute marginal and average product when given total product data.

6. Explain the relationship between total, marginal, and average product.

7. Distinguish between fixed, variable and total costs.

8. Explain the difference between average and marginal costs.

9. Compute and graph AFC, AVC, ATC, and marginal cost when given total cost data.

10. Explain how AVC, ATC, and marginal cost relate to one another.

11. Relate average product to average variable cost, and marginal product to marginal cost.

12. Explain what can cause cost curves to rise or fall.

13. Explain the difference between short-run and long-run costs.

14. State why the long-run average cost is expected to be U-shaped.

15. List causes of economies and diseconomies of scale.

16. Indicate relationship between economies of scale and number of firms in an industry.

17. Define and identify terms and concepts listed at the end of the chapter.

COMMENTS AND TEACHING SUGGESTIONS

1. Given the importance of the material presented in this chapter, instructors should devote considerable class time to a review of the different cost concepts. Students having difficulty should be encouraged to practice these concepts with end-of-chapter questions and the interactive microeconomics tutorial software that accompanies this text.

2. Students need to understand and be comfortable with the material in this chapter in order for them to be able to use it in the next three chapters.

3. Students must understand the meaning of "economic costs," what is included in "economic costs," and the relationship between "economic costs" and "economic profits."

4. The law of diminishing returns can be demonstrated in a brief classroom activity in which students "produce" any kind of product by adding an increasing number of variable inputs to fixed inputs. For example, have an increasing number of students share one pair of scissors and a felt-tip marker to "manufacture" paper pepperoni pizza or some similar product in a given period of time, such as one- or two-minute periods in a limited "factory" work-space.

   Emphasize the relationships between marginal product and marginal cost. Diminishing returns implies increasing cost. Drive this point home and the logic of the short-run cost condition is clear.

5. Use profit reports from the annual *Fortune 500* list to discuss whether these large firms appear to be making normal or economic profits or losses. Note the interindustry differences, the range of earnings from the ten highest to the ten lowest and the "all-500" composite return to stockholders' equity. Compare this to the current opportunity cost on invested capital as measured by interest rates paid on federally insured bonds or certificates of deposit that would represent a "normal" return. Profit reports also appear in *Business Week* annually.

6. To show the relationship between marginal and average values, use extreme (and therefore more humorous and memorable) examples. For example, assume the average height of students in the room is 5'8", but when one more student enters the room the average height rises to 6'6" or falls to 4'10". Have the class estimate the height of the "marginal" student in these two cases. More realistic illustrations include an estimate of their economics course grade (marginal) on their overall grade-point average, or the impact of one game on a hitter's batting average or temperatures at noon for a segment of a month.

STUDENT STUMBLING BLOCKS

1. Students are more familiar with average than with marginal concepts. Although they do not find the cost concepts in the chapter difficult to understand, in later chapters they inevitably become confused about the difference between average and marginal costs. Provide many opportunities for them to differentiate between these ideas now, so they won't be confused later.

2. The terms "economic costs," that include "normal profits," and "economic profits" that are not included in "economics costs" are often confusing. Using the term "excess or economic profits" helps.

3. The notion that the shut-down decision is determined by examining AVC and not AFC is counterintuitive to many students. Discuss Question 7 in class.

4. It is easy to neglect the long-term cost concepts because they appear at the end of the chapter. However, it is not possible to understand economies of scale without covering long-term costs carefully, and economies of scale become especially important in discussion of monopoly and oligopoly.

LECTURE NOTES

I. **Economic costs are the payments a firm must make, or incomes it must provide, to resource suppliers to attract those resources away from their best alternative production opportunities. Payments may be explicit or implicit. (Recall opportunity-cost concept in Chapter 2.)**

A. Explicit costs are payments to nonowners for resources they supply. In the text's example this would include cost of the T-shirts, clerk's salary, and utilities, for a total of $63,000.

B. Implicit costs are the money payments the self-employed resources could have earned in their best alternative employments. In the text's example this would include forgone interest, forgone rent, forgone wages, and forgone entrepreneurial income, for a total of $33,000.

C. Normal profits are considered an implicit cost because they are the minimum payments required to keep the owner's entrepreneurial abilities self-employed. This is $5,000 in the example.

D. Economic or pure profits are total revenue less all costs (explicit and implicit including a normal profit). Figure 22-1 illustrates the difference between accounting profits and economic profits. The economic profits are $24,000 (after $63,000 + $33,000 are subtracted from $120,000).

E. The short run is the time period that is too brief for a firm to alter its plant capacity. The plant size is fixed in the short run. Short-run costs, then, are the wages, raw materials, etc., used for production in a fixed plant.

F. The long run is a period of time long enough for a firm to change the quantities of all resources employed, including the plant size. Long-run costs are all costs, including the cost of varying the size of the production plant.

II. **Short-Run Production Relationships**

A. Short-run production reflects the law of diminishing returns that states that as successive units of a variable resource are added to a fixed resource, beyond some point the product attributable to each additional resource unit will decline.

1. Table 22.1 presents a numerical example of the law of diminishing returns.

2. Total product (TP) is the total quantity, or total output, of a particular good produced.

3. Marginal product (MP) is the change in total output resulting from each additional input of labor.

4. Average product (AP) is the total product divided by the total number of workers.

5. Figure 22.2 illustrates the law of diminishing returns graphically and shows the relationship between marginal, average, and total product concepts. (Key Question 4)

a. When marginal product begins to diminish, the rate of increase in total product stops accelerating and grows at a diminishing rate.

        b. The average product declines at the point at which the marginal product slips below average product.

        c. Total product declines when the marginal product becomes negative.

  B. The law of diminishing returns assumes all units of variable inputs—workers in this case—are of equal quality. Marginal product diminishes not because successive workers are inferior but because more workers are being used relative to the amount of plant and equipment available.

III.   Short Run Production Costs

  A. Fixed, variable and total costs are the short-run classifications of costs; Table 22.2 illustrates their relationships.

      1. Total fixed costs are those costs whose total does not vary with changes in short-run output.

      2. Total variable costs are those costs which change with the level of output. They include payment for materials, fuel, power, transportation services, most labor, and similar costs.

      3. Total cost is the sum of total fixed and total variable costs at each level of output (see Figure 22.3).

  B. Per unit or average costs are shown in Table 22.2, columns 5 to 7.

      1. Average fixed cost is the total fixed cost divided by the level of output (TFC/Q). It will decline as output rises.

      2. Average variable cost is the total variable cost divided by the level of output (AVC = TVC/Q).

      3. Average total cost is the total cost divided by the level of output (ATC = TC/Q), sometimes called unit cost or per unit cost. Note that ATC also equals AFC + AVC (see Figure 22-4).

  C. Marginal cost is the additional cost of producing one more unit of output (MC = change in TC/change in Q). In Table 22.2 the production of the first unit raises the total cost from $100 to $190, so the marginal cost is $90, and so on for each additional unit produced (see Figure 22.5).

      1. Marginal cost can also be calculated as MC = change in TVC/change in Q.

      2. Marginal decisions are very important in determining profit levels. Marginal revenue and marginal cost are compared.

      3. Marginal cost is a reflection of marginal product and diminishing returns. When diminishing returns begin, the marginal cost will begin its rise (Figure 22.6 illustrates this).

      4. The marginal cost is related to AVC and ATC. These average costs will fall as long as the marginal cost is less than either average cost. As soon as the marginal cost rises above the average, the average will begin to rise. Students can think of their grade-point averages with the total GPA reflecting their performance over their years in school, and their marginal grade points as their performance this semester. If their overall GPA is a 3.0, and this semester they earn a 4.0, their overall average will rise, but not as high as the marginal rate from this semester.

  D. Cost curves will shift if the resource prices change or if technology or efficiency change.

IV.   In the long-run, all production costs are variable, i.e., long-run costs reflect changes in plant size and industry size can be changed (expand or contract).

A. Figure 22.7 illustrates different short-run cost curves for five different plant sizes.

B. The long-run ATC curve shows the least per unit cost at which any output can be produced after the firm has had time to make all appropriate adjustments in its plant size.

C. Economies or diseconomies of scale exist in the long run.

    1. Economies of scale or economies of mass production explain the downward sloping part of the long-run ATC curve, i.e. as plant size increases, long-run ATC decrease.

        a. Labor and managerial specialization is one reason for this.

        b. Ability to purchase and use more efficient capital goods also may explain economies of scale.

        c. Other factors may also be involved, such as design, development, or other "start up" costs such as advertising and "learning by doing."

    2. Diseconomies of scale may occur if a firm becomes too large as illustrated by the rising part of the long-run ATC curve. For example, if a 10 percent increase in all resources result in a 5 percent increase in output, ATC will increase. Some reasons for this include distant management, worker alienation, and problems with communication and coordination.

    3. Constant returns to scale will occur when ATC is constant over a variety of plant sizes.

D. Both economies of scale and diseconomies of scale can be demonstrated in the real world. Larger corporations at first may successful in lowering costs and realizing economies of scale. To keep from experiencing diseconomies of scale, they may decentralize decision making by utilizing smaller production units.

E. Applications and illustrations:

    1. Recently there have been a number of start-up firms that have been able to take advantage of economies of scale by spreading product development costs and advertising costs over larger and larger units of output and by using greater specialization of labor, management, and capital.

    2. In 1996 Verson (a firm located in Chicago) introduced a stamping machine the size of a house weighing as much as 12 locomotives. This $30 million machine enables automakers to produce in 5 minutes what used to take 8 hours to produce.

    3. Newspapers can be produced for a low cost and thus sold for a low price because publishers are able to spread the cost of the printing equipment over an extremely large number of units each day.

    4. General Motors became so gigantic that many of its cost problems were blamed on diseconomies of scale. To offset this problem, the corporation has given its five divisions (Chevrolet, Buick, Pontiac, Oldsmobile, and Cadillac) more autonomy.

F. The concept of minimum efficient scale defines the smallest level of output at which a firm can minimize its average costs in the long run.

    1. The firms in some industries realize this at a small plant size: apparel, food processing, furniture, wood products, snowboarding, and small-appliance industries are examples.

    2. In other industries, in order to take full advantage of economies of scale, firms must produce with very large facilities that allow the firms to spread costs over an extended

range of output. Examples would be: automobiles, aluminum, steel, and other heavy industries. This pattern also is found in several new information technology industries.

    3. The Last Word discusses the fact that many industries have firms that are bigger than their estimated minimum efficient scale. Reasons for this may have to do with government policies, geographic location, mergers, and managerial ability rather than average costs.

V.   Irrelevancy of Sunk Costs

    A. Sunk costs should be disregarded in decision making.

        1. The old saying "Don't cry over spilt milk" sends the message that if there is nothing you can do about it, forget about it.

        2. A sunken ship on the ocean floor is lost, it cannot be recovered. It is what economists' call a "sunk cost."

        3. Economic analysis says that you should not take actions for which marginal cost exceeds marginal benefit.

        4. Suppose you have purchased an expensive ticket to a football game and you are sick the day of the game; the price of the ticket should not affect your decision to attend.

    B. In making a new decision, you should ignore all costs that are not affected by the decision.

        1. A prior bad decision should not dictate a second decision for which the marginal benefit is less than marginal cost.

        2. Suppose a firm spends a million dollars on R&D only to discover that the product sells very poorly. The loss cannot be recovered by losing still more money in continued production.

        3. If a cost has been incurred and cannot be partly or fully recouped by some other choice, a rational consumer or firm should ignore it.

        4. Sunk costs are irrelevant! Don't cry over spilt milk!

ANSWERS TO END-OF-CHAPTER QUESTIONS

22-1   Distinguish between explicit and implicit costs, giving examples of each. What are the explicit and implicit costs of attending college? Why does the economist classify normal profits as a cost? Are economic profits a cost of production?

Explicit costs are payments the firm must make for inputs to nonowners of the firm to attract them away from other employment, for example, wages and salaries to its employees. Implicit costs are nonexpenditure costs that occur through the use of self-owned, self-employed resources, for example, the salary the owner of a firm forgoes by operating his or her own firm and not working for someone else.

The explicit costs of going to college are the tuition costs, the cost of books, and the extra costs of living away from home (if applicable). The implicit costs are the income forgone and the hard grind of studying (if applicable).

Economists classify normal profits as costs, since in the long run the owner of a firm would close it down if a normal profit were not being earned. Since a normal profit is required to keep the entrepreneur operating the firm, a normal profit is a cost.

Economic profits are not costs of production since the entrepreneur does not require the gaining of an economic profit to keep the firm operating. In economics, costs are whatever is required to keep a firm operating.

22-2   (*Key Question*) Gomez runs a small pottery firm. He hires one helper at $12,000 per year, pays annual rent of $5,000 for his shop, and materials cost $20,000 per year. Gomez has $40,000 of his own funds invested in equipment (pottery wheels, kilns, and so forth) that could earn him $4,000 per year if alternatively invested. Gomez has been offered $15,000 per year to work as a potter for a competitor. He estimates his entrepreneurial talents are worth $3,000 per year. Total annual revenue from pottery sales is $72,000. Calculate accounting profits and economic profits for Gomez's pottery.

Explicit costs: $37,000 (= $12,000 for the helper + $5,000 of rent + $20,000 of materials). Implicit costs: $22,000 (= $4,000 of forgone interest + $15,000 of forgone salary + $3,000 of entreprenuership).

Accounting profit = $35,000 (= $72,000 of revenue - $37,000 of explicit costs); Economic profit = $13,000 (= $72,000 - $37,000 of explicit costs - $22,000 of implicit costs).

22-3   Which of the following are short-run and which are long-run adjustments? (a) Wendy's builds a new restaurant; (b) Acme Steel Corporation hires 200 more production workers; (c) A farmer increases the amount of fertilizer used on his corn crop; and (d) An Alcoa plant adds a third shift of workers.

    (a) Long-run, (b) Short-run, (c) Short-run, (d) Short-run

22-4   (*Key Question*) Complete the following table by calculating marginal product and average product from the data given. Plot total, marginal, and average product and explain in detail the relationship between each pair of curves. Explain why marginal product first rises, then declines, and ultimately becomes negative. What bearing does the law of diminishing returns have on short-run costs? Be specific. "When marginal product is rising, marginal cost is falling. And when marginal product is diminishing, marginal cost is rising." Illustrate and explain graphically.

Inputs of labor	Total product	Marginal product	Average product
0	0	____	____
1	15	____	____
2	34	____	____
3	51	____	____
4	65	____	____
5	74	____	____
6	80	____	____
7	83	____	____
8	82	____	____

Marginal product data, top to bottom: 15; 19; 17; 14; 9; 6; 3; -1. Average product data, top to bottom: 15; 17; 17; 16.25; 14.8; 13.33; 11.86; 10.25. Your diagram should have the same general characteristics as text Figure 22-2.

MP is the slope—the rate of change—of the TP curve. When TP is rising at an increasing rate, MP is positive and rising. When TP is rising at a diminishing rate, MP is positive but falling. When TP is falling, MP is negative and falling. AP rises when MP is above it; AP falls when MP is below it.

MP first rises because the fixed capital gets used more productively as added workers are employed. Each added worker contributes more to output than the previous worker because the firm is better able to use its fixed plant and equipment. As still more labor is added, the law of diminishing returns takes hold. Labor becomes so abundant relative to the fixed capital that congestion occurs and marginal product falls. At the extreme, the addition of labor so overcrowds the plant that the marginal product of still more labor is negative—total output falls.

Illustrated by Figure 22-6. Because labor is the only variable input and its price (its wage rate) is constant, MC is found by dividing the wage rate by MP. When MP is rising, MC is falling; when MP reaches its maximum, MC is at its minimum; when MP is falling, MC is rising.

22-5   Why can the distinction between fixed and variable costs be made in the short run? Classify the following as fixed or variable costs: advertising expenditures, fuel, interest on company-issued bonds, shipping charges, payments for raw materials, real estate taxes, executive salaries, insurance premiums, wage payments, depreciation and obsolescence charges, sales taxes, and rental payments on leased office machinery. "There are no fixed costs in the long run; all costs are variable." Explain.

The distinction can be made because there are some costs that do not vary with total output. These are the fixed costs that, fundamentally, are related to the scale or size of the plant. In the short run, by definition, the scale of the plant cannot change: The firm cannot bring in more machinery or move to a larger building. All costs that are related to the scale of the plant—costs that continue to be incurred even though the firm's output may be zero—are fixed costs. On the other hand, the firm can increase its output by using its plant—its fixed capital—more intensively, that is, by hiring more labor, or by using more materials. But by doing so, it will increase its operating costs, its variable costs.

Advertising expenditures: variable costs (although it may be reasonable to argue a fixed component). Fuel: variable costs. Interest on company-issued bonds: fixed costs. Shipping charges: variable costs. Payments for raw materials: variable costs. Real estate taxes: fixed costs. Executive salaries: fixed costs. Insurance premiums: fixed costs. Wage payments: variable costs. Depreciation and obsolescence charges: fixed costs. Sales taxes: variable costs. Rental payments on leased office machinery: fixed costs (although it is possible that short-term lease arrangements on some types of office equipment may rise or fall with output).

In the long run, the firm can, by definition, get out of paying all of its short-run fixed costs; its lease is up, it can fire its executives without penalty, the insurance has run out, and so on. All of its costs at this moment, then, are variable. It can decide to continue producing at the same scale and thus reassume all its previous fixed costs for the next short-run period; or it can decide to increase its scale and thus increase its fixed costs; or it can decide to go out of business and thus have no costs at all.

22-6   List several fixed and variable costs associated with owning and operating an automobile. Suppose you are considering whether to drive your car or fly 1,000 miles to Florida for spring break. Which costs—fixed, variable, or both—would you take into account in making your decision? Would any implicit costs be relevant? Explain.

Fixed costs associated with owning and operating an automobile include the price of the car (probably monthly payments); insurance; driver's license; car license; and depreciation.

Variable costs associated with owning and operating an automobile include gasoline, oil, lubricants; repairs; car wash; and depreciation, which is also in part a variable cost since the more the car is driven, the more it depreciates.

The costs of driving to Fort Lauderdale are the same variable costs (including depreciation) listed above. Going by plane, the variable cost is the cost of the ticket. It would probably be cheaper to drive but this would leave out the relevant implicit cost—my time and the wear and tear on myself of driving there and back. The plane would be faster. How much is it worth to me to arrive sooner and stay longer and be fresher on arrival? On the other hand, maybe I'd find the car useful around Fort Lauderdale, and having one's own car saves the variable cost of renting if one flies.

22-7 (Key Question) A firm has fixed costs of $60 and variable costs as indicated in the table below. Complete the table. When finished, check your calculations by referring to question 4 at the end of Chapter 23.

Total product	Total fixed cost	Total variable cost	Total cost	Average fixed cost	Average variable cost	Average total cost	Marginal cost
0	$___	$ 0	$___	$___	$___	$___	
1	___	45	___	___	___	___	___
2	___	85	___	___	___	___	___
3	___	120	___	___	___	___	___
4	___	150	___	___	___	___	___
5	___	185	___	___	___	___	___
6	___	225	___	___	___	___	___
7	___	270	___	___	___	___	___
8	___	325	___	___	___	___	___
9	___	390	___	___	___	___	___
10	___	465	___	___	___	___	___

a. Graph total fixed cost, total variable cost, and total cost. Explain how the law of diminishing returns influences the shapes of the total variable-cost and total-cost curves.

b. Graph AFC, AVC, ATC, and MC. Explain the derivation and shape of each of these four curves and their relationships to one another. Specifically, explain in nontechnical terms why the MC curve intersects both the AVC and ATC curves at their minimum points.

c. Explain how the locations of each of the four curves graphed in question 7b would be altered if (1) total fixed cost had been $100 rather than $60, and (2) total variable cost had been $10 less at each level of output.

The total fixed costs are all $60. The total costs are all $60 more than the total variable cost. The other columns are shown in Question 4 in Chapter 23.

(a) See the graph. Over the 0 to 4 range of output, the TVC and TC curves slope upward at a decreasing rate because of increasing marginal returns. The slopes of the curves then increase at an increasing rate as diminishing marginal returns occur.

(b) See the graph. AFC (= TFC/Q) falls continuously since a fixed amount of capital cost is spread over more units of output. The MC (= change in TC/change in Q), AVC (= TVC/Q), and ATC (= TC/Q) curves are U-shaped, reflecting the influence of first increasing and then diminishing returns. The ATC curve sums AFC and AVC vertically. The ATC curve falls when the MC curve is below it; the ATC curve rises when the MC curve is above it. This means the MC curve must intersect the ATC curve at its lowest point. The same logic holds for the minimum point of the AVC curve.

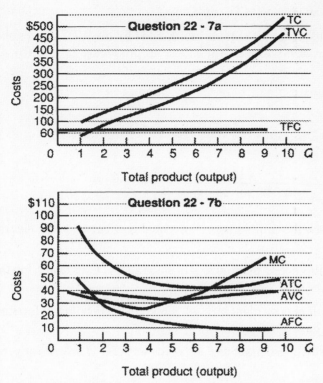

(c1) If TFC has been $100 instead of $60, the AFC and ATC curves would be higher—by an amount equal to $40 divided by the specific output. Example: at 4 units, AVC = $25.00 [= ($60 + $40)/4]; and ATC = $62.50 [= ($210 + $40)/4]. The AVC and MC curves are not affected by changes in fixed costs.

(c2) If TVC has been $10 less at each output, MC would be $10 lower for the first unit of output but remain the same for the remaining output. The AVC and ATC curves would also be lower—by an amount equal to $10 divided by the specific output. Example: at 4 units of output, AVC = $35.00   [= $150 - $10)/4], ATC = $50 [= ($210 - $10)/4]. The AFC curve would not be affected by the change in variable costs.

22-8   Indicate how each of the following would shift the (a) marginal-cost curve, (b) average-variable cost curve, (c) average-fixed-cost curve, and (d) average-total-cost curve of a manufacturing firm. In each case specify the direction of the shift.

a.   A reduction in business property taxes

b.   An increase in the nominal wages of production workers

c.   A decrease in the price of electricity

d.   An increase in the insurance rates on plant and equipment

e.   An increase in transportation costs

(a) MC no change; AVC no change; AFC shift down; ATC shift down.

(b) MC shift up; AVC shift up; AFC no change; ATC shift up.

(c) MC shift down; AVC shift down; AFC no change; ATC shift down.

(d) MC no change; AVC no change; AFC shift up; ATC shift up.

(e) MC shift up; AVC shift up; AFC no change; ATC shift up.

22-9   Suppose a firm has only three possible plant-size options represented by the ATC curves shown in the accompanying figure. What plant size will the firm choose in producing (a) 50, (b) 130, (c)

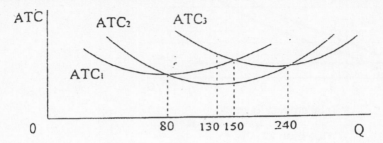

160, and (d) 250 units of output? Draw the firm's long-run average-cost curve on the diagram and define this curve.

(a) To produce 50 units, the firm will choose plant size #1, since its ATC is lower for this size firm in producing less than 80 units.

(b) To produce 130 units, the firm will choose plant size #2, since its ATC is lower for size #2 in producing between 80 and 240 units.

(c) To produce 160 units, the firm will choose plant size #2, since its ATC is lowest for producing between 80 and 240 units.

(d) To produce 250 units, the firm will choose plant size #3, since its ATC is lowest for production of more than 240 units.

The long-run average-cost curve drawn on this diagram would trace ATC_1 as far as 80 units, then ATC_2 between 80 and 240 units, then finally trace ATC3 from 240 units to the end of the graph. Students could reproduce the graph in the text and then use a heavy line or different color to show this tracing.

22-10   (*Key Question*) Use the concepts of economies and diseconomies of scale to explain the shape of a firm's long-run ATC curve. What is the concept of minimum efficient scale? What bearing may the exact shape of the long-run ATC curve have on the structure of an industry?

The long-run ATC curve is U-shaped. At first, long-run ATC falls as the firm expands and realizes economies of scale from labor and managerial specialization and the use of more efficient capital. The long-run ATC curve later turns upward when the enlarged firm experiences diseconomies of scale, usually resulting from managerial inefficiencies.

The MES (minimum efficient scale) is the smallest level of output needed to attain all economies of scale and minimum long-run ATC.

If long-run ATC drops quickly to its minimum cost which then extends over a long range of output, the industry will likely be composed of both large and small firms. If long-run ATC descends slowly to its minimum cost over a long range of output, the industry will likely be composed of a few large firms. If long-run ATC drops quickly to its minimum point and then rises abruptly, the industry will likely be composed of many small firms.

22-11 (*Last Word*) What is a sunk cost? Provide an example of a sunk cost other from this book. Why are such costs irrelevant in making decisions about future actions?

A sunk cost is one that cannot be partly or fully recouped by some choice. A person buys a ticket for a cruise and finds out that a hurricane is headed toward the Caribbean. A rational consumer or firm should ignore it. Economic analysis says that you should not take actions for which the marginal cost exceeds the marginal benefit. A firm that has spent millions of dollars developing a new product that bombs will not improve their situation by losing still more money in additional production.

CHAPTER TWENTY-THREE
PURE COMPETITION

CHAPTER OVERVIEW

This chapter is the first of three closely related chapters analyzing the four basic market models—pure competition, pure monopoly, monopolistic competition, and oligopoly. Here the market models are introduced and explained, which makes this the longest and perhaps most difficult of the three chapters.

Explanations and characteristics of the four models are outlined at the beginning of this chapter. Then the characteristics of a purely competitive industry are detailed. There is an introduction to the concept of the perfectly elastic demand curve facing an individual firm in a purely competitive industry. Next, the total, average, and marginal revenue schedules are presented in numeric and graphic form. Using the cost schedules from the previous chapter, the idea of profit maximization is explored.

The total-revenue—total-cost approach is analyzed first because of its simplicity. More space is devoted to explaining the MR = MC rule, and to demonstrating that this rule applies in all market structures, not just in pure competition.

Next, the firm's short-run supply schedule is shown to be the same as its marginal-cost curve at all points above the average-variable-cost curve. Then the short-run competitive equilibrium is discussed at the firm and industry levels.

The long-run equilibrium position for a competitive industry is shown by reviewing the process of entry and exit in response to relative profit levels in the industry. Long-run supply curves and the conditions of constant, increasing, and decreasing costs are explored.

Finally, the chapter concludes with a detailed evaluation of pure competition in terms of productive and allocative efficiency (P = minimum ATC, and P = MC).

WHAT'S NEW

There have been only a few modifications in this chapter since the previous edition. The "Qualifications" section at the end of the chapter has been omitted, a product (cucumbers) is used instead of Product X in the allocative efficiency section, and personal computers are used as the example in the discussion of a decreasing cost industry.

The two Web-Based Questions have been replaced.

INSTRUCTIONAL OBJECTIVES

After completing this chapter, students should be able to:

1. List the four basic market models and characteristics of each.

2. Describe characteristics of a purely competitive firm and industry.

3. Explain how a purely competitive firm views demand for its product and marginal revenue from each additional unit sale.

4. Compute average, total, and marginal revenue when given a demand schedule for a purely competitive firm.

5. Use both total-revenue—total-cost and marginal-revenue—marginal-cost approaches to determine short-run price and output that maximizes profits (or minimizes losses) for a competitive firm.

6. Find the short-run supply curve when given short-run cost schedules for a competitive firm.

7. Explain how to construct an industry short-run supply curve from information on single competitive firms in the industry.

8. Explain the long-run equilibrium position for a competitive firm using entry and exit of firms to explain adjustments from nonequilibrium positions.

9. Explain the shape of long-run industry supply curves in constant-cost and increasing-cost industries.

10. Differentiate between productive and allocative efficiency.

11. Explain why allocative efficiency and productive efficiency are achieved where P = minimum AC = MC.

12. Define and identify terms and concepts listed at the end of the chapter.

COMMENTS AND TEACHING SUGGESTIONS

1. Urge students to practice their understanding of this chapter's concepts with quantitative end-of-chapter questions and the relevant interactive microcomputer tutorial software. Assign and review in class numerical and graphical problems, so that students have "hands-on" experience in learning this material. It is essential for understanding the next several chapters and grasping the essence of marginal cost analysis.

2. Examples of "price-taking" situations are readily found in published quotations for commodity, stock, and currency markets. Such markets approximate the purely competitive model.

3. A useful example for demonstrating that profit maximization occurs where MR = MC, not where MR is much greater than MC, is to ask a student if she would trade $50 for $100 (of course), then $60 for $100 (of course), then $70 for $100, and so on up to $99.99 for $100. The student should want to trade as long as her additional "revenue" exceeds her marginal cost. In other words, if someone can make as much as $.01 more profit, the rational person will trade. It is not the profit per unit but the total profit that the seller is maximizing! This simple notion bears repeating several times in different ways, because some students will continue to be puzzled by this despite its simplicity.

4. Using the overhead for Table 23.4 and starting at output level "4," move to the next level of output while asking the students whether the next unit should be added by comparing MR and MC.

5. Review the short run cost concepts developed in Chapter 22, particularly MC, ATC and AVC and how they are related. Using a Key Graph (Figure 23.6), show how these costs can be used to evaluate a purely competitive firm's position in the short run. Each of the three cost concepts has a distinct contribution to make in the decision-making process.

    (a) MC determines the best Q of output. The point where MC = MR is always best, whether the firm is making an economic profit, breaking even, or operating at a loss.

    (b) ATC determines profit or loss. Have the students compare price and ATC at the best quantity of output. If price exceeds ATC, the difference is per unit profit. If Price = ATC the firm is breaking even and if price is less than ATC the firm is losing money.

    (c) AVC determines the shut down point. As long as price exceeds AVC the firm will continue to operate in the short run.

Review these three steps carefully, they can be used with each of the market structures. For the individual seller in pure competition, product price = MR. This is not the case in any of the other market structures. Stress this difference, it is the basis of the efficient outcome in the long run. (P = MC = minimum ATC)

6. Stress the importance of achieving both allocative efficiency (P = MC) and productive efficiency (P = minimum ATC). Pure competition delivers what people want at the lowest possible cost. This outcome will not be observed in other market structures. However, the three steps outlined above for decision making are the same in every case. This similarity can be used to reinforce the logic of the process and explain the difference in outcome in the other market structures.

STUDENT STUMBLING BLOCK

There are three fundamental skills that are necessary to engage successfully in economic reasoning. (1) The ability to use graphs and mathematical reasoning. (2) The ability to use abstract models and generalize. (3) The ability to use and apply the specialized vocabulary of economics. In this chapter, all students will find their skills being tested. Struggling students may be ready to bail out.

Using graphs to demonstrate the relationship between variables is a habit for economics instructors. The message the graph is sending is instantly received: the communication complete (for the teacher). Keep in mind that the curves you have drawn may not be "speaking" as clearly to the students. There are so many graphs in the chapters on market structure that the students can easily get lost. Take time to put numbers on the axis and work out the actual amount of total profit or loss in your examples. By taking a little extra time with the concepts in pure competition, the following discussion about other market structures will be easier for students to understand.

It must be emphasized in the analysis as to whether the focus of the discussion is on the individual firm or the industry; likewise, whether the focus is on the firm or industry in the short run or the long run.

Productive efficiency is relatively easy to explain and show graphically. Allocative efficiency is a more abstract concept to show.

Vocabulary in this chapter is also a problem. Students' "everyday" definition of competition is totally different from the narrow meaning that is applied in discussing the market structure of Pure Competition. Students are likely to question the usefulness of a model that is so far removed from actual business conditions. One helpful analogy is that we are, in a sense, creating a laboratory experiment that eliminates all outside influences and focuses on only one determining consideration, i.e. price. Similarly, a physicist might wish to create a vacuum to study the impact of gravity on a feather and a bowling ball.

LECTURE NOTES

I. **Four market models will be addressed in Chapters 23-25; characteristics of the models are summarized in Table 23.1.**

   A. Pure competition entails a large number of firms, standardized product, and easy entry (or exit) by new (or existing) firms.

   B. At the opposite extreme, pure monopoly has one firm that is the sole seller of a product or service with no close substitutes; entry is blocked for other firms.

   C. Monopolistic competition is close to pure competition, except that the product is differentiated among sellers rather than standardized, and there are fewer firms.

D. An oligopoly is an industry in which only a few firms exist, so each is affected by the price-output decisions of its rivals.

II. **Pure Competition: Characteristics and Occurrence**

    A. The characteristics of pure competition:

        1. Many sellers means that there are enough so that a single seller has no impact on price by its decisions alone.

        2. The products in a purely competitive market are homogeneous or standardized; each seller's product is identical to its competitor's.

        3. Individual firms must accept the market price; they are price takers and can exert no influence on price.

        4. Freedom of entry and exit means that there are no significant obstacles preventing firms from entering or leaving the industry.

        5. Pure competition is rare in the real world, but the model is important.

            a. The model helps analyze industries with characteristics similar to pure competition.

            b. The model provides a context in which to apply revenue and cost concepts developed in previous chapters.

            c. Pure competition provides a norm or standard against which to compare and evaluate the efficiency of the real world.

    B. There are four major objectives to analyzing pure competition.

        1. To examine demand from the seller's viewpoint,

        2. To see how a competitive producer responds to market price in the short run,

        3. To explore the nature of long-run adjustments in a competitive industry, and

        4. To evaluate the efficiency of competitive industries.

III. **Demand from the Viewpoint of a Competitive Seller**

    A. The individual firm will view its demand as perfectly elastic.

        1. Table 23.2 and Figures 23.1 and 23.7a illustrate this.

        2. The demand curve is not perfectly elastic for the industry: It only appears that way to the individual firm, since they must take the market price no matter what quantity they produce.

        3. Note from Figure 23.1 that a perfectly elastic demand curve is a horizontal line at the price.

    B. Definitions of average, total, and marginal revenue:

        1. Average revenue is the price per unit for each firm in pure competition.

        2. Total revenue is the price multiplied by the quantity sold.

        3. Marginal revenue is the change in total revenue and will also equal the unit price in conditions of pure competition. (Key Question 3)

IV. **Profit Maximization in the Short-Run: Two Approaches**

A. In the short run the firm has a fixed plant and maximizes profits or minimizes losses by adjusting output; profits are defined as the difference between total costs and total revenue.

B. Three questions must be answered.

   1. Should the firm produce?

   2. If so, how much?

   3. What will be the profit or loss?

C. An example of the total-revenue—total-cost approach is shown in Table 23.3. Note that the costs are the same as for the firm in Table 22.2 in the previous chapter.

   1. Firm should produce if the difference between total revenue and total cost is profitable, or if the loss is less than the fixed cost.

   2. In the short run, the firm should produce that output at which it maximizes its profit or minimizes its loss.

   3. The profit or loss can be established by subtracting total cost from total revenue at each output level.

   4. The firm should not produce, but should shut down in the short run if its loss exceeds its fixed costs. Then, by shutting down its loss will just equal those fixed costs.

   5. Graphical representation is shown in Figures 23.2a and b. Note: The firm has no control over the market price.

D. Marginal-revenue—marginal-cost approach (see Table 23.4 and Figure 23.3).

   1. MR = MC rule states that the firm will maximize profits or minimize losses by producing at the point at which marginal revenue equals marginal cost in the short run.

   2. Three features of this MR = MC rule are important.

      a. Rule assumes that marginal revenue must be equal to or exceed minimum-average-variable cost or firm will shut down.

      b. Rule works for firms in any type of industry, not just pure competition.

      c. In pure competition, price = marginal revenue, so in purely competitive industries the rule can be restated as the firm should produce that output where P = MC, because P = MR.

   3. Using the rule on Table 23.4, compare MC and MR at each level of output. At the tenth unit MC exceeds MR. Therefore, the firm should produce only nine (not the tenth) units to maximize profits.

   4. Profit maximizing case: The level of profit can be found by multiplying ATC by the quantity, 9 to get $880 and subtracting that from total revenue which is $131 x 9 or $1179. Profit will be $299 when the price is $131. Profit per unit could also have been found by subtracting $97.78 from $131 and then multiplying by 9 to get $299. Figure 23.3 portrays this situation graphically.

   5. Loss-minimizing case: The loss-minimizing case is illustrated when the price falls to $81. Table 23.5 is used to determine this. Marginal revenue does exceed average variable cost at some levels, so the firm should not shut down. Comparing P and MC, the rule tells us to select output level of 6. At this level the loss of $64 is the minimum loss this firm could

realize, and the MR of $81 just covers the MC of $80, which does not happen at quantity level of 7. Figure 23.4 is a graphical portrayal of this situation.

6. Shut-down case: If the price falls to $71, this firm should not produce. MR will not cover AVC at any output level. Therefore, the minimum loss is the fixed cost and production of zero. Table 23.5 and Figure 23.5 illustrate this situation, and it can be seen that the $100 fixed cost is the minimum possible loss.

E. Marginal cost and the short-run supply curve can be illustrated by hypothetical prices such as those in Table 23.6. At price of $151 profit will be $480; at $111 the profit will be $138 ($888-$750); at $91 the loss will be $3.01; at $61 the loss will be $100 because the latter represents the close-down case.

1. Note that Table 23.6 gives us the quantities that will be supplied at several different price levels in the short-run.

2. Since a short-run supply schedule tells how much quantity will be offered at various prices, this identity of marginal revenue with the marginal cost tells us that the marginal cost above AVC will be the short-run supply for this firm (see Figure 23.6).

F. Changes in prices of variable inputs or in technology will shift the marginal cost or short-run supply curve in Figure 23.6.

1. For example, a wage increase would shift the supply curve upward.

2. Technological progress would shift the marginal cost curve downward.

3. Using this logic, a specific tax would cause a decrease in the supply curve (upward shift in MC), and a unit subsidy would cause an increase in the supply curve (downward shift in MC).

G. Determining equilibrium price for a firm and an industry:

1. Total-supply and total-demand data must be compared to find most profitable price and output levels for the industry. (See Table 23.7)

2. Figure 23.7a and b shows this analysis graphically; individual firm supply curves are summed horizontally to get the total-supply curve S in Figure 23.7b. If product price is $111, industry supply will be 8000 units, since that is the quantity demanded and supplied at $111. This will result in economic profits similar to those portrayed in Figure 23.3.

3. Loss situation similar to Figure 23.4 could result from weaker demand (lower price and MR) or higher marginal costs.

H. Firm vs. industry: Individual firms must take price as given, but the supply plans of all competitive producers as a group are a major determinant of product price. (Key Question 4)

V. **Profit Maximization in the Long Run**

A. Several assumptions are made.

1. Entry and exit of firms are the only long-run adjustments.

2. Firms in the industry have identical cost curves.

3. The industry is a constant-cost industry, which means that the entry and exit of firms will not affect resource prices or location of unit-cost schedules for individual firms.

B. Basic conclusion to be explained is that after long-run equilibrium is achieved, the product price will be exactly equal to, and production will occur at, each firm's point of minimum average total cost.

   1. Firms seek profits and shun losses.

   2. Under competition, firms may enter and leave industries freely.

   3. If short-run losses occur, firms will leave the industry; if economic profits occur, firms will enter the industry.

C. The model is one of zero economic profits, but note that this allows for a normal profit to be made by each firm in the long run.

   1. If economic profits are being earned, firms enter the industry, which increases the market supply, causing the product price to gravitate downward to the equilibrium price where zero economic profits are earned (Figure 23.8).

   2. If losses are incurred in the short run, firms will leave the industry; this decreases the market supply, causing the product price to rise until losses disappear and normal profits are earned (Figure 23.9).

D. Long-run supply for a constant cost industry will be perfectly elastic; the curve will be horizontal. In other words, the level of output will not affect the price in the long run.

   1. In a constant-cost industry, expansion or contraction does not affect resource prices or production costs.

   2. Entry or exit of firms will affect quantity of output, but will always bring the price back to the equilibrium price (Figure 23.10).

E. Long-run supply for an increasing cost industry will be upward sloping as industry expands output.

   1. Average-cost curves shift upward as the industry expands and downward as industry contracts, because resource prices are affected.

   2. A two-way profit squeeze will occur as demand increases because costs will rise as firms enter, and the new equilibrium price must increase if the level of profit is to be maintained at its normal level. Note that the price will fall if the industry contracts as production costs fall, and competition will drive the price down so that individual firms do not realize above-normal profits (see Figure 23.11).

F. Long-run supply for a decreasing cost industry will be downward sloping as the industry expands output. This situation is the reverse of the increasing-cost industry. Average-cost curves fall as the industry expands and firms will enter until price is driven down to maintain only normal profits. (Key Question 8)

VI. **Pure Competition and Efficiency**

A. Whether the industry is one of constant, increasing, or decreasing costs, the final long-run equilibrium will have the same basic characteristics (Figure 23.12).

   1. Productive efficiency occurs where P = minimum AC; at this point firms must use the least-cost technology or they won't survive.

   2. Allocative efficiency occurs where P = MC, because price is society's measure of relative worth of a product at the margin or its marginal benefit. And the marginal cost of producing product X measures the relative worth of the other goods that the resources used

in producing an extra unit of X could otherwise have produced. In short, price measures the benefit that society gets from additional units of good X, and the marginal cost of this unit of X measures the sacrifice or cost to society of other goods given up to produce more of X.

3. If price exceeds marginal cost, then society values more units of good X more highly than alternative products the appropriate resources can otherwise produce. Resources are underallocated to the production of good X.

4. If price is less than marginal cost, then society values the other goods more highly than good X, and resources are overallocated to the production of good X.

5. Efficient allocation occurs when price and marginal cost are equal. Under pure competition this outcome will be achieved.

6. Dynamic adjustments will occur automatically in pure competition when changes in demand or in resource supplies or in technology occur. Disequilibrium will cause expansion or contraction of the industry until the new equilibrium at $P = MC$ occurs.

7. "The invisible hand" works in a competitive market system since no explicit orders are given to the industry to achieve the $P = MC$ result.

VII. **LAST WORD: Pure Competition and Consumer Surplus**

A. In almost all markets, consumers collectively obtain more utility (total satisfaction) from their purchases than the amount of their expenditures (product price x quantity).

B. Since pure competition establishes the lowest price consistent with continued production, it yields the largest sustainable amount of consumer surpluses.

ANSWERS TO END-OF-CHAPTER QUESTIONS

23-1 Briefly indicate the basic characteristics of pure competition, pure monopoly, monopolistic competition, and oligopoly. Under which of these market classifications does each of the following most accurately fit? (a) a supermarket in your home town; (b) the steel industry; (c) a Kansas wheat farm; (d) the commercial bank in which you or your family has an account; (e) the automobile industry. In each case justify your classification.

Pure competition: very large number of firms; standardized products; no control over price: price takers; no obstacles to entry; no nonprice competition.

Pure monopoly: one firm; unique product: with no close substitutes; much control over price: price maker; entry is blocked; mostly public relations advertising.

Monopolistic competition: many firms; differentiated products; some control over price in a narrow range; relatively easy entry; much nonprice competition: advertising, trademarks, brand names.

Oligopoly: few firms; standardized or differentiated products; control over price circumscribed by mutual interdependence: much collusion; many obstacles to entry; much nonprice competition, particularly product differentiation.

(a) Hometown supermarket: oligopoly. Supermarkets are few in number in any one area; their size makes new entry very difficult; there is much nonprice competition. However, there is much price competition as they compete for market share, and there seems to be no collusion. In this regard, the supermarket acts more like a monopolistic competitor. Note that this answer may vary by area. Some areas could be characterized by monopolistic competition while isolated small towns may have a monopoly situation.

(b) Steel industry: oligopoly within the domestic production market. Firms are few in number; their products are standardized to some extent; their size makes new entry very difficult; there is much nonprice competition; there is little, if any, price competition; while there may be no collusion, there does seem to be much price leadership.

(c) Kansas wheat farm: pure competition. There are a great number of similar farms; the product is standardized; there is no control over price; there is no nonprice competition. However, entry is difficult because of the cost of acquiring land from a present proprietor. Of course, government programs to assist agriculture complicate the purity of this example.

(d) Commercial bank: monopolistic competition. There are many similar banks; the services are differentiated as much as the bank can make them appear to be; there is control over price (mostly interest charged or offered) within a narrow range; entry is relatively easy (maybe too easy!); there is much advertising. Once again, not every bank may fit this model—smaller towns may have an oligopoly or monopoly situation.

(e) Automobile industry: oligopoly. There are the Big Three automakers, so they are few in number; their products are differentiated; their size makes new entry very difficult; there is much nonprice competition; there is little true price competition; while there does not appear to be any collusion, there has been much price leadership. However, imports have made the industry more competitive in the past two decades, which has substantially reduced the market power of the U.S. automakers.

23-2 Strictly speaking, pure competition never has existed and probably never will. Then why study it?

It can be shown that pure competition results in low-cost production (productive efficiency)—through long-run equilibrium occurring where P equals minimum ATC—and allocative efficiency—through long-run equilibrium occurring where P equals MC. Given this, it is then possible to analyze real world examples to see to what extent they conform to the ideal of plants producing at their points of minimum ATC and thus producing the most desired commodities with the greatest economy in the use of resources.

23-3 (*Key Question*) Use the following demand schedule to determine total and marginal revenues for each possible level of sales:

Product Price ($)	Quantity Demanded	Total Revenue ($)	Marginal Revenue ($)
2	0		
2	1		
2	2		
2	3		
2	4		
2	5		

a. What can you conclude about the structure of the industry in which this firm is operating? Explain.

b. Graph the demand, total-revenue, and marginal-revenue curves for this firm.

c. Why do the demand and marginal-revenue curves coincide?

d. "Marginal revenue is the change in total revenue." Explain verbally and graphically, using the data in the table.

Total revenue, top to bottom: 0; $2; $4; $6; $8; $10. Marginal revenue, top to bottom: $2, throughout.

(a) The industry is purely competitive—this firm is a "price taker." The firm is so small relative to the size of the market that it can change its level of output without affecting the market price.

(b) See graph.

(c) The firm's demand curve is perfectly elastic; MR is constant and equal to P.

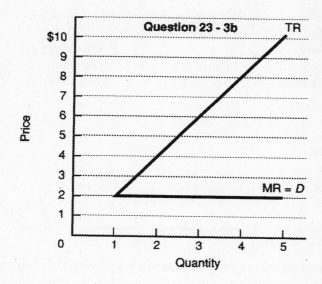

(d) Yes. Table: When output (quantity demanded) increases by 1 unit, total revenue increases by $2. This $2 increase is the marginal revenue. Figure: The change in TR is measured by the slope of the TR line, 2 (= $2/1 unit).

23-4 (*Key Question*) Assume the following unit-cost data are for a purely competitive producer:

Total Product	Average fixed cost	Average variable cost	Average total cost	Marginal cost
0				
1	$60.00	$45.00	$105.00	$45
2	30.00	42.50	72.50	40
3	20.00	40.00	60.00	35
4	15.00	37.50	52.50	30
5	12.00	37.00	49.00	35
6	10.00	37.50	47.50	40
7	8.57	38.57	47.14	45
8	7.50	40.63	48.13	55
9	6.67	43.33	50.00	65
10	6.00	46.50	52.50	75

Pure Competition

a. At a product price of $56, will this firm produce in the short run? Why, or why not? If it does produce, what will be the profit-maximizing or loss-minimizing output? Explain. What economic profit or loss will the firm realize per unit of output.

b. Answer the questions of 4a assuming that product price is $41.

c. Answer the questions of 4a assuming that product price is $32.

d. In the table below, complete the short-run supply schedule for the firm (columns 1 to 3) and indicate the profit or loss incurred at each output (column 3).

(1) Price	(2) Quantity supplied, single firm	(3) Profit (+) or loss (l)	(4) Quantity supplied, 1500 firms
$26	____	$____	____
32	____	____	____
38	____	____	____
41	____	____	____
46	____	____	____
56	____	____	____
66	____	____	____

e. Explain: "That segment of a competitive firm's marginal-cost curve which lies above its average-variable-cost curve constitutes the short-run supply curve for the firm." Illustrate graphically.

f. Now assume there are 1500 identical firms in this competitive industry; that is, there are 1500 firms, each of which has the same cost data as shown here. Calculate the industry supply schedule (column 4).

g. Suppose the market demand data for the product are as follows:

Price	Total quantity demanded
$26	17,000
32	15,000
38	13,500
41	12,000
41	10,500
56	9,500
66	8,000

47.14 + 7 = 329.95
322.00

450.00
$594.00
450.00

What will equilibrium price be? What will equilibrium output be for the industry? For each firm? What will profit or loss be per unit? Per firm? Will this industry expand or contract in the long run?

(a) Yes, $56 exceeds AVC (and ATC) at the loss—minimizing output. Using the MR = MC rule it will produce 8 units. Profits per unit = $7.87 (= $56 - $48.13); total profit = $62.96.

(b) Yes, $41 exceeds AVC at the loss—minimizing output. Using the MR = MC rule it will produce 6 units. Loss per unit or output is $6.50 (= $41 - $47.50). Total loss = $39 (= 6 □∞ $6.50), which is less than its total fixed cost of $60.

(c) No, because $32 is always less than AVC. If it did produce, its output would be 4—found by expanding output until MR no longer exceeds MC. By producing 4 units, it would lose $82 [= 4 ($32 - $52.50)]. By not producing, it would lose only its total fixed cost of $60.

(d) Column (2) data, top to bottom: 0; 0; 5; 6; 7; 8; 9, Column (3) data, top to bottom in dollars: -60; -60; -55; -39; -8; +63; +144.

(e) The firm will not produce if $P <$ AVC. When $P >$ AVC, the firm will produce in the short run at the quantity where P (= MR) is equal to its increasing MC. Therefore, the MC curve above the AVC curve is the firm's short-run supply curve, it shows the quantity of output the firm will supply at each price level. See Figure 23-6 for a graphical illustration.

(f) Column (4) data, top to bottom: 0; 0; 7,500; 9,000; 10,500; 12,000; 13,500.

(g) Equilibrium price = $46; equilibrium output = 10,500. Each firm will produce 7 units. Loss per unit = $1.14, or $8 per firm. The industry will contract in the long run.

23-5   Why is the equality of marginal revenue and marginal cost essential for profit maximization in all market structures? Explain why price can be substituted for marginal revenue in the MR = MC rule when an industry is purely competitive.

If the last unit produced adds more to costs than to revenue, its production must necessarily reduce profits (or increase losses). On the other hand, profits must increase (or losses decrease) so long as the last unit produced—the marginal unit—is adding more to revenue than to costs. Thus, so long as MR is greater than MC, the production of one more marginal unit must be adding to profits or reducing losses (provided price is not less than minimum AVC). When MC has risen to precise equality with MR, the production of this last (marginal) unit will neither add nor reduce profits.

In pure competition, the demand curve is perfectly elastic; price is constant regardless of the quantity demanded. Thus MR is equal to price. This being so, P can be substituted for MR in the MR = MC rule. (Note, however, that it is not good practice to use MR and P interchangeably, because in imperfectly competitive models, price is not the same as marginal revenue.)

23-6   (*Key Question*)   Using diagrams for both the industry and representative firm, illustrate competitive long-run equilibrium. Assuming constant costs, employ these diagrams to show how (a) an increase and (b) a decrease in market demand will upset this long-run equilibrium. Trace graphically and describe verbally the adjustment processes by which long-run equilibrium is restored. Now rework your analysis for increasing- and decreasing-cost industries and compare the three long-run supply curves.

See Figures 23.8 and 23.9 and their legends. See figure 23.11 for the supply curve for an increasing cost industry. The supply curve for a decreasing cost industry is below.

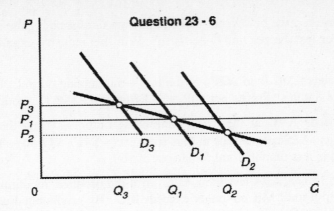

Question 23 - 6

23-7   (*Key Question*) In long-run equilibrium, P = minimum ATC = MC. Of what significance for economic efficiency is the equality of P and minimum ATC? The equality of P and MC? Distinguish between productive efficiency and allocative efficiency in your answer.

The equality of P and minimum ATC means the firms is achieving *productive efficiency;* it is using the most efficient technology and employing the least costly combination of resources. The equality of P and MC means the firms is achieving *allocative efficienc;*, the industry is producing the right product in the right amount based on society's valuation of that product and other products.

23-8   (*Last Word*) Suppose that improved technology causes the supply curve for oranges to shift rightward in the market discussed in this Last Word (see the figure there). Assuming no change in the location of the demand curve, what will happen to consumer surplus? Explain why.

A rightward shift of the supply curve with demand constant will lower the price and increase the quantity demanded. At the new equilibrium price more buyers will have entered the market. All of them will enjoy some amount of utility beyond their expenditures except the ones paying exactly the price they are willing to pay and not a cent more. The triangle representing consumer surplus will be larger because it includes an additional area between the original $4 price and the new lower price extending to a new larger quantity.

CHAPTER TWENTY-FOUR
PURE MONOPOLY

CHAPTER OVERVIEW

This chapter is divided into six basic sections: the characteristics of pure monopoly; the barriers to entry that create and protect monopolies; price and output determination under monopoly; the economic effects of monopoly; price discrimination under monopoly; and the regulation of monopolies.

The discussion of barriers to entry states at the outset that these barriers may occur to some extent in any form of imperfect competition, not just in a pure monopoly. The concept of a natural monopoly is addressed in this section.

Building on the analysis of the preceding chapter, the discussion of price-output decision making by monopoly firms points out that the marginal-revenue—marginal-cost rule still applies. Emphasis here is on the major difference between the determination of marginal revenue in pure competition and in pure monopoly. The misconceptions about monopoly pricing behavior are presented as well as a comparison of efficiency in pure competition and pure monopoly. This section ends with a discussion of effects of monopoly power in the U.S. economy and some policy alternatives.

The case of price discrimination and its effects are discussed along with the conditions necessary for it to occur. At the end of the chapter, the basic issues involved in the regulation of public service monopolies are reviewed.

WHAT'S NEW

In the introduction, the idea that "near" monopolies have a substantial amount of monopoly power in certain industries is presented. Throughout this chapter, current, front-page examples of firms with "near" monopoly power are used. The importance of R&D in creating barriers to entry and destroying monopoly power have been expanded in the "Legal Barriers to Entry", the "Pricing and Other Strategic Barriers to Entry," and the revised "Assessment and Policy Options" sections. The discussion of economies of scale has been expanded to include the effects of greater specialization of resources, product development costs, and learning-by-doing.

In the public utilities discussion there is an acknowledgement of the deregulation of the local telephone and electricity-provider industries in some states.

The Last Word, "De Beers' Diamonds: Are Monopolies Forever?", has been revised. The two Web-Based Questions have been changed.

INSTRUCTIONAL OBJECTIVES

After completing this chapter, students should be able to:

1. List the five characteristics of pure monopoly.

2. Explain the difference between a "pure" monopoly and a "near" monopoly.

3. List and give examples of the four barriers to entry.

4. Describe the demand curve facing a pure monopoly and how it differs from that facing a firm in a purely competitive market.

5. Compute marginal revenue when given a monopoly demand schedule.

6. Explain why the marginal revenue is equal to the price in pure competition but not in monopoly.

7. Determine the price and output level the monopoly will choose given demand and cost information in both table and graphic form.

8. Discuss the economic effects of pure monopoly on price, quantity of product produced, allocation of resources, distribution of income, and technological progress.

9. Give examples of how new technology has lessened monopoly power.

10. List three conditions necessary for price discrimination.

11. Explain why profits and output will be higher for a discriminating monopoly as compared to non-discriminating monopoly.

12. Identify two pricing strategies of monopoly regulation and explain the dilemma the regulators face in utilizing these strategies.

13. Define and identify terms and concepts listed at the end of the chapter.

COMMENTS AND TEACHING SUGGESTIONS

1. Ask students to list products that they believe are provided by a "pure" monopoly, or at least by firms with a high degree of monopoly power. Then ask them to list substitutes for the products sold by each of these "monopolies." Demonstrate how the relative "closeness" of the substitutes they listed determines, to a large degree, effective limits to the monopoly power of these firms.

2. Review what is meant by a firm versus the industry in pure competition and compare this with pure monopoly where the firm is the industry.

3. In addition to the example of patents discussed in the text, note how licenses, product safety requirements, zoning laws, environmental impact statements, price controls, etc.—all of which are enforced by various levels of government—can serve as barriers to entry in different situations.

4. Stress that the price-output decision is an either-or-decision, i.e., the monopolist can sell one unit at $162 or two units at $152. Ask how much of an increase in total revenue will occur if the second unit (one unit) is sold for $152: answer $152. Now ask how much total revenue will decrease if the price of the first unit is decreased from $162 to $152.

5. The ability to engage in price discrimination is based on differing price elasticities and demand among customers. There are many good examples given in this chapter. Telephone service, air travel, and electricity are all sold at various prices taking into account the customer's sensitivity to price. The more substitutes available to the buyer, the more elastic the demand. This is a good opportunity to review price elasticity and demonstrate the many applications of this measure.

6. Electrical utilities and telephone service were regulated monopolies for many years. Deregulation in both industries is a topic worthy of class discussion and student research. In addition to the basic dilemma facing regulators of natural monopolies covered in the text, discuss problems that result when regulators are not well-intentioned and attempt to maximize their own gains from such an elected or appointed position. The difficulty in finding impartial, yet knowledgeable, people to serve on regulatory commissions is a good topic for discussion, especially if there are any related issues affecting your community, such as an environmental or consumer group that may be challenging a ruling by a regulatory commission. Refer to the relevant summary of this material in chapter 32.

7. The Last Word in this chapter highlights the fact that monopolies do not necessarily last forever.

STUDENT STUMBLING BLOCK

In Chapter 23 the students learned that firms operating in a purely competitive setting equate marginal revenue to price. Now students learn that marginal revenue under imperfect competition is less than price. Students seem to grasp this initially, but because they first learned the identity of marginal revenue and price in a competitive setting, it is sometimes hard to unlearn that when analyzing other market structures. Some instructors avoid this problem by teaching the imperfect competition models first. Students learn to equate marginal revenue and marginal cost in seeking the profit-maximizing output level. Then they can use this rule in studying pure competition and treat the equality of price and marginal revenue as a special case. If you choose to present the material with Chapter 24 coming before Chapter 23, discuss the models in Table 23-1 before assigning this chapter on the monopoly model.

LECTURE NOTES

I. **Pure Monopoly: An Introduction**

   A. Definition: Pure monopoly exists when a single firm is the sole producer of a product for which there are no close substitutes.

   B. There are a number of products where the producers have a substantial amount of monopoly power and are called "near" monopolies.

   C. There are several characteristics that distinguish pure monopoly.

      1. There is a single seller so the firm and industry are synonymous.

      2. There are no close substitutes for the firm's product.

      3. The firm is a "price maker," that is, the firm has considerable control over the price because it can control the quantity supplied.

      4. Entry into the industry by other firms is blocked.

      5. A monopolist may or may not engage in nonprice competition. Depending on the nature of its product, a monopolist may advertise to increase demand.

   C. Examples of pure monopolies and "near monopolies":

      1. Public utilities—gas, electric, water, cable TV, and local telephone service companies—are pure monopolies.

      2. First Data Resources (Western Union), Wham-o (Frisbees) and the DeBeers diamond syndicate are examples of "near" monopolies. (See Last Word.)

      3. Manufacturing monopolies are virtually nonexistent in nationwide U.S. manufacturing industries.

      4. Professional sports leagues grant team monopolies to cities.

      5. Monopolies may be geographic. A small town may have only one airline, bank, etc.

   D. Analysis of monopolies yields insights concerning monopolistic competition and oligopoly, the more common types of market situations (see Chapters 25).

II. **Barriers to Entry Limiting Competition**

   A. Economies of scale constitute one major barrier. This occurs where the lowest unit costs and, therefore, lowest unit prices for consumers depend on the existence of a small number of large firms or, in the case of a pure monopoly, only one firm. Because a very large firm with a large market share is most efficient, new firms cannot afford to start up in industries with economies of scale (see Figure 22-9b and Figure 24-1).

1. Public utilities are known as natural monopolies because they have economies of scale in the extreme case where one firm is most efficient in satisfying existing demand.

2. Government usually gives one firm the right to operate a public utility industry in exchange for government regulation of its power.

3. The explanation of why more than one firm would be inefficient involves the description of the maze of pipes or wires that would result if there were competition among water companies, electric utility companies, etc.

B. Legal barriers to entry into a monopolistic industry also exist in the form of patents and licenses.

1. Patents grant the inventor the exclusive right to produce or license a product for seventeen years; this exclusive right can earn profits for future research, which results in more patents and monopoly profits.

2. Licenses are another form of entry barrier. Radio and TV stations, taxi companies are examples of government granting licenses where only one or a few firms are allowed to offer the service.

C. Ownership or control of essential resources is another barrier to entry.

1. International Nickel Co. of Canada controlled about 90 percent of the world's nickel reserves, and DeBeers of South Africa controls most of world's diamond supplies.

2. Aluminum Co. of America (Alcoa) once controlled all basic sources of bauxite, the ore used in aluminum fabrication.

3. Professional sports leagues control player contracts and leases on major city stadiums.

D. Monopolists may use pricing or other strategic barriers such as selective price-cutting and advertising.

III. **Monopoly demand is the industry (market) demand and is therefore downward sloping.**

A. Our analysis of monopoly demand makes three assumptions:

1. The monopoly is secured by patents, economies of scale, or resource ownership.

2. The firm is not regulated by any unit of government.

3. The firm is a single-price monopolist; it charges the same price for all units of output.

B. Price will exceed marginal revenue because the monopolist must lower the price to sell the additional unit. The added revenue will be the price of the last unit less the sum of the price cuts which must be taken on all prior units of output (Table 24-1 and Figure 24-2).

1. Figure 24-3 shows the relationship between demand, marginal-revenue, and total-revenue curves.

2. The marginal-revenue curve is below the demand curve, and when it becomes negative, the total-revenue curve turns downward as total-revenue falls.

C. The monopolist is a price maker. The firm controls output and price but is not free of market forces, since the combination of output and price that can be sold depends on demand. For example, Table 24-1 shows that at $162 only 1 unit will be sold, at $152 only 2 units will be sold, etc.

D. Price elasticity also plays a role in monopoly price setting. The total revenue test shows that the monopolist will avoid the inelastic segment of its demand schedule. As long as demand is elastic, total revenue will rise when the monopoly lowers its price, but this will not be true when demand becomes inelastic. At this point, total revenue falls as output expands, and since total costs rise with output, profits will decline as demand becomes inelastic. Therefore, the monopolist will expand output only in the elastic portion of its demand curve. (Key Question 4)

IV. **Output and Price Determination**

A. Cost data is based on hiring resources in competitive markets, so the cost data of Chapters 22 and 23 can be used in this chapter as well. The costs in Table 24-1 restate the data of Table 22-2.

B. The MR = MC rule will tell the monopolist where to find its profit-maximizing output level. This can be seen in Table 24-1 and Figure 24-4. The same outcome can be determined by comparing total revenue and total costs incurred at each level of production. (Key Question 5)

C. The pure monopolist has no supply curve because there is no unique relationship between price and quantity supplied. The price and quantity supplied will always depend on location of the demand curve.

D. There are several misconceptions about monopoly prices.

1. Monopolist cannot charge the highest price it can get, because it will maximize profits where total revenue minus total cost is greatest. This depends on quantity sold as well as on price and will never be the highest price possible.

2. Total, not unit, profits is the goal of the monopolist. Table 24-1 has an example of this, in which unit profits are $32 at 4 units of output compared with $28 at the profit-maximizing output of 5 units. Once again, quantity must be considered as well as unit profit.

3. Unlike the purely competitive firm, the pure monopolist can continue to receive economic profits in the long run. Although losses can occur in a pure monopoly in the short run (P>AVC), the less-than-profitable monopolist will shutdown in the long run (P>ATC). Figure 24-5 shows a short-run loss situation for a monopoly firm.

V. **Evaluation of the Economic Effects of a Monopoly**

A. Price, output, and efficiency of resource allocation should be considered.

1. Monopolies will sell a smaller output and charge a higher price than would competitive producers selling in the same market, i.e., assuming similar costs.

2. Monopoly price will exceed marginal cost, because it exceeds marginal revenue and the monopolist produces where marginal revenue and marginal cost are equal. The monopolist charges the price that consumers will pay for that output level.

3. Allocative efficiency is not achieved because price (what product is worth to consumers) is above marginal cost (opportunity cost of product). Ideally, output should expand to a level where price = marginal revenue = marginal cost, but this will occur only under pure competitive conditions where price = marginal revenue. (See Figure 24-6)

4. Productive efficiency is not achieved because the monopolist's output is less than the output at which average total cost is minimum.

B. Income distribution is more unequal than it would be under a more competitive situation. The effect of the monopoly power is to transfer income from the consumers to the business owners.

This will result in a redistribution of income in favor of higher-income business owners, unless the buyers of monopoly products are wealthier than the monopoly owners.

C. Cost complications may lead to other conclusions.

1. Economies of scale may result in one or two firms operating in an industry experiencing lower ATC than many competitive firms. These economies of scale may be the result of spreading large initial capital cost over a large number of units of output (natural monopoly) or, more recently, spreading product development costs over units of output, and a greater specialization of inputs.

2. X-inefficiency may occur in monopoly since there is no competitive pressure to produce at the minimum possible costs.

3. Rent-seeking behavior often occurs as monopolies seek to acquire or maintain government-granted monopoly privileges. Such rent-seeking may entail substantial costs (lobbying, legal fees, public relations advertising, etc.), which are inefficient.

D. Technological progress and dynamic efficiency may occur in some monopolistic industries but not in others. The evidence is mixed.

1. Some monopolies have shown little interest in technological progress.

2. On the other hand, research can lead to lower unit costs, which help monopolies as much as any other type of firm. Also, research can help the monopoly maintain its barriers to entry against new firms.

E. Assessment and policy options:

1. Although there are legitimate concerns of the effects of monopoly power on the economy, monopoly power is not widespread. While research and technology may strengthen monopoly power, overtime it is likely to destroy monopoly position.

2. When monopoly power is resulting in an adverse effect upon the economy, the government may choose to intervene on a case-by-case basis.

VI. **Price discrimination occurs when a given product is sold at more than one price and the price differences are not based on cost differences.**

A. Conditions needed for successful price discrimination:

1. Monopoly power is needed with the ability to control output and price.

2. The firm must have the ability to segregate the market, to divide buyers into separate classes that have a different willingness or ability to pay for the product (usually based on differing elasticities of demand).

3. Buyers must be unable to resell the original product or service.

B. Examples of price discrimination:

1. Airlines charge high fares to executive travelers (inelastic demand) than vacation travelers (elastic demand).

2. Electric utilities frequently segment their markets by end uses, such as lighting and heating. (Lack of substitutes for lighting makes this demand inelastic).

3. Long-distance phone service has higher rates during the day, when businesses must make their calls (inelastic demand), and lower rates at night and on week-ends, when less important calls are made.

4. Movie theaters and golf courses vary their charges on the basis of time and age.

5. Discount coupons are a form of price discrimination, allowing firms to offer a discount to price-sensitive customers.

6. International trade has examples of firms selling at different prices to customers in different countries.

C. Consequences of price discrimination:

1. More profits can be earned by the seller, since the price charged is what each buyer is willing to pay in perfect discrimination. The marginal revenue will be equal to price in the perfect discrimination case. (See Figure 24-8)

2. More production will occur with discrimination because as output expands, the reduced price applies only to the additional unit sold and not to prior units. Marginal revenue can now be equated to marginal cost to find the profit-maximizing level of output, and price of the last unit sold will equal that marginal revenue. End-of-chapter questions 5 and 6 allow comparison of the outcomes in nondiscriminating and discriminating cases.

VII. **Regulated Monopoly**

A. This occurs where a natural monopoly or economies of scale make one firm desirable.

B. As a result of changes in technology and deregulation in the local telephone and the electricity-providers industry, some states are allowing new entrants to compete in previously regulated markets.

C. In those markets that are still regulated, a regulatory commission may attempt to establish the legal price for the monopolist that is equal to marginal cost at the quantity of output chosen. This is called the "socially optimal price."

C. However, setting price equal to marginal cost may cause losses, because public utilities must invest in enough fixed plant to handle peak loads. Much of this fixed plant goes unused most of the time, and a price = marginal cost would be below average total cost. Regulators often choose a price equal to average cost rather than marginal cost, so that the monopoly firm can achieve a "fair return" and avoid losses. (Recall that average-total cost includes an allowance for a normal or "fair" profit.)

D. The dilemma for regulators is whether to choose a socially optimal price, where P = MC, or a fair-return price, where P = AC. P = MC is most efficient but may result in losses for the monopoly firm, and government then would have to subsidize the firm for it to survive. P = AC does not achieve allocative efficiency, but does insure a fair return (normal profit) for the firm. (Key Question 11)

VIII. **LAST WORD: De Beers' Diamonds: Are Monopolies Forever?**

A. De Beers Consolidated Mines of South Africa has been one of the world's strongest and most enduring monopolies. It produces about 50 percent of all rough-cut diamonds in the world and buys for resale many of the diamonds produced elsewhere, for a total of about 80 percent of the world's diamonds.

B. Its behavior and results fit the monopoly model portrayed in Figure 24-4. It sells a limited quantity of diamonds that will yield an "appropriate" monopoly price.

C. The "appropriate" price is well over production costs and has earned substantial economic profits.

D. How has De Beers controlled the production of mines it doesn't own?

1. It convinces producers that "single-channel" monopoly marketing is in their best interests.

2. Mines that don't use De Beers may find the market flooded from De Beers stockpiles of the particular kind of diamond they produce, which causes price declines and loss of profits.

3. Finally, De Beers purchases and stockpiles diamonds produced by independents.

E. Threats and problems face De Beers' monopoly power.

1. New diamond discoveries have resulted in more diamonds outside their control.

2. Russia, which has been a part of De Beers' monopoly, has been allowed to sell a part of its stock directly into the world market.

F. In mid-2000, De Beers abandoned its attempt to control the supply of diamonds.

G. The company is transforming itself into a company that sells "premium" diamonds and luxury goods under the De Beers label.

H. De Beers plans to reduce its stockpile of diamonds and increase the demand for diamonds through advertising.

ANSWERS TO END-OF-CHAPTER QUESTIONS

24-1 "No firm is completely sheltered from rivals; all firms compete for the consumer dollars. Pure monopoly, therefore, does not exist." Do you agree? Explain. How might you use Chapter 20's concept of cross elasticity of demand to judge whether monopoly exists?

Though it is true that "all firms compete for the dollars of consumers," it is playing on words to hold that pure monopoly does not exist. If you wish to send a first-class letter, it is the postal service or nothing. Of course, if the postal service raises its rate to $10 to get a letter across town in two days, you will use a courier, or the phone, or you will fax it. But within sensible limits, say a doubling of the postal rate, there is no alternative to the postal service at anything like a comparable price.

The same case can be made concerning the pure monopoly enjoyed by the local electricity company in any town. If you wish electric lights, you have to deal with the single company. It is a pure monopoly in that regard, even though you can switch to oil or natural gas for heating. Of course, you can use oil, natural gas, or kerosene for lighting too—but these are hardly convenient options.

The concept of cross elasticity of demand can be used to measure the presence of close substitutes for the product of a monopoly firm. If the cross elasticity of demand is greater than one, then the demand that the monopoly faces is elastic with respect to substitute products, and the firm has less control over its product price than if the cross elasticity of demand were inelastic. In other words, the monopoly faces competition from producers of substitute products.

24-2 Discuss the major barriers to entry into an industry. Explain how each barrier can foster monopoly or oligopoly. Which barriers, if any, do you feel give rise to monopoly that is socially justifiable?

Economies of scale are a barrier to entry because of the need for new firms to start big to achieve the low production costs of those already in the industry. However, not all industries need techniques of production that require large scale. In many industries the minimum efficient scale is only a small percentage of domestic consumption. Recall Chapter 22's Last Word on MES.

Natural monopolies give rise to monopoly that is socially justifiable. The economies of scale are sometimes such that having two or more firms serving the market would increase costs unreasonably. Two telephone companies, or gas companies, or water companies, or electricity companies in the same city would be highly inconvenient and costly as long as transmission requires wires and pipes. In such instances, it makes sense for government to grant exclusive franchises and then regulate the resulting monopoly to ensure the public interest is protected.

Patents and licenses are legal barriers to entry that also, to some extent, are justifiable. If inventions were not protected at all from immediate copying by those who bore none of the costs, the urge to invent and innovate would be lessened and the costly secrecy that is enforced already would have to be much greater and more costly. However, this does not mean that abuses do not exist in the present system and a case can be made for reducing the present seventeen years for which patents are granted.

Ownership of essential raw materials is the fourth barrier to entry. It has little social justification except to the extent that the hope of gaining a monopoly in the supply of an essential raw material leads to more prospecting. The Last Word on De Beers is an example.

Unfair competition is the last of the barriers and has no social justification at all, which is why price-cutting to bankrupt a rival is illegal. The problem here, though, is to prove that cutthroat competition truly is what it appears to be.

24-3   How does the demand curve faced by a purely monopolistic seller differ from that confronting a purely competitive firm? Why does it differ? Of what significance is the difference? Why is the pure monopolist's demand curve not perfectly inelastic?

The demand curve facing a pure monopolist is downward sloping; that facing the purely competitive firm is horizontal, perfectly elastic. This is so for the pure competitor because the firm faces a multitude of competitors, all producing perfect substitutes. In these circumstances, the purely competitive firm may sell all that it wishes at the equilibrium price, but it can sell nothing for even so little as one cent higher. The individual firm's supply is so small a part of the total industry supply that it cannot affect the price.

The monopolist, on the other hand, is the industry and therefore is faced by a normal downward sloping industry demand curve. Being the entire industry, the monopolist's supply is big enough to affect prices. By decreasing output, the monopolist can force the price up. Increasing output will drive it down.

Part of the demand curve facing a pure monopolist could be perfectly inelastic; if the monopolist put only a very few items on the market, it is possible the firm could sell them all at, say, $1, or $2, or $3. But it is the very fact that the monopolist could sell the same amount at higher and higher prices that would ensure that the profit-maximizing monopolist would not, in fact, sell in this perfectly inelastic range of the demand curve. Indeed, the monopolist would not sell in even the still slightly inelastic range of the demand curve. The reason is that so long as the demand curve is inelastic, MR must be negative, but since the MC of any item can hardly be negative also, the monopolist's profit must decrease if it produces here. To equate a positive MR with MC, the monopolist must produce in the elastic range of its demand curve.

24-4   (*Key Question*) Use the demand schedule that follows to calculate total revenue and marginal revenue at each quantity. Plot the demand, total-revenue, and marginal-revenue curves and explain the relationships between them. Explain why the marginal revenue of the fourth unit of output is $3.50, even though its price is $5.00. Use Chapter 20's total-revenue test for price elasticity to designate the elastic and inelastic segments of your graphed demand curve. What generalization can you make regarding the relationship between marginal revenue and elasticity of demand? Suppose that somehow the marginal cost of successive units of output were zero. What output would the profit-seeking firm produce? Finally, use your analysis to explain why a monopolist would never produce in the inelastic region of demand.

Price	Quantity Demanded	Price	Quantity Demanded
$7.00	0	$4.50	5
6.50	1	4.00	6
6.00	2	3.50	7
5.50	3	3.00	8
5.00	4	2.50	9

Total revenue, in order from Q = 0: 0; $6.50; $12.00; $16.50; $20.00; $22.50; $24.00; $24.50; $24.00; $22.50. Marginal revenue in order from Q = 1: $6.50; $5.50; $4.50; $3.50; $2.50; $1.50; $.50; -$1.50. See the accompanying graph. Because TR is increasing at a diminishing rate, MR is declining. When TR turns downward, MR becomes negative. Marginal revenue is below D because to sell an extra unit, the monopolist must lower the price on the marginal unit as well as on each of the preceding units sold. Four units sell for $5.00 each, but three of these four could have been sold for $5.50 had the monopolist been satisfied to sell only three. Having decided to sell four, the monopolist had to lower the price of the first three from $5.50 to $5.00, sacrificing $.50 on each for a total of $1.50. This "loss" of $1.50 explains the difference between the $5.00 price obtained on the fourth unit of output and its marginal revenue of $3.50. Demand is elastic from P = $6.50 to P = $3.50, a range where TR is rising. The curve is of unitary elasticity at P = $3.50, where TR is at its maximum. The curve is inelastic from then on as the price continues to decrease and TR is falling. When MR is positive, demand is elastic. When MR is zero, demand is of unitary elasticity. When MR is negative, demand is inelastic. If MC is zero, the monopolist should produce 7 units where MR is also zero. It would never produce where demand is inelastic because MR is negative there while MC is positive.

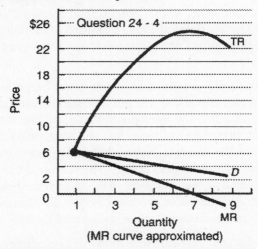

24-5   (*Key Question*) Suppose a pure monopolist is faced with the demand schedule shown below and the same cost data as the competitive producer discussed in question 4 at the end of Chapter 23. Calculate the missing total- and marginal-revenue amounts, and determine the profit-maximizing price and output for this monopolist. What is the monopolist's profit? Verify your answer graphically and by comparing total revenue and total cost.

Price	Quantity demanded	total revenue	Marginal revenue
$115	0	$___	
100	1	$___	$___
83	2	$___	$___
71	3	$___	$___
63	4	$___	$___
55	5	$___	$___
48	6	$___	$___
42	7	$___	$___
37	8	$___	$___
33	9	$___	$___
29	10	$___	$___

Total revenue data, top to bottom, in dollars: 0: 100; 166; 213; 252; 275; 288; 294; 296; 297; 290. Marginal revenue data, top to bottom, in dollars: 100; 66; 47; 39; 23; 13; 6; 2; 1; -7.

Price = $63; output = 4; profit = $42 [= 4($63 - 52.50)]. Your graph should have the same general appearance as Figure 24-4. At $Q = 4$, TR = $252 and TC = $210 [= 4($52.50)].

24-6   (*Key Question*) If the firm described in question 5 could engage in perfect price discrimination, what would be the level of output? Of profits? Draw a diagram showing the relevant demand, marginal-revenue, average-total-cost, and marginal-cost curves and the equilibrium price and output for a nondiscriminating monopolist. Use the same diagram to show the equilibrium position of a monopolist that is able to practice perfect price discrimination. Compare equilibrium outputs, total revenues, economic profits, and consumer prices in the two cases. Comment on the economic desirability of price discrimination.

Perfect price discrimination: Output = 6. TR would be $420 (= $100 + $83 + $71 + $63 + $55 + $48). TC would be $285 [= 6(47.50)]. Profit would be $135 (= $420 -$285).

Your single diagram should combine Figure 24-8a and 24-8b in the chapter. The discriminating monopolist faces a demand curve that is also its MR curve. It will sell the first unit at f in Figure 24-8b and then sell each successive unit at lower prices (as shown on the demand curve) as it moves to Q_2 units, where D (= MR) = MC. Discriminating monopolist: Greater output; total revenue, and profits. Some consumers will pay a higher price under discriminating monopoly than with nondiscriminating monopoly; others, a lower price. Good features: greater output and improved allocative efficiency. Bad feature: More income is transferred from consumers to the monopolist.

24-7   Assume a pure monopolist and a purely competitive firm have the same unit costs. Contrast the two with respect to (a) price, (b) output, (c) profits, (d) allocation of resources, and (e) impact upon the distribution of income. Since both monopolists and competitive firms follow the MC = MR rule in maximizing profits, how do you account for the different results? Why might the costs of a purely competitive firm and a monopolist *not* be the same? What are the implications of such cost differences?

With the same costs, the pure monopolist will charge a higher price, have a smaller output, and have higher economic profits in both the short run and the long run than the pure competitor. As a matter of fact, the pure competitor will have no economic profits in the long run even though it might have some in the short run. Because the monopolist does not produce at the point of minimum ATC and does not equate price and MC, its allocation of resources is inferior to that of the pure competitor. Specifically, resources are underallocated to monopolistic industries. Since a pure monopolist is more likely than the pure competitor to make economic profits in the short run and is, moreover, the only one of the two able to make economic profits in the long run, the distribution of income is more unequal with monopoly than with pure competition.

In pure competition, MR = P because the firm's supply is so insignificant a part of industry supply that its output has no effect on price. It can sell all that it wishes to at the price established by demand and the total industry supply. The firm cannot force the price up by holding back part or all of its supply.

The monopolist, on the other hand, is the industry. When it increases the quantity it produces, price drops. When it decreases the quantity it produces, price rises. In these circumstances, MR is always less than price for the monopolist; to sell more it must lower the price on all units, including those it could have sold at the higher price had it not put more on the market. When the monopolist equates MR and MC, it is not selling at that price: The monopolist's selling price is on the demand curve, vertically above the point of intersection of MR and MC. Thus, the monopolist's price will be higher than the pure competitor's.

Economies of scale may be such as to ensure that one large firm can produce at lower cost than a multitude of small firms. This is certainly the case with most public utilities. And in such industries as basic steelmaking and car manufacturing, pure competition would involve a very high cost. On the other hand, monopolies may suffer from X-inefficiency, the inefficiency that a lack of competition allows. Monopolies may also incur nonproductive costs through "rent-seeking" expenditures. For example, they may try to influence legislation that protects their monopoly powers.

The implications of the lower costs that economies of scale may give a monopolist are that a monopolist may not only produce at a lower cost than pure competitors but, in some cases, may also sell at a lower price. If such is the case, the misallocation of resources is reduced.

24-8   Critically evaluate and explain:

a. "Because they can control product price, monopolists are always assured of profitable production by simply charging the highest price consumers will pay."

b. "The pure monopolist seeks the output that will yield the greatest per-unit profit."

c. "An excess of price over marginal cost is the market's way of signaling the need for more production of a good."

d. "The more profitable a firm, the greater its monopoly power."

e. "The monopolist has a price policy; the competitive producer does not."

f. "With respect to resource allocation, the interests of the seller and of society coincide in a purely competitive market but conflict in a monopolized market."

g. "In a sense the monopolist makes a profit for not producing; the monopolist produces profits more than it does goods."

(a) The statement is false. If the monopolist charged the highest price consumers would pay, it would sell precisely one unit! (Conceivably, it might sell a little more than one if more than one consumer made matching bids for the first unit offered.) It is highly unlikely that the sale of one unit (or a very few) would cover the very high AFC of one or a very few units. And even a monopolist that does produce sensibly where MR = MC may still suffer a loss: P can be below ATC at all levels.

(b) The statement is false. The monopolist seeks the output that will yield the greatest profit. The profit equation is Q(P - ATC). It is not (P - ATC). If the monopolist sells one unit for $100 when ATC is $60, then its profit per unit and total profit is $40 (= $100 - $60). Nice, but if the same monopolist can sell 1,000 units for $40 when ATC is $39, then, though its per unit profit is a mere $1 (= $40 - $39), its total profit is $1,000 [= 1,000($40 - $39)]. And this is much better than $40.

(c) The statement is true. Price is the value society sets on the last item produced. Marginal cost is the value to society of the alternative production forgone when the last item is produced. When P>MC, society is willing to pay more than the opportunity cost of the last item's production.

(d) This statement can be true and probably usually is. Large profits allow expansion to gain economies of scale and thus prevent the late entry of smaller rivals. Large profits also enable the firm to price below cost, to engage (illegally) in a price war. Moreover, large profits in the short run are often associated with monopoly power. And in the long run, only a firm with monopoly power can gain economic profits; in pure competition such profits would invariably be competed away by new entry.

(e) The statement is true. The monopolist must equate MR and MC. Having determined at what quantity this equality occurs, the monopolist simultaneously sets price. This price differs at each output because the demand curve is downsloping. The pure competitor accepts the price given by total industry supply and demand. Knowing this externally given price, the competitor then equates it with the firm's MC and produces the amount determined by this equality.

(f) The statement is true. In pure competition, P = MC. This means that the value society sets on the last item produced (its price) is equal to the cost of the alternative commodities that are not produced because of producing the last item of the commodity in question (its MC). In monopoly, P>MC. This means that society values the last item produced more than its cost.

(g) The statement is true, "in a sense." If the nondiscriminating monopolist produced where P = MC, it would be producing more at a lower price—and gaining a lower profit. By producing instead where MR = MC, the monopolist gains a greater profit by producing less where P>MC. However, the monopolist does produce goods and can produce at a loss. The statement really should be: "The monopolist does its best to produce profits by restricting the output of goods as much as necessary to ensure the equality of MR and MC." Not as neat, but more accurate.

24-9 Assume a monopolistic publisher agrees to pay an author 15 percent of the total revenue from text sales. Will the author and the publisher want to charge the same price for the text? Explain.

The publisher is a monopolist seeking to maximize profits. This will occur at the quantity of output where MC = MR. (See Key Graph 24-4)

The author who will receive 15% of the total revenue will maximize his payment if the book is priced where MR = 0. This will occur where the price elasticity of demand is equal to 1 and total revenue is maximum. (See Figure 24-3)

The author would prefer a lower price than the publisher. Consult Key Graph 24-4 and compare the price charged where MC = MR and the price that would be necessary to maximize total revenue when MR = 0. This is a highly unlikely outcome since the publisher, whether economically literate or not, is certain to recognize the revenue maximizing price as disadvantageous.

24-10 Explain verbally and graphically how price (rate) regulation may improve the performance of monopolies. In your answer distinguish between (a) socially optimal (marginal-cost) pricing and (b) fair-return (average-total-cost) pricing. What is the "dilemma of regulation?"

Monopolies that are natural monopolies are normally subject to regulation. Because of extensive economies of scale, marginal cost is less than average total cost throughout the range of output. An unregulated monopolist would produce at Q_m when MC = MR and enjoy an economic profit. Society would be better off with a larger quantity. Output level Q_r would be socially optimal because MC = Price and allocative efficiency would be achieved. However, the firm would lose money producing at Q_r since ATC exceeds the price. In order for the firm to survive, public subsidies out of tax revenue would be necessary. Another option for regulators is to allow a fair-return price which would allow the firm to break even economically (cover all costs including a normal profit). Setting price equal to ATC would deliver Q_f output and only partially solve the underallocation of resources. Despite this dilemma regulation can improve on the results of monopoly from the social point of view. Price regulation (even at the fair-return price) can simultaneously reduce price, increase output, and reduce the economic profits of monopolies.

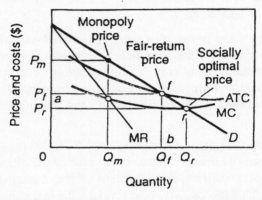

24-11 (*Key Question*) It has been proposed that natural monopolists should be allowed to determine their profit-maximizing outputs and prices and government should tax their profits away and distribute them to consumers in proportion to their purchases from the monopoly. Is this proposal as socially desirable as requiring monopolists to equate price with marginal cost or average total cost?

No, the proposal does not consider that the output of the natural monopolist would still be at the suboptimal level where P > MC. Too little would be produced and there would be an underallocation of resources. Theoretically, it would be more desirable to force the natural monopolist to charge a price equal to marginal cost and subsidize any losses. Even setting price equal to ATC would be an improvement over this proposal. This fair-return pricing would allow for a normal profit and ensure greater production than the proposal would.

24-12 (*Last Word*) How was De Beers able to control the world price of diamonds over the past several decades even though it produced only 50 percent of the diamonds? What factors ended its monopoly? What is its new strategy for earning economic profit, rather than just normal profit?

De Beers produces 50 percent of all rough-cut diamonds, but buys a large portion of the diamonds produced by other mines. As a result, it marketed over 80 percent of the world's diamonds.

New diamonds were discovered and mined in Angola, Canada, and Australia and some of these diamonds were leaking into the world market. In addition, Russia was allowed to sell a portion of its diamond stock directly into the world market.

De Beers' new strategy is to transform itself into a firm selling premium diamonds and other luxury goods. This new image will be portrayed in an advertising campaign.

CHAPTER TWENTY-FIVE
MONOPOLISTIC COMPETITION AND OLIGOPOLY

CHAPTER OVERVIEW

Pure competition and pure monopoly are the exceptions, not the rule, in the U.S. economy. In this chapter, the two market structures that fall between the extremes are discussed. Monopolistic competition contains a considerable amount of competition mixed with a small dose of monopoly power. Oligopoly, in contrast, implies a blend of greater monopoly power and less competition.

First, monopolistic competition is defined, listing important characteristics, typical examples, and efficiency outcomes. Next we turn to oligopoly, surveying the possible courses of price, output, and advertising behavior that oligopolistic industries might follow. Finally, oligopoly is assessed as to whether it is an efficient or inefficient market structure.

WHAT'S NEW

This chapter has been reorganized since it was introduced in the previous edition. There is greater stress on how products are differentiated and on the benefits of product variety. The discussion of "Cartels and Other Collusions" has been condensed with the focus on OPEC today rather than in the 1970s. Rather than referring to firms A, B, and C, hypothetical firms with names are used in the examples. Global Perspective 25.1 has been changed to the daily oil production of the 11 OPEC nations in 2001. Figure 25-7 and the discussion have been eliminated.

The Last Word has been revised. One of the Web-Based Questions is new.

INSTRUCTIONAL OBJECTIVES

After completing this chapter, students should be able to:

1. List the characteristics of monopolistic competition.

2. Explain how product differentiation occurs in similar products.

3. Determine the profit-maximizing price and output level for a monopolistic competitor in the short run when given cost and demand data.

4. Explain why a monopolistic competitor will realize only normal profit in the long run.

5. Identify the reasons for excess capacity in monopolistic competition.

6. Explain how product differentiation may offset these inefficiencies.

7. Describe the characteristics of an oligopolistic industry.

8. Differentiate between homogeneous and differentiated oligopolies.

9. Identify and explain the most important causes of oligopoly.

10. Describe and compare the concentration ratio and the Herfindahl index as ways to measure market dominance in an industry.

11. Use a profit-payoffs matrix (game theory) to explain the mutual interdependence of two rival firms and why oligopolists might tempt to cheat on a collusive agreement.

12. Identify three possible models of oligopolistic price-output behavior.

13. Use the kinked demand curve theory to explain why prices tend to be inflexible.

14. Explain the major advantages of collusion for oligopolistic producers.

15. List the obstacles to collusion behavior.

16. Explain price leadership as a form of tacit collusion.

17. Explain why oligopolies may prefer nonprice competition over price competition.

18. List the positive and negative effects of advertising.

19. Explain why some economists assert that oligopoly is less desirable than pure monopoly.

20. Explain the three ways that the power of olipogolists may be diminished.

21. Define and explain the terms and concepts listed at the end of the chapter.

COMMENTS AND TEACHING SUGGESTIONS

1. Since this chapter has combined the discussion of monopolistic competition and oligopoly, there are numerous possibilities for comparison. Have students make a list of businesses with which they are familiar. Ask them to decide whether they fit best in the model of oligopoly or monopolistic competition. What characteristics were most important in making their decision? Mutual interdependence is a key concept for students to understand in this chapter. It may be the most important determinant in deciding to which market structure a particular business belongs.

2. Students need to understand how market structures differ; but building a consistent method of evaluating a firm's position that is the same regardless of the market structure is helpful. Refer again to the three-step process outlined in Chapter 23 (Pure Competition) to determine a firm's situation in the short run. Using MC, ATC, and AVC consistently to determine the same information: (1) MC = MR determines the best quantity of production; (2) comparing ATC and price determines per unit profit or loss; and (3) if a loss is occurring should the firm shutdown? Compare AVC and price.

3. Review allocative and productive efficiency and compare the long run equilibrium outcome of pure competition with the corresponding models of monopolistic competition and oligopoly.

4. One activity that has been used successfully in small classes (up to 30 students) demonstrates the difficulty in predicting outcomes where collusive behavior is possible. There are several versions of the game, but one version is as follows. Tell the class that you are prepared to auction off a $20 bill with the highest bidder taking the prize. (Warning: You need to be prepared to lose $20!) Each student has to submit a written bid on a scrap of paper with his or her name. Then leave the room for five minutes on some excuse while the students decide on their bids. This will give them the opportunity to "collude," and the bright class will decide to have everyone except one person bid $.01 and the high bidder will submit $.02; then they'll divide the spoils. The interesting part of this game is both to see if the class thinks of colluding, and to see if anyone decides to cheat once the collusive agreement takes place – a "cheater" could win with $.03, knowing the collusive agreement.

    Other versions of this game make it less likely that you'll lose your whole $20. (1) Divide the class into two groups. Give one group the opportunity to talk, while you stand in the other half of the room next to the group that has been forbidden to talk. In this case you will award $10 to the high bidder in each group. The silent group will probably have bidders paying close to $10 for the $10 bill. The group with the opportunity to collude may get the $10 for $.02. (2) You could also use the original version above, but stipulate that while the winning bid will be announced, the winner's name will not and the money will be sent to the winner. This arrangement makes it easier for someone in the group to break the agreement in order to reap the entire reward. However, that person will have to bid more than the agreed upon $.02.

The goal of the game is to help students realize how difficult it is to predict pricing outcomes when collusive behavior is a possibility.

5. The OPEC cartel's changing strength is an excellent case study for demonstrating the factors that lead to successful collusive agreements and the factors that lead to their demise.

6. The beer industry (see Last Word section) and the soft-drink industry provide other good examples of familiar industries characterized by high concentration ratios. A good research topic or class debate topic is to evaluate whether these industries have "enough" competition or if consumers would benefit from more competition. The influence of microbreweries and imports complicate analysis of the beer industry.

7. The *Wall Street Journal*, Advertising Age, and *Business Week*, among other business periodicals, frequently have articles on industries that lend themselves to good group discussion topics. Other industries that are in the news frequently and would be suitable for discussion on whether they have become too concentrated are airlines, professional sports (any or all), college athletics, private colleges, and meatpacking.

STUDENT STUMBLING BLOCKS

Because the term "monopolistic competition" suggests monopoly, students seem to have a difficult time recalling that monopolistic *competition* is the market structure closest to pure competition. Stress the word competition in the title, and perhaps draw a yardstick diagram on the board to represent the spectrum of market models from one extreme to the other. If students visually see that monopolistic competition is near to pure competition, this may help them recognize the term later. Point out that monopolistic competition is an "oxymoron"; define the term and let the students have fun thinking of others: e.g., jumbo shrimp, pretty ugly, awfully good, etc. This may help them to understand the combination term, while the market structure is competitive there is also an element of monopoly present.

LECTURE NOTES

I.   **Review Table 23-1.**

II.   **Monopolistic Competition: Characteristics and Occurrence**

    A. Monopolistic competition refers to a market situation in which a relatively large number of sellers offer similar but not identical products.

       1. Each firm has a small percentage of the total market.

       2. Collusion is nearly impossible with so many firms.

       3. Firms act independently; actions of one firm are ignored by the other firms in the industry.

    B. Product differentiation and other types of nonprice competition gives the individual firm some degree of monopoly power that the purely competitive firm does not possess.

       1. Product differentiation may be physical (qualitative).

       2. Services and conditions accompanying the sale of the product are important aspects of product differentiation.

       3. Location is another type of differentiation.

4. Brand names and packaging lead to perceived differences.

5. Product differentiation allows producers to have some control over product prices.

C. Similar to pure competition, under monopolistic competition firms can enter and exit these industries relatively easily.

D. Examples of real-world industries that fit this model are found in Table 25.1.

III. **Monopolistic Competition: Price and Output Determination**

A. The firm's demand curve is highly, but not perfectly, elastic. It is more elastic than the monopoly's demand curve because the seller has many rivals producing close substitutes. It is less elastic than in pure competition, because the seller's product is differentiated from its rivals, so the firm has some control over price.

B. In the short-run situation, the firm will maximize profits or minimize losses by producing where marginal cost and marginal revenue are equal, as was true in pure competition and monopoly. The profit-maximizing situation is illustrated in Figure 25.1a, and the loss-minimizing situation is illustrated in Figure 25.1b.

C. In the long-run situation, the firm will tend to earn a normal profit only, that is, it will break even (Figure 25.1c).

1. Firms can enter the industry easily and will if the existing firms are making an economic profit. As firms enter the industry, this decreases the demand curve facing an individual firm as buyers shift some demand to new firms; the demand curve will shift until the firm just breaks even. If the demand shifts below the break-even point (including a normal profit), some firms will leave the industry in the long run.

2. If firms were making a loss in the short run, some firms will leave the industry. This will raise the demand curve facing each remaining firm as there are fewer substitutes for buyers. As this happens, each firm will see its losses disappear until it reaches the break-even (normal profit) level of output and price.

3. Complicating factors are involved with this analysis.

a. Some firms may achieve a measure of differentiation that is not easily duplicated by rivals (brand names, location, etc.) and can realize economic profits in the long run.

b. There is some restriction to entry, such as financial barriers that exist for new small businesses, so economic profits may persist for existing firms.

c. Long-run below-normal profits may persist, because producers like to maintain their way of life as entrepreneurs despite the low economic returns.

IV. **Monopolistic Competition and Economic Efficiency**

A. Review the definitions of allocative and productive efficiency:

1. Allocative efficiency occurs when price = marginal cost, i.e., where the right amount of resources are allocated to the product.

2. Productive efficiency occurs when price = minimum average total cost, i.e., where production occurs using the least-cost combination of resources.

B. Excess capacity will tend to be a feature of monopolistically competitive firms (Figure 25.2 or Figure 25.1c).

1. Price exceeds marginal cost in the long run, suggesting that society values additional units that are not being produced.

2. Firms do not produce the lowest average-total-cost level of output, as seen in Figure 25.2.

3. Average costs may also be higher than under pure competition, due to advertising and other costs involved in differentiation.

V. **Monopolistic Competition: Product Variety**

   A. A monopolistically competitive producer may be able to postpone the long-run outcome of just normal profits through product development and improvement and advertising.

   B. Compared with pure competition, this suggests possible advantages to the consumer.

      1. Developing or improving a product can provide the consumer with a diversity of choices.

      2. Product differentiation is the heart of the tradeoff between consumer choice and productive efficiency. The greater number of choices the consumer has, the greater the excess capacity problem.

   C. The monopolistically competitive firm juggles three factors—product attributes, product price, and advertising—in seeking maximum profit.

      1. This complex situation is not easily expressed in a simple economic model such as Figure 25.1. Each possible combination of price, product, and advertising poses a different demand and cost situation for the firm.

      2. In practice, the optimal combination cannot be readily forecast but must be found by trial and error.

VI. **Oligopoly: Characteristics and Occurrence**

   A. Oligopoly exists where a few large firms producing a homogeneous or differentiated product dominate a market.

      1. There are few enough firms in the industry that firms are mutually interdependent—each must consider its rivals' reactions in response to its decisions about prices, output, and advertising.

      2. Some oligopolistic industries produce standardized products (steel, zinc, copper, cement), whereas others produce differentiated products (automobiles, detergents, greeting cards).

   B. Barriers to entry:

      1. Economies of scale may exist due to technology and market share.

      2. The capital investment requirement may be very large.

      3. Other barriers to entry may exist, such as patents, control of raw materials, preemptive and retaliatory pricing, substantial advertising budgets, and traditional brand loyalty.

   C. Although some firms have become dominant as a result of internal growth, others have gained this dominance through mergers.

   D. Measuring industry concentration

      1. Concentration ratios are one way to measure market dominance. The four-firm concentration ratio gives the percentage of total industry sales accounted for by the four largest firms. The concentration ratio has several shortcomings in terms of measuring competitiveness.

a. Some markets are local rather than national, and a few firms may dominate within the regional market.

b. Interindustry competition sometimes exists, so dominance in one industry may not mean that competition from substitutes is lacking.

c. World trade has increased competition, despite high domestic concentration ratios in some industries like the auto industry.

d. Concentration ratios fail to measure accurately the distribution of power among the leading firms.

2. The Herfindahl index is another way to measure market dominance. It measures the sum of the squared market shares of each firm in the industry, so that much larger weight is given to firms with high market shares. A high Herfindahl index number indicates a high degree of concentration in one or two firms. A lower index might mean that the top four firms have rather equal shares of the market, for example, 25 percent each (25 squared x 4 = 2,500). A high index might be where one firm has 80 percent of the industry and the others have 6 percent each for a total of 6400 + (6 squared x 3) = 6,508.

3. Concentration tells us nothing about the actual market performance of various industries in terms of how vigorous the actual competition is among existing rivals.

VII. **Oligopoly Behavior: A Game Theory Overview**

A. Oligopoly behavior is similar to a game of strategy, such as poker, chess, or bridge. Each player's action is interdependent with other players' actions. Game theory can be applied to analyze oligopoly behavior. A two-firm model or duopoly will be used.

B. Figure 25.3 illustrates the profit payoffs for firms in a duopoly in an imaginary athletic-shoe industry. Pricing strategies are classified as high-priced or low-priced, and the profits in each case will depend on the rival's pricing strategy.

C. Mutual interdependence is demonstrated by the following: RareAir's best strategy is to have a low-price strategy if Uptown follows a high-price strategy. However, Uptown will not remain there, because it is better for Uptown to follow a low-price strategy when RareAir has a low-price strategy. Each possibility points to the interdependence of the two firms. This is a major characteristic of oligopoly.

D. Another conclusion is that oligopoly can lead to collusive behavior. In the athletic-shoe example, both firms could improve their positions if they agreed to both adopt a high-price strategy. However, such an agreement is collusion and is a violation of U.S. anti-trust laws.

E. If collusion does exist, formally or informally, there is much incentive on the part of both parties to cheat and secretly break the agreement. For example, if RareAir can get Uptown to agree to a high-price strategy, then RareAir can sneak in a low-price strategy and increase its profits.

VIII. **Three oligopoly models are used to explain oligopolistic price-output behavior. (There is no single model that can portray this market structure due to the wide diversity of oligopolistic situations and mutual interdependence that makes predictions about pricing and output quantity precarious.)**

A. The kinked-demand model assumes a noncollusive oligopoly. (See Key Graph 25.4)

1. The individual firms believe that rivals will match any price cuts. Therefore, each firm views its demand as inelastic for price cuts, which means they will not want to lower prices since total revenue falls when demand is inelastic and prices are lowered.

2. With regard to raising prices, there is no reason to believe that rivals will follow suit because they may increase their market shares by not raising prices. Thus, without any prior knowledge of rivals' plans, a firm will expect demand will be elastic when it increases price. From the total-revenue test, we know raising prices when demand is elastic will decrease revenue. So the noncolluding firm will not want to raise prices.

3. This analysis shows how prices tend to be inflexible in oligopolistic industries.

4. Figure 25.4a illustrates the situation relative to an initial price level of P. It also shows that marginal cost has substantial ability to increase at price P before it no longer equals MR; thus, changes in marginal cost will also not tend to affect price.

5. There are criticisms of the kinked-demand theory.

    a. There is no explanation of why P is the original price.

    b. In the real world oligopoly prices are often not rigid, especially in the upward direction.

B. Cartels and collusion agreements constitute another oligopoly model. (See Figure 25.5)

1. Game theory suggests that collusion is beneficial to the participating firms.

2. Collusion reduces uncertainty, increases profits, and may prohibit the entry of new rivals.

3. A cartel may reduce the chance of a price war breaking out particularly during a general business recession.

4. The kinked-demand curve's tendency toward rigid prices may adversely affect profits if general inflationary pressures increase costs.

5. To maximize profits, the firms collude and agree to a certain price. Assuming the firms have identical cost, demand, and marginal-revenue date the result of collusion is as if the firms made up a single monopoly firm.

6. A cartel is a group of producers that creates a formal written agreement specifying how much each member will produce and charge. The Organization of Petroleum Exporting Countries (OPEC) is the most significant international cartel.

7. Cartels are illegal in the U.S., so any collusion here is secret. Examples of these illegal, covert agreements include the 1993 collusion between dairy companies convicted of rigging bids for milk products sold to schools and, in 1996, American agribusiness Archer Daniels Midland, three Japanese firms, and a South Korean firm were found to have conspired to fix the worldwide price and sales volume of a livestock feed additive.

8. Tacit understanding or "gentlemen's agreement," often made informally, are also illegal but difficult to detect.

7. There are many obstacles to collusion:

    a. Differing demand and cost conditions among firms in the industry;

    b. A large number of firms in the industry;

    c. The temptation to cheat;

    d. Recession and declining demand;

    e. The attraction of potential entry of new firms if prices are too high; and

    f. Antitrust laws that prohibit collusion.

C. Price leadership is a gentleman's agreement that lets oligopolists coordinate prices legally; no formal agreements or clandestine meetings are involved. The practice has evolved whereby one firm, usually the largest, changes the price first and, then, the other firms follow.

   1. Several price leadership tactics are practiced by the leading firm.

      a. Prices are changed only when cost and demand conditions have been altered significantly and industry-wide.

      b. Impending price adjustments are often communicated through publications, speeches, and so forth. Publicizing the "need to raise prices" elicits a consensus among rivals.

      c. The new price may be below the short-run profit-maximizing level to discourage new entrants.

   2. Price leadership in oligopoly occasionally breaks down and sometimes results in a price war. A recent example occurred in the breakfast cereal industry in which Kellogg had been the traditional price leader.

IX.   **Oligopoly and Advertising**

   A. Product development and advertising campaigns are more difficult to combat and match than lower prices.

   B. Oligopolists have substantial financial resources with which to support advertising and product development.

   C. Advertising can affect prices, competition, and efficiency both positively and negatively.

      1. Advertising reduces a buyers' search time and minimizes these costs.

      2. By providing information about competing goods, advertising diminishes monopoly power, resulting in greater economic efficiency.

      3. By facilitating the introduction of new products, advertising speeds up technological progress.

      4. If advertising is successful in boosting demand, increased output may reduce long run average total cost, enabling firms to enjoy economies of scale.

      5. Not all effects of advertising are positive.

         a. Much advertising is designed to manipulate rather than inform buyers.

         b. When advertising either leads to increased monopoly power, or is self-canceling, economic inefficiency results.

X.   **The economic efficiency of an oligopolistic industry is hard to evaluate.**

   A. Allocative and productive efficiency are not realized because price will exceed marginal cost and, therefore, output will be less than minimum average-cost output level (Figure 25.5). Informal collusion among oligopolistics may lead to price and output decisions that are similar to that of a pure monopolist while appearing to involve some competition.

   B. The economic inefficiency may be lessened because:

      1. Foreign competition can make oligopolistic industries more competitive on a global scale.

      2. Oligopolistic firms may keep prices lower in the short run to deter entry of new firms.

3. Over time, oligopolistic industries may foster more rapid product development and greater improvement of production techniques than would be possible if they were purely competitive. (See Chapter 26)

XI.   LAST WORD: The Beer Industry: Oligopoly Brewing?

A. In 1947 there were 400 independent brewers in the U.S.; by 1967 the number had declined to 124; by 1987 the number was 33.

B. In 1947, the five largest brewers sold 19 percent of the nation's beer; currently, the big four brewers sell 87 percent of the total. Anheuser-Busch and Miller alone sell 69 percent.

C. Demand has changed.

1. Tastes have shifted from stronger-flavored beers to lighter, dryer products.

2. Consumption has shifted from taverns to homes, which has meant a different kind of packaging and distribution.

D. Supply-side changes have also occurred.

1. Technology has changed, speeding up bottling and can closing.

2. Large plants can reduce labor costs by automation.

3. Large fixed costs are spread over larger outputs.

4. Mergers have occurred but are not the fundamental cause of increased concentration.

5. Advertising and product differentiation have been important in the growth of some firms, especially Miller.

E. There continues to be some competition from imported beers and microbrewers.

ANSWERS TO END-OF-CHAPTER QUESTIONS

25-1   How does monopolistic competition differ from pure competition or pure monopoly? Explain fully what product differentiation involve. Explain how the entry of firms into its industry affects the demand curve facing a monopolistic competitor and how that, in turn, affects its economic profit.

In monopolistic competition there are many firms but not the very large numbers of pure competition. The products are differentiated, not standardized. There is some control over price in a narrow range, whereas the purely competitive firm has none. There is relatively easy entry; in pure competition, entry is completely without barriers. In monopolistic competition, there is much nonprice competition, such as advertising, trademarks, and brand names. In pure competition, there is no nonprice competition.

In pure monopoly there is only one firm. Its product is unique and there are no close substitutes. The firm has much control over price, being a price maker. Entry to its industry is blocked. Its advertising is mostly for public relations.

Product differentiation may only be in the eye of the beholder, but that is all a monopolistic competitor needs to gain advantage in a market if the consumer looks upon the assumed difference favorably. The real differences can be in quality, in services, in location, or even in promotion and packaging, which brings us back to where we started: possibly nonexistent differences. To the extent that product differentiation exists in fact or in the mind of the consumer, monopolistic competitors have limited control over price, for they have built up some loyalty to their brand.

When economic profits are present, additional rivals will be attracted to the industry because entry is relative easy. As new firms enter, the demand curve faced by the typical firm will shift to the left (fall). Because of this, each firm has a smaller share of total demand and now faces a larger number of close-substitute products. This decline firm's demand reduces its economic profit.

25-2   (*Key Question*) Compare the elasticity of the monopolistically competitor's demand curve with that of a pure competitor and a pure monopolist. Assuming identical long-run costs, compare graphically the prices and output that would result in the long run under pure competition and under monopolistic competition. Contrast the two market structures in terms of productive and allocative efficiency. Explain: "Monopolistically competitive industries are characterized by too many firms, each of which produces too little."

Less elastic than a pure competitor and more elastic than a pure monopolist. Your graphs should look like Figures 23.12 and 25.1 in the chapters. Price is higher and output lower for the monopolistic competitor. Pure competition: $P = MC$ (allocative efficiency); $P =$ minimum ATC (productive efficiency). Monopolistic competition: $P > MC$ (allocative efficiency) and $P >$ minimum ATC (productive inefficiency). Monopolistic competitors have excess capacity; meaning that fewer firms operate at capacity (where $P =$ minimum ATC) could supply the industry output.

25-3   "Monopolistic competition is monopoly up to the point at which consumers become willing to buy close-substitute products and competitive beyond that point." Explain.

As long as consumers prefer one product over another regardless of relative prices, the seller of the product is a monopolist. But in monopolistic competition this happy state is limited because there are many other firms producing similar products. When one firm's prices get "too high" (as viewed by consumers), people will switch brands. At this point our firm has entered the competitive zone unwillingly, which is why monopolistically competitive firms always try to find ways to differentiate their products more thoroughly and gain more monopoly price-setting power.

25-4   "Competition in quality and in service may be just as effective in giving the buyers more for their money as is price competition." Do you agree? Why? Explain why monopolistically competitive firms frequently prefer nonprice to price competition.

This can be true. And in a monopolistically competitive market the consumer can buy a substitute brand for a lower price, if the consumer prefers a lower price to better quality and service.

Monopolistically competitive firms often prefer nonprice competition to price competition. The latter can lead to a firm producing where $P =$ ATC, thus making no economic profit or, worse, short-run production where $P <$ ATC and losing money, possibly eventually going out of business.

Nonprice competition, on the other hand, if successful, results in more monopoly power: The firm's product has become more differentiated from now less-similar competitors in the industry. This increase in monopoly power allows the firm to raise its price with less fear of losing customers. Of course, the firm must still follow the MR = MC rule, but its success in nonprice competition has shifted both the demand and MR curves upward to the right. This results in simultaneously a larger output, a higher price, and more economic profits.

25-5   Critically evaluate and explain:

a.   "In monopolistically competitive industries economic profits are competed away in the long run. So there is no valid reason to criticize the performance and efficiency of such industries."

b.   "Long-run monopolistic competition leads to monopolistic price, but not monopolistic profits."

(a). The first part of the statement may well be true, but it does not lead logically to the second part. The criticism of monopolistic competition is not related to the profit level but to the fact that the firms do not produce at the point of minimum ATC and do not equate price and MC. This is the inevitable consequence of imperfect competition and its downward sloping demand curves. With $P >$ minimum ATC, productive efficiency is not attained. The firm is producing too little at too high a cost; it is wasting some of its productive capacity. With $P > MC$, the firm is not allocating resources in accordance with society's desires; the value society sets on the product (P) is greater than the cost of producing the last item (MC).

(b) The statement is often true, since competition of close substitutes tends to compete price of the average firm down to equality with ATC. Thus, there is no economic profit. However, the firm is producing where its (moderately) monopolistically downward-sloping demand curve is tangent to the ATC curve, short of the point of minimum ATC and thus at a higher than purely competitive price. In other words, it is at a "monopolistic" price.

26-6 Why do oligopolies exist? List five or six oligopolists whose products you own or regularly purchase. What distinguishes oligopoly from monopolistic competition?

Oligopolies exist for several reasons, the most common probably being economies of scale. If these are substantial, as they are in the automobile industry, for example, only very large firms can produce at minimum average cost. This makes it virtually impossible for new firms to enter the industry. A small firm could not produce at minimum cost and would soon be competed out of the business; yet to start at the required very large scale would take far more money than a nonestablished firm is likely to be able to raise before proving it will be profitable.

Other barriers to entry include ownership of patents by oligopolists and, possibly, massive advertising that thwarts would-be newcomers establishing a presence in the public's mind. Finally, there is the urge to merge. Mergers reduce competition and give the emerging oligopolists more monopoly power. They can result in economies of scale and increase that barrier to new entry.

Oligopolies with which I deal include manufacturers of automobiles, ovens, refrigerators, personal computers, gasoline, and courier services.

Oligopoly is distinguished from monopolistic competition by being composed of few firms (not many); by being mutual interdependent with regard to price (instead of control within narrow limits); by having differentiated or homogeneous products (not all differentiated); and by having significant obstacles to entry (not easy entry). Both engage in much nonprice competition.

25-7 (*Key Question*) Answer the following questions, which relate to measures of concentration:.

a. What is the meaning of a four-firm concentration ratio of 60 percent? 90 percent? What are the shortcomings of concentration ratios as measures of monopoly power?

b. Suppose that the five firms in industry A have annual sales of 30, 30, 20, 10, and 10 percent of total industry sales. For the five firms in industry B the figures are 60, 25, 5, 5, and 5 percent. Calculate the Herfindahl index for each industry and compare their likely competitiveness.

A four-firm concentration ration of 60 % means the largest four firms in an industry account for 60 % of sales; a four-firm concentration ratio of 90 % means the largest four firms account for 90 percent of sales. Shortcomings: (1) they pertain to the whole nation, though relevant markets may be localized; (2) they do not account for interindustry competition; (3) the data are for U.S. products, not imports; and (4) they don't reveal the dispersion of size among the top four firms.

Herfindahl index for A: 2,400 (= 900 + 900 + 400 + 100 + 100). For B: 4,300 (= 3,600 + 625 + 25 + 25 +25). We would expect industry A to be more competitive than Industry B, where one firm dominates and two firms control 85 percent of the market.

25-8 (*Key Question*) Explain the general meaning of the following profit payoff matrix for oligopolists C and D. All profit figures are in thousands.

a. Use the payoff matrix to explain mutual interdependence of oligopolistic industries.

b. Assuming no collusion between C and D, what is the likely pricing outcome?

c. In view of your answer to 8b, explain why price collusion is mutually profitable. Why might there be a temptation to chat on the collusive agreement?

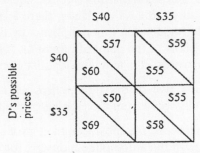

C's possible prices

The matrix shows 4 possible profit outcomes for two firms following two different price strategies. Example: If C sets price at $35 and D at $40, C's profits are $59,000, and D's $55,000.

(a) C and D are interdependent because their profits depend not just on their own price, but also on the other firm's price.

(b) Likely outcome: Both firms will set price at $35. If either charged $40, it would be concerned the other would undercut the price and its profit by charging $35. At $35 for both; C's profit is $55,000, D's, $58,000.

(c) Through price collusion—agreeing to charge $40—each firm would achieve higher profits (C = $57,000; D = $60,000). But once both firms agree on $40, each sees it can increase its profit even more by secretly charging $35 while its rival charges $40.

25-9 (*Key Question*) What assumptions about a rival's response to price changes underlie the kinked-demand curve for oligopolists? Why is there a gap in the oligopolist's marginal-revenue curve? How does kinked demand curve explain price rigidity in oligopoly? What are model weaknesses?

Assumptions: (1) Rivals will match price cuts: (2) Rivals will ignore price increases. The gap in the MR curve results from the abrupt change in the slope of the demand curve at the going price. Firms will not change their price because they fear that if they do their total revenue and profits will fall. Shortcomings of the model: (1) It does not explain how the going price evolved in the first place; (2) it does not allow for price leadership and other forms of collusion.

25-10 Why might price collusion occur in oligopolistic industries? Assess the economic desirability of collusive pricing. What are the main obstacles to collusion? Speculate as to why price leadership is legal in the United States, whereas price fixing is not.

Price wars are a form of competition that benefits consumers but is detrimental to producers. As a result, oligopolists are naturally drawn to the idea of price-fixing among themselves, i.e., colluding with regard to price. In a recession, it is nice to know whether one's rivals will cut prices or quantity, so that a mutually satisfactory solution can be reached. It is also convenient to be able to agree on what price to set to bankrupt any would-be interloper in the industry.

From the viewpoint of society, collusive pricing has no economic desirability. From the oligopoly's viewpoint it is highly desirable since, when entirely successful, it allows the oligopoly to set price and quantity as would a profit-maximizing monopolist.

Main obstacles to collusion are demand and cost differences resulting in different points of equality of MR and MC; number of firms; cheating (it pays to cheat by selling more below the agreed-on price provided other colluders do not find out); recession (when demand slumps, the urge to shave prices—to cheat—becomes much greater); potential entry (the above-equilibrium price that is the reason for collusion may entice new firms into this profitable industry—and it may be hard to get new entrants into the combine, quite apart from the unfortunate increase in supply they will cause); legal obstacles (for a century, antitrust laws have made collusion illegal).

Price leadership is legal because although others may follow a dominant firm's price, they are not forced. And the tacit agreement on price does not also include an agreement to control quantity and to divide the market.

25-11 (*Key Question*) Why is there so much advertising in monopolistic competition and oligopoly? How does such advertising help consumers and promote efficiency? Why might it be excessive at times?

Monopolistically competitive firms maintain economic profits through product development and advertising. Advertising can increase demand for a firm's product. An oligopolist would rather not compete on a basis of price. Oligopolists can increase market share through advertising financed with economic profits from past advertising campaigns. Advertising can act as a barrier to entry.

Advertising provides information about new products and product improvements to the consumer. It may result in an increase in competition by promoting new products and product improvements. Advertising may result in manipulation and persuasion rather than information. An increase in brand loyalty through advertising will increase the producer's monopoly power. Excessive advertising may create barriers to entry into the industry.

25-12 (Advanced analysis) Construct a game theory matrix involving two firms and their decisions on high advertising budgets even though both would be more profitable with low advertising budgets. Why won't they unilaterally cut their advertising budgets?

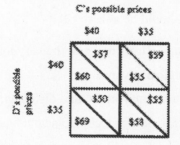

There are four possible combinations of strategies for the two firms relative to expenditures on advertising. (See the matrix above) Firms spend on advertising to increase the firm's market share, revenues, and profits. If Firm X promotes its product more than Firm Y, Firm Y will lose market shares and profits (cell C). Firm Y will respond by increasing its advertising budget to take back its market share. This will increase the profits to firm Y but decrease the profits to Firm X. Unless they collude, the firms will both end up with large advertising budgets and reduced profits.

25-13 (*Last Word*) What firm dominates the beer industry? What demand and supply factors have contributed to "fewness" in this industry?

Anheuser-Busch is the dominant firm in the industry. Demand-side, there is evidence that by the 1970s tastes changed in favor of lighter, drier beers produced by the larger brewers. Second, consumption in taverns lost out to home consumption, which means higher sales of packaged containers that can be shipped long distances.

On the supply side, technological advances increased bottling lines so that the number of cans filled per hour rose from 900 in 1965 to over 2000 in 1990s; large plants have been able to take advantage of economies of scale; television advertising also favors the large producers; and extensive product differentiation exists despite the smaller number of firms, which has enabled these firms to expand still further.

CHAPTER TWENTY-SIX
TECHNOLOGY, R&D, AND EFFICIENCY

CHAPTER OVERVIEW

This chapter introduces students to the importance of technical advances, R&D decisions, and innovation and brings these topics directly into the core microeconomic chapters. This chapter focuses explicitly on the effects of market structure on technological progressiveness.

We believe that R&D and innovation are simply too important to student understanding of modern industrial economies to disregard or relegate to a side bar. Therefore, we have integrated this material into the main flow of the theory of the firm. The instructor, however, can bypass this chapter without jeopardizing course continuity.

WHAT'S NEW

This chapter was first introduced in the previous addition. Some of the examples have been omitted and changed. Figure 26.2 has been deleted and the material has been included in the text.

The Last Word has been updated. The Web-Based Questions have been revised.

INSTRUCTIONAL OBJECTIVES

After completing this chapter, students should be able to:

1. Distinguish between the short run, the long run, and the very long run.
2. Describe the elements of technological advance.
3. Give a specific example of invention, innovation, and diffusion.
4. Compare and contrast the historical view of technological advance with the contemporary view.
5. Evaluate the role of entrepreneurs and other innovators in technological advancement.
6. Identify and explain how a firm's optimal amount of R&D spending is determined.
7. List the possible sources of R&D financing.
8. Explain how marginal utility theory can be used to determine the success or failure of a new product.
9. Explain how process innovation adds to a firm's profits.
10. Describe and give an example of the "fast-second" strategy.
11. Enumerate the protections and potential benefits for firms that take the lead with R&D and innovation.
12. Evaluate the strengths and weaknesses of each of the four basic market structures regarding the likelihood of R&D and innovation.
13. Describe the inverted U theory.
14. Evaluate the impact of technological advance on productive and allocative efficiency.
15. Describe, and give an example of "creative destruction."
16. Define and identify the terms and concepts listed at the end of the chapter.

COMMENTS AND TEACHING SUGGESTIONS

1. Student interest in this topic is likely to be high. Oral reports presenting recent newspaper or magazine articles on inventions, innovations or projections of new products, new materials or new processes should spark good discussion. *Scientific American* frequently devotes an issue to new technologies within a specific industry. In addition, *Discover, Popular Science*, weekly news magazines, and *Business Week* are all likely to feature reports on new technology.

2. Many craftsmen are natural innovators. Have the students interview someone that works in the building trades (carpenters, tile setters, plumbers, or welders). Each construction job is different and often special problems or conditions make doing the job a challenge. Many craftsmen have developed their own unique methods and are proud of both their efficient systems and the appearance of the finished projects. In some cases, this assignment could bring new appreciation for a parent or other family member who operates a business.

3. Ask students to describe an incident when they were faced with a task to complete without the proper or most convenient tools. How did they solve the problem? Did they fashion a new tool or use a tool designed for another purpose creatively?

LECTURE NOTES

I. **Technological Advance: Invention, innovation and diffusion.**

   A. In the short run it is assumed that technology, plant, and equipment are constant. In the long run, the size of the plant can change and firms can enter or leave the industry; in the very long run, technological advances can occur.

   B. Technological advance is a three-step process that shifts the economy's production possibilities curve outward-enabling more production of goods and services.

   1. The most basic element of technological advance is invention: The discovery of a product or process and the proof that it will work.

   2. Innovation is the first successful commercial introduction of a new product, the first use of a new production, or the creation of a new form of business enterprise.

   3. Diffusion is the spread of innovation through imitation or copying.

   C. Expenditures on research and development include direct efforts by business toward invention, innovation and diffusion. Government also engages in R&D, particularly for national defense.

   1. In 2000 total U.S. R&D expenditures (business plus government) were $264 billion, 2.64 percent of U.S. GDP. (See Global Perspective 26.1 for comparison.)

   2. American business spent $199 billion on R&D in 2000. (See Figure 26.1 for breakdown into categories.)

   D. The modern view of technological advance.

   1. For decades economists treated technological advances as an element largely external to the market system — a random outside force to which the economy adjusted.

   2. Contemporary economists see capitalism itself as the driving force of technological advance, providing the incentives and motives for firms and individuals to seek profitable opportunities.

II. **The role of entrepreneurs and other innovators.**

   A. The entrepreneur is an initiator, innovator, and risk bearer—the catalyst who uses resources in new and unique ways to produce new and unique goods and services.

B. Other innovators, who do not bear personal financial risk, include key executives, scientists, and others engaged in commercial R&D activities.

C. Often entrepreneurs form new companies called "start-ups", i.e., firms that focus on creating and introducing new products or employing a specific new production or distribution technique.

D. Innovators are also found within existing corporations supported by working conditions and pay incentives that foster creative thinking. Some firms have chosen to "spin off" the R&D function into new, more flexible and innovative companies.

E. Product innovation and development are creative endeavors with intangible rewards of personal satisfaction, but the "winners" can also realize huge financial gains. Success gives entrepreneurs and innovative firms access to more resources. The entrepreneurs are found in many different countries around the world.

F. Technological advance is supported by the scientific research of universities and government sponsored laboratories. Firms increasingly help to fund university research that relates to their products.

III. **The firm's optimal amount of R&D.**

A. Finding the optimal amount of R&D is an application of basic economics.

1. To earn the greatest profit, a firm should expand a particular activity until its marginal benefit equals its marginal cost.

2. The R&D spending decision is complex because the estimation of future benefits is highly uncertain while costs are immediate and more clearcut.

B. Interest rate cost of funds: Whatever the source of R&D funds, the opportunity cost of these funds is measurable by the current rate of interest. (See Figure 26.2) Possible sources include the following:

1. Bank loans

2. Bonds

3. Retained earnings

4. Venture capital

5. Personal savings

C. A firm's marginal benefit from R&D is its expected rate of return on the expenditures. The curve showing the expected rate of return slopes downward because of diminishing returns to R&D expenditures. (See Figure 26.3)

D. Optimal R&D expenditures occur when the interest rate cost of funds is equal to the expected rate of return. (See Figure 26.4)

1. Many R&D expenditures may be affordable but not worthwhile because the marginal benefit is less than the marginal cost.

2. Expenditures are planned on the basis of expected returns. R&D decisions carry a great deal of risk. There is no certainty of outcome.

IV. **Increased profit via innovation.**

A. Increased profit via product innovation.

1. Consumers will buy a new product only if it increases the total utility they obtain from their limited incomes. They purchase products that have the highest marginal utility per dollar. (Review Chapter 21 and Table 21.1)

   a. Consumer acceptance of a new product depends on both marginal utility and price.

   b. The expected return that motivates product innovation may not be realized. Expensive "flops" are common.

   c. Most product innovation consists of incremental improvements to existing products rather than radical inventions.

B. Reduced cost via process innovation.

   1. Firms can increase output by introducing better production methods or by using more productive capital equipment.

   2. An innovation that increases total product at each level of resource usage lowers the average total cost of a unit of output and thus enhances the firm's profit. (See Figure 26.5)

V. Imitation and R&D Incentives

A. A firm's rivals may deliberately employ the "fast-second strategy," allowing the originating firm to incur the high costs of R&D and then entering quickly if the product is a success.

B. There are protections, potential advantages, and benefits of being first.

   1. Some technological breakthroughs can be patented; they cannot be legally imitated for two decades. (See global perspective 26.2) Many holders of U.S. patents are citizens or firms of foreign nations.

   2. Copyrights and trademarks reduce the problem of direct copying.

   3. Along with trademark protection, brand name recognition may give the original innovator a marketing advantage.

   4. Trade secrets may prevent imitation of a product, and sometimes it is the process that is the key to success. The originating firm may also gain an advantage simply by learning on the job.

   5. Time lags between innovation and diffusion often permit originating firms to realize a substantial economic profit.

   6. A final advantage of being first is the potential for an attractive buyout offer. This allows the innovative entrepreneur to take their rewards immediately without the uncertainty of production and marketing on their own.

   7. There continue to be high levels of R&D that would not be the case if imitation consistently and severely depressed actual rates of return on these expenditures. (See Figure 26.6)

VI. Role of Market Structure

A. Market structure and technological advance.

   1. Pure competition—Although purely competitive firms may have an incentive to keep ahead of their competitors, the small size of the firms and the fact that there are no barriers to entry and therefore they can earn only a normal profit in the long run, leads to serious questions as to whether such producers can benefit from and finance substantial R&D programs.

2. Monopolistic competition—There is a strong profit incentive to engage in product development in this market structure. However, most firms remain small, which limits their ability to secure financing for R&D. Economic profits are usually temporary because there are few barriers to entry.

3. Oligopoly—The oligopolistic market structure is conducive to technical advance. Firms are large with ongoing economic profits, are protected by barriers to entry, and have large volume of sales. Although oligopolistic firms have the financial resources to engage in R&D, they are often complacent.

4. Pure monopoly—Pure monopolists have little incentive to engage in R&D. Since profits are protected by absolute barriers to entry, the only reason for R&D would be defensive, i.e., to reduce the risk of a new product or process that might destroy the monopoly.

B. Inverted-U Theory (Figure 26.7)

1. The inverted-U suggests that both very low concentration industries and very high concentration industries expend a relatively small percentage of their sales revenue on R&D.

2. The optimal market structure for technological advance seems to be an industry in which there is a mix of large oligopolistic firms (a 40 to 60 percent concentration ratio) with several highly innovative smaller firms.

3. Competitive firms are small, which makes it difficult for them to finance the R&D, and there is easy entry by competitors. Where firms have a substantial amount of monopoly power, monopoly profits are large and innovation will likely not add much more to the the firm's profits.

4. The level of R&D spending within an industry seems to be determined more by the industry's scientific character and "technological opportunities" than from its market structure.

VII. Technological Advance and Efficiency

A. Productive efficiency is improved when a technological advance involves process innovation and a reduction in costs. (Figure 26.5a and b)

B. Allocative efficiency is improved when a technological advance involves a new product that increases the utility consumers can obtain from their limited income.

C. Innovation can create monopoly power through patents or the advantages of being first, reducing the benefit to society from the innovation.

D. Innovation can also reduce or even disintegrate existing monopoly power by providing competition where there was none. In this case, economic efficiency is enhanced because the competition drives prices down closer to marginal cost and minimum ATC.

E. Creative destruction occurs when the innovation of new products or production methods destroys the monopoly positions of firms committed to existing products and their old ways of doing business.

VIII. Last Word: On the Path to the Personal Computer and Internet

Technological advance is clearly evident in the development of the modern personal computer and the emergence of the Internet. This is a brief history of these events.

ANSWERS TO END-OF-CHAPTER QUESTIONS

26-1   What is meant by technological advance, as broadly defined? How does technological advance enter into the definition of the very long run? Which of the following are examples of technological advance, and which are not: an improved production process; entry of a firm into a profitable purely competitive industry; the imitation of a new production process by another firm; an increase in a firm's advertising expenditures?

Technological advance is broadly defined as new and better goods and services and new and better ways of producing or distributing them. There is a distinction between the "long run" and the very "long run": In the long run, technology is constant but firms can change their plant sizes and are free to enter or exit industries. In contrast, the very long run is a period in which technology can change and in which firms can introduce entirely new products.

(a) An improved production process; Yes (innovation)

(b) Entry of a firm into a profitable purely competitive industry; No

(c) The imitation of a new production process by another firm; Yes (Diffusion)

(d) An increase in a firms advertising expenditures; No

26-2   Listed below are several possible actions by firms. Write INV beside those that reflect invention, INN beside those that reflect innovation, and DIF beside those that reflect diffusion.

a. An auto manufacture adds "heated seats" as a standard feature in its luxury cars to keep pace with a rival firm whose luxury cars already have this feature.

b. A television production company pioneers the first music video channel.

c. A firm develops and patents a working model of a self-erasing whiteboard for classrooms.

d. A maker of light bulbs becomes the first firm to produce and market lighting fixtures using halogen lamps.

e. A rival toy maker introduces a new Jenny doll to complete with Mattel's Barbie doll.

(a) DIF

(b) INN

(c) INV

(d) INN

(e) DIF

26-3   Contrast the older and modern views of technological advance as they relate to the economy. What is the role of entrepreneurs and other innovators in technological advance? How does research by universities and government affect innovators and technological advance? Why do you think some university researchers are increasingly becoming more like entrepreneurs and less like "pure scientists"?

The older view of technological advance was that it was external to the economy; a random outside force to which the economy adjusted. Scientific and technological advances were fortuitous and helpful but largely external to the market system. Most contemporary economists have a different view. They see capitalism itself as the driving force of technological advance. In this view, invention, innovation, and diffusion occur in response to incentives provided by the market. The motivation to seek new products and processes is driven by the expectation of new profit opportunities.

An entrepreneur is an initiator, innovator, and risk bearer—the catalyst who combines, land, labor and capital resources in new and unique ways to produce new goods and services. Historically, these were individuals. In today's more technologically complex economy, this role is just as likely to be carried out by entrepreneurial teams. Unlike entrepreneurs, other innovators do not bear personal financial risk. These people include key executives, scientists, and other salaried employees engaged in commercial R&D activities.

New scientific knowledge is highly important to technological advance, but scientific principles, as such, cannot be patented. For this reason entrepreneurs actively study the scientific output of university and government laboratories to find discoveries with commercial applications, obtaining information without paying for its development. Although, firms increasingly help fund university research that relates to their products, scientists increasingly realize their work may have commercial value.

26-4   (*Key Question*) Suppose a firm expects that a $20 million expenditure on R&D will result in a new product which will increase its revenue by a total of $30 million 1 year from now. The firm estimates that the production cost of the new product will be $29 million.

   a. What is the expected rate of return on this R&D expenditure?

   b. Suppose the firm can get a bank loan at 6 percent interest to finance its $20 million R&D project. Will the firm undertake the project? Explain why or why not.

   c. Now suppose the interest-rate cost of borrowing, in effect, falls to 4 percent because the firm decides to use its own retained earnings to finance the R&D. Will this lower interest rate change the firm's R&D decision? Explain.

   (a) 5 percent;

   (b) No, because the 5 percent rate of return is less than the 6 percent interest rate;

   (c) Yes, because the 5 percent the rate of return is now greater than the 4 percent interest rate.

26-5   (*Key Question*) Answer the lettered questions below on the basis of the information in this table:

Amount of R&D, millions	Expected rate of return on R&D, %
$10	16
20	14
30	12
40	10
50	8
60	6

   a. If the interest-rate cost of funds is 8 percent, what will be the optimal amount of R&D spending for this firm?

   b. Explain why $20 million of R&D spending will not be optimal.

   c. Why won't $60 million be optimal either?

   (a) $50 million, where the interest-rate cost of funds (i) equals the expected rate of return (r);

(b) at $20 million in R&D, *r* of 14 percent exceeds i of 8 percent, thus there would be an underallocation of R&D funds;

(c) at $60 million, *r* of 6 percent is less than i of 8 percent, thus there would be an overallocation of R&D funds.

26-6   (*Key Question*) Refer to Table 26-1 and suppose the price of new product C is $2 instead of $4. How does this affect the optimal combination of products A, B, and C for the person represented by the data? Explain: "The success of a new product depends not only on its marginal utility but also on its price."

(a) The person would now buy 5 units of product C and zero units of A and B;

(b) The MU/price ratio is what counts; a new product can be successful by having a high MU, a low price, or both relative to existing products.

26-7   Learning how to use software takes time. So once customers have learned to use a particular software package, it is easier to sell them software upgrades than to convince them to switch to new software. What implications does this have for expected rates of return on R&D spending for software firms developing upgrades versus those developing imitative products?

Expenditures on R&D carry a great deal of risk. Upgrading an existing product is likely to be less risky than developing an imitated product. Consumers value their time as well as money and are likely to prefer products that are familiar.

Imitating a successful product may save the cost of R&D for development, but there are significant protections that may end up costing the "copy cat" firm dearly. Patents, copyrights and brand name recognition all contribute to give the original innovator a major marketing advantage.

26-8   (*Key Question*) Answer the following questions on the basis of this information for a single firm: total cost of capital = $1,000; price paid for labor = $12 per labor unit; price paid for raw materials = $4 per raw-material unit.

a.   Suppose the firm can produce 5,000 units of output by combining its fixed capital with 100 units of labor and 450 units of raw materials. What are the total cost and average total cost of producing the 5,000 units of output?

b.   Now assume the firm improves its production process so that it can produce 6,000 units of output by combining its fixed capital with 100 units of labor and 45 units of raw materials. What are the total cost and average cost of producing the 6,000 units of output?

c.   In view of your answers to 8a and 8b, explain how process innovation can improve economic efficiency.

(a) Total cost = $4,000; average total cost = $.80 (= $4,000/5,000 units);

(b) Total cost = $4,000, average total cost = $.667 (= $4,000/6,000 units);

(c) Process innovation can lower the average total cost of producing a particular output, meaning that society uses fewer resources in producing that output. Resources are freed from this production to produce more of other desirable goods. Society realizes extra output through a gain in efficiency.

26-9   Why might a firm making a large economic profit from its existing product employ a fast-second strategy in relationship to new or improved products? What risks does it run in pursuing this strategy? What incentive does a firm have to engage in R&D when rivals can imitate its new products?

A dominant firm that is making large profits from its existing products may let smaller firms in the industry incur the high costs of product innovation while it closely monitors their successes and failures. In using this "fast, second strategy," the dominant firm counts on its own product improvement abilities, marketing prowess, or economies of scale to prevail.

A firm that attempts to imitate the new products of rival firms may encounter a variety of roadblocks. Patent rights for a secret process may stop the effort cold or lead to costly lawsuits.

Developing new products can be very profitable and there are several protections, and advantages to taking the lead including: patent protection, copyrights and trademarks, lasting brand name recognition, benefits from trade secrets and learning by doing, high economic profits during the lag time between a products introduction and its imitation, and the possibility of lucrative buyout offers from larger firms'.

26-10   Do you think the overall level of R&D would increase or decrease over the next 20 to 30 years if the lengths of new patents were extended from 20 years to, say, "forever"? What if the duration were reduced from 20 years to, say, 3 years?

If patent rights were extended indefinitely the motivation to spend on R&D could increase for two reasons. First the extended patent rights would add to their potential value and second, perpetual patent rights would provide an additional incentive to find a way around these rights. Firms would be motivated to seek other products and processes not covered by the endless patent restrictions.

If the restriction were reduced to a much shorter period of three years, the spending on R&D would be likely to decrease. The short period of protection would make it difficult to recover the costs of development.

26-11   Make a case that neither pure competition nor pure monopoly is very conducive to a great deal of R&D spending and innovation. Why is oligopoly more favorable to R&D spending and innovation than either pure competition or pure monopoly? What is the inverse-U theory and how does it relate to your answers to these questions?

For a purely competitive firm, the expected rate of return on R&D may be low or even negative. Because of easy entry, its profit rewards from innovation may quickly be competed away by existing or entering firms that also produce the new product or adopt the new technology. The small size of the firm would make it difficult to finance the R&D as well.

The pure monopoly market structure may provide the least incentive to engage in R&D. Absolute barriers prevent competition. The only incentive for R&D expenditures would be defensive, to reduce the risk of some new product or process that could destroy the monopoly.

The oligopoly market structure has many characteristics that are conducive to technological advance. First, the large size enables them to finance the often very expensive R&D costs associated with major product or process innovation. The typical firm in oligopoly is likely to realize ongoing economic profits, which provides a ready source of funds. The existence of barriers to entry gives some assurance that any economic profits earned from innovation can be maintained. The large volume of sales allows the firm to spread the cost of R&D over a great many units of output. The large size of the firms in oligopoly also make it easier to absorb the inevitable losses from "misses" while waiting for compensation from the "hits."

The inverted-U theory suggests that R&D expenditures as a percentage of sales rise with industry concentration until the four-firm concentration ratio reaches about 50%. Further increases in industry concentrations are associated with lower relative R&D expenditures. (See figure 26-8) The inverted-U theory reiterates the assessment made above regarding likely R&D spending and market structure.

26-12 Evaluate: "Society does not need laws outlawing monopolization and monopoly. Inevitably, monopoly causes its own self-destruction, since its high profit is the lure for other firms or entrepreneurs to develop substitute products."

Innovation can reduce or even disintegrate existing monopoly power by producing competition where there was none. According to Schumpeter, a new innovator will automatically displace any monopolist that no longer delivers superior performance. But many contemporary economists think this view reflects more wishful thinking than fact. Dominant firms have been known to persuade government to give them tax breaks, subsidies, and tariff protection to strengthen their market power. While innovation in general enhances economic efficiency, in some cases it can lead to entrenched monopoly power. Further innovation may eventually destroy this monopoly power, but the process of creative destruction is neither automatic nor inevitable.

26-13 (*Last Word*) Identify a specific example of each of the following in this Last Word:

   a. entrepreneurship,

   b. invention,

   c. innovation, and

   d. diffusion.

   (a) 1985- Ted Waitt starts a mail-order personal computer business (Gateway 2000) in his South Dakota barn.

   (b) 1947- AT&T scientists invent the "transfer resistance device" later known as the transistor. It replaces the less reliable vacuum tubes in computers.

   (c) 1981- Logitech commercializes the "x-y position indicator for a display system." Invented earlier by Douglas Engbart in a government funded research lab. Someone dubs it a "computer mouse" ... because it appears to have a tail.

   (d) 1982 Compaq Computer "clones" the IBM machines; others do the same. Eventually Compaq becomes the leading seller of personal computers.

CHAPTER TWENTY-SEVEN
THE DEMAND FOR RESOURCES

CHAPTER OVERVIEW

This chapter and the next two chapters survey resource pricing. The basic analytical tools involved in this survey are the demand and supply concepts of earlier chapters. While the present chapter focuses on resource demand, the following two chapters couple resource demand with resource supply in explaining the prices of human and property resources.

The two most basic points made in this chapter are closely related. First the MRP = MRC rule for resource demand is developed. Most students will recognize that the rationale here is essentially the one underlying the MR = MC rule of previous chapters, but that the orientation now is in terms of units of input rather than units of output. Second, the MRP = MRC rule is applied under the assumption that resources are being hired competitively to explain why the MRP curve is the resource demand curve.

Resource demand curves are developed for both purely competitive and imperfectly competitive sellers, but the emphasis is on the pure competition model in the hiring of resources. Also covered are changes in resource demand and the elasticity of resource demand.

The final section applies the equimarginal principle to the employment of several variable resources. An extended numerical example is used to help students understand and distinguish between the least-cost and profit-maximizing rules. Instructors who omitted the optional chapter on consumer behavior may want to ignore this final section of the chapter. Its omission will not disrupt ensuing chapters.

WHAT'S NEW

The section on "Real-World Applications" has been eliminated and a section called "Occupational Employment Trend" has been added, with new tables showing the ten fastest growing jobs in the U.S., and the ten U.S. occupations with the largest absolute job growth. Note that the tables have been renumbered.

The Last Word has been updated. The Web-Based Questions are new.

INSTRUCTIONAL OBJECTIVES

After completing this chapter, students should be able to:

1. Present four major reasons for studying resource pricing.

2. Explain the concept of derived demand as it applies to resource demand.

3. Determine the marginal-revenue-product schedule for an input when given appropriate data.

4. State the principle employed by a profit-maximizing firm in determining how much of a resource it will employ.

5. Apply the MRC = MRP principle to find the quantity of a resource a firm will employ when given the necessary data.

6. Explain why the MRP schedule of a resource is the firm's demand schedule for the resource in a purely competitive product market.

7. Explain why the resource demand curve is downward sloping when a firm is selling output in a purely competitive product market; an imperfectly competitive product market.

8. List the three determinants of demand for a resource and explain how a change in each of the determinants would affect the demand for the resource.

9. Explain what demand factors have influenced the growth of the occupations listed in Tables 27.4 and 27.5.

10. List four determinants of the price-elasticity of demand for a resource, and state how changes in each would affect the elasticity of demand for a resource.

11. State the rule for determining the least-cost combination of resources.

12. Find the least-cost combination of resources when given appropriate data.

13. State the rule used by a profit-maximizing firm to determine how much of each of several resources to employ.

14. When given necessary data, find the quantities of two or more resources a profit-maximizing firm will hire.

15. Explain the marginal productivity theory of income distribution and present two criticisms of it.

16. Define and identify terms and concepts listed at the end of the chapter.

COMMENTS AND TEACHING SUGGESTIONS

1. In many ways this chapter completes a circle of reasoning that was started in the early class meetings. It affords many opportunities to reinforce, and give examples of, principles that were introduced earlier in the semester.

2. Use a circular flow diagram to explain derived demand and illustrate the connection between the product and resource market. Review consumer sovereignty, stressing that it is the buyers of the final product that direct the resources, much like the conductor of a symphony orchestra directing the musicians on what and when to play.

3. Profit maximization occurs in the product market at the quantity of output where marginal cost equals marginal revenue. Show the students that in the resource market an analogous rule applies. Profit maximization occurs where the marginal resource cost of a factor of production is equal to its marginal revenue product. In terms of hiring it is a simple cost, benefit analysis. A numerical example is helpful to pull together the many important relationships.

4. The marginal revenue product of a factor of production traces that factor's demand schedule. The MRP is a marriage of MR and MP; this can be used to demonstrate the reasons for a change in demand for a resource. These shifts can be explained as affecting MP (the productivity of the resource) or MR (implying a change in the price of the final product).

The third explanation for a change in demand for a resource, a change in the price of a substitute or complementary resources allows an opportunity to review the same type of shifts in the product market. Be sure to point out the output effect for substitute resources. Price elasticity of demand can also be reviewed comparing the determinants of elasticity in the product market with the determinants in the resource market, stressing the differences and the reasons for them.

5. Finally, the least-cost rule is another example of the equimarginal principle first introduced in Chapter 21 (consumer behavior). Least-cost production of any specific level of output requires the last dollar spent on each resource to yield the same marginal product. Point out the analogous objective of the consumer to have the last dollar spent on each item yield equal marginal utility. Both are optimization problems and both are solved by requiring that the dollars do equal work at the margin.

STUDENT STUMBLING BLOCK

The similarity between product and resource markets is both a help and a hindrance. Students understand the concepts of market-determined equilibrium price and quantity. However, because the profit-maximizing relationship is so closely related to concepts in the product market, students must be reminded by repeated emphasis that resource markets are distinct and play a very different role in our economic system. The role that resource markets play in income determination cannot be emphasized enough, because it is the foundation for understanding the issues surrounding income inequality in later chapters (and in real life).

LECTURE NOTES

I.   Review the circular flow model (Figure 2-6).

II.   Resource Pricing

    A. Resources must be used by all firms in producing their goods or services; the prices of these resources will determine the costs of production.

    B. Significance of resource pricing:

        1. Money incomes are determined by resources supplied by the households. In other words, firm expenditures eventually flow back to the household in the form of wages, rent, and interest. (Figure 2-6)

        2. Resource prices determine resource allocation.

        3. Resource prices are input costs. Firms try to minimize these costs to achieve productive efficiency and profit maximization.

        4. There are ethical and policy issues concerning income distribution:

            a. Income distribution (Chapter 34);

            b. Income tax issues;

            c. Minimum wage law; and

            d. Agricultural subsidies.

III. Marginal productivity theory of resource demand: assuming that a firm sells its product in a purely competitive product market and hires its resources in a purely competitive resource market.

    A. Resource demand is derived from demand for products that the resources produce.

    B. The demand for a resource is dependent upon:

        1. The productivity of the resource;

        2. The market price of the product being produced.

    C. Discussion of Table 27.1:

        1. Review of the Law of Diminishing Returns;

        2. Review the significance of the fixed product price;

3. Determination of Total Revenue (TR) and Marginal Revenue Product (MRP); MRP is the increase in total revenue that results from the use of each additional unit of a variable input.

$$MRP = \frac{\text{Change in Total Revenue}}{\text{Change in Resource Quantity}}$$

4. MRP depends on productivity of input (recall that marginal product of inputs falls beyond some point in production process due to law of diminishing marginal returns).

5. MRP also depends on price of product being produced.

D. Rule for employing resources is to produce where MRP = MRC.

1. To maximize profits, a firm should hire additional units of a resource as long as each unit adds more to revenue than it does to costs. (MRC is the marginal-resource cost or the cost of hiring the added resource unit.) Equation form:

$$MRC = \frac{\text{Change in Total Resource Cost}}{\text{Change in Resource Quantity}}$$

2. Under conditions of pure competition in the labor market where the firm is a "wage taker," the wage is equal to the MRC.

3. MRP will be the firm's resource (labor) demand schedule in a competitive resource market because the firm will hire (demand) the number of resource units where their MRC is equal to their MRP. For example, the number of workers employed when the wage (MRC) is $12 will be 2; the number of workers hired when the wage (MRC) is $6 will be 5. In each case, it is the point where the wage (MRC of worker) equals MRP of last worker (Figure 27.1).

IV. **Marginal productivity theory of resource demand: assuming that a firm sells its product in an imperfectly competitive product market and hires its resources in a purely competitive resource market.**

A. Discussion of Table 27.2:

1. Note that the product price decreases as more units of output are sold.

2. TR = output x product price.

3. $MRP = \dfrac{\text{Change in Total Revenue}}{\text{Change in Resource Quantity}}$

B. MRP of imperfectly competitive seller falls for two reasons: Marginal product diminishes as in pure competition, and product price falls as output increases. Figure 27.2 illustrates this graphically.

V. **Market demand for a resource will be the sum of the individual firm demand curves for that resource.**

VI. **Determinants of Resource Demand:**

A. Changes in product demand will shift the demand for the resources that produce it (in the same direction).

B. Productivity (output per resource unit) changes will shift the demand in same direction. The productivity of any resource can be altered in several ways:

1. Quantities of other resources

2. Technical progress

3. Quality of variable resource.

C. Prices of other resources will affect resource demand.

   1. A change in price of a substitute resource has two opposite effects.

      a. Substitution effect example: Lower machine prices decrease demand for labor.

      b. Output effect example: Lower machine prices lower output costs, raise equilibrium output, and increase demand for labor.

      c. These two effects work in opposite directions—the net effect depends on magnitude of each effect.

   2. Change in the price of complementary resource (e.g., where a machine is not a substitute for a worker, but machine and worker work together) causes a change in the demand for the current resource in the opposite direction. (Rise in price of a complement leads to a decrease in the demand for the related resource; a fall in price of a complement leads to an increase in the demand for related resource). (See Table 27.3 for summary)

D. Occupational Employment Trends:

   1. Changes in labor demand will affect occupational wage rates and employment. (Wage rates will be discussed in Chapter 28.)

   2. Discussion of fastest growing occupations. (Table 27.5)

   3. Discussion of occupations with the greatest absolute job growth. (Table 27.6)

VII. Elasticity of resource demand is affected by several factors.

A. Formula of elasticity of resource demand:

$$\left(Erd = \frac{\text{percentage change in resource quantity}}{\text{percentage change in resource price}} \right)$$

measures the sensitivity of producers to changes in resource prices.

B. If Erd > 1, the demand is elastic; if Erd < 1, the demand is inelastic; and if Erd = 1, demand is unit-elastic.

C. Determinants of elasticity of demand:

   1. Rate of decline in marginal product: If MRP changes slowly as units of resource are added, the demand for resource will be elastic, because a small decline in price of resource will lead to a big increase in the quantity demanded; a small increase in resource cost will lead to a big decrease in quantity demanded.

   2. Ease of resource substitutability: The easier it is to substitute, the more elastic the demand for a specific resource

   3. Elasticity of product demand: The more elastic the product demand, the more elastic the demand for its productive resources.

   4. Resource-cost/total-cost ratio: The greater the proportion of total cost determined by a resource, the more elastic its demand, because any change in resource cost will be more noticeable.

VIII. **Optimal Combination of Resources**

    A. Two questions are considered.

       1. What is the least-cost combination of resources to use in producing any given output?

       2. What combination of resources (and output) will maximize a firm's profits?

    B. The least-cost rule states that costs are minimized where the marginal product per dollar's worth of each resource used is the same. Example: MP of labor/labor price = MP of capital/capital price. (Key Questions 4 and 5)

       1. Long-run cost curves assume that each level of output is being produced with the least-cost combination of inputs.

       2. The least-cost production rule is analogous to Chapter 21's utility-maximizing collection of goods.

    C. The profit-maximizing rule states that in a competitive market, the price of the resource must equal its marginal revenue product. This rule determines level of employment MRP(labor) / Price(labor) = MRP(capital) / Price(capital) = 1.

    D. See examples of both rules in Table 27.7.

IX. **Marginal Productivity Theory of Income Distribution**

    A. "To each according to what one creates" is the rule.

    B. There are criticisms of the theory.

       1. It leads to much inequality, and many resources are distributed unequally in the first place.

       2. Monopsony and monopoly interfere with competitive market results with regard to prices of products and resources.

X. **LAST WORD: Input Substitution: The Case of ATMs**

    A. Theoretically, firms achieve the least-cost combination of inputs when the last dollar spent on each makes the same contribution to total output; rule implies that firms will change inputs in response to technological change or changes in input prices.

    B. A recent real-world example of firms using the least cost combination of inputs is in the banking industry, in which ATMs are replacing human bank tellers.

       1. Between 1990-2000, 80,000 human tellers lost their jobs, and more positions will be eliminated in the coming decade.

       2. ATMs are highly productive: A single machine can handle hundreds of transactions daily, millions over the course of several years.

       3. The more productive, lower-priced ATMs have reduced the demand for a substitute in production.

ANSWERS TO END-OF-CHAPTER QUESTIONS

27-1 What is the significance of resource pricing? Explain how the factors determining resource demand differ from those underlying product demand. Explain the meaning and significance of the notion that the demand for a resource is a derived demand. Why do resource demand curves slope downward?

The Demand for Resources

All resources that enter into production are owned by someone, including the most important resource of all for most people, self-owned labor. The most basic significance of resource pricing is that it largely determines people's incomes. Resource pricing allocates scarce resources among alternative uses. Firms take account of the prices of resources in deciding how best to attain least-cost production.

Finally, resource pricing has a great deal to do with income inequality and the debate as to what government should or should not do to lessen this inequality. It is here that the factors that determine resource demand are most different from those that determine demand for products. Demand for products is a question of income and tastes. But resource demand is more passive in the sense that it is derived from the demand for the products the resource can produce. If a resource can't be used in production of a desired product, there will not be any demand for it. Additionally, resources are often less mobile than products, so their geographic location relative to demand for the output they produce may be an important factor determining demand for resources in particular geographic areas.

Resources, factors of production, are not hired or bought because their employer or buyer desires them for themselves. The demand for resources is entirely derived from what the firm believes the resources can produce. If there were no demand for output, there would be no demand for input.

The demand for a resource depends, then, on how productive it is in producing output and on the price of the output. The demand for a resource is downward sloping because of the diminishing marginal product of the resource (because of the law of diminishing returns) and, in imperfectly competitive markets, also because the greater the output, the lower its price.

27-2　(*Key Question*) Complete the following labor demand table for a firm that is hiring labor competitively and selling its product in a competitive market.

Units of labor	Total product	Marginal product	Product price	Total revenue	Marginal revenue product
0	0	____	$2	$____	
1	17	____	$2	____	$____
2	31	____	2	____	
3	43	____	2	____	____
4	53	____	2	____	____
5	60	____	2	____	____
6	65	____	2	____	____
					____

a.　How many workers will the firm hire if the going wage rate is $27.95? $19.95? Explain why the firm will not hire a larger or smaller number of workers at each of these wage rates.

b.　Show in schedule form and graphically the labor demand curve of this firm.

c.　Now again determine the firm's demand curve for labor, assuming that it is selling in an imperfectly competitive market and that, although it can sell 17 units at $2.20 per unit, it must lower product price by 5 cents in order to sell the marginal product of each successive worker. Compare this demand curve with that derived in question 2b. Which curve is more elastic? Explain.

Marginal product data, top to bottom: 17; 14; 12; 10; 7; 5. Total revenue data, top to bottom: $0, $34; $62; $86; $106; $120; $130. Marginal revenue product data, top to bottom: $34; $28; $24; $20; $14; $10.

(a) Two workers at $27.95 because the MRP of the first worker is $34 and the MRP of the second worker is $28, both exceeding the $27.985 wage. Four workers at $19.95 because workers 1 through 4 have MRPs exceeding the $19.95 wage. The fifth worker's MRP is only $14 so he or she will not be hired.

(b) The demand schedule consists of the first and last columns of the table:

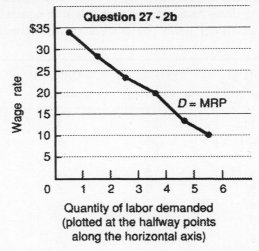

Quantity of labor demanded
(plotted at the halfway points
along the horizontal axis)

(c) Reconstruct the table. New product price data, top to bottom: $2.20; $2.15; $2.10; $2.05; $2.00; $1.95. New total revenue data, top to bottom: $0; $37.40; $66.65; $90.30; $108.65; $120.00; $126.75. New marginal revenue product data, top to bottom: $37.40; $29.25; $23.65; $18.35; $11.35; $6.75. The new labor demand is less elastic. Here, MRP falls because of diminishing returns *and* because product price declines as output increases. A decrease in the wage rate will produce less of an increase in the quantity of labor demanded, because the output from the added labor will reduce product price and thus MRP.

27-3 (Key Question) What factors determine the elasticity of resource demand? What effect will each of the following have on the elasticity or location of the demand for resource C, which is being used to produce product X? Where there is any uncertainty as to the outcome, specify the causes of the uncertainty.

a. An increase in the demand for product X.

b. An increase in the price of substitute resource D.

c. An increase in the number of resources substitutable for C in producing X.

d. A technological improvement in the capital equipment with which resource C is combined.

e. A decrease in the price of complementary resource E.

f. A decline in the elasticity of demand for product X due to a decline in the competitiveness of the product market.

Elasticity of demand for a resource is determined by: (1) the rate of decline of MP; (2) ease of resource substitutability; (3) elasticity of product demand; and (4) ratio of resource costs to total costs.

(a) Increase in the demand for resource C.

(b) Uncertainty relative to the change in demand for resource C; answer depends upon which is larger – the substitution effect or the output effect.

(c) Increase in the elasticity of resource C.

(d) Increase in the demand for resource C.

(e) Increase in the demand for resource C.

(f) Decrease in the elasticity of resource C.

27-4   (*Key Question*) Suppose the productivity of labor and capital are as shown in the accompanying table. The output of these resources sells in a purely competitive market for $1 per unit. Both labor and capital are hired under purely competitive conditions at $1 and $3, respectively.

Units of capital	MP of capital	Units of labor	MP of labor
1	24	1	11
2	21	2	9
3	18	3	8
4	15	4	7
5	9	5	6
6	6	6	4
7	3	7	1
8	1	8	1/2

a.   What is the least-cost combination of labor and capital to employ in producing 80 units of output? Explain.

b.   What is the profit-maximizing combination of labor and capital the firm should use? Explain. What is the resulting level of output? What is the economic profit? Is this the least costly way of producing the profit-maximizing output?

(a) 2 capital; 4 labor. $MP_L/P_L = 7/1$; $MP_C/P_C = 21/3 = 7/1$.

(b) 7 capital and 7 labor. $MRP_L/_L = 1 (= 1/1) = MRP_C/P_C = 1(= 3/3)$. Output is 142 (= 96 from capital + 46 from labor). Economic profit is $114 (= $142 - $38). Yes, least-cost production is part of maximizing profits. The profit-maximizing rule includes the least-cost rule.

27-5   (*Key Question*) In each of the following four cases MRP_L and MRP_C refer to the marginal revenue products of labor and capital, respectively, and P_L and P_C refer to their prices. Indicate in each case whether the conditions are consistent with maximum profits for the firm. If not, state which resource(s) should be used in larger amounts and which resource(s) should be used in smaller amounts.

a. $MRP_L = $8; P_L = $4; MRP_C = $8; P_C = 4

b. $MRP_L = $10; P_L = $12; MRP_C = $14; P_C = 9.

c. $MRP_L = $6; P_L = $6; MRP_C = $12; P_C = 12.

d. $MRP_L = $22; P_L = $26; MRP_C = $16; P_C = 19.

(a) Use more of both;

(b) Use less labor and more capital;

(c) Maximum profits obtained;

(d) Use less of both.

27-6   (*Last Word*) Explain the economics of the substitution of ATMs for human tellers. Some banks are beginning to assess transaction fees when customers use human tellers rather than ATMs. What are these banks trying to accomplish?

These banks are trying to produce using the least cost combination of resources. Given two resources, labor and capital, the least cost combination requires that the marginal product per dollar spent on each is equal.

$$\frac{MP_{Labor}}{P_{Labor}} = \frac{MP_{ATM} \ (Capital)}{P_{ATM} \ (Capital)}$$

With the introduction of the highly productive ATM machines, the MP/P of capital was greater than the MP/P of labor, to regain productive efficiency, (the least cost combination) the banks had to substitute capital for labor until the ratios are again equal.

$$\frac{MP_{Labor}}{P_{Labor}} < \frac{MP_{ATM} \ (Capital)}{P_{ATM} \ (Capital)}$$

Recall that using more of a resource lowers its marginal product and using less raises it.

27-7   Florida citrus growers say that the recent crackdown on illegal immigration is increasing the market wage rates necessary to get their oranges picked. Some are turning to $100,000 to $300,000 mechanical harvesters known as "trunk, shake, and catch" pickers, which vigorously shake oranges from trees. If widely adopted, what will be the effect on the demand for human orange pickers? What does that imply about the relative strengths of the substitution and output effects?

The effect of the adoption of the mechanical pickers will be to decrease the demand for human pickers. If this occurs, the substitution effect will have been greater than the output effect.

CHAPTER TWENTY-EIGHT
WAGE DETERMINATION

CHAPTER OVERVIEW

Building on the resource demand analysis of the previous chapter, this chapter provides a detailed supply and demand analysis of wage determination in a variety of possible labor market structures. Though the analysis may seem rigorous, it is little more than an application of supply and demand tools.

A discussion of the general level of real wages opens the chapter. The critical link between labor productivity and real wages merits emphasis as a theoretical and policy issue.

The section on wage determination in particular labor markets is the heart of the chapter. Competitive, monopsonistic, unionized, and bilateral monopoly market models are examined. Discussion of the effectiveness of unions in raising wages, and the complex issue of minimum wage laws follow.

Wage differentials are explained by the differences among worker characteristics, job characteristics, and lack of worker mobility. The chapter concludes with a discussion of pay schemes that link earnings to worker performance, their contributions to efficiency, and possible negative side effects.

WHAT'S NEW

The section on "Recent Stagnation of Real Wages" has been omitted. The graphs on Figure 28.3 have been transposed and the wage rate has been increased to $10. The section on monopsony discusses the monopsony power as well as pure monopsonies and updates some of the monopsony examples. The discussion of the minimum wage has been updated. A new Figure 28.9 has been added that shows how wage differentials are caused by supply and demand differences. "Stock options" has been added to the list of incentive pay devices. Global Perspective 28.2 has been eliminated.

One Web-Based Question has been revised and the other is new.

INSTRUCTIONAL OBJECTIVES

After completing this chapter, students should be able to:

1. Differentiate between nominal and real wages.

2. List those factors that have led to an increasing level of real wages in the U.S. historically.

3. Determine the equilibrium wage rate and employment level when given appropriate data for a firm operating in a purely competitive product and labor market; a firm operating in a monopolistically competitive product market and a purely competitive labor market; and a firm operating in a purely competitive product market and a monopsonistic labor markets.

4. Illustrate graphically how wage rates are determined in purely competitive and monopsonistic labor markets.

5. List the methods used by labor organizations to increase wages and the impact each has on employment. Give specific examples.

6. Illustrate graphically how an inclusive (industrial) union and an exclusive (craft) union would affect wages and employment in a previously competitive labor market.

7. Explain and illustrate graphically wage determination in the bilateral monopoly model.

8. Present the major points in the cases for and against the minimum wage.

9. Explain the demand factors that create wage differentials.

10. Explain the supply factors that create wage differentials.

11. Describe briefly salary systems in which pay is linked to performance rather than to time.

12. Describe the negative side effects of poorly planned incentive pay plans.

13. Define and identify terms and concepts listed at the end of the chapter.

COMMENTS AND TEACHING SUGGESTIONS

This chapter affords the opportunity for some community-based research.

1. Are local wages higher or lower than expected? Why? What factors contribute?

2. Is there a dominant industry in the community? Does it fit the monopsony model? Are the workers unionized?

3. Is the unemployment rate higher or lower than the current national average? Why?

4. If time permits a guest speaker such as a union leader and/or a director of human resources would be interesting.

(Last Word) Ask students to research the requirements for licensing and other barriers to entry to jobs that they would like to have. Have they, or a family member or friend, been turned down for employment because of a license, or certificate requirement? Are requirements in their field reasonable? Ask if they would favor dispensing with all professional licenses and government regulation of working conditions. Can they define what is "reasonable" in licensing requirements?

STUDENT STUMBLING BLOCK

The concept of monopsony hiring is not an easy one for students to grasp. However, the results of monopsony hiring make intuitive sense. It may be best to focus on the results first (fewer workers hired at a lower wage than would be the competitive outcome) and then address the theory. The results emphasize the importance of monopsony power in labor markets, which all students can grasp even if they have difficulty with the theory.

LECTURE NOTES

I.   **Introduction**

   A. Wage rates may be the most important price a student will encounter in his/her life.

   B. This chapter explores some of the factors behind the determination wage and wage differences. This is important since wages and salaries accounts for 80 percent of our national income when proprietors' income is included.

II. **Labor, Wages, and Earnings**

   A. Wages refer to the price paid for the use of labor.

      1. Labor may be workers in the popular sense of the terms blue-collar and white-collar workers.

      2. Labor also refers to professional people and owners of small businesses, in terms of the labor services they provide in operating their businesses.

B. Wages may take the form of bonuses, royalties, commissions, and salaries, but in this text the term "wages" is used to mean wage rate or price paid per unit of labor time.

C. It is important to distinguish between nominal and real wages.

1. Nominal wages are the amount of money received per hour, per day, per week and so on.

2. Real wages are the purchasing power of the wage, i.e., the quantity of goods and services that can be obtained with the wage. One's real wages depend not only on one's nominal wage but also on the price level of the goods and services that will be purchased.

3. Example: If nominal wages rise by 10 percent and there is a 5 percent rate of inflation, then the "real" wage rose only by 5 percent.

4. In this discussion, it is assumed that the price level is constant, and so the term "wages" is used in the sense of "real wages."

III. **The general level of wages differs greatly among nations, regions, occupations, and individuals. (See Global Perspective 28-1)**

A. Productivity plays an important role in determination of wages. Historically, American wages have been high and have risen because of high productivity. There are several reasons for this high productivity.

1. Capital equipment per worker is high—approximately $132,000 per worker.

2. Natural resources have been abundant relative to the labor force in the United States.

3. Technological advances have been generally higher in the U.S. than in most other nations, and work methods are steadily improving.

4. The quality of American labor has been high because of good education, health and work attitudes.

5. There are other, less tangible items underlying the high productivity of American workers.

a. Stable business, social and political environment.

b. Efficient, flexible management.

c. Vast size of the domestic market, which allows for economies of scale.

B. Real wages and productivity: real wages per worker can increase only at about the same rate as output per worker. This is illustrated historically for the U.S. in Figure 28.1.

C. There has been a long-term, secular growth pattern in real wages in the U.S. as seen in Figure 28.2.

IV. **A Purely Competitive Labor Market**

A. Analysis of the competitive labor market model.

1. Characteristics of a competitive labor market include:

a. Many firms competing to hire a specific type of labor,

b. Numerous qualified workers with identical skills available to independently supply this type of labor service, and

c. "Wage taker" behavior that pertains to both employer and employee; neither can control the market wage rate.

2. The market demand is determined by summing horizontally the labor demand curves (the MRP curves) of the individual firms, as suggested in Figure 28.3a (Key Graph).

3. The market supply will be determined by the amount of labor offered at different wage rates; more will be supplied at higher wages because the wage must cover the opportunity costs of alternative uses of time spent either in other labor markets or in household activities or leisure.

4. The market equilibrium wage and quantity of labor employed will be where the labor demand and supply curves intersect; in Figure 28.3a this occurs at a $10 wage and 1,000 employed. (Key Questions 3 and 4)

   a. Each individual firm will take this wage rate as given, and will hire workers up to the point at which the market wage rate is equal to the MRP of the last worker hired (according to the MRP = MRC rule). Note that the demand curve in Figure 28.3 is based on figures from Table 27.1 in the last chapter.

   b. For each firm, the MRC is constant and equal to the wage because the firm is a "wage taker" and by itself has no influence on the wage in the competitive model. (Table 28.1)

B. In the monopsony model, the firm's hiring decisions have an impact on the wage.

   1. Characteristics of the monopsony model:

      a. The firm's employment is a large portion of the total employment of a particular kind of labor.

      b. The type of labor is relatively immobile, either geographically or in the sense that to find alternative employment workers must acquire new skills.

      c. The firm is a "wage maker" in the sense that the wage rate the firm pays varies directly with the number of workers it employs.

   2. Complete monopsonistic power exists when there is only one major employer in a labor market; oligopsony exists when there are only a few major employers in a labor market. (Note: the root "sony" means "to purchase," whereas the root "poly" means "to sell.") The monopsonistic market is illustrated in Figure 28.4.

      a. The labor supply curve will be upward sloping for the monopsonistic firm; if the firm is large relative to the market, it will have to pay a higher wage rate to attract more labor.

      b. As a result, the marginal resource cost will exceed the wage rate in monopsony because the higher wage paid to additional workers will have to be paid to all similar workers employed. Therefore, the MRC is the wage rate of an added worker plus the increments that will have to be paid to others already employed. (See Table 28.2)

      c. Equilibrium in the monopsonistic labor market will also occur where MRC = MRP, but now the MRC is above the wage, so the wage will be lower than it would be if the market were competitive. As a result, the monopsonistic firm will hire fewer workers than under competitive conditions.

      d. Conclusion: In a monopsonistic labor market there will be fewer workers hired and at a lower wage than would be the case if that same labor market were competitive, other things being equal.

       e.   Illustrations: Nurses are paid less in towns with fewer hospitals than in towns with more hospitals. In professional athletics, players' salaries are held down as a result of the "player drafts" that prevent teams from competing for the new players' services for several years until they become "free agents." (Key Question 5)

C. Union models illustrate a different model of imperfect competition in the labor market where the workers are organized so that employers do not deal directly with the individual workers, but with their unions, who try to raise wage rates in several ways. There are three models of these methods.

    1. Unions prefer to raise wages by increasing the demand for labor. (Figure 28.5)

       a.   Unions may try to increase the demand for their products through advertising and through political lobbying to protect their jobs in various ways.

       b.   Unions sometimes increase productivity through training and joint labor-management committees designed to increase labor productivity.

       c.   Unions may try to increase the price of substitutes resources, thus increasing the demand for union workers, e.g., higher minimum wages.

       d.   Unions can increase the demand for their labor by supporting public actions that reduce the price of a complementary resource, e.g., utility prices.

    2. Exclusive or craft unions raise wages by restricting the supply of workers, either by large membership fees, long apprenticeships, or forcing employers to hire only union workers. (Figure 28.6)

    3. Occupational licensing requirements are another way of restricting labor supply in order to keep wages high. Six hundred occupations are licensed in the U.S.

    4. Inclusive or industrial unions do not limit membership but try (usually unsuccessfully) to unionize every worker in a certain industry so that they have the power to impose a higher wage than the employers would otherwise pay (Figure 28.7.) The bargained wage becomes the MRC for the employer between point "a" and point "e".

    5. Employers will hire fewer workers than they would if the workers were free to accept a lower wage.

       a.   Studies indicate that the size of the union advantage is between 10 and 15 percent.

       b.   The size of the unemployment effect will depend on certain factors.

          1. Growth in the economy—If demand is increasing, then this shift in labor demand can offset the unemployment effect of the union wage increase.

          2. If the demand for the product and/or labor is inelastic, the wage increase will not have as much effect on employment as it would if the demand were elastic.

D. Bilateral monopoly model occurs when a monopsonist employer faces a unionized labor force; in other words, both the employer and employees have monopoly power.

    1. In such a model, the outcome of the wage is indeterminate and will depend on negotiation (see Figure 28.8) and bargaining power.

    2. A bilateral monopoly may be more desirable than one-sided market power. In other words, if a competitive market does not exist, it may be more socially desirable to have power on both sides of the labor market, so that neither side exploits the other. This can be shown by comparing $Qu = Qm$ and Qc.

V. The minimum wage controversy concerns the effectiveness of minimum wage legislation as an antipoverty device. (Figure 28.7 and Figure 28.8 can be used by substituting the minimum wage for the bargained wage.)

A. The case against the minimum wage contains two major criticisms.

1. The minimum wage forces employers to pay a higher than equilibrium wage, so they will hire fewer workers as the wage pushes them higher up their MRP curve.

2. The minimum wage is not an effective tool to fight poverty. Most minimum wage workers are teens from affluent families who do not need protection from poverty.

B. The case for the minimum wage argues includes other arguments.

1. Minimum-wage laws occur in markets that are not competitive and not static. In a monopolistic market, the minimum wage increases wages with minimal effects on employment.

2. Increasing minimum wage may increase productivity.

a. Managers will use workers more efficiently when they have higher wages.

b. The minimum wage may reduce labor turnover and thus training costs.

C. Evidence and conclusions

1. During the 1980s, some unemployment resulted from the minimum wage, especially among teens, but the effect of increases during the 1990s were inconclusive.

2. Because many who are affected by the minimum wage are not from poverty families, an increase in the minimum wage is not as strong an antipoverty tool as many supports contend.

3. More workers are helped by the minimum wage than are hurt.

4. The minimum wage helps give some assurance that employers are not taking advantage of their workers.

VI. **Wage Differentials**

A. Table 28.3 gives a selection of wages in different occupations to illustrate the substantial differences among them.

B. Wage differentials can be explained by using supply and demand for various occupations.

1. Given the same supply conditions, workers for whom there is a strong demand will receive higher wages; given the same demand conditions, workers where there is a reduced supply will receive higher wages. (Figure 28.9)

2. The worker's contribution to the employer's total revenue (MRP) will depend upon the worker's productivity and the demand for the final product. (Figure 28.9 (a) and (b))

3. On the supply side, workers are not homogeneous, i.e., they are in noncompeting groups. These differences that determine these noncompeting groups are:

a. Ability levels differ among workers.

b. Education and training, i.e. "investment in human capital."

1. Figure 28.10 indicates that those with more years of schooling achieve higher incomes.

        2.   The pay gap between college graduates and high school graduates increased between 1980 and 2000.

        4.   Workers also will experience wage differentials partly due to "compensating differences" among jobs. These are the nonmonetary aspects of the job that may make some jobs preferable to others because of working conditions, location, etc. (Figure 28.9 (c) and (d))

D. Since market imperfections exist, labor markets are not perfectly competitive.

    1.   Workers may lack information about alternative job opportunities.

    2.   Workers may be reluctant to move to other geographic locations.

    3.   Artificial restraints on mobility may be created by unions, professional organizations, and the government.

    4.   Discrimination in certain labor markets may crowd women and minorities into certain labor markets and out of others.

VII.   Pay and performance are linked in many jobs, unlike the standardized wage rate per time unit.

A. When one considers workers as the firm's agents and the firm as the principal, the principal-agent problem emerges.

    1.   Both the workers and the firm want the firm to survive and be profitable.

    2.   If the agents do not perceive that the workers' and firm's interests are identical, there may be a problem, because workers will act to improve their own well-being, often at the expense of the firm. Some examples include loafing on the job, using company materials, and generally not working as hard as they might.

    3.   Some incentive methods of payment help to avoid the principal-agent problem.

        a.   With piece-rate payments, workers earn according to the quantity of output produced.

        b.   Commissions and royalties are payment schemes linked to the value of sales.

        c.   Bonuses, stock options, and profit sharing are other ways to motivate workers to have the same interests as the firm.

        d.   Efficiency wages are a way of providing incentives by paying workers above-equilibrium wages to encourage extra effort.

B. Pay for performance can help overcome the principle-agent problem and enhance worker productivity, but such plans can have negative side effects.

    1.   A rapid production pace can compromise quality and endanger workers.

    2.   Commissions may cause salespeople to exaggerate claims, suppress information, and use other fraudulent sales practices.

    3.   Bonuses based on personal performance may disrupt cooperation among workers.

    4.   Less energetic workers can take a "free ride" in profit sharing firms.

    5.   Firms paying "efficiency wages" may have fewer opportunities to hire the new workers who could energize the workplace.

VIII. LAST WORD: African-Style Hairbraiders and Stodgy Economists

A. Licensing requirements that are passed under the guise of protecting the "public interest" often benefit special interests by erecting barriers to entry in the marketplace.

B. The Example of Cornrows, Co. (a hairbraiding business) is a classic example of licensing as a barrier to entry. The license required a year of training in everything from manicures to eyebrow arching at a cost of thousands of dollars—but none of the classes covered hairbraiding techniques and other African styles.

C. Cornrows, Co. successfully challenged the city's outdated cosmetology code and was able to obtain a separate operating license with sensible training requirements.

ANSWERS TO END-OF-CHAPTER QUESTIONS

28-1   Explain why the general level of wages is higher in the United States and other industrially advanced countries. What is the single most important single factor underlying the long-run increase in average real-wage rates in the United States?

The general level of wages is higher in the United States and other industrially advanced nations because of the high demand for labor in relation to supply. Labor productivity is high in the U.S and other industrially advanced countries because: (1) capital per worker is very high; (2) natural resources are abundant relative to the size of the labor force particularly in the U.S.; (3) technology is advanced in the United States and other industrially advanced countries relative to much of the rest of the world; (4) labor quality is high because of health, vigor, training, and work attitudes compared to labor; (5) other factors contributing to high American productivity are the efficiency and flexibility of American management; the business, social, and political environment that greatly emphasizes production and productivity; and the vast domestic market, which facilitates the gaining of economies of scale.

The most important single factor underlying the long-run increase in average real wage rates in the United States is the increase in output per worker, that is, in productivity.

28-2   Why is a firm in a purely competitive labor market a wage taker? What would happen if it decided to pay less than the going market wage?

A firm in a purely competitive labor market is a wage taker because there are a large number of firms wanting to buy the labor services of the workers in that market and a large number of workers with identical skills wanting to sell their labor services. As a result, the individual firm has no control over the price of labor.

If a firm attempted to pay a wage below the going wage, no workers would offer their services to that firm.

28-3   (*Key Question*) Describe wage determination in a labor market in which workers are unorganized and many firms actively compete for the services of labor. Show this situation graphically, using W_1 to indicate the equilibrium wage rate and Q_1 to show the number of workers hired by the firms as a group. Show the labor supply curve of the individual firm, and compare it with that of the total market. Why the difference? In the diagram representing the firm, identify total revenue, total wage cost, and revenue available for the payment of nonlabor resources.

The labor market is made up of many firms desiring to purchase a particular labor service and of many workers with that labor service. The market demand curve is downward sloping because of diminishing returns and the market supply curve is upward sloping because a higher wage will be necessary to attract additional workers into the market. Whereas the individual firm's supply curve is perfectly elastic because it can hire any number of workers at the going wage, the market supply curve is upward sloping.

For the graphs, see Figure 28.3 and its legend.

28-4 *(Key Question)* Complete the accompanying labor supply table for a firm hiring labor competitively.

Units of labor	Wage rate	Total labor cost (wage bill)	Marginal resource (labor) cost
0	$14	$____	$____
1	14	____	____
2	14	____	____
3	14	____	____
4	14	____	____
5	14	____	____
6	14	____	____

a. Show graphically the labor supply and marginal resource (labor) cost curves for this firm. Explain the relationships of these curves to one another.

b. Plot the labor demand data of question 2 in Chapter 27 on the graph in part a above. What are the equilibrium wage rate and level of employment? Explain.

Total labor cost data, top to bottom: $0; $14; $28; $42; $56; $70; $84. Marginal resource cost data: $14, throughout.

(a) The labor supply curve and MRC curve coincide as a single horizontal line at the market wage rate of $14. The firm can employ as much labor as it wants, each unit costing $14; wage rate = MRC because the wage rate is constant to the firm.

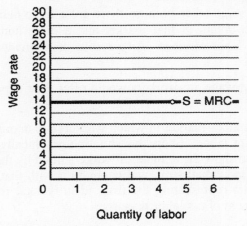

(b) Graph: equilibrium is at the intersection of the MRP and MRC curves. Equilibrium wage rate = $14; equilibrium level of employment = 4 units of labor. Explanation: From the tables: MRP exceeds MRC for each of the first four units of labor, but MRP is less than MRC for the fifth unit.

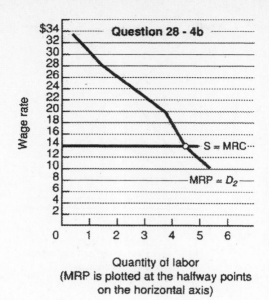

Quantity of labor
(MRP is plotted at the halfway points
on the horizontal axis)

28-5   Suppose that the formerly competing firms in question 3 form an employers' association that hires labor as a monopsonist would. Describe verbally the impact upon wage rates and employment. Adjust the market graph, showing the monopsonistic wage rate and employment level as W_2 and Q_2 respectively. Using this monopsony model, explain why hospital administrators frequently complain about a "shortage" of nurses. How might such a shortage be corrected?

The equilibrium wage in the monopsonistic market declines from the competitive market's W_1 rate to W_2. The employment level in this market will decline from Q_1 to Q_2. See Figure 28.4.

If there are only one or two hospitals in an area, there exists a monopsonistic market for nurses. Their wages would be less than those for nurses where there is competition among employers (numerous hospitals and/or clinics). Because hospitals prefer to hire more nurses at a wage W_2, they view the difference between Q_3 and Q_2 as a shortage. However, since their profits are maximized at W_2, they are unwilling to raise wages voluntarily. The hospital administrator might offer a higher wage, but this wage would not be profit maximizing. Another solution would be for nurses to organize and demand higher wages. This would allow nurses to earn wages closer to their MRP and as wages rise toward W_1, the shortage would disappear.

28-6   (Key Question) Assume a firm is a monopsonist that can hire the first worker for $6 but must increase the wage rate by $3 to attract each successive worker. Draw the firm's labor supply and marginal resource cost curves and explain their relationships to one another. On the same graph, plot the labor demand data of question 2 in Chapter 27. What are the equilibrium wage rate and level of employment? What will be the equilibrium wage rate and the level of employment? Why do these differ from your answer to question 4?

The monopsonist faces the market labor supply curve S—it is the only firm hiring this labor. MRC lies above S and rises more rapidly than S because all workers get the higher wage rate that is needed to attract each added worker. Equilibrium wage/rate = $12; equilibrium employment = 3 (where MRP = MRC). The monopsonist can pay a below -competitive wage rate by restricting its employment.

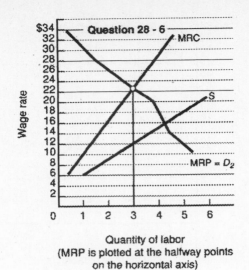

Question 28 - 6

Quantity of labor
(MRP is plotted at the halfway points
on the horizontal axis)

28-7 (*Key Question*) Assume a monopsonistic employer is paying a wage rate of W_m and hiring Q_m workers, as indicated in Figure 28.8. Now suppose that an industrial union is formed and that it forces the employer to accept a wage rate of W_c. Explain verbally and graphically why in this instance the higher wage rate will be accompanied by an increase in the number of workers hired.

The union wage rate Wc becomes the firm's MRC, which would be shown as a horizontal line to the left of the labor supply curve. Each unit of labor now adds only its own wage rate to the firm's costs. The firm will employ Q_c workers, the quantity of labor where MRP = MRC (= W_c); Qc is greater than the Q_m workers it would employ if there were no union and if the employer did not have any monopsonistic power, i.e., more workers are will to offer their labor services when the wage is Wc than Wm.

28-8 Have you ever worked for the minimum wage? If so, for how long? Would you favor increasing the minimum wage by a dollar? By two dollars? By five dollars? Explain your reasoning.

28-9 "Many of the lowest-paid people in society—for example, short-order cooks—also have relatively poor working conditions. Hence, the notion of compensating wage differentials is disproved." Do you agree? Explain.

Short-order cooks generally need few specific skills, i.e., practically anyone is thought to be capable of flipping burgers. Since the supply of unskilled workers is high relative to the demand for them, their wages are low. In this case, the concept of compensating wage differentials is swamped by the excess supply of low-wage workers.

28-10 What is meant by investment in human capital? Use this concept to explain (a) wage differentials, and (b) the long-run rise in real wage rates in the United States.

Investment in human capital is any action that improves a worker's the skills and abilities, i.e., increases the productivity of workers.

(a) Wage differentials are explainable to some extent through the concept of human capital investment. There is a strong positive correlation between time spent acquiring a formal education and lifetime earnings. Of course, it can be said that the brain surgeon who spent over twenty years in training, starting in grade 1, had the qualities to succeed in the labor market without spending over twenty years in school. Though this counter-argument has some merit, the point still is that this highly-skilled individual would never have become a brain surgeon without the over twenty years in school and might not have achieved the particular high income that goes with being a medical specialist.

(b) The long-run rise in real wage rates in the United States is positively correlated to investment in human capital. Without the increase in education and training of the American labor force that has occurred over the years, productivity (output per person per hour) would still have risen because of the investment in real capital, improved technology, and our abundant natural resource base. But the real wage would undoubtedly now be very much lower, because an unskilled labor force could not possibly have made efficient use of the material resources and advancing technology of the economy.

28-11 What is the principal-agent problem? Have you ever worked in a setting where this problem has arisen? If so, do you think increased monitoring would have eliminated the problem? Why don't firms simply hire more supervision to eliminate shirking?

Business owners who hire workers because they are needed to help produce the goods or services of the firm face the dilemma of the principal-agent problem. Workers are the agents; they are hired to promote the interests of the firm's owners (the principals). Owners and workers both have a common goal in the survival of the firm, but their interests are not identical. A principal-agent problem arises when those interests diverge. Workers may seek to increase their utility by shirking their responsibilities and providing less than the agreed upon effort. Owners of firms have a profit incentive to reduce or eliminate shirking. Hiring more supervisory personnel can be costly and there is no guarantee that it will eliminate the problem.

28-12 (*Last Word*) Do you think that African-style hairbraiders should be allowed to braid hair without a cosmetology license? If so, do you think that you would have the same view if you were a licensed cosmetologist?

Licensing requirements that are passed under the guise of protecting the "public interest" are often the work of special interest groups. Licensed cosmetologists benefit by limiting their numbers. Restrictions on entering the market allow the license holders to charge a higher price. Eliminating the barriers to entry will increase competition and lower the average compensation of the group. Economists are nearly unanimous in their opinion of trade barriers. They are against them.

CHAPTER TWENTY-NINE
RENT, INTEREST, AND PROFITS

CHAPTER OVERVIEW

In the preceding chapter, wages were accorded a lengthy discussion. In contrast, the discussions of the income shares—rent, interest, and profits—found in the present chapter are relatively brief. Because the theories of rent, interest, and profits are quite unsettled, and because together they constitute only 20 percent of national income, only the basic features of these income shares are covered.

The complete inelasticity of the supply of land and certain other natural resources is the foundation the analysis of economic rent. Related topics, such as differential rents and the single-tax movement, are presented.

The determination of the interest rate and its role in allocating loanable funds are briefly surveyed. In the discussion of profit, economic and accounting profits are differentiated. There is also an analysis of the sources and functions of profits. The chapter concludes with an overview of the relative shares of national income.

WHAT'S NEW

The chapter opener presents a number of questions. These questions are answered in the chapter discussion. The single tax discussion is presented as an application. The definition of interest has been expanded to include the idea that the lender is transferring purchasing power from the present to the future.

The two Web-Based Questions have been updated.

INSTRUCTIONAL OBJECTIVES

After completing this chapter, students should be able to:

1. Explain what determines economic rent.

2. Explain why economic rent is a surplus payment.

3. Explain the single-tax theory and its criticisms.

4. Explain what determines rent differentials.

5. Explain how rent functions as a cost to the individual firm.

6. Describe how the interest rate is determined.

7. Explain how business firms make investment decisions.

8. Distinguish between nominal and real interest rates.

9. State five factors which may cause interest rates to differ.

10. Distinguish between economic, normal, and accounting profits.

11. Explain why profits are received by some firms and not by others.

12. List three sources of economic profits.

13. Describe the general function of profits.

14. Summarize the current relative shares of national income.

15. Define and identify terms and concepts listed at the end of the chapter.

COMMENTS AND TEACHING SUGGESTIONS

1. To discuss the complexities of the ethical issues addressed by Henry George and the "single taxers," ask students whether income in the form of land rent is any more "unearned" than interest earned on inherited cash, stocks, bonds, and other financial resources, or the income of a well-coordinated 7'2" professional basketball player.

2. In classes of above-average students or business majors, a discussion of the time value of money and the procedures for calculating discounted present values may be useful. An investigation of the long-run relative constancy of real interest rates at about 3 percent may also be of interest, particularly in light of the fact that it has been higher than this in the recent past. Students might question why the rate has been constant and what might cause it to change.

3. The Last Word for this chapter is a pragmatic look at different methods of calculating interest rates. The Truth in Lending Act can be discussed here in terms of government reducing information costs to consumers. Also interesting is the "rule of 70," which allows savers to calculate the length of time it takes their savings to double if interest is compounded. Divide the rate of interest into 70 to get a close estimate of the number of years for doubling time, e.g., at 7 percent it would take 70/7 or 10 years for savings to double. The Federal Reserve System's catalog of *Public Information Materials* lists several relevant publications that are available in classroom quantities. The catalog is available from your regional Federal Reserve Bank. An example is the pamphlet, "The Arithmetic of Interest Rates," published by the Public Information Dept., Federal Reserve Bank of New York, 33 Liberty St., New York, NY 10045.

STUDENT STUMBLING BLOCKS

1. Because students are used to thinking in terms of labor income of various kinds, it is easy for them to dismiss the importance of rent, interest, and profits. One tip is to have students imagine an economic system in which these types of "capitalist" income did not exist. This was largely the case under the centrally planned system of the former Soviet economy. If rent and interest do not reflect resource scarcity, it is easy to imagine valuable (by our standards) pieces of property being used for low-priority uses. Such inefficient use of resources was common in planned socialist systems. Point to examples of the surge of entrepreneurial activity in Russia and other former Soviet states as illustrations of how the profit motive "works." It is easy for students to forget the importance of these "unearned" types of income for the smooth functioning of an economic system.

2. Students are notoriously ignorant about profits. Surveys of public knowledge about profits generally show that people believe the rate of profit on sales or equity may average as much as 50 percent. *They seem to confuse profits with retail markups.* It may be useful to have students examine corporate profits in more detail, using sources such as the Commerce Department's monthly, *Survey of Current Business*, publications by Standard and Poor's, or Moody's, or annual reviews of corporate performance in periodicals such as *Fortune* magazine's "Fortune 500." Discussion of the rate of profit relative to sales revenue and relative to owners' equity also furthers their understanding of the relative importance of profits.

LECTURE NOTES

I.   **Introduction**

A. Emphasis in previous two chapters was on labor markets, because wages and salaries account for about 70 percent of our national income. (If proprietors' income, which is largely labor income, is added to wages and salaries, the return to labor increases to 80 percent.)

B. This chapter focuses on the other three sources of income—rent, interest, and profits—which compose the remaining 20 percent of our national income.

C. This chapter will answer each of the following questions:

1. Why do different parcels of land in different locations receive different rent payments?

2. What factors determine interest rates and causes interest rates to change?

3. What are the sources of profits and losses and why do profits and losses change over time?

II. **Economic rent is the price paid for use of land and other natural resources that are fixed in supply. (Note that this definition differs from the everyday use of the term.)**

A. As presented in Chapter 27, the demand for land is downward sloping because of diminishing returns and the fact that producers must lower the price of the product to sell additional units of output.

B. Perfectly inelastic supply of the resource is one unique feature of the supply side of the market that determines rent. Land has no production cost; it is a "free and nonreproducible gift of nature." Its quantity does not change with price (with a few exceptions).

C. Changes in demand therefore determine the amount of rent. This will be determined by several factors. (See Figure 29.1)

1. The price of the product grown on the land,

2. The productivity of the land, and

3. The prices of other resources combined with the land for production.

D. Land rent is viewed as a surplus payment because it performs no incentive function to provide more supply; it is not necessary to ensure the availability of land.

E. Some argue that rent should be taxed away, since it is unearned, or that land should be nationalized and owned by the state.

1. Henry George's proposal for a single tax of up to 99 percent of land rent asserted that this tax could eliminate other taxes. Unlike the effect of a tax on other resources, the tax on land would not have a negative incentive effect.

2. Critics of the single-tax idea make several points.

a. Current levels of government spending are too great to be supported by rent taxes.

b. It is difficult to separate the rent component from other income resulting from the combined use of land with other resources.

c. Unearned income goes beyond land and land ownership; capital gains and interest income might also be considered unearned.

d. It is unfair to tax current owners, who may have paid a steep market price for the land and therefore find that the rent return is not high relative to that price.

E. Each parcel of land is not equally productive. More productive land will be in great demand and therefore will receive different rents. These different rent payments allocate land to its most productive use.

F. In reality, land has alternative uses and costs. From society's perspective, rent is a surplus; but an individual firm must pay rent to attract the land away from alternative uses. Without rent to allocate land among its various uses, there would be no market mechanism to make sure each piece of land was being utilized in its most valuable fashion. Therefore, rent does provide an important function to our economic system.

III. **Interest is the price paid for the use of money. It is usually viewed as the money that must be paid for the use of one dollar for one year.**

   A. Two aspects of interest are important.

     1. It is stated as a percentage, and the Truth in Lending Act of 1968 requires lenders to state the costs and terms of consumer credit in terms of an annualized interest rate.

     2. Money itself is not an economic resource, but it is used to acquire capital goods, so in hiring money capital, businesses are ultimately buying the use of real capital goods.

   B. The loanable funds theory of interest.

     1. The supply of loanable funds is an upward-sloping curve—a larger quantity of funds will be made available at high interest rates than at low interest rates. Most individuals prefer present consumption and must be paid to defer consumption by saving.

     2. The demand for loanable funds is inversely related to the rate of interest. At higher interest rates fewer investment projects will be profitable since fewer projects yield the high rate of return needed to compensate for the high interest cost.

     3. Economists disagree about the responsiveness of the quantity of investment funds supplied to changes in interest rates. Most economists believe that saving is relatively insensitive to interest rate changes and believe the supply of funds is inelastic.

     4. Whether the curves are elastic or inelastic, the equilibrium interest rate equates the quantities of loanable funds supplied and demanded. (See Figure 29-2)

     5. Households rarely lend savings directly to businesses. Households place their savings in financial institutions and receive an interest payment. Businesses borrow funds from financial institutions and pay an interest payment.

     6. Changes in the supply of funds may occur as a result of changes in tax policy or social insurance benefits.

     7. Anything that changes the rates of return on potential investments, such as improvements in technology or a decrease in the demand of the final product, will change the demand for funds.

     8. Both households and businesses operate on both the supply and demand sides of the market for loanable funds. While households supply loanable funds, they may also borrow to finance large purchases and education. Similarly, businesses may save in the market for loanable funds, and governments may borrow to finance deficits.

   C. Banks and other financial institutions not only gather and make available the savings of households, but also create funds through the lending process.

   D. There are many different interest rates with different names and they vary for many reasons. (See Table 29.1)

     1. Varying degrees of risk (riskier loans carry higher rates),

     2. Differing maturities on the loan (higher rates usually on longer-term loans),

     3. The size of the loan (larger loans have lower rates),

4. Taxability (interest on some local and state bonds is tax-free; the interest would be lower, since lenders don't have to pay federal taxes on that interest income),

5. Market imperfections play a role, because some banks in smaller towns have more market power than banks that have a lot of competition.

E. Economists usually refer to what is called the "pure rate of interest," which is best approximated by the interest paid on long-term, riskless bonds such as the long-term bonds of the U.S. government. In spring 2001 this rate was 5.5 percent. The current rate can be found in the third section of the daily *Wall Street Journal* and other publications.

F. The role of the interest rate is important because it affects both the level and composition of investment and R&D spending.

1. The level of investment varies inversely with the interest rate. The Federal Reserve System will increase and decrease the money supply and thus influence interest rates. Changes in investment will affect the level of GDP.

2. Interest rates will also have an effect on borrowing for R&D. Again, R&D depends upon the cost of borrowing money as compared to the expected rate of return on the R&D project.

3. Nominal interest rates are those stated in terms of current dollars; the "real" interest rate is the rate of interest expressed in terms of dollars of constant or inflation-adjusted value. The real interest rate is the nominal rate minus the rate of inflation.

5. It is the real interest rate, not the nominal rate, that businesses should consider in making their investment and R&D decisions.

G. Application: Usury laws specify maximum interest rate that can be charged on loans. The purpose is to make borrowing more accessible to low-income borrowers. However, Figure 29-2 demonstrates several problems with usury laws.

1. There will be a shortage of credit if the usury rate is below the market rate. Riskier borrowers may be excluded from borrowing from established financial institutions.

2. Credit-worthy borrowers will be able to borrow at below-market "prices."

3. Lenders will receive less than market rates of return on the funds loaned.

4. Funds will not be allocated to their most efficient use.

IV. **Economic profits are what remains of a firm's total revenue after it has paid individuals and other firms for materials, capital and labor supplied to the firm (the explicit costs) and allowed for payment to self-employed resources (the implicit costs).**

A. The role of the entrepreneur is most important in a capitalist economy. Profits are the reward paid for entrepreneurial ability, which includes taking initiative in combining resources for production, making nonroutine policy decisions, introducing innovations in products and production processes, and taking risks associated with the uncertainty of all of the above functions.

1. A normal profit is the minimum required to retain the entrepreneur in some specific line of production.

2. An economic profit is any profit above the normal profit. This residual profit also goes to the entrepreneur. This residual profit does not exist under pure competition in a static economy. It occurs because of the dynamic nature of real-world capitalism and the presence of monopoly power.

B. There are several sources of economic profits, but they would not occur in a static, unchanging economy. Thus, the first prerequisite is that the economy be dynamic.

   1. In a dynamic economy, the future is uncertain and some risks cannot be insured against.

   2. Uninsurable risks stem from three general sources:

      a. Changes in the general economic environment

      b. Changes in the structure of the economy; and

      c. Changes in government policy.

   3. Some or all of the economic profit in a real, dynamic economy may be compensation for risk taking.

   4. Some of the economic profit may be compensation for dealing with the uncertainty of innovation.

   5. Monopoly power is a less desirable source of economic profits because such profits stem from a misallocation of resources.

C. The functions of profits include the following:

   1. The expectation of profits encourages firms to innovate, which stimulates new investment. This will expand output and employment.

   2. Profits allocate resources among alternative lines of production. Resources leave unprofitable ventures and flow to profitable ones, which is where society is signaling it wants these resources to be allocated.

V. **Labor income is the dominant type of income, with wages and salaries constituting about 70 percent of national income. If one adds in a part of proprietors' income, which is probably largely labor income, the share rises to about 80 percent. Therefore, the "capitalists'" share of income is only about 20 percent. These percentages have remained remarkably stable in the U.S. since 1900.**

VI. **LAST WORD: Determining the Price of Credit**

A. To determine the interest rate, one compares the interest paid with the amount borrowed: If you borrow $10,000 and agree to repay that amount plus $1,000 at the end of the year, the interest rate is 10 percent.

$$r = \$1,000/\$10,000 = 10\%$$

B. In some cases a lender will discount the interest payment at the time the loan is made, so the borrower would pay the $1,000 and receive the remaining $9,000 for an 11 percent rate of interest.

$$r = \$1,000/\$9,000 = 11\%$$

C. In other cases the financial institution uses a 360-day year instead of 365 days to calculate the interest rate, because it is simpler to calculate monthly rates (twelve 30-day months), but this does reduce interest paid.

D. If the loan is paid back in installments, the process becomes more complicated because on average the borrower had only half the loan for the full year, so $r = \$1,000/\$5,000 = 20$ percent on an annual basis.

E. Another fact that influences the effective interest rate is whether or not it is compounded. If it is, then interest is added on to the deposit as it is earned and the new amount earns interest. Compound interest on deposits is effectively more than simple interest. The more often it is compounded, the more the effective rate will be.

F. "Let the buyer beware" is a fitting motto in the world of credit.

ANSWERS TO END-OF-CHAPTER QUESTIONS

29-1   How does the economist's use of the term "rent" differ from everyday usage? Explain: "Though rent need not be paid by society to make land available, rental payments are very useful in guiding land into the most productive uses."

In everyday usage, "rent" is the term used to describe the payment that must be paid for the legal borrowing of some good or service. One pays rent for the use of a house or apartment; or one rents a tool from the equipment rental company. When paying this rent one is paying for part of the capital cost of the commodity, plus its maintenance, plus a share of the taxes on it, plus profit to the owner.

An economist defines rent much more restrictively: Economic rent is the price paid for the use of land and other natural resources which are completely fixed in total supply.

Land is completely fixed in total supply. No matter how high the rent, no more can be brought into use. Thus rent serves no incentive function; the same amount of land will be available no matter how high the rent. But the resulting argument that rent is a surplus that could be eliminated without reducing the supply is to look at it from the viewpoint of society only.

The fact is that land has alternative uses. To get land into its most productive use, individuals and firms must compete and the winners are those who will pay the highest rent. It only makes sense to outbid someone else for any particular land if the winner expects to make more profitable use of it than the losers, that is, employ it in its most productive use.

29-2   (*Key Question*) Explain why economic rent is a surplus to the economy as a whole but a cost of production from the standpoint of individual firms and industries. Explain: "Rent performs no incentive function in the economy."

Land is completely fixed in total supply. As population expands and the demand for land increases, rent first appears and then grows. From society's perspective this rent is a surplus payment unnecessary for ensuring that the land is available to the economy as a whole. If rent declined or disappeared, the same amount of land would be available. If it increased, no more land would be forthcoming. Thus, rent does not function as an incentive for adding land to the economy.

But land does have alternative uses. To get it to its most productive use, individuals and firms compete and the winners are those who pay the highest rent. To the high bidders, rent is a cost of production that must be covered by the revenue gained through the sale of the commodities produced on that land.

29-3   If money capital is not an economic resource, why is interest paid and received for its use? What considerations account for the fact that interest rates differ greatly on various types of loans? Use these considerations to explain the relative size of the interest rates charged on the following.

a.   A 10-year $1000 government bond

b.   A $20 pawnshop loan

c.   A 30-year mortgage loan on a $145,000 house

d. A 24-month $12,000 commercial bank loan to finance the purchase of an automobile

e. A 60-day $100 loan from a personal finance company

Though money is not in itself productive, it is useful for acquiring resources that are productive. In borrowing money, businesses get the use of it to buy factories, machines, and equipment that are productive and with which the businesses hope to make a profit. Thus, it makes economic sense to pay for the use of money. It would make no economic sense to lend money without charging interest, for the lender has the alternative of buying productive real capital or consumer goods with it.

There are many considerations involved in the fact that interest rates differ greatly on various types of loans. (1) Risk: The greater the chance the borrower will not repay, the higher the interest rate. (2) Maturity: The longer the term of the loan, the higher the interest rate to compensate the lender for the risk of being without the use of the money for an extended period of time. (3) Loan size: The smaller the loan, the higher the interest rate because the administrative costs of large and small loans are about the same absolute amounts. (4) Taxability: The interest payments on certain state and municipal bonds being nontaxable, the interest that lenders require as payment is lower. (5) Market imperfections: The small firm in a small town with only one bank will likely pay a higher interest rate on a loan than the large corporation with access to the world money markets, even though the smaller firm may well represent less of a risk of default than the large corporation. The market simply cannot assess the credit-worthiness of the small firm, which is not able, in any event, to shop around in New York, London, or Tokyo.

(a) A 10-year $1000 government bond will have a relatively low rate of interest because it is riskless: The Federal government cannot default (since its promise to repay is in currency that the government can have printed). However, the term to maturity normally would lead to a higher interest rate than a shorter-term government bond. The loan size is irrelevant here because the government pays the same interest regardless of the bond's denomination.

(b) A $20 pawnshop loan will have a high rate of interest. There's good chance the good pawned will not be redeemed but, in this case, the pawnbroker is not really at risk. The pawned article undoubtedly has a resale value greater than $20. The high interest rate in fact helps ensure that the good will not be redeemed—to the pawnbroker's benefit. The high interest rate also compensates for the small size of the loan.

(c) Mortgages are generally large loans at a relatively low interest rate. The loan is for a very long term and the house is pledged as collateral. Under certain circumstances, the loan may qualify for a government-subsidized mortgage insurance program, which insures the lender against default. Additionally, the borrower may deduct the interest from his/her taxable income. These contrasting considerations result in a lower interest rate than most types of long-term loans.

(d) A 24-month $12,000 commercial bank loan to finance the purchase of an automobile will certainly have a higher interest rate than a government bond, but its risk is reduced by the fact that the automobile serves as collateral for the loan. However, the bank would rather get its money back than a used car, so the bank certainly does not consider the loan riskless. The loan is of a relatively large size; this will tend to lower the interest rate. The outcome of these conflicting considerations is an interest rate lower than for a straight, unsecured, consumer loan but higher than for a loan to a well-established business.

(e) A 60-day $100 loan from a personal finance company will have the highest rate of all, except possibly for the pawnshop loan. Though it is very short term, it is considered relatively high risk, because otherwise the borrower would have gotten the loan from a bank; and the loan size is very small, making the administrative costs high in relation to the loan size. Also, the fact that it is a personal loan implies there is no collateral like a car or home to back it up.

29-4   (*Key Question*) Why is the supply of loanable funds upsloping? Why is the demand for loanable funds downsloping? Explain the equilibrium interest rate. List some factors that might cause it to change.

(a) The supply of loanable funds is upsloping because savers will make more funds available at higher interest rates than lower interest.

(b) The demand of loanable funds is downsloping because there are few investment and R&D projects that yield a high rate of return and many more that will yield a lower rate of return.

(c) The equilibrium interest rate is determined where the interest rate (cost of borrowing the funds) is equal to the expected rate of return (the expected benefit from borrowing the funds and engaging in the investment or R&D project). The supply of loanable funds may change because of a change in households' attitudes about saving (tax policies, macroeconomic conditions) or changes in Federal Reserve policies relative to the money supply. The demand for loanable funds could change as a result a change in technology or a change in the demand for the final product. If there is either a change in supply of or demand for loanable, the interest rate will change.

29-5   What are the major economic functions of the interest rate? How might the fact that many businesses finance their investment activities internally affect the efficiency with which the interest rate performs its functions?

There are two major economic functions of the interest rate. (1) Interest rates affect the level of domestic output as the monetary authorities deliberately vary them by changing the money supply. Low interest rates encourage investment, and this tends to expand the economy. High interest rates discourage investment and this tends to restrain inflation or contract the economy. (2) Interest rates allocate capital to its most productive uses. When interest rates are, say, at 10 percent, a project that expects to earn 8 percent after the payment of all costs will not be undertaken, because the cost of the borrowed money is greater than the return expected on it. This is true even if the firm is using its own money. Why make 8 percent on the project with the firm's money when lending it will earn 10 percent? On the other hand, all projects that are expected to return more than the interest rate will be undertaken. The interest rate thus allocates money capital to those investments that are most productive, that is, which have the highest rate of return.

To the extent that firms truly are profit maximizers, the internal financing of investment should make no difference to the investment decision. One invests if the expected rate of return is greater than the rate of interest; one does not if the rate of interest is greater. However, firms are probably somewhat less anxious about what happens to money that they do not have to pay back. In other words, the efficiency with which the interest rate performs its functions is probably lessened the more firms finance their investments internally.

29-6   (*Key Question*) Distinguish between nominal and real interest rates. Which is more relevant in making investment and R&D decisions? If the nominal interest rate is 12 percent and the inflation rate is 8 percent, what is the real rate of interest?

The nominal interest rate is the interest rate stated in dollars of current value (unadjusted for inflation). The real interest rate is the nominal interest rate adjusted for inflation (or deflation). The real interest rate is more relevant for making investment decisions—it reflects the true cost of borrowing money. It is compared to the expected return on the investment in the decision process. Real interest rate = 4 percent (= 12 percent -8 percent).

29-7   Historically, usury laws which put below-equilibrium ceilings on interest rates have been used by some states on the grounds that such laws will make credit available to poor people who could not otherwise afford to borrow. Critics of such laws contend that it is poor people who are most likely to be hurt by such laws. Which view is correct?

The critics are probably closer to the truth than the legislators. The relatively high interest rates charged in a free market to those with little or no collateral to put up as security on a loan is demanded by banks and other legitimate lending institutions because of the additional risk of nonrepayment involved. No doubt, banks are sometimes a little more hardhearted with the poor than is necessary to keep the banks viable; they may well charge a little more than the risks really require. However, when laws are passed preventing banks and other legitimate lending institutions from charging the rate they think is justified, these institutions simply stop lending to the poor entirely.

So, the poor, who were supposed to be helped, end up going to loan sharks and others outside the law, who charge truly usurious interest rates running into the hundreds of percent a year and who demand an arm and a leg as security. Sometimes literally!

29-8   (*Key Question*) How do the concepts of accounting profits and economic profits differ? Why are economic profits smaller than accounting profits? What are the three basic sources of economic profits? Classify each of the following in accordance with these sources:

a.   A firm's profits from developing and patenting a new medication that greatly reduces cholesterol and thus diminishes the likelihood of heart disease and stroke.

b.   A restaurant's profit that results from construction of a new highway past its door.

c.   The profit received by a firm benefiting from an unanticipated change in consumer tastes.

Accounting profit is what remains of a firm's total revenues after it has paid for all the factors of production employed by the firm (its explicit costs) but not for the use of the resources owned by the business itself. Economists also take into consideration implicit costs—the payment the owners could have received by using the resources they own in some other way. The economist adds these implicit costs to the accountant's explicit costs to arrive at total cost. Subtracting the total cost from total revenue results in a smaller profit (the economic profit) than the accountant's profit.

Sources of economic profit: (1) uninsurable risks; (2) innovations; and (3) monopoly.

(a) Profit from assuming the uncertainities of innovation, as well as monopoly profit from the patent.

(b) Monopoly profit arising from its locational advantage.

(c) Profit from bearing the uninsurable risk of a change in demand (the change could have been unfavorable).

29-9   Why is the distinction between insurable and uninsurable risks significant for the theory of profits? Carefully evaluate: "All economic profits can be traced to either uncertainty or the desire to avoid it." What are the major functions of profits?

An insurable risk does not fatally affect the profit and loss of a firm. The firm insures against fire and theft and so on and then goes about its business, secure in the knowledge that it cannot suffer an irreparable loss if one of the insured-against events occurs.

Economic profit (and serious loss) occurs when the firm takes uninsurable risks. Such risks relate to uncontrollable and unpredictable changes in demand and supply conditions. An insurance company is most unlikely to insure against a serious recession occurring in the next year or so or against the price of oil skyrocketing—or, if one did, the premium the insurance company would demand would be greater than the profit a firm could expect to make by forecasting these events correctly. Thus, firms must risk that the demand for their products in the future will give them adequate revenue to cover their future costs that, too, they must take the risk of estimating. If the firms are successful, they have earned their economic profits.

"All economic profits can be traced to either uncertainty or the desire to avoid it." A considerable amount of economic profits can be traced to either uncertainty or the desire to avoid it, but not all. There is clearly uncertainty in trying to estimate future demand and supply conditions. A firm cannot be sure what it will get for its output, what the input will cost, and the consequent economic profit or loss. There is also much uncertainty with regard to innovation. Will it fly (literally) or in the sense of being able to convince people to buy the new or redesigned product? Or will all of the revenue needed to pay back the development costs be gained before freeloading copiers come on the market with their versions?

However, though monopoly economic profits may be the product of the same types of uncertainty just discussed, they are by no means entirely so. It is De Beers' tight control of the supply of diamonds that has ensured its continuing economic profits, not favorable changes in the public's demand for diamonds.

The major functions of profits include providing an incentive for entrepreneurial initiative in combining resources to produce a good or service; for innovation in the form of new products or production processes; and for taking the risks which the entrepreneur bears by operating in a dynamic and uncertain environment. Profits also allocate resources among alternative lines of production. Entrepreneurs seek profits and shun losses, which means industries will expand as long as they experience economic profits and contract when they experience losses.

29-10 Explain the absence of economic profit in a purely competitive, static economy. Realizing that the major function of profits is to allocate resources according to consumer preferences, describe the allocation of resources in such an economy.

A static economy is changeless; everything is constant. There is no innovation; there is no economic uncertainty. There is no question of uninsurable risks that entrepreneurs can take in the hope of gaining economic profits. There are no uninsurable risks to be taken. Moreover, since the economy is also purely competitive, there can be no economic profit gained through monopoly power.

The allocation of resources in a static, changeless, purely competitive economy would be in accordance with whatever the consumer preferences were when the economy became static.

29-11 What is the rent, interest, and profit share of national income if proprietors' income is included within the labor (wage) share?

If proprietors' income is included within the labor share of income, wages would be almost 80 percent of national income. That leaves about 20 percent of the national income in the form of rent, interest and profit—a relatively small share and a share that has been remarkably stable in the United States since 1900.

29-12 (*Last Word*) Assume you borrow $5,000 and pay back the $5,000 plus $250 in interest at the end of the year. What is the interest rate? What would the interest rate be if the $250 of interest had been discounted at the time the loan was made? What would the interest rate be if you were required to repay the loan in 12 equal monthly installments?

Simple interest in the first case is 5 percent. ($250 / $5000 × 100)

In the second case the amount received at the time of borrowing would be $4750, so the interest rate is slightly higher at 5.26%. ($250 / $4750 × 100)

If you repaid the loan in twelve monthly installments and the interest payments still were equal to $250, then you have repaid $5250 total, but you have repaid part of the principal each month. Therefore, you did not borrow the entire $5000 for the whole year. Without having the exact equation to solve this problem, you could estimate that you borrowed on average $2500 for the whole year, since you would have paid back about half by the sixth month and reduced the principal by about 1/12 for every month thereafter. This means that the $250 is about 10 percent of the average amount borrowed.

CHAPTER THIRTY
GOVERNMENT AND MARKET FAILURE

CHAPTER OVERVIEW

Chapter 5 covered the economic functions of government, some facts about government expenditures and taxes, and the growth of the public sector. The present chapter extends and deepens our understanding of government's role in a market-oriented economy. In the process, the authors identify some of the problems the government faces in carrying out its economic functions.

The chapter begins by examining the topic of market failure. Through marginal analysis, there is a fuller discussion of public goods and externalities than is found in Chapter 5. Various approaches for limiting negative externalities are also presented. The growing pollution problem, including global warming, is discussed.

The end of the chapter addresses the problem of information failures in the private sector and possible government solutions to this problem.

WHAT'S NEW

The chapter material has been tightened and reorganized. Much of the section "A Closer Look at Pollution" has been eliminated; some of the material is dealt with in the discussion of externalities. The discussion on "Solid Waste Disposal and Recycling" has been retained and a discussion on "Global Warming " has been added. The term "benefit-cost analysis" has been changed to "cost-benefit analysis". A new cost-benefit example is used in Table 30.2.

The Last Word is new. One Web-Based Question has been revised and the other is new.

INSTRUCTIONAL OBJECTIVES

After completing this chapter, students should be able to:

1. Describe graphically the collective demand curve for a particular public good and explain this curve.

2. Explain why the supply curve for public goods is upward sloping and explain how the optimal quantity of a public good is determined.

3. Identify the purpose of cost-benefit analysis and explain the major difficulty in applying this analysis.

4. Explain what is meant by spillovers or externalities.

5. Describe graphically and verbally how an overallocation of resources results when spillover costs are present and how this can be corrected by government action.

6. Describe graphically and verbally how an underallocation of resources occurs when spillover benefits are present and how this can be corrected by government action.

7. Explain the Coase theorem, its significance, and the three conditions necessary for it to work.

8. Describe three policies that would reduce negative externalities.

9. Use an example to explain a market for pollution rights and how this market would lead to a better allocation of resources.

10. Relate the law of conservation of matter and energy to the pollution problem.

11.   Using supply and demand diagrams, explain the economics of recycling.

12.   Discuss the predicted effects of global warming and how cost-benefit could be used to determine international policies and goals

13.   Give two examples of how inadequate information about sellers can create a market failure.

14.   Explain the moral hazard and adverse selection problems faced by sellers.

15.   Define and identify terms and concepts listed at the end of the chapter.

COMMENTS AND TEACHING SUGGESTIONS

1.   The difficulties, yet importance, of using cost-benefit analysis can be demonstrated through class role-playing exercises in which students consider the costs and benefits of various proposals for public investment projects under consideration in their community, state, or region. Even national projects can be considered. Citizens and legislators often consider only the costs of a proposed project without considering the benefits (or the reverse). Have students identify an actual issue in which benefit-cost analysis would be appropriate, analyze if it has been used, and, if so, discuss the outcome. A debate over whether it is appropriate to use an efficiency standard (using benefit-cost) or a safety standard in regulation will be interesting as this is an ongoing issue.

2.   The concept of selling pollution rights is generally an unfamiliar and interesting topic for class discussion. It highlights the economic advantages of this type of pollution control over blanket regulation. Since the use of pollution rights is expanding and they are actually traded now on commodity exchanges, it would be a good topic for students to research in recent periodicals.

3.   Another activity useful for illustrating concepts in this chapter is the budget game. You can devise your own version of the game by taking major categories from the federal, state, or local budget and creating a worksheet whereby the students have the actual budget figures for each of perhaps, ten categories. Then tell them that the budget must be cut by a certain dollar figure or by a certain percentage and have them decide which categories must be reduced and which have priority for maintaining current spending (or even increasing current levels). This can be a group or individual exercise, but at the end of the exercise, have each student or each group explain their decision. This usually leads to some lively discussion as groups will undoubtedly have different priorities. Be sure to emphasize cost-benefit thinking during this exercise.

STUDENT STUMBLING BLOCKS

1.   External costs and benefits are not easy concepts for students to grasp because our systems of economic measurement (national income accounts, etc.) traditionally ignore them. For example, the average person thinks of investment in pollution control as a cost having no productive return. However, once students grasp the concept of external benefits, they can understand that not all positive production is measured officially. Yet the benefits from investment in pollution control are real and often can and should be measured. The difficult point to grasp is that markets do fail and that the public sector can have a positive role to play when this happens.

2.   Students easily confuse the concept of "public goods" as defined by economists with the goods and services that are provided by the public sector. The two are not necessarily synonymous. For example, electric power is provided by the public sector in some areas and by private corporations in other areas. This provides a good example of the fact that goods and services provided by the government do not necessarily fit the definition of "public goods and services."

Government and Market Failure: Public Goods, the Environment, and Information

LECTURE NOTES

I.   Introduction

    A. We all use the goods and services that are provided by government.

    B. The questions to be answered are why the private sector does not provide these goods and services efficiently and what is the role of government in bringing about a better allocation of resources.

II.   Public Goods

    A. Unlike private goods, public goods are those goods that are indivisible and for which the exclusion principle does not apply. (Recall that the exclusion principle refers to the characteristic of private goods that allows the purchaser of the good to consume or use that product with the ability to exclude others from using it.)

    B. Public goods suffer from the free-rider problem, where a consumer can enjoy the benefit of the good without having to pay for the benefit.

    C. The demand for public goods differs from the market demand for private goods.

        1. It is a "phantom" demand since the consumers will not be making individual purchases.

        2. To find the collective demand schedule for a public good, we add the prices people collectively are willing to pay for the last unit of the public good at each quantity demanded (Table 30.1).

        3. Figure 30.1 is a graphical illustration of this table. A collective demand curve is the vertical sum of the individual demand curves for the public who want that good. (Key Question 1)

        4. Recall that the market demand for a private good was a horizontal summation of the individual demand curves.

    D. The supply curve for any good is its marginal cost curve. As with private goods, the law of diminishing returns applies to the supplying of public goods.

    E. The optimal quantity of a public good can be determined by comparing the collective demand curve with the supply (marginal cost) curve to determine their point of intersection or by looking at the demand and supply (marginal cost) schedules to see at what price and quantity marginal benefit equals marginal cost.

    F. Cost-benefit analysis is a technique for decision making in the public sector.

        1. The concept involves comparing the benefit of providing incremental units of public goods with the costs of providing these additional units. Note that the comparison is a marginal one, i.e., the comparison is made between the costs and benefits of additional amounts of a public good or service.

        2. Table 30.2 illustrates this concept in determining the scope of a national highway construction project. Four possible phases of projects are considered, with costs and benefits compared. By comparing the marginal costs and benefits as one moves from the least expensive phase to the most-expensive phase, we see Plan C is the optimal choice.

        3. The rule for this decision-making technique is to use the marginal benefit = marginal cost rule; if the marginal cost exceeds the marginal benefit, that part of the project should not be included.

4. The problem with this technique is the difficulty in measuring costs and benefits. Benefits are particularly difficult to estimate, because there are so many related aspects that are not easily calculated. Nevertheless, this method is widely used. (Key Question 3)

III. **Externalities revisited**

A. Figures 30.2a and 30.2b, respectively, illustrate that an overallocation of resources occurs when spillover costs are present and an underallocation of resources occurs when spillover benefits are present.

1. Spillover costs occur when producers are able to shift some of their costs onto the community.

2. Spillover benefits occur when the benefits of a good are received by others in the community although they did not pay for them. These benefits are not reflected in the individual demand curve.

B. One approach to reducing the externality or misallocation problem is the market approach of individual bargaining.

1. The Coase theorem, named after Nobel prize-winning economist Ronald Coase, suggests that spillover costs and benefits will not occur and government intervention is not necessary when property rights are clearly defined, the number of people involved is small, and bargaining costs are negligible.

2. Government's role should be to encourage bargaining wherever possible, rather than to get involved in direct restrictions or subsidies.

3. The extended example in the text looks at the owner of a forest who wants to contract with a logging company to clear-cut his land. The land surrounds a lake with a nationally known resort, which depends on the beauty of the forest for its success. Should the state or government intervene?

    a. The Coase theorem would assign property rights over the issue and let both parties negotiate a solution. Since the forest owner has the right over the trees, the resort should negotiate to reduce the logging impact because it has economic incentive to do so. The resort owner should be willing to pay the forest owner to avoid or minimize the spillover cost.

    b. The Coase theorem argues that it doesn't matter which party is assigned the property rights. If the resort owner had been assigned the right to prevent logging, the forest owner would have to negotiate and pay the resort owner for the right to cut the forest. Both parties would have an economic incentive to eliminate the externality in this situation also. In the unlikely event that this were the case, the resort owner's property would have been much more valuable in the first place, because it included the rights over the logging permission.

4. Limitations exist with the Coase theorem, because many problems involving externalities affect many people and bargaining is too costly and inefficient to accomplish solutions effectively.

C. A second approach is by the assignment of liability through lawsuits. If one property owner damages another, a private lawsuit may settle the dispute by assessing damage liability on the violator. Once again, however, this solution is limited to cases in which the damaged parties can afford to initiate the suit, or in the case of many people, can organize to sue.

D. A third approach is to apply direct government controls or taxes to reduce negative externalities or spillover costs, or to provide subsidies or government provision where spillover benefits exist.

1. Direct controls place limits on the amount of the offensive activity that can occur. Clean air and water legislation are examples. The effect is to force the offenders to incur costs associated with pollution control. This should shift the product supply curve leftward and reduce the equilibrium quantity. Therefore, it should reduce the resource allocation in a socially optimal way.

2. Specific taxes can be levied on pollutors. The tax payment will increase costs to the producer, shifting the product supply curve leftward, and reducing resource allocation to this type of production as desired. (See Figure 30.3)

3. Subsidies and government provision suggest three options.

   a. Buyers may be subsidized. For example, new parents may be given coupons to receive inoculations at reduced prices for their children. This would increase the number of vaccinations and eliminate the underallocation of resources (Figure 30.4 a and b).

   b. Producers could be subsidized so that producers' costs are reduced, thus shifting the supply curve rightward, increasing equilibrium output, and eliminating the underallocation shown in Figure 30.4c.

   c. The government could provide the product as a public good where spillover benefits are extremely large. An example would be administering free vaccines to all children in India to end smallpox. (Key Question 4)

E. A fourth corrective approach is the development of markets for externality rights. This is the latest policy innovation for dealing with pollution abatement.

1. A pollution-control agency decides the acceptable amount of pollution in a particular region and creates rights that firms can purchase to allow them to pollute. Each right will allow a certain amount of pollution. The total supply of rights is perfectly inelastic (Figure 30.5).

2. The demand for rights should be downward sloping. At high prices, polluters will either stop polluting or pollute less by acquiring pollution-abatement equipment, which is more attractive when the rights are more expensive.

3. With the given supply of rights, and a demand for rights, an equilibrium price will be established for each right to pollute.

4. There are several advantages to this system.

   a. It reduces society's costs because pollution rights can be bought and sold. Some firms will find it cheaper to buy the rights than to acquire abatement equipment; other firms can sell their rights because they may be able to reduce pollution at a lower cost; in both situations, the firms reduce their cost below what the cost would have been under direct controls.

   b. Conservation groups as well as producers can buy rights. If conservation groups are unhappy with the existing amount of pollution, they can acquire pollution rights and hold them.

   c. The revenue from the sale of pollution rights could be used to improve the environment.

        d. The rising cost of pollution rights should lead to improved pollution-control techniques.

        e. A market for air pollution rights has emerged and is expanding.

F. Table 30.3 reviews the methods for correcting externalities.

G. Society's optimal amount of externality reduction is not necessarily total elimination.

    1. The cost of reducing spillover costs increases with each additional unit of reduction. The benefit received from each additional unit of reduction decreases due to diminishing marginal utility.

    2. In general, the marginal benefit of reducing pollution should equal the marginal cost. At this point, society has found its optimal amount of pollution abatement (Figure 30.6).

    3. In reality it is difficult to measure benefits as well as costs, but this analysis demonstrates that some degree of pollution may be socially efficient.

H. Solid-waste disposal and recycling problems occur with increasing frequency in crowded urban areas where there is high opportunity cost involved in the use of land for landfills. There is an ongoing demand for more recycling of solid wastes.

    1. The root of the problem with solid-waste disposal is the law of conservation of matter, i.e., matter can be transformed into other matter or energy but it never vanishes.

    2. Figure 30.7 illustrates the economics of recycling from a market perspective, indicating the demand and supply of recyclable items.

    3. Government policies with regard to recycling take two forms.

        a. Demand incentives include: (1) placing taxes on non-recycled substitute resources, thus increasing the demand for recyclable materials; and (2) requiring recycled products be used in goods purchased by the government.

        b. Supply incentives include encouraging recycling by providing low-cost or free pickup of household recyclable goods.

I. Global warming

    1. The global warming problem is an example of how cost-benefit analysis can be used to establish policies that will deal with a global environmental problem.

    2. Scientific evidence suggests that carbon dioxide and other gas emissions are creating a greenhouse effect.

    3. It is predicted that all regions of the world will experience climatic changes.

    4. Industrially advanced countries agreed in the Kyoto Protocol of 1997 to reduce their gas emissions 6 to 8 percent below 1990 levels by 2012.

    5. In setting policies and goals, the costs and benefits of the reduction in gas emissions must be considered.

IV. **Information failures are another form of market failure. Buyers or sellers have incomplete or inaccurate information and the cost of obtaining better information is often prohibitive.**

A. Inadequate information about sellers—two examples:

    1. Assume that the gasoline market exists in an absurd situation in which there is no system of weights and measures established by law. In such a world, the station could advertise

high-octane gas that was actually low-octane gas; pumps could register more gallons than were actually being pumped. Without government regulation, one could imagine some incentive for some stations to cheat in such ways. Government intervenes in such markets to prevent such cases of market failure. This provides reliable information to buyers and also helps sellers through enforcement of fair sales practices.

2. Licensing of surgeons is another example in which the consumer would find it difficult to gather information about a physician's expertise without government licensing standards. Such standards set minimum standards for competence. There will still be physicians of varying abilities, but the consumer can be confident that basic standards were met.

B. Inadequate information about buyers may lead to potential problems for sellers.

1. The moral hazard problem occurs when there is a tendency of one party to a contract to alter his/her behavior in ways that are costly to the other party. Examples include the driver who behaves more recklessly after obtaining insurance; guaranteed contracts for athletes, which may reduce their performance; unemployment compensation insurance, which may discourage incentives to work.

2. The adverse selection problem arises when information known by the first party to a contract is unknown to the second and, as a result, the second party incurs major costs. Examples include those in poor health who take out health insurance, the person planning an arson attempt who takes out fire insurance, and the person whose marriage is failing who takes out the book's hypothetical "divorce" insurance. In areas where insurance is traditionally underprovided, the government has provided insurance or subsidized insurance.

3. Workplace safety becomes a problem if workers do not know particular occupations or workplaces are less safe than others. Without accurate information about employers (buyers), workers will not demand higher wages for less-safe jobs. This is a market failure involving information about buyers (employers) where the government has intervened.

    a. Government can directly provide information to workers.

    b. Policies can mandate that firms provide information.

    c. Standards of workplace safety can be set.

4. Qualification: There are private methods of overcoming lack of information problems.

    a. Product warranties overcome lack of information about the seller or product.

    b. Franchising helps set uniform standards, so that most McDonalds or Holiday Inns have similar quality.

    c. Firms have specialized in providing information to buyers and sellers; consumer reports, travel guides, and credit-checking agencies are some examples.

V. **LAST WORD: Lojack: A Case of Positive Externalities**

A. Lojack is a device that can be installed in a car. If activated by police, it gives the police the car's precise location.

B. Not only has this device resulted in benefits to the owners of the cars who have installed the device by increasing the retrieval rate from 60 percent to 95 percent, it has had a positive spillover effect upon other car owners.

C. Police have been able to intercept cars while the thieves are still driving them. Police have been able to trace the cars with the device to "chop shops."

D. Some state have mandated a reduction in insurance premium for car owners who have installed the device in order to encourage an increase in sales of the device.

E. Ayres and Leavitt contend that the current levels of insurance discounts are too small to correct for the underallocation of the product that results from the positive externalities created by Lojack.

ANSWERS TO END-OF-CHAPTER QUESTIONS

30-1   (*Key Question*) On the basis of the three individual demand schedules below, and assuming these three people are the only ones in the society, determine (a) the market demand schedule on the assumption that the good is a private good, and (b) the collective demand schedule on the assumption that the good is a public good. Explain the differences, if any, in your schedules.

Individual #1		Individual #2		Individual #3	
Price	Q_d	*Price*	Q_d	*Price*	Q_d
$8	0	$8	1	$8	0
7	0	7	2	7	0
6	0	6	3	6	1
5	1	5	4	5	2
4	2	4	5	4	3
3	3	3	6	3	4
2	4	2	7	2	5
1	5	1	8	1	6

(a) Private good, top to bottom: P = $8, Q = 1; P = $7, Q = 2; P = $6, Q = 4; P = $5, Q = 7; P = $4, Q = 10; P = $3, Q = 13; P = $2, Q = 16; P = $1, Q = 19. (b) Public good, top to bottom; P = $19, Q = 1; P = $16, Q = 2; P = $13, Q = 3; P = $10, Q = 4; P = $7, Q = 5; P = $4, Q = 6; P = $2, Q = 7; P = $1, Q = 8. The first schedule represents a horizontal summation of the individual demand curves; the second schedule represents a vertical summation of these curves. The market demand curve for the private good will determine—in combination with market supply—an actual price-quantity outcome in the marketplace. Because potential buyers of public goods do not reveal their individual preferences in the market, the collective demand curve for the public good is hypothetical or needs to be determined through "willingness to pay" studies.

30-2   (*Key Question*) Use your demand schedule for a public good determined in question 1 and the following supply schedule to ascertain the optimal quantity of this public good. Why is this the optimal quantity?

Optimal quantity = 4. It is optimal because at 4 units the collective willingness to pay for the final unit of the good (= $10) matches the marginal cost of production (= $10).

P	Qs
$19	10
16	8
13	6
10	4
7	2
4	0

30-3   (*Key Question*) The following table shows the total costs and total benefits in billions for four different antipollution programs of increasing scope. Which program should be undertaken? Why?

Program	Total Cost	Total Benefit
A	$ 3	$ 7
B	7	12
C	12	16
D	18	19

Program B since the marginal benefit no longer exceeds marginal cost for programs that are larger in scope. Plan B is where net benefits—the excess of total benefits over total costs—are maximized.

30-4   (*Key Question*) Why are spillover costs and spillover benefits also called negative and positive externalities? Show graphically how a tax can correct for a spillover cost and a subsidy to producers can correct for a spillover benefit. How does a subsidy to consumers differ from a subsidy to producers in correcting for a spillover benefit?

Spillover costs are called negative externalities because they are *external* to the participants in the transaction and *reduce* the utility of affected third parties (thus "negative"). Spillover benefits are called positive externalities because they are *external* to the participants in the transaction and *increase* the utility of affected third parties (thus "positive"). See Figures 30-3 and 30-4. Compare (b) and (c) in Figure 30-4.

30-5   An apple-grower's orchard provides nectar to a neighbor's bees, while a beekeeper's bees help the apple grower by pollinating the apple blossoms. Use Figure 30.2b to explain why this situation might lead to an underallocation of resources to apple growing and to beekeeping. How might this underallocation get resolved via the means suggested by the Coase theorem?

Using Figure 30.2b in the text the following can be said. The market demand curves for apples and honey, D_a and D_h, would not include the spillover benefits accruing to the production of the other good. The total benefits associated with the consumption and production of each good could be shown by D_{at} prD_{ht} and the optimal outputs for each good would be Q_{ao} and Q_{ho}. Both of these outputs are greater than equilibrium outputs, Q_{ae} and Q_{he}, leading to an underallocation of resources to both apple-growing and beekeeping.

Using the Coase theorem, we note that it will be to the advantage of individual apple growers and beekeepers to negotiate so that beekeepers (whose hives can be moved) locate their production in or near orchards. This negotiation will occur as long as property ownership is well defined, only a few people are involved, and bargaining costs are low. For example, an apple grower who owns an orchard could allow a beekeeper to use a portion of his or her land, charging below-market rents so that both parties gain from the agreement.

30-6   Explain: "Without a market for pollution rights, dumping pollutants into the air or water is costless; in the presence of the right to buy and sell pollution rights, dumping pollution creates an opportunity cost for the polluter." What is the significance of this fact to the search for better technology to reduce pollution?

The rights to air and water are held in common by society. Without markets for the use of these rights, private individuals will not restrict their polluting activities because there is no monetary incentive to do so. Once these markets are established, the right to pollute will be restricted and have a positive price associated with it. The price represents an explicit monetary cost to polluters, providing them with a tangible incentive to seek ways to cut pollution. This will create potential profits for those who can successfully develop new types of pollution-abatement equipment, accelerating the rate of technological development in this area.

30-7 (Key Question) Explain the following statement, using the MB curve in Figure 30.6 to illustrate: "The optimal amount of pollution abatement for some substances, say, water from storm drains, is very low; the optimal amount of abatement for other substances, say, cyanide poison, is close to 100 percent."

Reducing water flow from storm drains has a low marginal benefit, meaning the MB curve would be located far to the left of where it is in the text diagram. It will intersect the MC curve at a low amount of pollution abatement, indicating the optimal amount of pollution abatement (where MB = MC) is low. Any cyanide in public water sources could be deadly. Therefore, the marginal benefit of reducing cyanide is extremely high and the MB curve in the figure would be located to the extreme right where it would intersect the MC curve at or near 100 percent.

30-8 Relate the law of conservation of matter and energy to: (a) the air pollution problem and (b) the solid-waste disposal problem. What is the tragedy of the commons as it relates to pollution?

(a) Fuel burned to produce energy for one productive purpose will be transformed into smoke and heat. In other words, the fuel is not destroyed but merely transformed. Smoke contains particles that are absorbed by the air and can become dangerous to the health of residents in the region who breathe that air; smoke can also be transformed into a toxic liquid when mixed with rain.

(b) The solid-waste disposal problem is similar. For example, when we consume food, we produce garbage and sewage. Similar by-products result from consumption of virtually every material—new cars become junk cars, stoves become scrap iron, etc. These are solid wastes which will be deposited somewhere. The problem of how to treat these wastes and where to locate them constitutes the so-called solid-waste disposal problem.

The so-called "tragedy of commons" is the tendency for society to overuse and thus abuse common resources when no one holds property rights. A common pasture in which anyone can graze cattle will quickly be overgrazed. Profit-seekers will choose the least-cost combination of inputs and bear only unavoidable costs. If they can dump waste without paying for proper disposal individuals, firms—and even government agencies—are likely to do so, because it is cheap and convenient.

30-9 What is the global-warming problem? How is it being addressed? Using an example other than the one in the text, explain how global warming might hurt one industry, particular region, or country but help another.

Scientific evidence suggests that carbon dioxide and other gas emissions are accumulating and causing the average temperature of the atmosphere to increase. In the Kyoto Protocol, the industrialized nations agreed to cut emissions 6 to 8 percent below 1990 by 2012. Flooding may occur in some regions, thus decreasing the land upon which the population lives, whereas temperatures in the northern parts of the globe may moderate and make these areas more habitable.

30-10 Explain how marketable emissions credits add to overall economic efficiency, compared to across-the-board limitations on maximum discharges of air pollutants by firms.

If company A can reduce pollution by 1 ton at less cost than company B, then company B should buy emission credits from company A. In doing this, society is using fewer resources (spending fewer dollars) to achieve the same level of pollution reduction.

30-11 Explain why there may be insufficient recycling of products when the externalities associated with landfills and garbage incinerators are not considered. What demand and supply incentives might the government provide to promote more recycling? Explain how there could be too much recycling in some situations.

If the externalities are not considered, then the true economic cost of waste disposal has not been accurately measured. If only the explicit costs of the landfill or incinerator are considered, the cost of waste disposal will be underestimated and the amount of recycling will be less than optimal.

On the demand side, the government could levy specific taxes on materials that are substitute inputs for recycled materials. This would raise the cost of the raw materials and increase the demand for the recycled inputs. Government could purchase goods made with recycled inputs and require government contractors to do the same. Environmental awareness and education have expanded consumer demand for goods that use recycled inputs.

Supply incentives might include curbside pickup of recyclable goods at lower fees than normal garbage, or requiring deposits on bottles and cans to provide incentives for consumers to return the empty containers.

30-12 Why is it in the interest of new homebuyers and builders of new homes to have government building codes and building inspectors?

The reason is related to the lack of information and education on the part of most new homebuyers and builders with regard to every aspect of home construction. To make sure that a new building conforms to adequate safety and construction standards, building codes have been created. The government inspectors provide impartial third-party expertise to assure the buyer that the codes have been met. Such inspections also provide information to builders about the electrical and plumbing installation that is usually done by subcontractors. Without building codes and inspections, the market for new homes might be severely hampered. Builders thus also benefit from codes and inspectors.

30-13 (*Key Question*) Place an M beside items in the following list which describe a moral hazard problem; place an A beside those that describe an adverse selection problem.

a. A person with a terminal illness buys several life insurance policies through the mail.

b. A person drives carelessly because he or she has insurance.

c. A person who intends to "torch" his warehouse takes out a large fire insurance policy.

d. A professional athlete who has a guaranteed contract fails to stay in shape during the off-season.

e. A woman anticipating having a large family takes a job with a firm that offers exceptional child-care benefits.

Moral hazard problem: (b) and (d). Adverse selection problem: (a), (c), and (e).

30-14 (*Last Word*) Explain how a global-positioning antitheft device installed by one car owner can produce a positive spillover to thousands of others in the city.

If a car with the device is stolen, police can track the stolen car, possibility arresting the theft and preventing him/her from stealing other cars. Also, the police might be able to track the car to a "chop shop," thus putting an entire ring of thefts out of business.

CHAPTER THIRTY-ONE
PUBLIC CHOICE THEORY AND TAXATION

CHAPTER OVERVIEW

This chapter includes a study of public choice theory, an economic analysis of government decision making, and selected topics related to public expenditures and tax revenues. The theoretical discussion includes an examination of the inefficiency of voting outcomes, interest-group influence, political logrolling, and the paradox of voting outcomes. The median-voter model is considered. Also examined is public sector failure, or the failure of public decisions to promote the general welfare.

Attention is then focused on how public goods are financed. The ability-to-pay vs. the benefits-received principles of taxation are evaluated. Progressive, proportional, and regressive taxes are defined and illustrated with examples. The concepts of tax incidence and efficiency loss are also reviewed. This chapter concludes with a discussion of the relationship between the size and power of government and individual freedom.

WHAT'S NEW

There are only a few changes in this chapter except for updating the statistics. A discussion of "logrolling" has been added to the section on pork-barrel politics. The discussion of the social security tax clarifies that the 6.2 percent applies to the first $76,200 whereas the Medicare tax of 1.45 percent applies to all earned income. The section in the previous edition on the flat tax and the VAT has been omitted.

The Last Word has been updated. One Web-Based Question has been revised, the other is new.

INSTRUCTIONAL OBJECTIVES

After completing this chapter, students should be able to:

1. Explain the problems created with majority voting and the median-voter outcome.

2. State four reasons given by public choice theorists for government's inefficiency in providing public goods and services.

3. Differentiate between the benefits-received and ability-to-pay principles of taxation.

4. Identify which taxes are progressive, proportional, and regressive.

5. Describe how elasticities of demand and supply are related to the incidence of a sales or excise tax.

6. Explain the relationship between the elasticities of demand and supply and the efficiency loss of a particular tax.

7. Describe the probable incidence of the personal income tax, corporate income tax, sales and excise taxes, and property tax.

8. Explain the U.S. structure relative to the progressivity or regressivity of Federal, state, and local taxes.

9. Outline the conservative and liberal positions on the size of government spending and an individual's freedom.

10. Define and identify the terms and concepts listed at end of the chapter.

COMMENTS AND TEACHING SUGGESTIONS

1. Have students investigate the use of special-interest lobbyists. They may be shocked by their findings; some may even discover a new career objective since some lobbyists are extremely well paid. The sheer number of interest groups that hire lobbyists to represent them may also be surprising to students. The process of lobbying legislatures is itself a big business. Point out that state legislatures are under the same kind of pressure from interest groups as the Senate and the House of Representatives.

2. The IRS has regional Taxpayer Education Coordinators who will provide informational materials and/or speakers on the subject of federal taxes. Contact your local IRS office for information on how to reach the coordinator for your area. Most state revenue departments also have public information departments that may provide speakers and/or materials on the subject of state taxes. Finally, many states have independent tax research councils who provide information to interested parties. These organizations are good sources of unbiased materials because their support usually depends on their providing good information about the impact of various taxes and proposed taxes.

3. If you are covering this chapter near tax-filing season, an interesting exercise is to look at the tax tables for the federal income tax and have students identify various tax "loopholes" differences between tax on same income for married, head-of-household, and single individuals; the difference between a deduction and a tax credit; and other items that may be of interest to you or your students. It is then fun to have students try to discover or imagine the reasons behind various tax breaks or to design a tax system that would be more fair in their view. This is also a good group exercise.

4. Students could be asked to come up with their own examples of public sector failures after reading this chapter and, in each case, identify the cause of the "failure."

STUDENT STUMBLING BLOCK

Because government programs are currently viewed with a great deal of suspicion by many citizens, it may be difficult to focus the students' attention on the theoretical aspects of this chapter, as opposed to the emotional reaction that government is inherently wasteful and inefficient. While there is a focus on public sector failure in this chapter, recall that there are also market failures that led to the need for government action in the first place. How to balance the public and private sectors is a question that deserves attention at this point.

LECTURE NOTES

I. **Introduction**

    A. In the last chapter we examined some examples of market failure in the private sector and the government policies designed to remedy them. This chapter examines more closely the public sector and its failures that elicit disenchantment.

    B. This chapter deals with two main topics:

        a. "Public choice theory" is the economic analysis of government decision making that helps us to understand public sector problems.

        b. The economics of taxation.

II. **Revealing society's preferences through majority voting is the way collective decisions are made in a democracy.**

A. Majority voting can lead to inefficient outcomes; that is, the majority can defeat a proposal that would have provided greater benefits than costs and adopt one that costs more than the benefits it provides (Figure 31.1).

   1. Illustration of an inefficient "no" vote result: Suppose there are 3 voters who each will have to pay $300 in tax if a proposal is adopted. It is worth $700 to one, $250 to the second and $200 to the third. The second and third voters will vote "no" and defeat the proposal despite the fact that the total benefits ($1150) exceed the $900 cost.

   2. Illustration of an inefficient "yes" vote result: Take the same three voters as above and the same level of taxation. Now the proposal is worth $100 to the first voter and $350 to each of the others. The vote will be 2 to 1 in favor of the proposal even though the total benefit of $800 is less than the $900 cost.

   3. Conclusion: The problem is that the one-person one-vote rule does not measure intensity of preferences, so the result may not be economically efficient.

B. Interest groups may improve the economic efficiency of results by registering intense feelings with elected representatives or by organizing major efforts to get the vote to go their way.

C. Logrolling or vote trading may also secure favorable decisions for those who feel strongly about certain issues, but it may also negate an efficient outcome in favor of a special interest group where the value of the benefits received does not justify the cost. The efficiency of the outcome will depend on the circumstances.

D. The paradox of voting is that society may not be able to rank its preferences consistently through majority voting.

   1. Table 31.1 demonstrates a situation in which three voters have expressed their rankings of three public projects; each has a different ranking. If voting is done on pairs of projects, it can be shown that national defense will win over roads, and roads will win over weather warning systems. But the logical conclusion that the community prefers national defense to weather warning systems is not the case—they would each get the same number of points (if points were awarded for a 1st, 2nd, and 3rd choice). In other words, if one choice must receive a majority of the votes, there will not be a consistent outcome in this case unless somehow the strengths of the rankings can be measured.

   2. Government might find it difficult to provide the "correct" public goods by acting in accordance with majority voting.

E. The median-voter model suggests that under majority rule the median voter will in a sense determine the outcomes of elections. The median voter is the person holding the middle position on an issue.

   1. The textbook example has three voters deciding among three types of weather warning systems. The first is willing to spend $400; the second, $800; the third, $300. The median-voter model suggests that the $400 proposal will win. In a choice between the $400 and $800 proposal, the first and third will vote for the $400 type. In a choice between the $400 and $300, the first and second will vote for the $400 type. In other words, both extreme voters prefer the median choice rather than the other extreme, so the median voter will tend to predominate.

   2. Real-world examples occur in political positions where candidates seem to aim their appeal at the median voters within each party to get the nomination and later at the middle of the population in an effort to win the election.

   3. Implications of the median-voter model:

a. Many people will be dissatisfied by the extent of government involvement in the economy.

b. Some people may "vote with their feet" by moving into political jurisdictions where the median voter's preferences are closer to their own.

c. Median preferences can change over time.

III. **Government failure can occur as well as market or private sector failure. The fact that the latter exist does not mean that the public sector improves efficiency.**

A. Special interests and "rent seeking" may promote the interests of a small group at the expense of society at large.

1. The special-interest effect refers to the situation where a small number of people will receive large gains at the expense of a much larger number of people who individually suffer small losses. The small group will be well informed and highly vocal on the issue and press politicians for approval. The large numbers who will each suffer small losses will not have the incentive to be informed or feel strongly. The result is that the politician will support the special-interest program, whose supporters will notice the vote in their favor, and ignore the majority who don't feel strongly.

2. Pork-barrel politics is an example of the special-interest effect. In this case, the benefit goes to a single political district and to the politician from that political district. The cost of the project is spread out to many individuals who will never receive the benefits. Pork-barrel politics is often combined with logrolling.

3. Rent-seeking behavior occurs when a transfer of wealth at someone else's or society's expense occurs through government action. Here the term "rent" means any payment to a resource supplier, business, or other organization above that which would accrue under competitive market conditions. Examples include tax loopholes that benefit only certain groups; public works projects that cost more than the benefits they yield; and occupational licensing that requires more than is necessary to protect consumers.

B. Clear benefits, hidden costs (or the reverse, immediate costs and future more vague benefits) are another dilemma for politicians trying to decide on public programs. Where the benefits are recognizable and popular, the politician may vote for the program even if the costs exceed these benefits if the costs are diffuse or hidden.

C. Limited choice is another problem with public goods. The voter must choose between a few candidates who will have the power to select the public goods and services to be financed by the voter's tax money. In the private sector, the consumer has a multitude of choices available.

D. Bureaucracy and inefficiency can be another problem in the public sector because there is not the profit motive or competitive pressure to perform efficiently. Ironically, the typical response of government to a program's failure may be to increase its budget and staff.

1. Government employees together with the special-interest groups they serve often have the political clout to block attempts to pare down or eliminate their agencies.

2. There is a tendency for government bureaucracy to justify continued employment by looking for and eventually finding new problems to solve.

E. Imperfect institutions exist in both the public and private sectors, which often makes it difficult to decide which institutions would perform best in the production of certain goods and services.

IV.   **Apportioning the tax burden and deciding how the public sector should be financed is also a complex question.**

A. Benefits received vs. ability to pay principle of taxation.

1. The benefits-received principle asserts that households and businesses should be taxed in relationship to the services they receive. For example, gasoline taxes are earmarked for highway construction and maintenance.

a. How can the government decide which citizens receive how much benefit from less divisible   public goods like national defense?

b. Government efforts to redistribute income would be self-defeating if the benefits-received principle of taxation were applied universally—welfare recipients would have to pay for their welfare at the extreme version of this.

2. The ability-to-pay principle asserts that the tax burden should rest more heavily on those with greater income and wealth. The rationale is that those people with much income or wealth will value their marginal dollars less than those with low incomes, where each dollar is very meaningful.

B. Progressive, proportional, and regressive taxation systems relate to the above issues. (Key Question 9)

1. A tax is progressive if its average rate increases as income increases; the tax grows absolutely with income and also proportionately.

2. A tax is proportional if its average rate remains the same; the tax payment grows absolutely with income but remains the same proportionate to income.

3. A tax is regressive if its average rate declines as income increases; the tax may or may not increase in the absolute amount, but it declines in proportion to income.

C. Applications in existing tax structure:

1. The federal personal income tax is mildly progressive, with marginal tax rates ranging from 15 to 39.6 percent. Certain deductions that favor high-income groups erode the progressivity of this tax.

2. Sales taxes are not as proportional as they seem if they are on all goods. A general sales tax is regressive because, although everyone pays the same percent on expenditures, the rich tend to spend a much smaller fraction of their incomes, while the poor may spend all of their incomes. Therefore, the rich will pay a smaller overall proportion of their income in sales taxes.

3. The federal corporate income tax is essentially a flat-rate tax with a set rate, but if it is passed on to consumers in the form of higher prices it may actually be regressive in its impact.

4. Payroll taxes are regressive. The social security portion of the tax (6.2 percent) is not applied to income above a certain level ($76,200 in 2000). On the other hand, the Medicare portion of the tax is applied to all wage income. A person making $100,000 paid the same amount of social security tax as the person making $76,200, i.e. 6.2 percent times $76,2000 or $4,724. The tax payment would be 7.65 percent of the $76,200 income, but about 4.7 percent of the $100,000 income.

5. Property taxes tend to be regressive because landlords pass along this cost to tenants who have lower incomes; housing costs are a larger proportion of income for the poor than for

the rich, so economists estimate that the property tax on that housing would end up being a greater proportion of low incomes than of high incomes.

V.   **Tax Incidence and Efficiency Loss**

A. Tax incidence refers to who actually bears the economic burden of a tax (Figure 31.2).

1. The division of the burden is not obvious. Figure 31.2 shows the impact of a $1 per-bottle tax on wine that was priced at $4 per bottle before the tax.

2. S is the no-tax supply situation and St is the after tax supply curve. The new equilibrium price rises to $4.50, not $5 as one might expect with the $1 tax.

a. Consumers pay $.50 more per bottle.

b. Producers receive $.50 less per bottle.

3. In this example, consumers and producers share the burden of the tax equally. The incidence is not completely on either one.

B. Elasticities of demand and supply explain the incidence of an excise or sales tax.

1. Given supply, the more inelastic the demand for the product, the larger the portion of the tax is shifted forward to consumers (Figure 31.3b). Figure 31.3a shows the situation if demand is more elastic.

2. Given demand, the more inelastic the supply (Figure 31.4b), the larger the portion of the tax borne by producers or sellers. Figure 31-4a shows the situation if supply is more elastic.

C. Efficiency loss is one result of an excise or sales tax.

1. Figure 31.5 illustrates the concept of efficiency loss, which occurs as a result of an excise tax or sales tax. The efficiency loss is the reduction of well-being that occurs because there will be less produced at the higher price caused by the tax. It is the sacrifice of net benefit accruing to society because consumption and production of the taxed product are reduced below their allocatively efficient levels.

2. Elasticities play a role in determining the extent of the efficiency loss. Other things being equal, the greater the elasticities of supply and demand, the greater the efficiency loss of a particular tax.

3. Qualifications to the analysis relate to the idea that the goals of tax policy may be more important than the goal of minimizing efficiency losses from taxes. Two examples are given.

a. Redistributive goals—Excise taxes placed on luxury items in the 1990s resulted in efficiency losses, but the benefits from redistributing income from the wealthier consumers who buy luxury items may have been worth the loss in efficiency. However, these luxury taxes were unpopular and have been repealed.

b. Reducing negative externalities—If there is less alcohol and tobacco consumption as a result of excise taxes, the taxes may have socially desirable consequences.

D. Probable incidence of U.S. taxes is estimated for various taxes.

1. The personal income tax generally falls on the individual except for those who can control the price of their labor services and pass on the cost of the tax through higher fees.

2. The incidence of the corporate income tax is uncertain. Some corporations may be able to shift the burden by charging higher prices; others may find there is decreased profitability and the burden is then borne by stockholders.

3. Excise taxes can be shifted to the consumer where demand is inelastic. This is true generally with the small range of products on which excise taxes are levied (gasoline, cigarettes, and alcoholic beverages). However, because sales taxes cover such a wide range of products, the incidence of sales taxes is just as likely to fall on the seller—it depends on the respective elasticities of demand and supply for the product.

4. The incidence of property taxes may fall on the property owner, or in the case of rental and business property, the tax would be largely shifted onto the tenant or the customer.

5. Global Perspective 31.1 indicates that the U.S. is less dependent upon sales and excise taxes than many other industrialized nations.

E. Table 31.2 summarizes the discussion of the shifting and incidence of taxes.

VI. **The U.S. Tax Structure**

A. It is difficult to determine the overall progressivity or regressivity of the American tax structure. Disagreement among economists persists.

B. The Federal tax system: The system is progressive.

1. In 1999, the average Federal tax rate for the 20 percent of taxpayers with the lowest incomes was only 4.6 percent. The tax rate for the 20 percent of the taxpayers with the highest income was 29.1 percent. The tax rate was 30.6 percent for the top 10 percent of tax payers and 34.4 percent for the top 1 percent. The top 5 percent of all taxpayers paid 50 percent of the total Federal income tax collected.

2. This progressivity is offset by the social security tax, which is regressive. Because of the cap of $76,200, taxpayers who earn more, pay a lower percent of their income as tax than do lower and middle income earners.

C. The state and local tax system: State and local tax structures are largely regressive as a percentage of income. Both sales and property taxes fall as a proportion of income when income rises.

D. Combined Tax Structure: Overall, the American tax structure is slightly progressive. The American system of transfer payments does reduce income inequality and is estimated to quadruple the incomes of the poorest one-fifth, which makes the tax-transfer system more progressive than the tax system alone.

VII. **The issue of freedom: the relationship between the role and size of government and personal freedom.**

A. The conservative position asserts that apart from the costs of the public sector, individual freedom is reduced by a growth in government.

1. One argument is that "power corrupts" and the more power given to government, the more individual freedoms are restricted.

2. Second, private spending allows much more freedom of choice than does public spending, where taxpayers generally relinquish their power to spend to their elected representatives.

3. Finally, freedom is enhanced if governmental power is decentralized rather than centralized at the Federal level.

B. The liberal position asserts that the conservative view is based on the so-called fallacy of limited decisions. That is, the more decisions made by government, the fewer available to individual consumers. They assert that it is not a zero-sum game, but that government spending extends the range of free choice by giving society opportunities that would not be available in the absence of government. They argue that government is important in the areas of education, employment policy, reduction of poverty, crime, disease, discrimination, and other ills. Also, the government purchases many of its goods through private enterprise; for example, the highway system is built by private contractors. The quote by Paul Samuelson at the end of the chapter is a classic statement of the liberal position.

IX.   **LAST WORD: "Public Sector Failure" in the News**

A. It took 23 Federal employees to approve the purchase of laptop computers costing $3,500 each. The same computers were priced at $1,500 each in a retail store.

B. The Federal government paid $333.000 for a two-hole restroom facility in a national recreation area that did not work in the winter months.

C. In 1998, the Congress contracted to buy 20 transport planes for $1 billion that the Air Force did not request.

D. As a part of a radiation cleanup project, the EPA spent an average of $651,700 to custom-build 10 new homes that replaced old houses that were valued at $147,000 each.

E. There are Congressional provisions that require the government to purchase certain equipment from a single firm.

F. Appropriations bills sometime contain riders that are unrelated to the bill itself.

G. The omnibus appropriations bill for fiscal 1999 was 4,000 pages long and weight 40 pounds.

H. Appropriations bills for 2,000 contained hundreds of special projects that bypassed the appropriate budget review process.

ANSWERS TO END-OF-CHAPTER QUESTIONS

31-1   Explain how affirmative and negative majority votes can sometimes lead to inefficient allocations of resources to public goods. Is this problem likely to be greater under a benefits-received or an ability-to-pay tax system? Use the information in Figure 31-1a and b to show how society might be better off if Adams were allowed to buy votes.

The problem arises because the one-person one-vote rule does not allow voters to register the strength of their preferences. In the text's example, three people—Adams, Benson, and Conrad— have preferences with regard to the benefits of national defense as follows: It is worth $700 to Adams, $250 to Benson, and $200 to Conrad for a total of $1,150 worth of benefits. The national defense program would cost $900 to be borne by each voter equally, or $300 each. This program would lose a majority vote because neither Benson nor Conrad would be willing to pay $300 for it. However, the total benefit to society in this three-voter world would have been $1,150. A "no" vote is therefore inefficient in the economic sense.

On the other hand, suppose the program was worth $100 to Adams, but $350 each to Benson and Conrad for a total benefit of $800. In this case the program would win because both Conrad and Benson would vote for it, but Adams would not. The $900 spending program would be approved even though it was worth only $800 to society. In this case a "yes" vote is inefficient in the economic sense.

In Figure 31-1a, we can see that society would be better off if Adams had been allowed to pay enough to Benson to get Benson's "yes" vote. Benson should be willing to vote "yes" for any amount above $50, because then his benefits would exceed the $300 cost of the defense program. Let's say Adams paid him $75 to vote "yes." Then, Benson receives $75 plus $250 worth of defense benefits for a total benefit of $325 for which he pays $300 in taxes. Meanwhile, Adams has received his $700 worth of defense benefits for a cost of $300 in taxes and $75 payment to Benson.

In Figure 31-1b, Adams could pay $75 to Benson again to vote "no." Now Adams incurs only $75 cost rather than the $200 cost differential between his cost and benefits from the defense program in Figure 31-1b. If the program had passed, Benson would have gained $50 in net benefits, but without the program and with Adams' payment he has gained $75 in net benefits.

31-2   (*Key Question*) Explain the paradox of voting through reference to the accompanying table which shows the ranking of three public goods by voters Larry, Curley, and Moe.

Public Good	Larry	Curley	Moe
Courthouse	2d choice	1st choice	3d choice
School	3d choice	2d choice	1st choice
Park	1st choice	3d choice	2d choice

The paradox is that majority voting does not always provide a clear and consistent picture of the public's preferences. Here the courthouse is preferred to the school and the park is preferred to the courthouse, so we would surmise that the park is preferred to the school. But paired-choice voting would show that the school is preferred to the park.

31-3   (*Key Question*) Suppose that there are only five people in a society and that each favors one of the five flood-control options shown in Table 30.2 (include no protection as one of the options). Explain which of these flood control options will be selected using a majority rule. Will this option be the optimal size of the project from an economic perspective?

Project B (small reservoir wins) using a paired-choice vote. There is no "paradox of voting" problem here and B is the preference of the median voter. The two voters favoring No reservoir and Levees, respectively, will prefer Small reservoir—project B—to Medium or Large reservoir. The two voters preferring Large reservoir or Medium reservoir will prefer Small reservoir to Levees or No reservoir. The median voter's preference for B will prevail. However, the optimal size of the project from an economic perspective is C—it would provide a greater net benefit to society than B.

31-4   (*Key Question*) How does the problem of limited and bundled choice in the public sector relate to economic efficiency? Why are public bureaucracies alleged to be less efficient than private enterprises?

The electorate is faced with a small number of candidates, each of whom offers a broad range or "bundle" of proposed policies. Voters are then forced to choose the individual candidate whose bundle of policies most resembles their own. The chances of a perfect identity between a particular candidate's preferences and those of any voter are quite slim. As a result, the voter must purchase some unwanted public goods and services. This represents an inefficient allocation of resources.

Government bureaucracies do not function on the basis of profit, so the incentive for holding down costs is less than in the private sector. Also, because there is no profit-and-loss test of efficiency, it is difficult to determine whether public agencies are operating efficiently. Nor is there entry of competing entities to stimulate efficiency and develop improved public goods and services. Furthermore, wasteful expenditures can be maintained through the self-seeking lobbying of bureaucrats themselves, and the public budgetary process can reward rather than penalize inefficiency.

31-5   Explain: "Politicians would make more rational economic decisions if they weren't running for reelection every few years." Do you favor term limits for elected officials?

Because political officeholders must seek voter support every few years, they favor programs with immediate and clear-cut benefits and with vague or deferred costs. Conversely, politicians will reject programs with immediate and easily identifiable costs but with long term, less measurable benefits. Such biases can lead politicians to reject economically justifiable programs and to accept programs which are economically irrational.

Politicians may make these and other irrational decisions in order to curry favor with the voters. But what kind of irrational decisions might be made by politicians who did not have to face the voters again and stand for reelection?

31-6   Distinguish between the benefits-received and the ability-to-pay principles of taxation. Which philosophy is more evident in our present tax structure? Justify your answer. To which principle of taxation do you subscribe? Why?

The benefits-received principle holds that governments should supply public goods and services in much the same manner as does private business. Those who make use of government services should pay for them. This principle is at work in the gasoline tax, with the proceeds going to the building and upkeep of roads, and in the sale of postage stamps. However, even here the principle is hardly fully respected. Some drivers get paved highways, while others who drive just as much do so on dirt roads. And the same first-class postage stamp will move a letter ten miles or three thousand.

The redistribution of income by government—transfer payments—would be impossible on the benefits-received principle. People on welfare receive benefits because they need more from government than they could possibly contribute in taxes.

The ability-to-pay principle of taxation takes account of this fact and assesses tax liability based on a person's ability to pay: The higher one's income, the higher the tax and the higher the percentage of one's income paid in tax. The objection to this principle is that it cannot be decided in principle how much more a wealthy person should pay than one of restricted means. The decision then becomes a political one—with the decision everywhere being not to make the wealthy pay fully in accordance with their ability to pay. In summary, it seems that the ability-to-pay principle is the one of the most, if half-heartedly, respected in the United States.

31-7   (*Key Question*) Suppose a tax is such that an individual with an income of $10,000 pays $2,000 of tax, a person with an income of $20,000 pays $3,000 of tax, a person with an income of $30,000 pays $4,000 of tax, and so forth. What is each person's average tax rate? Is this tax regressive, proportional, or progressive?

Average tax rates: 20; 15; and 13.3 percent. Regressive.

31-8   What is meant by a progressive tax? A regressive tax? A proportional tax? Comment on the progressivity or regressivity of each of the following taxes, indicating in each case your assumption concerning tax incidence:

a.   The Federal personal income tax

b.   A 4 percent state general sales tax

c. A Federal excise tax on automobile tires

d. A municipal property tax on real estate

e. The Federal corporate income tax

A progressive tax is one whose average rate increases as income increases. One pays in tax a larger proportion of one's income as income increases.

A regressive tax is one whose average rate declines as income increases. One pays in tax a smaller and smaller proportion of one's income as income increases, though it is possible for the absolute amount to increase.

A proportional tax is one whose average rate remains the same regardless of the size of income.

(a) Mildly progressive ("mildly" because of loopholes). Incidence is usually on the taxpayer. However, those who charge a fee for services (that is, the self-employed) may be able to increase their fees enough to have the fee-payer in effect pay the tax. Also, some unions may be able to get big enough wage increases to pay increased income tax.

(b) Regressive. The poor spend all their income, mostly on commodities subject to the sales tax. Thus the sales tax is, in effect, on all their income. The wealthier one is, the smaller the proportion of one's income is spent on commodities subject to the sales tax. (Stocks and bonds and real estate are not subject to this tax.) Thus, the average tax rate declines as income increases. The incidence of the tax is mostly on the consumers who buy the taxed commodities.

(c) Regressive for the same reasons as for state general sales taxes. The incidence, again, is mostly on the buyer. There are no substitutes for automobile tires (assuming one does not give up driving a car).

(d) The incidence is on (1) owners in the case of an owner-occupied residence or land; (2) tenants if the property is rented; (3) consumers if the property is used in business. In the case of (1) and (2), the tax tends to be proportional since the tax is based on the value of the property, and the lower one's income, the lower the value of the property one owns or rents. In the case of (3), the tax will be regressive for the same reasons the state general sales tax is regressive.

(e) The incidence is probably shared between the corporation's shareholders and the buyers of the corporation's products. To the extent it is on the shareholders, the tax is proportional. To the extent it is on the consumers, it is regressive for the same reasons the general sales tax is regressive.

31-9 (*Key Question*) What is the incidence of an excise tax when demand is highly inelastic? Elastic? What effect does the elasticity of supply have on the incidence of an excise tax? What is the efficiency loss of a tax, and how does it relate to elasticity of demand and supply?

The incidence of an excise tax is likely to be primarily on consumers when demand is highly inelastic and primarily on producers when demand is elastic. The more elastic the supply, the greater the incidence of an excise tax on consumers and the less on producers.

The efficiency loss of a sales or excise tax is the net benefit society sacrifices because consumption and production of the taxed product are reduced below the level of allocative efficiency which would occur without the tax. Other things equal, the greater the elasticities of demand and supply, the greater the efficiency loss of a particular tax.

31-10 Advanced analysis: Suppose the equation for the demand curve for some product X is $P = 8 - .6Q$ and the supply curve is $P = 2 + .4Q$. What is the equilibrium price and quantity? Now suppose an excise tax is imposed on X such that the new supply equation is $P = 4 + .4Q$. How much tax revenue will this excise tax yield the government? Graph the curves and label the area of the graph which represents the tax collection TC and the area which represents the efficiency loss of the tax EL. Briefly explain why area EL is the efficiency loss of the tax but TC is not.

Demand is $P = 8 - .6Q_d$, therefore $Q_d = (40 - 5P)/3$

Original supply is $P = 2 + .4Q_s$, therefore $Q_s = (5/2)P - 5$

In equilibrium, $Q_d = Q_s$:

$(40 - 5P) = 3((5/2)P - 5)$ or

$40 - 5P = (15/2)P - 15$

$55 = (25/2)P$ or $25P = 110$ and $P = 22/5 = 4.4$

Substituting this value in either Q_d or Q_s:

$Q_d = (40 - 5(22/5))/3 = 18/3 = 6$

$Q_s = (5/2)(22/5) - 5 = 11 - 5 = 6$

An excise tax of $2 is imposed, and the vertical intercept of the supply equation increases by 2 units:

New supply is $P = 4 + .4Q_s$, therefore $Q_s = (5/2)P - 10$

Again using the equilibrium condition, $Q_d = Q_s$:

$(40 - 5P) = 3((5/2)P - 10)$

$40 - 5P = (15/2)P - 30$

$70 = (25/2)P$ or $P = (28/5) = 5.6$

(Substituting in either Q_d or Q_s:)

$Q_d = (40 - 5(28/5))/3 = 12/3 = 4$

$Q_s = (5/2)(28/5) - 10 = 14 - 10 = 4$

The total revenue yielded by this tax is $8, and is found by multiplying the per unit yield ($2) by the number of units sold after the tax is imposed.

The area EL represents the loss to society that results from the reduction in consumption and production of good X. The loss occurs because the fifth and sixth units are no longer produced.

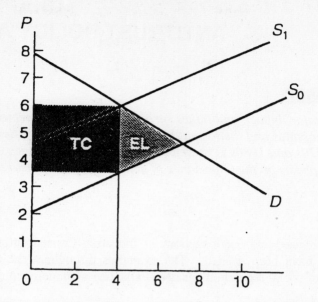

31-11 (*Last Word*) How do the concepts of "pork-barrel" politics and "logrolling" relate to the items listed in the Last Word?

Both of these political techniques are examples of special interest effects. "Pork-barrel" politics refers to the practice that congressional representatives follow when they obtain unneeded benefits for their own districts, and "logrolling" is a related practice whereby one group of legislators helps another with the understanding that at some point in the future they, in turn, will be helped.

The Last Word contains some examples of public spending that undoubtedly resulted from such practices. These include the purchasing of equipment that is not asked for by the military and buying equipment from a single firm both to benefit particular Congressional districts; building projects that are outlandishly costly; and appropriations bills that are so large, contain so much detail, with provisions that benefit small groups or individuals.

CHAPTER THIRTY-TWO
ANTITRUST POLICY AND REGULATION

CHAPTER OVERVIEW

Antitrust laws, their major impact, and issues surrounding their enforcement, are presented in the chapter. Natural monopolies and their regulation are discussed and critically evaluatde. Information on deregulation in the 1970s and 1980s is presented. The chapter concludes with an analysis of social regulation with an emphasis on the importance of determining its optimal level through cost-benefit analysis.

WHAT'S NEW

The chapter has been revised and major sections – "Industrial Concentration: Beneficial or Harmful?" and "Industrial Policy" – have been deleted. The examples throughout the antitrust discussion have been updated. The section of social regulation has been expanded with more emphasis on its costs and benefits.

The Last Word is new. One of the Web-Based Questions has been changed and the other is new.

INSTRUCTIONAL OBJECTIVES

After completing this chapter, students should be able to:

1. Outline the major provisions of each of the following: Sherman Act, Clayton Act, Federal Trade Commission Act, and Celler-Kefauver Act.

2. Identify major issues in antitrust enforcement by reviewing decisions in U.S. Steel, Alcoa, and DuPont cellophane Supreme Court cases.

3. Identify three current economic goals that may conflict with strict enforcement of antitrust laws.

4. Analyze effectiveness of antitrust laws by noting how they have been applied to existing market structures, mergers, and price fixing.

5. Distinguish between three types of merger.

6. Explain how the Herfindahl index is used as a guideline by the government in deciding whether to permit horizontal mergers.

7. Identify the options that government might use when a natural monopoly exists.

8. Explain why a regulated monopoly does not have an incentive to reduce costs.

9. Explain two major problems encountered in regulating natural monopolies.

10. State the major arguments for and against social regulation.

11. Define and identify terms and concepts listed at the end of the chapter.

COMMENTS AND TEACHING SUGGESTIONS

1. Instructors who feel pressed for time may wish to include some of the content of this chapter in a unit with the market structures—Chapter 24 monopoly—or with Chapter 5 (the six economic functions of government). This chapter could be used in discussing the deregulation of utilities,

telephone service and electrical transmission and its impact on businesses and consumers. To what extent have regulatory agencies subsidized one set of buyers at the expense of others?

2. A guest speaker familiar with anti-trust issues, a lawyer or business person would be an interesting addition to the class at this point. Local utilities often have a speaker's bureau you could use as well.

3. Strict enforcement of Section 1 of the Sherman Act (see text) isn't really possible since many contracts and business arrangements clearly restrain trade. The key is to find "unreasonable" restraints of trade such as anticompetitive mergers, price fixing, bid rigging, and other such conspiracies. Often, there may be local examples of businesses charged with violating the Sherman Act. Such cases make this section more relevant to students who may be far from industrial or financial centers of power. Speculation regarding whether colleges and universities violate antitrust price-fixing prohibitions is always fascinating to students. A 1991 court decision in a case involving some Ivy League schools, and their practice of not competing in their financial aid offers to students applying to several of these schools, challenged the applicability of antitrust law to "nonprofit" institutions. Students may question the tuition practices of area schools, or whether the food service may have a "tying contract" for soda machines, for example.

4. Have the students research a merger of two large companies that have been competing with each other. Ask the students to analyze the merge as to whether the merger resulted in positive or negative effects upon others firms in the industry and the industry's customers.

5. Have the students write critical reviews on news articles dealing with social regulation.

STUDENT STUMBLING BLOCK

There seem to be few stumbling blocks in this chapter. However, some students do not understand the relationship between court decisions and the interpretation and implementation of laws. Spend some time emphasizing the importance of the Supreme Court decisions presented in the text in terms of their importance for the future implementation of antitrust laws.

LECTURE NOTES

I. **Antitrust Laws**

   A. Historical background is rooted in the decades following the Civil War, when the corporate form of business began to develop and "trusts" or monopolies were formed in industries such as petroleum, meatpacking, railroads, sugar, lead, coal, whiskey, and tobacco.

   B. Questionable tactics were used by some of these trusts, and popular sentiment turned against them. Two mechanisms for dealing with monopolies were developed.

      1. Regulatory agencies were formed to control "natural" monopolies.

      2. Antitrust legislation was passed to inhibit or prevent the growth of monopolies in other industries.

   C. As a result of public resentment against trusts, the Sherman Act was passed 1890.

      1. It contains two major provisions:

         a. Contracts or combinations in restraint of trade or commerce among the several states or with foreign nations is illegal.

      b. Every person who shall monopolize or attempt to monopolize any part of the trade or commerce among the states or with foreign nations shall be deemed guilty of a misdemeanor.

  2. Today, the U.S. Department of Justice, the Federal Trade Commission, injured private parties, or state attorney generals can bring suits against alleged violators of the act.

  3. Firms found violating either provision of the act could be ordered dissolved by the courts, or prohibited from engaging in the unlawful practices. Fines and imprisonment were possible, and injured parties could sue for triple damages.

D. The Clayton Act of 1914 is an elaboration of the Sherman Act, which was often not explicit enough to be effective. The Clayton Act strengthened the Sherman Act in several ways.

  1. It outlaws anticompetitive price discrimination among purchasers when the price differentiation is not based on cost and if it lessens competition.

  2. It forbids exclusive or tying contracts in which a producer forces purchasers of one of its products to acquire other products from the same seller or producer.

  3. Acquisition of stock in competing corporations is forbidden if it lessens competition

  4. Interlocking directorates are not allowed where directors of one firm are also on the board of a competing firm.

E. Also in 1914, Congress passed the Federal Trade Commission Act. This act created the Federal Trade Commission (FTC), an agency designed to enforce antitrust laws and the Clayton Act in particular.

  1. FTC investigates unfair competitive practices and, when appropriate issues cease-and desist orders.

  2. Additionally, the Wheeler-Lea Act in 1938 gave the FTC power to police "deceptive acts or practices in commerce."

F. The Celler-Kefauver Act of 1950 amended Section 7 of the Clayton Act, which prohibits firms from acquiring the stock of competitors when this would reduce competition. This section had a loophole whereby firms could accomplish their purpose by acquiring the physical assets rather than stock of a competing company, and the Celler-Kefauver bill closed this loophole.

II.   **Antitrust issues and their impact have varied throughout the history of antitrust law.**

A. There are two distinct approaches to the application of antitrust law—one based on the structure of an industry and the other on the behavior of firms in an industry. Two landmark cases reveal the dilemma.

  1. The 1920 Supreme Court decision on the U.S. Steel case led to the application of the "rule of reason." The Court decided that not every monopoly is illegal if the firm(s) involved did not gain that power unreasonably.

  2. In the 1945 Alcoa case the Court held that, even though a firm's behavior might be legal (Alcoa had control over bauxite reserves, the raw material needed for aluminum), mere possession of monopoly power (90 percent of the aluminum market) violated antitrust laws.

  3. These two cases point to a continuing controversy in antitrust policy: Should industries be judged by their behavior or structure?

   a. Structuralists claim that monopolists will behave like monopolists, and this economic performance is undesirable.

   b. Behavioralists argue that the relationship between structure and performance is unclear.

4. In recent years, the rule of reason has been more dominant. In 1982 the government dropped its 13-year-long case against IBM, deciding that IBM had not unreasonably restrained trade. Most recently, the government alleged that Microsoft violated the Sherman Act, not because of its dominance in the industry, but because of its behavior.

B. Defining what is the relevant market is important in antitrust Court decisions.

1. If the market is defined broadly, then a firm's market share will appear to be smaller.

2. If the market is defined narrowly, then a firm's market share may seem large.

3. In the Alcoa case, the court used a narrow definition of the relevant market - the aluminum ingot market.

4 The court defined the market broadly in the DuPont cellophane case of 1956 to include all "flexible packaging materials," waxed paper, aluminum foil, etc. and therefore DuPont, which had a monopoly in cellophane, was not found to violate the law.

C. Other desirable economic goals may conflict with antitrust enforcement.

1. Balance of trade: Should firms be allowed to merge if the merged firm is domestically dominant but is more competitive internationally?

2. Defense cutbacks: Should the government allow defense industry firms that may be losing government funding to merge in order to maintain profitability and employment of workers, despite the concentration such mergers would involve?

3. Emerging new technologies: Should the government permit large firms in several overlapping industries, like entertainment, communications, software, and computer industries, to merge, particularly if these merged firms will hasten development and improve U.S. industrial competitiveness?

D. The effectiveness of antitrust laws is difficult to judge. The government has generally been lenient in applying antitrust laws to firms that have grown "naturally."

1. Antitrust laws have generally not been applied unless a firm has more than 60 percent of the relevant market and there is evidence the firm used abusive conduct to achieve or maintain its market dominance. An example of a significant case was the 1982 settlement out of court by the government and AT&T (the telephone company). It was charged with violating the Sherman Act by engaging in several anticompetitive actions to keep its domestic monopoly in telephone communications. AT&T agreed to divest itself of its 22 regional phone-operating companies, but was allowed to keep its long-distance service operations.

2. In 2000, a Federal district court found Microsoft guilty of violating the Sherman Act. The court's remedy was to split Microsoft into two companies and to prohibit each from in engaging in anticompetitive behavior. Microsoft has appealed the decision to a higher court.

3. Mergers are treated differently, depending on the type of merger and the effect on the industry. There are three types of mergers:

a. Horizontal mergers are between companies selling similar products in the same market. Examples are Chase Manhattan's merger with Chemical Bank, Boeing's merger with MacDonell Douglas, and Exxon's merger with Mobil.

b. Vertical mergers are between firms at different stages of the production process in the same industry. Pepsico's merger with restaurant chains that it supplies with beverages is an example. (This merger did not prove to be successful and thus Pepsico spun off the restaurant part of the business.)

c. Conglomerate mergers are between firms in unrelated industries, such the merger between Walt Disney Company and the American Broadcasting Company, and the merger between America Online and Time Warner.

4. The Hefindahl index is used as a guideline by the Federal government to decide whether the merger will be allowed. Recall from Chapter 25 that this index is the sum of the squared market shares of the firms in the industry 10,000 would be the index for a pure monopoly (100 squared). Generally, the post-merger index must be above 1800 and significantly changed by the merger for the government to challenge a horizontal merger. Other factors, such as economies of scale, the degree of foreign competition, the ease of entry of new firms, and whether one of the merging firms is under major financial stress are also considered. Two examples of recently blocked horizontal mergers are the mergers between Staples Office Depot and between WorldCom and Sprint.

5. Vertical mergers are usually ignored unless they are between two firms who are each in highly concentrated industries. A proposed merger between Barnes & Noble and Ingram Book groups was abandoned when it appeared that the FTC was going to take action.

6. Conglomerate mergers have generally been permitted.

7. Price fixing is treated strictly. Evidence of price fixing, even by small firms, can elicit antitrust action. Such violations are called per se violations because they are illegal in and of themselves; they are not subject to the rule of reason. There are several recent examples.

a. Archer Daniels Midland (ADM) admitted to fixing the price of an additive to livestock feed, a sweetener made from corn, and citrus acid.

b. ConAgra and Hormel paid $21 million to settle their roles in a nationwide price-fixing of catfish.

c. Reebok paid $10 million in damages in a lawsuit in which they were accused by fixing the minimum price that retailers could charge for its footwear.

d. UCAR International was fined $110 million for scheming with competitors to fix prices and divide up the graphite electrode market.

e. Seven international makers of vitamins agreed to pay $1.2 billion to settle a lawsuit that alleged the producers engaged in a 9-year conspiracy to artificially inflate vitamin prices.

8. The Federal government also has strictly enforced the Clayton Act's prohibition of tying contracts. The government has stopped movie distributors from forcing theaters to "buy" the projection rights to a full package of films as a condition of showing a blockbuster movie. Tying contracts, such as Microsoft "bundling" its Internet Explorer browser with its Windows operating software, was declared illegal.

E. Has U.S. antitrust policy been effective in achieving its goal of promoting competition and efficiency?

1. Antitrust policy has not been effective in restricting the rise of or breaking up of monopolies or oligopolies resulting from internal expansion.

2. Antitrust laws have been more effective against predatory or abusive monopoly power, but the effectiveness has been slowed because of the legal process.

3. Antitrust policy has been effective in blocking anticompetitive merges and prosecuting price fixing and tying contracts.

F. Most economists conclude that antitrust policy has been moderately effective in promoting competition and efficiency. Others, though, believe that with the era of rapidly changing technology, U.S. antitrust policy is anachronistic.

III. Industrial Regulation

A. Natural monopoly

1. A natural monopoly exists when economies of scale are so extensive that a single firm can supply the entire market at lower unit cost than would be achieved by a number of smaller, competing firms. Public utilities, such as electricity, water, gas, local telephone service, and cable TV are examples.

2. Two possible alternatives exist for protecting society in such cases.

   a. Public ownership, as occurs with the Postal Service, water systems, many municipal electric systems, etc., is one solution.

   b. Public regulation has been the option pursued most extensively in the U.S. Regulatory commissions regulate the prices charged by monopolies.

3. The rationale for public ownership or industrial regulation is that uncontrolled monopoly power can be abused. This is the public interest theory of regulation. The goal of industrial regulation is to allow the public to benefit from the lower costs of a natural monopoly while avoiding the reduction in output associated with an unregulated monopoly.

4. Regulators seek to establish rates that will cover production costs and yield a "fair" return to the enterprise, i.e., price = ATC.

B. Problems with industrial regulation:

1. An unregulated firm has the incentive to reduce its production cost. If a regulated firm lowers its operating costs, the increase in profits will lead the commission to lower its rates so as to reduce profit.

2. Higher production costs are passed on to the consumers in the form of higher rates. A regulated firm might give higher salaries for its workers without an increase in marginal productivity.

3. Although natural monopoly reduces cost through economies of scale, industrial regulation fosters considerable X-inefficiency.

4. Industrial regulation can lead to continuing monopoly power after the conditions of natural monopoly are gone.

   a. Technological changes create potential competition for the regulated industry (trucks compete with trains; cell phones compete with regular phones).

       b. Regulatory commissions may protect regulated firms out of the belief that new-entrant competitors would serve only select customers, thus resulting in higher rate for those who do not "pay their way."

       c. Regulators, by blocking entry, may perpetuate a monopoly where natural conditions no longer exist. The beneficiaries of outdated regulation are the regulated firms, their employees and, possibly, some of their customers.

  C. Legal Cartel Theory

    1. Proponents of this theory contend that regulators guarantee a return to the regulated firms while blocking entry and dividing up the market – activities that would be illegal in unregulated markets.

    2. Occupational licensing is an example of this theory in certain labor markets.

IV. Deregulation

  A. Deregulation came about in the 1970s and 1980s as a result of the greater acceptance of the legal cartel theory, increasing evidence of inefficiency in regulated industries, and the contention that government was regulating potentially competitive industries.

  B. Industries that were deregulated included airline, trucking, banking, railroad, natural gas, television broadcasting, and telecommunications.

  C. Controversy surrounds deregulation:

    1. One view asserts that deregulation will bring lower prices, more output, and greater efficiency.

    2. The opposing view fears that deregulation may lead to excessive competition and industry instability and that vital services may be withdrawn from smaller communities. There is also the fear that lower safety standards may result.

  D. Outcomes of deregulation.

    1. Benefits to society through lower prices, lower costs, and increased output are estimated at $50 billion annually. The gains come primarily from airlines, railroads, and trucking.

    2. Deregulation has lead to technological advances in new and improved products.

    3. Past deregulation has led to calls for further deregulation in other industries, for example electricity.

V. Social regulation

  A. Social regulation differs from industrial regulation in that it is concerned with the conditions under which production occurs, the impact of production on society, and the physical qualities of the goods produced. Table 32.2 lists the main Federal regulatory commissions engaged in social regulation.

  B. There are a few distinguishing features of social regulation.

    1. Social regulation is applied "across the board" to many or all industries and affects many people.

    2. Social regulation involves government in the details of production. Regulation often dictates the design of products, the conditions of employment, and the nature of the production process.

3. This type of legislation has expanded rapidly in last two decades, one example being the Equal Opportunity Commission that enforces laws against workplace discrimination on the basis of age, race, sex, disabilities, etc.

C. The optimal level of social regulation.

1. While most economists agree on the need for social regulation and that cost-benefit analysis should be used in determining the optimal level, there is disagreement on how to measure the marginal cost and marginal benefit of a particular regulation.

2. In support of social regulation:

a. Although the cost of social regulation is high, the appropriate test is to determine whether the cost exceeds the benefit.

b. The benefits are difficult to measure and are often realized only after time has passed.

c. There are continuing problems that can best be addressed through additional social regulation, for example, greater regulation of certain food products and health care services and insurance.

3. Criticism of social regulation:

a. Many standards are uneconomic in that marginal costs exceed marginal benefits leading to over regulation.

b. Many regulations are poorly written resulting in regulation beyond the original intent.

c. Many rules have unintended side effects, such as lighter fuel-efficient cars having higher fatality rates.

d. Overzealous, anti-market personnel often work for these agencies.

D. Two reminders:

1. There are costs to social regulation. Social regulation can produce higher prices, stifle competition, and reduce competition.

2. Social regulation can increase economic efficiency and society's well-being by improving working conditions, removing unsafe products, and reducing pollution.

X. **LAST WORD: The Microsoft Antitrust Case**

A. In May 1998, the U.S. Justice Department, 19 individual states, and the District of Columbia (the government) filed antitrust charges against Microsoft under the Sherman Antitrust Act.

B. The government charged that Microsoft had violated Section 2 of the act by taking a series of actions that were designed to maintain its "Windows" monopoly;

C. Microsoft denied the charges, arguing that it had achieved success through product innovation and lawful business practices. It also pointed out that monopoly was transitory because of rapid technological advances.

D. In June 2000, the district court ruled that Microsoft's share of the software used to operate Intel-compatible personal computers was 95 percent of the market, which clearly gave Microsoft monopoly power.

E. Although being a monopoly is not illegal, the court stated that Microsoft had violated the Sherman Act by using anticompetitive means to maintain and broaden its monopoly power.

These actions were taken against Netscape's Navigator and Sun's Java programming language. The court ruled that Microsoft had illegally tied the Microsoft browser, Internet Explorer, to Windows and provided Internet Explorer at no charge.

F. The court concluded that Microsoft had mounted an attack on competitors and had used actions that trammeled the competitive process through which innovation occurs.

G. The court ordered Microsoft to be split into two companies. These companies were prohibited from entering into joint ventures with one another.

H. In late 2000, Microsoft filed an appeal with a U.S. court of appeals.

ANSWERS TO END-OF-CHAPTER QUESTIONS

32-1   Both antitrust policy and industrial regulation deal with monopoly. What distinguishes the two approaches? How does government decide to use one form of regulation rather than the other?

One of the goals of government in a market economy is to promote competition as a way of achieving efficiency. One approach is to maintain competition by using antitrust laws to discourage the creation of excess monopoly power such as through mergers or by taking action against a firm that is abusing its monopoly power. The other approach, particularly in cases where there is a natural monopoly, is for the government to regulate the firm. The government will choose an approach by analyzing the structure of the industry, the cost structure of the firm, the impact of the firm's actions on its competitors and customers, industry technology, and the likelihood of new competitors entering the industry.

32-2   (*Key Question*)   Describe the major provisions of the Sherman and Clayton acts. What government entities are responsible for enforcing those laws? Are firms permitted to initiate antitrust suits on their own against other firms?

Sherman Act: Section 1 prohibits conspiracies to restrain trade; Section 2 outlaws monopolization. Clayton Act (as amended by Celler-Kefauver Act of 1950): Section 2 outlaws price discrimination; Section 3 forbids tying contracts; Section 7 prohibits mergers which substantially lessen competition; Section 8 prohibits interlocking directorates. The acts are enforced by the Department of Justice, Federal Trade Commission, and state attorneys general. Private firms can bring suit against other firms under these laws.

32-3   Identify the basic issues involved in the U.S. Steel, Alcoa, and Du Pont cellophane cases. What issues in antitrust enforcement are implicit in these cases?

The main issue in the landmark U.S. Steel case was whether the mere possession of monopoly power was sufficient cause to convict a company, or whether illegal acts had to be proved. In other words, the courts had to decide whether an industry should be judged on the basis of its structure or behavior. The courts accepted the behaviorist position, thereby implementing a precedent known as the "rule of reason" because it stated that U.S. Steel had behaved reasonably in obtaining its market power. The Alcoa case decades later dealt with the same basic issue as the U.S. Steel case. This time, however, the courts reversed the U.S. Steel case precedent and accepted the position that monopoly structure was sufficient for violation of the law; illegal acts did not have to be proven to successfully prosecute a firm for antitrust violations. The issue in the du Pont cellophane case was how widely to define an industry for the purposes of measuring market power. In this case the courts chose a broad definition of the relevant market—flexible wrapping materials rather than cellophane—and ruled that du Pont had not monopolized the market.

The common issue in all of these cases revolved around how to define illegal monopoly power.

32-4 Explain how strict enforcement of the antitrust laws might conflict with (a) promoting exports to achieve a balance of trade; (b) easing burdens in the defense industry; and (c) encouraging new technologies. Do you see any dangers of using selective antitrust enforcement as part of an industrial policy?

Strict enforcement of the antitrust laws could mean that a merger of two large firms would be prohibited or a dominant manufacturer in an industry might be broken up. (a) The targeted firms could be weakened, which might reduce their ability to compete successfully with strong foreign firms in sales abroad. This in turn conflicts with the goal of expanding American exports. (b) Recent government military spending cuts have weakened major defense suppliers. The Defense Department and antitrust regulators have reached an informal agreement to ease the way for consolidation of some of these defense industry firms. (c) Major mergers involving companies in entertainment, telecommunications, computer manufacturers and software producers have led to questions of how strict antitrust enforcement should be in these industries, where emerging technology may benefit from industry restructuring. Hastening the development of the "information superhighway" could also benefit U.S. exports of these services, which would strengthen our trade balance.

Selective enforcement of antitrust laws is a type of government industrial policy that interferes with the market process to the extent that it favors some industries by easing the way for concentration in some industries and strictly limiting consolidation in others. Selective enforcement encourages rent seeking and self-interest lobbying efforts, which may dictate policy more than the technological merits warrant.

32-5 (*Key Question*) How would you expect antitrust authorities to react to (a) a proposed merger of Ford and General Motors; (b) evidence of secret meetings by contractors to rig bids for highway construction projects; (c) a proposed merger of a large shoe manufacturer and a chain of retail shoe stores; and (d) a proposed merger of a small life insurance company and a regional candy manufacturer.

(a) They would block this horizontal merger (violation of Section 7 of the Clayton Act). (b) They would charge these firms with price fixing (violation of Section 1 of the Sherman Act). (c) They would allow this vertical merger, unless both firms had very large market shares and the resultant merger substantially lessens competition. (d) They would allow this conglomerate merger.

32-6 Suppose a proposed merger of firms will simultaneously lessen competition and reduce unit costs through economies of scale. Do you think such a merger should be allowed?

Abstracting from other issues (for example, the relative sizes of the two firms in the market), such a merger should only be allowed if it can be shown that price reductions associated with the decrease in unit costs will outweigh the probable increase in price associated with the reduced level of competition in the industry.

32-7 In the 1980s, Pepsico Inc., which then had 28 percent of the soft drink market, proposed to acquire the Seven-Up Co. Shortly thereafter the Coca-Cola Company, with 39 percent of the market, indicated it wanted to acquire the Dr. Pepper Company. Seven-Up and Dr. Pepper each controlled about 7 percent of the market. In your judgment, was the government's decision to block these mergers appropriate?

The government's decision was justified. Each of the proposed merged companies would have resulted in a Herfindahl index of well over 1800, the guideline used by the federal government for horizontal mergers. Furthermore, the mergers would have significantly increased the level of concentration in the soft-drink industry, with only two firms effectively controlling four-fifths of the market. Proponents of the merger might argue that economies of scale in the industry necessitate the formation of large firms such as Pepsico and Coca-Cola, but this is unlikely. (Note: Later Dr. Pepper and Seven-Up merged and in 1995 were in turn purchased by a Canadian firm.)

32-8   "The antitrust laws serve to penalize efficiently managed firms." Do you agree? Why or why not?

Opponents of antitrust legislation contend that by restricting the operations of those firms that are most successful in a particular market these laws reduce efficiency, penalizing well-managed firms and allowing for the continued existence of badly managed companies. Proponents of antitrust legislation argue that firms subject to the laws still have a strong incentive to produce efficiently—the profit motive. Furthermore, firms with monopoly power allocate resources inefficiently by restricting output below the point where marginal benefits to society equal marginal costs and often act in a predatory way toward competitors and potential competitors. By reducing monopoly power antitrust laws therefore enhance economic efficiency. Correctly applied, antitrust legislation probably serves to increase efficiency overall.

32-9   "The social desirability of any given business enterprise should be judged not on the basis of its market share but on the basis of its conduct and performance." Make a counterargument, referring to the monopoly model in your statement.

Market share is a good indication of a firm's monopoly power. A firm with substantial monopoly power will likely use the power to restrict output, charge high prices, generate excessive profits, and act in predatory ways toward competitors and potential competitors. The mere fact that a firm has significant monopoly power is a strong indication that it is violating antitrust laws.

32-10   (*Key Question*) What types of industries, if any, should be subjected to industrial regulation? What specific problems does industrial regulation entail?

Industries composed of firms with natural monopolies conditions are most likely to be subjected to industrial regulation. Regulation based on "fair-return" prices creates disincentives for firms to minimize costs since cost reductions lead regulators to force firms to change a lower price. Regulated firms may also use "creative" accounting to boost costs and hide profits. Because regulatory commissions depend on information provided by the firms themselves and commission members are often recruited from the industry, the agencies may in effect be controlled by the firms they are supposed to oversee. Also, industrial regulation sometimes is applied to industries that are not, or no longer are, natural monopolies. Regulation may lead to the conditions of a cartel, conditions that are illegal in an unregulated industry.

32-11   In view of the problems in regulating natural monopolies, compare socially optimal (marginal-cost) pricing and fair-return pricing by referring again to Figure 24-9. Assuming a government subsidy might be used to cover any loss entailed by marginal-cost pricing, which pricing policy would you favor? What problems might this subsidy entail?

Many of the regulatory problems associated with fair-return pricing also apply to a policy of marginal-cost pricing. In the unlikely case that a marginal-cost pricing policy does not entail public subsidies, it is subject to fewer regulatory problems. While there is an incentive for firms to artificially inflate marginal-cost estimates, there is no disincentive to contain costs and inefficient substitutions of capital for labor are not encouraged. Some of these conclusions do not hold in the more likely case where public subsidies are required.

Because marginal-cost pricing fosters allocative efficiency, it is preferable to fair-return pricing. However, if the firm requires public subsidies to produce at the socially optimal point, the same disincentive exists to minimize actual and estimated unit costs as with fair-return pricing, since cost reductions will simply lead to a lower subsidy. Inefficient substitutions of capital for labor are not encouraged, since regulators are not attempting to enforce a stipulated rate of return. While public subsidies to ensure allocative efficiency can be worthwhile from an economic perspective, they are usually politically unpopular, since voters are reluctant to provide large monopolistic firms with scarce public funds.

32-12   (*Key Question*) How does social regulation differ from industrial regulation? What types of costs and benefits are associated with social regulation?

Industrial regulation is concerned with prices, output, and profits specific industries, whereas social regulation deals with the broader impact of business on consumers, workers, and third parties. Benefits: increased worker and product safety, less environmental damage, reduced economic discrimination. Two types of costs: administrative costs, because regulations must be administered by costly government agencies, compliance costs, because firms must increase spending to comply with regulations.

32-13   Use economic analysis to explain why the optimal amount of product safety may be less than the amount that would totally eliminate risks of accidents and deaths. Use automobiles as an example.

To produce an automobile that would totally eliminate the risk of accidents and death would be extremely expensive in terms of materials. Additionally, the cost of operating such a vehicle would likely be expensive because of the weight of the car. As additional design changes are considered, engineers should balance the marginal cost of providing the extra units of safety with the expected marginal benefit received from the design change.

32-14   (*Last Word*) Under what law and on what basis did the Federal government find Microsoft guilty of violating the antitrust laws? What was the government's proposed remedy? In mid-2000, Microsoft appealed the district court ruling to a higher court. Update the Microsoft story, using the Internet browser. What is the current status of that appeal? Is it still pending? Did Microsoft win its appeal? Or was the district court's decision upheld?

Microsoft was found guilty of violating the Sherman Act. The court ruled that Microsoft had taken unlawful actions to maintain its Windows monopoly by tying the Internet Explorer to Windows at no charge. Also under license from Sun, Microsoft developed Windows-related Java software that made Sun's own software incompatible with Windows. The court's remedy was to break Microsoft into two companies that were prohibited from entering into joint ventures.

CHAPTER THIRTY-THREE
AGRICULTURE: ECONOMICS AND POLICY

CHAPTER OVERVIEW

This chapter represents a case study of agriculture, one of the most important sectors of the U.S. economy. The long-standing, low-income farm problem continues to be a timely issue. This problem is surveyed with a look at some of the short-run and long-run causes.

Public policies toward agriculture are described in some detail and critically evaluated, including their international implications. The 1996 Freedom to Farm Act is discussed. The Last Word section focuses on an international economic analysis of the sugar program.

WHAT'S NEW

This chapter has been significantly revised. A new Figure 33.3 has been added that shows U.S. farm exports as a percentage of farm output. Old Figure 33.3 showing inflation-adjusted prices received by farmers has been replaced by Figure 33.4 that shows inflation-adjusted prices for selected agricultural commodities. Table 33.3 has been changed to show farm employment rather than farm population. The discussion of the 1996 Freedom to Farm Act and the transition from price supports and acreage allotments to free-market agriculture has been expanded. Recent agricultural developments of 1998 and 1999 have been included.

The Last Word has been updated. One Web-Based Question has been updated and the other is new.

INSTRUCTIONAL OBJECTIVES

After completing this chapter, students should be able to:

1. Describe both the long-run and short-run farm problems.
2. State four causes of the short-run farm problem.
3. State four causes of the long-run farm problem.
4. Explain the rationale for the past government farm policies.
5. Define and explain the significance of parity.
6. Explain price supports verbally and graphically.
7. State seven effects of price supports.
8. Describe two government policies used to limit surpluses.
9. Present four criticisms of the past U.S. farm policy.
10. Use public choice theory to explain the contradictions in U.S. farm policy.
11. Explain how the politics of the farm-subsidy program has changed.
12. Describe the world trade impact of current farm programs in the European Union and the U.S.
13. State the goals of the Freedom to Farm Act.
14. Define and identify terms and concepts listed at the end of the chapter.

COMMENTS AND TEACHING SUGGESTIONS

1. This chapter can be used in several ways. It can be used (a) as a real-world case study to demonstrate analytical concepts, especially elasticity, pure competition, and government interference with market-determined prices; or (b) to illustrate a problem with complex interrelationships among social, political, economic, and global issues.

2. Have students research the agricultural industry in the state in which their college is located. Which crops are most important? Where is the farming industry located? Are family farms typical in their state or is it dominated by large corporations? What is the rank of the agricultural industry in the state? Is it important or minor? Do government subsidies contribute substantially to the farm income of the state? Which crops? Is there a department of agriculture at their college? Pay a visit and find out more!

3. Land use conflicts form the basis of many economic issues. In many cities urban sprawl is taking over valuable farmland. Debate the necessity for government planning versus allowing market forces to determine land use. Is an unplanned city livable? What are the long-term consequences of allowing unplanned growth on the edge of towns? The battle over water rights for farming or urban use can also be used.

4. Biotechnology is a very important growth industry. There are moral and ethical issues involved, in addition to economic considerations. The genetic engineering of plants holds much potential for meeting the needs of the growing population of the world. Are there any potential dangers? Will the cloning of animals revolutionize agriculture?

STUDENT STUMBLING BLOCK

Most students have few connections to rural areas and thus may not be initially interested in this topic. The chapter covers so many of the topics discussed in microeconomics that it is a good way of relating the theories to a real world problem. Any students who are interested in the political process will relate to the political aspects of the establishment and maintaining of agricultural policy.

LECTURE NOTES

I. **Introduction: American agriculture is economically important for a number of reasons.**

   A. Agriculture is a large industry. Consumers allocated about 14 percent of their personal consumption expenditures to food. Gross farm income was about $245 billion in 2000.

   B. Agriculture, in the absence of government farm programs, is a real world example of pure competition (see Chapter 23), many firms selling a virtually standardized product.

   C. Agriculture provides evidence of the intended and *unintended* effects of government policies that interfere with market forces.

   D. Farm policies are excellent illustrations of Chapter 31's special interest effect and rent- seeking behavior.

   E. Agriculture reflects the increasing globalization of markets.

   F. This chapter examines the economics of agriculture as well as examining the problems with government intervention programs and recent changes in government farm policies.

II. **The economics of agriculture**

   A. The short-run problem: Price and income instability result from several factors.

1.   There is an inelastic demand for agricultural products. The price elasticity of demand is low since there are few substitutes for agricultural products in general, and diminishing marginal utility occurs rapidly in wealthier societies (Figure 33.1).

2.   There are fluctuations in output: Weather is an important factor in production, as is the competitive nature of farming. Both of these result in the individual farmer having little control over the amount of output. Coupled with an inelastic demand this means that relatively small changes in output can lead to relatively large changes in farm prices and incomes. A bumper crop can result in a loss of revenue and income because of the inelasticity of demand (Figure 33.1).

3.   Fluctuations in domestic demand can lead to sharp changes in farm incomes (Figure 33.2) but not farm production, due to the fact that farmers' fixed costs are high when compared with their variable costs.

4.   Some of the volatility of demand is caused by unstable foreign demand that is dependent to some extent on weather and crop conditions in the countries that buy U.S. agricultural products. The increased importance of exports has increased the instability of farm incomes (Figure 33.3). (Key Question 1)

5.   Figure 33.4 shows the volatility in prices of select agricultural commodities.

B.   The long-run problem is a declining industry.

1.   Over time, technology has led to a rapidly increasing supply keeping the pressure on lower prices. Government-sponsored research has been the source of much of the technological advance.

2.   Demand has not grown as fast as supply.

3.   Demand for agricultural products is relatively income inelastic—the quantity demanded doesn't rise proportionately as incomes rise.

4.   Population growth has not been enough to allow demand to keep pace with increases in supply.

5.   Figure 33.5 is a graphical portrayal of the long-run situation. Given the inelastic price and income demand for farm products, an increase in the supply of farm products relative to the demand for them has created persistent tendencies for farm incomes to fall relative to nonfarm incomes. (Key Question 3)

6.   Low farm incomes have resulted in an out migration of agricultural workers who worked on small, high-cost farms, a consolidation of smaller farms, and the emergence of huge agribusiness producers.

7.   The recent increase in farm household incomes has been partially because of members of farm households taking nonfarm jobs.

III.   **The Economics of Farm Policy**

A.   The "farm program," which began in the 1930s, involves six basic policies.

1.   Subsidies to support prices, incomes, and output;

2.   Soil and water conservation;

3.   Agricultural research;

4.   Farm credit;

5. Crop insurance;

6. Subsidized sale of farm products in world markets.

B. This program has been viewed by farmers and politicians as primarily a program to prop up prices and incomes.

C. Rationale for farm subsidies: A variety of arguments have been made over the years to justify farm subsidies.

1. Many farmers earn relatively low incomes.

2. The "family farm" is an American institution that should be preserved.

3. Farms are highly competitive, but their suppliers have considerable market power which puts farmers at an unfair advantage (Figure 33.6).

C. The parity concept was established by the Agricultural Adjustment Act of 1933. Parity suggests that the relationship between the prices received by farmers for their output and the prices they must pay for goods and services should remain constant at the prosperous level of 1910-1914 base period. The parity ratio is the ratio of prices received by farmers divided by the prices paid by farmers and today is a fraction of the parity concept. This indicates that prices received must rise dramatically for farmers to achieve parity.

Parity ratio = prices received by farmers / prices paid by farmers

D. The concept of parity provides the rationale for government price floors on farm products; these minimum prices are called price supports. Many different price support programs have been tried; they all tend to have similar effects.

1. Support prices tend to cause surplus output because private consumers cut back the quantity purchased at the higher support price, and sellers offer a greater quantity than at the lower market equilibrium price.

2. Farmers gain from price supports as their gross revenues increase (Figure 33.7).

3. Consumers lose because they must pay the higher price and receive less. In some cases the difference between world market prices and support prices can be great. For example the U.S. price of sugar is more than two times the world market price.

4. There is an overallocation of resources to agriculture, which represents an efficiency loss. The competitive market would produce less output at a lower price.

5. There are other social losses.

   a. Taxpayers pay higher taxes to finance the government's purchase of the surplus.

   b. Government's intervention entails administrative costs.

   c. "Rent-seeking" activity by farm groups involves considerable sums to sustain political support for price supports and other programs to enhance farm incomes.

6. Environmental costs result from the extra production.

   a. Greater use of fertilizer and pesticides occurs.

   b. More land is cultivated, including "marginal" land that is erodable and wetlands that support wildlife habitat.

7. There are international costs of farm price supports (see Last Word).

a. Inefficient use of resources extends worldwide as U.S. limits imports of foreign products.

b. Government-caused surpluses are "dumped" on world markets which depresses world market prices for these products.

E. How do the government and farmers cope with surpluses that occur with price supports?

1. Restricting supply: One policy is called "set aside" or acreage allotment programs that accompany price supports. Farmers agree to limit planting in exchange for the supported prices. "Soil bank" programs pay farmers not to grow any crops, but conserve land for a period of time.

2. Bolstering demand is another way to erase or reduce surpluses.

a. Finding new uses for agricultural products is one way to raise demand—one such use is gasohol, a gasoline-grain alcohol fuel blend.

b. Augmenting domestic and foreign demand also is done through programs like food stamps for low-income families to buy more food and the Food for Peace program, a government program for less developed countries to buy our surplus farm products.

IV. **Criticism, Politics, and Reform**

A. Sixty years of experience with government price support programs suggested that the goals and techniques of farm policy needed to be reexamined and revised. In 1996 Congress ended the price support programs for several farm commodities.

1. Agricultural subsidies were designed to treat the symptoms of farm problems, not the causes.

2. The root cause of the problem is a misallocation of resources. There have been too many farmers relative to the rest of the economy.

3. Price and income supports have kept people in agriculture who otherwise would have moved to nonfarm occupations.

4. Price support and subsidy programs benefit farmers who need it least. In 1996, 6 percent of farms with $250,000 in sales or more received 46 percent of the payments; the poorest 61 percent of farmers received only 4 percent of direct subsidy payments.

5. Some believe that it would have been a better use of the money to provide direct-income supports to low-income farmers and to provide retraining to those who decided to leave agriculture.

B. Policy contradictions:

1. Subsidized research is aimed at increasing farm productivity, while farmers take land out of production to reduce supply.

2. Price supports for crops mean increased feed costs for ranchers and higher meat prices for consumers.

3. Tobacco farmers are subsidized while the costs of medical care soar higher.

4. Import quotas on sugar conflict with our free trade policies.

C. Public choice theory can help explain the contradictions in farm policy. (See Chapter 31)

1. Rent-seeking behavior occurs when a group (a union, a firm in an industry, or farmers producing a particular crop) uses political means to transfer income or wealth to itself at the expense of another group or society as a whole.

2. The special-interest effect involves promoting a policy or program whereby a small group of farmers realizes large benefits, and the individual taxpayer's and consumer's costs are largely hidden and relatively small.

3. Logrolling occurs to get representatives from rural states to vote on urban issues.

4. Large agribusinesses that sell chemicals and machinery to farms, as well as Department of Agriculture employees, also lobbied for the continuation of the programs.

D. There has been a change in politics of farm subsidies.

1. The farm population continues to decline and is now less than 2 percent of the population.

2. Urban congressional representatives have been critically examining the effects of the farm policies on consumers' grocery bills.

3. More farms resent the Federal government intrusion into their decision making.

E. World trade consideration

1. The U.S. has taken the lead in reducing trade barriers on agricultural products.

2. Nations of the European Union (EU) and many other nations continue to provide agricultural price support. They then try to rid themselves domestic surpluses on the world markets.

3. These trade barriers hinder American farmers, first because of the trade barriers hinder U.S. farmers from selling in the EU and second because the subsidized exports depress world agricultural prices.

4. These policies distort both world agricultural trade and the international allocation of agricultural resources. Agricultural subsidies shift production away from what would occur based on comparative advantage.

   a. Artificially high prices in industrially advanced nations encourage more farm output than would otherwise occur.

   b. Farmers in developing countries then face artificially low prices for their exports, discouraging output.

5. In 1994, the world's trading nations agreed to reduce farm price-support programs and barriers on imported farm products.

VI. **Recent Reform: Freedom to Farm.**

A. In 1996, Congress passed the Freedom to farm Act, which:

1. Ended price supports and acreage allotments for wheat, corn, barley, oats sorghum, rye, cotton and rice, thus allowing farmers to respond to changing crop prices;

2. Provided guaranteed annual transition payments to farmers through 2002; these payments are based upon the subsidies formerly received by the farmer and not on crop prices or the farmer's current income.

B. Economists expect the act will increase the overall agricultural output in the U.S., but also the variability of agricultural prices and farm incomes.

C. To protect themselves against the volatility of prices and income, farmers can be expected to use more tools to manage risk.

D. During 1998 and 1999 when commodity and pork prices severely declined, the government provided emergency relief in the form of farm-income assistance and crop disaster relief.

E. Clearly, the Federal government is not out of the farm-subsidy area.

VII. **LAST WORD: The Sugar Program: A Sweet Deal**

A. Price supports for U.S. sugar producers has kept U.S. sugar prices twice the world price for an estimated cost to consumers of $1.9 billion per year. The effect is regressive because poor households spend a larger percentage of their income on food than do high-income households. Also, sugar growers receive benefits that are estimated to be twice the nation's average family income. In one recent year, a single producer received $30 million in benefits while many sugar producers receive more than $1 million each year.

B. Import quotas have been imposed to keep low-priced foreign sugar out of the U.S. market so that price supports can be maintained. In 1975, 30 percent of U.S. sugar was imported; today imports are about 16 percent comes from abroad.

C. Important foreign markets in less developed countries have been harmed. The decline in potential sugar revenue has hurt the Philippines, Brazil, and a number of Central American countries.

1. Decline in export revenues hurts their ability to repay foreign debt.

2. The sugar that could have been sold in the U.S. is dumped on world markets, where the world price is then further depressed.

3. The U.S. could become an exporting country. This would increase competition for the sugar producer of the developing world.

D. The General Accounting Office estimates that U.S. sugar producers receive a benefit of $1 billion annually while the sugar program costs consumers $1.9 billion. This loss of efficiency has resulted from an over-allocation of resources to the production and processing of sugar in the U.S.

E. Price supports have caused a shifting of resources to less efficient U.S. producers away from more efficient, low-cost foreign producers.

ANSWERS TO END-OF-CHAPTER QUESTIONS

33-1   (*Key Question*) Carefully evaluate: "The supply and demand for agricultural products are such that small changes in agricultural supply will result in drastic changes in prices. However, large changes in farm prices have modest effects on agricultural output." (*Hint*: A brief review of the distinction between supply and quantity supplied may be of assistance.) Do exports increase or reduce the instability of demand for farm products? Explain.

First sentence: Shifts in the supply curve of agricultural goods (*changes in supply*) relative to fixed inelastic demand curves produce large changes in equilibrium prices. Second sentence: But these drastic changes in prices produce only small changes in equilibrium outputs (where *quantities demanded* equals *quantities supplied*) because demands are inelastic.

Because exports are volatile from one year to the next, they increase the instability of demand for farm products.

33-2   What relationship, if any, can you detect between the fact that the farmer's fixed costs of production are large and the fact that the supply of most agricultural products is generally inelastic? Be specific in your answer.

Because fixed costs are a significant portion of total costs, average variable costs for agricultural producers will tend to be small, and shut-down points will occur only at relatively low prices. As long as prevailing prices exceed these levels, farmers will produce close to capacity to recoup as much of their fixed costs as possible.

33-3   (*Key Question*) Explain how each of the following contributes to the farm problem: (a) the inelasticity of the demand for farm products, (b) rapid technological progress in farming, (c) the modest long-run growth in the demand for farm commodities, and (d) the volatility of export demand.

(a) Because the demand for most farm products is inelastic, the frequent fluctuations in supply brought about by weather and other factors have relatively small effects on quantity demanded, but large effects on equilibrium prices of farm products. Farmers' sales revenues and incomes therefore are unstable. (b) Technological innovations have decreased production costs, increased long-run supply for most agricultural goods, and reduced the prices of farm output. These declines in prices have put a downward pressure on farm income. (c) The modest long-run growth in the demand for farm products has not been sufficient to offset the expansion of supply, resulting in stagnant farm income. (d) Foreign demand has been unpredictable. Any change in demand will affect farm prices but farmers cannot easily adjust production.

33-4   The key to efficient resource allocation is shifting resources from low-productivity to high-productivity uses. In view of the high and expanding physical productivity of agricultural resources, explain why many economists want to divert additional resources from farming to achieve allocative efficiency.

Economic efficiency is only partly a matter of high productivity or low marginal costs. Allocative efficiency depends on the requirement that the marginal benefit to society of producing another unit of a particular good exceeds the marginal cost. Even though total benefits to society from the production of most agricultural goods are high, low marginal costs are matched by low marginal benefits. In the case of agricultural markets subject to support prices, marginal costs at prevailing production levels exceed marginal benefits as measured by free market prices. This is the reason many economists contend resources should be moved out of these sectors.

33-5   Explain and evaluate: "Industry complains of the higher taxes it must pay to finance subsidies to agriculture. Yet the trend of agricultural prices has been downward, while industrial prices have been moving upward, suggesting that on balance agriculture is actually subsidizing industry."

According to this statement, one can distinguish transfers of income by using the concept of price parity. Since the parity ratio for farmers has declined they have necessarily been subsidizing industry. Changes in relative prices cannot be used to make these sorts of statements. Agricultural prices have declined relative to industrial prices largely because of decreases in costs in agriculture. Subsidies to agriculture have also increased the supply of many agricultural products. Lower agricultural prices are therefore partially the result of subsidies from industry to agriculture.

33-6   "Because consumers as a whole must ultimately pay the total incomes received by farmers, it makes no real difference whether this income is paid through free farm markets or through supported prices supplemented by subsidies financed out of tax revenues." Do you agree?

This argument is fallacious for two reasons. First, not all consumers of a particular good are taxpayers or vice versa. Taxpayers are forced to fund price-support programs for agricultural goods (e.g., peanuts or sugar) whether or not they choose to consume these particular items.

Second, and more important, price-support programs do not allow us to subsidize through taxation what we would otherwise be spending at the checkout counter since these programs increase both prices and taxes as well as taking resources away from more efficient domestic uses, lessening the rate of exodus from farming and distorting world agricultural markets.

33-7   If in a specific year the indexes of prices received and paid by farmers were 120 and 165 respectively, what would the party ratio be? Explain the meaning of this ratio.

Prices received by farmers would have increased by 20 percent since the base year (1910) whereas price paid by farmers would have increased by 65 percent during the same time period.

Parity ratio = prices received by farmers/prices paid by farmers = 120/165 = 73 percent

In this year, a unit of farm output can buy only 73 percent of could it could have in the base year.

33-8   (*Key Question*) Explain the economic effects of price supports. Explicitly include environmental and global impacts in your answer. On what grounds do economists contend that price supports cause a misallocation of resources?

Price supports benefit farmers, harm consumers, impose costs on society, and contribute to problems in world agriculture. Farmers benefit because the prices they receive and the output they produce both increase, expanding their gross incomes. Consumers lose because the prices they pay for farm products rise and quantities purchased decline. Society as a whole bears several costs. Surpluses of farm products will have to be bought and stored, leading to a greater burden on taxpayers. Domestic economic efficiency is lessened as the artificially high prices of farm products lead to an overallocation of resources to agriculture. The environment suffers: the greater use of pesticides and fertilizers contributes to water pollution; farm policies discourage crop rotation; and price supports encourage farming of environmentally sensitive land. The efficient use of world resources is also distorted because of the import tariffs or quotas, which such programs often require. Finally, domestic overproduction leads to supply increases in international markets, decreasing prices and causing a decline in the gross incomes of foreign producers.

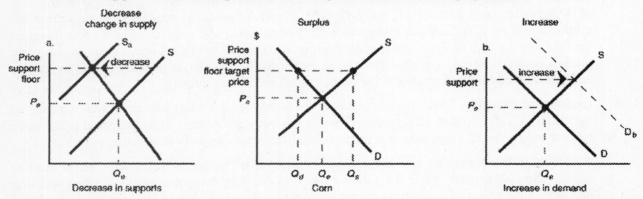

33-9   Use supply and demand curves to depict equilibrium price and output in a competitive market for some farm product. Then show how an above-equilibrium price floor (price support) would cause a surplus in this market. Demonstrate in your graph how government would reduce this surplus through a policy that (a) changes supply or (b) changes demand. Identify each of the following actual government policies as primarily affecting the supply of, or the demand for, a particular farm product: acreage allotments, food stamp program, Food-for-Peace program, a government buyout of diary herds, export promotion.

    (See graphs above)

    Average allotments: decrease supply

Food stamp program: increase demand

Food-for-Peace: increase demand

Government buyout of dairy herds: decrease in supply

Export promotion: increase in demand

33-10 Do you agree with each of the following statements? Explain why or why not.

   a. "The problem with American agriculture is that there are too many farmers. This is not the fault of farmers, but the fault of government programs."

   b. "The Federal government ought to buy up U.S. farm surpluses and give them away to developing nations."

   c. "All industries would like government price supports if they could get them; agriculture got price supports only because of its strong political clout."

(a) Yes, historically the problem has been one of too many farmers, and public policy has been oriented toward supporting farm prices and incomes rather than fixing the resource allocation problem. Further, price and income supports have kept people in agriculture who otherwise would have moved to nonfarm occupations.

(b) No, this is not the best way for the U.S. to provide foreign aid. This policy would contribute to the misallocation of resources in the U.S. and prevent a more efficient solution. Farmers elsewhere in the world who might have a comparative advantage over American farms would be harmed, perhaps forcing them to leave the industry.

(c) While strong political clout has played a role in the price supports given to farmers, there were other more important factors. Government has subsidized American agriculture since the 1930s. Agricultural prices and incomes are more volatile than in most other industries. Small changes in farm output translate into a relatively large change in price because the demand for these products is price inelastic. In the absence of government intervention, agricultural markets are highly competitive and farmers have no control over the price they receive for their goods. However, farmers must buy their supplies and capital equipment in markets where producers have a high degree of control over price. This disparity and disadvantage along with a variety of other arguments has been used to justify farm subsidies over the years. Likewise, government support programs come with government intervention into management decisions by farmers.

33-11 What are the effects of farm subsidies such as those of the United States and the European Union on (a) domestic agricultural prices; (b) world agricultural prices; (c) the international allocation of agricultural resources?

Domestic agricultural prices are obviously higher than they would be in the absence of subsidies. The reason for the subsidies in the first place is that market equilibrium prices were lower than farmers believed they should be. Without subsidies farm product prices would initially fall to the lower equilibrium price. It is also argued that subsidies protect inefficient farmers, and without such programs only the efficient, low-cost producers would remain. To the extent that this is true, farm prices would remain lower than the current support prices that exist for many products.

The situation on world markets is somewhat more complex because the European Union (EU) subsidizes its exports of agricultural products on world markets. Thus, the supply of these products is greater than it would be under competitive market conditions, and the world prices of many products are depressed.

There is an international misallocation of agricultural resources. Wherever there is a farm subsidy program without programs restricting supply, there will be an expansion of production in response to the above-market price supported. Without such restrictions, continuing farm subsidies would mean that more than the efficient amount of resources is devoted to production of subsidized products. The over-allocation occurs both within and among countries. Farmers in countries that might more efficiently import agricultural products and use these resources more productively in other pursuits are encouraged to remain in agriculture as long as their governments subsidize this type of production. Meanwhile, farmers in countries without farm programs face artificially depressed world market prices and find it is not profitable to raise farm products for export. In a free-market world, they might be more efficient producers than their subsidized neighbors.

33-12 Use public choice theory to explain the persistence of farm subsidies in the face of major criticisms of these subsidies. If the special-interest effect is so strong, then what factors made it possible in 1996 for government to end price supports and acreage allotments for several crops?

Rent-seeking behavior occurs when a group (a labor union, a firm in a specific industry or farmers producing a particular crop) uses political means to transfer income or wealth to itself at the expense of another group or society as a whole. The special-interest effect involves a program or policy that benefits a small group greatly, while a much larger group individually suffers relatively small losses. Farmers have been relatively successful in both rent-seeking and special interest legislation. A combination of factors has led to a change in the politics of farm subsidies. As the farm population has declined, agriculture's political power has also diminished. Also, more farmers have become resentful of government intrusion into their decision-making.

Today large corporations dominate the production of some crops and land owners may live in distant countries with no direct connection to the farm operation.

Agricultural subsidies distort both world trade and the international allocation of agricultural resources. The United States made such a strong case against price supports in world trade negotiations in 1994 that it undoubtedly altered the domestic debate on the subject as well.

33-13 What is the major intent of the Freedom to Farm Act of 1996? Do you agree with this intent? Why or why not? Why have there been recent calls for repeal of the act?

The intent of the Freedom to Farm Act of 1996 was to allow markets, not government programs, to determine what products farmers grow, where they are grown, and their total outputs. To ease the transition away from farm subsidies, farmers were to receive guaranteed, but declining, annual "transition payments" through 2002.

I agree that market allocation of resources is more efficient than the use of government programs. The overall output of agricultural products is likely to increase although prices are likely to be more volatile. This will increase the risk to farmers, but will benefit consumers and tax payers.

During 1998 and 1999, agricultural prices were low and farm incomes fell. Farmers, who had gotten used to financial help from the government-support programs, realized that there was a downside to allowing the market to determine prices and, therefore, farm incomes.

33-14 (*Last Word*) Who benefits and who loses from the U.S. sugar subsidy program?

The benefits accrue to the sugar producers in the United States, but the costs are heavy on U.S. consumers and foreign producers. The estimated cost to U.S. consumers is about $1 billion per year in terms of higher sugar prices. As a result of import quotas, foreign sugar imports have declined from 30 percent of our sugar consumption in 1975 to about 3-4 percent today. Foreign producers in less developed countries have suffered with export earnings declining as much as $7 billion per year which, in turn, means lower incomes in these poor countries. Also, the sugar barred from sale in the U.S. contributes to larger supplies on world markets, depressing the world price for sugar and further lowering foreign producer incomes. That situation may worsen because the U.S. subsidies have caused U.S. sugar production to increase to the point where we may become a sugar exporter and add to the competitive situation abroad. Further losses are incurred with such a misallocation of the world's resources and a shift of demand toward corn-based and artificial sweeteners. This shift has contributed to an estimated 7000 lost jobs in the last decade in sugar refineries in this country and American candy manufacturers may add to the losses as they consider moving abroad where sugar is less expensive.

CHAPTER THIRTY-FOUR
INCOME INEQUALITY AND POVERTY

CHAPTER OVERVIEW

The statistical information, analytical concepts, and discussions of public policy alternatives can help students find their way through the maze of controversial topics and issues concerning income distribution and poverty.

The chapter begins by surveying some basic facts concerning the distribution of income in the United States and the Lorenz Curve that gives a graphic representation of the distribution. Next, the major causes of income inequality are considered, as well as historical trend information. Third, the debate over income inequality and the tradeoff between equality and efficiency implied by this debate is examined. Fourth, the poverty problem in America is analyzed. Finally, the social insurance programs and new public-assistance programs are outlined and discussed.

WHAT'S NEW

That chapter has been reorganized. The section on the historical trends in inequality and the causes of these trends is now discussed after the general discussion of the causes of income inequality. The maximum income level at each quintile has been added to Table 34.2. Table 34.4 has been expanded to include the earned income credit. The discussion on welfare reform has been revised to include effects of the Personal Responsibility Act of 1996.

The Last Word is new. One of the Web-Based Question is new the other has been revised.

INSTRUCTIONAL OBJECTIVES

After completing this chapter, students should be able to:

1. Describe the distribution of income in the United States by personal income categories by families and quintile distribution by families.

2. Explain how a Lorenz curve is used to describe income inequality.

3. Discuss the impact of income mobility on income distribution data.

4. Explain the broadened concept of income, which includes the effects of taxes and transfer payments, and how this affects the extent of inequality of income and poverty in the U.S.

5. List seven causes of an unequal income distribution.

6. Describe changes and causes for the changes in inequality through the 1929-47, 1947-69, and 1969-96 periods.

7. State and evaluate the cases for and against income inequality, using the equality vs. efficiency argument.

8. Define poverty as the Federal government does.

9. Identify the rate of poverty in the U.S., and the incidence of poverty for blacks, Hispanics, and female-headed families; identify some of the reasons for the poverty of each group.

10. Identify the "invisible" poor and give three reasons for this invisibility.

11. Contrast social insurance and public assistance (welfare) programs.

12. Describe the major social insurance programs.

13. Describe and evaluate the major public assistance (welfare) programs.

14. Explain the differences between social insurance programs and public assistance programs.

15. Describe and evaluate the goals and conflicts inherent in public assistant programs.

16. Explain the criticisms of the old welfare system.

17. Describe the major provisions of the Personal Responsibility Act of 1996.

18. Define and identify terms and concepts listed at the end of the chapter.

COMMENTS AND TEACHING SUGGESTIONS

1. Help students find a way to generalize the myriad facts presented here. Trends and "ballpark" figures are more important than exact statistics, which change from year to year.

2. Several topics in this chapter illustrate the tradeoffs inherent in the "economic way of thinking." For example, the goal is not perfect equality or inequality, but an acceptable degree of inequality. What degree is best? How much efficiency is society willing to give up for more equality? What is the minimum standard of living that a person should have to endure? Should we strive for equality of opportunity or equality of results?

3. Nearly every community has some poverty. Encourage students to discover the realities of local poverty through visits to a local social welfare agency, speaker presentations, or by having students discuss their own experiences.

4. Changing concerns over poverty and income inequality might be illustrated by assigning students to find newspaper or magazine articles on this topic from each of the three periods discussed in the text.

5. The Economic Report of the President and Statistical Abstract of the United States has much data dealing with topics covered in this chapter. Also, the reports based upon the 2000 census will provide current income distribution information.

STUDENT STUMBLING BLOCK

Much of the material in this chapter is descriptive and not difficult for students to comprehend. The difficulty comes in trying to separate emotional views of poverty and welfare programs from the facts. This is a good time to discuss the difference between positive and normative economics. Good debate topics are found in this chapter, and both state and Federal welfare reform programs can be presented for evaluation. Remind students that government "welfare" in the form of tax benefits and subsidies exists for middle-income and upper-income groups (education subsidies, home mortgage interest deductions from taxable income, farm subsidy programs and others).

This can be an emotional issue for a variety of reasons. Some students may hold strong beliefs that have little basis in fact. There may be students in your class who are desperately struggling to escape from poverty. There may be some current or former welfare recipients in your class who do not wish to reveal this to others. Discussion on this topic leads through a minefield with loaded cannons perched on each side.

LECTURE NOTES

I.   **Income inequality facts**

Income Inequality and Poverty

A. In 1999, over 32 million Americans—11.8 percent of the population—lived in poverty, 500,000 were estimated to be homeless, and George Lucas earned $400 million.

B. Personal income distribution is shown in Tables 34-1 and 34-2.

  1. Average family income in 1999 was $62,636.

  2. Seven percent of the families had annual incomes of less than $15,000 annual income while 15 percent had annual incomes of $100,000 or more.

  3. The top 20 percent of the families received nearly half (47 percent) of all income, more than ten times as much as the lowest 20 percent of families.

C. The Lorenz curve depicts income distribution graphically. Figure 34.1.

  1. If income were distributed perfectly equally, the Lorenz curve would be the straight-line diagonal line.

  2. The extent to which the actual income distribution varies from the line of perfect equality is the measure of inequality; the greater the distance of the curve from the line of equality, the more unequal the distribution of income.

  3. The extreme would be a line that follows the horizontal axis to the right until it meets the right vertical axis and then turns upward along that axis.

  4. The Lorenz curve can be used to compare changes in the curve over time or to compare income distributions across countries.

D. Income Mobility: The Time Dimension

  1. The income accounting period of a year is too short to be meaningful in judging income inequality. Over a period of time—several years, a decade, or a lifetime—earnings might be more equal.

  2. If Brad earns $1,000 in year 1 and $100,000 in year 2, while Jenny earns $100,000 in year 1 and $1000 in year 2, income distribution looks unequal in a single year, but appears equal over the two-year period.

  3. There is considerable "churning around" in the distribution of income over time.

  4. Most income receivers start at a low level, peak during middle age, and then decline. As a result, considerable income inequality will exist in any specific year because of age differences.

  5. Individuals and families will move up to higher quintile groups or move down to lower quintile groups. This is called income mobility.

  6. A recent Dallas Federal Reserve Bank study traced income mobility of individuals from their 1975 quintile to their 1991 quintile.

    a. Ninety-five percent of the people in the lowest quintile in 1975 had moved to a higher quintile by 1991.

    b. Almost 30 percent of the lowest quintile jumped to the richest quintile.

    c. Nearly 2/3 of the middle quintile changed to another quintile between 1975 and 1991.

    d. For the highest income quintile in 1975, 37 percent had fallen to a lower quintile by 1991.

E. Effect of Government on Redistribution

1. The income date in Tables 34-1 and 34-2 show before-tax, cash income, including earnings (wages, salaries, dividends, interest) and cash transfers (social security, unemployment compensation, welfare payments).

2. The figures do not take into account outlays for personal income taxes and payroll (social security) taxes. Nor do they include in-kind (noncash) transfers such as Medicare, Medicaid, food stamps or housing subsidies.

3. Government significantly redistributes income from higher to lower income households through taxes and transfers.

    a. Without government redistribution, the lowest 20 percent of households would have received only 1.1 percent of total income. With distribution they receive 4.9 percent.

    b. Because the American tax system is only modestly progressive, transfer payments are the most important method of redistribution. They account for more than 75 percent of the income of the lowest quintile.

II.   **Income Inequality: Causes**

A. Ability differences lead to differences in earnings.

B. Education and training correlate closely with differences in earnings. In general, the more education, the higher the income.

C. Discrimination in education, hiring, training, and promotions contributes to income inequality.

    1. If women and minorities are restricted to certain occupations, there will be an oversupply of workers relative to demand and wages and incomes will be low.

    2. If women and minorities are restricted from entering white-male occupations, there will be an undersupply of workers relative to demand and wages and incomes will be high.

D. Differences in tastes and risk preferences lead to different incomes.

    1. Workers who are willing to work long hours at arduous jobs will tend to earn more.

    2. Those who are willing to assume risk, e.g., entrepreneurs, are likely to earn more income.

E. Unequal distribution of wealth:

    1. Wealth is a "stock," reflecting at a particular moment the financial and real assets an individual has accumulated over time. A retired person may have little income but vast amounts of accumulated wealth.

    2. Ownership of wealth in the United States is more unequal than the distribution of income. In 1998, the wealthiest 10 percent of households owned 69 percent of total net wealth.

    3. This inequality of wealth leads to inequality in rent, interest and dividends, which contributes to income inequality.

F. Market power in the product market can lead to a firm receiving monopoly profits. A union or professional organization may be able to restrict the supply of labor, thus leading to higher than competitive wages and incomes.

G. Luck, connections, and misfortune are other forces explaining income differences. (Key Question 5)

III.   **Trends in inequality.**

A. Absolute incomes have risen over time, while the relative distribution by quintile has been changing.

B. Table 34.3 examines the relative income distribution by quintiles for selected years: 1929, 1935-36, 1947, 1955, 1969, 1985 and 1999.

1. During the 1929-47 time period, income inequality decreased as the share going to bottom fifth grew slightly, and share going to the top fifth declined significantly from 54 to 43 percent.

2. During the 1947-69 period, income inequality decreased very slightly as the share going to the bottom fifth grew by a fraction of a percent from 5 to 5.6 percent, and the share going to the top fifth declined slightly from 43 to 40.6 percent.

3. Since 1969, the trend has been in the other direction, that is, toward increased inequality as the share going to the bottom fifth has declined from 5.6 to 4.3 percent, and the share going to the top fifth has risen from 40.6 to 47.2 percent. It should be noted that the shares going to the second, third, and fourth quintiles has decrease as well. Today, the top fifth earns nearly ten times as much before-tax personal income as the bottom fifth.

C. Causes of growing inequality.

1. Firms have increased their demand for highly skilled and well-educated workers. Because the demand for these workers continues to exceed the supply, wages have been bid up. Between 1980 and 1999, the wage difference between college graduates and high school graduates increased. The growth of income to business, athletic, and entertainment "superstars" has increased income inequality.

2. In terms of demographics, large numbers of less-experienced and less-skilled "baby boomers" entered the labor force during the 1970s and 1980s, thus contributing to greater inequality during those decades. When high earnings potential men and women marry, the income to the highest quintile will likely increase. An increase in the number of families headed by single women has lead to greater inequality.

3. More international competition has reduced the demand for less-skilled, high-paid and often union workers in manufacturing industries in the U.S. An upsurge in immigration of unskilled workers.

4. Two cautions: First, all quintiles have grown in terms of absolute income, but growth was fastest in the top quintile. Second, increased income inequality is not unique to the U.S.

5. Global Perspective 34-1 indicates that there is more inequality in other nations.

IV. **Equality vs. Efficiency**

A. The case for equality is based on the idea that more equal distribution will maximize utility. If income is subject to diminishing marginal utility, then people at the high end of the income scale receive less utility per dollar of income than people at the low end. The argument is that utility would be raised if low-income people were given more by taking it from the high-income groups. The high-income earners would lose less utility than the low-income groups would gain. This idea is illustrated in Figure 34.3, which assumes that money incomes are subject to diminishing marginal utility (Chapter 21). If this is true, utility would be maximized when each has the same amount of income dollars.

B. The case for inequality is that inequality is an important determinant of the amount of income produced and available for distribution overall. In other words, inequality provides an incentive for people to work harder and more efficiently.

C. The equality-efficiency tradeoff is the belief that society sacrifices some efficiency when it tries to achieve more egalitarianism. The "leaky-bucket" analogy presumes that money must be transferred from the rich to the poor in a leaky bucket. The leak represents the efficiency loss due to the loss of incentives to work, to save and invest, and to accept risk. It also reflects the resources that must be diverted to bureaucracies that administer the tax-transfer system. How much of a leakage is there? And how much should society accept? The answers to these questions are not clear. Studies about the extent of tradeoff do not all agree, but the estimated loss ranges from a cost equal to the amount of the dollars given to the poor to as high as three times the amount of the dollars given to the poor.

V. **The Economics of Poverty**

    A. The degree of income inequality will not predict the amount of poverty in a society.

    B. Poverty is defined as a situation in which a family's basic needs are greater than its means of satisfying them. The poverty-level income is defined officially by government agencies based on family size. In 1999 poverty-level income was $8501 for a single person; $17,029 for a family of four; and $22,727 for a family of six. Over 32 million people or 11.8 percent of the population lived in poverty in 1999 according to this definition. Note that while the figures include cash transfers, they do not include in-kind transfers like medical care, housing assistance, and food stamps.

    C. The poor are not homogeneous, nor are they randomly distributed. Figures 34.4 and 34.5 provide details about the incidence of poverty among different groups in our society.

        1. Blacks and Hispanics bear a disproportionate share of poverty compared to whites (23.6, 22.8, and 9.8 percent, respectively, in 1999).

        2. The incidence of poverty is extremely high among female-headed families, foreign born people who are not citizens, and children under 18 years of age.

        3. Although there has been considerable movement out of poverty, poverty is much more long-lasting among black and Hispanic families, families headed by women, persons with little education and few labor market skills, and people who are personally and socially dysfunctional.

    D. Poverty Trends

        1. Figure 34.4 shows that total poverty fell between 1959 and 1969 and then rose in the early 1980s. Between 1993 and 1999, the poverty rate fell from 15.1 to 11.8 percent.

        2. Many who live in poverty are "invisible."

            a. Research shows that as many as half of those in poverty are poor for only one or two years and thus are not as visible as permanently downtrodden and needy.

            b. Permanently poor people are increasingly isolated geographically in depressed areas of large cities and rural areas of Appalachia, the deep South and the Southwest.

            c. The poor are politically invisible. They do not belong to advocacy groups and they have very little direct voice in U.S. politics.

VI. **The Income Maintenance System (Table 34.4)**

    A. The reduction in poverty is a widely accepted goal of public policy. Despite recent attempts to slow the upward trend in spending on these programs, enormous amounts of money are being spent.

    B. The U.S. income-maintenance system consists to two kinds of programs: social insurance and public assistance. Both types are entitlement programs.

C. Social insurance programs are viewed as earned rights because the beneficiaries have paid into them. Social security, unemployment compensation, and Medicare fit this category.

1. Old Age, Survivors, and Disability Health Insurance (OASDHI), or "social security" for short, is financed by a payroll tax of 7.65 percent levied on both the worker and the worker's employer on the first $76,200 of wage income. Currently, over 90 percent of the labor force is covered by this system. In 2000, over 45 million people received OASDHI benefits averaging about $804 per month.

2. Medicare is part of social security for the elderly and disabled. It also includes a low-cost voluntary insurance, which helps pay doctor fees.

3. Unemployment compensation is sponsored in all fifty states in cooperation with the Federal government. The size of payments and the number of weeks of coverage vary from state to state. Benefits averaged about $200 per week in 1999.

D. Public assistance programs provide benefits for those who are unable to earn income because of permanent handicaps or having no or very low incomes and also having dependent children. The Federal government finances about two-thirds of the welfare program expenditures, the rest being paid by the states.

1. Supplemental Security Income (SSI) is a program for people who are unable to work because of disability and who do not qualify for other programs.

2. Temporary Assistance for Needy Families (TANF) is state-administered but partly financed with federal grants. It provides aid to families with children and also seeks to reduce welfare dependency by providing job preparation and work.

3. The food stamp program is for low-income Americans who may qualify for coupons that are redeemable for food. The number of coupons received depends on a family's size and income.

4. Medicaid helps finance medical expenses of individuals in SSI and TANF programs.

5. The Earned Income Tax Credit (EITC) is a refundable tax credit for low-income working families with children, which reduces income taxes owed or provides the families with a cash payment if the credit exceeds their tax liability. The purpose of the credit is to offset social security taxes paid by low-wage earners. EITC is a wage subsidy that can pay as much as $2 per hour for the lowest-paid workers with families. Twenty million recipients qualified for the program in 1999 and the total cost was $30 billion.

VII. **Welfare: Goals and Conflicts**

A An ideal public assistance program would achieve three goals simultaneously:

1. The plan should be effective in getting individuals and families out of poverty.

2. It should provide adequate incentives for the able-bodies to work.

3. Its cost should be reasonable.

4. Unfortunately, these three goals conflict, causing tradeoffs and necessitating compromises.

B. Common features: consider three hypothetical welfare plans (see Table 34.5).

1. In each of the three plans there is a minimum annual income that the government will provide.

2. Each plan has a benefit-reduction rate that reduces benefits as income is earned.

C. Comparing the three plans on minimum annual income and benefit reduction rate, respectively: Plan 1 $8,000, 50%; Plan 2 $8,000, 25%; and Plan 3 $12,000, 50%.

D. Conflicts among goals:

1. Plan 1 keeps cost down but is not very effective in eliminating poverty and the high benefit reduction rate weakens work incentives.

2. Plan 2 has stronger work incentives, but is more costly and would pay benefits to more families.

3. Plan 3, when compared to Plan 1, is more effective in eliminating poverty, weakens work incentives, and is more costly because of the higher guaranteed income.

VIII. **Welfare Reform**

A. In 1996, the Personal Responsibility Act was passed. The concern was that the number of people living in poverty had increased and that the AFDC program was creating dependency on government and thus robbing individuals and family members of motivation and dignity.

B. The 1996 act ended the government's guarantee of cash assistance for poor families. Instead, the Federal government now pays each state a lump sum to operate its own welfare and work program. The lump-sum payments are called Temporary Assistance for Needy Families (TANF).

C. Other features of TANF are:

1. A lifetime limit of 5 years on receiving TANF benefits and a requirement that able-bodied adults work after receiving assistance for 2 years.

2. An end to food-stamp eligibility for able-bodied person 18 to 50 (with no dependents) who are not working or engaged in job training.

3. A tightening of the definition of "disabled children" as it applies for eligibility SSI assistance.

4. Establishing a 5-year waiting period on public assistance for new immigrants who have not become citizens.

D. Assessment of TANF

1. Supporters of TANF point to the decrease in the number of individuals receiving assistance. About half of the decrease experts attribute to welfare reform, and the other half to the strong U.S. economy.

2. Critics of the reform point out that nearly two-thirds of those receiving welfare are children, and that the reforms penalize children for their parents' shortcomings. There is also a concern about what will happen when the economy experiences recession and widespread unemployment. To maintain their work requirements, states will have to expand their very expensive "public employment" programs.

3. Relative to the reform results, it is generally agreed by economists that economic growth is a power antipoverty force and program incentives (and disincentives) matter.

IX. **LAST WORD: Some Facts on U.S. Wealth and Its Distribution**

A. In 2000, the Federal Reserve reported that household wealth (net worth) in the U.S. increased between 1989 and 1998, but that its distribution became more unequal.

B. Median income and average income, adjusted for inflation, was considerably higher in 1998 than in 1989.

C. In 1998, the wealthiest 10 percent of the households owned 68.7 percent of the wealth and the wealthiest 1 percent owned 34 percent; this compares with 62.9 percent and 30.2 percent respectively in 1989.

D. The bottom 90 percent of the households owned 32.7 percent of the wealth in 1989 and 30.2 percent in 1998. The bottom 40 percent of the households had negative net worth in 1998.

E. The major source of the growing wealth for the wealthiest 1 percent and 10 percent was a rise in the value of business assets and stockholdings, of which few of the bottom 90 percent own.

F. Good news/bad news: While median and average wealth rose substantially, the bottom 25 percent of the households experienced average declines in wealth.

G. There are various public policy questions that arise from this latest wealth information, including whether the estate tax should be eliminated.

ANSWERS TO END-OF-CHAPTER QUESTIONS

34-1   Using quintiles, briefly summarize the degree of income inequality in the United States. What criticisms have been made of standard Census Bureau data on income inequality? How and to what extent does government contribute to income equality?

The income share received by the highest 20 percent was 47.2 percent in 1999, which is more than ten times the 4.1 percent received by the lowest 20 percent. The middle three quintiles receive under 50 percent of the total before-tax income. The top two quintiles receive twice as much as the bottom three quintiles combined; in fact, the top 20 percent receives almost as much as the bottom 80 percent.

One common criticism of the bureau's data is that its definition of income is too narrow. While wages, salaries, dividends, interest, and government cash transfers are included in the census figures of household income, other possible sources are not included. One can argue that capital gains and government subsidies, such as in-kind transfers and education, represent income to households just as much as wages or social security payments do. Another major criticism relates to the bureau's time specification of household income. It is argued that by measuring incomes annually the census figures conceal the significant variations that tend to occur over the lifetime of families. The distributions of total lifetime earnings are thus less unequal than the bureau's annual figures indicate.

The effect of government on the distribution of income occurs through both taxes and transfer payments. The total effect of federal, state, and local taxes on income distribution is mildly progressive in that high-income households pay a somewhat higher proportion of their incomes in taxes than low-income families. But about 80 percent of government's contribution to income equality takes place through transfer programs. This contribution is particularly significant for those in the lowest quintile, for whom government transfer payments comprise over 75 percent of total income.

These statistics do not necessarily mean that the contribution of government in furthering equality is entirely positive. To the extent that transfer programs aimed at lower-income households decrease the incentive to work, the earned incomes of these households will be less than otherwise. Also, some transfer programs go to the non-poor. For example, most farm subsidies go to the wealthiest farmers, and higher education funding tends to benefit middle to high-income students. The Last Word illustrates some of these programs.

34-2   (*Key Question*)   Assume Al, Beth, Carol, David, and Ed receive incomes of $500, $250, $125, $75, and $50 respectively.   Construct and interpret a Lorenz curve for this five-person economy. What percentage of total income is received by the richest and by the poorest quintiles?

See the figure on the next page.   In this simple economy each person represents a complete income quintile—20 percent of the total population.   The richest quintile (Al) receives 50 percent of total income; the poorest quintile (Ed) receives 5 percent.

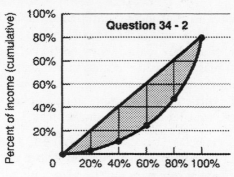

34-3   Why is the lifetime distribution of income more equal than the distribution in any specific year?

The disparity of incomes in a single year reflects the income distribution at a point in time.   The very young and very old will receive lower incomes, while the middle-aged tend to receive higher incomes, giving a picture of great inequality.   However, if we view these same groups over time, there is considerable income mobility both up and down the income quintile groups, suggesting that income is more equally distributed over a five-, ten-, or twenty-year period for these same households.   A Treasury Department study confirmed that the longer the time period considered, the more equal the distribution of income because there is "significant household income mobility over time."

34-4   (*Key Question*)   Briefly discuss the major causes of income inequality.   With respect to income inequality, is there any difference between inheriting property and inheriting a high IQ?   Explain.

The reasons for income inequality are: differences in abilities and talents among individuals, differences in the amount of education and training an individual obtains, labor market discrimination, differences in tastes and preferences toward work and job attributes, inequality in the distribution of wealth, the ability to use market power to transfer income to oneself, luck, connections, and misfortune.

A high IQ normally does not lead to high income unless it is combined with personal initiative and favorable social circumstances.   Inherited property—as long as it is competently managed—provides income irrespective of one's character and personal attributes.   Both factors are largely a matter of the luck of being born into a family with good ability genes and/or wealth.   What one does with the genes or wealth is up to the recipient.

34-5   What factors have contributed to increased income inequality since 1969?

Several factors have contributed to the increase in income inequality since 1969. The overriding factor is the structural changes that have occurred in the U.S. economy.   There has been an increase in the demand for high-skill and well-educated workers relative to lesser-skilled workers. During the 1970s and 1980s less experienced, younger people entered the labor force in large numbers, thus reducing their incomes. There also was a rise in the number of single mothers with children, but few labor market skills. More recently, there has been a tendency for well-educated men and women to marry, thus placing these families in the highest quintile and increasing the income to those in that quintile. Increased divorce rates have tended to push female-headed households into poverty. Other structure changes include more import competition resulting in a reduction in the demand for and employment of less-skilled workers who used to command high-paying, often union, jobs in manufacturing and an increased the immigration of unskilled workers.

34-6   Use the "leaky-bucket analogy" to discuss the equality-efficiency tradeoff. Explain how welfare reform (TANF) has reduced the leak.

Most economists argue that whenever incomes are redistributed from some members of society to others, economic efficiency will be adversely affected in two ways. Affluent individuals will have less reason to earn income, since they realize that a portion of the income will be taken from them, and the poor will have less reason to work because of the guarantee of government subsidies. The bucket used to bring about this shift in income therefore has two separate leaks. According to conservatives, both may be difficult, if not impossible, to plug. In addition, administrative costs involved in implementing the transfer constitute another leak.

While some economists concede the existence of the first problem associated with the income-earning behavior of the affluent, they contend that in the long run redistribution programs will increase economic efficiency by providing the poor with sufficient resources to increase their own earning potential or that of their offspring. The need for the leaky bucket will therefore be decreased over time.

The TANF program does continue cash assistance to families with children, but it also places a time limit on the cash assistance and requires that recipients participate in job preparation programs that will lead to work. Although the program continues to be expensive both in terms of cash transfers and administrative costs, the goal is less cash transfers and more self-sufficiency.

34-7   Should a nation's income be distributed to its members according to their contributions to the production of that total income or to members' needs? Should society attempt to equalize income or economic opportunities? Are the issues of equity and equality in the distribution of income synonymous? To what degree, if any, is income inequality equitable?

The answer to this question is inextricably tied to value judgments, but most of us probably favor a combination of the two types of income distribution. A purely capitalist system, in which incomes are determined exclusively by the market mechanism, would mean that those who, for whatever reason, are unable to contribute to production would have to depend exclusively on private charity for their livelihood. A (hypothetical) communist state also leads to a seemingly intractable problem—if income is to be distributed purely on the basis of need, why would anyone engage in production? Most modern societies attempt to seek a compromise of one sort or another between these two extremes. The compromise that is actually found often differs markedly from what prevailing political rhetoric in that society might suggest. Socialist economies, which historically have had large differences in income distribution, also have wider-ranging government transfer programs than most capitalist economies.

Conservatives contend that because of the tradeoff between equality and efficiency, society should content itself with attempting to ensure equality of opportunity. Liberals argue that income redistribution is essential since equality of economic opportunity is impossible in an economy with wide differences in income, especially when these differences are related to the inheritance of property.

Income equity refers to how fairly income is distributed. One can argue that some inequality of income is not only necessary for reasons of efficiency but is fairer than an equal distribution of income, since those who produce more deserve to be rewarded for their efforts. But unequal incomes are not necessarily related to differences in individual ability or effort. It is difficult to defend the inequalities that result from market power and discrimination as being equitable. The justness of inherited wealth is also questionable. Liberals argue that by creating inequality of opportunity, property inheritance is inherently unjust. Conservatives contend that allowing individuals to pass on wealth to whom they wish is much fairer than having wealth appropriated by the government.

34-8   Analyze in detail: "There need be no tradeoff between equality and efficiency. An 'efficient' economy that yields an income distribution that many regard as unfair may cause those with meager income rewards to become discouraged and stop trying. So, efficiency may be undermined. A fairer distribution of rewards may generate a higher average productive effort on the part of the population, thereby enhancing efficiency. If people think they are playing a fair economic game and this belief causes them to try harder, an economy with an equitable income distribution may be efficient as well."

It is hard to imagine that the disincentive effects on both high- and low-income earners of income redistribution will be swamped by an increased interest on the part of some of the poor in "playing the economic game." Without the prospect of higher incomes, few individuals in an economy—including the poor—would choose to increase their productivity. What would increase individual effort and hence aggregate efficiency is the perception that opportunities for all are equal in every respect. In other words, it is not so much an unequal distribution of income that causes some members of society to become discouraged and stop participating in the market, but rather the wide-ranging perception that the deck is stacked against them. Many feel they can never earn incomes commensurate with their abilities and efforts because of a lack of financial resources, restricted access to education, or barriers in the workplace.

34-9   Comment on or explain:

a. Endowing everyone with equal income will make for very unequal enjoyment and satisfaction.

b. Equality is a 'superior good'; the richer we become, the more of it we can afford.

c. The mob goes in search of bread, and the means it employs is generally to wreck the bakeries.

d. Some freedoms may be more important in the long run than freedom from want on the part of every individual.

e. Capitalism and democracy are really a most improbable mixture. Maybe that is why they need each other—to put some rationality into equality and some humanity into efficiency.

f. The incentives created by the attempt to bring about a more equal distribution of income are in conflict with the incentives needed to generate increased income.

(a) No distribution of income can ensure equal enjoyment. Using marginal utility theory, it can be argued that by equalizing incomes in an economy, there is the probability of maximizing total utility for all individuals. This assumes that everyone has identical diminishing-marginal-utility-of-money schedules.

(b) The lessening of poverty provides a host of indirect benefits to affluent members of society—social peace, physical security, and perhaps the intangible satisfaction of living in a more equitable society. The better off the affluent become, the more they are willing to spend in order to purchase these benefits.

(c) Mobs commonly exhibit a marked preference for present over future consumption. Many conservatives contend that the income redistribution schemes resulting from democratic decision making suffer from a similar failing by decreasing the incentive to accumulate capital in order to provide present consumption to the poor. Is this view valid? Perhaps. Does this mean that such redistribution schemes are misguided? Not necessarily.

(d) This is a common conservative view, that civil and political liberties are more important than the universal eradication of poverty. Liberals are likely to contend that ensuring universal freedom from want does not necessarily detract from these fundamental freedoms.

(e) The principles underlying the two systems can be summarized as follows: Each dollar has a vote in the marketplace, and each person has a vote at the ballot box. These principles are similar enough that the presence of one often leads to the other. They are dissimilar enough so that the type of society that arises from a combination of the two represents a workable social compromise.

(f) Incentives created in the attempt to bring about more equal distribution of income may cause a tradeoff in decreased economic efficiency. Higher marginal taxes may reduce the efforts of those at the top to work harder and produce more. Greater benefits to those at the bottom may reduce their incentive to do the same as they receive benefits without the productive effort. In so far as this tradeoff occurs, there will be a reduction in economic growth and therefore, damage to incentives leading to increased incomes.

34-10 What are the essential differences between social insurance and public assistance programs? Why is Medicare a social insurance program, whereas Medicaid is a public assistance program? Why is the earned-income tax credit considered to be a public assistance program?

Social insurance programs provide aid to those who are retired or suffering from temporary distress. They are usually financed through payroll levies and are viewed to be earned rights because they are paid for by recipients. Public assistance programs provide benefits for those who are unable to earn income because of permanent handicaps or who have no or very low income and have dependent children. To receive assistance, an individual must pass a "means" test. The cash payments are paid for out of general tax revenues. Most of these revenues come from individuals other than the recipients.

The Medicare program is a part of the Social Security program and is financed with a 2.9 percent tax on wage and salary earnings. Those who have reached 65 years of age are eligible to participate in the program. Medicaid is a program for individuals who are participating in the SSI and TANF programs. It is financed from general tax revenues and is available only to qualified individuals.

The earned-income tax credit is considered a public assistance program because it is targeted at low-income families.

34-11 (*Key Question*) The table following contains three hypothetical public assistance plans.

Plan One Earned income	NIT subsidy	Total income	Plan Two Earned income	NIT subsidy	Total income	Plan Three Earned income	NIT subsidy	Total income
$ 0	$4,000	$4,000	$ 0	$4,000	$ 4,000	$ 0	$8,000	$ 8,000
2,000	3,000	5,000	4,000	3,000	7,000	4,000	6,000	10,000
4,000	2,000	6,000	8,000	2,000	10,000	8,000	4,000	12,000
6,000	1,000	7,000	12,000	1,000	13,000	12,000	2,000	14,000

a. Determine the basic benefit, the benefit-reduction rate, and the break-even income for each plan.

b. Which plan is the most costly? The least costly? Which plan is most effective in reducing poverty? The least effective? Which plan embodies the strongest disincentive to work? The weakest disincentive to work?

c. Use your answers in part b to explain the following statement: "The dilemma of public assistance is that you cannot bring families up to the poverty level and simultaneously preserve work incentives (without work requirements) and minimize program costs."

(a) Plan 1: Minimum income = $4,000; benefit-reduction rate = 50 percent; break-even income = $8,000 (= $4,000/.5). Plan 2: Minimum income = $4,000; benefit-reduction rate = 25 percent; break-even income = $16,000 (= $4,000/.25). Plan 3: Minimum income = $8,000; benefit-reduction rate = 50 percent; break-even income = $16,000 (= $8,000/.5).

(b) Plan 3 is the most costly. Plan 1 is the least costly. Plan 3 is most effective in reducing poverty (although it has a higher benefit-reduction rate than Plan 2, its minimum income is higher). Plan 1 is least effective in reducing poverty. Plan 3 has the strongest disincentive to work (although it has the same benefit-reduction rate as Plan 1, its higher minimum income discourages work more). Plan 2 has the weakest disincentives to work (its minimum income and benefit-reduction rates are low).

(c) The only way to eliminate poverty is to provide a minimum income high enough to lift everyone from poverty, including people who cannot work or choose not to work. But this large minimum income reduces the incentive to work, expands the number of people receiving transfer payments, and substantially boosts overall program costs.

34-12 What major criticisms of the U.S. welfare system led to its reform in 1996 (via the Personal Responsibility Act)? How did this reform try to address these criticisms? Do you agree with the general thrust of the reform and with its emphasis on work requirements and time limits on benefits?

The major criticisms of the old welfare system (AFDC) was that it was not ending poverty although billions of dollars were being spent, that the number of people in poverty was increasing, and that it was creating a dependency on the government by those participating in the program.

The new program (TANF) sets a 5-year lifetime limit on the participants and requires able-bodied adults to work after receiving assistance for 2 years. It ended food-stamp eligibility for able-bodied person aged 18 to 50 years (with no dependents) who are not working or engaged in a job-training program. It tightened the definition of "disabled children" relative to eligibility for SSI assistance. And finally, it established a 5-year waiting period for new immigrants who are not citizens to receive assistance.

Economic security and self-sufficiency are two goals that are best for individuals as well as for the economy as a whole. The new TANF will help to achieve both of these goals, hopefully without causing undue hardship particularly for children

34-13 (*Last Word*) Go to Table 1 in the Last Word and compute the ratio of average wealth to median wealth for each of the 4 years. What trend do you find? What is your explanation for the trend? The Federal estate tax redistributes wealth in two ways: by encouraging charitable giving, which reduces the taxable estate, and by heavily taxing extraordinarily large estates and using the proceeds to fund government programs. Do you favor repealing the estate tax? Explain.

The average wealth was 4.0 percent times than median wealth in 1989, 3.8 times greater in 1992, 3.6 times greater in 1995, and 3.9 times greater in 1998. There was some decrease in the inequality of wealth between 1989 and 1995, but since 1995, the wealthiest 10 percent have experienced a disproportionate increase in their wealth when compared to the other 90 percent. Although the bottom 25 percent of the households has an absolute smaller amount of wealth in 1998 when compared to 1995, the next 25 percent must have experienced some increase in the median wealth for the median wealth amount to have increased..

Just as public assistance programs can have a disincentive on work, inheritance, or even the hope for inheritance, can have a negative incentive effect on the likely recipients. On the other hand, those who have worked hard and saved believe that they should be able to pass this wealth on to their heirs. Rather than repealing the tax, changes in the tax might be preferable. Such reform might include increasing the amount of wealth that can to inherited before the estate tax is applied.

CHAPTER THIRTY-FIVE
LABOR MARKET ISSUES:
UNIONISM, DISCRIMINATION,
AND IMMIGRATION

CHAPTER OVERVIEW

This chapter focuses on three important labor market issues: unionism, discrimination, and immigration. Although not necessarily related to one another, each issue is significant in its own right. Instructors may choose to treat the three topics selectively without any loss of continuity.

The first part of the chapter looks at labor unions. We first see who belongs to unions, examine collective bargaining, and discuss the reasons for unionism's recent decline. Then we assess the affect of unions on wages, efficiency, and productivity. Second, we discuss the types and costs of discrimination, economic theories of discrimination, and current antidiscrimination policies. The last part of the chapter examines immigration: the inflow of people (workers) to the United States from abroad. Here we focus on the size of both legal and illegal immigration and its economic effects.

WHAT'S NEW

In the previous edition, this was chapter 36; it is now chapter 35. Besides the renumbering of the chapter and updating some of the statistics, there are very few changes from the previous edition.

The Web-Based Questions are new.

INSTRUCTIONAL OBJECTIVES

After completing this chapter, students should be able to:

1. Identify the industries and occupations with the highest percentage of union members.
2. Identify two factors that have led to the decline of unionism.
3. List and explain the major clauses in a work agreement.
4. Summarize/evaluate positive and negative views of union influence on efficiency and productivity.
5. Describe four types of labor market discrimination.
6. Illustrate graphically the cost of discrimination.
7. Explain how an employer's taste-for-discrimination is reflected in the value of "d," the discrimination coefficient.
8. Give two examples of statistical discrimination.
9. Explain the crowding model of occupational discrimination.
10. List three major antidiscrimination laws and policies that involve direct government intervention.
11. Contrast and evaluate the views of supporters and opponents of affirmative action.
12. Illustrate graphically the predicted economic effects of migration, and then discuss four complications relevant to this model.
13. Define and identify terms and concepts listed at the end of the chapter.

Labor Market Issues: Unionism, Discrimination, and Immigration

COMMENTS AND TEACHING SUGGESTIONS

1. The three topics in this chapter may be treated or may be introduced earlier in combination with the chapter on wage determination, or the section on immigration could be included with the international trade topics.

2. All three of these topics lend themselves well to lively class debates. They are also good topics for outside speakers, especially in urban areas where union representatives are available to talk to classes, and civil rights and women's organizations or state/city equal opportunity agencies have speakers. Recent concerns over the economic impact of immigrants in several states have received much publicity, and many reports have been published, which provide contradictory evidence on this issue. The text provides a framework for further study on each of these issues.

3. In discussing collective bargaining, stress that: (a) It is a process of decision making with a system of consistent work rules. It is not simply a wage bargain. (b) Although public attention is focused only on the negotiations phase, the result is an agreement that determines working conditions over a period of time, usually one to three years. (c) Most labor agreements contain no-strike clauses during the life of the agreement. In exchange, a grievance procedure is established. (d) Business firms have the certainty of knowing what their wage rates will be, what their competitors' wage rates will be, and that there will be no work stoppage during the contract period. This reduction in uncertainty helps productivity.

4. The AFL-CIO has an Education Department that publishes materials on the labor movement and labor issues that are suitable for use in a principles course. Most are free or very low in cost. Write AFL-CIO Dept. of Education, 815 Sixteenth St., NW, Washington, DC, 20006 (Ph. 202-637-5000). The AFL-CIO has a website that provides information on many topics of concern to organized labor.

STUDENT STUMBLING BLOCK

The potential stumbling block in this chapter is that of preconceived ideas about the economic impact of unions, discrimination, and immigration. This chapter presents a brief overview of some of the facts, but by no means gives a comprehensive picture of these three topics. Further reading is advised.

LECTURE NOTES

I. **Unionism in America**

    A. About 13.5 percent (16 million) U.S. workers belong to unions; most of the unions are voluntarily affiliated with the American Federation of Labor and Congress of Industrial Organizations (AFL-CIO). (Global Perspective 35-1 compares U.S. union members with other industrialized nations.)

    B. In the United States, unions have generally adhered to a philosophy of business unionism.

        1. Concerned with the practical short-run economic objectives of higher pay, shorter hours, and improved working conditions.

        2. Union members have not organized into a distinct political party.

    C. The likelihood of union membership depends mainly on the industry: Membership is high in government, transportation, construction, manufacturing and mining; low in agriculture, finance, insurance, real estate, services, wholesale and retail trade. (See Figure 35.1a and b)

    D. The decline of unionism.

1. Since the mid-1950s union membership has not kept pace with the growth of the labor force. Union membership has declined both absolutely and relatively.

2. The structural-change hypothesis says that changes unfavorable to union membership have occurred in both the economy and the labor force.

   a. Employment patterns have shifted away from unionized industries. Consumer demand has shifted from unionized U.S. producers of manufactured goods to foreign producers. Also demand has shifted from highly organized "old-economy" unionized firms to "high-tech" industries.

   b. A higher proportion of the increase in employment recently has been concentrated among women, youths and part time workers; groups that harder to organize.

   c. A geographic shift of industrial location away from the northeast and midwest (traditional union country) to the south and southwest.

   d. Union success in gaining higher wages for their workers may have given employers an incentive to substitute away from the expensive union labor in a number of ways.

      i. Substituting machinery for workers,

      ii. Subcontracting more work to nonunion suppliers,

      iii. Opening nonunion plants in less industrialized areas, and

      iv. Shifting production of components to low-wage nations.

   E. Relatively high-priced union produced goods would encourage consumers to seek lower-cost goods produced by non-union workers.

   F. The managerial-opposition hypothesis argues that union firms are less profitable than nonunion firms.

      1. One aggressive managerial strategy has been to employ labor-management consultants who specialize in mounting anti-union drives.

      2. Confronted with a strike, management is more likely to hire permanent strikebreakers.

      3. Management may also improve working conditions and personnel policies to discourage union organization.

II. **Collective Bargaining**

   A. The goal of collective bargaining is to establish a "work agreement" between the firm and the union.

   B. Union status and managerial prerogatives.

      1. In a closed shop, a worker must be (or become) a member of the union before being hired. This is illegal except in transportation and construction.

      2. In a union shop, an employer may hire nonunion workers, but they must join in a specified period of time.

      3. An agency shop requires nonunion workers to pay dues or donate a similar amount to charity.

      4. Twenty states have right-to-work laws that prohibit union shops and agency shops.

5. In an open shop, the employer may hire union or nonunion workers. Workers are not required to join the union or contribute; but the "work agreement" applies all worker – union and nonunion.

6. Most work agreements contain clauses outlining the decisions reserved solely for management; these are called managerial prerogatives.

C. The focal point of any bargaining agreement is wages and hours.

1. The arguments most frequently used include for wage increases are:

a. "What others are getting";

b. Employer's ability to pay based on profitability;

c. Increases in the cost of living; and

d. Increases in labor productivity.

2. In some cases, unions win automatic cost-of-living adjustments (COLAs).

3. Hours of work, voluntary and mandatory overtime, holiday and vacation provisions, profit sharing, health plans, and pension benefits are other contract issues.

D. Unions stress seniority as the basis for worker promotion and for layoff and recall and sometimes seek means to limit a firm's ability to subcontract work or to relocate production facilities overseas.

E. Union contracts contain grievance procedures to resolve disputes.

F. The bargaining process.

1. Collective bargaining on a new contract usually begins about 60 days before the existing contract expires.

2. Hanging over negotiations is the "deadline" which occurs at the expiration of the old contract, at which time a strike (union work stoppage) or a lockout (management forbids workers to return) can occur.

3. Bargaining, strikes and lockouts occur within a framework of Federal labor law, specifically the National Labor Relations Act (NLRA).

III. **Economic Effects of Unions**

A. The union wage advantage is verified by studies that suggest that unions do raise the wages of their members relative to comparable nonunion workers; on average, this pay differential over the years is estimated to have been about 15 percent.

1. The overall average level of wages of all workers has probably not been affected by unions (Figure 35.2).

2. Union workers seem to gain at the expense of nonunion workers.

3. Real wages overall still depend on productivity. (See Figure 28.1)

B. Efficiency and productivity are affected both positively and negatively by unions.

1. The negative view has three major points.

a. Featherbedding and work rules make it difficult for management to be flexible and to use their workers in the most efficient ways.

    b.   Strikes, while rare, do constitute a loss of production time and affect certain industries more than others.

    c.   Labor misallocation might occur as a result of the union wage advantage, but studies suggest that the efficiency loss is minimal—perhaps only a fraction of one percent of U.S. GDP.

  2. The positive view has three major points as well.

    a.   Managerial performance may be improved when wages are high because managers are forced to use their workers in more efficient ways. This is called the shock effect.

    b.   Worker turnover may be reduced where workers feel they can voice dissatisfaction and have some bargaining power.

    c.   Seniority promotes productivity because workers do not fear loss of jobs, and informal training may occur on the job because workers do not compete with one another in a seniority-based system.

  3. Research findings have been mixed. Some have found a positive effect of unions on productivity, while an almost equal number have found a negative effect of unions on productivity.

IV. Labor Market Discrimination

A. We saw in Chapter 34 that blacks, Hispanics, and women bear a disproportionately large burden of poverty. Their low incomes are a result of the operation of the labor market, and this includes the impact of discrimination.

B. Economic discrimination occurs when female or minority workers, who have the same abilities, education, training, and experience as white male workers, are accorded inferior treatment with respect to hiring, occupational access, promotion, or wage rate. Table 35.1 provides data suggesting the presence of racial discrimination.

C. Types of discrimination.

  1. Wage discrimination occurs when minority workers or women are paid less than white males for doing the same work. This practice violates Federal law, but it can be subtle and difficult to detect.

  2. Employment discrimination takes place when women or minority workers receive inferior treatment in hiring, promotions, layoffs, or permanent discharges. This type of discrimination also includes sexual and racial harassment.

  3. Occupational discrimination occurs when women or minority workers are arbitrarily restricted or prohibited from entering the more desirable, high-paying occupations. Historically, craft unions have effectively barred blacks from membership and, thus, from employment.

  4. Human-capital discrimination occurs when investments in education and training are less and inferior to that of whites.

D. Cost of discrimination.

  1. Discrimination does more than simply transfer benefits from women, blacks, and Hispanics to men and whites; where it exists, discrimination actually diminishes the economy's output and income.

2. The effects of discrimination can be depicted as a point inside the economy's production possibilities curve. (See Figure 35.3)

3. Rough estimates suggest the U.S. economy would gain $325 billion per year by eliminating racial and ethnic discrimination and $180 billion per year by ending gender discrimination.

V. **Economic Analysis of Discrimination**

    A. Taste-for-discrimination model.

        1. The model assumes that, for whatever reason, prejudiced employers experience a subjective and psychic cost—a disutility—whenever they must interact with those they are biased against.

        2. The amount of this cost is reflected in a discrimination coefficient d, measured in monetary units.

        3. The cost of employing the preferred worker is the workers wage rate, W_w (in the example the preferred worker is white).

        4. The employer's perceived "cost" of employing the worker, against whom he/she is prejudiced (in the example the worker is black) is the black worker's wage rate, W_b plus the cost of d, or $W_b + d$.

        5. The prejudiced employer will not refuse to hire blacks under all conditions. They will, in fact, prefer blacks if the actual white-black wage difference in the market exceeds the value of d.

    B. Prejudice and the market black-white wage ratio.

        1. For a particular supply of black workers, the actual black-white wage ratio will depend on the collective prejudice of white employers. (See Figure 35.4)

        2. An increase in white employer prejudice, i.e., a decrease in the demand for black workers, reduces the black wage rate and thus the black-white wage ratio.

        3. A decrease in white employer prejudice, i.e., an increase in the demand for black workers, increases the black wage rate and thus the black-white wage ratio.

    C. The taste-for-discrimination model suggests that competition will reduce discrimination in the very long run.

        1. The actual black-white wage difference for equally productive workers allows nondiscriminating employers to hire blacks for less than whites and, therefore, gain a cost advantage over discriminating competitors.

        2. The lower costs will allow nondiscriminators to underprice prejudiced employers, eventually driving them out of the market.

        3. Critics of the implication of the model note that progress in eliminating prejudice has been modest. (See Key Question 7)

    D. Statistical discrimination

        1. People are judged on the basis of the average characteristics of the group to which they belong, rather than on their own personal characteristics or productivity.

2. The firm practicing statistical discrimination is not being malicious in its hiring behavior (although it may be violating antidiscrimination laws). The decision it makes will be rational and profitable.

   a. In hiring, an employer wants to find the best person for the job, but collecting all of the information on each possible candidate can be expensive.

   b. Employers may reduce the cost of hiring by using the average characteristics of women and minorities in determining whom to hire; the employer is using crude indicators of gender, race, or ethnic background as a measure of production-related attributes.

   c. By reducing hiring costs, the use of statistical discrimination may increase the employer's profits.

E. Occupational discrimination can cause crowding or an oversupply of workers in the few occupations that are left to the class of workers experiencing discrimination. This theory helps to explain the relatively low wages of women relative to men. (Figure 35.5 explains this in supply and demand diagrams.)

   1. The crowding model illustrated in Figure 35.5 includes the following assumptions: the number of male and female (or black and white) workers is equal; the economy has three occupations; the two groups of workers have identical labor force characteristics—anyone could fill a position equally well.

   2. There are several effects of crowding.

      a. Wages will be lower in the few occupations where women are not discriminated against because most women are "crowded" into these occupations. The supply is unnaturally large relative to demand.

      b. Eliminating discrimination will shift women from the low-wage occupations into higher-wage occupations, bringing about an equilibrium wage that should be the same in all occupations requiring similar types of workers without respect to gender.

   3. The conclusion is that society will gain from a more efficient allocation of resources when discrimination is abandoned. (Key Question 9)

VI. **Antidiscrimination Policies and Issues**

A. Government might attack the problems of discrimination in several ways.

   1. Promote a strong economy: higher wages increase the cost of discrimination, tight labor markets help overcome stereotyping.

   2. Improve the education and training opportunities of women and minorities.

   3. Direct government intervention: The U.S. government has outlawed certain practices in hiring, promotion and compensation and required government contractors to take affirmative action to ensure that women and minorities are hired at least up to the proportions of the labor force. (See Table 35.2)

B. The affirmative action controversy.

   1. Affirmative action consists of special efforts by employers to increase employment and promotion opportunities for groups that have suffered past discrimination and continue to experience discrimination.

   2. Supporters of affirmative action contend that merely removing the discrimination burden does nothing to close the present socioeconomic gap.

a. Because of historical discrimination, women and minorities find themselves in an inferior position economically to white men.

b. The results of past discrimination continue due to seniority layoff plans and inferior education and training of women and minorities.

c. Something more than equal opportunity, i.e., preferential treatment, is necessary to counter the inherent bias in favor of white men.

3. Those against affirmative action claim that affirmative action goes beyond aggressive recruitment.

a. Preferential treatment has forced employers to hire less-qualified women and minority workers.

b. Preferential treatment, if it causes the hiring of less-qualified women and minority employees, may result in resentment by majority workers who have been passed over for jobs and promotions and reinforce stereotypical views of women and minorities that will negatively affect highly-qualified women and minorities.

C. Recent developments.

1. A series of important Supreme Court decisions in 1986 and 1987 upheld the constitutionality of affirmative action programs, but more recent decisions have undermined some specific programs.

2. In 1996 Congress debated legislation restricting affirmative action, and the Clinton administration halted several Federal programs designed to give preference in Federal contracting to minorities. Californians voted in favor of a state constitutional amendment ending all state programs that give preferences.

VI. Immigration

A. Number of immigrants.

1. The annual flow of legal immigrants has increased from roughly 250,000 in the 1950s to about 850,000 per year in the 1990s. About one-third of recent annual population growth in the United States is the result of immigration. (See Global perspective 35.2)

2. The Census Bureau estimates the net inflow of illegal immigrants is now about 100,000 per year, most coming from Mexico, the Caribbean, and Latin America.

B. The economics of immigration.

1. One theoretical model is a variation of the crowding model of discrimination (Figure 35.5). The immigration model is portrayed in Figure 35.6. It assumes that workers migrate from Mexico to the U.S. where technology is more sophisticated and labor demand stronger; it also assumes that full employment exists in both countries. Theoretically, workers will migrate to the U.S. until wage rates in the two countries are equalized. The elimination of barriers to immigration should enhance economic efficiency, as workers from low productivity countries move to where they have higher levels of productivity. U.S. business will benefit from migration while Mexican business will lose as they end up paying higher wages to a diminished supply of workers.

2. Business incomes in the U.S. should improve and those in Mexico should fall. America is receiving the "cheap" labor and Mexico loses this "cheap" labor. This explains why, historically, American employers have sometimes actively recruited immigrants.

3. Complications and modifications to this model change the conclusions somewhat.

a. There are costs to migration, so wages will always remain higher in the U.S. as migrants consider the costs compared to the benefits.

b. Many migrants come temporarily and either return or send money home, which causes a redistribution of the net gain between the countries involved.

c. Mexico will gain if its unemployed and underemployed migrate to the U.S. If the migrants become unemployed in the U.S., the U.S. will lose.

d. Although the fiscal impact of immigrants is debatable, the consensus has been that they are probably net contributors to the fiscal system of the host country. They are more often young people with skills who are productive and tend not to bring children with them. On the other hand, immigrants since the 1970s may have lower levels of education and skills and may require several years of public or philanthropic aid to assimilate. Immigrants now make up 10 percent of the Supplemental Security Income (SSI) rolls as compared with only 3.3 percent a decade earlier. The 1996 welfare reform denies benefits to new immigrants for their first five years in the United States. (Key Question 12)

C. There are two views of immigration.

1. One view is that economic benefits occur in the host country from young, skilled workers when the economy is robust and growing.

2. The counterview is that benefits may not occur if immigrants are unskilled and illiterate, and our economy has high unemployment. Racial problems may be worsened; poverty may increase.

3. From a strictly economic perspective nations seeking to maximize net benefits from immigration should expand immigration until its marginal benefits equals it marginal costs. (MB = MC) There can be too few immigrants as well as too many.

VII: **LAST WORD: Orchestrating Impartiality**

A. There have long been allegations of discrimination against women in the hiring process in some occupations.

B. The introduction of "blind" musical auditions in which "screens" were used to hide the identity of candidates affected the success of women in obtaining positions in major symphony orchestras.

1. In 1970 only 5 percent of the members of the top five orchestras in the United States were women.

2. The change to screens during the audition process increased by 50 percent the probability that a woman would be advanced from the preliminary rounds.

3. Without the screens about 10 percent of all hires were women, but with the screens about 35 percent were women.

4. Today about 25 percent of the membership of top symphony orchestras are women. The screens explain from 25 to 45 percent of the increases in the proportion of women members of the orchestras studied.

5. Researchers Goldin and Rouse examined information on turnover and leaves of orchestra members for the period 1960-1996 in an effort to determine the cause of past discrimination.

a. If this was an example of statistical discrimination there should have been a difference in the rate of turnover by gender. This was not the case.

b. Instead, the discrimination in hiring seemed to reflect a taste for discrimination by musical directors. A positive discrimination coefficient d was present; they simply preferred male musicians.

ANSWERS TO END-OF-CHAPTER QUESTIONS

35-1 Other things equal, who is more likely to be a union member: Stephen, who works as a salesperson at a furniture store, or Susan who works as a machinist for an aircraft manufacturer? Explain.

Union membership as a percentage of employed wage and salary workers varies considerably from one industry to another. The union membership of machine operators is much higher than retail sales persons. Therefore, it is more likely that Susan is a union member than Stephen. (See Figure 35.1)

35-2 Contrast the structural-change and managerial-opposition hypotheses as they relate to the decline in unionism. Which view do you think is more convincing?

According to the first hypothesis, unions' relative decline in the past thirty years can be attributed to changes in the structure and composition of the American economy and labor force. There has been a significant shift in demand from the unionized manufacturing sector to the relatively nonunionized service sector. Domestic consumers have shifted their demand for manufactured products from U.S. firms to foreign producers. There has also been a significant migration of firms and labor from the unionized "Rustbelt" to the relatively nonunionized "Sunbelt." Finally, women and young people, who have traditionally been difficult to organize, have been increasing their participation in the labor force.

The second hypothesis focuses on employers' efforts to become or remain nonunion. Businesses have mounted concerted antiunion campaigns, encouraged decertification elections, and engaged in antiunion tactics that, though illegal, are difficult to prosecute. Employers have also improved wages and benefits to make the workers less likely to approach a union.

While the factors highlighted by the managerial-opposition hypothesis are no doubt relevant in many instances, the first hypothesis would seem to be a more valid explanation. While managerial antiunion activity is important, particularly in certain industries, economy-wide structural changes are continuous and wide-ranging.

35-3 Suppose that you are the president of a newly established local union about to bargain with an employer for the first time. List the basic areas you would want covered in the work agreement. Why might you begin with a larger wage demand than you actually are willing to accept?

Areas to be included in a work agreement:

1. Wage rates with automatic increases over time, preferably in the form of a cost-of-living adjustment

2. Regulations governing hours of work which ensure employees are entitled to paid vacation time and the choice to engage in overtime work at a substantial premium

3. A liberal fringe-benefits package provided by the firm, including pension plans and job security provisions

4. Rules governing promotions, layoffs and recalls that are based on worker seniority

5. A stipulated grievance procedure with mandatory union participation in rulings.

6. A provision that requires all worker to join or monetarily support the union.

Asking for a higher-than-expected wage increase is a tactical decision. The law requires that bargaining must occur. The higher-than-expected-wage demand allows for the give-and-take of bargaining and for compromises in other areas of the initial proposal.

35-4   (*Key Question*) What is the estimated size of the union wage advantage? How might this advantage diminish the efficiency with which labor resources are allocated?

Fifteen percent. The higher wages that unions achieve reduce employment, displace workers, and increase the marginal revenue product in the union sector. Labor supply increases in the nonunionized sector, reducing wages and decreasing marginal revenue production there. Because of the lower nonunion marginal revenue product, the workers added in the nonunion sector contribute less to GDP than they would have in the unionized sector. The gain of GDP in the nonunionized sector does not offset the loss of GDP in the unionized sector so there is an overall efficiency loss.

35-5   Explain the logic of each of the following statements:

a. By constraining the decisions of management, unions inhibit efficiency and productivity growth.

b. As collective-voice institutions, unions increase productivity by reducing worker turnover, inducing managerial efficiency, and enhancing worker security.

(a) Unions can and do inhibit efficiency in several ways. Featherbedding, regulations that force firms to promote on the basis of seniority rather than productivity, and rules barring particular employees from engaging in tasks they could perform most productively, all decrease productive efficiency. More generally, the existence of a union in the workplace can restrict the firm's use of productivity-enhancing techniques. Furthermore, work stoppages decrease production directly and can adversely affect other industries or sectors, although such disruptions are relatively infrequent. Finally, the fact that wages in unionized sectors are higher than those in nonunionized sectors can mean that the marginal revenue products in these sectors differ. Total output would be increased if these wage differentials were eradicated.

(b) Unions can provide a convenient voice mechanism for workers, enhancing the resolution of worker grievances with management and decreasing employee turnover. Some empirical evidence suggests the presence of unions plays a significant role in reducing worker turnover. Managerial efficiency can be enhanced through the effects of wage increases and higher production costs brought on by unionization. Finally, by enhancing security of employment and decreasing competition for particular jobs, unions encourage informal on-the-job training of newer workers by senior employees.

35-6   Explain how discrimination reduces domestic output and income. Demonstrate this loss using production possibilities analysis.

Discrimination actually diminishes the economy's output and income; like any other artificial barrier to free competition, it decreases economic efficiency and reduces production. It arbitrarily blocks certain groups of people from making their maximum contribution to the economy's output.

Discrimination represents a failure to achieve productive efficiency, on the production possibilities curve. The cost of discrimination to society is the sacrificed output associated with a point such as *D* inside the nation's production possibilities curve, compared with points such as *X*, *Y*, and *Z* on the curve.

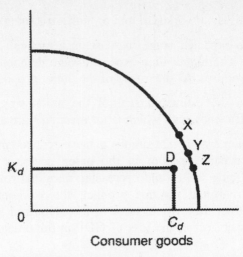

Consumer goods

35-7   (Key Question) The labor demand and supply data in the following table relate to a single occupation. Use them to answer the questions that follow. Base your answers on the taste-for-discrimination model.

Quantity of Hispanic labor demanded, thousands	Hispanic wage rate	Quantity of Hispanic labor supplied, thousands
24	$16	52
30	14	44
36	12	36
42	10	28
48	8	20

a.   Plot the labor demand and supply curves for Hispanic workers in this occupation.

b.   What are the equilibrium Hispanic wage rate and quantity of Hispanic employment?

c.   Suppose white wage rate in this occupation is $16. What is the Hispanic-to-white wage ratio?

d.   Suppose a particular employer has a discrimination coefficient d of $5 per hour. Will that employer hire Hispanic or white workers at the Hispanic-white wage ratio indicated by part c? Explain.

e.   Suppose employers as a group become less prejudiced against Hispanics and demand 14 more units of Hispanic labor at each Hispanic wage rate in the table. What are the new equilibrium Hispanic wage rate and level of Hispanic employment? Does the Hispanic-white wage ratio rise or fall? Explain.

f.   Suppose Hispanics as a group increase their labor services in this occupation, collectively offering 14 more units of labor at each Hispanic wage rate. Disregarding the changes indicated in part e, what are the new equilibrium Hispanic wage rate and level of Hispanic employment? Does the Hispanic-white wage ratio rise, or does it fall?

(a)

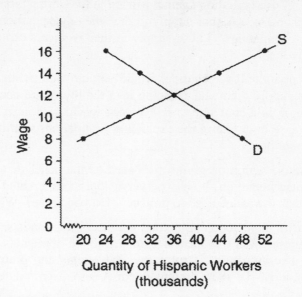

Quantity of Hispanic Workers
(thousands)

(b) The equilibrium Hispanic wage rate is $12; the equilibrium quantity of Hispanic employment is 36,000 workers.

(c) The Hispanic-to-white wage ratio is .75   (= $12/$16).

(d) The employer will hire only white workers because the $5 discrimination coefficient exceeds the $4 difference between the wage rates of whites and Hispanics.

(e) The new equilibrium Hispanic wage rate is $14 and the new equilibrium quantity of Hispanic employment is 44,000 workers. The Hispanic-white wage ratio rises to .875 (= $16/$14) because of the increased demand for Hispanic labor in relation to the unchanging supply of Hispanic labor.

(f) The new equilibrium Hispanic wage rate is $10 and the new equilibrium quantity of Hispanic employment is 20,000. This Hispanic-white wage ratio falls to .625 (= $10/$16).

35-8   Males under the age of 25 must pay far higher auto insurance premiums than females in this age group. How does this fact relate to statistical discrimination? Statistical discrimination implies that discrimination can persist indefinitely, while the taste-for-discrimination model suggests that competition might reduce discrimination in the long run. Explain the difference.

Statistical discrimination occurs when people are judged on the basis of the average characteristics of the group to which they belong. Insurance companies base auto insurance premiums on the statistical information available, and the consequent discrimination will continue as long as there is a difference in accident rates by gender in this age group.

The taste-for-discrimination model suggests that competition will reduce discrimination in the long run. Firms that do not discriminate will have lower actual wage costs per unit of output and lower average total costs than will the firms that discriminate. These lower costs will allow nondiscriminating firms to charge lower prices. This should eventually drive the discriminating firms out of the market.

35-9   (*Key Question*) Use a demand and supply model to explain the impact of occupational segregation or "crowding" on the relative wage rates and earnings of men and women. Who gains and who loses from the elimination of occupational segregation? Is there a net gain or net loss to society? Explain.

See Figure 35-5. Discrimination against women in two of the three occupations will crowd women into the third occupation. Labor supply in the "men's occupations" (*X* and *Y*) decreases, making them high-wage occupations. Labor supply in the "women's occupation" (*Z*) increases creating a low-wage occupation.

Eliminating occupational segregation would entice women into the high-wage occupations, increasing labor supply there and reducing it in the low-wage occupation. The wage rates in the three occupations would converge to *B*. Women would gain, men would lose. Society would gain because the increase in output in the expanding occupations would exceed the loss of output in the contracting occupation.

35-10 "Current affirmative action programs are based on the belief that to overcome discrimination, we must practice discrimination. That perverse logic has created a system that undermines the fundamental values it was intended to protect." Do you agree? Why or why not?

Supporters of affirmative action argue that job discrimination is so pervasive that it will persist for decades unless preferential treatment is extended to job applicants who are members of the groups subject to past discrimination. Critics say that quotas and preferential treatment are a form of reverse discrimination. To show preference for A is to discriminate against B.

The nature of a market economy includes competition for the best jobs. Government cannot possibly insure equal outcomes for all individuals in the economy. Attempting to do so would require a degree of government control that would approach central planning and destroy important incentives that promote productivity. A better course of action would be to improve opportunities for disadvantaged groups by supporting additional education and training to level the playing field. While government cannot insure equal outcome, it can contribute greatly to equal opportunity.

35-11 Suppose Ann and Becky are applicants to your university and that they have *identical* admission qualifications (SAT score, high school GPA, etc.). Ann is black, growing up in a public housing development; Becky is white, growing up in a wealthy suburb. You can admit only one of the two. Which person would you admit and why? Now suppose that Ann is white and Becky is black, all else equal. Does this change your selection? Why or why not?

The real issue in this question is not the color of the applicant, but the advantages or disadvantages the students have had during their high school preparation. If the two applicants are equal in other respects, the student growing up in a public housing development should be selected, rather than the student from the wealthy suburb.

35-12 (*Key Question*) Use graphical analysis to show the gains and losses resulting from the migration of population from a low-income country to a high-income country. Explain how your conclusions are affected by (a) unemployment, (b) remittances to the home country, (c) backflows of migrants to their home country, and (d) the personal characteristics of the migrants. If the migrants are highly skilled workers, is there any justification for the sending country to levy a "brain drain" tax on emigrants?

See Figure 35.6. Migration of labor from the low- to high-income country increases labor supply in the high-income country and decreases it in the low-income country. Wages are equalized at *We*. Output and business income increase in the receiving country; decline in the sending country. World output increases: The output gain in the receiving country exceeds the output loss in the sending country.

(a) The gains to the receiving country will not materialize if the migrants are unemployed after they arrive; there may be gains in the low-income country if the immigrant had been unemployed prior to moving. (b) Remittances to the home country will decrease the income gain in the receiving country and reduce the income loss in the sending country. (c) If migrants who return to their home country have enhanced their skills, their temporary departure might be to the long-run advantage of the home country. (d) Young, skilled migrants will increase output and likely be the net taxpayers in the receiving country, but the sending country will experience a "brain drain." Older or less skilled workers who are not so easily assimilated could be net recipients of government services.

In view of the sometimes large investments which sending countries have made in providing education and skills, there is a justification for levying a departure tax on such migrants. But if this tax were too high, it would infringe on a basic human right: the right to emigrate.

35-13   If a person favors the free movement of labor within the United States, is it then inconsistent to also favor restrictions on the international movement of labor? Why or why not?

If one is just as concerned with the economic well-being of citizens of foreign countries as one is with the welfare of one's national compatriots, then to argue for free labor mobility nationally but not internationally is logically inconsistent. Arguments in favor of restrictions on international labor mobility take account of the fact that immigration can lead to a loss of income for some domestic residents. While total output in the host country is increased, wage rates will fall, hurting laborers already working in that country. The loss of economic welfare for these individuals is often considered to be more important than the benefits accruing to businesses and the migrants themselves, even though the total benefits exceed losses in the host country.

35-14   Evaluate: "If the United States deported, say, 1 million illegal immigrants, the number of unemployed workers in the United States would decline by 1 million."

This statement is false. The presence of illegal aliens supplements aggregate expenditure in the economy. If 1 million were deported, total spending would fall, decreasing the demand for labor and creating less than 1 million available positions. Furthermore, it is possible that workers will not be found to fill all these jobs because of low wages or poor working conditions. Therefore national unemployment will decline by considerably less than 1 million.

35-15   (*Last Word*) What two types of discrimination are represented by the discrimination evidenced in this chapter's Last Word?

The two models of discrimination discussed were taste-for-discrimination and statistical discrimination. Economists Claudia Goldin and Cecilia Rouse examined evidence of discrimination in hiring musicians for major symphony orchestras. If the past discrimination in hiring was an example of statistical discrimination, they would expect to observe a higher turnover rate among women. Since this proved not to be the case, the evidence suggests that male musical directors had a taste for discrimination.

CHAPTER THIRTY-SIX
THE ECONOMICS OF HEALTH CARE

CHAPTER OVERVIEW

This chapter addresses one of the most prominent economic and political issues of our time. Providing health care is an economic issue, and the American public's concern ranges from the problem of rising health care costs, to gaps in health insurance coverage, to government insurance programs draining Federal and state budgets. The debate over the desirability of more government involvement in providing health insurance continues.

Chapter 36 examines the economic aspects of our health care problems, offers a demand and supply analysis to explain rapid increases in health care costs, and evaluates some methods of containing increases in health care costs.

WHAT'S NEW

There are few changes with the exception that this chapter was chapter 35 in the previous edition. Some of the statistics have been updated. There are discussions of the "patients' bill of rights" and the inclusion of prescription drugs in the Medicare program.

The Last Word has been revised. Both of the Web-Based Questions have been revised.

INSTRUCTIONAL OBJECTIVES

After completing this chapter, students should be able to:

1. Describe what is meant by the health care industry and approximate its size with relevant data.
2. Identify the problem connected with rising health care costs.
3. Give the negative effects associated with rising health care costs.
4. Explain what is meant by the overallocation of resources to the health care industry.
5. Describe the extent of the problem regarding a lack of health insurance coverage.
6. Identify four special characteristics of the health care market.
7. Give four factors that have contributed to the rise in the demand for health care.
8. Explain the role of physicians in increasing the demand for health care.
9. Explain the "moral hazard" problem arising from health insurance coverage.
10. Explain how the Federal income tax structure subsidizes health care demand.
11. Identify three basic reform proposals designed to increase access to health care.
12. Explain what National Health Insurance is.
13. Present the arguments for and against National Health Insurance.
14. Explain how insurance company deductibles, copayments, and preferred provider organizations might help contain health care costs.
15. Outline the recent laws passed by Congress and some of proposals before Congress.
16. Define and identify terms and concepts listed at the end of the chapter.

COMMENTS AND TEACHING SUGGESTIONS

1. There is a wealth of information available on this health care in the popular press. This topic provides an excellent opportunity for student debates, papers, and presentations. Because it is an issue that concerns so many of us, you can easily get students to relate their personal experiences to the economics of health care. Once you have their interest, you can relate their concerns to many of the theoretical and structural concepts raised in microeconomics.

2. The National Issues Forum has some excellent teaching materials that provide a focus for discussing some of the major issues. Related to this chapter are two of their topics, "The Health Care Cost Explosion: Why It's So Serious, What Should Be Done, " and "Health Care for the Elderly: Moral Dilemma, Mortal Choices." This organization also has units that focus on "Coping with AIDS" and "The Drug Crisis," which may be useful supplements in a more interdisciplinary course. For more information about their issue books, audiocassette tapes, and videocassettes, call 1-800-433-7834 or write to them at 100 Commons Road, Dayton, Ohio 45459-2777.

3. The Nebraska Council on Economic Education has an excellent set of activities, suitable for secondary or college-level classes, which revolve around the economics of health care and are available for about $10. They also have a video, "Code Blue," of a teleconference panel highlighting some of the major issues. For more information call 1-800-328-2854 or 402-472-2333 or FAX 402-472-9700.

4. The health care industry can be analyzed from the perspective of market structure, which reinforces what students have just learned about the different market models, from perfect competition to pure monopoly. How do the markets for various types of health care services fit the various market models? If the market being examined does not fit the competitive model, or if consumers pay indirectly through prepaid insurance plans, does it make sense to talk about market solutions? If market solutions are possible, should reforms be aimed at enhancing competition? The health care industry, or particular components of it, provide excellent opportunities for using the case-study method to teach economic concepts.

5. Price elasticity and income elasticity of demand both play an important role in the problems of the health care industry. Most health care services are a necessity with few substitutes, making the demand for them relatively price-inelastic. This fact means that rising costs of production which decrease supply will have more impact on the price of health care than on the quantity purchased. Health care is a normal good which means that as incomes rise the demand for health care will also increase. Employing this chapter as a demonstration when studying the theory of elasticity in Chapter 20 can be an effective combination.

STUDENT STUMBLING BLOCKS

Do not assume your younger students know anything about health insurance coverage, even at the personal level. Unless they have encountered some problem, it is probably one of those economic costs that they have ignored, since they are covered by their parents' insurance or university health center. The students who have encountered some problem with coverage will help you "open other students' eyes."

LECTURE NOTES

I.   **Introduction**

A. The high costs of health care in the United States are frequently the subject of news reports.

1. People without health insurance.

2. Federal and state budgets strained by health care costs.

3. Labor dispute over health insurance.

4. Insurance companies dictating the medical care doctors can provide.

5. Ethical questions concerning the acutely or terminally ill.

B. This chapter focuses on several issues.

1. The United States system of health care.

2. The economics health care costs.

3. Actual and proposed reforms.

II. The Health Care Industry

A. Government's definition of this far-reaching industry includes many aspects.

1. Services provided in hospitals, nursing homes, labs, physicians' and dentists' offices,

2. Prescription and nonprescription drugs, artificial limbs, and eyeglasses,

3. Services of many nontraditional practitioners, but not fitness club services, or health foods.

B. The size of the industry is immense.

1. Nine million are employed in the industry, including 700,000 physicians.

2. There are over 6,000 hospitals with over 1 million beds.

3. Health care accounts for more than 14 percent of GDP.

III. Twin problems: cost and access

A. Health care costs include the "price" of health care as well as the "quantity" of health care services provided.

B. Health care costs have been rising rapidly because of higher prices and an increase in the quantity of services provided. The price of medical care has been increasing far faster than the overall price level.

C. Efforts to reform health care have focused on controlling costs and increasing accessibility. A dual system of health care (one for those who can afford to pay and the other for those who cannot) may be evolving.

IV. High and rising health care costs.

A. Health care spending in the U.S. is rising in absolute terms, as a percentage of domestic output and on a per capita basis.

B. Figure 36.1 shows major types of spending and major sources of funds for these expenditures.

1. Thirty-three cents of each health care dollar is spent on hospitals; 20 cents goes to physicians; and 26 cents pays for other health care services.

2. About 80 percent of expenditures are paid for by public and private insurance; the remaining amount is paid by the health-care consumer.

C. Health care absorbed 5.1 percent of GDP in 1960, 13.9 percent in 1999, and is projected to increase to 16.2 percent by 2008. (Figure 36.2).

D. Global Perspective 36.1 shows that per capita spending on health care is higher in the U.S. than in any other major industrialized nation.

E. Quality of care: Are we healthier?

1. Medical care in the U.S. is probably the best in the world, but not our health.

2. As a result of medical research, the incidence of certain diseases has been declining and the quality of treatment has been improving in the U.S. But the U.S. has a lower life expectancy, higher maternal mortality and infant mortality rates, an AIDS epidemic that has claimed over 480,000 lives; and an increase in tuberculosis.

3. The U.S. Office of Technology Assessment has concluded that the U.S. ranks low internationally on may health indicators.

F. There are economic implications of rising costs.

1. The increase in health care costs is the main reason for rising health care spending.

2. Increased health care costs have other effects as well.

   a. Fewer uninsured can afford health care; fewer employers can offer health insurance to workers.

   b. Adverse effects on labor markets exist.

      i. Wages grow more slowly because health care benefits are taking a larger share of the "compensation" package.

      ii. Employers use more part-time and temporary workers to avoid the high cost of health insurance coverage for workers. Employer may contract-out the work of low-paid workers to avoid paying health care costs.

   c. Government budgets at all levels are having to deal with spiraling health care expenditures.

      i. Medicare and Medicaid has been the fastest growing segment of the Federal budget.

      ii. Higher taxes or reductions in other budget components (national defense, education, environmental programs) must be used to cover the increases.

      iii. States are finding it difficult to cover their share of Medicaid costs and must reduce other expenditures (infrastructure, education, and welfare).

      iv. Local governments face similar strains.

G. A basic allocation problem.

1. Most industries are happy to have increased spending. Why are we alarmed about more spending on health care?

2. Experts are concerned that at the margin, the consumption of health care is worth less than the alternative goods and services that could otherwise have been produced with those resources. In other words, there is an overallocation of resources to health care, which imposes a real economic cost on society.

V. **Limited access: Many are uninsured.**

1. In 1999 about 43 million households (16 percent of population) had no health insurance for the entire year. This is a growing number.

2. Which groups have no insurance?

a. Fifty percent of the uninsured are families where the head works full time, the family income is too high to qualify for Medicaid, but the earned income is not enough to afford health insurance.

b. Young people with excellent health choose not to buy health insurance.

c. The chronically ill find it impossible or too costly to obtain insurance because of the likelihood they will incur substantial costs in the future.

d. The unemployed lack insurance because most policies accompany employment.

e. Workers for small firms are unlikely to have insurance because high administrative costs make it costly for small business employers to offer this benefit.

f. Part-time and low-wage workers are also less likely to be insured.

3. The uninsured will sometimes pay directly, but often wait until their illness is so critical that the hospital emergency room is the only alternative, and this adds to hospitals' uncompensated health care burdens, estimated at over $10 billion per year. Hospitals are forced to shift these costs to other health-care customers.

VI. Why the rapid rise in costs?

A. Health care market is unique.

1. Ethical and equity considerations are intertwined. Society regards much of health care as a right and is reluctant to ration it solely on the basis of who can afford it.

2. Information is asymmetric: Physicians and other caregivers possess more information about the product than the consumer. Often the provider orders the service for the consumer or patient.

3. Spillover or external benefits exist. Healthy individuals make the entire society more productive and contribute to general prosperity and well-being.

4. Third-party payment or payment by the insurance company means that the consumer has little or no direct out-of-pocket expenditure for health care services. Therefore, the consumer does not seek out the lowest cost alternative.

B. Demand for health care has been increasing.

1. Health care is a "normal" good, so when incomes rise, the demand for health care rises proportionately. Elasticity with respect to income is estimated about 1 and may be as high as 1.5 in the U.S.

2. Demand for most health care is believed to be price "inelastic," which means that the quantity demanded does not decline with rising prices.

a. Most health care is a necessity.

b. There are few substitutes for most health care services.

c. Consumers do not "shop around" for doctors in most cases.

d. Patients with insurance do not care much about the price of each service received since they prepay for the total package.

3. The population is aging. By 1999 the proportion those over age 65 had risen to 15 percent from 9 percent thirty years earlier. Those over 65 consume 3 1/2 times more health care services as those between 19 and 64. By 2030 the proportion of the population over age 65 will be almost 20 percent.

4. Unhealthy lifestyles, particularly substance abuse, are common, although smoking is declining.

5. The role of physicians may increase the demand for health care.

   a. Asymmetric information exists, meaning that doctors possess more information about health care needs than do their patients (consumers) and doctors order the services for them. Also doctors are paid on a "fee-for-service" basis, which encourages them to order more services, and patients seldom have advance information on the cost or necessity of these services.

   b. Defensive medicine is common in that doctors err on the side of being overly cautious to avoid any charges of malpractice. They often order many procedures that may not be necessary.

   c. Medical ethics cause doctors to use the "best practice" to serve their patients and to try to sustain human life regardless of cost.

6. Insurance pays over 79 percent of health care costs. While this is positive in providing security against devastating losses, it creates a "moral hazard" problem.

   a. Insured may seek more health care and engage in more damaging behavior than the uninsured.

   b. Overconsumption occurs because people regard health care as "free," since they have prepaid for their services.

   c. Price provides a direct incentive to restrict use of a product, but insurance coverage, removes the consumer's budget constraint when he or she decides to consume health care.

7. Employer-financed health insurance constitutes a "tax subsidy" because the health benefits are exempt from both federal income tax and payroll (social security) taxation.

8. Figure 36.3a gives graphic portrayal of a competitive health care market (on the demand side) that might exist if all consumers were uninsured. Allocative efficiency occurs only when we pay in full for a product. In Figure 36.3b we see the effect of health insurance paying half the price of health care, so the consumer's bill for the service is the same as half price. Therefore, the quantity consumed will be Q_i rather than Q_u and there is more health care consumed than would be justified by the total cost of this amount of care to society. Figure 36.3b illustrates this "welfare loss" be the area abc.

9. "Equity-efficiency" tradeoff is illustrated here. The dilemma is if we provide social insurance that is believed equitable, then overconsumption will occur, which is inefficient. Efficiency may be achieved when less insurance is provided, but this may be inequitable.

C. Supply factors also cause rising costs.

1. Some believe that the supply of physicians has been restricted artificially, but the evidence for this argument is not strong, since the number of physicians per 100,000 people has increased over the years. But the increase in the supply of physicians has not kept up with the increase in demand for services provided.

2. Physicians' incomes are high in part because of the high costs incurred during their education. Although doctors have high rates of return on their educational expenses, these returns are below those for lawyers and business school graduates.

3. Productivity growth has been slow in health care because it is labor intensive and there is no strong incentive to raise productivity in a fee-for-service system.

4. Changes in medical technology have often caused rising costs, because private and public insurance pays for new technology regardless of costs. Some studies estimate that this accounts for as much as one-half of the growth of health care expenditures.

D. Relative importance.

1. Health care costs have escalated because of both demand and supply side factors as enumerated above; however some factors are more important than others.

2. Most experts attribute the relative rise in health care spending to the following:

   a. Advances in medical technology.

   b. The medical ethic of providing the best treatment available.

   c. Private and public health insurance (the presence of third party-payers).

   d. Fee for service physician payments.

V. Reforming the Health Care System

A. Again, the two goals of health care reform are containing costs and increasing access. There are tradeoffs between these two goals.

B. Achieving universal access is one goal. Three proposals have been considered.

1. "Play or pay" is the name given to a proposal in which employers would be required to provide a basic health insurance program for their workers and their dependents (play) or pay a special payroll tax to provide health insurance for uninsured workers (pay).

   a. This may lower real wages on the one hand.

   b. It may also lead to more job mobility on the other hand.

   c. Some fear it could lead to a rise in unemployment for low-wage workers.

2. Tax credits or vouchers offer another approach. Tax credits would be given to low-income families to purchase health care coverage, or a voucher would be issued to the poorest.

3. National health insurance is the most far-reaching proposal. It is not "socialized" medicine because the government would not provide health care services, only insure them.

   a. Proponents say it is the simplest and most direct way to provide universal access, it allows patient choice; it reduces administrative costs (administrative costs are 5 percent of total health care costs in Canada, while they are currently about 17 percent of health care costs in U.S.); it increases labor mobility, since health insurance is not tied to the job; and it would give government power to contain costs.

   b. Opponents argue that government price ceilings will not contain costs—-doctors would have too many loopholes; that Canada's system has waiting lists for certain types of procedures and that technology is not as available as in U.S. today; that the Federal government does not contain costs in other areas very successfully; and that health insurance coverage would become a sort of progressive tax benefit program, since low-income groups would pay little and workers in other industries might find themselves with more take-home income if their employers saved with national insurance.

C. Cost containment: One solution is to alter incentives.

   1. Deductibles and copayments reduce the overconsumption problem, since the insured have higher out-of-pocket costs. Administrative costs have been reduced by eliminating small claims.

   2. Managed-care organizations are those in which medical services are controlled or coordinated by insurance companies or health care organizations in order to reduce health care expenditures.

      a. In 1999, 60 percent of U.S. workers received health care through managed-care arrangements.

      b. Preferred provider organizations (PPOs) give breaks to insurance companies, which rewards the insured for using members of PPO with smaller copayment requirements.

      c. Health maintenance organizations (HMOs) offer prepaid health plans, which give incentives to the organization to hold costs down, and encourage preventive care.

      d. With both PPOs and HMOs, medical services and spending by physicians and hospitals are monitored.

      e. The disadvantages of managed care from the patient's perspective is the focus on reducing costs by denying expensive but effective treatment. Because of bi-partisan support, it is likely that a "patients' bill of rights" will be passed by the Congress.

   3. Medicare reimburses hospitals based on categories of procedures that characterize a patient's condition rather than on what the physician or hospital say is needed regarding length and type of hospital care. This is known as diagnosis-related-group (DRG) system.

D. Recent laws and proposals:

   1. Although Congress has rejected major reforms, it has made some modest changes and is discussing others.

      a. The Health Insurance and Portability Act of 1996 ensures that workers with a group health plan can continue to buy health insurance when they change jobs or become self-employed and prohibits group insurance plans from dropping coverage of a sick employee or of a business that has a sick employee.

      b. Medical savings accounts were introduced in 1996 on a trial basis. These tax deductible accounts can be used for routine medical expenses and include a catastrophic health insurance plan for large medical expenses. Critics contend that the accounts create an adverse selection problem by pulling the healthiest and wealthiest away from the general insurance market.

      c. Prescription drugs are not currently covered by Medicare, but the coverage has growing Congressional support. There are several reasons for this increased support:

         i.   Prescription drugs are becoming a larger portion of health care spending particularly for the elderly.

         ii. Politicians are aware of the popularity of a prescription-drug benefit among the Americans on Medicare.

         iii. Federal budget surpluses make it possible to provide this benefit.

VI. **LAST WORD: A Market for Human Organs?**

    A. Advances in medical technology make it possible for surgeons to replace some human body parts with donated "used parts." But not everyone who needs a transplant can get one.

    B. Why shortages?

        1. No market exists for human organs.

        2. The demand curve for human organs would resemble others in that a greater quantity would be demanded at low prices than at higher prices.

        3. Donated organs that are rationed by a waiting list have a zero price. The existing supply is perfectly inelastic and is the fixed quantity offered by willing donors.

        4. There is a shortage of human organs because at a zero price the quantity demanded exceeds the quantity supplied.

    C. Using a market.

        1. A market for human organs would increase the incentive to donate organs. The higher the expected price of an organ, the greater would be the number of people willing to have their organs sold at death.

        2. The shortage of organs would be eliminated, and the number of organs available for transplanting would rise.

    D. Objections.

        1. The first is a moral objection that turning human organs into commodities commercializes human beings and diminishes the special nature of human life.

        2. An analytical critique based on the elasticity of supply, suggests that the likely increase in the actual number of usable organs for transplants would not be great.

        3. A health-cost concern suggests that a market for body organs would greatly increase the cost of health care.

    E. A worldwide, $1 billion-per-year illegal market in human organs has emerged.

ANSWERS TO END-OF-CHAPTER QUESTIONS

36-1 Why would increased spending on, say, household appliances or television sets in a particular economy be regarded as economically desirable? Why, then, is there so much concern about rising expenditures as a percentage of the GDP on the health care?

Increasing expenditures on goods such as household appliances or television sets is regarded as desirable because production is expanding under relatively competitive market conditions. Thus, not only are output and employment expanding, but presumably these are happening because of allocative efficiency. Consumers are choosing to buy appliances or televisions because they are willing to pay the price for these goods.

There is concern about the same rising expenditures in the health care industry because of the unique factors that characterize the market for health care services. On the demand side, there is imperfect competition in that buyers do not have good information about the services needed or the fees that will be charged for the services; doctors control much of this information and, in fact, order the services for the consumer in most cases. Third-party insurance companies pay the direct costs of most health care on a fee-for-service basis, and therefore the consumer pays less than the full price at the time of consumption, leading to overconsumption; overconsumption by the insured may also be encouraged by the "moral hazard" problem. On the supply side, technology is encouraged without much regard for its cost by insurance providers; doctors also control much of the provision of health care in an imperfectly competitive supply structure, since they really don't compete on the basis of price. In other words, many of the unique factors of the health care market lead economists to believe that overconsumption is occurring and that society is losing because resources are not being allocated efficiently in a way that maximizes society's welfare.

36-2 (*Key Question*) What are the "twin problems" of the health care industry? How are they related?

The "twin problems" are rising prices for all and limited access (lack of insurance) for about 16 percent of the population. The problems are related since rising costs make insurance unaffordable for many individuals and families and make it difficult for some businesses to insure their workers.

36-3 Briefly describe the main features of Medicare and Medicaid, indicating how each is financed.

Medicare is a nationwide Federal health care program available to social security beneficiaries and the disabled. It consists of a hospital insurance program and certain other coverage for post-hospital care. It also includes a subsidized medical insurance portion ($41.10 per month in 1994) for physician services, lab tests, and other outpatient services. The hospital portion is covered through payroll taxes, the same as social security. The medical portion is covered as stated, with about three-fourths of the cost being covered by the government.

Medicaid provides payment for medical benefits to certain low-income people, including the elderly, blind, disabled, children, and adults with dependent children who qualify. Nevertheless, it covers less than half of those in poverty.

36-4 What are the implications of rapidly rising health care costs for (a) the growth of real wage rates, and (b) government budgets? Explain.

The real total compensation package, wages plus benefits, can only rise as fast as productivity does. If health insurance benefits rise more rapidly than productivity, then the real wage component of the compensation package is squeezed and it must fall. Workers feel the burden of rising health care costs as their take-home wages fall.

Government budgets are also stretched by rising health care costs, because social security recipients qualify for federally financed Medicare benefits, which grow as a result of higher health care costs and a greater proportion of the population qualifying for these benefits. All levels of government are affected by Medicaid payments, which are financed by a combination of state and federal funds. Finally, local governments may also be affected through their support of public hospital and other health care facilities, because the uninsured and underinsured need to have their health care costs subsidized.

36-5 Who are the main groups without health insurance?

One group of uninsured is the working poor, who make too much to qualify for Medicaid but not enough to afford health insurance. Both they and their employers find it difficult to support this cost for minimum-wage and other low-income workers. Another group includes part-time workers and those who work for small firms, or who are self-employed in small businesses or farms. Those who believe they are healthy and can avoid accidents, such as young adults, may refuse to spend money on insurance, and on the opposite extreme, the chronically ill, who are unable to get insurance coverage at all or at any reasonable price, are often without insurance.

36-6 List the special characteristics of the U.S. health care market, and specify how each affects our health care problems.

The health care market has many characteristics that differentiate it from a perfectly competitive market. (1) There are ethical questions connected with health care services that don't arise when

447

people are unable to afford other types of goods and services—in general, society regards access to basic health care as a right. (2) Buyers of health care typically have little information about the services they need and should acquire, creating the unusual situation in which the doctor (supplier) orders the services for the patient (consumer). (3) There are significant spillover or external benefits connected with health care, suggesting that society should be willing to pay more than the amount coming from the private sector alone. (4) Third-party payments are common because the patient (consumer) has prepaid for insurance benefits, and about three-fourths of all health care expenses are paid in this way. Consumers directly pay lower "out-of-pocket" expenses than if they were not insured, which causes them to overconsume.

36-7 (*Key Question*) What are the estimates of the income and price elasticities of demand for health care? How does each relate to rising health care costs?

Income elasticity is 1.0 suggesting that health care spending will rise proportionately with income. Some studies indicate the it might be 1.5 in the U.S. Price elasticity is only 0.2, meaning higher prices for health care services will increase total health care spending.

36-8 Briefly discuss the demand and supply factors which contribute to rising health costs. Specify how (a) asymmetric information, (b) fee-for-service payments, (c) defensive medicine, and (d) medical ethics, might cause health care costs to rise.

(a) Asymmetric information refers to the fact that consumers of health care often have very little understanding or access to the information about the health care services that they need. Therefore, they must depend on health care professionals to order the services for them. This creates the unusual market situation in which producers have the power to create demand for what they produce. Even when patients understand and do create the demand, it is difficult for them to find price information about health care services. Obviously this situation is not a competitive one on the production side, and consequently there is less pressure to keep prices low, as would be the case in a competitive industry.

(b) Fee-for-service payments can contribute to rising health care costs by making it possible for providers to increase their incomes by simply ordering more services for the patient. If an attempt were made to legally control prices, for example, the provider could simply require the patient to purchase more tests, more exams, etc. The administrative costs of billing on a fee-for-service basis are also higher than would be the case if there were other types of reimbursement for services.

(c) Defensive medicine refers to the practice that physicians follow to avoid malpractice charges. To defend against such concerns, they may order more tests and procedures than would be warranted medically or economically.

(d) Medical ethics, which require the "best practice" techniques, may result in the use of costly medical practices with only marginal benefits. Also, the values that promote the support of a human life as long as possible, regardless of the cost or condition of life, add to the cost of health care.

36-9 "Health care expenditures have been rising principally because of the technological transformation of medical care." Do you agree? Explain.

Significant advances in medical technology have occurred and have been encouraged by the willingness of public and private insurance to pay for new treatments without regard to cost. There appears to be an interplay among the availability of new medical technology, increases in health care costs, increases the demand for health insurance, and finally increases in the demand for the new services. This process is continuous. One illustration of this occurred when Medicare programs agreed to pay for magnetic resonance imaging (MRI) scans in 1985; the sales of such scanners then rose dramatically.

Many experts agree that as much as one-half of the increase in health care expenditures is the result of advances in medical technology.

36-10 (*Key Question*) Using the concepts in Chapter 21's discussion of consumer behavior, explain how health care insurance results in an overallocation of resources to the health care industry. Use a demand and supply diagram to specify the resulting efficiency loss.

Health care insurance removes or greatly lessens a person's budget restraint at the time health care is purchased, raising health care utility per dollar spent and causing an overconsumption of health care. In Figure 35-3b, insurance reduces the price of health care at the time of purchase from P_u to P_i, increasing the quantity consumed from Q_u to Q_i. At Q_i the marginal cost of health care is represented by point b and exceeds the marginal benefit represented by c, indicating an overallocation of resources. The efficiency loss is area *cab*.

36-11 How is the moral hazard problem relevant to the health care market?

The moral hazard problem is relevant to the health care market in two basic ways. First, the insured individual may neglect preventive health care, knowing that the costs of illness and/or injury are covered. Second, when health care is needed, the insured may overconsume, because the out-of-pocket expense for any single service is subsidized by the insurance. Providers may also be encouraged to order more tests or treatments than are really necessary when the patient is not having to bear the entire cost directly.

36-12 What is the rationale for exempting a firm's contribution to its workers' health insurance from taxation as worker income? What is the impact of this exemption on allocative efficiency in the health care industry?

The underlying rationale is that spillover benefits exist from a healthy, productive workforce. Therefore, it is appropriate to make health care more widely available to workers and their families. The impact of the exemption is to make private health care insurance more accessible to more people, but it also contributes to the overconsumption problem. Workers in the 28 percent marginal tax bracket can essentially receive $1.00 worth of insurance for a contribution of $.72, which is the after-tax value of that $1.00 in income spent on health insurance. The tax subsidy costs the Federal government an estimated $65 billion in forgone revenue and boosts private health insurance spending by about one-third. Health care spending may be 10-20 percent higher than it would be without the tax break.

36-13 Comment on or explain:

a. "Providing health insurance to achieve equity goals creates a tradeoff with the efficient allocation of resources to the health care industry."

b. "Improved health habits are desirable, but would not necessarily reduce health care costs. For example, the deaths of many smokers are from sudden and lethal heart attacks and are therefore medically inexpensive."

c. "If government were to require employer-sponsored health insurance for all workers, the likely result would be an increase in the unemployment of low-wage workers."

(a) If equity means that society has a right to decent health care and universal access is a goal, then there will be a tradeoff with the efficient allocation of resources. Under every universal access proposal, there is some incentive toward overconsumption of health care resources, since by definition of universal access, some people are being provided with access to health care they would otherwise not care to purchase. By providing universal access, all who have coverage find health care available at a lower "out-of-pocket" price than would be the case if there were no insurance and health care prices were determined on the private market. Thus, the quantity demanded will be greater than that justified by the cost of providing the services.

(b) This statement is true only for those few who may die from sudden, lethal heart attacks. Poor habits, such as smoking, lead to increased health care costs for the majority who do follow healthy lifestyles. Long-term health care problems, which lead to absenteeism and lower productivity in the work force, spells of hospitalization from other illnesses, and heart problems that do not result in sudden death, may occur. In considering smoking specifically, there is also the potential for causing damage to the health of others through secondhand smoke in the air.

(c) This statement is based on the view that many low-wage workers have low productivity, and their employers are paying them according to the theory of marginal revenue productivity—in other words, the low wage is equivalent to the value each contributes to the employer's output. To require health insurance coverage, is, in effect, raising the cost of each worker and the employer could not afford this without some increase in the worker's marginal revenue product. While the statement seems true on the surface, if every employer faced the same requirement, it may have the same result as minimum wage laws, and that is that only a very small increase in unemployment results.

36-14 Briefly describe (a) "play or pay"; (b) tax credits and vouchers; and (c) national health insurance as means of increasing access to health care. What are the major criticisms of national health insurance?

(a) "Play or pay" refers to the proposal whereby employers must either provide health insurance to their employees (play) or pay a tax into a public insurance fund for those employees not insured (pay).

(b) The tax credit or voucher proposal is to give access to those who cannot now afford private insurance. Low-income households would be given a credit to use for health insurance, thus reducing their tax by the cost of the insurance. The poorest households, for whom a credit would not apply, would be given vouchers to use in purchasing private health insurance in much the same way as food stamps are used to purchase food.

(c) National health insurance would provide a basic package of health care to every citizen at no direct charge or at a low-cost sharing level. It would be financed by tax revenues. Private insurers could continue to offer health coverage for procedures not covered by the national health insurance package.

Critics of national health insurance charge that government-controlled fees are not likely to control costs, since providers can circumvent the low fees by ordering more procedures, more frequent visits, and so forth. They also point to excess demand for health care in countries where national health insurance exists. In Canada, the government's efforts to control costs have resulted in a shortage of technology and other services available to meet the demand. Critics argue that the Federal government does not have a good track record in cost containment. Finally, they fear some of the redistributional effects of national health insurance, which would, by and large, result in a more progressive tax-subsidy structure, as low-income people would receive more benefits and high-income groups would pay more into the system than the value of the benefits they receive.

36-15 What are (a) preferred provider organizations and (b) health maintenance organizations? Explain how each is designed to alleviate the overconsumption of health care.

(a) Preferred provider organizations (PPOs) are collective agreements among hospitals, doctors, and insurance companies in which the providers (hospitals and doctors) agree in advance to provide discounts on their services in exchange for receiving the business of those insured by the company in question. Policy holders are given a list of those cooperating hospitals, clinics, and physicians and will receive greater reimbursement by patronizing those members of the PPO. Usually, the patient has a choice to receive care elsewhere, but at a lower insurance reimbursement level.

(b) Health maintenance organizations (HMOs) are organizations which contract with employers, insurance companies, labor unions, or other groups to provide medical care for their members. HMOs alter the traditional fee-for-service arrangement by providing prepaid health plans, which usually cover preventive care as well as sickness and injury.

PPOs lower costs by the agreement to lower fees in exchange for the contract from the insurance company. The use of one organization can also lower administrative costs substantially ,as uniform medical forms and bills are streamlined. HMOs are considered "managed care" systems, because utilization and spending are "managed" or controlled by close monitoring of physician and provider behavior to eliminate unneeded tests and treatments, since HMOs operate on a fixed budget. The existence of a budget for HMOs, which don't charge on a fee-for-service basis, provides an incentive to economize on services offered to each patient. Furthermore, by encouraging patients to receive preventive care, HMOs might also reduce the higher cost of the hospitalization of ill patients.

36-16 Do you think prescription drugs should be covered under Medicare? Are you willing to pay a higher social security/Medicare tax to pay for this added benefit? Do you think the prescription-drug benefit should go to everyone covered by Medicare, including those who can easily afford to pay for the prescription drugs out of packet?

Prescription drugs are becoming a more significant part of health care costs and are claiming a larger share of the income of older Americans. Some older Americans must sacrifice necessities to pay for prescription drugs or choose to do without the drugs even when they are required to maintain health. Personally, I am willing to pay a higher Medicare tax. As with social security and Medicare, the benefit should be considered a social insurance program and be available to all who are Medicare eligible.

36-17 (*Last Word*) Do you favor the establishment of a market for "donated" human organs? Why or why not?

Advances in medical technology make it possible for surgeons to replace some human body parts with donated organs. However, not everyone who needs a transplant can get one. There are shortages of donated organs available for transplant. A market for human organs might eliminate the present shortage, but there are many serious objections to turning human body parts into commodities for purchase and sale.

Some people die while on a waiting list; creating a market for human organs would increase the incentive to donate. In such a market an individual could specify in a legal document that they were willing to sell one or more usable organs upon death. The person could specify where the money from the sale would go, for example, to a family member or a charity. The higher the expected price of an organ the greater would be the number of people willing to have their organs sold at death. Market processes are impersonal and efficient, rationing what is scarce, and providing incentives to supply more of what is desired. The shortage of organs would be eliminated and the number of organs available for transplanting would rise. This means more lives would be saved and enhanced than under the current donor system.

The objections to such a market in human body parts fall into three categories: moral, analytical, and cost concerns. Critics say it is unseemly to buy or sell body organs as if they were bushels of wheat or ounces of gold. Human organs should not be treated as commodities; the nature of human life is special. The market would also ration the available organs and only those with health insurance for transplants or private means could afford them. An analytical critique suggests that a market price for organs might increase the number of potential donors but would have no effect on the death rate of those individuals. Thus the number of available organs might not increase very much. Finally, a market for body organs could increase the cost of health care dramatically. Rather than obtaining freely donated organs, insurance companies would have to pay market prices. As transplant procedures are further perfected, the demand could increase greatly relative to supply and the increase in the price of organs would continue to escalating health care costs.

CHAPTER 37
INTERNATIONAL TRADE

CHAPTER OVERVIEW

This chapter builds on Chapter 6, providing more analysis of international trade and protectionism. First, it reviews important facts about world trade. Second, it examines how international specialization based on comparative advantage can mutually benefit participating nations. Third, supply and demand analysis is used to help students understand prices and quantities of imports and exports. Fourth, the economic impact of trade barriers is examined, followed by the arguments for protectionism. Finally, the chapter discusses the costs of protectionism and some continuing international trade controversies.

WHAT'S NEW

A section on the World Trade Organization replaces the "International Trade Policies" section in 14th edition. Otherwise changes are mainly editorial and revisions, making the text more concise.

INSTRUCTIONAL OBJECTIVES

After completing this chapter, students should be able to:

1. Summarize the importance of international trade to the U.S. in terms of overall volume.

2. List the major imports and exports of the United States.

3. State two economic points that explain why nations trade.

4. Compute, when given appropriate data, the relative costs of producing two commodities in two countries and determine which nation has the comparative advantage in each good.

5. Compute, when given appropriate data, the range for the terms of trade.

6. Calculate the potential gains from trade and specialization for each nation and the world when given appropriate data.

7. State the economist's case for free trade.

8. Explain the relationship between world prices and American export supply curve, and the relationship between world prices and American import demand curve.

9. Explain international equilibrium price and quantity using a two-nation market model for import demand and export supply.

10. Identify four types of trade barriers.

11. Describe the economic impact of tariffs, including both direct and indirect effects.

12. Contrast the economic impact of a quota with that of a tariff.

13. List seven arguments in favor of protectionist barriers, and critically evaluate each.

14. Identify the costs of protectionist policies and their effects on income distribution.

15. Describe the major provisions of the WTO.

16. Define and identify terms and concepts listed at the end of the chapter.

COMMENTS AND TEACHING SUGGESTIONS

1. Students can be made more aware of the extent of international trade with some simple exercises such as the following: (a) list all the things that the student owns that were made in another country, and name the countries; (b) list all of the foods eaten that day (week, month) that were imported and name the sources; (c) list all of the friends and relatives you have who are working for an export industry, or for a foreign-owned firm, or all the foreign-owned firms in your city or town; (d) if you have several students who always wear baseball caps, have them look at the label. Despite outward appearances, most caps are manufactured outside the U.S.

2. Numerical examples help students to understand the principle of comparative advantage. Using state names instead of country names can help them to see the benefits from trade without the antiforeign bias that may exist initially.

3. Tell students to assume that tariffs and quotas are enacted only when national defense is affected by the imported good. Then ask them to develop creative arguments to convince Congress that sugar, scissors, textiles, alcoholic beverages, and other products now covered by tariffs or quotas might be essential to national defense. In other words, they are to assume the role of lobbyists for these industries.

4. The "Buy American" campaign is a good topic for class discussion, presentations, or short papers. It is interesting to focus on the automobile industry to illustrate the various aspects to this issue. One question might address the desirability of buying American in the first place. Another question concerns the difficulty in defining what is "American" when it comes to automobiles and many other products. For example, many "Japanese" vehicles are now manufactured in varying degrees in the U.S., while many automobiles produced by the "Big Three" U.S. auto corporations are manufactured outside this country. Which of these can be considered to be American? The Last Word for Chapter 6 is a humorous look at this issue, but it makes a serious point. Robert Reich's "The Work of Nations" and Thomas Friedman's "The Lexus and the Olive Tree" are good books on the issue of globalization.

5. The Last Word for this chapter is Bastiat's famous "Petition of the Candlemakers"—a favorite reading for introductory classes in economics since the 1800s. Note that the real concern is both employment and living standards.

6. "International Economics," an amusing but very informative comic book explanation of the theory of comparative advantage and also the principles of foreign exchange, can be ordered from the New York Federal Reserve Bank's Public Information Department. 35 copies of the comic-book explanations, four duplicating activity masters, and one teacher's guide can be obtained free for classroom use. (Write or call them at FRB New York, Public Information Dept., 33 Liberty Street, New York, NY 10045, Ph. 212-791-6134.) Other Federal Reserve Banks publish other educational booklets on international trade and exchange topics.

STUDENT STUMBLING BLOCK

The principle of comparative advantage is not an easy concept to grasp. Where absolute advantage is involved, the principle is understandable, but it is tougher to grasp a situation such as that in the text example where the U.S. has an absolute advantage in both wheat and coffee production. Work through this example carefully with students. A short, soft-cover book, "The Choice" by Russell Roberts illustrates the principle of comparative advantage in story form and does an excellent job. If you assign a supplementary reading, this is recommended. Another idea is to demonstrate comparative advantage at the personal level. A lawyer may be the best gardener and house painter in town (has an absolute advantage). Still it is to the lawyer's comparative advantage to specialize in law and hire gardeners and painters.

LECTURE NOTES

I.   **Facts of International Trade: Highlights**

A. Exports of goods make up about 12% of total U.S. output.

B. The U.S. leads the world in the volume of exports and imports with about 1/8 of total.

C. Since 1975 U.S. exports and imports have more than doubled as a percentage of GDP.

D. In 1999 the U.S. had a goods and services trade deficit of $265 billion dollars.

E. The principal exports of the U.S. are computers, chemicals, semiconductors, consumer durables, and aircraft. Its main imports are petroleum, automobiles, computers, and clothing.

F. The U.S. exports many of the "same" goods it imports.

G. The bulk of U.S. trade is with other industrialized nations.

H. Improved transportation and communication has contributed greatly to international trade since WWII.

I. Although the U.S. still dominates world trade, there are emerging nations around the world that collectively generate substantial international trade such as South Korea, Taiwan, Singapore and China. Conditions in one nation affect many others.

J. International trade and finance link economies.

K. International trade is often at the center of U.S. economic policy.

II. **The Economic Basis for Trade**

A. International trade is a way nations can specialize, increase the productivity of their resources, and realize a larger total output than they otherwise would.

B. Two points amplify the rationale for trade.

1. The distribution of economic resources among nations is uneven.

2. Efficient production of various goods requires different technologies or combinations of resources.

3. Products are differentiated among nations and some people prefer imports.

C. Interaction of these points can be illustrated.

1. Japan has a large, well-educated labor force and can specialize in labor-intensive commodities.

2. Australia has an abundance of land relative to human and capital resources and can cheaply produce land-intensive agricultural products.

3. Industrially advanced nations (including Japan) are in a position to produce capital-intensive goods.

D. As national economies evolve, the resource base may be altered affecting the relative efficiency with which nations can produce various goods and services.

III. **Graphical Analysis of the Principle of Comparative Advantage**

A. The basic principle of comparative advantage rests on differing opportunity costs of producing various goods and services.

B. An example of comparative advantage is developed in Figure 37-1 and Table 37-1 comparing an imaginary example using the U.S. and Brazil.

1. Before trade, both nations are self-sufficient in wheat and coffee and produce at the levels shown in Figure 37-1.

2. The principle of comparative advantage says that total output will be greatest when each good is produced by the nation that has the lower opportunity cost. The U.S. has a comparative advantage in wheat production and should specialize in wheat, and Brazil should specialize in coffee as one would expect.

3. Note in Table 37-1 that after specialization there will be more coffee and more wheat in total than the totals before specialization. Total wheat production rose from 26 units of wheat to 30 units of wheat; coffee production rose from 16 to 20.

4. Since each nation would like some of both goods, they will now have to trade. The terms of trade will be limited by the original cost conditions in each country. For example, in the U.S. 1 wheat =1 coffee, so the U.S. will not give up more than 1 wheat for each coffee. Similarly, in Brazil 1 wheat = 2 coffee, so Brazil will not trade more than 2 coffee for 1 wheat. These two facts set the limits to the terms of trade. The rate of exchange will be somewhere between 1 and 2 coffees for each wheat (Figure 37-2 illustrates these possibilities graphically). The actual terms of trade within these limits will depend on each country's negotiating power and world demand and supply conditions for these products.

5. The gains from trade can be shown by selecting any trade ratio within the limits. The text selects 1W = 1-1/2C. If the U.S. chooses to trade 10 tons of wheat for 15 tons of coffee, both nations will be better off than they were when they were self-sufficient. Specialization and trade have improved the productivity of their resources.

6. As a result of specialization and trade, both countries can have more of both products.

7. The above example assumes constant cost industries, which would not be the case in the real world. Rather, as the U.S. begins to expand wheat production, its relative costs will rise and likewise with costs of coffee production in Brazil. The effect of increasing costs is that complete specialization will probably not occur with many products.

C. The case for free trade is restated in the text: Through free trade, based on the principle of comparative advantage, the world economy can achieve a more efficient allocation of resources and a higher level of material well-being. See Figure 37.2 (Key Graph)

1. One side benefit from free trade is that it promotes competition and deters monopoly power.

2. Another side benefit may occur as specialization increases the production possibility curve by raising the productivity of the resources devoted to producing certain goods.

3. Try Quick Quiz 37.2.

IV. **Supply and Demand Analysis of Exports and Imports**

A. This analysis helps us understand how prices and quantities of exports and imports are determined in world markets.

1. The equilibrium world price derives from the interaction of world supply and demand.

2. The equilibrium domestic price is determined by domestic supply and demand. It is the price that would prevail in a closed economy with no international trade.

3. When economies are open to trade, differences between world and domestic prices form the basis for exports or imports.

B. Supply and demand in the U.S.

1. Assume first that there are no trade barriers, that Canada is the only other nation in the world, that aluminum is the product in question, and that there are no international transportation costs, to keep the analysis simple.

2. Figure 37.3a shows the domestic supply and demand curves for aluminum in the U.S. with an equilibrium price of $1 per pound and an equilibrium quantity of 100 million pounds.

3. If the world price exceeds $1, American firms will increase production and export the excess output to the rest of the world (Canada).

a. If the world price is $1.25, then American producers will supply 50 million pounds for export. (See Figure 37.3)

b. If the world price rises to $1.50, Americans will have 100 million pounds to export, because domestic consumers will buy only 50 million pounds at that price.

c. The American export supply curve is found in Figure 37.3b by plotting the domestic surpluses occurring at world prices above the $1 domestic equilibrium price. When world prices rise relative to American domestic prices, U.S. exports rise.

4. U.S. import demand will be shown by the Figure 37.3b plot of the excess domestic demand created if prices fall below the $1 domestic equilibrium price. The downsloping curve shows the amount of aluminum imported by the U.S. at prices below the $1 American domestic price. When world prices fall relative to domestic prices, American imports rise.

C. Supply and demand of aluminum in Canada can be depicted in a similar manner, as shown in Figure 37.4. The prices have been converted into U.S. dollar equivalents using the exchange rate mechanism discussed in Chapters 6 and 38.

1. Canada's import demand curve represents domestic shortages in Canada when the world price falls below the $.75 domestic Canadian price.

2. Canada's export supply curve represents domestic surpluses in Canada when the world price is above the $.75 Canadian domestic price.

D. Determination of the equilibrium world price, of exports and imports is illustrated in Figure 37.5.

1. Equilibrium occurs in this two-nation model where one nation's import demand curve intersects another nation's export supply curve. In this example, this occurs at a price of $.88.

2. At the $.88 world price, the domestic prices in both Canada and the U.S. will also be $.88.

E. Canada will export aluminum to gain earnings to buy other goods, such as computer software, that are made in the United States. These exports enable Canadians to acquire imports that have greater value to them than exported aluminum. Otherwise, they would be willing to pay more than $.88 per pound for aluminum. (Key Question 8)

V. **Trade Barriers: Barriers to free trade do exist.**

A. Types of barriers:

1. Tariffs are excise taxes on imports and may be used for revenue purposes, or more commonly as protective tariffs that protect domestic producers from foreign competition by raising import prices.

2. Import quotas specify the maximum amounts of imports allowed in a certain period of time. Low import quotas may be a more effective protective device than tariffs, which do not limit the amount of goods entering a country.

3. Nontariff barriers refer to licensing requirements, unreasonable standards, or bureaucratic red tape in customs procedures.

4. Voluntary export restrictions are agreements by foreign firms to "voluntarily" limit their exports to a particular country. Japan has voluntary limits on its auto exports to the United States.

B. The economic impact of tariffs is shown in Figure 37.6. With free trade, consumption will take place at the world price P_w, and domestic production will be 0a with imports making up the difference, ad. There are 4 direct effects.

1. When the tariff is imposed, domestic consumption declines to 0c as the price rises to P_t.

2. Domestic production will rise to 0b because the price has risen.

3. Imports fall to bc from ad.

4. Government tariff revenue will represent a transfer of income from consumers to government.

5. One indirect effect also may occur in that relatively inefficient industries are expanding and relatively efficient industries abroad have been made to contract.

C. The economic impact of quotas is similar to tariffs, but worse because no revenue is generated for the government; the higher price results in more revenue per unit for the foreign producer. After the quota, the price will rise to P_t as with the tariff, but the entire amount of revenue generated by the higher price will go to the foreign and domestic producers supplying the product at price P_t. Also, there is no possibility for consumers to obtain more than the allowed quota, even at higher prices.

VI. **The Case for Protection: A Critical Review**

A. Military self-sufficiency may be a valid political-economic argument for protecting industries that are critical to national defense. The argument is that the country cannot be dependent on other countries for its national defense. However, the problem with this rationale is that nearly every industry is critical in one way or another. It is difficult to select strategic industries to protect. Also, most goods are produced in many places, so dependency on one is not likely.

B. Increasing domestic employment is the most popular reason for protection, but there are important shortcomings associated with this reasoning.

1. Imports may eliminate some jobs, but they create others in the sales and service industries for these products.

2. The fallacy of composition applies here. The imports of one nation are the exports of another. By achieving short-term employment goals at home, the trading partner may be made weaker and less able to buy the protectionist nation's products.

3. Retaliation is a risk that occurred in the 1930s when high tariffs were imposed by the U.S. Smoot-Hawley Tariff Act of 1930. Protectionism against American goods will hurt our

export industries. Such trade wars still erupt today although the WTO helps to eliminate the problem.

    4. Long-run feedbacks relate to the fact that continued excess of exports over imports leads to a shortage of dollars abroad, which foreigners need to purchase more American goods and services; a nation must import in order to export.

C. Diversification for stability may be a legitimate reason for a nation to protect certain industries until they become viable. For example, Saudi Arabia may not always be able to depend on oil exports nor Cuba on sugar exports. They need to develop other industries.

    1. This argument does not apply to the U.S. or other diversified economies.

    2. The economic costs of diversification may be great and not worth the protection.

D. The infant-industry argument is similar to the diversification argument for protection. New industries allegedly may need "temporary" protection to gain productive efficiency. But qualifications must be noted.

    1. It is difficult to determine which industries are the best to protect.

    2. Protection may persist after industrial maturity is realized.

    3. Direct subsidies may be preferable to international protection.

E. Strategic trade policy has been successful in Japan and South Korea, but there is still a danger of retaliation by affected nations. Affected nations can implement tariffs in response.

F. Protection against "dumping" is another argument for tariffs when nations "dump" excess products onto U.S. markets at below cost.

    1. These firms may be trying to drive out U.S. competition.

    2. Dumping can be a form of price discrimination.

    3. Dumping is a legitimate concern and is prohibited under U.S. trade law. The Federal government has the right to impose antidumping duties (tariffs) on the goods that were "dumped," but it may be difficult to prove the below-cost sales in the first place.

G. Protection is said to be needed against the competition from cheap foreign labor. However, this argument is not valid. It is mutually beneficial for rich and poor to trade with one another. By not trading, we don't raise our living standards at all, but we will decrease them by shifting labor into inefficient areas where the foreign labor could have produced the items more efficiently.

H. A summary of arguments suggests that only two arguments for protection are really valid and they are tough to apply. The infant-industry argument and the military self-sufficiency argument may be justifiable on political grounds. Most other arguments are based on emotional half-truths or outright fallacies. Evidence of the results of protectionism shows that it has not had positive effects.

I. Summing Up:

    1. Within the U.S., the Constitution says states cannot prevent trade, so we have a prosperous, huge free-trade area.

    2. The European Union has prospered as trade barriers have been eliminated.

    3. The world economy has grown under the trend toward more tariff reduction since the mid-1930s.

4. High tariffs were a factor in causing the Great Depression.

5. Nations with high protectionist policies have slower growth than those with no barriers.

VII. **The World Trade Organization**

A. Inefficiencies of protectionism have led nations to seek ways to promote free trade.

B. In 1994 the more than 120 member nations of the World Trade Organization (WTO) agreed to implement several policies by 2005. These policies include:

1. Reduce tariffs worldwide.

2. New rules to promote service trade.

3. Reduction in agricultural subsidies that protect less efficient farmers.

4. New protection for intellectual property.

5. Phasing out of quotas on textiles and clothing replacing them with gradually declining tariffs.

C. These policies are predicted to boost trade by 8% or $6 trillion.

D. WTO today.

1. 138 nations belong in 2000.

2. Organization oversees provisions of agreement and resolves disputes.

3. Has become a protest target of groups who are against various aspects of globalization.

E. Economists favor free trade with labor and environmental protections.

VIII. **LAST WORD: The Petition of the Candlemakers, 1845**

A. This satire points out the absurd extreme logic of protectionism.

B. Candlemakers are urging laws to eliminate a free source of light, sunlight! They argue for laws requiring shutting off all sources of daylight in order to encourage French manufacturers of candles, candle wax, etc.

C. The point is that even if French manufacturers were made wealthier by shutting out sunlight, the overall standard of living in the nation would be much worse.

ANSWERS TO END-OF-CHAPTER QUESTIONS

37-1   Quantitatively, how important is international trade to the United States relative to other nations?

Our exports of goods and services are about 12 percent of GDP, which is small relative to the proportion in many other industrialized nations. For example, the percentage is 56 percent in the Netherlands, 29 percent in United Kingdom, 29 percent in New Zealand, and 41 percent in Canada. However, total U.S. exports and imports have more than doubled as a percent of GDP since 1975.

37-2   Distinguish among land-, labor- and capital-intensive commodities, citing an example of each. What role do these distinctions play in explaining international trade?

Land-intensive commodities include agricultural products such as corn and wheat. Labor-intensive commodities require much skilled labor in production, such as transistor radios and clothing.

Capital-intensive products are produced with a large amount of capital equipment and include manufactured items such as aircraft and automobiles.

These distinctions are important because if a nation has an abundant supply of particular type of resources, it can produce items that are intensive in these resources with a comparative cost advantage. On the other hand, if it has a relative scarcity of certain resources, such as land, then it will be relatively expensive to produce land-intensive products such as corn and wheat. The difference in relative resource abundance among nations leads to a difference in comparative costs of production, which is the basis for international trade and specialization.

37-3   Suppose nation A can produce 80 units of X by using all its resources to produce X or 60 units of Y by devoting all its resources to Y. Comparative figures for nation B are 60 of X and 60 of Y. Assuming constant costs, in which product should each nation specialize? Why? Indicate the limits of the terms of trade.

The cost ratio for the two goods in nation A is 2 units of X for each unit of Y; in nation B it is 1 unit of X for each unit of Y. The opportunity cost of producing each unit of X is lower in A (1/2 unit of Y) than it is in B (1 unit of Y). Conversely, the opportunity cost of producing Y is lower in B (1 unit of X) than it is in A (2 units of X). Nation A should produce X since it has a comparative cost advantage in the production of this good, and B should produce Y in which it has a comparative advantage.

The limits of the terms of trade for the two goods are the cost ratios in the two countries; this will be between 1X and 2X for each unit of Y. B will sell Y for 1-to-2 X units.

37-4   (*Key Question*) Below are the hypothetical production possibilities tables for New Zealand and Spain.

New Zealand's production possibilities table (millions of bushels)

Product	Production alternatives			
	A	B	C	D
Apples	0	20	40	60
Plums	15	10	5	0

Spain's production possibilities table (millions of bushels)

Product	Production alternatives			
	R	S	T	U
Apples	0	20	40	60
Plums	60	40	20	0

Plot the production possibilities data for each of the two countries separately. Referring to your graphs, answer the following: (a) What is each country's cost ratio of producing plums and apples. (b) Which nation should specialize in which product? (c) Show the trading possibilities lines for each nation if the actual terms of trade are 1 plum for 2 apples. (d) Suppose the optimum product mixes before specialization and trade were alternative B in New Zealand and S in Spain. What would be gains from specialization and trade?

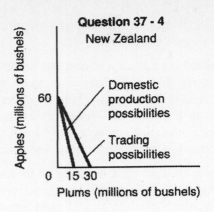

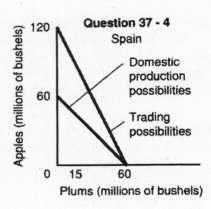

(a) New Zealand's cost ratio is 1 plum = 4 apples (or 1 apple = 1/4 plum). Spain's cost ratio is 1 plum = 1 apple (or 1 apple = 1 plum). See the graphs.

(b) New Zealand should specialize in apples, Spain in plums.

(c) See the graphs.

(d) Total production before specialization and trade: 40 applies (20 + 20) and 50 plumbs (10 + 40). After specialization and trade: 60 applies and 60 plums. Gain = 20 applies and 10 plums.

37-5   "The United States can produce product X more efficiently that can Great Britain. Yet we import X from Great Britain." Explain.

Trade is based on comparative rather than absolute cost advantages. The United States may have an absolute advantage in the production of good X yet still import it from another country because its cost advantage in the production of another good Y is even greater. By producing Y and importing X from Great Britain, Americans are devoting resources to their most productive use, even though an isolated analysis of the international production of X might suggest otherwise.

37-6   (*Key Question*) Refer to Figure 3.5 (Chapter 3). Assume the graph depicts the U.S. domestic market for corn. How many bushels of corn, if any, will the United States export or import at a world price of $1, $2, $3, $4, and $5? Use this information to construct the U.S. export supply curve and import demand curve for corn. Suppose the only other corn-producing nation is France, where the domestic price is $4. Which country will export corn; which will import it?

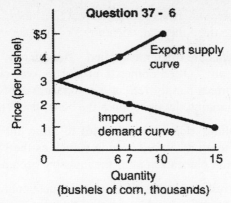

At $1: import 15,000. At $2: import 7,000. At $3: no imports or exports. At $4: export 6,000. At $5: export 10,000.

The United states will export corn, France will import it.

37-7   (Key Question) Draw a domestic supply and demand diagram for a product in which the United States does not have a comparative advantage. What impact do foreign imports have on domestic price and quantity?. On your diagram show a protective tariff which eliminates approximately one-fourth the assumed imports. What are the price-quantity effects of this tariff to (a) domestic consumers, (b) domestic producers, and (c) foreign exporters? How would the effects of a quota that creates the same amount of imports differ?

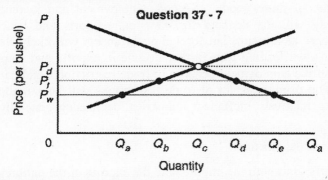

See the graph. The United States does not have a comparative advantage in this product so the world price Pw is below the U.S. domestic price of Pd. Imports will reduce the domestic price, increasing consumption from nontrade Qc to Qe and decreasing domestic production from Qc to Qa. See the graph. A tariff of $PwPt$ (a) harms domestic consumers by increasing price from Pw to Pt and decreasing consumption from Qe to Qd; (b) aids domestic producers through the increase in price from Pw to Pt and the expansion of domestic production from Qa to Qb; (c) harms foreign exporters by decreasing exports from $QaQe$ to $QbQd$.

An import quota of $QbQd$ would have the same effects as the tariff, but there would be no tariff revenues to government from these imports; this revenue would effectively go to foreign producers.

37-8   "The potentially valid arguments for tariff protection are also the most easily abused." What are those arguments? Why are they susceptible to abuse? Evaluate the use of artificial trade barriers, such as tariffs and import quotas, as a means of achieving and maintaining full employment.

Trade barriers may be defended as being necessary to protect domestic firms from foreign dumping, to protect so-called infant industries, and to ensure adequate production levels in sectors deemed to be essential in the event of war. (The arguments relating to supposed increases in domestic employment, protection from foreign low-wage labor, and economic diversification are not valid or are irrelevant to the American economy.)

Each of these valid arguments are often misapplied. Dumping by foreign firms in the United States are difficult to prove and rare. Often domestic producers will claim their foreign competitors are dumping when the lower prices simply reflect a comparative advantage in foreign production. If this is true the use of antidumping duties reduces the benefits of trade.

The protection of new "infant" domestic industries to allow them to develop efficient production techniques is questionable in an advanced economy such as the United States. There is a tendency for trade barriers to remain in place even after the industry becomes established.

The argument relating to military self-sufficiency is questionable when applied to sectors other than those directly related to defense. Almost all industries can claim to play a role in a wartime economy. As a rule, direct government subsidies are a more equitable means of protecting military security than trade protection, since taxpayers as a whole, rather than just consumers of protected industries will shoulder the burden. Direct subsidies also make the costs of these programs obvious rather than hiding them in the form of higher import prices.

Trade barriers on imports will cause consumers to partially substitute domestically produced items now for the higher-priced imported items, leading to a short-run increase in domestic output and employment in an economy experiencing a recession. These barriers will have several indirect effects, however, which tend to counteract this short-term rise in employment. First, a decrease in imports will lower employment in sectors that use these goods as inputs or are involved in the distribution and sale of these goods. Second, employment and income in other countries will decrease. Not only will the demand for American exports and hence domestic employment automatically decrease as a result, but foreign governments will likely retaliate by imposing trade restrictions of their own, leading to a further decline in exports and employment. These indirect effects severely limit the employment benefits of trade restrictions, and can completely cancel them in the long run. The primary result of trade restrictions will be a reallocation of American and foreign resources to relatively inefficient industries, decreasing generally long-term national and world output.

37-9 Evaluate the following statements:

a. "Protective tariffs limit both the imports and the exports of the nation levying tariffs."

b. "The extensive application of protective tariffs destroys the ability of the international market system to allocate resources efficiently."

c. "Unemployment can often be reduced through tariff protection, but by the same token inefficiency typically increases."

d. "Foreign firms that 'dump' their products onto the American market are in effect providing bargains to the country's citizens."

e. "In view of the rapidity with which technological advance is dispersed around the world, free trade will inevitably yield structural maladjustments, unemployment, and balance of payments problems for industrially advanced nations."

f. "Free trade can improve the composition and efficiency of domestic output. Competition from Volkswagen, Toyota and Honda forced Detroit to make a compact car, and only foreign success with the oxygen process forced American steel firms to modernize."

g. "In the long run foreign trade is neutral with respect to total employment."

(a) This statement is true. Protective tariffs increase domestic prices of imported goods, decreasing quantity of demand for these products, limiting import volumes, and causing real incomes in producing countries to fall. This decline in incomes will cause foreigners to demand fewer goods and services, including exports from the nation that originally imposed the tariff. Other countries may also retaliate, decreasing export volumes of the tariff-levying nation even further.

(b) This statement is true. Extensive protective tariffs dampen every trading country's ability to export, and since exports ultimately pay for imports, each country's ability to import is hampered as well. As trade flows decrease, countries will be forced to devote scarce resources to the production of goods in which they do not have a comparative advantage, decreasing both world output and real incomes in each nation.

(c) This statement is true. While tariffs directly increase domestic employment in sectors that compete with foreign exporters, there will be indirect employment losses in other sectors. Not only will jobs be lost in the tariff-levying country's own export industries, as incomes and import levels in foreign countries decrease, but also in industries that distribute or use imported goods because of rises in price and unit cost.

(d) This statement is true, at least in the short run. Dumping by foreign firms causes prices in American markets to decline, increasing quantities purchased by domestic consumers and enhancing economic welfare. In the long run, the price wars caused by dumping may force some firms out of the market, restricting competition in domestic markets and allowing foreign firms to raise prices. If this occurs, the welfare of American consumers will decline, and remaining domestic producers will benefit, but there is virtually no evidence that foreign firms raise prices even after domestic competition disappears.

(e) This statement is true in the short run. Industrially advanced nations have erected many trade barriers for manufactured exports from less developed countries, given the cost advantage these countries possess because of their adoption of modern production techniques and the availability of low-wage labor. If these trade barriers were removed, not only would manufactured exports from these countries immediately increase, but entrepreneurs in both industrially advanced and less developed countries would find it profitable to set up additional production facilities in these countries, raising exports even more in the long run. These low-priced exports could cause short-term harm to manufacturing industries in industrially advanced countries that use predominantly unskilled labor. Output and employment levels in these sectors would fall, and import levels in industrially advanced countries would rise, leading to the possibility of short-run balance of payments deficits in countries maintaining fixed exchange rates. In the long run, however, industrially advanced economies will benefit from free trade, as resources move to sectors in which these countries have a comparative advantage. Moreover, future exports to previously less developed countries will increase as real incomes in these countries rise.

(f) This statement is true. Not only does free trade increase efficiency in the short run by allowing countries to specialize in those products in which they possess a comparative advantage, but by increasing levels of competition and the size of potential markets it acts as a spur to technological innovation and enhanced product quality in the long run.

(g) This statement is true. While changes in levels of foreign trade can cause temporary effects on employment through fluctuations in the net export component of aggregate expenditures, in the long run total employment levels in trading nations are determined by domestic macroeconomic policies and labor-market conditions. Foreign trade, however, has a significant effect on the allocation of labor among various industries in an economy, shifting employment into sectors in which a particular economy has a comparative cost advantage.

37-10 Between 1981-1985 the Japanese agreed to a voluntary export restriction, which reduced U.S. imports of Japanese automobiles by about 10 percent. What would you expect the short-run effects to have been on the U.S. and Japanese automobile industries? If this restriction were permanent, what would be its long-run effects in the two nations on (a) the allocation of resources, (b) the volume of employment, (c) the price level, and (d) the standard of living?

In the short run, the limitation on imported Japanese automobiles would cause a domestic shortage of these items. Japanese companies can respond to this shortage in two ways. They can maintain prices at current levels and ration sales through delivery delays, or they can increase prices for their products in the American market. The latter response will cause a long-term decrease in the firms' American market shares, but the longer the import limitations are in effect the more probable it becomes, since the increase in unit profits that results from higher prices will partly counteract the effects of sales losses.

No matter which policy is followed, some prospective purchasers will shift their demand to other goods, including domestically produced automobiles. Profits for American producers will rise either through increases in sales or in price.

(a) Resource allocation will be less efficient in both the U.S. and Japan. U.S. automobile firms will devote scarce resources to the production of units in which they do not have a comparative advantage. As for Japan, decreased exports will lead to a fall in imports in the long run, and resources will be moved to sectors in which Japan's comparative advantage is less.

(b) Employment in each country will not change appreciably in the long run, although there could be a temporary increase in American employment as automobile production rises and a corresponding decrease in Japan as production declines.

(c) Automobile prices in the United States will rise in the long run, boosting the general price level. Other prices will rise as costs for car-using firms increase and American consumers purchase fewer automobiles and more of other goods and services. The decrease in Japanese exports to the United States, meanwhile, will cause a drop in the supply of American dollars being exchanged for yen, leading to an appreciation of the yen price of the dollar (see Chapter 40). Prices of American imports in Japan therefore rise. Other Japanese prices increase as costs for import-using firms rise and consumers shift spending to other products.

(d) Because voluntary quotas decrease trade flows between the U.S. and Japan, some of the benefits from specialization are lost, decreasing total output and real incomes in both countries.

37-11 (*Key Question*) What is the WTO, and how does it relate to international trade? What problems, if any, arise when too many extraneous efforts are tied to efforts to liberalize trade?

The WTO is the World Trade Organization with 138 member nations in 2000. It was established in 1994 by some 120 nations who had been supporters of GATT (General Agreement on Trade and Tariffs), which preceded WTO. The organization promotes reduction in trade barriers and helps to enforce the agreement signed by its nation members.

If too many extraneous issues are tied to efforts to liberalize trade, the liberalization process is slowed down. For example, tying human rights protection to free trade policies might be a very difficult political process, which could take much longer to change than trade policy.

37-12 (*Last Word*) What point is Bastiat trying to make with his petition of the candlemakers?

He is providing an exaggerated example of protectionism to illustrate the point that trade restrictions may help a few producers, but they serve to reduce the overall standard of living. How ridiculous it would be to eliminate natural sunlight in order to protect the makers of products that provide artificial light.

CHAPTER THIRTY-EIGHT
EXCHANGE RATES,
THE BALANCE OF POWER,
AND TRADE DEFICITS

CHAPTER OVERVIEW

This chapter addresses several important aspects of international trade. The chapter begins with a brief discussion of how trade is financed. Next the balance of payments is explained and examined. Exchange rate systems and balance of payments adjustments under each system are then analyzed. The section concludes with a discussion of the advantages and disadvantages of each. The history of major policies is summarized, beginning with the gold standard, continuing through the Bretton Woods system, and concluding with the periods of managed float and of freely floating exchange rates. Finally, the chapter looks at the trade deficits of recent years and examines the causes and effects of these deficits.

WHAT'S NEW

This chapter has been tightened considerably; it is perhaps 1 to 2 pages shorter than the 14th edition chapter. While the consolidation occurs throughout, the main areas of tightening are in elimination of balance sheets that explained import and export financing and Global Perspective 38-2. Otherwise the revision consists of updating and editorial changes to improve clarity.

INSTRUCTIONAL OBJECTIVES

After completing this chapter, students should be able to:

1. Explain how U.S. exports create a demand for dollars and a supply of foreign exchange; and how U.S. imports create a demand for foreign exchange and a supply of dollars.

2. Explain and identify the various components of the balance of payments.

3. Identify trade and balance of payments deficits or surpluses when given appropriate data.

4. Explain how a nation finances a "deficit" and what it does with a "surplus."

5. Explain how exchange rates are determined in a flexible system.

6. Explain how flexible exchange rates eliminate balance of payments disequilibria.

7. List five determinants of exchange rates.

8. List three disadvantages of flexible exchange rates.

9. List three ways a nation could control exchange rates under a fixed-rate system.

10. Describe a system based on the gold standard, the Bretton Woods system, and a managed float exchange rate system.

11. Describe two effects of a trade deficit.

12. Define and identify terms and concepts listed at the end of the chapter.

COMMENTS AND TEACHING SUGGESTIONS

1. *The Wall Street Journal* reports exchange rates daily. A good exercise is to have students learn to use these tables. There is great disparity among students' understanding of such information. Those who have traveled in other countries understand the basics of foreign exchange, while others have not thought about the idea before.

2. New instructors often have difficulty relating international trade concepts such as the principle of comparative advantage and exchange rate determination. Remember: Exchange rates are an application of supply and demand. If you carefully label the axes on your graph during the lecture, you can avoid confusing students. Try to focus on the demand side of only one currency at a time, and don't jump back and forth from looking at the exchange rate for dollars and another currency at the same time. For example, if the focus is on the dollar, measure the exchange rate or price in "foreign currency per dollar" on the vertical axis, and quantity of dollars on the horizontal axis. That is, treat dollars like apples or any other commodity. When the demand shifts rightward, the price or exchange rate will rise; when the demand shifts leftward, the price or exchange rate will decline. Conversely, if the supply shifts rightward, the exchange rate will fall, and if the supply shifts leftward, the exchange rate will rise.

3. A good topic for discussion or essay centers on the following questions. Is a trade deficit bad or good? Is foreign investment in the U.S. harmful or beneficial? It should be easy for students to find thoughtful, current articles on both sides of these issues in newspapers, magazines, and journals available in most college libraries.

STUDENT STUMBLING BLOCKS

1. Some students seem to have great difficulty in understanding that units of other countries' currencies are not equivalent to our dollar. For example, when some students hear that they can receive 120 yen for one dollar, they believe that means they would be very rich in Japan. Many have difficulty comprehending that one yen is worth about one cent. The confusion seems to lie in their belief that the basic units of exchange should have equivalent values across countries. That is, some seem to believe that a yen is a dollar is a franc is a mark, etc. Several examples are necessary before the basics of exchange are understood.

2. There is a common belief that trade deficits are bad or "unfavorable" and that being a debtor nation is always a problem. As with so much in economics, it is necessary to point out that this evaluation depends on the situation and on whose point of view is being expressed. Trade deficits may be good for consumers if they arise because Americans are obtaining quality imports at low prices. Foreign investment that entails the selling of U.S. assets can be beneficial to U.S. future economic growth and productivity. The effects of balance of payments deficits are not easy to understand or analyze, and news articles that suggest alarm that the U.S. is the world's largest debtor nation may add to the confusion. During the 1800s and our greatest industrial expansion, the U.S. was also a debtor nation, and it had very beneficial effects.

LECTURE NOTES

I. **Financing International Trade**

   A. Foreign exchange markets enable international transactions to take place by providing markets for the exchange of national currencies.

   B. An American export transaction is explained below.

      1. U.S. firm is selling $300,000 worth of computers to British firm.

2. Imagine the exchange rate is $2 = 1 Br. pound, so the British firm must pay 150,000 pounds.

3. The British firm will draw a check on its deposit at a London bank for 150,000 pounds, and will send it to the U.S. exporter.

4. The exporter sells the British check to an American bank for $300,000 in exchange for the British check, and the exporter's account is credited.

5. The American bank will deposit the 150,000 pounds in a correspondent London bank for future sale.

6. Note the major points here.

   a. Exports create a demand for dollars and a supply of foreign money, in this case British pounds.

   b. The financing of an American export reduces the supply of money (demand deposits) in Britain and increases it in the U.S.

C. An American import transaction example illustrates how a British exporter is paid in pounds while the importer pays dollars.

   1. A U.S. firm is buying 150,000 pounds worth of compact discs from Britain.

   2. The exchange rate remains at $2 = 1 Br. pound, so the American purchaser must exchange its $300,000 for 150,000 Br. pounds at an American bank—perhaps the same one as in the export example.

   3. The American bank will give up its 150,000 pounds in the London bank to the importer, who will pay the British compact discs exporter, who will deposit the money in the exporter's bank.

   4. Again note the major points.

      a. The financing of American imports reduces the supply of money (demand deposits) in the U.S. and increases it in the exporting country, Britain.

      b. Imports create a demand for foreign currency (pounds in this case) and a supply of U.S. currency.

II. **The Balance of Payments (Table 38.1 summarizes the balance for 1999)**

A. A nation's balance of payments is the sum of all transactions that take place between its residents and the residents of all foreign nations. These transactions include merchandise exports and imports, tourist expenditures, and interest plus dividends from the sale and purchases of financial assets abroad. The balance of payments account is subdivided into three components: the current account, the capital account, and the official reserves account.

B. Current Accounts is shown in top portion of Table 38.1. The main entries are:

   1. The current account summarizes U.S. trade in currently produced goods and services.

   2. The merchandise trade balance is the difference between its exports and imports of goods.

   3. The balance on goods and services, shown in (line 7) Table 38.1 is the difference between U.S. exports of goods and services (items 1 and 4) and U.S. imports of goods and services (items 2 and 5).

   4. Balance on the current account is found by adding all transactions in the current account (item 10, Table 38.1).

     5. Global Perspective 38.1 gives trade balance for other nations.

  C. Capital Account:

     1. The capital account summarizes the flows of payments (money "capital") from the purchase or sale of real or financial assets.

     2. For example, a foreign firm may buy a real asset, say an office tower in the U.S., or a U.S. government bond. Both kinds of transactions involve the "export" of the ownership of U.S. assets from the United States in return for payments of foreign currency (money "capital") inflows.

     3. The balance in the capital account was $322 billion in 1999. (Line 12, Table 38-1)

  D. Official Reserves Account:

     The third account in the overall balance of payments is the official reserves account. The central banks of nations hold quantities of foreign currencies called official reserves. These reserves can be drawn on to make up any net deficit in the combined current and capital accounts (much as you would draw on your savings to pay for a special purchase). In 1999 this was $9 billion (Line 10 minus Line 13).

  E. Payments Deficits and Surpluses: (See Lines 10 minus Line 13 in Table 38.1)

     1. A drawing down of official reserves measures a nation's balance of payments deficit; a building up of official reserves measures its balance of payments surpluses. Adding to foreign reserves would occur if there is a surplus.

     2. A balance of payments deficit is not necessarily bad, nor is a balance of payments surplus necessarily good. However, persistent payments deficits would ultimately deplete the foreign exchange reserves.

     3. To correct its balance of payments deficit, a nation might implement a major depreciation of its currency or other policies to encourage exports.

III.   **Flexible Exchange Rates**

  A. Freely floating exchange rates are determined by the forces of demand and supply. Figure 38.1 (Key Graph) illustrates the exchange rate (price) for British pounds in American dollars.

     1. The demand for any currency is downsloping because as the currency becomes less expensive, people will be able to buy more of that nation's goods and, therefore, want larger quantities of the currency.

     2. The supply of any currency is upsloping because as its price rises, holders of that currency can obtain other currencies more cheaply and will want to buy more imported goods and, therefore, will give up more of their currency to obtain other currencies.

     3. As with other commodities, the intersection of the supply and demand curves for a currency (pounds in Figure 38.1) will determine the price or exchange rate. In the example it is $2 to 1 pound.

  B. Depreciation means the value of a currency has fallen; it takes more units of that country's currency to buy another country's currency. $3 for 1 pound would be a depreciation of the dollar, compared to the original example of $2 per pound.

  C. Appreciation means the value of a currency or its purchasing power has risen; it takes less of that currency to buy another country's currency. $1 = 1 pound would be an appreciation of the dollar relative to the pound.

D. Determinants of exchange rates are the forces that cause the demand or supply curves to shift.

1. Changes in tastes or preferences for a country's products would shift the demand for the currency as well.

2. Relative income changes will cause changes in the demand and supply of currencies. Rising incomes increase the demand for imports, which increases the supply of that country's currency and the demand for other country's currencies.

3. Relative price changes will cause changes in the demand and supply of currencies. If American prices rise relative to British prices, this will increase the demand for British goods and pounds; conversely, it will reduce the supply of pounds as British purchase fewer American goods. The theory of purchasing power parity asserts that exchange rates will change to maintain a uniform price in one currency, e.g., dollars, for each product across countries.

4. Changes in relative real interest rates will affect the demand and supply of currencies. Higher U.S. interest rates attract foreign savings; hence, they raise the demand for dollars and reduce the supply of dollars as U.S. investment dollars may remain in this country.

5. Speculation is another determinant. If one believes the value of a currency is about to fall, it will increase the supply of that currency and reduce its demand. Likewise, if one believes the value of a currency is about to rise, it will increase its demand and reduce its supply as people want to hold that currency. Note that such predictions can be self-fulfilling prophecies, since the change in demand is in the direction of the prediction. (Table 38.2)

E. Theoretically, flexible rates have the virtue of automatically correcting any imbalance in the balance of payments. If there is a deficit in the balance of payments, this means that there will be a surplus of that currency and its value will depreciate. As depreciation occurs, prices for goods and services from that country become more attractive and the demand for them will rise. At the same time, imports become more costly as it takes more currency to buy foreign goods and services. With rising exports and falling imports, the deficit is eventually corrected (Figure 38.2 illustrates this).

F. There are some disadvantages to flexible exchange rates.

1. Uncertainty and diminished trade may result if traders cannot count on future prices of exchange rates, which affect the value of their planned transactions. (However, see Last Word for this chapter for ways in which traders can avoid risk.)

2. Terms of trade may be worsened by a decline in the value of a nation's currency.

3. Unstable exchange rates can destabilize a nation's economy. This is especially true for nations whose exports and imports are a substantial part of their GDPs.

IV. Fixed Exchange Rates

A. Fixed exchange rates are those that are pegged to some set value, such as gold or the U.S. dollar.

B. Official reserves are used to correct an imbalance in the balance of payments, since exchange rates cannot fluctuate to bring about automatic balance. This is called currency intervention.

C. Trade policies directly controlling the amount of trade and finance might be used to avoid imbalance in trade and payments.

D. Exchange controls and rationing of currency have been used in the past but are objectionable for several reasons.

    1. Controls distort efficient patterns of trade.

    2. Rationing involves favoritism among importers.

    3. Rationing reduces freedom of consumer choice.

    4. Enforcement problems are likely as "black market" rates develop.

E. Domestic macroeconomic adjustments may be more difficult under fixed rates. For example, a persistent deficit of trade may call for tight monetary and fiscal policies to reduce prices, which raises exports and reduces imports. Such contractionary policies can also cause recessions and unemployment, however.

V. International Exchange Rate Systems

A. The gold standard was the international system used during the 1879-1934 period. It provided for fixed exchange rates in terms of a certain amount of currency for an ounce of gold. Under this system, each nation must:

    1. Maintain a fixed relationship between the stock of gold and the money supply.

    2. Gold flows would maintain the fixed rate. If the dollar appreciated, gold would flow into the U.S.; if it depreciated, gold would flow out. These flows would keep the value of the currencies at their fixed rates.

    3. Figure 38.2 helps explain the domestic macroeconomic adjustments that would occur. If gold flowed into a country, its money supply would increase because the gold/money ratio is fixed. Therefore, when the dollar appreciated, the U.S. money supply would increase proportionately to the gold increase. A rise in the money supply would cause U.S. incomes and prices to rise and would increase our demand for foreign goods, while the demand for U.S. exports declined. Such a change in the balance of trade would cause the dollar to depreciate again. In other word, a gold standard causes domestic adjustments. This is its major disadvantage.

    4. The advantages are stable exchange rate and automatic adjustments in balance of payments.

    5. The worldwide Depression of the 1930s ended the gold standard, because improving economic conditions became the main goal of national policies.

B. The Bretton Woods system was enacted following World War II by the leading industrialized western nations. It had two main features.

    1. The International Monetary Fund (IMF) was created to hold and lend official reserves. Included in official reserves was a new kind of international governmental currency called Special Drawing Rights (SDRs).

    2. Pegged exchange rates were initiated, which were adjustable when a fundamental imbalance was recognized. The rates were maintained by government intervention in the supply and demand of currencies.

       a. Governments could spend or purchase currencies directly.

       b. Gold could be bought or sold by governments.

       c. IMF borrowing could take place from the required accounts that nations had at the International Monetary Fund.

3. The pegged rates could be changed (adjusted) when there were persistent problems with the balance of payments using the existing rate. A persistent deficit could lead to devaluation (depreciation).

4. The Bretton Woods system was abandoned as nations acquired more and more dollars, and the U.S. abandoned its pledge to convert dollars into gold in 1971. This led to a flexible exchange rate for the dollar and, therefore, flexible rates for every other major currency that was related to the dollar.

C. The current system is really a "managed float" exchange rate system in which governments attempt to prevent rates from changing too rapidly in the short term. For example, in 1987, the G-7 nations—U.S., Germany, Japan, Britain, France, Italy, and Canada—agreed to stabilize the value of the dollar, which had declined rapidly in the previous two years. They purchased large amounts of dollars to prop up the dollar's value. Since 1987 the G-7 has periodically intervened in foreign exchange markets to stabilize currency values.

1. In support of the managed float.

a. Trade has expanded and not diminished under this system as some predicted it might.

b. Flexible rates have allowed international adjustments to take place without domestic upheaval when there has been economic turbulence in some areas of the world.

2. Concerns with the managed float.

a. Much volatility occurs without the balance of payments adjustments predicted.

b. There is no real system in the current system. It is too unpredictable.

VI. **Recent U.S. Trade Deficits**

A. In 1999 the current account deficit in U.S. was $331 billion. (Figure 38.3)

B. Causes of the trade deficit.

1. Since 1992 the U.S. economy has grown more rapidly than the economies of several major trading nations. This growth of income has boosted U.S. purchases of foreign goods. In contrast, Japan, some European nations, and Canada have suffered recessions or slow income growth during this period.

2. Also, a declining savings rate in the U.S. has contributed to U.S. trade deficits and an increase in foreign investment in U.S.

C. Implications of U.S. trade deficits

1. A trade deficit means that the U.S. is receiving more goods and services as imports from abroad than it is sending out as exports. The gain in present consumption may come at the expense of reduced future consumption.

2. A trade deficit is considered "unfavorable" because it must be financed by borrowing from the rest of the world, selling off assets or dipping into foreign currency reserves. In 1999, foreigners owned $1.5 billion more assets in U.S. than Americans owned in foreign assets.

3. Therefore, the current consumption gains delivered by U.S. trade deficits mean permanent debt, permanent foreign ownership, or large sacrifices of future consumption. But it could also mean higher economic growth as foreign investment expands our capital base.

VII. **LAST WORD: Speculation in Currency Markets**

A. Are speculators a positive or a negative influence? Speculators sometimes contribute to exchange rate volatility. The expectation of currency appreciation or depreciation can be self-fulfilling.

   1. If speculators expect the Japanese yen to appreciate, they sell other currencies to buy yen. The increase in demand for yen and in supply of other currencies will boost its value, which may attract still other speculators to buy yen. The rise in yen value is partly a result of expectations.

   2. Eventually, the yen's value may soar too high relative to economic realities, the speculative "bubble" bursts, and the yen can plummet for the same self-fulfilling reasons, as speculators sell yen to buy other currencies.

B. Speculation can have positive effects in foreign exchange markets.

   1. Speculators may be useful in smoothing out temporary fluctuations. If there is a temporary decline in demand, speculators take advantage of the dip in value by buying the currency; this props up demand, strengthening the value again. If there is a temporary strong demand, which artificially raises the value of a currency, speculators will sell to take advantage of the price hike, and this will reduce the inflated value.

   2. Speculators also absorb risks that others do not want to bear. International transactions in goods and services can be risky if exchange rates change. Buyers and sellers in international trade can reduce the risk of exchange rate changes in foreign transactions by hedging or buying the needed currency with forward contracts. This is where a buyer or seller protects against a change in future exchange rates in the futures market. Foreign exchange is bought or sold at contract prices fixed now, for delivery at a specified future date.

   3. The example given is of an American importer who agrees to buy 10,000 Swiss watches to be delivered and paid for in three months. The price is 75 francs per watch, or $50 per watch at the exchange rate on the date of the sale. If the franc were to appreciate from 1.5 francs per dollar to 1 franc per dollar in three months, the importer would have to pay $75 per watch instead of $50 per watch.

      a. Hedging can reduce the importer's risk of having the franc appreciate.

      b. The importer can purchase the 750,000 francs needed by signing a futures contract, agreeing to pay a specified amount (maybe $500,000 plus some allowance for fees) for those francs in three months.

      c. Speculators accept such contracts. In this case, the speculator would be betting that the value of the franc would fall vs. the dollar, and at the end of the three months, the speculator would take the $500,000 and obtain more than the 750,000 francs for it. The importer will have the 750,000 francs, and the speculator will have profited by having excess francs. Of course, if the franc appreciates, the speculator loses on this deal. In other words, the speculator has assumed the risk from the importer—and as a result may profit or lose.

ANSWERS TO END-OF-CHAPTER QUESTIONS

38-1 Explain how a U.S. automobile importer might finance a shipment of Toyotas from Japan. Trace the steps as to how a U.S. export of machinery to Italy might be financed. Explain: "U.S. exports earn supplies of foreign currencies, which Americans can use to finance imports."

The American importer can purchase a check made out in yen from its American bank. The bank buys the yen by decreasing its yen-denominated deposit with a Japanese bank and receives payment by reducing the importing firm's dollar-denominated deposit. Once Toyota receives the check, it will deposit it in its yen-denominated account at a Japanese bank.

An Italian importer of American machinery can purchase lira or a lira-denominated check from its Italian bank. The bank takes payment by decreasing the firm's lira-denominated bank account. Once the American exporter receives the lira, it will sell it to an American bank, receiving payment through an increase in its dollar-denominated deposit. The American bank deposits the lira in its account with an Italian bank for later use.

American exports lead to an increase in the foreign-currency bank deposit holdings of Americans. These holdings will be decreased through American purchases of imports. Hence, the foreign-currency assets earned through exports can be used to finance imports.

38-2 (*Key Question*) Indicate whether each of the following creates a demand for, or a supply of, European euros in foreign exchange markets:

a. A U.S. airline firm purchases several Airbus planes assembled in France.

b. A German automobile firm decides to build an assembly plant in South Carolina.

c. A U.S. college student decides to spend a year studying at the Sorbonne.

d. An Italian manufacturer ships machinery from one Italian port to another on a Liberian freighter.

e. The United States economy grows faster than the French economy.

f. A United States government bond held by a Spanish citizen matures, and the loan is paid back to that person.

g. It is widely believed that the Swiss franc will fall in the near future.

A demand for euro's is created in (a),(c),(e),(f) and (g) but see note below for e and g. A supply of francs is created in (b) and (d).

Note: Answer for (e) assumes U.S. demand for French goods will grow faster than French imports of U.S. goods; (g) assumes some franc holders will buy euros instead (Switzerland is not in EU).

38-3 (*Key Question*) Alpha's balance of payments data for 2001 are shown below. All figures are in billions of dollars. What are (a) the balance of trade, (b) the balance on goods and services, (c) the balance on current account, and (d) the balance on capital account? Does Alpha have a balance of payments deficit or surplus? Explain.

Merchandise exports	+$40	Net Transfers	+$10
Merchandise imports	- 30	Foreign purchases of U.S. assets	+ 10
Service exports	+ 15		
Service imports	- 10	U.S. purchases of foreign assets	- 40
Net investment income	- 5		
		Official reserves	+ 10

Balance of trade = $10 billion surplus (= exports of goods of $40 billion minus imports of goods of $30 billion). Note: This is goods balance only – uses narrow definition of trade balance. Balance on goods and services = $15 billion surplus (= $55 billion of exports of goods and services minus $40 billion of imports of goods and services). Balance on current account = $20 billion surplus (= credits of $65 billion minus debits of $45 billion). Balance on capital account = $30 billion deficit (= Foreign purchases of assets in the United States of $10 billion minus U.S. purchases of assets abroad of $40 billion). Balance of payments = $10 billion deficit. Therefore, U.S. must export official reserves = $10 billion.

38-4   "A rise in the dollar price of yen necessarily means a fall in the yen price of dollars." Do you agree? Illustrate and elaborate: "The critical thing about exchange rates is that they provide a direct link between the prices of goods and services produced in all trading nations of the world." Explain the purchasing power parity theory of exchange rates.

If the yen appreciates relative to the dollar, it takes more dollars to purchase one yen. At the same time, it takes fewer yen to buy a dollar, meaning that the yen price of dollars has fallen.

Through exchange rates, residents of all trading nations can express the prices of goods and services in other trading nations in terms of their domestic currencies. A change in the exchange rate between any two countries will automatically lead to an adjustment in the prices of all goods and services in both countries in terms of the other's currency. The determination of these price conversions represents the most basic and visible function of exchange rates. For example, the recent realignment of the yen and the dollar values has appreciably increased the dollar prices of all Japanese goods and services. This represents a significant decrease in purchasing power for American consumers of Japanese products. Similarly, the yen prices of all American goods and services have decreased, increasing purchasing power of Japanese consumers for American products.

The purchasing power parity theory of exchange rates holds that exchange rates change to equal the ratios of the nations' price levels. If a certain item costs $100 in the U.S. and 22,900 yen in Japan, then the exchange rate should be $1 = 229 yen. It should take the same amount of dollars to buy the item anywhere in the world if exchange rates adjust to maintain purchasing power parity.

38-5   Suppose a Swiss watchmaker imports watch components from Sweden and exports watches to the United States. Also suppose the dollar depreciates, and the Swedish Krona appreciates, relative to the Swiss franc. Speculate as to how this would hurt the Swiss watchmaker.

If the dollar depreciated relative to the franc, this means that it took more dollars to get the francs necessary to buy a watch. In other words, the watch becomes more expensive in dollar terms which would cause a decline in imported watches purchased in the United States. Second, if the krona appreciated relative to the Swiss franc, this is the same thing as saying that the franc depreciated relative to the krona. In other words, it took more Swiss francs to buy parts in Sweden than it did previously. As a result, the imported components for the watches became more expensive to the Swiss company. The Swiss Watchmaker was hurt twice. Its costs rose while its export sales declined.

38-6   (Key Question) Explain why the U.S. demand for Mexican pesos is downsloping and the supply of pesos to Americans is upsloping. Assuming a system of floating exchange rates between Mexico and the United States, indicate whether each of the following would cause the Mexican peso to appreciate or depreciate:

a.   The United States unilaterally reduces tariffs on Mexican products.

b.   Mexico encounters severe inflation.

c.   Deteriorating political relations reduce American tourism in Mexico.

d.   The United States' economy moves into a severe recession.

e.   The U.S. engages in a high interest rate monetary policy.

f.   Mexican products become more fashionable to U.S. consumers.

g.   The Mexican government encourages U.S. firms to invest in Mexican oil fields.

h.   The rate of productivity growth in the United States diminishes sharply.

The U.S. demand for pesos is downsloping: When the peso depreciates in value (relative to the dollar) the United States finds that Mexican goods and services are less expensive in dollar terms and purchases more of them, demanding a greater quantity of pesos in the process. The supply of pesos to the United States is upsloping: As the peso appreciates in value (relative to the dollar), US. goods and services become cheaper to Mexicans in peso terms. Mexicans buy more dollars to obtain more U.S. goods, supplying a larger quantity of pesos.

The peso appreciates in (a), (f), (g), and (h) and depreciates in (b), (c), (d), and (e).

38-7   Explain why you agree with the following statements:

a.   "A country that grows faster than its major trading partners can expect the international value of its currency to depreciate.

b.   "A nation whose interest rate is rising more rapidly than interest rates in other nations can expect the international value of its currency to appreciate."

c.   "A country's currency will appreciate if its inflation rate is less than that of the rest of the world."

(a) This statement is true. If high rates of economic growth mean that the real incomes of a country's citizens are rising more rapidly than in other countries, its imports will rise more than its exports. The demand for foreign currency by its citizens will increase more than the supply of foreign currency, causing the value of the domestic currency to decline.

(b) This statement is true. If domestic real interest rates are increasing more quickly than those in other countries, foreign financial investment will be attracted to the country, causing a rise in the supply of foreign currency and therefore an appreciation of the country's currency.

(c) This statement is true. If a country's inflation rate is lower than rates in other countries, the foreign prices of its products will decline relative to foreign-made products, increasing exports and the supply of foreign currency. And the domestic prices of foreign imports will increase relative to domestically made goods, decreasing the demand for foreign currency. Both factors will cause the country's currency to appreciate.

38-8   "Exports pay for imports. Yet in 1999 the nations of the world exported about $346 billion more worth of goods and services to the United States than they imported from the United States." Resolve the apparent inconsistency of these two statements.

Exports pay for imports in the long run. In the short term, a country can import more goods and services than it exports through external borrowing or the sale of domestic assets to foreigners. Both activities increase the country's capital account balance and cause an inflow of foreign currency that can be used to finance import purchases. Depletion of a country's official reserves can also be used as a short-term measure to finance imports, since the sale of foreign monies for domestic currency has the same financial effect as an export transaction. See Table 38.1 for 1999 figures.

38-9   (*Key Question*) Diagram a market in which the equilibrium dollar price of one unit of fictitious currency Zee is $5 (the exchange rate is $5 = Z1). Then show on your diagram a decline in the demand for Zee.

a. Referring to your diagram, discuss the adjustment options the United States would have in maintaining the exchange rate at $5 = Z1 under a fixed exchange-rate system.

b. How would the U.S. balance of payments surplus that is created (by the decline in demand) get resolved under a system of flexible exchange rates?

See the graph illustrating the market for Zees.

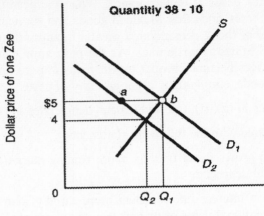

Quantity of Zee

(a) The decrease in demand for Zees from D_1 to D_2 will create a surplus (*ab*) of Zees at the $5 price. To maintain the $5 to Z1 exchange rate, the United States must undertake policies to shift the demand-for-Zee curve rightward or shift the-supply-of Zee curve leftward. To increase the demand for Zees, the United States could use dollars or gold to buy Zees in the foreign exchange market; employ trade policies to increase imports to U.S. from Zeeonia; or enact expansionary fiscal and monetary policies to increase U.S. domestic output and income, thus increasing imports from Zeeonia and elsewhere. Expansionary monetary policy could also reduce the *supply* of Zees: Zeeons could respond to the lower U.S. interest rates by reducing their investing in the United States. Therefore, they would not supply as many Zees to the foreign exchange market.

(b) Under a system of flexible exchange rates, the *ab* surplus of Zees (the U.S. balance of payments surplus) will cause the Zee to depreciate and the dollar to appreciate until the surplus is eliminated (at the $4 = Z1 exchange rate shown in the figure) because U.S. would import more from Zeeonia and they would buy less from U.S. since Zee's lost value.

38-10 Compare and contrast the Bretton Woods system of exchange rates with that of the gold standard. What caused the collapse of the gold standard? What caused the demise of the Bretton Woods system?

Under both systems gold was used as means of fixing exchange rates. Under the gold standard nations defined their currency in terms of a quantity of gold. For example, if the U.S. defines $1 as worth 25 grains of gold and Britain defines 1 pound is worth 50 grains of gold, then a British pound is worth 2 ∞ 25 grains, or $2.00.

The exchange rate cannot change under the gold standard and the way governments deal with balance of payments surpluses or deficits is through domestic adjustments. That is, under the gold standard a nation's money supply is altered by changes in supply and demand in currency markets. If the United States, for example, was experiencing declining output and incomes, the loss of gold under the gold system would reduce the U.S. money supply, which might cause higher interest rates, lower borrowing and spending, and worsen declines in output and income.

The Bretton Woods system, like the gold standard, defined currencies in terms of gold, establishing exchange rates. But, unlike the gold standard, the Bretton Woods system had created the (IMF). Nations were required to make contribution to the IMF based on their income, population, and volume of trade. If necessary, the U.S. could borrow pounds on a short-term basis from the (IMF) by supplying its own currency as collateral.

Also the Bretton Woods system recognized that from time to time a nation may be confronted with persistent and sizable balance of payments problems that could not be corrected by traditional means. The Bretton Woods remedy was an "orderly" reduction of the nation's pegged exchange rate. For example, a depreciation of the dollar would increase U.S. exports and lower U.S. imports, correcting its persistent payments deficits.

The end of gold standard was brought on by the Great Depression of the 1930s. Nations enacted protectionist policies to reduce imports. In effect, nations deliberately devalued their currency ending the gold standard. The demise of the Bretton Woods system developed because the U.S. began having persistent payments deficits in the 1950s and 1960s. The system had fixed the price of gold at $35 an ounce and the U.S. was making deficit payments in dollars. Foreign nations with large quantities of dollars began demanding gold at $35 an ounce. In 1971 the government saw that its gold supply was too small and it would be impossible to meet the demand. The U.S. ended its 37-year policy of exchanging gold for dollars.

38-11   Describe what is meant by the term "managed float." Did the managed float system precede or follow the adjustable-peg system? Explain.

The managed float international exchange rate system came into being at the end of Bretton Woods adjustable peg system (1971). Exchange rates among major currencies are free to float to their equilibrium market levels, but nations occasionally intervene in the foreign exchange market to stabilize or alter market exchange rates. Thus, the term "managed" floating exchange rates. Governments might purchase a currency whose value is falling too rapidly or sell if a currency is rising too dramatically. However, government intervention has not been able to prevent long-term depreciation or appreciation of currencies.

Some nations peg their currencies to the dollar and allow their currencies to fluctuate with it against other countries. These systems exist together with the managed float conducted by major economic powers.

38-12   What have been the causes of the large U.S. trade deficits since 1992? What are the major benefits and costs associated with trade deficits? Explain: "A trade deficit means that a nation is receiving more goods and services from abroad than it is sending abroad." How can that be called "unfavorable?"

Causes:

(1) The U.S. economy has grown more rapidly than the economies of several major trading nations. Thus U.S. exports have not kept pace with the rise in U.S. imports. (2) Until very recently the U.S. had large federal deficits. These deficits required the Federal government to compete with the private sector for financing, bidding up interest rates. The demand for U.S. dollars makes exports relatively more expensive to foreigners. (3) Finally, a declining savings rate in the U.S. (while investment has remained stable) has also contributed to the trade deficit.

A trade deficit allows the Unites States to consume outside its production possibilities curve. But, the gain in current consumption comes at the expense of reduced future consumption.

A trade deficit is considered "unfavorable" because it must be financed by borrowing from the rest of the world, selling off assets and dipping into foreign currency reserves. Financing of the U.S.

trade deficit has resulted in a larger foreign accumulation of claims against U.S. financial and real assets than the U.S. claim against foreign assets.

38-13   (*Last Word*) Suppose Winter Sports—a French retailer of snowboards—wants to order 5,000 snowboards made in the United States. The price per board is $200, the present exchange rate is 1 euro = 1 dollar, and payment is due in dollars when the boards are delivered in three months. Use a numerical example to explain why exchange rate risk might make the French retailer hesitant to place the order. How might speculators absorb some of Winter Sports' risk?

Because payment is due in three months in dollars, the French retailer might worry that his anticipated price, which today is 1 million euros (5,000 boards ∞ $200 ∞ 1 euro per dollar), might rise if the euro loses value relative to the dollar. For example, at the end of three months the euro could fall in value to 1.5 euros = 1 dollar, and it would take 300 to obtain $200 rather than 200 euros. For 5,000 snowboards, this increases the retailer's cost from 1,000,000 euros to 1,500,000 euros. To protect against this risk, the retailer could purchase dollars forward—agreeing to pay a specified price for dollars in three months. The retailer would know exactly what was owed at the end of the three-month period, which would depend on the three-month forward exchange rate, which may or may not be higher than the current rate. But at least the retailer would know exactly how many euros will be needed at the end of three months to obtain the $1 million for the snowboards.

Who would be willing to sign such a contract? It could be a speculator who is betting that the value of the euro will rise against the dollar rather than fall. Therefore, the speculator would be happy to sign a contract giving $1,000,000 for 1 million euros (or whatever the forward agreement is), with the expectation that these 1 million euros will be worth more than $1,000,000 in three months. Then, the speculator will have made a profit, and the retailer will have eliminated the risk of not knowing how many euros will be needed to obtain the $1 million for the snowboards. It is the speculator who has assumed the risk in this example.

CHAPTER THIRTY-NINE
THE ECONOMICS OF DEVELOPING COUNTRIES

CHAPTER OVERVIEW

It is sometimes difficult for affluent Americans to realize that hunger, squalor, and disease are commonplace for most of the world's population. The problem of raising the standard of living in these countries is the central issue of this chapter. The chapter begins by identifying the developing countries and discuss their characteristics. Then we discuss why these countries have such low standards of living emphasizing the obstacles to economic growth. Next, we examine the potentials and pitfalls of government's role in economic development. We also examine private money flows from the advanced industrial countries (IACs) to the developing countries and assess the debt problem the developing countries face including a discussion of possible debt foregiveness. Finally, we distill a list of possible policies which might help developing countries increase their growth rates.

WHAT'S NEW

A few changes made in this chapter, mainly to update information. Former Global Perspective 39-1 is replaced by Figure 39-2, which is new and shows the big population growth in developing world. A new Global Perspective 39-1 demonstrates levels of corruption around the globe.

The section on the debt crisis has been deleted. A new section discusses debt forgiveness.

INSTRUCTIONAL OBJECTIVES

After completing this chapter, students should be able to:

1. Distinguish between industrially advanced and two categories of developing countries (DVCs).
2. Identify factors that characterize DVCs.
3. Describe the growth rates of IACs, middle-income DVCs, and low-income DVCs.
4. Enumerate some human implications of poverty in the DVCs.
5. State the two basic avenues for growth for a nation.
6. Describe the four primary obstacles to growth in the DVCs.
7. Illustrate by diagram the vicious circle of poverty.
8. State five features of the positive role of government in development.
9. Explain the problems of public sector involvement in development.
10. Describe three aspects of the role of advanced nations in development assistance.
11. Describe the extent of DVC debt, consequences, and possible solutions including debt forgiveness.
12. List and describe nine policies for promoting economic growth in the DVCs.
13. Define and identify terms and concepts listed at the end of the chapter.

COMMENTS AND TEACHING SUGGESTIONS

1. Current data are important for the discussion of economic growth and underdevelopment. Good sources include the World Bank's annual *World Development Report*, the *World Bank Atlas*, and the International Monetary Fund's annual *World Economic Outlook*. Data can also be found in a free monthly publication, *International Economic Conditions*, which can be obtained from the Federal Reserve Bank of St. Louis, PO Box 442, St. Louis 63166 and the periodical magazine, *The Economist*.

2. The world population problem is a challenging issue for most students and it can be explored by recalling the Malthusian model summarized in most texts on the history of economic thought. One such text is Robert Heilbroner's *The Worldly Philosophers*, which has a chapter on Malthus.

LECTURE NOTES

I. **The Rich and the Poor**

   A. Industrially advanced countries (IACs) include the U.S., Canada, Australia, New Zealand, Japan, and most of western Europe. They have developed market economies based on large stocks of capital goods, advanced technologies, and a well-educated labor force. They have a high per capita output, as seen in Figure 39-1.

   B. Developing countries (DVCs) are 107 unindustrialized nations heavily committed to agriculture. They have low rates of literacy, high unemployment, rapid population growth, and their exports are largely agricultural or raw materials. Capital equipment is scarce, production technologies are primitive, and productivity is low. More than 60 percent of the world's population lives in these nations, which can be divided into two groups (Figure 39-1).

      1. The first group consists of "middle-income" DVCs with an average annual per capita output in 1999 of $2,000, but with a range from $756 to $9,265 per capita.

      2. The low-income group is the poorest with average output per capita of only $410 and a range to $755. Dominating this group are India, China, and the sub-Saharan African nations.

   C. Comparisons highlight income disparities.

      1. U.S. 1999 GDP was more than the total output of the poorest 109 countries combined.

      2. The U.S. has 5 percent of the population but produces 27 percent of the world's output.

      3. The largest U.S. corporations have sales greater than most DVC nations' output. General Motors had sales greater than the output value of all but 22 lower-income nations of the world.

      4. The assets of the three wealthiest people in the world exceeded the combined GDPs of the 48 poorest nations.

   D. Growth, Decline, and Income Gaps

      1. DVCs such as China, Malaysia and Thailand have achieved high annual growth rates in their GDPs in recent decades. Several previous DVCs, such as South Korea, Singapore, and Hong Kong have achieved IAC status. But many DVCs, such as those in sub-Saharan Africa, have experienced declining GDPs per capita.

      2. The absolute income gap between rich and poor nations has been widening. For example, if per capital income is $400 a year in a DVC, a 2% growth rate means an $8 increase in

income. Where per capita income is $20,000 per year in an IAC, the same 2% growth rate translates into a $400 increase in income.

E. Human realities are difficult. Implications are great in terms of poverty and the human condition as dramatized by the excerpt from Michael Todaro's book in the text. Table 39-1 highlights other socioeconomic differences.

II. **Obstacles to Economic Development**

A. Natural resources must be used more efficiently and their supplies expanded. Resource distribution is very uneven as is evidenced by the wealth of the OPEC countries. Often ownership of natural resources is an issue if they belong to corporations in industrially advanced countries. However, weak resource bases are not necessarily impossible to overcome, as Switzerland, Israel, and Japan have shown.

B. Human resources in DVCs have three characteristics

1. Overpopulation is the rule. An annual population growth of approximately 1.8 percent in these countries means that their populations double approximately every 35 years. This compares to an average 0.7 percent rate of population growth in advanced countries. It means that economic growth must be very rapid to make any gain on population; DVC per capita incomes are lagging behind the IACs (see Table 39-2).

   a. Population growth accelerates with economic growth as better living conditions extend life.

   b. Birth rates remain high as medical care and sanitation cut infant mortality.

   c. Population growth hinders development because large families create obstacles to development. They reduce the ability of households to save, more investment is required to keep up with increases in the labor force, an overuse of agricultural land may occur, and massive urban problems are generated.

   d. Other reasons exist in explaining why expansion hinders development.

   e. Possible solutions include China's "one-child" program, but many nations have religious and sociocultural reasons to oppose contraception or birth control.

   f. Three additional points are worth noting.

      i. The relationship between population and economic growth is not as clear as it seems. Japan and Hong Kong are densely populated, but wealthy. Did the wealth come before or after population growth rates declined?

      ii. Population growth rates for the DVCs in general have declined in recent decades.

      iii. The traditional view is that reduction in population growth leads to economic development. But the "demographic transition" theory maintains that rising incomes lead to slower population growth. Children are viewed more as economic liabilities as the wealth of a country becomes greater. (Key Question 6)

2. High unemployment and underemployment are characteristics of DVCs with rates in the vicinity of 15 to 20 percent. This may become worse as rural populations migrate to cities in the hope of finding jobs that are not there. Underemployment occurs when workers are employed less time than desired or at jobs that do not fully utilize their skills.

3. Low labor productivity occurs because there has not been enough investment in physical or human capital. Furthermore, often there is no entrepreneurial class. Higher education is

often oriented toward the humanities rather than technical areas, and some of the best workers have migrated from their home countries, causing what is called the "brain drain."

C. Capital accumulation is an important focus.

1. All DVCs suffer from a lack of capital goods—factories, machinery and equipment, public utilities, etc. Better equipped workers would improve productivity.

2. Increasing the stock of capital goods is crucial because of the very limited possibility of increasing the supply of arable land.

3. Once begun, the accumulation of capital may be cumulative if it can raise output faster than the population grows.

4. Domestic capital formation must come as a result of domestic saving. A nation cannot consume everything it produces if it wants to invest in the future.

5. Savings potential is not promising in the poorest countries and may require foreign investment in these countries.

6. Another concern has been capital flight, which occurs when citizens who have been able to save transfer their savings to the IACs for safety and higher returns. This is a quantitatively significant problem.

7. Obstacles to investment include the lack of investors but also the lack of incentive to invest. Education and skilled workers as well as an adequate infrastructure are needed to encourage private investment.

8. One potential bright spot is in-kind or nonfinancial investment in the form of surplus labor working on the improvement of the infrastructure and other capital improvements.

D. Technological advance is a somewhat separate process from capital formation. In some cases DVCs are able to transfer new technologies that are capital-saving. Technological borrowing has aided the rapid growth of Pacific Rim region; OPEC nations have benefited in similar ways and the former Soviet bloc countries and republics are seeking western technology. On the other hand, DVCs often require technology appropriate to their resource mixes and must develop their own.

E. Sociocultural and institutional factors: One intangible ingredient is the "will to develop."

1. Sociocultural obstacles to growth exist.

a. Tribal allegiances may take precedence over national identity.

b. Religious beliefs and observances may restrict the length of the productive workday.

c. A caste system may allocate labor inefficiently.

2. Institutional obstacles also exist, especially the problem of land reform in these predominantly agricultural countries.

III. **The Vicious Circle of Poverty**

A. Poverty makes it difficult to grow. The obstacles to development listed in this chapter seem to arise from poverty. How can a country break the cycle of poverty?

B. Increasing the rate of capital accumulation may help, but only if the rate of population growth is somehow slowed at the same time. (Key Question 13)

IV. **The Role of Government**

A. A positive role exists for government, according to one perspective.

1. Government provides law and order.

2. The absence of entrepreneurship means that government may have to substitute in spearheading investment.

3. The infrastructure like education, highways, and other government services, depend on adequate public investment in these projects.

4. Forced saving and investment may also require government intervention.

   a. Increasing taxes is one alternative.

   b. Government can cause inflation by creating and spending new money on public projects and by selling bonds to banks and spending the proceeds. The resulting inflation is like an arbitrary tax on the economy, but there are objections to creating investment in this way.

5. Social-institutional problems like land ownership and population growth can be alleviated by government policy.

B. Public sector problems exist in the DVCs.

1. Entrepreneurial ability is lacking in the public sector, too.

2. Many DVCs have histories of government corruption and poor administration and much of these economies is state-owned or state-controlled.

V. **Role of the Advanced Nations**

A. Expanding trade may be the simplest way to benefit DVCs, and IACs can lower trade barriers against DVC products. However, many countries need basic capital and assistance to produce export.

B. Foreign aid can take several forms.

1. Public loans and grants from governments: In the last decade, U.S. aid has averaged about $10 to 14 billion per year, mostly administered by the Agency for International Development (AID). Total IAC has been $40-60 billion per year. (Global Perspective 39.2)

2. The World Bank Group, supported by about 180 member nations including the U.S., lends out capital funds to DVC governments and also sells bonds and guarantees and insures private loans.

   a. The World Bank is a "last resort" lending agency whose loans are limited to productive projects for which private funds are not available.

   b. Many World Bank loans are for basic development projects, such as infrastructure that is needed to attract private capital.

   c. The World Bank also provides technical assistance.

   d. Two World Bank affiliates supplement the Bank's activities: The International Finance Corp. invests in private corporations in the DVCs; The International Development Association (IDA) makes "soft loans" to the poorest DVCs on more liberal terms than the World Bank.

    C. Criticism of foreign aid to DVCs takes several forms.

        1. A basic charge is that foreign aid, like welfare programs, creates dependency.

        2. The recipients of much foreign aid end up being the bureaucracy and centralized governments of the receiving country.

        3. Corruption and misuse characterize too much foreign aid. Many of the beneficiaries are IAC-based consultants and multinational corporations.

        4. Foreign aid declined from $58 billion in 1990 to $40 billion in 1999.

    D. Private capital flows mostly from large corporations, and private banks also enter DVCs, rising from about $50 billion in 1990 to $250 billion in 1999.

VI. Where from here?

    A. DVC policies for promoting growth.

        1. Establishing and strengthening the rule of law. Clearly defined and enforced property rights bolster economic growth by ensuring that individuals receive and retain the fruits of their labor.

        2. Opening economies to international trade.

        3. Controlling population growth.

        4. Encouraging foreign direct investment.

        5. Building human capital, programs which increase basic literacy, education, and labor-market skills help enhance economic growth.

        6. Making peace with neighboring countries.

        7. Establishing independent central banks.

        8. Establishing realistic exchange rate policies.

        9. Privatizing many state run industries.

    B. IAC policies for fostering DVC growth.

        1. Directing foreign aid to the poorest DVCs, much of foreign aid from IACs is strongly influenced by potential and military considerations. Only one-fourth of foreign aid goes to those 10 countries whose population constitutes 70 percent of the world's poorest people.

        2. Reducing tariffs and import quotas.

        3. Providing debt relief to DVCs.

        4. Admitting temporary workers while discouraging brain drains.

        5. Discouraging arms sales to the DVCs.

VIII. LAST WORD: Famine in Africa

    A. Famine is not uncommon and caused about 300,000 deaths of children in Somalia in early 1990s; in 2000 an estimated 12 million people in 10 African countries are threatened by famine.

    B. Immediate cause of famine is drought, but other causes are a more complex interaction of civil strife, overpopulation, soil erosion, and counterproductive public policies.

1. Civil strife has torn many countries for decades. Somalia is one example.

2. Population growth has outstripped food production; population growth in Africa averages 2.2% per year but only .6% per year in IACs.

3. Ecological degradation has occurred in countries struggling to employ marginal land for crop production.

4. Ill-advised public policies and large international debt are other causes:

   a. Some governments spend four times as much on arms as they do on agriculture.

   b. Many African governments have followed the policy of establishing prices of agricultural goods at low levels to provide cheap food, but it diminishes incentives to produce.

5. External debt of about $230 billion in 1999 force sub-Saharan countries to cut back on needed domestic programs.

ANSWERS TO END-OF-CHAPTER QUESTIONS

39-1 What are the characteristics of a developing nation? List the two basic avenues of economic growth available to such a nation. State and explain the obstacles that face DVCs in breaking the poverty barrier. Use the "vicious circle of poverty" to outline in detail steps a DVC might take to initiate economic development.

Developing countries have relatively small industrial sectors, a significant portion of resources employed in agriculture, and exports consisting primarily of unprocessed agricultural goods and raw materials. Illiteracy rates and rates of unemployment and population growth are often high, and there is usually a critical shortage of capital equipment, leading to the use of labor-intensive production methods and low productivity levels.

In order to achieve high rates of economic growth, DVCs, like IACs, must allocate existing resources more efficiently; invest in improving the productivity of labor and expanding the base of capital; and adopt new types of production methods.

The DVCs face a complex assortment of obstacles in attaining economic prosperity. The operation of the so-called vicious circle of poverty means that the potential for economic growth is often severely hampered by the problems associated with current poverty. In particular, low levels of savings and investment restrict capital accumulation, limiting growth in labor productivity and in real incomes.

Low real income levels, coupled with the large family sizes associated with rapid population growth, cause saving rates to be low in most DVCs. The lack of domestic saving is often exacerbated by the foreign flight of financial capital, as citizens seek to shield their savings from the uncertainty created by unstable political and economic circumstances within these countries.

Rapid population growth requires high rates of capital formation to maintain current per capita supplies, but even when savings are found to fund private capital accumulation, more will likely be needed to supplement the inadequate public infrastructure. Private investment is further hampered by a shortage of entrepreneurs willing to take on associated risks. The perceived benefits of capital formation are often limited by political and economic volatility, low domestic demand for nonagricultural goods, the difficulties producers face competing in foreign markets, shortages of skilled labor (worsened by the brain drain of trained workers to the IACs), and deficiencies in the existing public infrastructure.

Because of these obstacles, per capita supplies of real capital do not increase rapidly. Combined with low rates of investment in human capital and the exhaustion of natural resources often associated with rapid population growth, this leads to low productivity levels. The relative abundance of labor also causes high unemployment rates in urban areas and underemployment in rural areas.

While productivity levels can be increased through the adoption of new types of technology, new methods usually require large amounts of capital and skilled labor, which most DVCs do not possess. Citizens of DVCs may not be receptive to new production techniques. Growth in many DVCs is hampered by a series of sociocultural and institutional obstacles. The costs of political and economic instability have already been mentioned. Religious beliefs, while offering spiritual comforts to the impoverished, often contribute to rapid population growth and social stratification; beliefs that foster the so-called "capricious universe" doctrine may also detract from accumulative behavior. The lack of institutional and national development can cause widespread corruption, the imposition of inefficient and inequitable tax systems, and the possibility of destructive civil discord. Quasi-feudal systems of land ownership provide even further economic disincentives for the mass of rural populations.

The circle of poverty can be broken through significant rates of savings that are used for rapid capital accumulation. Coupled with moderate rates of population growth, this capital accumulation can lead to increases in both labor productivity and output; eventually, countries reach a point at which the development process becomes self-sustaining through the high saving rates associated with large incomes.

39-2 Explain how the absolute per capita income gap between rich and poor nations might increase, even though per capita income (or output) is growing faster in DVCs than it is in IACs.

Because base incomes are so much higher in IACs than in DVCs, slower growth as a proportion of GDP in these countries can still translate into higher absolute gains in per capita living standards, causing the absolute per capita income gap between IACs and DVCs to increase rather than decline. For example, 1 percent of $10,000 per capita is more than 3 percent of $2,000 per capita.

39-3 (Key Question) Assume an DVC and an IAC presently have real per capita outputs of $500 and $5,000 respectively. If both nations have a 3 percent increase in their real per capita outputs, by how much will the per capita output gap change?

Rise in per capital output gap = $135 (= 3% ∞ $5,000 - 3% ∞ $500).

39-4 Discuss and evaluate:

a. "The path to economic development has been clearly blazed by American capitalism. It is up to the DVCs to follow this trail."

b. "The problem with the DVCs is that income is too equally distributed. Economic inequality promotes saving, and saving is prerequisite of investment. Therefore, greater inequality in the income distribution of the DVCs would be a spur to capital accumulation and growth."

c. "The core of economic development involves changing human beings more than it does altering a nation's physical environment."

d. "The U.S. 'foreign aid' program is a sham. In reality it represents neocolonialism—a means by which the DVCs can be nominally free in a political sense but remain totally subservient in an economic sense."

e. "The biggest obstacle facing poor nations in their quest for development is the lack of capital goods."

(a) The first statement is false. Modern economic development was pioneered by Great Britain during the Industrial Revolution in the latter half of the eighteenth century. At this time the North American colonies—later the United States and Canada—engaged in trade with Britain much like that between modern DVCs and IACs, exporting primarily raw materials in return for imported manufactured goods. It was only in the nineteenth century that the United States, along with other nascent IACs, underwent a process of industrialization similar to that of Great Britain.

The second statement is also false. Countries that have successfully undergone rapid industrialization in recent years have not all followed the model of decentralized development provided by the history of American capitalism. Citing the most obvious example, postwar Japan underwent a highly successful process of economic development in which government planning and coordination played a central role.

(b) Increases in inequality will raise domestic saving only if the foreign flight of financial capital can be stemmed. Forced government saving can be just as effective in stimulating capital investment, as long as problems associated with public sector decision making can be overcome. Increasing inequality also has effects on general incentives to work and engage in risk-taking. While some inequality of income can stimulate economic activity, excessive concentrations of wealth can also hinder the development process, worsening the cycle of poverty for a large portion of the country's population.

While theory provides some arguments concerning the desirability of income inequality in stimulating development, much empirical evidence conflicts with this view. For example, newly industrialized countries, such as Taiwan, South Korea, Singapore, and Hong Kong all exhibit low levels of income inequality in comparison to most other DVCs.

(c) Because of the higher incomes in IACs, average propensities to save are also relatively high. While these high rates of saving are essential in supporting rapid capital accumulation, they represent a leakage of potential spending from the income-expenditures stream and dampen output and employment in the short run. Low incomes in the DVCs, on the other hand, mean that average propensities to save are relatively low, limiting the potential for capital accumulation and productivity growth. The problems IACs face because of high saving rates are short-term and subject to amelioration; the problem of undersaving for DVCs is a crucial long-term restriction on the potential for economic growth.

(d) Changes in prevailing social, cultural, and institutional patterns in DVCs are probably the most significant prerequisite of economic development. Countries have managed in the past to initiate development in the face of tremendous shortages of physical resources—for example, many economies ravaged by the Second World War—but accomplishing this feat in the absence of amenable sociocultural and institutional circumstances is a virtual impossibility.

(e) There is no doubt that bilateral foreign aid, such as that provided by the United States, is often made for self-serving as well as altruistic reasons. The Food for Peace program can be viewed as a component of domestic agricultural policy, and other types of "tied" aid benefit American producers. While these forms of aid can sometimes have overtones of neocolonialism, it is hard to imagine that these aspects represent the overriding purpose of American foreign aid. If DVCs are economically dependent on IACs, this is more often the result of existing trade patterns, external debt, and foreign corporate ownership.

39-5   Studies indicate that, in general, landlocked countries tend to have lower per capita income levels than surrounding nations that border on oceans and seas. Why do you think this is the case? Use Global Perspective 39-1 to identify a major exception to this generalization. Why do you think this exception exists?

Exporting and importing goods without access to major ports increases the cost of foreign as well as domestic trade. Nations and empires of the past one thousand years have depended extensively on shipping to increase the wealth of its people.

Switzerland is completely landlocked but has one of the highest GDPs' per capital on earth.

39-6   (*Key Question*)   Contrast the "demographic transition" view of population growth with the traditional view that slower population growth is a prerequisite for rising living standards in the DVCs.

Demographic transition view: Expanded output and income in developing countries will result in lower birthrates and slower growth of population. As incomes of primary family members expand, they begin to see the marginal cost of a larger family exceeding the marginal benefit. The policy emphasis should therefore be on economic growth; population growth will realize. Traditional view: Developing nations should reduce population growth as a first priority. Slow population growth enables the growth of per capita income.

39-7   (*Key Question*) Because real capital is supposed to earn a higher return where it is scarce, how do you explain the fact that most international investment flows to the IACs (where capital is relatively abundant) rather than to the DVCs (where capital is very scarce)?

Capital earns a higher return where it is scarce, *other things equal*. But, when comparing investment opportunities between IACs and DVCs, other things equal. Advanced factors filled with specialized equipment require a productive work force. IACs have no abundance of educated, experienced workers; these workers are scarce in DVCs. Also, IACs have extensive public infrastructures which increase the returns on private capital. Example: a network of highways makes it more profitable to produce goods that need to be widely transported. Finally, investment returns must be adjusted for risk. IACs have stable governments and "law and order," reducing the risk of capital being "nationalized" or pilfered by organized crime.

39-8   Do you think that the nature of the problems the DVCs face require governmentally directed as opposed to a private-enterprise-directed development process? Explain why or why not.

Positive government contributions to development are evident in Japan, South Korea, and Taiwan. In contrast, Mobutu's Zaire, Somoza's Nicaragua, Marcos' Philippines, and Haiti under the Duvaliers are examples of corrupt and inept governments that functioned as impediments to economic progress. The revolutionary transformations of the former Soviet Union away from communism and toward market-oriented economies make clear that central planning is no longer recognized as an effective mechanism for development. Therefore, government focus should be in fostering an environment of economic incentives. Promoting competition among economic players for the purpose of sustainable growth.

39-9   What were the trends relating in government-provided foreign aid versus private capital flows to the DVCs in the 1990s? Why do you think those trends occurred?

Government provided foreign aid to developing countries is declining. In 1990 IACs provided $58 billion of foreign aid; by 1999 government aid dropped to $40 billion. Although government aid is declining, private capital flows have been increasing in the 1990s. Private capitals flows to DVCs was $50 billion in 1990 and increased to $250 billion in 1999.

The major reason that private capital flows have increased is due to debt negotiations. Heavily indebted DVCs agreed to reform their economies to promote growth and avert future debt crisis. DVCs have made major efforts to reduce deficits and control inflation. One of the main reasons for the decline in foreign aid by governments is the end of the cold war. Nations such as Cuba, Ethiopia and North Korea that adhered to communist principles received substantial foreign aid from the Soviet Union. The United States in turn, lavished foreign aid on developing nations such as Egypt, Israel, Mexico, Thailand, Turkey, and Chile that tended to support U.S. policies. But with the disintegration of the former Soviet Union, the political-military rationale for foreign aid has lost much of its force.

39-10 Do you favor debt forgiveness to all the DVCs, just the poorest ones, or none at all? What incentive problem might debt relief create? Would you be willing to pay $20 a year more in personal income taxes for debt forgiveness? How about $200 dollars? How about $2,000 dollars?

Debt forgiveness to the poorest nations may allow them to devote these interest payments to needed social programs – especially investment in human capital programs like education. Countries requesting forgiveness could be required to submit a plan for using these funds for productive purposes before the debt is forgiven. Debt relief might reduce incentives for careful borrowing and saving for future growth. If countries believe loans are gifts, it might encourage reckless spending.

The answers to the last 3 questions are based on personal views, but students should realize that the U.S. currently grants $10-14 billion per year in total foreign aid or about $40 per person per year.

39-11 What types of products do the DVCs typically export? How do those exports relate to law of comparative advantage to explain the character of these exports. How do tariffs by the IACs reduce the standard of living of DVCs?

DVCs export primarily raw materials and agricultural goods to IACs in return for imported manufactured goods and services. This pattern of trade follows from the law of comparative advantage. As far as the extraction of nonrenewable resources is concerned, past depletion of deposits in the IACs has meant that DVCs are often the lowest-cost producers of these goods. As for renewable resources such as agricultural products, the production of these goods is usually labor intensive. The large pools of low-wage labor in DVCs give them a comparative advantage in many of these products.

It is important to note that the law of comparative advantage does not necessarily consign DVCs to be raw materials exporters forever. The production of many manufactured goods is also fairly labor-intensive, giving DVCs an opportunity to become low-cost producers and hence exporters of these products. Many have already begun to develop thriving manufacturing sectors based on this cost advantage, and if trade barriers in IACs continue to be lowered this trend will be intensified, living standards will rise and more efficient use of world resources results.

39-12 Do you think that IACs such as the United States should open their doors wider to immigration of low-skilled DVC workers to help the DVCs develop? Do you think that it is appropriate for students from DVC nations to stay in IAC nations to work and build careers?

IACs could help the DVCs by accepting more temporary workers from the DVCs. Temporary migration is not only an outlet for surplus DVC labor, but also a source of income in the form of migrant remittance to their families in the home country.

If the goal of IACs is to encourage development in the DVCs, then the IACs should discourage "brain drains" from the DVCs. If IACs recruit the best and brightest students from DVC nations and try to train these students in the workforce, DVCs human capital stock will be drained. In the long run the DVCs development will be slowed.

39-13 (*Key Question*) Use Figure 39-2 (changing box labels as necessary) to explain rapid economic growth in a country such as Chile or South Korea. What factors other than those contained in the figure might contribute to growth?

To describe countries such as Chile and South Korea, we would need to change labels on three boxes, leading to a change in the "results" boxes. "Rapid" population growth would change to "low" rate of population growth; "low" level of saving would change to "high" level of saving; "low" levels of investment in physical and human capital would change to "high" levels of investment in physical and human capital. These three changes would result in higher productivity and higher per capita income, which would produce a rising level of demand. Other factors: stable national government; homogeneous population; extensive investment in infrastructure; "will to develop"; strong private incentives.

39-14 (*Last Word*) Explain how civil wars, population growth, and public policy decisions have contributed to periodic famines in Africa.

Civil conflicts divert resources from civilian uses, destroy institutions, and complicate the distribution of famine and developmental aid. They also discourage investment in the productive sector due to the uncertain political and economic base. Population in Africa is growing more rapidly than food production, and this grim arithmetic suggests declining living standards and per capita food supplies. Population growth also contributes to ecological degradation, which depresses the ability to produce food still further. Finally, public policy decisions have exacerbated the problem. The average African government spends four times as much on armaments as it does on agriculture. Governments frequently control food prices at low levels, which discourages production and encourages wasteful consumption. Dependence on foreign aid complicates the problem still further by providing temporary relief from food shortages and discouraging local self-sufficiency. Finally, the sub-Saharan African nations are burdened by large-scale external debt, forcing them to cut back on domestic spending programs and further worsening their economic conditions.

BONUS WEB CHAPTER
TRANSITION ECONOMIES:
RUSSIA AND CHINA

CHAPTER OVERVIEW

Two of the most profound events of the past two decades are the collapse of communism in the Soviet Union and the rapid emergence of the market system in China. Russia and China are perhaps the world's most significant developing economies: Together they constitute 20 percent of the world's surface area and 24 percent of the world's population.

In this final chapter, we first briefly look at Marxist (communist) ideology that gave rise to the command economies. Then we examine the institutions and techniques of central planning common to both the Soviet Union and pre-reform China.

Next, we discuss the coordination and incentive problems that central planning created. Finally, our attention turns to Russia and China's transition to market economies.

WHAT'S NEW

Few major changes from the 14th edition were made. However, this chapter now appears only on the Internet and not in the print version of the text's 15th edition. www.mhhe.com./economics/mcconnell15

Updating and editing has been done in the sections on Russia and China. There is a new Last Word on the difficulties of privatization in Russia.

INSTRUCTIONAL OBJECTIVES

After completing this chapter, students should be able to:

1. Summarize the Marxist ideology, especially the concepts of the labor theory of value.

2. Identify two major institutional features of the former Soviet system and the pre-reform Chinese economy.

3. List six characteristics of Soviet and Chinese central planning.

4. Describe the coordinating problem found in central planning.

5. Describe the difficult problem of incentives faced by central planners.

6. Explain the causes of the failure of the Soviet centrally planned economic system.

7. Describe the components necessary for the transition to a market system.

8. Compare market reform in China with the reform process in Russia and explain how it has differed.

9. Identify three institutions developed in China for the support and control of market activity.

10. Identify the problems and accomplishments of Russian economic reform.

11. Identify three problems that have slowed the transition process in China.

12. Contrast the pessimist's and the optimist's view of Russia's future.

13. Define and identify terms and concepts listed at the end of the chapter.

COMMENTS AND TEACHING SUGGESTIONS

1. This chapter can be assigned near the beginning of the principles course, after students have been introduced to the operation of a capitalist market system. The contrast between central planning and a capitalist system seems to help students realize that the market system we often take for granted is something worth studying after all. In learning about the problems with a centrally planned system, students begin to appreciate the market forces and freedoms of a capitalist system. However, it is worth returning to this chapter after a thorough grounding in the microeconomics of the preceding chapters.

2. Current economic problems in the former Soviet republics and China are the focus of many news stories and offer an opportunity to discuss how our system deals with such problems, if they exist here. Or, if the problems don't exist in the U.S., students can discuss why not. Another possible assignment would be to examine the published problems and have students design solutions for them. Ask students to identify specific types of problems relating to property rights, coordination of economic activity and the presence or lack of economic incentives.

3. *Business Week* and other magazines have run extensive articles on the transition of the Chinese economy and the recent change in the status of Hong Kong. *Business Week* has a CD-ROM available for educators to conveniently store and access articles. Using the Internet is a good way for students to access articles from major newspapers.

    A recent article in the *Los Angeles Times*, April 18, 1998 "China's New Tenants Won't Buy Excuses" by Rone Tempest is an entertaining example of what can happen when foreign investors bring consumer rights, a sense of entitlement, and a more sophisticated view of property rights— along with their money.

4. Above-average classes might be interested in discussing Oskar Lange's ideas on the possibility of central planers duplicating market efficiencies with rational pricing methods. Market socialism is discussed in most texts on comparative economic systems.

STUDENT STUMBLING BLOCK

Students confuse Russia with the whole former Soviet Union. A map showing the size (stretching eleven time zones) of Russia and its location relative to the fifteen former republics, which are now independent countries, is a good lesson in economic geography. A source of confusion related to this chapter is the common misperception that any government involvement in an industry is "socialism." In learning about a centrally planned socialist system, students may be more aware of what the Soviet brand of socialism was like and less about the Chinese system.

LECTURE NOTES

I.   **Ideology and Institutions**

   A. History

   1. The Russian Revolution of 1917 produced a dictatorship under Vladimir Lenin and later Joseph Stalin.

   2. China's communist takeover took place in 1947 under Mao Zedong

   3. Both nations viewed centrally planned socialism as a solution to the instability of what they believed were chaotic market systems.

   B. Marxian ideology was the basis for the Communist Party's power and economic system.

1. Marx's labor theory of value holds that all value was determined by the amount of labor time required for its production. However, capitalists owned the means of production and had power over the workers whom they employed.

2. Workers were exploited by the capitalists, who bought the labor for a low wage and got full-time service from each worker. The value of workers' production exceeded their wages, and this led to the capitalist earning what Marx called "surplus value."

3. Communism's function was to overthrow the capitalist control of the means of production so that the worker had control and would no longer be exploited. The Party viewed itself as the vanguard of the working class, but in fact it was a strong dictatorship.

C. There were two major institutional characteristics of the previous economies of Russia and China.

1. There was state ownership of all property, transportation and communication facilities, banking institutions, virtually all industry including retail and wholesale enterprises, and most urban housing structures.

2. There was also central economic planning, which meant that the economy was directed by the government rather than by decentralized market mechanisms.

II. **Central planning and its problems**

A. Planning goals and techniques.

1. Industrialization and military strength had the highest priority in terms of resource allocation in the Soviet Union. In China emphasis was placed on developing small-scale industries scattered throughout the rural areas. Both countries neglected consumer goods industries.

2. Resources were overcommitted, planners committed more resources than were available, so there were persistent shortages.

3. Resources were initially mobilized to achieve rapid economic growth and this was successful through the 1950s. Both China and the Soviet Union induced or coerced a larger proportion of the population into the labor force.

4. Allocation of inputs was done by directive.

5. Government fixed prices of virtually all inputs and outputs, but prices did not reflect the relative scarcity of the resource or product.

6. The Soviet Union and China aimed at self-sufficiency and avoided trade with western countries if possible.

7. Macroeconomic policies were passive, meaning that money and prices accommodated output plans but did not play a role in influencing their outcome.

B. Problems of central planning were serious.

1. The coordination problem was massive; outputs of some industries are inputs in others, so problems in any single sector would immediately be felt in many. There was no price mechanism to provide incentives to eliminate bottlenecks, as is true in a market economy. Planners had to coordinate inputs and outputs for thousands of production enterprises. Bottlenecks were common and had historical roots dating to the early 1960s or before.

2. The incentive problem.

a. In a market system, profits and losses signal success and failure and provide incentives to increase or decrease production. In central planning managers are rewarded for meeting assigned goals and have no incentive to respond to product shortages or surpluses.

b. The centrally planned system also lacked entrepreneurship. Without profit there is no reward for innovation or enterprise.

c. In centrally planned systems business is essentially a government owned monopoly with no reward for improving product quality or developing more efficient production techniques.

d. Workers lack motivation because there are few material incentives.

III.   **The Collapse of the Soviet Economy: The Soviet Union ceased to exist by that name in November of 1991, and became 15 separate nations.**

A. After rapid economic growth through the 1950s and 1960s (about 6 percent reported per year, compared to 3 percent in the U.S.), the rate fell to less than 3 percent in the 1970s, and by late 1980s the Soviet GDP was actually declining.

B. The quality of goods was below international standards, the selection of consumer goods was extremely limited, and technology was primitive by world standards. Shortages of basic goods were common, leading to long lines, black markets, and corruption in product distribution.

C. The lack of ability to fulfill consumer needs contributed to the fall of communism.

D. There was a huge military burden: 15 to 20 percent of GDP was devoted to military as compared with 6 to 7 percent of a much larger GDP in the U.S.

E. The agricultural sector experienced great inefficiency and consumed 25 percent of annual investment. It employed 30 percent of the labor force while still not producing enough for the population to feed itself. Output per farm worker was 10-25% that of U.S. farm workers.

IV.   **The Russian Transition to a Market System.**

A. Privatization

1. Since 1992 more than two-thirds of former state owned enterprises have been privatized, including 90% of small companies and 80% of service sector companies.

2. In the first phase government gave vouchers to 40 million Russian citizens, which could be pooled and used to purchase enterprises.

3. The second phase allowed state enterprises to be purchased for cash, which enabled foreign investors to buy Russian enterprises, providing much needed direct investment from abroad.

4. In 1995 wealthy lenders were given shares in many companies in exchange for loans.

5. Land reform has progressed more slowly. It will take many years to develop a functional market for farm land.

B. Price Reform

1. Prices in the former Soviet system bore no relationship to the economic value of either products or resources.

2. Because input prices did not measure the relative scarcity of resources, it was impossible for a firm to minimize real production costs.

3. Prices of many consumer items were fixed at artificially low levels and shortages existed for many of these goods. (See Figure Web-1)

4. In January 1992, the government decontrolled about 90% of all prices including the Russian currency. Domestic prices surged and the international value of the Russian ruble sank.

5. The decontrolled prices began to more closely reflect the marginal cost of producing goods, which helped reallocate resources to best suit consumer wants.

C. Promotion of competition.

1. The former Soviet Union consisted of large state-owned enterprises—monopolies that produced 30 to 40 percent of total industrial output.

2. Russian reformers realized an efficient market economy requires competition, but only limited change has occurred.

3. Joint ventures between Russia and foreign companies are one possible way to increase competition and recent legislation has opened the door for firms to invest directly in Russia.

D. Joining the world economy by making the ruble convertible.

1. The Soviet economy was largely isolated from the world economy for over 75 years, joining required making the ruble a convertible currency.

2. The plunging value of the ruble has been detrimental to Russia's world trade. The international value of the ruble has been more stable since its crash in 1998. It traded at about 17 rubles to $1 in 2000.

E. Price level stabilization. (See Table Web-1)

1. The transition to free markets brought hyperinflation.

2. "Ruble overhang"—or hoarding of rubles—existed as Russian households had huge amounts of currency and bank deposits waiting for consumer goods to be more abundant.

3. Large government deficits were financed by increases in the money supply.

   a. Privatization of state enterprises caused the government to lose profits.

   b. The uncertainty of transition led to general disorder and widespread tax evasion.

   c. The government extended massive subsidy credits to both industry and agriculture.

   d. Pensions and welfare spending was increased by printing more money.

4. Russia's economic reforms included the creation of an independent central bank that implemented anti-inflationary monetary policy, reducing inflation from 1,353 percent in 1992 to 14 percent in 1997.

F. Other major problems of the transition:

1. Real output began its fall in the 1980s but the decline accelerated during the reforms; the magnitude resembles that associated with the Great Depression in the United States. Causes of the declined include:

   a. Rapid inflation, which caused an uncertain environment.

   b. Unraveling trade relationships with former Soviet Bloc trading partners.

    c.   Bankruptcy and closing of many former state-owned enterprises.

    d.   Massive reallocation of resources including major cuts in military spending.

2.   Because real output equals real income, the Russian living standard has declined dramatically; at least 30,000 scientists have left Russian to work elsewhere.

3.   Economic inequality has increased during the transition. While some new wealth has been created through entrepreneurship, others have enriched themselves via corruption and illegal activities.

4.   The major disruptions, swift changes, and lack of regulatory oversight created major opportunities for organized crime.

5.   Greater economic freedom has brought greater economic insecurity; medical and educational services have declined, alcohol abuse has increased.

G. Future prospects.

1.   A remaining concern about the transition to markets in Russia is the weakness of government in law enforcement, particularly the collection of taxes.

2.   Declining tax revenue cripples the central government's ability to perform basic functions and provide a safety net for its citizens.

3.   The most severe economic dislocations seem to have ended, but the transition to a fully functioning market economy will require additional time.

V.   **Market Reforms in China**

A. China has taken a different path to market reform than Russia. The reforms began earlier, were more gradual, and allowed the old systems to function along with the new.

B. Market reform began in agriculture in 1978. The key elements were the leasing of land to individual farmers and the establishment of a two-track price system (lower prices for government orders and market prices for the surplus). Responding to the profit motive, individual farmers increased their productivity and agricultural output soared.

C. The success of reforms in agriculture led the central government to extend the reforms to state-owned enterprises (SOEs) in urban areas.

1.   The two-track price system was again employed, gradually increasing the portion of inputs and outputs that could be sold at market prices.

2.   The government also encouraged the formation of urban collectives—enterprises owned jointly by managers and their workforces. The urban collectives experienced explosive growth, some at the expense of the SOEs. However, the competition spurred productivity advance and innovation in many of the SOEs.

D. In 1980 China created special economic zones (SEZs) open to foreign investment, private ownership, and international trade.

E. Reforms in China also included building institutions to facilitate the market system and its macroeconomic control.

1.   A central bank, a stock market and currency exchange facilities were established.

2.   China replaced the system of "profit transfers" from state enterprises to the central government with an enterprise tax system.

F. Transformation of the SOEs.

1. In the 1990s the market reforms continue as the Communist Party operatives running the SOEs are replaced with professional business managers.

2. In a competitive environment many SOEs found that they were producing the wrong goods, in the wrong amounts, using the wrong combinations of inputs. In short they were inefficient, in both production techniques and in allocation of resources. Some will be allowed to fail, others will issue stock with the government holding a controlling interest.

VI. Outcomes and Prospects

A. China's economic growth rate in the past two decades is among the highest on record for any country during any period of world history. (See Table Web-2)

B. The growth of per capita income in China has resulted from increased use of capital, improved technology and shifts of labor away from lower-productivity toward higher productivity uses.

C. Rapid expansion of international trade from $5 billion in 1978 to $195 billion in 1999 took place.

D. China still faces some significant economic problems in its transition to the market system.

1. Outright ownership of farm land is still prohibited and this inhibits investment in farm equipment and capital improvements on the land.

2. The financial and monetary control systems in China are still weak and inadequate. Many unprofitable SOEs owe colossal sums of money on loans made by banks.

3. China still has much work to do to fully integrate its economy into the world's system of international finance and trade.

4. There is great regional unevenness in China's economic development.

VII. Conclusion

A. China's greadual path has been more successful so far, but questions remain about future prospects.

B. Once Russia stabilizes, it may be in a stronger position than China because it has become more democratic.

VIII. LAST WORD: Police Smash Down Smirnov's Doors

A. In November 2000, masked police smashed through the doors of one of Russia's leading vodka makers while factory workers threw bottles at the police.

B. Reports said the police were enforcing a court decision naming a new director of the company, but its head, Boris Smirnov, said that the court's decision was illegal.

C. The conflict arose with a claim by one of the leading industrial banking groups, Alfa-Eco, that it had obtained 50% of Smirnov shares. Smirnov claimed that these shares were false.

D. Related disputes also continue:

1. Smirnov Vodka is fighting a court battle in U.S. with UDV North American Co.'s Smirnoff Vodka, the world's leading brand, over the use of the name. UDV says it acquired the name in 1934 when its predecessor company Heublein bought the name from Russian émigré Rudolf Kunett who bought it originally from a Smirnov founder.

2. Another dispute in Russia in August 2000, was over control of Moscow's Kristall distillery, which makes Stolichnaya and other brands of vodka. Two men who both

claimed to be the manager occupied the executive offices with their private security guards. A court decided the dispute in September.

3. Because privatizations are often questioned, workers seized a paper mill in Russia to protest foreign ownership and a worker was shot by police. In another case, rival factions fought for control of a chemical plant in Yekaterinburg.

ANSWERS TO END-OF-CHAPTER QUESTIONS

Web-1 Compare the economic ideology of the former Soviet and pre-reform China with that of the capitalist economies as to the (a) source and role of profits, (b) ownership of capital, and (c) method of allocating resources.

The ideology of the former Soviet economy and pre-reform China was based on the theories of Karl Marx and their first leaders, Vladimir Lenin, and China's Mao Zedong. They envisioned their system as a successor to capitalism, which they believed was doomed to collapse. To communists the market system is chaotic, unstable and inequitable. (a) Communists accept the "labor theory of value," which is the idea that the value of any good is determined by the amount of labor required for its production. In their view capitalists exploit workers by paying them a wage below the value of their output. In market economies individual ownership of property resources requires that payment be made for all factors of production. (b) In the former Soviet Union and China the state owned all enterprises and physical resources in the country, with few exceptions. (c) All economic activity in the Soviet Union and pre-reform China with few exceptions was subject to a complex system of central planning and represented for all intents and purposes a command economy.

In contrast, the United States and other capitalist economies are characterized by the private ownership of resources and the use of decentralized markets to direct and coordinate most economic activity. Government involvement, while significant, is restricted to areas in which private markets are deemed to be inefficient or unworkable.

In the United States, it is consumer preferences communicated through private markets that determine the nature of production and resource allocation. In the former Soviet Union and China, it was government decisions communicated through the mechanism of central plans that motivated production and determined the allocation of scarce resources—at least as far as legally sanctioned economic activity was concerned.

Web-2 What does the term "central economic planning" mean? Describe the coordination problem faced by central planners in the Soviet Union and pre-reform China. Explain how a planning failure can cause a chain reaction of additional failures.

Planners must not only set output targets for each industry and enterprise, but they must allocate inputs to each of these enterprises so that their output targets can be met. Because the outputs of many industries are inputs to other industries, the failure of any single industry to fulfill its plan is likely to cause a whole chain of adverse repercussions. For example, if the iron mines fail to supply the steel industry with enough iron, then the steel industry will not be able to supply steel-using industries, such as automobiles, tractors, and transportation, with their needed inputs. Bottlenecks are thus created in many related industries. In a market system, prices would rise to provide incentives to break such bottlenecks, but in a planned economy, price incentives exist only outside the official system.

Web-3 Why were new product introductions and the use of new methods of production so uncommon in the Soviet Union and pre-reform China compared to in such capitalist economies as the United States, Japan and Germany?

In the capitalist system profits and losses signal success and failure, they also act as powerful incentives. The centrally planned system lacks entrepreneurship, it does not allow the profit motive and does not reward innovation and enterprise.

The route for getting ahead in the centrally planned economies of the Soviet Union and China was by movement up the political hierarchy of the communist party. Moving up the hierarchy meant better housing, better access to health care, and the right to shop in special stores. Meeting planning targets and skillfully maneuvering through the minefields of party politics measured success in "business." A definition based solely on political savvy is not conducive to technological advance, which is often disruptive to existing products, production methods, and organizational structures.

Web-4 What factors contributed to the collapse of the Soviet economy?

In 1991, the Soviet Union broke into several newly independent states, the largest of which is the Russian Republic. The collapse of the Soviet Union was caused by a number of economic problems stemming from the failures of central planning. The Soviet growth rate, at least measured by their statistics, was impressive during the 1950s and 1960s, fell during the 1970s and 1980s, but then broke down, falling sharply. In addition the quality of the goods produced was generally poor, with technology lagging behind the other major industrial producers. Consumer goods were both of poor quality and in short supply. The Soviet military expenditures were a serious burden, representing 15 to 20 percent of domestic output compared to the 6 percent absorbed by the military in the larger United States economy. Finally, the Soviet Union had an agricultural sector that required 30 percent of the labor force and about one fourth of the annual capital investment. Many of these problems were the result of serious errors in planning and administration, but perhaps most important was the lack of an effective incentive system.

Web-5 (*Key Question*) Use a supply and demand diagram to explain why persistent shortages of many consumer goods occurred under central planning in the Soviet Union and in prereform China. Why were black markets common in each country?

See Figure Web-1. Because Russia and China set prices and did not allow them to change as supply or demand shifted, prices were below the equilibrium price for most goods and services. When the fixed price, *Pf*, is below the equilibrium price, *Pe*, there will be a shortage since the quantity demanded will exceed the quantity supplied.

Black markets are common where prices are fixed below equilibrium levels. People can buy goods at the fixed government prices (or pay off clerks to save such goods to sell to them), and because of the shortages at the low fixed price, resell these goods at a much higher price to those unable to find the goods in government stores at the controlled prices. This reselling is said to occur on the black market.

Web-6 (*Key Question*) What have been the major components of economic reform in Russia? What is meant when these reforms are described as "shock therapy"? How successful has Russia been thus far in its reforms?

Privatization of state-owned businesses; market-determined prices; promotion of competition; integration with the world economy; and price-level stabilization. These reforms are referred to as shock therapy because they were dramatic and quick rather than phased in over many years. Russia's reform has nominally privatizied much of the economy (but property rights are still not clearly defined), establishing market-determined prices, and setting the stage for future prosperity. But the transition has resulted in declining living standards for many and increasing income inequality. Also, the government still does not have a successful program for collecting taxes.

Web-7 In what general respects have Chinese economic reforms differed from those of Russia? Do you believe that these differences account for China's higher growth rate? Why?

China has taken a different path than Russia in its transition to a market economy. Russia pursued a "shock therapy" approach to reform in 1992, attempting to achieve "irreversibility" of its reforms through a rapid and radical transformation to private property and free markets.

China's market reforms began far earlier—1978—and have been more gradual. Russia concluded that its political apparatus, the Communist Party, was an obstacle to economic reform. China, in contrast, has sought economic reform under the strong direction of its Communist Party. China feels that communist dictatorship and markets are compatible. China has protected the existence and development of its state owned enterprises while simultaneously encouraging the creation of competing private enterprises. Deng Xiaping, Mao Zedong's successor recognized that the profit incentives of a market economy could increase China's standard of living.

Agriculture was "decollectivized" and a two-track price system was adopted. Gradually the percentage of farm products sold in competitive markets was increased until by 1990 it had reached 80 percent. Agricultural output increased dramatically. The success of reforms in agriculture led the central government to extend the reforms to state-owned enterprises (SOEs) in urban areas. In 1980 China created special economic zones (SEZs) open to foreign investment, private ownership, and international trade. The success of these special regions eventually undercut support for central planning.

The reforms in China also included the building of institutions to facilitate the market system and its macroeconomic control. Among these institutions were a central bank, a stock market and a currency exchange. China also replaced the system of "profit transfers" from state enterprises to the central government with an enterprise tax system.

China's economic growth rate in the past two decades is among the highest in the world. The rapid expansion of China's international trade has accompanied the expansion of real output. These exports have provided the foreign currency needed to import consumer goods and capital goods. The growth of per capita income in China has resulted from increased use of capital, improved technology and the shifts of labor away from lower-productivity toward higher productivity uses. These shifts were made possible by the gradual introduction of market reforms allowing market price rather than central planning to coordinate most of the economic activity.

Web-8 (*Key Question*) Relate each of the following items to the success of market reform in China: (a) leasing farm land, (b) price reform, (c) private rural and urban enterprises, (d) special economic zones, and (e) corporatization of state-owned enterprises.

  (a) Leasing of land resulted in individually operated rather than collectivized farms; this greatly increased production incentives and boosted farm output.

  (b) Price reform established market-based prices. These higher-than-government prices provided incentives for enterprises to expand output; they also enabled market-determined allocation of resources to replace inefficient central planning.

  (c) Private rural and urban enterprises absorbed workers released by greater productivity in China's agricultural sector and established competition for China's state-owned enterprises.

  (d) The special economic zones—with their private corporations, free trade, and foreign investment—established the workability and benefits of "near-capitalism."

  (e) Corporatization focused the goals of state-owned enterprises on providing high-quality, minimum per-unit cost goods desired by consumers.

Web-9 What progress has China achieved in its transition to a market economy? What problems remain?

China has made considerable progress in its transition to a market economy. These significant but gradual reforms were outlined in answer to question 7.

China still faces some significant economic problems in its transition to a market system. After initial surges in the 1980s productivity in agriculture has stagnated. The possible reason may be that property rights are incomplete. The government policy has been to lease land for 15-year periods. But without outright ownership many farmers are reluctant to invest in farm equipment and capital improvements on the land. There is the possibility of macroeconomic instability, partly because of investment booms that have resulted in too much spending relative to production capacity and partly due to the inadequacy of the monetary control system. Many unprofitable SOEs owe colossal sums of money on loan from owned banks.

China still has much to do to fully integrate its economy into the world's system of international trade and finance. China's record of protecting intellectual property rights such as copyrights, trademarks, and patents is particularly poor. Finally, there is great regional unevenness in China's economic development.

Web-10   Do you think that China's economic reforms will eventually result in the demise of the Communist Party in China? Explain your answer.

The history of economic reform in China has been one of gradual adaptation to changing conditions. China's leadership often acts pragmatically using methods that show results, discarding less effective means slowly over time. The Communist Party in China has continued to keep social and political control in the country even as market reforms have been implemented. I certainly would not anticipate a sudden demise of the Communist Party based upon the tendency of the Chinese system to adjust slowly after allowing seemingly incompatible methods to be used simultaneously.

Web-11   "Paradoxically, Russia's disorder may provide a firmer base for future growth than China's order." Do you agree or disagree? Explain.

China has experienced very high rates of economic growth, while Russia has suffered years of declining output and income because of its swift transformation to capitalism. One could view this as placing Russia in a stronger position to succeed in the future. The Communist Party in China has been able to maintain power as market reforms have taken place but this may in fact be a "forced order" that cannot be contained indefinitely. History suggests that economic freedom usually creates demand for political freedom: free speech, freedom of peaceful assembly, freedom to organize political parties, and free elections. Is it possible that China's period of disorder is still to come? Forecasts, tea leaves or crystal balls, we have no solid answer to this question.

Web-12   (*Last Word*) In what way does the subject of this Chapter's Last Word relate to (a) the profit motive, (b) the importance of clear property rights to a market economy, (c) the privatization process in Russia, including control by the oligarchs?

The dispute over management and control over Smirnov Co. and others indicates that the profit motive is alive and well as control over the plant will also mean control over profit income. These disputes highlight the importance of clear property rights. When ownership is not clear, it can lead to the type of chaos reported, and also, it will make future investors cautious about investing when their efforts may be seized by someone else claiming ownership. One possible source of these disputes is the problem resulting from the program of providing shares for loans. If wealthy and maybe corrupt oligarchs demand ownership when they make loans, they may then try to seize control over the companies to which they made these loans. While it wasn't mentioned in the Smirnov case, it does seem to be true in the August case involving production of Stolichnaya vodka.